Moral Controversies
in
American Politics

Moral Controversies in American Politics

Cases in Social Regulatory Policy

Raymond Tatalovich
Byron W. Daynes, editors

With a foreword by **Theodore J. Lowi**

M.E. Sharpe
Armonk, New York
London, England

Library of Congress Cataloging-in-Publication Data

Moral controversies in American politics: cases in social regulatory policy / edited by
Raymond Tatalovich and Byron W. Daynes.
p.   cm.
Rev. and expanded ed. of: Social regulatory policy. 1988.
Includes bibliographical references and index.
ISBN 1-56324-993-6 (alk. paper).   ISBN 1-56324-994-4 (pbk. : alk. paper)
1. Public policy (Law)—United States. 2. United States—Social policy—Case studies.
3. Social norms—Case studies. 4. Civil rights—United States—Case studies.
5. Social values—United States—Case studies.   I. Tatalovich, Raymond.
II. Daynes, Byron W.   III. Social regulatory policy.
KF450.P8M67   1998
320.973—dc21   97-35839
CIP

Printed in the United States of America

The paper used in this publication meets the minimum requirements of
American National Standard for Information Sciences—
Permanence of Paper for Printed Library Materials,
ANSI Z 39.48-1984.

BM (c)   10   9   8   7   6   5   4   3   2   1
BM (p)   10   9   8   7   6   5   4   3   2   1

To our mentor,
Theodore J. Lowi,
who inspires us
as his teachings continue to guide us

R.T.
B.W.D.

Contents

— About the Editors and Contributors

RAYMOND TATALOVICH (Ph.D., University of Chicago) is a professor of political science at Loyola University of Chicago, where he specializes in American politics and the study of moral conflicts in public policy. Among his most recent publications are *The Politics of Abortion in the United States and Canada* (M.E. Sharpe, 1997) and *Nativism Reborn: The Official English Language Movement and the American States* (1995).

BYRON W. DAYNES (Ph.D., University of Chicago) is professor of political science at Brigham Young University. He has coauthored five books with Raymond Tatalovich (including Social Regulatory Policy, the precursor of the present collection) and written some fifty articles on the American presidency, public policy, and the Supreme Court.

THEODORE J. LOWI is John L. Senior professor of American Institutions at Cornell University.

GARY C. BRYNER is professor of political science at Brigham Young University.

MARGARET ELLIS is assistant professor of political science at James Madison University.

TED G. JELEN is professor of political science and chairman at the University of Nevada at Las Vegas.

ROBERT J. SPITZER is distinguished service professor of political science at State University of New York College at Cortland.

MARY ANN E. STEGER is professor of political science at Northern Arizona University.

BRENT S. STEEL is associate professor of political science at Washington State University in Vancouver.

RUTH ANN STRICKLAND is associate professor of political science and criminal justice at Appalachian State University.

List of Tables and Figures

Tables

Figures

Foreword

New Dimensions in Policy and Politics

Theodore J. Lowi

Public policy can be defined simply as an officially expressed intention backed by a sanction. Although synonymous with law, rule, statute, edict, and regulation, public policy is the term of preference today probably because it conveys more of an impression of flexibility and compassion than the other terms. But no citizen, especially a student of political science, should ever forget that *policy* and *police* have common origins. Both come from "polis" and "polity," which refer to the political community itself and to the "monopoly of legal coercion" by which government itself has been defined. Consequently, all public policies must be understood as coercive. They may be motivated by the best and most beneficent of intentions, and they may be implemented with utmost care for justice and mercy. But that makes them no less coercive.

There are multitudes of public policies because there are multitudes of social arrangements and conduct that people feel ought to be controlled by coercive means if public order is to be maintained and people are to be able to pursue their private satisfactions in peace. Consequently, some kind of categorization is necessary if meaningful policy analysis is to take place. If the editors and authors of this volume had a particular reason for inviting me to participate in their important project by the writing of this foreword, it was probably because I was young and foolish enough twenty-five years ago to attempt to provide a categorization of public policies and, somewhat

Figure 1. **Types of Coercion, Types of Policy, and Types of Politics**

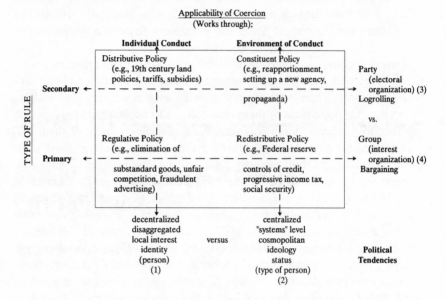

Applicability of Coercion
(Works through):

	Individual Conduct	Environment of Conduct	
Secondary	Distributive Policy (e.g., 19th century land policies, tariffs, subsidies)	Constituent Policy (e.g., reapportionment, setting up a new agency, propaganda)	Party (electoral organization) (3) Logrolling
			vs.
Primary	Regulative Policy (e.g., elimination of substandard goods, unfair competition, fraudulent advertising)	Redistributive Policy (e.g., Federal reserve controls of credit, progressive income tax, social security)	Group (interest organization) (4) Bargaining

TYPE OF RULE

decentralized disaggregated local interest identity (person) (1) versus centralized "systems" level cosmopolitan ideology status (type of person) (2)

Political Tendencies

Source: Adapted from Theodore J. Lowi, "Four Systems of Policy, Politics, and Choice," *Public Administration Review* (July-August 1972), p. 300.

later, to describe the logic underlying the categories. If there had been a second reason for involving me it was probably because they found the scheme uncomfortable as well as useful. In brief, I began the categorization with a simple question: If all policies are coercive, is it possible that we can develop a meaningful, small set of policy categories by asking a prior question of jurisprudence: How many kinds of coercion are there? Leaving aside the fine points of definition, I identified four logically distinguishable ways that government can coerce, and I then attempted to demonstrate, with some degree of acceptance in the field, that each of these types of coercion underlies a type of identifiable public policy. The source of each type of policy was, therefore, so close to state power itself that each, I reasoned, should be located in history and that each would, over time, tend to develop its own distinctive political structure. I was attempting to turn political science on its head (or back on its feet) by arguing that "policy causes politics."

The four categories were given the most appropriate names I could con-trive at the time: Distributive Policy (or as I have come more recently to call it, Patronage Policy), Regulatory Policy, Redistributive (and Welfare) Pol-icy, and Constituent Policy. (Figure 1 is the four fold formulation.) Lately I have grown accustomed to a modification of the names of the categories in order to emphasize the intimacy of the historical association between the type of policy and the type of politics that tends to be associated with it: The Distributive (or Patronage) State, the Regulatory State, the Redistributive (or Welfare) State, and the State within the state.

During the very decade (roughly 1964–1974) that these categories were being developed, the national government was going through a virtual second New Deal. There was an explosion of new regulatory and welfare programs. Although most of these new policies fit comfortably enough into the four fold scheme, there *was* something new about many of them that was not being captured by the scheme. Every scheme of categorization (of anything) sacrifices informational detail and nuance in order to gain analytic power, but is there a point where the sacrifice is too great? Students of these 1960s and 1970s policies referred to them as "new regulation," "social policy," and "social regulation" in order to convey an emerging sense that there is indeed something about these policies that does not fit comfortably into existing categories. Tatalovich, Daynes, and associates do a valiant job of trying to catch the meaning of the "new" and the "social" and why these policies somehow don't fit into any preexisting scheme. In the opinion of these authors, the only way to preserve the four-fold scheme is to add, in effect, a fifth category, which they call "social regulatory policy."

There is no need to take issue directly with the definition of this fifth category. I will try instead to *subsume* it. I recognize at the outset that there are cases of regulatory policy in my terms; if they don't seem to fit comfortably it is because the *politics* of the "new" or "social" regulation looks a lot more like what is to be expected with the politics of redistributive policy. The authors discover in their cases that the observed political behavior is more ideological, more moral, more directly derived from fundamental values, more intense, less utilitarian, more polarized, and less prone to compromise.

However, while granting these authors their empirical findings, I hesitate to create a new category to fit the findings until all ways of maintaining the four-fold scheme have been exhausted. This position is one part ego but at least four parts bona fide concern not to destroy the simplicity and, more importantly, the logic of the analysis. For one cannot solve the problem by merely adding a new category. Addition of a category weakens the logic altogether. The fifth category won't work entirely until its logic has been worked out and until a probable sixth is coupled with it to give the new scheme a reasonable symmetry.

In the spirit of trying to preserve the four-fold scheme and at the same time trying to give the new findings their due, I will try an alternative. Some people will agree with me that it is a way to preserve the four-fold scheme.

Others will say that I am being too accommodating and will destroy the four-fold scheme by turning it not merely into a six- or eight-fold scheme but in fact (as in Figure 4) into a twelve-fold scheme. Either way, the effort will enhance and dramatize the value of the case materials presented in this volume.

For several years I have shared with these authors a concern for how to make sense of the "new politics" of the public-interest groups on the left and the right in the United States and in Europe. Although these groups seem to be seeking policies that could be categorized as (largely) regulatory or redistributive, they refused to join what most of us would consider mainstream political processes, insisting instead on trying to convert political issues into moral polarities, claims into rights, legislation into litigation, grays into blacks and whites, and campaigns into causes and crusades. If there is confusion among analysts about all this, it is because there is an obvious, age-old fact that we have all been overlooking: that for every type of mainstream politics, there is a *radical politics*. Policies can remain the same, insofar as the type of coercion involved is regulatory, or redistributive, or whatever. But just as some mainstream strategies will pay off and some will not (giving each policy type its political distinctiveness) so will radicalization as a strategy sometimes pay off and sometimes will not pay off. When it does pay off, there is likely to be an intensification of all the political elements without necessarily transforming the patterns altogether. And, to repeat, the policy at issue can remain in the same category even as its politics is being radicalized.

Figure 2, a first step toward a new scheme, is an attempt to define radical in relation to mainstream in politics. The *Oxford English Dictionary* defines radical as "of or pertaining to a root or roots." That is also the meaning in mathematics and the origin of the term in politics. It is associated with extremes precisely because people who insist on getting to the root of things are likely to express themselves intensely, rejecting the rules and procedures designed to produce compromise—in other words, rejecting mainstream or ordinary politics. However, as soon as the two dimensions, radical and mainstream, are put side by side it becomes obvious that they are not a simple dichotomy because it is in the nature of radical politics to be so much more ideological that radicalism is at least dichotomous within itself. (I say "at least" because a full-scale analysis of radicalism would require more distinctions than the simple two needed here.) Ideology is not absent in mainstream politics, but lower intensity permits mainstream politicians to practice their skill, which is to obtain practical consensus on goals and to reduce differences to a point where political conflict becomes political competition, strategy becomes tactic, and compromise is possible because the

Figure 2. **Public Philosophy: Mainstream and Radical**

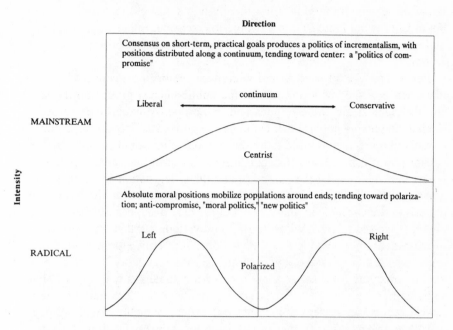

Direction

Consensus on short-term, practical goals produces a politics of incrementalism, with positions distributed along a continuum, tending toward center: a "politics of compromise"

continuum

Liberal ⟵————————————⟶ Conservative

MAINSTREAM

Centrist

Absolute moral positions mobilize populations around ends; tending toward polarization; anti-compromise, "moral politics," "new politics"

Left

Right

RADICAL

Polarized

Intensity

stakes are incremental. To the radical, mainstream means trivialization, and that is absolutely true. Figure 2 attempts to capture this evaluation for the mainstream by placing relevant ideologies on a continuum, with the concentration of positions towards the center, where the frontier between left and right is very fuzzy.

This is precisely where radicalism differs most: What is a rather fuzzy frontier for the mainstream is a formalized border between radicals of the left and the right. Intensity of commitment demands an underlying logic, and logic demands some degree of consistency, reinforced by a conscious affiliation. Positions are distributed accordingly, in what can best be illustrated in Figure 2 as a bimodal distribution. So consistently is radical politics polarized that this distribution has to be maintained in any diagrammatic analysis. (This is why in Figure 4 we go from four mainstream to eight radical categories.)

Figure 3 moves the analysis one step further by attempting to specify the general substantive orientations of the two dimensions. The basic four policy categories are maintained (across the top and extending through both Mainstream and Radical dimensions). The cells contain brief descriptions of the general political orientation for each of the eight resulting patterns. In this diagram, the left-right direction of ideology is disregarded for the sake

Figure 3. How Policy Problems are Defined in Mainstream and in Radical Politics

	Regulative (Policy toward conduct)	Distributive (Policy toward facilities)	Redistributive (Policy toward status)	Constituent (Policy toward structures)
MAINSTREAM	Control the *consequences* of conduct, consequences defined in purely instrumental terms. Orientation of the discourse is: ERROR	Goals defined instrumentally or denotatively, without a governing rule. Orientation of the discourse is: UTILITY	Class and status relations are specified but redistributive effect minimized by spreading benefits upward and obligations downward. Exclusiveness softened with equities. Orientation of discourse is: ENTITLEMENT	A process definition of the Constitution and rights; a representation definition of government; the good administrator is neutral, obedient to elected officials; decision by competition. Orientation of discourse is: ACCOUNTABILITY
RADICAL	Control of conduct as good or bad *in itself*; consequences defined in moral absolutes; stress particularly on bad conduct. The orientation of discourse is: SIN	Goals defined in terms of consequences but moral consequences, such as improvement of character (right) or defense against capitalism (left). The orientation of discourse is: CIVIC VIRTUE	Class and status relations are exclusive, imbedded in absolutes that transcend policy. Property rights (right) and welfare rights (left); social definitions of rights (left), individualist definitions of rights (right). Orientation of discourse is: RIGHTS	A substantive definition of the Constitution. Good government is commitment to a substantive definition of justice. The good administrator is committed to the program (left) or to good moral character (right). The orientation of discourse is: COMMITMENT

of simplicity, based on the assumption that even radicals can, in the words of Carl Friedrich, "agree on what to disagree about." A word of explanation is needed mainly for the concept in boldface. These were the best available words to connote the general orientation; the prose in each box is an effort to spell that out. Note, for example, the distinction between ERROR and SIN; this is an antinomy, which is intended to suggest how differently the two types view the same regulatory issue. The mainstream approach to regulation is as close to instrumental as human beings can get. Mainstream political actors avoid taking a moral posture toward the conduct to be regulated; conduct is to be regulated only because *it is injurious in its consequences*. Though privately the mainstreamer may consider prostitution immoral, the mainstream public position would be that prostitution should be regulated as to its potential for disease or its association with drugs and abduction. The radical would define the conduct moralistically; i.e., for the radical, conduct is to be regulated because *it is good or bad in itself*. From the radical left, prostitution is a sinful product of a sinful economic system; for the radical right it is a sinful expression of bad character. But radicals take a moral posture toward it while mainstreamers can take it as a conduct in need of modification. Regulation is itself a mainstream word, coming from the French, *régle* (rule), so that *réglementation* means "to impose rules upon" or to regularize. From the radical, moralistic standpoint, something like elimination would be a more accurate description.

There is no need to treat the three remaining categories too extensively, since the phenomenon of concern in their book is regulation. Suffice it to say that the boldface concepts in each of the categories were also selected as antinomies that distinguish most clearly between mainstream and radical discourse, with radicals of both sides agreeing with each other on what to disagree about. Thus, even on something as commonplace as distributive policy (patronage), radicals can be quite moralistic: Railroads should be public corporations because capitalism is bad; museums should be built because art is good. In contrast, for mainstreamers, the whole point of resorting to patronage policies is its UTILITY, its complete amorality; patronage policy is a way to displace conflict, not confront it. For redistributive policy, the near antinomy between ENTITLEMENT and RIGHTS should be close to self-evident. Description in the boxes might help marginally. The constituent policy categories may cause a bit more of a problem, but that need not be a burden for us here. The best way to think about this category is through the history of American approaches to the "good administrator." The mainstream ideal was the "common man"; the modern version of this is the individual trained in the appropriate skills but loyal to majority rule and to the elected representatives of that majority, presumably whatever the "goal." To the radical, majorities and skills are not irrelevant, but they are subordinate to character. Administrators are good if they are committed to virtue (on the right) or "program" (on the left).

We can now turn to Figure 4, the main point and purpose of this enterprise. Figure 4 combines features of Figures 1–3 and joins them to actual policy issues. The antinomies from Figure 3 are repeated in boldface to evoke (without space to be explicit) a sense of the political patterns to be expected.

Figure 4 is a variation on an earlier effort to make sense of environmental policies, which are so rich in "new politics."[1] Only one-quarter of the figure (the Regulatory column, therefore put first) is relevant to the cases in this volume, but the comprehensive (and I hope exhaustive) presentation in the figure makes a productive linkage to the findings in this book and puts these findings in an inherently comparative context.

I like this figure, as revised, not merely because it might preserve my scheme. It confirms my own confidence that policy categorization (not necessarily mine) will in the long run be the route to the new political theory because it arises out of some fundamental political truths: (1) that there are inherent limits to the ways a state can control society, no matter how powerful that state my be; (2) that each of these ways is so fundamental that it has enough of a history and a regularity to become in itself a kind of regime; and (3) that every regime tends to produce a politics consonant with itself. This particular effort has perhaps added a fourth truth: that political leaders can radicalize politics by adding a moral dimension to policy. Radicalizing the policy (i.e., adding the moral dimension) will almost certainly change the political patterns, but even radicalized political patterns will probably vary according to the particular policy category (regime) in question.

Since Tatalovich, Daynes, and associates have concentrated on the regulatory category, I will hold my elaboration of this now two-dimensional scheme to the regulatory quadrant alone. But this should not mask the fact that if we had cases here of radicalized policies in, say, the redistributive category, the political pattern, though radicalized, would probably differ from the pattern observed in the radicalized regulatory cases.

Virtually all regulatory policy, as we know it from the familiar economic regulatory programs of the national government, approaches conduct in an almost purely instrumental way. It arises largely out of concern for conduct deemed good or bad *only in its consequences.* (See Figure 4, upper left corner.) The very term regulation or regulatory policy, as suggested above, became the term of choice by lawyers, economists, and policymakers because the goal of most of these policies is not so much to eliminate the

Figure 4. **Policies and Politics in Two Dimensions**

POLICY TYPE

DIMENSION OF POLITICS	1 Regulatory	2 Distributive	3 Redistributive	4 Constituent
MAINSTREAM	**ERROR** Standards of conduct Economic sector regulation Regulation to maintain competition Regulatory taxes Licensing to enforce standards	**UTILITY** Public works Defense installations and stockpiling R & D Sales of public property or access to it Unconditional licensing	**ENTITLEMENT** "Social costs" Income taxation Economic policy through the tax system ("tax expenditure") Social Security Monetary policies	**ACCOUNTABILITY** "Causal theory" Liberal, value-free education Policies restricting state action Administrative reform for neutral, scientific decisionmaking
RADICAL	**SIN** **Left** Right to results of regulation (suits to force regulation) Cost-oblivious economic regulation Affirmative action Capitalism as morally suspect **Right** Right to public order & self-defense Regulation for moral guidance Victimless crimes Capitalism as a moral good	**CIVIC VIRTUE** **Left** Public ownership of essential service Displacement of corporate power Planning for national use of resources Convert distributive to redistributive **Right** Public works for private market Subsidies to industry for the public good Convert distributive to moral regulation	**RIGHTS** **Left** Progressive income taxation exclusively Anti-wealth taxes (estate, luxuries, etc.) Welfare as a right **Right** Sales taxes and other regressive taxes exclusively Punitive taxes ("sin" taxes to discourage alcohol, tobacco, etc.) Welfare as a moral lesson	**MORAL GOVERNMENT** **Left** "Class theory" Socialization education Bill of Rights (complete nationalization) Participatory democracy (judicially enforced) Programmatic administrator Party executive **Right** "Obligation theory" Moral education State rights Republicanism ("rightly understood") Good administrator Commander-in-chief executive

conduct in question but to reduce it, channel it, or otherwise constrain it so that the conduct might persist but with fewer of the injuries (or in some instances, more of the benefits) attributed to it. But there is another whole reality of regulatory policies, and those policies are concerned with conduct *deemed good or bad in itself* (lower left corner in figure). Call the first C_1 and the second C_2. The first type, instrumental regulation, will be abbreviated as C_1. The second, moral regulation, will be referred to as C_2. Most C_2 regulation in the United States has escaped the recent attention of most political scientists (until this volume) because it has been the province of state government. Examples include the criminal law, all the sex and morality laws, most family and divorce laws, the basic compulsory education laws, and the fundamental property laws. The intrinsic moral orientation of this kind of policy accounts also for the fact that state politics in the nineteenth century (when most of these policies were being enacted as a matter of positive, statute law) was far more radical, often violent, than the politics of regulation at the national level. But note well, the descriptions of state politics will reveal that they were dominated not by political parties but by interest groups and movements. Some of those interest groups engaged in mainstream politics—lobbying, bargaining, and compromise like the interest group patterns we associate with the national government. But those groups engaged in "direct-action politics," "single-issue politics," and "social movement politics" to a far greater extent than is found at the national level, except during the epoch of what we now are calling "new politics."

In contrast, the regulatory policies at the national level have not only been quite recent (most of them dating from the New Deal) but have been almost exclusively of the C_1 type. To repeat, the politics is mainstream—dominated by organized interest groups and engaging in lobbying and all the patterns associated with pluralism—and, in a word, regulatory. However, it is an obvious point, though made significant within the context of the cases and my Figure 4, that this standard type of national regulatory policy *can be radicalized by the addition of moral* (C_2) *considerations*.

An example of radicalization by degree would be civil rights, and specifically the 1964 Civil Rights Act. Going back to Abraham Lincoln, I do not think that anyone was more committed to the idea that slavery was a moral evil, but Lincoln's *first* effort to emancipate the slaves was "compensated emancipation," where he was going to float a large bond issue to buy the slaves their freedom, thereby reducing the issue to an instrumental one that would permit normal political treatment. Slaves would get their freedom and slave owners would convert *slavery as capital* into plain old ordinary money.

Almost a century later, the ironic thing about *Brown v. Board of Education* is that the Supreme Court, under the wisdom of Chief Justice Warren, tried their best to ward off the radicalizing aspects of what they were deal- ing with. People who have never read *Brown* would be surprised at how instrumental and nonmoral (i.e., how mainstream liberal) the Supreme Court argument was. The Court avoided denouncing legal segregation as a moral evil, even though all of them agreed that it was. What they did instead was to deal with the problem *instrumentally*. Segregation was de- clared unconstitutional because it was inherently unequal, and it was inher- ently unequal because of the *effect it was having on the black children in the schools*. Note how they turned it into an instrumental argument, an argument about consequences, not about good and evil.

Now consider the 1964 Civil Rights Act. Most of the titles were by and large of the C_1 type. Following the spirit of *Brown v. Board of Education*, Congress reasoned that separate schools and public facilities and separate criteria of employment were inherently unequal in their consequences, un- constitutional because they gave minorities a badge of inferiority and tended to render minority individuals in actual fact unequal in their ability as well as their opportunity to enjoy what society had to offer.

Although this same utilitarian, C_1 rationale, was sufficient to win a con- gressional majority in favor of the historic 1964 Act, it was far from the full argument the civil rights movement itself was making. Happy as the move- ment was to have such a historic law, the leaders of the movement had good reason to be frustrated by the public debates and by the modesty of the message and the sanctions in the regulatory provisions of the Act. The *moral* case against all forms of discrimination was overwhelming, and there was equally strong moral justification not only for stronger and more unilat- eral sanctions eliminating all discrimination but also for more direct com- pensatory policies to overcome the effects of past discrimination—in other words, affirmative action. This amounts, as the critics say, to positive and group discrimination that contradicts the individualist definition of rights as comprehended by the Constitution and also contradicts the explicit wish of Congress, as expressed, for example, in the following passage from the employment provisions (Title VII) prohibiting "preferential treatment to any individual or group . . . on account of an imbalance which may exist with respect to the total or percentage of persons of any race, color, religion, sex, or national origin. . . ." The civil rights movement (note the form: a movement) sought what amounted to a radicalization of the civil rights laws and, if not the laws, the implementation of the laws by the agencies and courts. To the extent that civil rights policy embodied a moral dimension, it both reflected and contributed to a "new politics"—the politics of morality, of movements, of polarization, and of what the authors in this book call "social regulatory policymaking."

Though *Brown* itself was not radical, it is precisely the rights orientation triggered by *Brown* that contributed to the radicalization of politics in the 1960s, and would have done so even if there had been no Vietnam War. In many respects, that is a desirable contribution to politics, but it is tragic in that it can so quickly be carried too far, undermining politics and therefore interfering with precisely the outcomes the rights movement seeks. The main function of politics is to trivialize demands, while the main need of a movement is to intensify demands. These have to come into some kind of balance, but we have to understand the nature of radicalization in politics so that we can fear it even as we deal with it.

Many of the same persons who have decried what I have described here as the radicalization of civil rights share responsibility not only for radicalizing the opposition to civil rights but also for radicalizing other important policies in other subject matter areas. Thus, anything can be radicalized, depending on how the issue is defined. A good example of this is the effort of environmentalists to convert environmental protection into a great moral cause. There have been a number of instances where they succeeded in defining an environmental or ecological issue in moral terms, and they definitely radicalized the politics to that extent.

Another example is the early history of AIDS. Tremendous credit goes to C. Everett Koop and the Public Health Service for their role in redefining AIDS as a social and policy problem. When it was first diagnosed and associated with homosexual life-styles, it was immediately given a moral definition. That has been true of most new diseases that become epidemics, treated as a visitation from God. It has been the wonderful role of the public health profession to redefine diseases in order to remove the moral stigma. The best case in our lifetime is AIDS. Removing the moral stigma also removed much of the radicalization of the politics surrounding efforts to make policies toward AIDS treatment, AIDS research, AIDS prevention. AIDS is a perfect case of radical politics, as seen by the effort to de-radicalize. Redefining the disease removed the moral stigma, which removed much of the radicalization of the politics surrounding efforts to make policy toward AIDS treatment, AIDS research, and AIDS prevention. The consequence of this was to deradicalize a particular definition and a particular demand flowing from it.

Although the list is longer than the cases in this volume, all the cases here belong to such a list. And note well the several following characteristics of these cases:

1. Each C_2 policy had once been the almost exclusive province of state government power;

2. Each policy experienced radical politics almost any time the issue got on state policy agendas, in the nineteenth or the twentieth centuries;
3. All but gun control were removed altogether or in substantial part from state jurisdiction by the Supreme Court;
4. Each in recent years was then nationalized altogether or in substantial part.

Thus, none of the politics flowing from these issues was "new." If the politics appeared new, it was relatively new merely to the *national* government. All of the laws and proposals in these cases qualify as "social" in that their focus and preoccupation were not on economic activities as such, even when companies and employers were the main objects of regulation. But now we can get a better sense of what people have been trying to convey by calling policies new or social. If people only meant that these policies were non-economic, that wouldn't add much to our understanding of policies *or* politics.

Although all the issues in this volume involve sociological conflicts at their core, economic as well as non-economic policies can become radicalized by moralistic fervor. A better distinction that lends more light to policy is between moral and instrumental. The fact is that the national government, in its effort to regulate things, dealt with problems that were fairly patently economic problems and economic issues. But having said that, that only helps to explain why and how the politics of these issues was most often instrumental. The regulated parties tried their best to make moral issues out of this, by accusing the national government of communism, or by talking about property rights that are being infringed upon. But they fairly quickly lost this battle, because most of the people, including their colleagues, began dealing with this material instrumentally. So it doesn't really matter for analytic purposes whether the policy dispute involves so-called economic or non-economic substance.

If we take *social* to indicate that the policy is aiming at the moral base of conduct, then we have opened an entirely new dimension or have put an old dimension into a new and more useful context. That is at least what I intend to convey by the concept of radicalization. George Will, a self-defined man of the right, provides the distinction between mainstream and radical that I am striving for here: "In a famous opinion in a famous case . . . Justice Felix Frankfurter wrote: 'Law is concerned with external behavior and not with the inner life of man.' I am not sure what Frankfurter meant. I am sure what he said cannot be true. The purpose of this book is to say why that proposition is radically wrong."[2] Taken in moderation, Will's position may be mainstream, simply toward the far right of the mainstream continuum.

But embraced to the fullest extent, by our taking Will literally on the desirability of using law to reach "the inner life of man," the continuum becomes a circle, turning downward toward the radical half of Figures 2, 3 or 4. But note well that moral, C_2, considerations can also be introduced from the left, pushing the left side of the continuum in a circular turn downward toward radicalization. In the world of morality and radicalization, the left and the right are a unity of opposites, together as one, logically and empirically apart from the mainstream.

This formulation will, I hope, make a contribution to theory in political science in at least three ways. First, it may make cases like the ones in this volume more interesting and significant by rendering their findings more cumulative, due to their demonstrated membership in a common framework. Second, introduction of the second dimension of policy may contribute to overcoming a long-standing embarrassment in political science: our difficulty in dealing with political radicalism in U.S. history except as something exceptional, sporadic, and temporary. Radical politics is as regular as mainstream, even if less frequent. Some policies are radical from the start, but any area of policy can be radicalized. It depends upon the way the policy or policy proposal is constructed and the severity of the sanctions provided.

Third, success on the first two points would be good for theory in political science. But my hopes expressed in this third point are even more ambitious. Taking away the "new" from the so-called new politics could lead to a richer sense of the historic relation between society and the state in the United States. Radical elements are inevitable in a society as dynamic as ours, and the society would be less healthy and less productive without the radical. The question for the study of political development is how radicalized forces interact with governmental institutions, whether they are channeled into progressive changes, and how they make a place for themselves within the constitutional structure. Was the U.S. system lucky or successful in the great transition through the New Deal to the "Second Republic"?[3] Everyone will agree that the Depression had radicalized an unusually large segment of U.S. society. Yet, it is clear from this analysis that most of the New Deal policies were of the C_1 type. Imagine, if possible, what the outcome would have been if the radicalized groups and movements of the 1930s had succeeded in radicalizing the policies. If there had been in the 1930s a large number of cases at the national level like the cases in this volume, we would not be talking here about the political system as it is today.[4]

Tatalovich, Daynes, and their colleagues have given us not only cases and findings, but more. They have provided an agenda for a new policy analysis appropriate to the new politics.

Notes

1. Theodore J. Lowi, "The Welfare State, The New Regulation and the Rule of Law," in Allan Schnaiberg et al., *Distributional Conflicts in Environmental Resource Policy* (London, England: Gower Publishing Co., Ltd., 1986), p. 113. My thanks to Schnaiberg for suggesting, albeit for different purposes, the first antimony between error and sin.

2. George Will, *Statecraft as Soulcraft* (New York: Simon and Schuster, 1983), p. 20.

3. A formulation of mine in *The End of Liberalism* (New York: W.W. Norton, 1979).

4. A more extended version of the latter pages of this revised foreword will be found in Theodore J. Lowi, *The End of the Republican Era* (Norman, OK: University of Oklahoma Press, 1995), and that book owes a lot to the original version of this foreword.

Introduction

Social Regulations and Moral Conflict

Raymond Tatalovich and Byron W. Daynes

In a now classic article, Theodore J. Lowi argued that government enacts three different types of economic policy: distributive policy (government subsidies), regulatory policy (government controls on business), and redistributive policy (government welfare programs).[1] Later he added a fourth type, constituent policy, by which Lowi meant changes in the political system itself (for example, the current movement to impose term limits on legislators likely qualifies as constituent policy).[2]

Lowi did not attempt to describe policies that erupt from moral conflicts, which led T. Alexander Smith to define yet another policy of "emotive symbolism," which "generate[s] emotional support for deeply held values, but unlike the other [Lowi] types . . . the values sought are essentially noneconomic."[3] In our early study of abortion, we originally used the term *lifestyle* to characterize why that conflict was grounded in a debate over values, not economics, though at the time we believed that moral conflicts represented a "variant" of regulatory policy making as described by Lowi.[4] Moral conflicts, we still believe, are policies (1) based on noneconomic values, (2) which are politicized by single-issue groups, and (3) where the federal judiciary, notably the Supreme Court, is the primary decision maker.

We then hypothesized in the first edition of this work, and here, how moral conflicts affect policy making insofar as the judicial, legislative, and executive branches, plus the federal bureaucracy, states and localities, interest groups, and public opinion, interact to formulate and implement "social" regulations.[5] The term *regulation,* as Lowi employed it, is generally associated with government controls on businesses, from the auto industry to the stock market, that stimulate or restrict competition, protect the consumer and worker, and ensure a stable legal environment for economic transactions. With "social" regulations, what is being regulated is not an economic transaction but a social relationship. But changing social relationships may give rise to demands from citizens that legal authority be used to affirm the traditional normative order, or modify it, or sanction entirely new standards of behavior.

In our previous volume we argued that the federal judiciary was the key policy maker because aggrieved citizens bent on changing social norms would petition the courts on civil rights and liberties grounds. We assumed that legal authority would be an agent for change in society. While we still largely adhere to that belief, the current debate over enacting "official English" laws illustrates once again how concerned citizens may also resort to legal sanctions to affirm traditional values. Thus we offer this slightly altered definition of social regulatory policy: *the exercise of legal authority to affirm, modify, or replace community values, moral practices, and norms of interpersonal conduct.*

Status Anxiety and Identity Politics

Sociologist Neil Smelser defines one type of collective behavior as the "norm-oriented" movement that attempts "to restore, protect, modify, or create norms" by people who "demand a rule, a law, a regulatory agency, designed to control the inadequate, ineffective, or irresponsible behavior of individuals."[6] Such movements are generated by four types of structural "strain" in society, of which two seem especially relevant to our analysis: (1) disharmony between existing normative standards and actual social conditions and (2) real or apparent loss of wealth, power, or prestige by groups.

The first would seem to be a prerequisite for activating groups that promote social change. When people who were socially disenfranchised develop group consciousness and become organized, the politics of identity has commenced. It is unlike the normal course of American politics, as Button, Rienzo, and Wald explain: "Identity politics is rooted in groups based on 'race, ethnicity, gender and sexuality' rather than the traditional group divisions associated with politics—economic classes, interest groups, industries, labor unions, and the like."[7] The case studies in this volume on abortion, gay rights, affirmative action, and official English are the purest examples of identity politics by women, homosexuals, African-Americans, and Spanish-speakers. Contemporary usage reserves the concept of identity politics for change-oriented groups who attack the normative status quo. But some of the constituencies who now engage in identity politics at one time were latent interests (what pluralist David Truman called "potential" groups) that were not formally organized for political action.[8] Here feminism comes to mind.

Smelser's second type of "strain" seems to give rise to "status anxiety," which often is manifested in single-issue politics. The National Right-to-Life Committee, Morality in Media, and U.S. English are single-issue groups who believe that our traditional values with regard to abortion, obscenity, and language are under siege, just as the National Rifle Association can be viewed as representing a gun culture at odds with modernity. There also can be latent interests that cling to traditional norms but have not counterorganized. The so-called angry white man opposed to racial quotas represents a potentially huge latent interest regarding affirmative action.

During the 1950s social scientists believed that people with psychological insecurities and without social ties to established institutions were attracted to radical causes and charismatic leaders offering solutions to what such people perceived to be harmful changes in society.[9] At that time historian Richard Hofstadter joined a group of sociologists to first apply the term *status politics* to explain the rise of the radical right and popular support for Senator Joseph McCarthy's (R-WI) anti-Communist crusade.[10] But that concept originated with Max Weber's distinction between status groups, "communities based upon the sharing of similar claims to social honor and prestige," and social classes, which have "similar economic capacity to command scarce resources and life chances."[11]

Studies have linked status anxieties to many social issues, including some considered here. Gusfield applied status theory in researching the Women's Christian Temperance Union.[12] Analysis of antiobscenity campaigns led to the conclusion that "a primary function of the symbolic crusade is to provide those individuals whose life style is being threatened by social change with a way to reinforce that style."[13] Status politics explains why some people opposed the Equal Rights Amendment[14] and may account for periodic anti-immigrant "nativist" outbursts over the course of U.S. history.[15]

Status theory is also applied in research on religious fundamentalism. A study of the Kanawha County, West Virginia, textbook controversy found that "the protestors are adherents of a life style and world view which are under threat from . . . the educational system, the mass media, the churches—fundamentally from every socialization agency beyond their immediate control which impinges on their lives."[16] Moen agreed that "[p]eople support prayer because they are religious, but even more so because they see in modern society a threat to their cherished values and their established way of life."[17] Wald, Owen, and Hill showed that "status discontent proved to be a significant predictor of orientation to the Christian Right," although status anxiety alone may not be enough unless accompanied by mobilizing forces:

> To suggest that contemporary moral reform movements can be explained solely by resentment over social devaluation ignores both the proximate causes of discontent and the additional mechanisms necessary to channel it toward political action. The resentment may grow out of deeply-held social values inculcated in traditionalist environments, may be articulated and channeled by entrepreneurial elites with ties to evangelical churches, and may become part of a more generalized conservative syndrome. That combination of factors showed up in our analysis in the manifold paths of influence leading to NCR [New Christian Right] support. Whatever the role of status discontent, it does not provide a complete explanation for the strength of moral reform movements.[18]

Nor does status anxiety necessarily explain why public opinion is generally conservative on social regulations. It stretches the imagination to believe that status insecurities preoccupy the thinking of the majority of citizens who express traditional values when asked about religion, capital punishment, official English, and racial quotas. However, status anxiety may be relevant as a mobilizing force for single-issue activists who emerge to defend community norms.

America is in the midst of profound social change, says Ronald Inglehart, who argues that all industrial societies will experience a "culture shift" from materialistic values to such postmaterialist values as belongingness and self-actualization as industrialization fades.[19] In this new milieu, economic conflicts will be displaced by issues such as civil rights, environmental protection, alternative lifestyles, and peace. A less optimistic scenario about the postindustrial era is posited by Scott Flanagan, who says that new social cleavages may emerge between "the New Left issues agenda, including liberalizing abortion, women's lib, gay rights and other new morality issues" and "the New Right issue agenda, which includes right-to-life, anti–women's lib, creationism, antipornography, and support for traditional moral and religious values. . ."[20]

The political dangers inherent in moral conflicts always pose a challenge to our system of government; abolitionism and Prohibition rocked the nation to its philosophical foundations. However, they were exceptional episodes from the normal course of policy making; looking ahead, the past may not be prologue. Moral conflicts over social regulation, or any public policy, may become endemic in the postmaterialist society of the twenty-first century, and the preface by Theodore J. Lowi warns us that moral discourse can radicalize any and all types of policy.

Notes

1. Theodore J. Lowi, "American Business, Public Policy, Case Studies, and Political Theory," *World Politics* 16 (July 1964), pp. 677–715.

2. Theodore J. Lowi, "Four Systems of Policy, Politics and Choice," *Public Administration Review* 32 (July-August, 1972), pp. 298–310. Among the other scholars who applied Lowi's typology to economic and foreign policies are Robert J. Spitzer, *The Presidency and Public Policy: The Four Arenas of Presidential Power* (University: University of Alabama Press, 1983) and his "Promoting Policy Theory: Refining the Arenas of Power," *Policy Studies Journal*, vol. 15 (June 1987), pp. 675–689; William Zimmerman, "Issue Area and Foreign-Policy Process," *American Political Science Review* (December 1973), pp. 1204–1212; Randall B. Ripley and Grace A. Franklin, *Congress, the Bureaucracy, and Public Policy*, 5th ed. (Belmont, CA: Wadsworth Publishing Company, 1991).

3. T. Alexander Smith, *The Comparative Policy Process* (Santa Barbara, CA: Clio Press, 1975), p. 90.

4. Raymond Tatalovich and Byron W. Daynes, *The Politics of Abortion* (New York: Praeger, 1981).

5. Raymond Tatalovich and Byron W. Daynes, *Social Regulatory Policy: Moral Controversies in American Politics* (Boulder, CO: Westview, 1988).

6. Neil J. Smelser, *Theory of Collective Behavior* (New York: Free Press, 1962), pp. 270 and 109.

7. James W. Button, Barbara A. Rienzo, and Kenneth D. Wald, *Private Lives, Public Conflicts: Battles over Gay Rights in American Communities* (Washington, DC: CQ Press, 1997), p. 5.

8. David B. Truman, *The Governmental Process: Political Interests and Public Opinion* (New York: Alfred A. Knopf, 1960), p. 506.

9. William Kornhauser, *The Politics of Mass Society* (Glencoe, IL: Free Press, 1959).

10. Richard Hofstadter, "The Pseudo-Conservative Revolt" and "Pseudo-Conservatism Revisited," in Daniel Bell, ed., *The Radical Right* (New York: Doubleday Anchor, 1964), pp. 75–103. This collection of essays was an expanded and updated version of Daniel Bell, ed., *The New American Right* (New York: Criterion, 1955).

11. Max Weber, *Economy and Society* (New York: Bedminster, 1968), pp. 302–307, 901–940. Also see Gerard A. Brandmeyer and R. Serge Denisoff, "Status Politics: An Appraisal of the Application of a Concept," *Pacific Sociological Review* 12 (1969), pp. 5–11.

12. Joseph R. Gusfield, *Symbolic Crusade: Status Politics and the American Temperance Movement* (Urbana: University of Illinois Press, 1963).

13. Louis A. Zurcher Jr., R. George Kirkpatrick, Robert G. Cushing, and Charles K. Bowman, "The Anti-Pornography Campaign: A Symbolic Crusade," *Social Problems* 19 (Fall 1971), p. 236.

14. J. Wilbur Scott, "The Equal Rights Amendment as Status Politics," *Social Forces* 64 (December 1985), pp. 499–506.

15. John Higham, "Another Look at Nativism," *Catholic Historical Review* 44 (July 1958), pp. 151–152.

16. Ann L. Page and Donald A. Clelland, "The Kanawha County Textbook Controversy: A Study of the Politics of Life Style Concern," *Social Forces* 57 (September 1978), p. 279.

17. Matthew C. Moen, "School Prayer and the Politics of Life-Style Concern," *Social Science Quarterly* 65 (December 1984), p. 1070.

18. Kenneth D. Wald, Dennis E. Owen, and Samuel S. Hill Jr., "Evangelical Politics and Status Issues," *Journal for the Scientific Study of Religion* 28 (1989), pp. 13–14.

19. Ronald Inglehart, *Culture Shift in Advanced Industrial Society* (Princeton, NJ: Princeton University Press, 1990).

20. Scott C. Flanagan, "Changing Values in Industrial Societies Revisited: Towards a Resolution of the Values Debate," *American Political Science Review* 81 (1987), p. 1306.

Moral Controversies
in
American Politics

1

Abortion: Prochoice versus Prolife

Ruth Ann Strickland

January 22, 1998, marked the twenty-fifth anniversary of the watershed decision *Roe v. Wade*. Seven of the nine original *Roe* justices have died or retired, which may result in modification or even reversal of this controversial decision. The plaintiff, Norma McCorvey, who authored a book titled *I Am Roe*, quit her job at a Dallas abortion clinic in 1995, was born again, joined Operation Rescue, and now serves as a poster child for prolife advocates. The landmark *Roe* decision leaves behind unanswered questions such as "When does life begin?" and "When should the fetus be given the chance to develop and thrive?" It pushes society to ponder reproductive privacy, the degree of bodily integrity guaranteed to women, and the extent to which abortion is an individual right necessary for self-actualization. The abortion issue divides people into seemingly irreconcilable camps—"those who sponsor family values and life" versus "those who champion civil liberties and choice."

Arguably *Roe*, by subverting the normal political process (i.e., not allowing the prochoice and prolife forces to battle for support and legitimacy of their proposals on a state-by-state basis), may have prompted a "tidal wave of abortion restrictions."[1] The framing of the issue as a "right" also may have undercut an emerging consensus that favored abortions for therapeutic or medical purposes. There is no doubt, however, that the trimester formula in the *Roe* ruling opened the door to the viability issue and intensified the moral debate over when a fetus becomes a person and therefore obtains due-process rights. Because the issue has been framed in the United States as a question of a woman's right to bodily integrity and privacy versus a

3

fetus's right to life, common ground and compromise in the political arena have been almost impossible to attain. Prochoice and prolife forces still battle at the state and federal levels of government over the abortion issue.

Historical Evolution of the Abortion Issue

Abortion was not considered an offense under either Roman or Catholic canon law. Throughout most of the 1800s there were no national legal restrictions on obtaining an abortion in the first few months of pregnancy. The standard of "quickening" (or the first notice of fetal movement by a pregnant woman) was used to determine whether abortion was permitted in any given case. Common law throughout most of the nineteenth century did not recognize fetal rights in criminal prosecutions until quickening.[2]

The quickening standard became controversial in 1821 when Connecticut—a predominantly Catholic state—enacted the first statute making abortion illegal after quickening. Missouri (1825), Illinois (1827), and New York (1828) followed suit, but New York's law was unique by its "therapeutic" qualification, legalizing abortions necessary to save a mother's life. Sixteen more states adopted restrictive abortion laws between 1830 and 1849, mostly making abortion a crime after quickening. Maine's law made any method of abortion a crime except if the mother's life was in danger.[3] During the period between 1840 and 1870, estimates hold that there was one abortion for every five to six live births. Abortion was a highly visible, frequently performed, commercial procedure from 1800 through 1870.[4]

A chilly climate toward the abortion procedure was created during the mid-nineteenth century by the medical community, which mobilized to oppose abortion on moral grounds and fears that abortions were not being performed safely.[5] The American Medical Association lobbied against abortions obtained without a physician's designation that the abortion was "therapeutic."[6] Dr. Horatio Storer, an obstetrician and gynecologist, led a movement to criminalize all abortions and eventually persuaded the AMA to pass a resolution in 1859 that urged state legislatures to forbid all abortions. As a result, most abortions were outlawed in most states during the Civil War period.[7] Abortions were permitted only if, in the opinion of the physician, a woman's life was at stake. Ten states required the concurring opinion of a second physician.[8]

In 1873 Congress passed the Comstock Act, which aided and abetted the antiabortion agitation. This law contained various antiobscenity provisions but also included a ban on any drug, medicine, or object that could be used for abortion or contraceptive purposes being transported in the mails and a prohibition on mailing advertisements of such items.[9] In effect, the Comstock Act stifled dissemination of information and discussions about birth control or abortion.

The historical record is important to the modern abortion controversy, especially the rationales offered for why antiabortion restrictions emerged. According to prochoice advocates and some feminists, antiabortion laws were the culmination of a separatist ideology that sought to promote homemaking as a full-time vocation, particularly among middle-class women. This perspective is supported by estimates purporting that by 1900 it was unwed lower-class women or immigrant wives who sought and obtained abortions, not married, middle-class, Protestant women.[10]

One prolife viewpoint is that abortions were banned in order to save women from themselves. Early surgical abortion procedures exposed women to risks, and possibly death. Another prolife argument rests on the desire to protect not only the mother but the fetus, holding that under the Fourteenth Amendment the unborn had due-process rights.[11] Still another perspective held that antiabortion laws were the result of concerns over falling birthrates as well as public and medical community disgust at the commercial spectacle and large profits earned from performing abortions.[12]

Once federal and state antiabortion laws were in place, a period of quietude reigned from 1900 through 1950, at least on the surface of the American social and political landscape. Data on illegally obtained abortions during this period suggest that women continued to obtain abortions at roughly the same rate, despite the newly enacted restrictions.[13] During the 1950s, U.S. hospitals established abortion committees to process requests for abortions and to designate whether, in the judgment of the physician, the abortion was necessary to save the mother's life.[14] In 1955 Planned Parenthood sponsored a conference on abortion, promising to keep the event "quiet." For the first time since the criminalization of abortion, physicians and other professionals who attended the conference called for repeal of existing laws and reforms that would make "therapeutic" abortion a matter between patient and physician.[15]

In 1959, one year after the Planned Parenthood conference proceedings were published, the American Law Institute (ALI), alarmed by illegal abortions in unsanitary conditions and deaths in the "back alley," proposed legalized abortions when the physical or mental health of the mother was at stake or where the child would be born with serious physical or mental defects.

The case of Sherry Finkbine in 1962 further highlighted problems with existing antiabortion laws. Finkbine, an Arizona mother of four, chose to have an abortion after learning that the drug thalidomide, which she had taken early in her pregnancy, caused gross birth defects. She asked an

Arizona hospital to provide her an abortion (the hospital had routinely allowed such abortions in the past under a liberal interpretation of Arizona's abortion statute). Because her story made the headlines in newspapers across the country, the local prosecutor threatened the assisting physician with arrest, and subsequently the hospital canceled the surgery. Also in 1962, in Grove, Oklahoma, Dr. W.J. Bryan Henrie was convicted of a crime—performing abortions—and was sentenced to two years in jail. After serving his sentence, Dr. Henrie began a solo campaign to liberalize abortion laws.[16]

In the mid-1960s, Lawrence Lader, author of a book on Margaret Sanger, started pushing for abortion law reform. Two prochoice groups—the Association for the Study of Abortion (New York–based) and the Parents' Aid Society—were created in 1964. Patricia Maginnis, founder of the Society for Humane Abortion (based in San Francisco) in 1965, advocated repeal of all abortion restrictions and sought to place women rather than physicians in control of the abortion decision rather than physicians. Maginnis also established an underground operation that reportedly sent thousands of women to Mexico, Japan, Sweden, and other less hostile environments for abortions.[17]

In 1968 the National Association for the Repeal of Abortion Laws was formed (originally known as the New York Abortion Rights Action League and later becoming the National Abortion Rights Action League, or NARAL). In the late 1960s the liberalization movement began to develop a national base of support. In 1967 the National Organization for Women adopted a plank demanding the right of women to control their reproductive capacities and repealing restrictions on access to abortion. In March 1968 the American Civil Liberties Union (ACLU), a national interest group, also called for the repeal of all criminal abortion laws. The Planned Parenthood Federation reversed its earlier position and gave its full endorsement of abortion rights in 1969.

The liberalization movement resulted in eighteen states reforming their original antiabortion statutes. Beginning in 1966 Mississippi added rape as another therapeutic exception. In 1967 Colorado was the first state to adopt the American Law Institute guidelines proposed in 1959. North Carolina and California adopted the ALI model shortly thereafter. By 1972 fourteen other states had liberalized their abortion laws, with some going beyond therapeutic abortions and simply making abortion an elective procedure (Table 1.1). Instead of basing those reform laws on a woman's right to bodily integrity or a right to privacy, the early reformers justified the changes on "health" grounds (saving the life or preserving the mental or physical health of the mother).[18]

Roe v. Wade, 410 U.S. 113 (1973), galvanized the prolife movement.

Table 1.1

States Reforming Original Antiabortion Laws, 1966–1872

Year	State
1966	Mississippi
1967	Colorado
1967	California
1967	North Carolina
1968	Georgia
1968	Maryland
1969	Arkansas
1969	Delaware
1969	Kansas
1969	New Mexico
1969	Oregon
1970	Alaska*
1970	Hawaii*
1970	New York*
1970	South Carolina
1970	Virginia
1970	Washington*
1972	Florida

Source: Raymond Tatalovich and Byron W. Daynes, *The Politics of Abortion: A Study of Community Conflict in Public Policymaking* (New York: Praeger, 1981), p. 24.

Note: An asterisk indicates that a state repealed its original antiabortion law and made abortion an elective procedure.

The National Right to Life Committee was founded in Detroit in June of 1973, and the National Conference of Catholic Bishops (NCCB) issued a statement that any Catholic involved in any phase of abortion would be excommunicated. The NCCB also supported a constitutional amendment to outlaw abortion. The U.S. Catholic Conference funded and created the National Committee for a Human Life Amendment for that objective.[19] Following *Roe,* prolife organizations sprang up around the country in every state. Every year on January 22, the anniversary of *Roe,* prolife groups still march on the Capitol steps, carrying signs and making speeches.

Judiciary

When the Supreme Court in *Griswold v. Connecticut,* 381 U.S. 479 (1965), struck down that state's law banning the sale of birth control information and devices, it ruled that a right to privacy could be inferred from a penumbra of several guarantees found in the Bill of Rights. The right to privacy, therefore, was created implicitly by the First Amendment's freedom-of-association provision, the Third Amendment's ban on forced quartering of soldiers in private dwellings, the Fourth Amendment's protection from unreasonable searches and seizures, the Fifth Amendment's prohibition of coerced confessions, and the Ninth Amendment's guarantee that rights not specifically mentioned in the Constitution might still exist.

The first abortion ruling by a federal court occurred in the 1969 case of *United States v. Vuitch* (305 F. Supp. 1032 D.D.C.). Judge Gehard Gesell found the therapeutic exception phrase void for vagueness and held that the state had no compelling interest in regulating abortions. At the same time, Judge Gesell urged the government to appeal his decision, which it did. In 1971 *United States v. Vuitch* (402 U.S. 62) was the first abortion decision of the U.S. Supreme Court. Unlike the lower courts, the Supreme Court upheld the District of Columbia's abortion statute, clarified the meaning of a mother's life and health to include not only her physical well-being but also her psychological well-being, but declined to pronounce that abortion was a fundamental right.[20]

Roe v. Wade

The central question in *Roe* was the constitutionality of the 1857 Texas statute that criminalized abortion except to save a woman's life. Justice Harry Blackmun, writing for the majority, declared the statute unconstitutional and ruled that the right to privacy encompassed a woman's decision to end her pregnancy—in effect establishing a constitutional right to abortion. Blackmun devised a trimester formula that would be used to balance these competing interests. In the first trimester (three months) of pregnancy, the abortion decision is left to the medical judgment of the woman's attending physician in consultation with his patient. In the second trimester, the state may regulate the abortion procedure in the interest of the mother's health. During the third trimester, when fetal viability is an issue, the state may regulate or even prohibit abortions to protect the life of a fetus and may allow abortions when necessary to protect the life or health of the mother.[21]

Roe struck down forty-six state laws and superseded the repeal laws in the other four states. By issuing this sweeping decision, the Court began national debate and forever changed political discourse about this issue. It mobilized the right-to-life movement and temporarily lulled prochoice proponents into a false state of security. It shifted the locus of responsibility on abortion policy to the federal government and Washington, and by the 1980s all three branches of government would be embroiled in the issue.[22]

From Roe to Webster (1973–1989)

Including *Roe,* nineteen abortion cases reached the Supreme Court through 1989.[23] With the exception of four rulings that allowed governments to ban public funding and use of public facilities for abortions—*Beal v. Doe* (1977), *Maher v. Roe* (1977), *Poelker v. Doe* (1977), and *Harris v. McRae* (1980)—the Court has conceded very little to prolife interests. The fundamental underpinnings of *Roe* remain intact.

When the Court decided *City of Akron v. Akron Center for Reproductive Health,* 462 U.S. 416 (1983), it involved the most restrictive city ordinance of any municipality in the nation. This ordinance mandated that all second- and third-trimester abortions be performed in a hospital; unmarried minors under age fifteen obtain parental consent or a court order before obtaining an abortion; physicians give all patients antiabortion information, including telling them that "the unborn child is a human life from the moment of conception"; patients must wait twenty-four hours after this lecture before obtaining an abortion; and physicians must dispose of fetal tissue and remains in an unspecified "humane and sanitary manner." By a 6–3 vote, the Court struck down all these provisions, holding that no city or state regulation could "interfere with physician-patient consultation or with the woman's choice between abortion and childbirth." In particular, the requirement that second- and third-trimester abortions be performed in hospitals was struck down as an unreasonable infringement on a woman's right to an abortion, placing undue hardships and costs on her.[24]

Three years later the Court, in *Thornburgh v. American College of Obstetricians and Gynecologists,* 476 U.S. 747 (1986), voted 5–4 to strike down a Pennsylvania statute that required physicians: to give patients antiabortion information including pictures of fetuses at various stages of development; to publicly identify the attending physician and provide information about the woman obtaining an abortion; to use a degree of care necessary to preserve the life and health of any unborn child in a postviability abortion that would favor the life of the fetus at a risk to the mother's health; and the mandated presence of a second physician in postviability abortions except in a medical emergency.[25]

However, some restrictions have been allowed. For example, the Court has ruled that under certain circumstances a state may require a minor woman to get parental permission or notification before obtaining an abortion (*Bellotti v. Baird [I],* 428 U.S. 132 [1976]; *H.L. v. Matheson,* 450 U.S. 398 [1981]; *Planned Parenthood Association of Kansas City, Mo. v. Ashcroft,* 462 U.S. 416 [1983]). Also, the Court upheld restrictions on public funding of abortions at both the state and federal levels when there was no threat to the health or life of the mother (*Poelker v. Doe,* 432 U.S. 519 [1977]; *Harris v. McRae,* 448 U.S. 297 [1980]). The Court has also affirmed requirements that a second physician be present during a postviability abortion and provisions that require physicians to perform second-trimester abortions in a licensed hospital (which includes outpatient hospitals) to promote the health of women obtaining abortions (*Planned Parenthood Association of Kansas City, Mo. v. Ashcroft,* 462 U.S. 416 [1983]).

The pivotal case, *Webster v. Reproductive Health Services,* 492 U.S. 490 (1989), gave prolife activists hope that the Court might reverse *Roe.* An abortion clinic challenged a Missouri statute that banned the performance of abortions in public institutions, even when the woman paid for her abortion. This restrictive law also included a preamble that declared that life began at conception, a regulation that required physicians to conduct viability tests prior to performing abortions, a two-parent notification requirement for minors with a procedure for judicial waiver, a forty-eight-hour waiting period for minors, and a prohibition on public funding of abortion counseling. By upholding the viability testing and the prohibition on the use of public facilities or public personnel in the performance of abortions, the Court moved away from strict scrutiny and toward Justice O'Connor's "unduly burdensome" standard, which she articulated in *Akron* and *Thornburgh.* For the first time since 1973, only a minority of Supreme Court justices—four—voted to reaffirm *Roe.*

From **Webster** to **Madsen** *(1989–1994)*

Webster, reflecting a change in Court composition and sending a signal to state governments that the Court would consider abortion restrictions that did not strictly meet controlling judicial precedents, "refederalized" abortion. In only a short period of time (July 1989 to July 1990), 351 bills were introduced in state legislatures about abortion policy.[26] *Webster* energized prolife advocates, while prochoice proponents feared its repercussions.[27]

In 1990 two related cases were heard, *Hodgson v. Minnesota,* 497 U.S. 417 (1990), and *Ohio v. Akron Center for Reproductive Health,* 497 U.S. 417 (1990), which dealt primarily with the issue of a parental notification requirement for minors. Both rulings, by a vote of 5–4 and 6–3 respectively, upheld parental notification requirements as long as a procedure for judicial waiver existed. By 1989, thirty-one states had passed legislation requiring teenagers under age eighteen to either notify their parents before getting an abortion or obtain parental consent. These decisions validated the movement in the states toward parental involvement in a minor's abortion decision, and the 1992 case of *Planned Parenthood of Southeastern Pennsylvania v.*

Casey, 505 U.S. 833 (1992), in which the Court upheld a one-parent consent requirement for minors with a judicial bypass, gave further legitimacy to state parental involvement regulations. As of May 1996, twenty-eight states enforced these mandatory parental involvement laws. In 1997 the Supreme Court upheld a Montana parental notification law that required an unmarried minor to notify one parent forty-eight hours before having an abortion. A judge could grant a waiver if convinced that the minor is mature enough to make the decision on her own or if notification would harm her best interests.[28]

In 1991 the Court entered another abortion dispute. The Reagan administration imposed a gag rule that banned any discussion of abortion in federally funded family planning clinics, even if a woman's health or life was at stake. Later President Bush instructed his solicitor general, Kenneth Starr, to defend the gag rule, which was challenged in 1991 by a physician at a clinic receiving federal money. About four thousand clinics receive Title X money, and millions of women depend on these clinics for health care and family planning information. In another 5–4 vote on an abortion issue (but this time intermingled with freedom of speech), the Court upheld the gag rule, arguing that Congress's intent on whether to allow such funding was vague.

In 1992 *Casey* presented another possible challenge to *Roe.* Under the disputed Pennsylvania Abortion Control Act, additional restrictions were placed on abortion, including a mandatory twenty-four-hour waiting period, parental consent, spousal notification, an informed-consent provision, and reporting/public disclosure requirements. Although the Rehnquist Court reaffirmed the central holding in *Roe,* upholding all the provisions except spousal notification, it explicitly overruled the *Akron* and *Thornburgh* cases and abandoned strict scrutiny in favor of the less stringent "undue burden" standard.

Prolifers blockading entrances to abortion clinics (so-called abortion rescues) in addition to threatened or actual violence led prochoice advocates to strike back with federal lawsuits and injunctions, claiming that these tactics violated the civil rights of women who try to obtain abortions.[29] A coalition of prochoice groups—NOW, Planned Parenthood of Metropolitan Washington, and several Virginia abortion clinics—filed suit under the Ku Klux Klan Act of 1871 and 42 U.S.C. Sec. 1985(3), which was enacted to prevent conspiratorial efforts to deny any group their civil rights. In *Bray v. Alexandria Women's Health Clinic,* 506 U.S. 616 (1993), the plaintiffs argued that the KKK Act should be used to stop clinic blockades by Operation Rescue and the Bray family. Under the KKK Act, however, plaintiffs had to show that the defendants acted with "class-based, invidiously discriminatory animus." In its 5–4 decision, the Supreme Court held that the act did not protect women from prolife health clinic blockades and, further, that the prolife blockades did not constitute sex-based discrimination.[30]

Prochoice activists turned to another statute that they hoped would curtail clinic blockades—the Racketeer Influenced and Corrupt Organizations (RICO) Act. Originally enacted by Congress in 1970, it prohibited racketeering by employees or associates of any enterprise. In *National Organization for Women v. Scheidler,* 510 U.S. 249 (1994), NOW and two women's health care centers argued that the defendants (a coalition of antiabortion groups called Pro-Life Action Network, and Joseph Scheidler) had conspired to engage in illegal activities (including intimidation, bombings, vandalism, and other violent acts) aimed at putting the health care centers out of business, in violation of RICO. The defendants contended that Congress intended RICO to apply only to profit-seeking ventures and that application of RICO to their activities would violate their First Amendment rights. By a vote of 9–0, the Court rejected the defendants' claims and allowed NOW and a group of women's health centers to pursue civil suits against the clinic blockaders under RICO.[31]

Madsen v. Women's Health Center, 114 S.Ct. 2516 (1994), further limited the activities of antiabortion protesters. *Madsen* specifically addressed a state judge's injunction prohibiting antiabortion protesters from blocking or obstructing access to an abortion clinic in Melbourne, Florida; congregating, picketing, or demonstrating within thirty-six feet of the property line of the clinic; approaching within a three-hundred-foot radius of the clinic any person seeking its services or its staff; physically abusing, harassing, or crowding persons trying to leave the clinic; and threatening any clinic personnel.[32]

In its 5–4 decision, the Supreme Court upheld parts of the Florida injunction including the thirty-six-foot buffer zone and prohibitions on noisemaking by antiabortion protesters that was disruptive and could be heard by patients in the clinic during hours in which surgical procedures were performed. Justices Kennedy, Thomas, and Scalia dissented vigorously, claiming that "the judicial creation of a 36-foot zone in which only a particular group, which has broken no law, can not exercise its rights of speech, assembly, and association, and the judicial enactment of a noise prohibition, applicable to that group and that group alone, are profoundly at odds with our First Amendment precedents and traditions."[33]

Of twenty-six major abortion cases to reach the Supreme Court between 1972 and 1994, twenty-four were split decisions, and seven of these were 5–4 decisions. The number of splintered decisions indicates the lack of consensus on the Court about abortion policy and also reflects a change in Court composition. Vacancies on the Supreme Court enabled Presidents

Reagan and Bush to alter the Court's composition and mold it to suit a prolife agenda.

Reagan's first opportunity arose in 1981 with Sandra Day O'Connor, who had a prolife reputation and replaced Justice Potter Stewart (who had voted with the majority in *Roe*). Two years after Reagan's reelection, Warren Burger retired and Reagan was able to nominate Associate Justice William H. Rehnquist to replace him; to fill Rehnquist's vacancy, Reagan subsequently nominated a conservative Roman Catholic, U.S. Court of Appeals Judge Antonin Scalia.[34] Later in 1988 Reagan replaced Lewis Powell with Anthony M. Kennedy. In 1990 President George Bush was able to appoint David Souter to replace William Brennan—a core supporter of abortion rights. Although Souter refused to comment on his views on abortion during his confirmation hearing, prochoice advocates avidly opposed his appointment. Still, he was easily confirmed. When Justice Thurgood Marshall resigned during the 1990–1991 term of the Court, President Bush nominated Clarence Thomas, an African-American conservative with decidedly prolife views.

[handwritten margin notes: Sandra Day had o prolife rep; Antonin Scalia; Thomas prolife]

However, when Justice Byron White (who dissented in *Roe*) retired in 1993 at the beginning of President Bill Clinton's first term, he was replaced by Judge Ruth Bader Ginsburg. Ginsburg specifically stated in her confirmation hearings that the right to privacy was central to a woman's dignity and abortion was a decision a woman should make for herself. Stephen Breyer—another Clinton appointee—ascended to the Court in 1994 upon Harry Blackmun's retirement and took a judicially restrained position. When Strom Thurmond of the Senate Judiciary Committee asked him about the constitutional status of abortion rights, Breyer responded by stating, "That's the law."[35]

[handwritten margin notes: Ginsburg; Blackmun]

Although the Rehnquist Court under Reagan and Bush was decidedly more conservative than the Warren Court and demonstrated a willingness to modify or even overturn *Roe,* the election of Bill Clinton to the presidency in 1992 and 1996 and his subsequent appointments to the Court may stymie efforts aimed at significantly reversing abortion rights. A splintered Court may be the wave of the future. Note that a 5–4 prolife majority upheld abortion restrictions in the 1989 *Webster* case but, with new justices today, a 5–4 prochoice majority placed restrictions on antiabortion protesters in the 1994 *Madsen* case (Table 1.2).

Public Opinion

Since 1965 national public opinion polling on abortion has been frequent. The National Opinion Research Center (NORC) has asked a set of ques-

Table 1.2

Votes on Key Abortion Cases: Impact of Changes in Supreme Court Makeup

Justices	1973 Roe PC	PL	1983 Akron PC	PL	1986 Thornburgh PC	PL	1989 Webster PC	PL	1994 Madsen PC	PL
Burger	X		X			X	—		—	
Brennan	X		X		X		X		—	
Marshall	X		X		X		X		—	
Stewart	X		—		—		—		—	
Blackmun	X		X		X		X		—	
Powell	X		X		X		—		—	
Douglas	X		—				—		—	
Stevens	—		X		X		X			X
Rehnquist		X		X		X		X	X	
White		X		X		X		X	—	
O'Connor	—			X		X		X	X	
Scalia	—		—		—			X		X
Kennedy	—		—		—			X		X
Souter	—		—		—		—		X	
Thomas	—		—		—		—			X
Ginsburg	—		—		—		—		X	
Breyer	—		—		—		—		X	

Note: PC = a prochoice vote; PL = a prolife vote; a dash indicates that this justice was not on the Court to render a decision.

tions about whether a woman should be able to obtain abortion under six different circumstances. From 1965 to 1973 support for access to abortion in all categories grew, with much more approval for abortions when a woman's health is at stake, the pregnancy resulted from rape, or the baby might be born with a serious defect. Support leveled off in the mid- to late 1970s and declined slightly during the 1980s. Yet by the 1990s the trend reversed and support picked up slightly again.[36] Support of abortion for any reason rose to 39 percent by 1982, fell to 37 percent in 1988, and peaked in 1990 at 42 percent (Table 1.3).

Some polls have been framed bimodally and ask: "In general, do you favor or oppose the U.S. Supreme Court decision making abortions up to three months of pregnancy legal?" In 1969 40 percent of those interviewed favored abortion, while 50 percent were opposed. Eighteen years later, in a 1986 Gallup poll, with virtually the same question being asked, 45 percent said yes, 45 percent said no, and 10 percent held no opinion. By 1989, at the time of the *Webster* ruling, 56 percent favored *Roe* and

Table 1.3

Public Support for Abortion Under Certain Circumstances

Percentage of Respondents Favoring the Right to an Abortion Under the Following Circumstances

	1965	72	73	74	75	76	77	78	80	82	84	85	87	88	90	96
Mother's Health	71	83	91	90	88	89	88	88	88	89	87	87	85	89	89	82
Rape	56	74	81	83	80	80	80	80	80	83	77	78	85	81	81	77
Fetal Defect	55	74	82	84	80	82	83	80	80	81	77	76	77	78	78	54
Low Income	21	46	52	52	51	50	52	45	50	50	44	42	43	42	45	32
Unmarried	18	41	47	48	46	48	47	39	46	47	43	40	40	40	43	—
No More Children	15	38	46	45	44	45	44	40	45	46	41	39	40	40	43	—
Any Reason	—	—	—	—	—	—	36	32	39	39	37	36	38	37	42	—

Sources: National Opinion Research Center (NORC) data; General Social Surveys; Gallup Report, February 1989. Selected years of data are reported in Raymond Tatalovich, *The Politics of Abortion in the United States and Canada: A Comparative Study* (Armonk, NY: M.E. Sharpe, 1997), p. 112. Data for 1996 was drawn from the *Gallup Poll Monthly*, August 1996, p. 32.

42 percent opposed it, with only 2 percent undecided (Table 1.4).

Another way to divide public opinion is to ask respondents whether abortion should be legal under any circumstances, legal under certain circumstances, or illegal under all circumstances, or whether they are undecided or have no opinion on this issue. When framed this way, opinions on the abortion issue appear much more moderate, with 50 percent or more of respondents supporting abortion under certain circumstances from 1975 through 1996. These data, combined with the NORC polls, suggest that support for therapeutic abortions has increased or remained stable. When socioeconomic reasons are cited, however, the public is more reluctant to give approval, although in 1990 and 1991 support for nontherapeutic abortions increased slightly (Table 1:5).

Recent trends in public opinion do not bode well for parts of the prolife agenda. After the *Rust v. Sullivan* decision was issued in 1991, 74 percent of Americans indicated opposition to the ruling by favoring the right of the doctor to advise his patient over the ability of government to withhold financial aid in order to dictate policy.[37] In 1996 a majority of Americans considered themselves prochoice (53 percent) rather than prolife (39 percent). As a single-issue factor in the voting decisions of Americans, abortion's saliency has declined, with just 16 percent saying they would vote only for a candidate who shares their views on abortion, and a majority (51 percent) saying that they consider a candidate's position on abortion as just one of many important factors when voting.[38] Opposition to a constitutional amendment to ban abortions has fluctuated, with 49 percent opposing such an amendment in 1976, 71 percent opposing it in 1981, and 56 percent opposing it in 1984.[39] Twelve years later, in 1996, by a margin of 59 percent to 38 percent, respondents opposed a constitutional amendment to ban abortion.

The prolife activists may be heartened by the fact that an overwhelming majority (71 percent) in 1996 opposed "partial birth" or late-term abortions. Similarly, large majorities supported under-eighteen parental consent, twenty-four-hour waiting periods, and spousal notification provisions. Eighty percent supported a law requiring doctors to inform patients about alternatives to abortion before performing the procedure.[40] Because opinion toward abortion has been relatively stable and coherent, policymakers do not have to worry about erratic shifts and unpredictability.

Interest Groups

The debate about abortion, a decades-long struggle, is characterized by the rhetoric of war.[41] The *Roe* decision did not bring a truce; instead, it simply

Table 1.4

A Bimodal Distribution of Public Opinion on Abortion

Year	Favor	Oppose	No Opinion/Not Sure
1969	40%	50%	10%
1972	46%	45%	9%
1973	52%	41%	7%
1974	47%	44%	9%
1976	60%	31%	9%
1981	56%	41%	3%
1985	50%	47%	3%
1986	45%	45%	10%
1989	56%	42%	2%

Sources: Gallup Reports, 1969, 1972, 1974 and 1986; Harris Poll, 1989. Question asked: "In general, do you favor or oppose the U.S. Supreme Court decision making abortions up to three months of pregnancy legal?"

redefined the rules of engagement. The abortion debate in the 1990s is still largely defined by the prolife and prochoice advocates rather than by public opinion.

Prochoice Coalition

Consisting of a loose coalition of women's groups, health care associations, local abortion reform and repeal groups, population movement activists, religious denominations, and traditional "liberal" groups, the movement was overawed by the sweeping rulings in *Roe* and *Doe*. Before becoming well organized or even powerful, the prochoice movement paradoxically had already won one of its most coveted victories.[42]

Prior to 1973, local single-issue groups (e.g., the Association for the Study of Abortion and the Abortion Rights Association of Illinois) dominated the movement initially. Eventually, however, single-issue groups combined with multi-issue organizations to create the National Association for the Repeal of Abortion Laws. Support from established organizations such as Planned Parenthood and the American Civil Liberties Union was crucial, since these larger groups possessed badly needed institutional expertise on how to lobby Congress.

After the *Roe* decision, liberal Protestant churches such as the Presbyterian and United Methodist churches, reformed Jewish synagogues, and a splinter group of Catholics joined the prochoice cause. In 1973 the Religious Coalition for Reproductive Choice (formerly known as the Religious

Table 1.5

Multimodal Distribution of Opinion on Legal Conditions for Abortion

Percentage of Respondents:

	1975	77	79	80	81	83	88	89	90	91	92	93	94	95	96
Legal under any circumstances	21	22	22	25	23	23	24	28	31	33	33	32	33	31	25
Legal under certain circumstances	54	55	54	53	52	58	57	51	53	50	51	51	51	53	58
Illegal under all circumstances	22	19	19	18	21	16	17	17	12	33	33	32	13	12	15

Source: Gallup Reports as reported in Neil Nevitte, William P. Brandon, and Lori Davis, "The American Abortion Controversy: Lessons from Cross-National Evidence," *Politics and the Life Sciences* 12 (February 1993), p. 21. The 1993 data are from *Gallup Poll Monthly* (April 1993), p. 38, and the 1994–1996 data are from *Gallup Poll Monthly* (August 1996), p. 31.

Coalition for Abortion Rights) was formed largely in response to efforts aimed at overturning *Roe v. Wade*. By 1995, thirty-eight Protestant, Jewish, and other faith groups in more than fifty state and local affiliates had organized to explain to the public and elected officials how abortion could be a moral and religiously responsible decision. Catholics for a Free Choice (CFFC)—also formed in 1973—supports family planning and abortion, contrary to the position of the Catholic Church.

The American Civil Liberties Union (ACLU) and the National Organization for Women (NOW) have taken a leadership role in defending abortion rights. The Reproductive Freedom Unit of the ACLU, founded in 1973, makes protection of the right to privacy and reproductive choice its primary purpose. NOW first called for abortion rights in 1967, but the *Webster* ruling caused a rejuvenation of activity by women's groups, including the 1990 Freedom Caravan for Women's Lives—a state-by-state campaign to bring in volunteers and promote prochoice candidates in the 1990 elections. A spin-off organization of NOW, the Feminist Majority (and Feminist Majority Fund) is a multi-issue organization generally oriented toward getting women in positions of power. Its lobbying seeks to end various abortion restrictions, such as parental notification, and spearheads the National Clinic Defense Project, which seeks to protect abortion and family planning clinics from antiabortion activities.[43]

Medical interest groups have also gotten involved, as the American College of Obstetricians and Gynecologists (ACOG) supports legal, safe, accessible, and publicly funded abortions. The Planned Parenthood Federation of America has also run prochoice television ads. Medical Students for Choice, founded in 1995, encourages medical students to become abortion providers.[44] The National Abortion Federation (NAF), founded in 1977, is an association of abortion providers that issues fact sheets and collects data on incidents of violence and disruption against abortion providers.

Founded in 1969, the National Abortion Rights Action League (NARAL) is the premier prochoice single-issue national organization. With a grassroots network of thirty-five state affiliates and half a million members nationwide, it is also the largest organization devoted entirely to defending abortion rights. In 1993 it was ranked among the top three effective lobbying groups on Capitol Hill in the O'Leary/Kamber Reports.[45] NARAL has done much to professionalize the prochoice movement by hiring staff, using paid political consultants, engaging in polling, and employing technologies, such as focus groups, normally used by political parties.[46]

In general, the prochoice coalition has viewed the federal judiciary as an ally in the battle to protect reproductive freedom. A study of federal district court abortion cases decided between 1973 and 1990 reveals that involvement of prochoice interest groups in the case increases the probability that the judges will enter a prochoice decision. Abortion litigation on the prochoice side is dominated by civil liberties groups (especially the ACLU) and Planned Parenthood. These groups have a much higher success rate than other organizational litigants in federal district court, with civil liberties groups prevailing in 87 percent of the cases they participated in and Planned Parenthood winning in 82.4 percent of its cases.[47]

Prochoice Arguments

Central to the prochoice movement is the idea that decisions about abortion should be a private matter between physician and patient. Therefore, women should be allowed to terminate an unwanted pregnancy without external interference, not because abortion is desirable but because it is important to their privacy. They accuse their opponents of trying to substitute the judgment of clergy or governmental officials for that of women and their physicians.

Prochoice feminists put forward the "container" or "vessel" argument, which dismisses the claim that an embryo is a person. Putting fetal rights before those of the woman who carries the fetus makes the woman a second-class citizen. To elevate the fetus to "independent" personhood is to ignore the interdependency between mother and fetus. The fetus therefore is a part of her body, not a mere inhabitant ready to come out and survive under any conditions. The fetus also affects her health. When the rights of the fetus are elevated above the mother's rights, a woman may be asked to sacrifice her health and well-being for the survival or well-being of another.

Prolife Lobby

Prolife interest groups are more single-issue-oriented, focusing almost entirely on abortion, unlike the prochoice coalition, which has garnered the support of more multi-issue interest groups.[48] Unlike the prochoice coalition, which was led by secular interest groups, the Roman Catholic Church spearheaded the right-to-life movement and used the National Conference of Catholic Bishops (NCCB) to organize the National Right to Life Committee (NRLC). The Mormon Church and Southern Baptists have consistently opposed abortion. Christian evangelicals were first mobilized by the Christian Action Council, founded by Billy Graham in 1975, and Dr. C. Everett Koop, later appointed as surgeon general by President Reagan. By 1978 the Moral Majority (consisting primarily of Christian evangelicals and led by Jerry Falwell) made its presence felt, pouring money into congressional races and distributing "family ratings" on members of Congress. Among Falwell's top goals was a constitutional amendment that would ban abortion.

In 1989 Moral Majority closed down due to declining revenues, but it was quickly replaced by the Christian Coalition, led by televangelist Pat Robertson, who used his *700 Club* viewership to further the Christian Coalition's political goals as well as his own presidential aspirations. The Christian Coalition's political savvy became crystal clear in the 1992 and 1996 Republican National Conventions, when they weighed in on the abortion issue and prevented prochoice Republicans from moderating the anti-abortion plank.[49]

Medical prolife groups also surfaced. The American Association of Pro Life Obstetricians and Gynecologists (AAPLOG) was begun in 1973 by Dr. Matthew J. Bulfin to try to persuade their colleagues to oppose abortion. Doctors for Life, founded in 1978, consists of physicians who believe that human life begins at conception and refuse to participate in or assist in abortions or euthanasia.

The first national, nonsectarian prolife organization was founded in 1971—the Americans United for Life Legal Defense Fund. Devoted to defending human life, it has engaged in vigorous educational campaigns. In addition to this, it provides legal defense counsel to parties who seek to protect prolife laws and testifies in support of prolife legislation. It also drafts model state legislation that contains numerous abortion restrictions, and it writes and files amicus curiae briefs for submission to the Supreme Court and lower courts.[50]

The largest and most recognized prolife organization is the National Right to Life Committee (NRLC). With over three thousand local chapters, it has played a leading role in securing the passage of restrictive abortion laws from state legislatures across the country. Affiliate groups created from the NRLC include the National Right to Life PAC (formed to elect prolifers to public office), American Victims of Abortion, Black Americans for Life, and National Teens for Life.

Frustrated by the slow, incremental change that occurred through traditional NRLC lobbying efforts and by the steady abortion rate, new antiabortion groups emerged in the late 1970s and mid-1980s. Operation Rescue National, the Pro-Life Action League (PLAL), and the Prolife Nonviolent Action Project (PNAP) began the practice of abortion "rescues"—protesters sing and pray, creating human blockades that give prolife counselors a chance to dissuade women from either entering the clinics or obtaining abortions. Modeled on civil disobedience, over twenty-nine thousand prolife advocates were arrested between 1987 and 1991. These prolife extremists believe that the only way to end abortion is to put abortion providers out of business.[51]

By 1994 more-radical prolife activists called the killing of doctors and staff who participated in providing abortion services justifiable homicide, and a year later disgruntled Operation Rescue members splintered and formed their own organization, the American Coalition of Life Activists. This group began to target for violence and intimidation well-known physicians who performed abortions. In the 1990s the well-publicized murders of Michael Griffin, David Gunn, George Tiller, John Britton, James Barrett, Shannon Lowney, and Leanne Nichols, committed by antiabortion zealots, created a backlash against the prolife movement, prompting legislative and judicial action. As of 1997, the prolife movement has not completely recovered from the public relations debacle as well as the prochoice victories that followed.[52]

Between 1973 and 1990 prolife litigation in federal district courts was sporadic (with 10 percent of cases involving a prolife group, as opposed to 65 percent with a prochoice group). During that period federal district courts adopted a prolife position in only 23 percent of abortion cases. In comparison to prochoice groups, prolife organizations are less professionalized, have fewer resources and allies, and tend to be one-shotters.[53]

Prolife Arguments

Prolifers believe that the life of a baby begins long before birth and that a new human being is growing in the womb from the moment of fertilization. They support their belief that the fetus is a human life with medical facts. For instance, at six weeks, there are brain waves; at ten to eleven weeks, the fetus is sensitive to touch; one nineteen-week baby born prematurely survived. They believe this proves that the fetus is a living being, a person.[54]

By comparing abortion to genocide and slavery, they depict abortion as a threat to basic American values. If abortions continue, they believe, it will lead to an anchorless, godless society with no "family values."[55] Abortions not only subvert the sanctity of life but inflict "moral pain" on antiabortionists, who are "horrified by the death of unborn children, disgusted that other persons are committing acts that their religion regards as mortal sins, or fear that legal abortion will reduce their numbers, significance and influence of their racial group."[56]

The National Right to Life Committee flaunts statistics showing that from 1973 through 1996 over thirty-five million Americans have been legally "killed."[57] To support their stance they cite scripture, such as "Thou shalt not murder" (Exodus 20:13) or "Whoever shed man's blood, by man his blood shall be shed, for in the image of God, He made man" (Genesis 9:6). Pope Pius IX in 1869 declared that the fetus, "although not ensouled, is directed to the forming of man. Therefore, its ejection is anticipated homicide." Consequently, he prohibited abortions under all circumstances.[58]

Prochoice/Prolife Activists

There is only a small number of intense activists on each side of the abortion debate. Twenty-two percent of prolife advocates view abortion as critical to their vote, while only 12 percent of prochoice voters feel this strongly about the abortion issue. Still, 34 percent of those committed prolifers intended to vote for Bill Clinton, a prochoice candidate, while 15 percent of prochoicers, who said the issue was critical to them, indicated they would support prolife candidate Bob Dole.[59]

In a study of California abortion activists, prolife activists were more likely to be politically inexperienced and were predominantly women homemakers (63 percent). In contrast, 94 percent of female prochoice activists worked outside the home.[60] Antiabortion activists, then, had more time for letter writing, picketing, and other grassroots activities.[61] This demographic difference gives abortion opponents a grassroots mobilization advantage.

Presidency

Abortion has been a partisan issue between Democrats and Republicans officially since 1976, when the party platforms began to take opposing stances. The Democratic party is captured by prochoice interests and the Republican party is controlled by prolife interests when the party planks are written on abortion.

Before *Roe,* President Nixon in 1971 asserted that abortion on demand and as a method of population control was unacceptable and that "the unborn have rights also." His Democratic presidential opponent, George McGovern, countered that abortion was a private matter between a woman and her physician. After *Roe,* abortion became a more salient issue, and in 1976 it played a more prominent role in presidential politics. Although both Gerald Ford and Jimmy Carter preferred to ignore the issue, repeated questions on the campaign trail forced them to address it. Both gave fence-straddling responses, with Ford opposing abortion on demand and favoring state control of the procedure, but also recognizing the need for it in exceptional cases. Carter, a born-again Christian, personally opposed abortion and federal funding for abortions but also opposed any constitutional amendment to overturn *Roe*. The 1976 party platforms reflected the tentative steps each party was taking toward polarization. The Democratic party acknowledged the divisive religious and ethical nature of the issue but opposed any effort to overturn *Roe*. The Republican party endorsed a position on abortion that valued human life and supported the efforts of those who sought a constitutional amendment to protect the unborn. These murky responses were not very satisfying to the prolife or prochoice advocates.[62]

During Carter's presidency, an ambivalent attitude toward abortion prevailed as Carter tried to placate prochoicers and prolifers. He did not make any attempts to reverse *Roe* (which offended prolife interests), but he opposed federal funding of abortion (which put off prochoice groups). Carter was challenged by Edward Kennedy (a prochoice advocate) in the primary. Ronald Reagan, on the other hand, aggressively supported the antiabortion position, taking a hard-line prolife stance. The party platforms diverged more sharply in 1980 with the Democrats supporting *Roe* and rejecting any constitutional amendment to restrict or overturn it and the Republicans favoring a constitutional amendment to protect the unborn and restrictions on federal funding of abortion. By 1984 the parties were absolutely polarized, as Republicans in their platform recognized for the first time that the unborn have a fundamental right to life and Democrats recognized reproductive freedom as a fundamental human right.[63]

Reagan transformed the abortion debate. His administration tried to reverse *Roe,* screened candidates for federal judgeships and nominated prolifers to those positions, and enacted restrictive regulations that affected the availability of abortions. Although Reagan promoted the prolife agenda, some have argued that his rhetoric did not match his actions. Abortion was not a priority item early in Reagan's presidency, and only later, in his second term, did Reagan issue the gag rule on abortion counseling and limit funding of organizations and clinics that performed abortions.[64] His successor, George Bush, was initially prochoice, but during his election bid in 1988, following in Reagan's footsteps, he called for the criminalization of abortion. Michael Dukakis, his Democratic opponent, defended abortion rights. Both party platforms remained diametrically opposed on the abortion issue.[65]

Bush defeated Dukakis and basically continued the Reagan administration policies. He looked to the federal courts for more abortion restrictions, and his Justice Department filed an amicus curiae brief in the *Webster* case, asking the Court to use it as a vehicle for overturning *Roe*. In 1990, however, after President Bush delivered a message to antiabortion protesters on the anniversary of Roe, his press secretary told reporters that Bush's views were personal and based on his conscience and that the Republican party was big enough to accommodate varying points of view. Lee Atwater, then Republican national chairman, relayed a similar sentiment when he spoke to the Republican National Committee by stressing his commitment to an umbrella party that would allow both sides of the abortion issue to coexist.[66]

In 1992 George Bush faced Bill Clinton, who stressed his moderate "new Democrat" values. In 1992, in contrast to 1976, 1980, and 1984, all the Democratic candidates for the presidency were prochoice. Clinton and Gore carefully controlled their convention, going so far as to prevent Governor Robert Casey (D-PA), a prolifer, from making an antiabortion speech to the convention. The Democratic party platform more forcefully backed *Roe* and supported the right to choose regardless of ability to pay. The Republican party national convention, although well orchestrated, was inundated with the remarks from favorites of the Christian Coalition and the extreme right wing of the party. In sharp contrast to the Democratic party platform, the GOP platform adamantly opposed abortion and reaffirmed support for a human life amendment.

When Clinton sought reelection in 1996, he was opposed by Republican Bob Dole, who faced a field of several primary challengers for the nomination. Ironically, in 1974 Dole had used the abortion issue to defeat Dr. William Roy in a narrow reelection victory to his congressional seat. Confronted by abortion again in a 1976 primary presidential debate, Dole flip-flopped, at first saying he opposed all abortions and later saying he supported abortions in certain circumstances such as rape, incest, or if the life of the mother was endangered by carrying the pregnancy to term. Once again, in 1996, a prochoice president with a prochoice agenda was elected to office. But Clinton faced GOP majorities in both houses of Congress, which also shifted favor toward prolife interests.

Bureaucracy

The election of Bill Clinton to the White House, the first prochoice president since 1976, represented a sharp change in executive treatment of abortion politics. On January 22, 1993, President Clinton issued five executive orders overturning antiabortion initiatives that had been in force during the Reagan and Bush administrations. One of his executive orders overturned the "gag rule" issued by President Reagan's Department of Health and Human Services (HHS) that prohibited professionals at Title X clinics from counseling or providing information about abortion and from referring patients to abortion services even when women requested such information. Congress had attempted to overturn the gag rule in 1991 and 1992, but these efforts were countered by presidential vetoes.

Next Clinton lifted the ban on RU486 (mifepristone). RU486 is a pill that induces abortion when followed by a dose of another drug, prostaglandin. Although medical complications are rare, it may not be an option for every woman, particularly older women with cardiovascular problems. RU486 and other abortion-inducing drugs are currently undergoing clinical trials.[67]

Many believe that these abortion-inducing drugs could reshape the abortion landscape by making the abortion decision a much more private matter. Research suggests that RU486 could replace 30 to 50 percent of clinical legal abortions and that abortifacient vaccines could replace 90 percent of them. President Clinton has made his support of the drugs clear by making fast-track approval of them a priority.[68]

A third executive order lifted the ban on fetal tissue research. This order violated the sensibilities of prolifers who oppose funding of fetal tissue transplantation research because the tissue is obtained from abortions. The ban was instituted by Reagan in 1988 and upheld by Bush in 1992 when he vetoed legislation that would have lifted the ban. The ban limited research that showed promise for developing cures for sufferers of Parkinson's, Alzheimer's, and Huntington's diseases as well as AIDS, strokes, and spinal cord injuries. President Clinton also lifted a ban on the performance of privately funded abortions at military hospitals that had been put into place by Reagan. Under the 1988 Reagan ban, women could not receive abortions at U.S. military facilities anywhere in the world, even if paid for by the patient and even if these services were not available where a woman or her husband was stationed. Abortion would only be allowed, under the Reagan ban, if the life of the woman would be endangered by carrying the pregnancy to term. President Clinton lifted the ban with the proviso that abortion services would be allowed as long as no Department of Defense funds were used.[69]

The last Clinton executive order reversed another Reagan/Bush policy that disallowed U.S. aid to any international family planning programs that included abortion counseling. Under this policy, developed in 1984 at a United Nations Conference on Population in Mexico City, all Agency for International Development funds were barred from nongovernmental organizations that promoted abortion as a method of family planning in other nations. Clinton believed that this international "gag rule" undercut U.S. efforts to promote family planning abroad and so he rescinded it.[70]

The controversy over abortion policy has touched at least twenty-two agencies and programs within the federal government, including law enforcement agencies (the U.S. Customs Service, FBI, Bureau of Alcohol, Tobacco, and Firearms, and U.S. Marshals Service); family planning grants

through the Office of Population Affairs and the National Center for Family
Planning Services within HHS; health care overseers including the FDA,
surgeon general, Centers for Disease Control, and the Health Care Financ-
ing Administration (responsible for the federal share of Medicaid spending
on health care for the poor); and foreign aid activities of the Agency for
International Development within the State Department.[71]

During the Reagan and Bush presidencies, prolifers within the administrations carefully screened prospective nominees for the position of secretary of health and human services, the surgeon general of the United States,
director of the National Institutes of Health (because of the administrations'
opposition to using fetal tissue in research), and the head of the Office of
Population Affairs, which disperses Title X (of the 1970 Family Planning
Services and Population Research Act) family planning grants to several
hundred Planned Parenthood clinics.

Congress still plays a very critical role in shaping and defining abortion
policy and in micromanaging its implementation. In the 1970s Congress
banned the Legal Services Corporation (LSC) from bringing abortion-related
lawsuits against governmental authorities and precluded abortion policy
from the jurisdiction of the U.S. Civil Rights Commission.[72] Since Congress today is dominated by members who call themselves prolife, Clinton
going into his second term faces a formidable foe on his abortion policies.

Congress

Once the *Roe* decision was announced, Congress became the logical flash
point, especially for prolife interest group activity. Significant attempts to
legislate abortion policy began in 1973, with nearly 10 percent of congressional representatives sponsoring or cosponsoring antiabortion legislation or
constitutional amendments. By 1976 more than fifty different varieties of
prolife constitutional amendments had been introduced in Congress, but
none were passed.[73]

One major success story for the prolife movement was the Hyde Amendment. Originally it allowed use of Medicaid funds for an abortion only if the
mother's life was endangered. Subsequent legal challenges held up implementation and for a few years Medicaid abortions were allowed in cases
of rape and incest. But in 1981 the Hyde Amendment returned to its original
language of permitting abortions only to save the mother's life. This state of
affairs did not change for thirteen years until in 1994 the 103rd Congress
reenacted coverage for cases of rape and incest.[74]

Legislative riders to bills barred the use of funds in programs that used
abortion as a method of family planning (Family Planning Services and

Population Act of 1970), prevented judges or public officials from ordering recipients of federal funds to perform abortions (Health Program Extension Act of 1973), and barred Legal Aid lawyers from giving legal assistance on how to obtain nontherapeutic abortions (Legal Services Corporation Act of 1974). An avalanche of restrictions, too numerous to mention, were attached to appropriations bills. All of the following were banned, except to save the mother's life: abortion services at military hospitals, use of federal funds for abortions in the District of Columbia (and the District's use of its own funds), and use of federal health benefits to pay for abortions.[75]

Studies of voting behavior patterns on abortion indicate that ideology, not party, is the most important predictor of congressional votes.[76] When a partisanship variable is used (which combines party affiliation with ideology), the more partisan and liberal Democratic senators also vote prochoice and the more partisan and conservative Republican senators vote prolife more frequently.[77] Evidence drawn from the 101st and 102nd Congresses (through 1991) indicated a slight shift in favor of a prochoice legislative strategy. Out of seventeen key House votes on abortion from these two Congresses, prolifers won in only six (or 35 percent) roll call votes.[78] Prochoice forces in the 1990s, although still defensive and placed in a position where they must fend off the most restrictive bills, have started going on the offensive by introducing some prochoice legislation, such as the 1991 Freedom of Choice Act, which did not pass, and the 1993 Freedom of Access to Clinics Act (FACE), which was enacted.

Passing by a 241–174 margin in the House and a 69–30 margin in the Senate, FACE was supported by both prolife and prochoice advocates. FACE, prompted by violence directed against women's health centers and abortion providers across the country, criminalized blockades of reproductive health facilities as well as the use of force or threats of force against those using the facilities. This measure, signed by Clinton in May 1994, has proven to be a deterrent: data show that under FACE violent incidents directed at abortion providers have decreased from 3,429 in 1993 to 1,815 in 1995.[79]

Prolifers in Congress struck back in 1995 and 1996 with two initiatives—a proposed law banning the "partial birth" (late-term) abortion procedure and a proposed law banning abortion information on the Internet or on-line services. In 1995 the House of Representatives voted to ban the specific late-term abortion procedure the bill's sponsors call "partial birth" abortion. Later that year, the Senate passed the House bill but amended it to allow the procedure if the mother's life was endangered.[80] The proposed act banned the "partial birth" abortion procedure and subjected a physician who violates the ban to possible fines, civil suits, and/or a maximum of two years imprisonment. The final version, however, did not include the amendment to permit the procedure if the mother's life was endangered. It was vetoed by President Clinton on April 10, 1996.

In 1997 Senate Minority Leader Tom Daschle (D-SD) proposed a compromise that would ban most abortions after the fetus reached viability except if a woman's life was endangered or she was faced with grievous injury to her health. Clinton signaled support for this bill, but it was defeated in a floor vote.[81] Prolifers were given some help in late May of 1997 when the American Medical Association (AMA) endorsed a ban on a specific "partial birth" abortion procedure—the D&E, or dilation and extraction. The new measure protected doctors from prosecution when they intend to deliver a baby but are forced to use D&E to protect the mother's life. The American College of Obstetricians and Gynecologists opposed the ban, arguing that it allows legislators to make decisions best left to medical professionals. This bill passed in both houses with no exception but to save the mother's life, although the president has promised a veto.[82]

A less emotional issue was raised in 1996 by Representative Henry J. Hyde (R-IL), a longtime abortion opponent who successfully buried a little-noticed provision in the Telecommunications Act of 1996. This proviso criminalized use of interactive computer systems to provide or receive information about abortion. First Amendment proponents and abortion rights groups challenged the measure in court, where a United States attorney told federal district judge Charles P. Sifton that the Justice Department considered it unconstitutional and not enforceable. The judge held that it was unnecessary to issue an injunction restraining implementation of the measure until actual harm to speech was incurred.[83]

Although Congress has enacted significant restrictions on abortion (especially abortion funding) and historically has been dominated by prolife advocates, the main goal of prolifers—to overturn *Roe* by constitutional amendment—has not been accomplished.

Federalism

Between 1973 and 1989 the states enacted nineteen types of antiabortion regulations, including conscience clauses (thirty-five states), postviability requirements (twenty-nine states), postviability standards of care (twenty-nine states), abortion funding limits (twenty-five states), fetal tissue experimentation bans (twenty-three states), parental notification (eighteen states), informed consent (seventeen states), parental consent (seventeen states), second trimester hospitalization requirements (seventeen states), insurance restrictions that allow for maternity benefits but exclude abortion (ten states), spousal notification (seven states), and a requirement that women be noti-fied that the fetus experiences pain in second-trimester abortions (one state).[84]

The *Webster* ruling officially passed the "hot potato" issue of abortion back to the states. Between 1989 and 1992 new abortion restrictions were generated. Premier among them were efforts to ban "birth control" abortions (all abortions, they say, except those necessary to save the mother's life or in cases of rape, incest, or gross fetal abnormality).[85] By the end of 1991 nine states had passed new restrictions on abortion. Michigan, Nebraska, and South Carolina, which had already enacted parental notification for minors seeking abortions prior to *Webster,* added the necessary judicial bypass pro-vision. Mississippi, North Dakota, and Ohio passed waiting-period and "right to know" statutes, the latter of which required a discussion on alterna-tives to abortion and the dangers of the procedure before it could be per-formed. Louisiana and Utah enacted the most restrictive laws, modeled after the centerpiece of the post-*Webster* antiabortion movement; both banned birth control abortions. On the prochoice side, four states (Connecticut, Maryland, Nevada, and Washington) passed liberalizing abortion laws that in essence wrote *Roe* into state law. Still, prolifers by the end of 1991 walked away with a 9–3 victory scorecard. Given impetus by the 1992 *Casey* deci-sion, eleven states—Idaho, Kansas, Louisiana, Mississippi, Nebraska, North Dakota, Ohio, Pennsylvania, South Carolina, South Dakota, and Utah—en-acted mandatory waiting periods.

In a six-year time frame, from 1990 until 1996, twelve more states passed bans on abortion after the fetus is "viable." The viability time period, when specified, varies from twenty to twenty-four weeks. Of the forty-one states that have postviability bans, twelve require that a second physician be present at a postviability abortion to give medical attention to the fetus. From 1993 through 1995 six more states passed "women's right to know" or "informed consent" statutes, with a total of thirty states requiring this in 1996. By June of 1996, thirty-seven states mandated parental consent or notice for abortion. Though declared unconstitutional in a number of states, the laws are enforced in at least thirty states. As of 1994, federal law required all states to pay for life-saving abortions or abortions that resulted from rape or incest. Fifteen states publicly fund abortion for low-income women on the same terms as other pregnancy-related health services.[86] In 1995 and 1996 various states passed thirty-two antichoice laws, compared to sixteen laws in 1993 and 1994; prochoice advocates became alarmed, since a majority of state legislatures have indicated a willingness to restrict abortion beyond the limits put forward in *Roe.*[87]

Following the lead of prolifers in Congress, state legislators have also proposed bans on "partial birth" abortions. As of May 1997, forty states have taken up this issue. Three states—Michigan, South Carolina, and Utah—have bans in effect. Seven other states—Alaska, Arizona, Arkansas, Georgia, Mississippi, Montana, and South Dakota—have bans that take effect later in 1997. The bans in Ohio and Michigan have been challenged in court, and federal judges have declared the language of the laws too vague and broad. Prochoice groups fear that this is an attempt to build momentum toward the ultimate goal of prolifers, which is to ban all abortions.[88]

State restrictions on abortion are likely to continue. Public opinion evidence at the state level indicates that the populace is generally supportive of more restrictions on abortion availability.[89] In addition, support for additional restrictions may depend on political cycles of liberalism and conservatism. In the post-*Webster* era in particular, political factors were important in explaining abortion restrictiveness in the states, illustrating how the dominance of conservatism may heighten partisan conflict over abortion.[90]

Summary

Roe's legalization of abortion has led to legislative backlashes at the federal and state level. Although prochoice advocates obtained a powerful ally in the federal judiciary, they face tremendous problems in Congress and state legislatures. The abortion debate also has been transformed by the Reagan and Clinton presidencies—one a prolife president, the other a prochoice president. In many ways, they symbolize how the extremes at both ends of the abortion debate control the agenda. Both presidents have championed the cause for and against the liberalization of abortion more ardently than any other presidents.

The prolife lobby is also experiencing growing pains as it transforms into a coalition. The National Women's Coalition for Life, founded in 1992, has set up an umbrella organization for national women's groups that oppose abortion. This effort may ameliorate some of the perceived weaknesses of the prolife lobby—that it is composed of single-issue, one-shot litigators without cooperative litigation strategies. The prochoice coalition, on the other hand, paradoxically faces the opposite challenge—mobilizing more effectively at the grassroots level and keeping the abortion issue salient to affected and interested constituencies.

Attempts to find common ground are under way between both sides of the abortion debate. The Common Ground Network for Life and Choice, founded in 1989, has established local groups in Cleveland, Buffalo, Denver, Washington, and Baltimore to promote dialogue on this most divisive issue. Areas of common interest include more emphasis on adoption, reduction of pregnancy among teenagers, and an end to violence outside abortion clinics and providers. The network also has plans to set up a data bank of facts on which both sides agree, such as the annual number of abortions and when the fetus's heartbeat begins.[91] Such talks represent a beginning, and public opinion polls of Americans from 1965 to the present indicate that this direction is where the majority would like the abortion debate to go.

Notes

1. Neal Devins, *Shaping Constitutional Values: Elected Government, the Supreme Court, and the Abortion Debate* (Baltimore and London: Johns Hopkins University Press, 1996), p. 145.

2. James C. Mohr, *Abortion in America: The Origins and Evolution of National Policy, 1800–1900* (New York: Oxford University Press, 1978).

3. Marie Costa, *Abortion: A Reference Handbook* (Santa Barbara, CA: ABC-CLIO, 1996), p. 6.

4. Nanette J. Davis, *From Crime to Choice: The Transformation of Abortion in America* (Westport, CT: Greenwood Press, 1985), p. 211.

5. Ibid., p. 211.

6. Karen O'Connor, *No Neutral Ground? Abortion Politics in an Age of Absolutes* (Boulder, CO: Westview Press, 1996), p. 21.

7. Linda Gordon, *Woman's Body, Woman's Right: Birth Control in America* (New York: Penguin, 1990), pp. 50–60.

8. Laurence H. Tribe, *Abortion: The Clash of Absolutes* (New York: W.W. Norton, 1990), p. 34.

9. Carroll Smith-Rosenberg, *Disorderly Conduct: Visions of Gender in Victorian America* (New York: Alfred A. Knopf, 1985), p. 222.

10. Davis, *From Crime to Choice*, p. 213.

11. Raymond Tatalovich, "Abortion: Prochoice Versus Prolife," in Raymond Tatalovich and Byron W. Daynes, eds., *Social Regulatory Policy: Moral Controversies in American Politics* (Boulder, CO: Westview Press, 1988), p. 178.

12. Davis, *From Crime to Choice*, pp. 212–213.

13. See the following sources for estimates of illegal abortions obtained from 1900 through 1950: Marie E. Kopp, *Birth Control in Practice: Analysis of Ten Thousand Case Histories of the Birth Control Clinical Research Bureau* (New York: Arno Press, 1972), pp. 121–127, 207; F.I. Taussig, *Abortion, Spontaneous and Induced* (St. Louis: C.V. Mosby, 1936), pp. 387–388; Raymond Pearl, *The Natural History of the Population* (London: Oxford University Press, 1939), pp. 202–203; and Daniel Callahan, *Abortion: Law, Choice and Morality* (New York: Macmillan Co., 1970).

14. Costa, *Abortion: A Reference Handbook*, p. 12.

15. Leslie J. Reagan, *When Abortion Was a Crime: Women, Medicine, and Law in the United States, 1867–1973* (Berkeley, CA: University of California Press, 1997), pp. 219–220.

16. Costa, *Abortion: A Reference Handbook*, p. 11.

17. Reagan, *When Abortion Was a Crime*, p. 224.

18. O'Connor, *No Neutral Ground? Abortion Politics in an Age of Absolutes*, p. 29.

19. Barbara Hinkson Craig and David M. O'Brien, *Abortion and American Politics* (Chatham, NJ: Chatham House, 1993), pp. 43–44.

20. See Raymond Tatalovich and Byron W. Daynes, *The Politics of Abortion: A*

Study of Community Conflict in Public Policy Making (New York: Praeger, 1981), p. 27, and Tatalovich, "Abortion: Prochoice Versus Prolife," pp. 180–181.

21. David J. Garrow, *Liberty and Sexuality: The Right to Privacy and the Making of Roe v. Wade* (New York: Macmillan, 1994), pp. 591–594.

22. Mary C. Segers and Timothy A. Byrnes, "Introduction: Abortion Politics in American States," in Mary C. Segers and Timothy A. Byrnes, eds., *Abortion Politics in American States* (Armonk, NY: M.E. Sharpe, 1995), p. 5.

23. The nineteen cases decided during 1973–1989 were: *Roe v. Wade, District Attorney of Dallas County,* 410 U.S. 113 (1973); *Doe v. Bolton,* 410 U.S. 179 (1973); *Bigelow v. Virginia,* 421 U.S. 809 (1975); *Connecticut v. Menillo,* 423 U.S. 9 (1975); *Bellotti v. Baird (I),* 428 U.S. 132 (1976); *Planned Parenthood of Central Missouri v. Danforth,* 428 U.S. 52 (1976); *Maher v. Roe,* 432 U.S. 464 (1977); *Beal v. Doe,* 432 U.S. 438 (1977); *Poelker v. Doe,* 432 U.S. 519 (1977); *Colautti v. Franklin,* 439 U.S. 379 (1979); *Bellotti v. Baird (II),* 443 U.S. 622 (1979); *Harris v. McRae,* 448 U.S. 297 (1980); *Williams v. Zbaraz,* 448 U.S. 358 (1981); *H.L. v. Matheson,* 450 U.S. 398 (1981); *City of Akron v. Akron Center for Reproductive Health,* 462 U.S. 416 (1983); *Planned Parenthood Association of Kansas City, Mo. v. Ashcroft,* 462 U.S. 476 (1983); *Simopoulos v. Virginia,* 462 U.S. 506 (1983); *Thornburgh v. American College of Obstetricians and Gynecologists,* 476 U.S. 747 (1986), and *Webster v. Reproductive Health Services,* 492 U.S. 490.

24. Tatalovich, "Abortion: Prochoice Versus Prolife," p. 183.

25. National Abortion Rights Action League, (n.d.). NARAL Factsheets: Supreme Court Decisions Concerning Reproductive Rights: A Chronology: 1965–1995," n.d., *NARAL Home Page,* http://www.naral.org/publications/facts/sup.html (May 1, 1997).

26. Segers and Byrnes, "Introduction: Abortion Politics in American States," p. 7.

27. Irene Davall, "Which Way After Webster?: Throughout the U.S., Six-Hour Drives Are Not Uncommon for Women Needing Abortions," *On the Issues* 17 (Winter 1990), pp. 8–9, 40–41.

28. American Civil Liberties Union, "Parental Involvement Laws," *American Civil Liberties Union Reproductive Rights Page,* 1996, http://www.aclu.org/libraryparent. html (May 9, 1997). Also see: American Civil Liberties Union, "Parental Rights Legislation," *American Civil Liberties Union Reproductive Rights Page,* 1996, http://www. aclu.org/library/parentrt.html (May 9, 1997), and Allison Beth Hubbard, "The Erosion of Minors' Abortion Rights: An Analysis of *Hodgson v. Minnesota* and *Ohio v. Akron Center for Reproductive Health,*" *UCLA Women's Law Journal* 1 (Spring 1991), pp. 227–244. For information on the Montana parental notification law, see CNN, "Court Upholds Montana Abortion Notification Law," *CNN/Time Home Page,* 1997, http://cnn.com/US/8703/31/scotus.wrap/index.html (April 2, 1997).

29. David A. Gardey, "Federal Power to the Rescue: The Use of Section 1985(3) Against Anti-Abortion Protestors," *Notre Dame Law Review* 67 (1992), pp. 707–743.

30. Lissa Shults Campbell, "A Critical Analysis of *Bray v. Alexandria Women's Health Clinic* and the Use of 42 U.S.C. Section 1985(3) To Protect a Woman's Right to an Abortion," *University of Kansas Law Review* 41 (Spring 1993), pp. 569–589.

31. Amy L. Mauk, "RICO—Abortion Protesters Subject to Civil RICO Actions— *National Organization for Women, Inc. v. Scheidler,* No. 92–1780, 1994 U.S. LEXIS 1143 (Jan. 24, 1994)," *Suffolk University Law Review* 28 (Spring 1994), pp. 288–297. Also see Michelle R. Moretti, "Using Civil RICO to Battle Anti-Abortion Violence: Is the Last Weapon in the Arsenal a Sword of Damocles?" *New England Law Review* 25 (Summer 1991), pp. 1363–1414.

32. Jennifer J. Seibring, "If It's Not Too Much to Ask, Could You Please Shut Up?:

Madsen v. Women's Health Ctr., Inc., 114 S. Ct. 2516 (1994)," *Southern Illinois University Law Journal* 20 (Fall 1995), pp. 205–222.

33. Linda Greenhouse, "High Court Backs Limits on Protest at Abortion Clinic," *New York Times* (July 1, 1994).

34. Tatalovich, "Abortion: Prochoice Versus Prolife," pp. 185–186.

35. Devins, *Shaping Constitutional Values: Elected Government, the Supreme Court and the Abortion Debate,* p. 92. Also see Rachael K. Pirner and Laurie B. Williams, "Roe to Casey: A Survey of Abortion Law," *Washburn Law Journal* 32 (Winter 1993), pp. 166–189.

36. Craig and O'Brien, *Abortion and American Politics,* p. 249.

37. *Gallup Poll Monthly* (June 1991), pp. 36–39.

38. *Gallup Poll Monthly* (August 1996), p. 29.

39. Ann McDaniel, "The Future of Abortion," *Newsweek* (July 17, 1989), p. 15; *The Gallup Report* (October 1989), p. 17.

40. *Gallup Poll Monthly* (August 1996), pp. 34–35.

41. Craig and O'Brien, *Abortion and American Politics,* p. 35.

42. Suzanne Staggenborg, *The Pro-Choice Movement: Organization and Activism in the Abortion Conflict* (New York: Oxford University Press, 1991), p. 3.

43. Costa, *Abortion: A Reference Handbook,* p. 199.

44. Ibid., pp. 190, 203, and 212–213.

45. National Abortion Rights Action League, "About NARAL," *NARAL Home Page,* n.d., http://www.naral.org/naral/about.html (May 22, 1997).

46. Staggenborg, *The Pro-Choice Movement,* p. 145.

47. Barbara M. Yarnold, *Abortion Politics in the Federal Courts: Right Versus Right* (Westport, CT: Praeger, 1995), pp. 22–23, 116.

48. Raymond Tatalovich and Byron W. Daynes, "The Lowi Paradigm, Moral Conflict, and Coalition-Building: Pro-Choice Versus Pro-Life," *Women and Politics* 13 (1993), pp. 39–66.

49. O'Connor, *No Neutral Ground? Abortion Politics in the Age of Absolutes,* pp. 84–85, 146–147.

50. Costa, *Abortion: A Reference Handbook,* pp. 192–193.

51. Keith Cassidy, "The Right to Life Movement: Sources, Development, and Strategies," *Journal of Policy History* 7 (1995), pp. 128–159.

52. Charles S. Clark, "Abortion Clinic Protests: Is Violence Changing the Abortion Debate?," *CQ Researcher* 5 (April 7, 1995), pp. 297–320; Jill Petty, "Enemies of Choice," *Ms.* (May/June 1995), pp. 44–47; National Abortion Rights Action League, "Justifiable Homicide and the Anti-Choice Movement," *NARAL Factsheets,* 1996, http:www.naral.org/publications/facts/shooting.html (May 1, 1997).

53. Yarnold, *Abortion Politics in the Federal Courts,* pp. 23, 117.

54. National Right to Life, "When Does Life Begin?," *NRLC: Abortion Information,* n.d., http://www.nrlc.org/abortion/index.html (May 1, 1997).

55. Gary Leber, "We Must Rescue Them," in Robert M. Baird and Stuart E. Rosenbaum, eds., *The Ethics of Abortion: Pro-Life vs. Pro-Choice,* rev. ed. (Buffalo, NY: Prometheus Books, 1993), p. 139.

56. Mark A. Graber, *Rethinking Abortion: Equal Choice, the Constitution, and Reproductive Rights* (Princeton, NJ: Princeton University Press, 1996), p. 24.

57. National Right to Life Committee, "Over 35 Million Abortions in U.S. from 1973 through 1996," *National Right to Life: Abortion in the United States,* n.d., http://www.nrlc.org/abortion/aboramt.html (May 1, 1997).

58. Leber, "We Must Rescue Them," p. 139; Jeffrey L. Sheler, "The Theology of Abortion," *U.S. News Online: Citizen's Toolbox,* 1992, http:www.usnews.com/usnews/wash/theology.htm (May 1, 1997).

59. *The Gallup Poll Monthly* (August 1996), pp. 29–30.
60. Kristin Luker, *Abortion and the Politics of Motherhood* (Berkeley, CA: University of California Press, 1984), p. 145.
61. Craig and O'Brien, *Abortion and American Politics,* p. 46.
62. Ibid., pp. 158–159.
63. Tatalovich, "Abortion: Prochoice Versus Prolife," p. 198.
64. Craig and O'Brien, *Abortion and American Politics,* pp. 169–170; Tatalovich, "Abortion: Prochoice Versus Prolife," p. 200.
65. O'Connor, *No Neutral Ground? Abortion Politics in an Age of Absolutes,* pp. 116–119.
66. Raymond Tatalovich, *The Politics of Abortion in the United States and Canada: A Comparative Study* (Armonk, NY: M.E. Sharpe Publishers, 1997), pp. 157–158.
67. Lawrence Lader, *A Private Matter: RU486 and the Abortion Crisis* (Amherst, NY: Prometheus Books, 1995), pp. 115–117; Karen Freeman, "Planned Parenthood to Test 2 Abortion Drugs," *New York Times* (September 12, 1996), p. A10; Tamar Lewin, "Abortion Group to Advise Doctors on Drug Used to End Pregnancy," *New York Times* (March 30, 1996), pp. 1, 10.
68. Philip J. Hilts, "Giving Push to the Abortion Pill, A Second Group Will Test It," *New York Times* (March 14, 1996), p. A9; National Abortion Rights Action League, "Mifepristone (RU486) and the Impact of Abortion Politics on Scientific Research," *NARAL Factsheets,* 1997 (May 1, 1997).
69. National Abortion Rights Action League, "Executive Orders," *NARAL Factsheets.* http://www.naral.org/publications/facts/ru486fin.html.
70. O'Connor, *No Neutral Ground? Abortion Politics in an Age of Absolutes,* p. 151.
71. Tatalovich, *The Politics of Abortion in the United States and Canada,* p. 169.
72. Ibid., 184–186.
73. O'Connor, *No Neutral Ground? Abortion Politics in an Age of Absolutes,* p. 67.
74. Tatalovich, *The Politics of Abortion in the United States and Canada,* p. 98.
75. Craig and O'Brien, *Abortion and American Politics,* pp. 112–113.
76. Raymond Tatalovich and David Schier, "The Persistence of Ideological Voting on Abortion Legislation in the House of Representatives, 1973–1988," *American Politics Quarterly* 21 (1993), pp. 125–139.
77. Mark J. Wattier and Raymond Tatalovich, "Senate Voting on Abortion Legislation Over Two Decades: Testing a Reconstructed Partisanship Variable," *American Review of Politics* 16 (1995), pp. 167–183.
78. Raymond Tatalovich and David Schier, "The Persistence of Ideological Cleavage in Voting on Abortion Legislation in the House of Representatives, 1973–1988," in Malcolm L. Goggin, ed., *Understanding the New Politics of Abortion* (Newbury Park, CA: Sage, 1993), pp. 118–119.
79. Robert Pear, "Abortion Clinic Protests Drop Under New Law," *New York Times* (September 24, 1996), p. A13; "The ACLU's Role in Stopping Clinic Violence," *American Civil Liberties Union Reproductive Rights,* 1996, http:www.aclu.org/library/clinicvi.html (May 9, 1997).
80. Jerry Gray, "White House Says Clinton Plans to Veto Bill Banning Late-Term Abortions," *New York Times* (October 27, 1995), p. A8.
81. Katherine Q. Steelye, "Three Bills Offered to Settle Debate on Late-Term Abortions," *The New York Times,* 1997, http://www.nytimes.com/yr/mo/day/news/washpol/senate-abortion.html. (May 15, 1997); Darlene Superville, "Defeats Democratic Late-Term Abortion Proposals," *The Associated Press,* 1997, http://www.nando.net/newsroom/ntn/politics/051697/politics8_4470.html (May 16, 1997).
82. AllPolitics, "AMA Recommends Alternatives to So-Called 'Partial Birth' Abor-

tions," *AllPolitics: CNN/Time,* 1997, http://AllPolitics.com/1997/05/14/ama.abortion/ (May 15, 1997); Darlene Superville, "Abortion Bill, With Slight Changes, Wins AMA Endorsement," *The Associated Press,* 1997, http://www.nando.net/newsroom/ntn/politics/052097/politicst_28841.html (May 20, 1997); AllPolitics, "Senate OKs Late-Term Abortion Ban: But a 64–26 Margin Once Again Leaves It Vulnerable to Clinton's Veto," *AllPolitics: CNN/Time,* 1997, http://allpolitics.com/1997/05/20/abortion.vote/ (May 25, 1997).

83. The Center for Reproductive Law and Policy, "Women's Health Advocates Challenge Gag on Abortion Information on the Internet," *Reproductive Freedom News,* 1996, http://www.echonyc.com/comstop/rfn/v-03.html (May 15, 1997); The Center for Reproductive Law and Policy, "Women's Health Care Advocates Win Government Assurance that Internet Abortion Gag Won't Be Enforced," *Reproductive Freedom News,* 1996, http://www.echonyc.com/comstop/rfn/v-04.html (May 15, 1997); Pamela Mendels.

84. Glen A. Halva-Neubauer, "The States After *Roe*: No 'Paper Tigers,' " in Malcolm L. Goggin, ed., *Understanding the New Politics of Abortion* (Newbury Park, CA: Sage, 1993), pp. 186–189.

85. Ibid., p. 179.

86. National Abortion Rights Action League, "State Post-Viability Bans," *NARAL Factsheets,* http://www.naral.org/publications/facts/post-viability.html (May 1, 1997); Life Action Advocates, "Women's Right to Know Statutes," *Prolife.ORG,* 1995, http://www.prolife.org/ultimate/stateleg.html (May 9, 1997); National Abortion Rights Action League, "Parental Rights Legislation Alert," *NARAL Factsheets,* 1996, http://www.naral.org/publications/facts/pra.html (May 1, 1997); National Abortion Rights Action League, "Mandatory Waiting Periods and the Freedom to Choose"; National Abortion Rights Action League, "Mandatory Parental Consent and Notice Laws and the Freedom to Choose," *NARAL Factsheets,* 1995, http://www.naral.org/publications/facts/parental.html (May 1, 1997); American Civil Liberties Union, "Access Denied: The Scarcity of Public Funding for Abortion," *American Civil Liberties Union: Reproductive Rights,* 1996, http://www.aclu.org/library/aborfund.html (May 9, 1997).

87. Linda Feldmann, "Abortion Foes Push Restrictions in Legislatures Across the Country," *Christian Science Monitor* (January 22, 1997), p. 4.

88. Katherine Q. Seelye, "States Move to Ban Controversial Abortion Procedure," *New York Times,* May 5, 1997, http: //www.nytimes.com/yr/mo/day/news/national/abort-states.html (May 5, 1997); National Abortion Rights Action League, "Late Term Abortion Ban," *NARAL Factsheets,* 1997, http://www.naral.org/publications/facts/lateban.html (May 1, 1997).

89. Malcolm L. Goggin and Christopher Wlezian, "Abortion Opinion and Policy in the American States," in Malcolm L. Goggin, ed., *Understanding the New Politics of Abortion* (Newbury Park, CA: Sage, 1993), p. 201.

90. Ruth Ann Strickland and Marcia Lynn Whicker, "Political and Socio-Economic Indicators of State Restrictiveness Toward Abortion," *Policy Studies Journal* 20 (1992), pp. 598–617.

91. Life Support Advocates, "Grass-Roots Dialogue Explores Common Ground in Abortion Debate," *Prolife.ORG,* n.d., http://www.prolife.org/ultimate/un4.html (May 26, 1997).

Affirmative Action: Minority Rights or Reverse Discrimination?

Gary C. Bryner

Affirmative action is a tremendously important issue in American politics for at least two reasons. First, it is a symbolic and highly visible manifestation of the enduring problem of race in America and the problems facing the country in dealing with its history of discrimination and inequality. Second, affirmative action is representative of some of the efforts aimed at improving the economic and social opportunities for African Americans (as well as other people of color and women). The controversy surrounding affirmative action threatens to engulf the progress that has been made during the past forty years of civil rights; some argue that it has already had that effect. The rancorous debate highlights significant differences between the ways in which blacks and whites view political, economic, and social questions in America; the rancor itself threatens the goal of affirmative action to serve as a means to a color-blind society and equal opportunity for all.

Equal employment opportunity generally has been understood to mean that decisions concerning the selection, promotion, termination, and treatment of individuals in employment must be free of considerations of race, color, national origin, religion, and sex. Equal employment opportunity rests upon the idea of nondiscrimination—that these kinds of considerations are unconstitutional and morally unacceptable. Affirmative action is defined here, following the U.S. Civil Rights Commission, as having three components. First, it is remedial: affirmative action denotes efforts that take race, sex, and national origin into account for the purpose of remedying discrimination and its effects. Second, affirmative action seeks ultimately to bring about equal opportunity: affirmative action assumes that "race, sex or national origin [must be considered] in order to eliminate considerations of race, sex and national origin," that "because of the duration, intensity, scope and intransigence of the discrimination women and minority groups experience, affirmative action plans are needed to assure equal employment opportunity."[1] Third, affirmative action specifies what racial groups are to be considered part of the "protected class" covered by its policies.

In practice, there is no agreement over how to define affirmative action; the term represents a range of public policies that stretch along a continuum from outreach and recruitment of candidates, remedial efforts to "make whole" victims of past discrimination, racial diversity as one of several factors in making decisions, flexible goals for increasing the percentage of blacks in certain position, devices such as separate admission tracks or contract set-asides that treat minority and white candidates differently in order to increase minorities' participation rates, and numerical quotas. There is little controversy surrounding the outliers: almost everyone is in favor of outreach programs to increase the pool of qualified minority candidates but is opposed to quotas.

Nor is there clear agreement about which groups are to benefit from affirmative action. Under Title IV of the 1964 Civil Rights Act, the primary equal employment opportunity statute, minority groups include blacks, Hispanics, Asian or Pacific islanders, and Native Americans or Alaskan natives. Under public works legislation that sets aside 10 percent of funds for minority-run enterprises, groups included are "blacks, Spanish-speaking persons, Orientals, Native Americans, Eskimos, and Aleuts." Federal agencies with policy responsibility in this area define protected groups as blacks (all racial groups of Africa except North Africa), Hispanics (Mexicans, Puerto Ricans, Cubans, Central or South Americans, and members of other Spanish cultures), Asian/Pacific Islanders (from the Far East, Southeast Asia, the Indian subcontinent, and Pacific Islands), and Native Americans (original people of North America who maintain their tribal identity).

There is little agreement over how to think about affirmative action. For some, it is an attempt to establish an equality of results rather than of opportunity, or a means of ensuring that the distribution of employment opportunities mirrors the distribution of groups in society. Others call affirmative action "reverse discrimination" (racial discrimination against whites). Still others emphasize the concept of "preferential treatment" and view it either as an imperative to overcome the effects of past discrimination or as an evil that perpetuates race consciousness and injustice.[2] Affirmative action is rejected by others, including some blacks, for undermining the self-respect of those who are the action's intended beneficiaries and denigrating the progress and advancement achieved by blacks.[3] Proponents argue that affirmative action has increased the percentage of minority students, especially those from middle-class families, in selective colleges. A movement away from affirmative action—to, say, granting preference only to persons from low-income families—would at best be likely to produce a decline in racial diversity. From one point of view, while injustice persists, some progress has been made: "While discrimination for most blacks is an unfortunate fact of life, it is no longer . . . the central fact of life."[4] While affirmative action will not eliminate discrimination, proponents believe it is naive to believe that it is no longer needed. These competing views about affirmative action underlie the differences in the evolution of policies pursued by different policy makers.

Federalism

After World War II, some states began to enact laws and programs to protect the civil rights of blacks. New York was the first state to use the term *affirmative action* in providing for remedies to victims of employment discrimination. A 1964 study by the U.S. Department of Labor (done in response to the passage of Title VII of the Civil Rights Act) found that twenty-five states had fair-employment laws that prohibited private employers from discriminating on the basis of race, color, creed, and national origin in decisions relating to hiring or discharging employees, wages, and other conditions of employment.[5] None of these twenty-five states was in the South, however. The Labor Department study concluded that twenty-two of the twenty-five state laws were essentially compatible with the provisions of the Civil Rights Act.

Title VII of the 1964 Civil Rights Act encouraged states to enact and implement their own fair employment laws and assumed that much of the enforcement of Title VII would take place in state agencies. In 1965 the Equal Employment Opportunity Commission (EEOC) agreed to permit agencies in some twenty-two states to begin enforcing the federal law, including the 1964 law. Title VII clearly was aimed at the southern states that had no laws protecting blacks from discrimination. As support for affirmative action began to unravel politically and legally in the 1990s, opponents began to push state initiatives to end affirmative action in several states, including California, Colorado, Florida, Illinois, Oregon, and Washington. The University of California Board of Regents voted in 1995 to end the use of applicants' race as a factor in applications, and reviewed the outreach programs. The board issued guidelines in July 1995 for pursuing ethnic and racial diversity, requiring schools to admit 50 percent of applicants solely on academic achievement; the other half are to be evaluated based on "special circumstances" such as whether the applicant has shown unusual persistence and determination, needs to work, is from an educationally or socially disadvantaged background, or comes from a difficult family situation. Critics argued that the process of deciding which applicants were disadvantaged would be burdensome and imprecise, but the regents rejected appeals to reinstate the traditional affirmative action program. In February 1996 the Board of Regents voted to delay the implementation of the new admissions program until spring 1998.[6]

The most visible efforts were ballot initiatives and legislative proposals to end affirmative action in state and local governments. Ten states considered legislation or ballot initiatives in 1995 to abolish affirmative action, but none was enacted. By March 1996 ballot initiatives to end affirmative action had been proposed in six states, and seventeen state legislatures were considering similar bills.[7] But most of the attention focused on California. Two professors started a petition drive to roll back affirmative action because it had shifted from voluntary outreach to a system of quotas and mandates. Proposition 209, the California Civil Rights Initiative, provides that the state of California "shall not discriminate against or grant preferential treatment to any individual or group on the basis of race, sex, color, ethnicity, or national origin in the operation of public employment, public education or public contracting."[8] But the drive was faltering by the end of 1995. Governor Pete Wilson suggested that Ward Connerly, a black Sacramento businessman who as a member of the Board of Regents had led the fight for ending affirmative action in California universities, take over the drive.[9] Connerly's organizational and fund-raising abilities paid off; the Republican National Committee took over the signature gathering process; and the measure qualified for the ballot in February when Governor Wilson turned in the final batch of petitions.[10] By February, some one hundred groups had joined the coalition opposing the initiative, including the YWCA, the National Organization for Women, the NAACP Legal Defense and Education Fund, the Feminist Majority, and the Mexican American League. Students from a hundred colleges throughout the nation agreed to spend their summers working in California to oppose the measure.[11] Proponents of the initiative spent an estimated $6 million, including $2.5 million donated by the Republican Party. Its opponents, Stop Prop 209, raised about $2.5 million.[12]

California voters passed Proposition 209 in November 1996 by a 54 to 46 percent margin. Critics of the measure immediately filed lawsuits challenging the initiative.[13] The American Civil Liberties Union challenged the constitutionality of Proposition 209, claiming it eliminated protection for women and minorities in violation of the equal protection clause, and in December 1996 a federal judge issued an injunction prohibiting its implementation until the challenge can be heard.[14] The appeals court overturned the district court decision in 1997, but the Supreme Court could still hear the case.[15] Several cities in California vowed to continue affirmative action programs until the legal challenges to the initiative have been completed.[16]

Despite their success in California, opponents of affirmative action have had little success elsewhere.[17] In some states, such as New Jersey, Republican governors and leaders support affirmative action. In many southern states, minority legislators have blocked repeal efforts. In conservative western states, the minority population is so small that affirmative action is not an issue.[18]

Congress

As the peaceful, nonviolent civil rights protests and demonstrations by ad hoc groups of students and community activists in the late 1950s were transformed into violent confrontations in the early 1960s, civil rights groups and political activists, trade unions, civil liberties associations, and religious leaders joined together in a broad-based social movement to lobby Congress and the Kennedy administration for decisive action.[19] This outpouring of support for civil rights, combined with lobbying and political activities under the umbrella of the Leadership Conference on Civil Rights, founded in 1949 to coordinate such efforts, resulted in significant civil rights planks in the platforms of both parties in 1960.[20]

President John Kennedy did not actively pursue civil rights legislation until 1963; his hesitation has been attributed to concerns that opposition to such initiatives by southern chairmen of important committees would spill over to defeat his other New Frontier programs. Much of the basis for legislative initiatives arose from the recommendations of the Civil Rights Commission, which had been established in 1957. In its 1961 report, the commission recommended that Congress create a new agency similar to the President's Committee on Equal Employment Opportunity or empower that agency to enforce a policy of nondiscrimination in all employment decisions where federal funds or contracts were involved. Unions would be prohibited from discriminatory practices in accepting or discharging members or in segregating them. Congress also was encouraged to provide for job training programs that would ensure that members of minority groups, and especially teenagers, have access to vocational education and apprenticeship opportunities. In 1963 the commission recommended that fair employment legislation be extended to employment practices related to interstate commerce and that all employment from federal grants, loans, and other spending take place in a nondiscriminatory manner.[21]

The Civil Rights Act of 1964

By the middle of 1963, debate in Congress focused on public accommodations provisions of the civil rights bills that were before it, because great attention had been generated by the sit-ins and demonstrations directed at restaurant and hotel operators who refused to serve black customers. No bill was enacted before President Kennedy's assassination. Lyndon Johnson, five days after Kennedy's death, addressed Congress and urged passage of this civil rights bill: "No memorial oration or eulogy could more eloquently honor President Kennedy's memory than the earliest possible passage of the civil rights bill for which he fought so long."[22] The assassination was perhaps more responsible than anything else for the passage of the bill at that time, although Johnson also likely saw it as an opportunity to extend his constituency; he had no real record on civil rights, and some civil rights leaders believed he was unsupportive of earlier legislative efforts.[23]

The House version of the legislation passed in 1964 was rejected as too extreme by Republican leaders, who negotiated with leaders of both parties and with Justice Department officials and eventually softened the bill enough to gain solid bipartisan support and overcome southern opposition. Some compromises led to less federal involvement than had been proposed and permitted local governments to attempt solving problems before federal authorities intervened. There was particular opposition to the sections on equal employment opportunity and access to public accommodations, both of which were amended. The amendment that prohibited discrimination on the basis of sex eventually became the most important change from the original bill. Contrary to the hopes of the amendment's sponsor, who saw the proposal as an opportunity to generate opposition to the whole package, the amendment passed and generated additional support for the entire bill.

In the Senate, opponents blocked legislative action through a filibuster conducted by eighteen southern Democrats and one southern Republican that featured a twenty-four-hour-long speech by then Democrat Strom Thurmond of South Carolina. Southern opposition focused mainly on the sections of the proposed legislation that provided for a cutoff of federal funds for discriminatory practices and set up a fair practices commission. At the same time that southern Democrats tried to block the legislation, Republicans worked to gain concessions on the provisions they were most concerned about—access to public accommodations and fair employment practices. Ultimately the negotiators agreed to provisions that permitted government suits only for egregious cases of discrimination (where there was a clear "pattern or practice" of discriminatory behavior), that required the administrative agency created to enforce the law to seek *voluntary* compliance with the law, and that permitted individuals to sue in federal courts for redress. The filibuster finally was cut off on June 10. Southerners then presented a large number of amendments that were soundly defeated; northern Democrats grew weary and decided not to call up strengthening amendments as planned. The House agreed not to tamper with the fragile Senate compromise and passed the bill.[24]

Title VII of the Civil Rights Act of 1964, the fair employment practices section of the act, contained five major provisions. First, it prohibited hiring, firing, disciplinary, and other employment and union practices on the basis of race, color, religion, national origin, or sex. Second, Title VII extended coverage to those employees and union members in organizations of greater than twenty-five individuals. (The act eventually was amended to reach organizations with fifteen or more members.) Third, Title VII provided exemptions from coverage for individuals who required security clearances for government employment; for individuals who were hired for educational functions by educational institutions or religious activities by religious groups; for cases where employees of a particular religion, national origin, or sex were part of a bona fide occupational qualification; and for Native Americans hired on or near reservations. Fourth, Title VII created an independent agency, the Equal Employment Opportunity Commission, and charged it with the responsibility to investigate claims brought by aggrieved individuals; to attempt to negotiate resolutions; and to provide technical assistance to employers and unions seeking to comply with the law. The attorney general was empowered to bring suits for widespread (pattern or practice) discrimination, and individuals also could bring suit should EEOC conciliatory efforts fail. Finally, the title defined as permissible seniority systems, merit systems, tests used in application procedures, and different standards of compensation or work responsibilities as long as these practices were not used with the intent to discriminate.

Title VII also expressly rejected the imposition of quotas in the hiring of members of minority groups or women. Section 703(j) of the act was added in response to criticisms that the law would require hiring quotas; this section prohibited "preferential treatment to any individual or group . . . on account of an imbalance which may exist with respect to the total or percentage of persons of any race, color, religion, sex, or national origin employed . . . in any comparison with the total number or percentage in any community, state, section or other area or in the available workforce in any community." Sponsors maintained that the law "does not require an employer to achieve any sort of racial balance in his workforce by giving preferential treatment to any individual or group." "What the bill does," explained one sponsor, "is to simply make it an illegal practice to use race as a factor in denying employment."[25]

Once Title VII was enacted, proponents of the legislation began pressing for action to strengthen the Equal Employment Opportunity Commission. Legislation was introduced in 1965 that would have given the EEOC the authority to bring charges against employers who discriminated, to issue cease-and-desist orders in order to end prohibited practices, and to order employers to hire or reinstate victims of discrimination. In the House, the proposal won broad bipartisan support. In the Senate, however, southern Democrats teamed with other members who responded to lobbying by business groups that feared increased governmental intervention in their decision making to defeat the proposal.[26]

Equal Employment Opportunity Act of 1972

In late 1971 legislation to amend Title VII of the 1964 Civil Rights Act was passed by a Senate committee; this legislation granted to the EEOC cease-and-desist powers. The Nixon administration opposed the transfer of power from the Justice and Labor Departments to the EEOC, while the NAACP, the Commission on Civil Rights, and the AFL-CIO backed the transfer. The opposition was led by Sam Ervin (D-NC) and James Allen (D-AL), who argued that such authority would render the EEOC "prosecutor, judge and jury" and would prevent employers from enjoying the rights of due process. Ervin and Allen favored the Nixon administration's proposal for empowering the EEOC to bring suits against violators of Title VII provisions. Three times the Senate voted, by slim margins, to reject the Ervin-Allen alternative; Senator Allen threatened to filibuster in order to block a final vote on the amendments to Title VII. Proponents, failing to find sufficient votes to invoke cloture and prevent the filibuster, agreed to compromise. The court-enforcement alternative eventually was passed by the Senate along with another major point of controversy—bringing state and local government employees under Title VII, expanding coverage to firms with fifteen or more employees, and maintaining the power to bring pattern or practice suits by the attorney general rather than by the EEOC.

In the House, it became clear that organized labor favored the transfer of power to the EEOC as a way to weaken the Labor Department and the Philadelphia Plan. The labor–civil rights coalition was reformed to lobby for the proposal, yet was split over the desired outcome of the transfer. House and Senate conferees eventually agreed on most of the Senate positions but gave to the EEOC authority to bring pattern or practice suits against employers, brought employees of educational institutions under coverage (these employees had been exempted in the 1964 act), and created the Equal Employment Opportunity Coordinating Council to facilitate cooperation between the EEOC, the Office of Federal Contracts Compliance (OFCC), and other agencies.

The passage of the Equal Employment Opportunity Act of 1972 was a clear defeat for civil rights groups, whose major goal had been to empower the EEOC to issue cease-and-desist orders against discriminatory employment practices. One civil rights leader described the act as a "slap in the face, but not a knockout punch" for the civil rights movement.[27] It is clear from the tortuous history of the 1972 amendments to Title VII of the 1964 act that Congress as a whole was quite willing to rely on the federal courts as the primary forum for the implementation of equal employment opportunity. For southern members of Congress, this was an attractive alternative because federal judges were residents of the areas over which they presided and to some extent were screened and approved by senior members of Congress before being appointed by the president.

For others in Congress, federal bureaucrats who were free from local prejudices were viewed as more appropriate enforcers of the law, but federal judges at least might provide some independence and would be preferable to a reliance on state and local officials to implement antidiscrimination laws. Congress also was willing to defer to judicial judgments in defining substantive provisions. In a section-by-section analysis of the 1964 Civil Rights Act and the 1972 amendments, sponsors of the legislation stated that "in any area where the new law does not address itself, or in any areas where a specific contrary intention is not indicated, it was assumed that the present case law as developed by the courts would continue to govern the applicability and construction of Title VII."[28]

Debate concerning the 1972 amendments to Title VII included a claim, unchallenged by proponents of affirmative action, that "to hire a negro solely because he is a negro is racial discrimination just as much as a white only policy. Both forms of discrimination are prohibited by Title VII." At the same time, the Senate rejected an amendment that would have prohibited government agencies from requiring employers to practice reverse discrimination by hiring applicants of a particular race or sex in order to reach a quota.[29]

Congress amended Title VII in 1978 to reverse a Supreme Court decision, *General Electric v. Gilbert,* 429 U.S. 125 (1976), where the Court had ruled that an employer's exclusion of pregnancy benefits from a disability plan was not gender-based discrimination but was motivated only by economic considerations. Women's, labor, and civil rights groups were very outspoken in their criticism of this decision and began pressuring Congress for action, although the issue became mired in disputes about how abortions were to be provided for. Title VII thus was amended in 1978 (92 Stat. 2076) to read that all pregnancy-based distinctions were to be considered gender-based discrimination and that pregnancy was to be treated the same way as any other temporary disability in employee benefit programs, and employers were free to exempt from coverage for medical payments elective abortions unless the life of the mother was threatened.

In legislation passed in the 1970s, Congress began requiring affirmative action by state agencies that received federal funds to employ and promote handicapped persons and by federal agencies for veterans. In the Public Works Employment Act of 1977, Congress required 10 percent of the grants to state and local governments for public works to be directed toward "minority business enterprises," businesses owned and controlled by U.S. citizens from the following minority groups: "Negroes, Spanish-speaking persons, Orientals, Indians, Eskimos, and Aleuts."

The Civil Rights Act of 1991

Changes in the composition of the Supreme Court and strong opposition to preferential treatment in employment decisions, admission to professional programs, and granting of government contracts in the Reagan and Bush administrations came together in the mid- to late 1980s in a number of Supreme Court cases that either narrowly interpreted civil rights laws or appeared to reverse decisions issued during the previous fifteen years. Six Supreme Court decisions issued in 1989, in particular, resulted in demands on Capitol Hill for legislation to overturn these holdings: *Patterson v. McLean Credit Union*, 491 U.S. 164 (1989): *Wards Cove Packing Co. v. Antonio*, 490 U.S. 642 (1989); *Price Waterhouse v. Hopkins*, 490 U.S. 228 (1989); *Lorance v. AT&T Technologies, Inc.*, 490 U.S. 900 (1989); *Martin v. Wilks*, 490 U.S. 755 (1989); *Jett v. Dallas Independent School District*, 491 U.S. 701 (1989); *and Independent Federation of Flight Attendants v. Zipes*, 491 U.S. 754 (1989).

The Civil Rights Act of 1990 was introduced in January of that year and passed both chambers by the summer. President Bush's threat of a veto and the lack of votes in either chamber to override it led to intense negotiations by the conference committee to try to salvage the bill. One of the compromises agreed to in order to win the administration's support was to put a cap of $150,000 on punitive damages that could be sought by victims of intentional discrimination. Unlike most of the other provisions of the bill, this one represented an expansion of civil rights law. (Under 42 U.S.C. @ 1981, unlimited punitive damages can be sought by victims of intentional racial discrimination; the 1990 law extended damage claims to other kinds of discrimination.) Business groups opposed the expansion of their potential liability. In addition to that concern, the Bush administration argued that the provision of the bill requiring that employment decisions producing a disparate impact on women and minorities be justified by a strict showing of "business necessity" would result in employers simply setting up quotas to ensure that the disparate impact didn't occur. The negotiations failed, the Civil Rights Act of 1990 was passed on October 17, 1990, with broad, bipartisan support; it was vetoed by President Bush less than a week later because it was a "quota" bill; and the veto override attempt failed in the Senate by one vote.[30]

Members of Congress and White House staff continued negotiations in 1991 in an attempt to find some common ground, but both sides resisted a softening of positions until other events provided the breakthrough, primarily the victory of former Klan leader David Duke in the Louisiana Republican gubernatorial election, and the hearings of Supreme Court nominee Clarence Thomas. Political damage control apparently moved the administration to drop its opposition to the legislation. The law was passed by Congress on November 7, 1991, and signed by President Bush on November 21 (105 Stat. 1071).

The four purposes of the act included: (1) to provide appropriate remedies for intentional discrimination and unlawful harassment in the workplace; (2) to codify the concepts of "business necessity" and "job-related" enunciated by the Supreme Court in *Griggs v. Duke Power Co.,* 401 U.S. 424 (1971), and in the other Supreme Court decisions prior to *Wards Cove Packing Co. v. Antonio* (1989); (3) to confirm statutory authority and provide statutory guidelines for the adjudication of disparate-impact suits under title VII; and (4) to respond to recent decisions of the Supreme Court by expanding the scope of relevant civil rights statutes in order to provide adequate protection to victims of discrimination.

In a typical disparate-treatment case brought under Title VII, plaintiffs have the burden of proof to show that there is a prima facie case of different treatment. The employer may explain how the decision rested on nondiscriminatory grounds; the plaintiff must then prove that the explanation is a mere pretext and that the employer actually intended to discriminate. In some situations, however, plaintiffs may show that employment decisions were based on a combination of lawful and unlawful motives. In *Price*

Waterhouse v. Hopkins (1989) the Court found that these "mixed motives" cases were to proceed differently. The plaintiff has a higher initial burden of showing that the employer intended to discriminate. Once that is shown, the burden then shifts to the employer to show, by a preponderance of the evidence, that the same decision would have been made absent the discriminatory motivation. The Court found that an employment decision that was in part motivated by prejudice was not a violation of Title VII because the employer showed that he would have made the same decision absent the discriminatory factor. The 1991 act overturned *Price Waterhouse v. Hopkins* by amending section 703 of the Civil Rights Act of 1964 to clarify the prohibition against impermissible consideration of race, color, religion, sex, or national origin in employment practices. A complaining party need only show that "race, color, religion, sex, or national origin was a motivating factor for any employment practice, even though other factors also motivated the practice." Once that is shown, the court "may grant declaratory relief, injunctive relief . . . and attorney's fees and costs demonstrated to be directly attributable only to the pursuit of a claim under section 703(m) [but] shall not award damages or issue an order requiring any admission, reinstatement, hiring, promotion, or payment" (section 107).

The Court has regularly given civil rights laws restrictive holdings during the past fifteen years, only to see those decisions reversed by Congress. In every case, Congress has broadened the coverage or reach of the civil rights statutes in the face of narrow Court holdings.[31] Congress largely saw itself, in enacting these statutes, as reaffirming its original purposes, rather than enacting new legislation. Despite the large number of cases reversed, Congress's reversal of these cases in the 1991 act was similar to what earlier Congresses had done in response to civil rights decisions of the Court. But the new Congress in 1994 took a much different approach.

The Republican Congress

The new Republican majority that was elected in 1994 appeared poised to make changes in affirmative action a high priority. Majority Leader Robert Dole cosponsored a repeal of all race and gender preferences in 1995 with Rep. Charles T. Canady (R-FL).[32] Sen. Phil Gramm, as part of his campaign for the Republican nomination, tried to attach to appropriations bills amendments prohibiting minority set-aside programs but was blocked by a coalition of moderate Republicans and Democrats. Efforts soon ground to a halt, however, as the bill stalled in the Senate, awaiting Sen. Dole's decision about whether to push the issue forward. The Clinton administration opposed the bill.[33]

In the House, Speaker Newt Gingrich blocked consideration of a repeal bill until Republicans could pass "empowerment" legislation to help minorities and the poor. In March 1996 Rep. Canady began pushing his bill, and the Dole-Canady bill was approved by the House Judiciary Committee's Constitution Subcommittee on an 8–5 vote.[34] The purpose of the bill, according to Canady, was to "prohibit the Federal Government from intentionally discriminating against, or granting a preference to, any person or group based in whole or in part on race, color, national origin or sex, in three specific areas—Federal contracting, Federal employment, and the administration of other federally-conducted programs." The bill also sought to prevent the federal government from "requiring or encouraging Federal contractors to discriminate or grant preferences based on race or sex." The bill would permit affirmative action programs such as outreach and recruitment efforts that sought to increase the pool of women and minority candidates, as long as "at the decision stage, all applicants are judged in a nondiscriminatory manner—that is, without regard to their race or sex."[35] Part of the reason for the slow movement in anti-affirmative-action legislation was the position of big business. Many corporations were afraid of offending women and minorities and uninterested in dismantling their own affirmative action programs. As a result, the rollback movement went nowhere in 1995, and Clinton administration opposition to major changes in affirmative action ensured no action in 1996.[36] In 1997, opponents of affirmative action in Congress identified some 150 provisions in federal law granting preferential treatment and proposed legislation or amendments to eliminate them.

Judiciary

The Supreme Court assumed a major role in grappling with important issues that sprang from the implementation of Title VII. First, the Court tried to provide criteria for determining when discrimination could be adjudged to have occurred. Second, the Court sought to define appropriate remedies once discrimination had been demonstrated. Third, the Court attempted to interpret actions of employers as required by Title VII and to indicate which employees, employers, and employment practices were exempt from coverage.

Proving Employment Discrimination

Title VII specified various prohibited employment practices; these included limiting, classifying, or segregating applicants or employees on the basis of race, color, religion, sex, or national origin in making hiring decisions, determining compensation and other conditions of employment, or discharging employees. Two kinds of discriminatory employment practice became apparent: those that treated individual employees differently and thus were violations of the law and those that resulted in disparate impacts among different employee groups.

In this first area of concern, the Court tried to define, through a series of cases between 1973 and 1981, the nature of the burden of proof required in proving disparate treatment. In *McDonnell Douglas Corp. v. Green,* 411 U.S. 792 (1973), the Court ruled that the employee who claims to be a victim of discrimination must first show that "(i) he belongs to a racial minority; (ii) that he applied and was qualified for a job for which the employer was seeking applicants; (iii) that, despite his qualifications, he was rejected; and (iv) that, after his rejection, the position remained open and the employer continued to seek applicants from persons of [the employee's] qualifications." If these conditions are met, the burden then shifts to the employer to "articulate some legitimate, nondiscriminatory reason for the employee's rejection." Finally, the employee then could seek to show that the employer's justification was merely a "pretext for discrimination."

The *McDonnell Douglas* decision resulted in a variety of interpretations by lower courts in subsequent cases. These courts attempted to grapple with the question of how extensive the burden of proof had to be—what the Court meant by "articulate" (rather than "prove") and whether "one" or "some" legitimate reasons were sufficient defense. Five years later, in *Furnco Construction Corp. v. Waters,* 438 U.S. 567 (1978), the Court tried to provide additional guidance for resolving these questions. Here the Court concluded that "in the absence of any other explanation it is more likely than not that those actions were bottomed on impermissible considerations." Furthermore, the employer then should be allowed "some latitude to introduce evidence which bears on his motive" for his actions.

In a subsequent case, *Board of Trustees of Keene State College v. Sweeney,* 439 U.S. 295 (1978), the Court ruled that lower courts that had required employers to rebut prima facie cases of discrimination by "articulating some legitimate, nondiscriminatory reason" and "proving absence of discriminatory motive" had erred because the former standard was sufficient. However, the lower federal courts still continued to render conflicting decisions, thus forcing the Court to try again to define clearly the issues. In *Texas Department of Community Affairs v. Burdine,* 450 U.S. 248 (1981), the Court again addressed the nature of the proof required of employers charged with a prima facie case of discrimination. The decision of a lower court, which imposed the requirement that employers "prove by a preponderance of the evidence the existence of nondiscriminatory reasons" for taking the actions in question, was rejected by the high court; an employer so charged "bears only the burden of explaining clearly the action."

In a related area of concern, the determination of whether employment decisions have resulted in a disproportionate impact on minorities or women, cases also have centered on the burden of proof. In one of its first Title VII cases, *Griggs v. Duke Power,* 401 U.S. 424 (1971), the Supreme Court ruled that employment practices resulting in an adverse impact on minority applicants were illegal. At issue here was the employer's use of a general intelligence test and the requirement of a high school diploma in determining promotions from one division of the Duke Power Company to another. Black employees, who had effectively been prevented from transferring to other divisions and the higher-paying jobs within those divisions, brought suit against their employer. The court of appeals upheld the use of the test because the court found no intent to discriminate; the Supreme Court rejected that view in arguing that "good intent or absence of discriminatory intent does not redeem employment procedures or testing measures that operate as 'built-in headwinds' for minority groups and are unrelated to measuring job capability."

The justices argued that in Title VII, Congress had authorized the use of "any professionally developed ability test" except those that were "designed, intended or used to discriminate because of race" (Section 703[h]). The Court found that because members of minority groups failed to qualify for employment positions at a greater rate than did nonminority applicants as a result of employer selection devices, the burden of proof then fell upon the employer to show that the selection devices were reasonably related to job performance and not intended to discriminate against minorities. If the employer could demonstrate that tests were job-related, then the burden was shifted back to the party initiating the complaint to show that the selection devices or tests would be just as useful in choosing qualified employees without producing the disparate impact.

Proving that tests and other selection devices measure job-related skills is a very difficult and expensive procedure and has caused some employers to initiate their own hiring or promotion quotas in order to avoid the cost of validating selection devices and to protect against litigation. Criticism of the *Griggs* ruling has called it inconsistent with legislative intent. Sponsors of Title VII emphasized that an intent to discriminate was to be determinative: "Inadvertent or accidental discrimination will not violate the Title. . . . It means simply that the respondent must not have intended to discriminate."[37] In response to concerns that employers might be required to achieve racial balance and be forced to give preferential treatment to minorities, Title VII was amended to prohibit "preferential treatment to any individual or group . . . on account of an imbalance which may exist with respect to the total or percentage of persons of any race, color, religion, sex, or national origin employed" (Section 703[j]). The Supreme Court refined its *Griggs* position in a 1977 case, *International Brotherhood of Teamsters v. U.S.*, 431 U.S. 324 (1977), where the Court ruled that a statistical disparity alone was insufficient proof of discrimination and that it must be accompanied by other evidence. Yet the Court still maintained that such a standard was consistent with congressional intent and argued that a reliance on proof of intent would render Title VII useless.

Remedies for Employment Discrimination

In the second area of judicial policy making—providing for remedies once discrimination has been shown—the Court assumed a more conservative stance relative to congressional intent. In *Albemarle v. Moody*, 422 U.S. 405 (1975), the Supreme Court ruled that once discriminatory activity was proven, back pay was generally to be awarded in order to "make whole" victims of illegal behavior. Retroactive seniority also was awarded to victims of Title VII violations in *Franks v. Bowman Transportation Co.*, 424 U.S. 747 (1976). Both decisions were justified by the Court as consistent with the power of the courts under Title VII to grant equitable relief, and specifically to award back pay, although Title VII clearly indicates that such remedies can be awarded only "if the court finds that the [employer] has intentionally engaged in or is intentionally engaging in an unlawful employment practice" (Section 706[g]).

In *Memphis Fire Department v. Stotts*, 104 S.Ct. 2576 (1984), the Supreme Court maintained its view that "bona fide" seniority systems could not be interfered with in trying to protect the jobs of minorities who, as last to be hired, were first to be fired or laid off by cities or other employers suffering from financial constraints. That decision was reinforced in *Wygant v. Jackson Board of Education*, 476 U.S. 267 (1986). The Court reaffirmed the majority position taken in earlier cases that race-conscious actions must meet three conditions: there must be a "compelling state interest" that requires a response; the action taken must be "narrowly tailored"; and there must be evidence of prior discrimination. The Court rejected the argument that the value of having minority teachers as role models outweighed the commitment to the seniority system.

The Responsibilities of Employers

The third area of important judicial influence is that of determining the general extent of employer responsibility under Title VII. In *United States v. Weber,* 433 U.S. 193 (1979), the Supreme Court upheld an affirmative action agreement embodied in a collective bargaining agreement that reserved 50 percent of the openings in a training program for black employees. A nonminority employee challenged the agreement as a violation of Title VII's prohibition against preferential treatment (Section 703[j]). The plan in question here was upheld by the Court for three reasons. First, although Section 703 prohibited government from requiring preferential treatment in response to a racial imbalance, the section did not interdict a voluntary effort. Second, the plan was temporary and was "not intended to maintain a racial balance but simply to eliminate a manifest racial imbalance." Third, the plan did not "unnecessarily trample the interests of white employees," nor did it "require the discharge of white workers and their replacement with new black hirees."

In cases related to Title VII and affirmative action, the Court has provided a variety of hints at what would and would not be acceptable interpretations of affirmative action. In *Fullilove v. Klutznick,* 448 U.S. 448 (1980), the Supreme Court upheld a 1977 federal works program enacted by Congress that set aside 10 percent of the provided funds for "minority business enterprises." The Court concluded that Congress need not act in a "wholly color-blind fashion" in remedying discrimination, but that such action could be justified only under the broad remedial powers of Congress. In *United Jewish Organization v. Carey,* 443 U.S. 144 (1978), a case involving the redrawing of voting district lines, the Court ruled that the state legislature could consider the impact of redistricting on racial groups even though there had been no finding of discrimination in previous redistricting decisions. In *Regents of the University of California v. Bakke,* 438 U.S. 265 (1978), the Court rejected the university's medical school admission policy, which set aside sixteen admissions for minority applicants. In 1995, however, a Federal Court of Appeals struck down the University of Texas Law School's affirmative action program that was based on the *Bakke* ruling because it violated the constitutional rights of nonminority applicants.[38]

In *Local 28 of the Sheet Metal Workers' International Association v. EEOC,* 478 U.S. 421 (1986), the Court upheld race-conscious relief as a remedy for past discrimination and ruled that remedial action need not be limited to actual victims of discrimination. The lower court's imposition of a goal of 29.23 percent for black membership in the union was upheld by the Supreme Court as a narrowly tailored and reasonable response to a "history of egregious violations" of Title VII. The remedy was temporary; it did not "unnecessarily trample the interests of white employees." It was consistent with congressional intent and was not invoked "simply to create a racially balanced work force."

In the Court's third 1986 case, *Local Number 93, International Association of Firefighters v. City of Cleveland,* 478 U.S. 501 (1986), the Court upheld a consent decree adopted by a lower court that required a fixed number of goals for the promotion of minority employees. The city of Cleveland had negotiated with an organization of black and Hispanic firefighters a set of promotion goals that was submitted to a federal court as a proposed consent decree. The court approved the decree in 1983, over the objections of the union. The Supreme Court found that even though the plan benefited individuals who were not actual victims of discrimination, the Congress had intended to encourage voluntary agreements between unions and employers to end discriminatory practices. Consent decrees were characterized by the Court as essentially voluntary, thus exempting them from the restrictions placed by Congress on judicially imposed remedies for Title VII violations.

In two key decisions issued in 1987, the Supreme Court ruled that federal courts may impose promotion quotas to bring the percentage of qualified minority employees up to the level of minority participation in the relevant labor force, given a long history of discrimination and resistance to court orders (*U.S. v. Paradise,* 480 U.S. 149 [1987], a case involving discrimination in the Alabama State highway patrol). In *Johnson v. Transportation Agency,* 480 U.S. 616 (1987), the Court indicated that female employees who possessed the requisite qualifications for promotion could be given preferential treatment where there was an "obvious imbalance" of men and women. Even absent legal findings of past discrimination, the Court sanctioned preferential treatment that was a "moderate, flexible, case-by-case approach to effecting a gradual improvement in the representation of minorities and women in the Agency's work force."

The Court made it more difficult for governments to undertake affirmative action programs in several cases such as *City of Richmond v. Croson,* 488 U.S. 469 (1989), where it held that courts should apply strict scrutiny in assessing all race-based classifications devised by state and local governments. Richmond had required prime contractors for city construction projects to subcontract at least 30 percent of their contracts to minority-owned businesses. The Court then struck down the plan because of the city's failure to show a history of discrimination that compelled a remedial effort; a general claim of past discrimination in the construction industry as a whole was insufficient. The Court relied on its holding in *Wygant v. Jackson Board of Education,* 476 U.S. 267 (1986), that strict scrutiny of a state's race-based classification was required, and that remedying past discrimination, if convincing evidence was available, was a compelling governmental interest.

In *Metro Broadcasting Inc. v. FCC,* 497 U.S. 547 (1990), at 566, the Court applied an intermediate standard of judicial scrutiny to the federal agency's policy of favoring minority ownership of radio and television broadcast stations. The policy's goal of "promoting programming diversity" was an "important" government interest and the agency's specific efforts were "substantially related" to achieving that goal. The Court found that it was of "overriding significance" that the program had been mandated by Congress. In *Adarand Constructors, Inc. v. Pena,* 115 S.Ct. 2097 (1995), at 2113, the Court applied the strict scrutiny standard, arguing that any racial classification by any governmental body and regardless of the race of those burdened or benefited, must be "narrowly tailored measures that further compelling governmental interests," and rejected minority set-aside programs in federal highway grants. The case was brought by the owner of a company that was a low bidder for guardrails on a federally funded highway project but lost the bid to a Hispanic-owned company.

The Supreme Court's affirmative action jurisprudence is a moving target. As of October 1997, the Supreme Court's current interpretation of constitutional and statutory law seemed to be that preferential treatment is limited to remedial efforts to cure the effects of past discrimination for which the institution giving the preference is responsible.

Presidency

The earliest attempts of the federal government to encourage fair employment practices originated in the executive branch. In the 1940s and 1950s, there was some pressure exerted by black leaders for governmental action, but the response of presidents from Franklin Roosevelt to John Kennedy was to limit efforts to the employment practices of federal contractors. Such a limited scope of coverage was politically noncontroversial; it also was consistent with general expectations of limited presidential power and with the idea that federal funds should not be used to subsidize discriminatory actions.

President Roosevelt issued Executive Orders 8802, 9001, and 9346, which were the first in a series of important presidential initiatives for equal employment opportunity. Under the orders, defense contractors were prohibited from discrimination in hiring and other employment practices on the basis of race, color, creed, or national origin. The Fair Employment Practices Committee (FEPC) was created to monitor compliance.[39] President Truman also issued a series of executive orders that transferred responsibility for FEPC activities to the Defense Department, granted authority to other agencies that contracted for defense-related goods and services to require nondiscrimination in the employment decisions of their contractors, and created the Committee on Government Contract Compliance to monitor compliance with the government's fair employment policy and to study the effectiveness of previous efforts.[40] President Eisenhower issued an executive order in 1953 that established the President's Committee on Government Contracts and, for the first time, extended nondiscrimination requirements to all companies that contracted with the federal government. One year later, a second Eisenhower order extended coverage to subcontractors.[41]

It was not until the Kennedy administration that the executive branch began to consider taking a more vigorous and aggressive role in pursuing equal employment opportunity. Two months after he took office, President Kennedy issued Executive Order 10925, which continued to require fair employment practices of contractors with federal agencies and created the President's Committee on Equal Employment Opportunity. Chaired by Vice President Lyndon Johnson, the committee was given jurisdiction over all complaints of discriminatory behavior by contractors, was empowered to conduct compliance reviews and to require that contractors supply hiring data and other employment records, and was authorized to cancel existing contracts and debar firms violating the executive order from future contracts.[42] For the first time there was a general acceptance of the power of agencies to cancel contracts if companies engaged in unfair employment practices. Of more importance, however, was the requirement that all contracts include the following clause: "The contractor will take affirmative action to ensure that applicants are employed, and that employees are treated during employment without regard to their race, creed, color or national origin" (Part III, Section 301 [1]).

One of the most important actions affecting the affirmative action efforts of the federal government was the issuance of Executive Order 11246 by Lyndon Johnson in 1965. This order delegated to the secretary of labor authority to issue regulations implementing the order; the rules that were issued subsequently included the requirement that construction contractors and subcontractors who received federal contracts must comply with goals and timetables for female and minority employees in job categories where both groups had been "underutilized" in the past. In 1967, discrimination on the basis of sex was added to the prohibited practices.[43]

The Ford administration was roundly criticized by civil rights groups for its lack of interest in equal employment opportunity. Black leaders attacked budget cuts in health, education, and welfare programs; a lack of initiatives to combat black unemployment; and a general attitude of "benign neglect" to the concerns of blacks.[44]

The Carter administration came to office with a strong commitment to civil rights. In 1978 Carter reorganized the executive branch's equal employment opportunity efforts and consolidated power and responsibility in the Equal Employment Opportunity Commission and the Office of Federal Contracts Compliance Programs (OFCCP). In the important Supreme Court cases decided between 1977 and 1980, the Justice Department was a vigorous proponent of affirmative action in the cases it litigated as well as in those where it filed briefs.[45]

The Reagan administration promised to make dramatic changes in equal employment opportunity policy..The Reagan administration reversed many of the Carter administration's enforcement initiatives and ordered industry-wide targeting to be dropped and the EEOC to concentrate on cases where it could readily prove discrimination. The administration joined in litigation to overturn decisions by federal courts and state and local governments that imposed hiring and promotion goals. In 1984, after the Memphis fire-fighters case, Assistant Attorney General Reynolds proclaimed that the "era of racial quotas has run its course" and that EEOC and OFCCP officials no longer would require employers to develop numerical hiring goals in order to increase minority employment.[46] The Supreme Court's two 1986 decisions upholding hiring goals, however, dampened these efforts. The Reagan Justice Department also proposed that Executive Order 11246 be rewritten to prohibit the use of hiring and promotion goals, but never made the change.

During the first two years of the Clinton administration, White House and executive branch officials debated what its position should be. In a major address in July 1995, Clinton largely defended affirmative action, arguing that the country should "mend it, don't end it." He appealed to whites even as he argued that they were still guilty of discrimination, and to blacks even as he said the problems facing blacks cannot all be blamed on white America. But there was little subsequent effort by the president to build support for affirmative action.[47] In October 1995 the Clinton administration ended a $1 billion Defense Department minority contract set-aside program, the only step taken by the federal government to actually reduce affirmative action.[48] The program was challenged by a Minneapolis-based builder, McCrossan Construction Co., who argued in federal court that huge percentages of construction work in some areas were reserved for minority contractors. The Defense Department, applying the strict scrutiny test that the Supreme Court had ordered in 1995, concluded that the program was not narrowly tailored to satisfy a compelling state interest.[49]

In 1996 the administration suspended for three years all government contract set-aside programs for women- and minority-owned companies, but allowed agencies to give preference to these companies on a case-by-case basis. The decision was an attempt to find middle ground by eliminating the kind of affirmative action the administration felt was closest to quotas. The administration's new guidelines for affirmative action set as a goal the awarding of 5 percent of federal contracts to minority-owned firms. That goal had been unanimously approved by both houses of Congress in 1994 while the Democrats still controlled Congress. Agencies are first required to take racially neutral steps such as outreach in recruitment. They are to commission "disparity studies" to determine the available pool of women and minority contractors and how large that pool would be if no demonstrable discrimination had occurred, and use those studies to set goals for the percentage of women and minority contractors the agencies should have. The further the agency is from the goal, the more preferential treatment they can engage in, culminating, only in egregious situations, in set-asides.[50] Some $12 billion in annual federal procurement decisions are affected by the guidelines.[51]

In 1996 the Justice Department issued a memorandum to federal agencies that argued, in response to the Supreme Court's 1995 *Adarand* holding, that the "application of strict scrutiny should not require major modifications in the way federal agencies have been properly implementing affirmative action policies," but that to protect themselves against reverse discrimination lawsuits, agencies should be able to show a "compelling" need for race-based policies. That showing could come through "historical evidence" of agency discrimination, "statistical evidence" of underrepresentation of minorities in job categories, or "operational needs" such as having a diverse workforce. In any case, no absolute preference is to be given on the basis of race, but race could be one of several factors involved in hiring decisions.[52]

Bureaucracy

The evolution of employment policy from equal opportunity to affirmative action and preferential treatment has occurred within the partnership of the courts, the Equal Employment Opportunity Commission, the Office of Federal Contracts Compliance (later retitled the Office of Federal Contracts Compliance Programs), and the president. Much of the current controversy regarding EEO can be traced to actions taken by the OFCC during this time. The director of OFCC in 1967, Edward C. Sylvester Jr., explained that "in a general way, affirmative action is anything that you have to do to get results. But this does not necessarily include preferential treatment. The key word here is 'results.' . . . Affirmative action is really designed to get employees to apply the same kind of imagination and ingenuity that they apply to any other phase of their operation."[53]

The OFCC issued regulations in 1968 that for the first time required all contractors with fifty or more employees and contracts of at least $50,000 to have a written affirmative action plan.[54] The OFCC eventually issued additional regulations, known as Order No. 4, that provided instructions for contractors in complying with Executive Order 11246. These guidelines became the basis for almost all subsequent efforts related to affirmative action. Order No. 4 defined an affirmative action program as a "set of specific and result-oriented procedures to which a contractor commits himself to apply every good-faith effort. The objective of those procedures plus such efforts is equal employment opportunity."[55] The key components of an affirmative action plan were to include an "analysis of areas within which the contractor is deficient in the utilization of minority groups, and further, goals and timetables to which the contractor's good faith efforts must be directed to correct the deficiencies and thus to achieve prompt and full utilization of minorities at all levels and in all segments of his work force where deficiencies exist."[56] The OFCC was careful to insist that preferential treatment of any kind was not required; rather, the order required action "necessary to assure that all persons receive equal employment opportunity."

During this period, the OFCC also shifted from a policy of encouraging voluntary compliance with fair employment practices to enforcement activities including debarment of contractors. In 1969, for the first time, contracting agencies began reporting to Congress that they had canceled or suspended contracts with contractors who failed to comply with EEO requirements and that some contractors had been debarred from future contracts.

The first area of contracting activity to be subjected to specific affirmative action requirements was the construction industry. Concerned about past discriminatory practices that had restricted minority membership in construction crafts, the OFCC instituted its Philadelphia Plan, a program of goals and timetables for increasing minority employment in the construction industry, named after the city in which it was first put into effect. The Philadelphia Plan empowered the Department of Labor's Office of Federal Contracts Compliance to set hiring quotas for minority workers that then were to be applied to federal contractors bidding for jobs in the Philadelphia area. Labor Department officials found that because of discrimination in craft trade unions, blacks had been employed in construction projects in extremely small numbers. The Labor Department established goals for the employment of minority ironworkers, plumbers and pipefitters, and electrical and other workers that would have increased black employment in these crafts from less than 5 percent to between 19 and 26 percent by 1973.[57]

The Nixon administration defended the Philadelphia Plan against its critics in Congress, who proposed in 1969 that no funds be appropriated for efforts to require contractors to meet minority employment goals. The White House urged members of Congress to defeat this proposal as "the most important civil rights issue in a long, long time."[58] Attorney General John Mitchell defended the Labor Department's policy by arguing that "it is now well recognized in judicial opinions that the obligation of nondiscrimination . . . does not require, and in some circumstances may not permit obliviousness or indifference to the racial consequences of alternative courses of action which involve the application of outwardly neutral criteria."[59] The Labor Department hailed its policy as a "major breakthrough in the fight for equality of opportunity in employment." Enforcement efforts could not rest on findings of discriminatory intent, because evidence for such motivations was so difficult to uncover. The reliance on statistical disparity as evidence of discrimination was an extremely important development in the shift toward preferential treatment, as proponents argued that enforcement activity in response to such disparities was

> grounded on the common-sense proposition that the underrepresentation of minority and women in any area of economic or professional enterprise is an indication that discrimination may exist. . . . Apparently rational arguments can mask discriminatory behavior and even neutral efforts can unintentionally cause discriminatory results. In such circumstances, the best available means for detecting the possible presence of discriminatory processes is to examine their statutory outcome.[60]

Perhaps the most important factor in this shift was the difficulty in measuring progress in gaining compliance. A related difficulty was the use of data to demonstrate progress in achieving policy objectives. For equal employment opportunity, the number of suspended contracts or debarred contractors became convenient indicators of policy effectiveness, even though there was no clear correlation between such figures and increased opportunities for minorities.

Finally, it should be noted here that the OFCC rather than the EEOC was primarily responsible for bureaucratic initiatives for affirmative action. During much of the late 1960s and into the 1970s, the Equal Employment Opportunity Commission spent much of its time trying to get organized. During the EEOC's first three years of operation, one or two of the five commissioner slots were vacant for more than half the time. There was no chairperson for four months in 1966, and there was a high turnover because the first five commissioners were appointed for terms of five, four, three, two, and one year to assure a future distribution of appointments.[61]

From its conception the Equal Employment Opportunity Commission has been described as understaffed, underfunded, and weak. The number of complaints filed with the commission grew from 60,000 in 1990 to 92,000 in 1995, but the number of staff members actually fell during those same years from 2,853 to 2,183, and the backlog of cases waiting to be addressed grew from 40,000 to nearly 100,000. Part of the increase in cases filed was due to cases filed under the Americans with Disability Act passed in 1992. As the backlog grows, the agency files fewer cases: in FY 1990, it filed 643 individual and class action cases; in FY 1996, only 160.[62] Other federal agencies filed 95 job bias cases. Less than 25 percent of these cases were class action suits. Private law firms now handle about 98 percent of the job discrimination cases filed. In 1991 private firms filed 8,140 job discrimination cases; in 1995, 19,059.[63] The average EEOC investigator handled 123 cases in 1995, more than double the average 55 cases she had in 1990. The backlog forces thousands of people who have alleged job discrimination to wait before they can take their case to court, since the EEOC must first dismiss, settle, pursue, or pass the case before the courts hear it.[64]

The Office of Federal Contracts Compliance Programs is the other major federal agency involved in implementing equal employment opportunity policy. The agency enforces the nondiscrimination and affirmative action requirements imposed on government contractors under executive orders through compliance reviews and by responding to complaints. In FY 1994 it conducted four thousand compliance reviews and investigated more than eight hundred complaints. When problems are found, the agency works with the contractor to form a conciliation agreement that may include back pay, job offers, seniority credit, promotions, or "other make-whole remedies to those who have been discriminated." If there is evidence of underutilization of minority and women contractors, the agreement may include outreach and other recruitment efforts and other affirmative action efforts. If conciliation agreements fail to solve the problem, the case may be turned over to the Labor Department for administrative hearings that can terminate in loss of contracts and disbarment from future awards. The OFCCP was responsible for overseeing more than $161 billion in 176,000 contracts to 192,500 companies in FY 1993. According to testimony given to Congress in 1995, the agency does not require contractors to hire or promote women or minorities on the basis of race or sex, but only requires "outreach and other efforts to broaden the pool of qualified applicants to include groups previously excluded"; an employer "is never required to hire a person who

does not have the qualifications needed to perform the job successfully."
Goals are neither a "ceiling or a floor for the employment of particular
groups."[65] The Small Business Administration's (SBA) minority set-aside
program has also come under fire for helping companies that are not advan-
taged.[66]

Interest Groups

The civil rights movement was instrumental in awakening the nation to
racial injustices and forcing the Congress to consider major legislation,
including the Civil Rights Act of 1964. By the early 1970s, when affirmative action programs became firmly entrenched in the federal bureaucracy
and courts, group opposition to the programs began to mount. This development caused a deep split among groups that had been allies in the civil
rights movement. Organized labor, which had banded together behind civil
rights legislation, now was divided about affirmative action. Affirmative
action was rejected by virtually all major Jewish groups.[67] A third source of
opposition came from groups representing "white ethnic" voters, who believed that they, too, suffered from discrimination.

This conflict was illustrated by the organizations filing amicus briefs in
the major affirmative action cases to reach the Supreme Court during the
late 1970s. This pattern was best illustrated by the case of *Regents of the
University of California v. Bakke,* 438 U.S. 265 (1978), which addressed the
constitutionality of quotas aimed at increasing minority student enrollment
in medical school. Some 116 organizations submitted amicus briefs in this
case. The most important division reflected in these data was between
groups representing blacks, Spanish-speaking persons, Asians, and Native
Americans and those speaking for the Jewish community and "white ethnic" nationalities. Racial minorities are the protected groups under most
affirmative action programs, whereas religious and ethnic minorities do not
benefit from such programs even though religion is mentioned along with
race, color, and sex in the 1964 Civil Rights Act. No Jewish or white ethnic
group (for example, those with Italian, Ukrainian, Greek, or Polish memberships) endorsed affirmative action in an amicus brief; and no black,
Spanish-speaking, Asian, or Native American group allied itself with
Bakke's position. Although no single-issue group filed amicus briefs, it is
noteworthy that racial and ethnic groups within multi-interest organizations
from legal, health/medical, and academic sectors were mobilized on this
question. These groups included the American Indian Bar Association, the
Puerto Rican Legal Defense and Education Fund, the Hellenic Bar Association of Illinois, and the black National Medical Association.

Public Opinion

Surveys point to three conclusions about how the public views equal employment opportunity and affirmative action. First, there has been a gradual shift during the past two decades toward more racial tolerance among both northern and southern whites. One study by Tom W. Smith and Paul B. Sheatsley constructed a racial tolerance index.[68] Smith and Sheatsley also found that there has been a significant evolution in opinion concerning employment opportunity, as demonstrated in opinion surveys between 1942 and 1972. In response to the question, "Do you think (Negroes/Blacks) should have as good a chance as white people to get any kind of job, or do you think white people should have the first chance at any kind of job?" 42 percent of the respondents in 1942 indicated that there should be equal treatment. By 1963, 83 percent favored equal treatment, and by 1972, the figure was 96 percent.

Some polling data show only limited support even for affirmative action as remedial policy: 85 percent of respondents opposed "preferential hiring and promotion of blacks" and more than half of the white respondents said it "is not the government's business" to redress cases where blacks have not received "fair treatment in jobs." Opposition to affirmative action and opposition to welfare often go hand in hand. "Racial resentment," one study concluded, is the "most potent force in white public opinion today."[69]

Eighty percent of the public typically agrees with statements that the government should fight discrimination, promote equal opportunity, and treat everyone fairly. When asked if they support affirmative action, usually 40 to 50 percent agree. When asked if they favor special treatment or preferences for blacks, only about a third agree; when the word *quotas* is used, support falls to about 20 percent. A January 1995 *Los Angeles Times* poll, for example, asked respondents for their views on affirmative action: 39 percent said such programs "go too far," 32 percent said they are "adequate now," and 23 percent said they "don't go far enough." But when asked if Congress should ban "preferential treatment in hiring," 73 percent agreed.[70] For fifteen years, polls have shown strong opposition to prefererential hiring and race-based college admissions.[71] After reviewing the survey data on this issue, Seymour Lipset and William Schneider concluded:

> Policies favoring quotas and numerical goals for integration . . . violate traditional conceptions of the meaning of equality of opportunity. Americans will accept the argument that race and sex are disadvantages deserving of compensation. . . . They will go along with special compensation up to the

point where it is felt that resources have been roughly equalized and the initial terms of competition are once again fair. But the data show that every attempt to introduce any form of absolute preference . . . meets with stiff and determined resistance from the vast majority of Americans.[72]

Opposition to affirmative action among white males seemed to peak in the mid-1990s, according to a *Wall Street Journal*/NBC News poll: in 1991, 44 percent of white men said they opposed affirmative action, 67 percent opposed it in 1995, and 52 percent were against affirmative action in late 1996. The decline in opposition seemed to be a result of Supreme Court decisions that made defending affirmative action more difficult, and many companies have slowed their hiring and promotion of women and minorities.

Affirmative action programs often fail to satisfy anyone. White males complain about reverse discrimination, but women and minorities continue to argue that few opportunities are given them. More support for affirmative action came from business executives who developed such programs in response to OFCCP regulations on contractors. The director of public affairs for Time, for example, indicated that Time's affirmative action efforts "didn't change when Reagan came to power" and that efforts "have redoubled in the last four years."[73] A Mountain Bell executive stated that its minority and female workforce was a "gold mine" for good managers, but had it not been for hiring goals imposed on the company by a court decree, Mountain Bell would not have made such efforts on its own.[74]

Affirmative action has been used by Republicans for three decades to try to splinter the Democratic base of women, minorities, and working-class white males. The Nixon administration sought to pit white workers against black recipients of affirmative action, and peel off the angry white males from the Democratic Party and encourage them to vote Republican. The strategy was successful in the 1972 presidential election, and much more so in appealing to the "Reagan Democrats."[75] By the 1980s Republicans could run against the programs they had created in order to appeal to the white working class. That strategy continued into the 1990s. Republican presidential primary candidate Pat Buchanan led the party's appeal to "angry white males" by making affirmative action and opposition to illegal immigration central planks of his platform. Bob Dole and Jack Kemp, who had been supporters of affirmative action earlier in their congressional careers, reversed position when they ran as Republican presidential and vice presidential nominees in 1996.[76] Dole acknowledged that he had once supported affirmative action but concluded that it did not work: "We ought to do away with preferences," he said in a speech billed as a statement on affirmative action, "it ought to be based on merit. This is America!"[77] Kemp had initially opposed Proposition 207 in California, but announced his support for the initiative during the summer of 1996.[78] Republicans have largely been successful in achieving that goal. What was once a policy with bipartisan support and a united Democratic party has come to pit unions against minority advocates and to alienate Jewish and white ethnic groups.

The fragmented policy-making process has produced unreasonable expectations for affirmative action. It is expected to eliminate the effects of past discrimination, end racism, reduce poverty, and create opportunities for people of color. It should be no surprise that it has failed to so. Affirmative action programs that simply set goals for increased opportunities by women and minorities are much easier to devise and cheaper to implement than the policies necessary to address root problems like improving public schools, reducing crime and substance abuse, strengthening families, encouraging responsible fatherhood, discouraging out-of-wedlock pregnancy, reducing economic isolation, improving housing, and remedying the other ills that plague so many Americans, and disproportionately affect African Americans. Affirmative action is, in the short-run, sometimes a zero-sum game. In the long-run, however, an integrated, diverse society will be more humane and productive.

Has affirmative action increased racism and resentment among whites who believe their opportunities have been compromised? Apparently it has. Has it encouraged victimization and dependency on the part of recipients? Some blacks argue so. And even if it produces such outcomes, others make constitutional claims for it that cannot be dismissed on the grounds that the outcomes are unfortunate for some. It is doubtful that we would really want to pursue a policy that actually harms its intended beneficiaries, but few policy makers are seeking definitive answers to the question.

Moral policies are enveloped by a political discourse that emphasizes absolutes—clear positions that are enshrined in simple slogans such as "the Constitution is color-blind." We generally applaud principled policy making and encourage appeals to fundamental ideals, but this ignores reality. Preferential treatment cannot be contrasted with employment and admissions decisions that are strictly based on objective standards of merit, for such decisions rarely occur. It ought to be compared with the variety of existing criteria used in making employment decisions and the real barriers women and minorities face in employment. Quotas have dominated policy debate about affirmative action, with too little attention given to educational reforms, job training, and outreach programs designed to help minorities compete more effectively in the job market. What is needed is more attention to the costs and benefits of affirmative action and a careful examination of policy alternatives, not a continued debate about moral absolutes.

Notes

1. U.S. Commission on Civil Rights, *Affirmative Action in the 1980s: Dismantling the Process of Discrimination,* (Washington, D.C.: U.S. Commission on Civil Rights, 1981), pp. 3–5.

2. See Morris Abram, "Affirmative Action: Fair Shakers and Social Engineers," *Harvard Law Review* 99 (1986), pp. 1312–1326.

3. Quoted in Carl Cohen, "The DeFunis Case, Race, and the Constitution," *The Nation* (February 8, 1975), pp. 135–145.

4. Ellis Close, *Color-Blind: Seeing Beyond Race in a Race-Obsessed World* (New York: HarperCollins Publishers, 1997).

5. They were Alaska, California, Colorado, Connecticut, Delaware, Hawaii, Idaho, Illinois, Indiana, Iowa, Kansas, Massachusetts, Michigan, Missouri, New Jersey, New Mexico, New York, Ohio, Oregon, Pennsylvania, Rhode Island, Vermont, Washington, and Wisconsin. Bureau of National Affairs, *State Fair Employment Laws and Their Administration* (Washington, D.C.: BNA, 1964), p. ii.

6. "University's Leaders Are Torn by Affirmative-Action Ban," *The New York Times* (January 28, 1996), p. A8; B. Drummond Ayres, Jr., "California Regents Postpone a Ban on Affirmative Action," *The New York Times* (February 16, 1996), p. A11.

7. Kathryn Wexler, "The Fight Over Affirmative Action," *The Washington Post National Weekly Edition* (March 11–17, 1996), p. 33.

8. B. Drummond Ayres, Jr., "Foes of Affirmative Action Complete California Drive," *The New York Times* (February 22, 1996), p. A7.

9. B. Drummond Ayres, Jr., "Foes of Affirmative Action Are Gaining in Ballot Effort," *The New York Times* (February 6, 1996), p. A8.

10. Paul M. Barrett and G. Pascal Zachary, "Affirmative Action Foes Advance in California," *The Wall Street Journal* (February 21, 1996).

11. Wexler, "The Fight Over Affirmative Action."

12. William Claiborne, "The Dulling of a Cutting-Edge Issue," *The Washington Post National Weekly Edition* (June 17–23, 1996), p. 12.

13. Sam Howe Verhovek, "Vote in California Is Motivating Foes of Anti-bias Plans," *The New York Times* (November 10, 1996), p. A1.

14. R. Drummond Ayres, Jr., "U.S. Judge Blocks Voters' Initiative on Job Preference," *The New York Times* (November 28, 1996), p. A1.

15. Peter Schmidt, "A Federal Appeals Court Upholds California Measure Barring Racial Preferences," *The Chronicle of Higher Education* (April 18, 1997), p. A28.

16. G. Pascal Zachary, "Some Major Cities Thumb Their Noses At California Ban on Affirmative Action," *The Wall Street Journal* (November 15, 1996), p. A8.

17. Ayres, "U.S. Judge Blocks Voters' Initiative on Job Preference."

18. Verhovek, "Vote in California is Motivating Foes of Anti-bias Plans."

19. Congressional Quarterly, *Congress and the Nation,* vol. 1 (Washington, D.C.: Congressional Quarterly, 1964), p. 1634.

20. Ibid., p. 1629.

21. Ibid., p. 1610.

22. Ibid., p. 1635.

23. See, generally, Charles and Barbara Whalen, *The Longest Debate: A Legislative History of the 1964 Civil Rights Act* (New York: New American Library, 1985), especially chapter 3.

24. Congressional Quarterly, *Congress and the Nation,* vol. 1, pp. 93a, 96a, and 1637.

25. See Gary Bryner, "Congress, Courts, and Agencies: Equal Employment and the Limits of Policy Implementation," *Political Science Quarterly* 96 (1981), pp. 411–430.

26. Congressional Quarterly, *Congress and the Nation,* vol. 2 (Washington, D.C.: Congressional Quarterly, 1969), p. 174.

27. Ibid., p. 503.

28. Quoted in *Washington v. Davis,* 426 U.S. 229 (1976).

29. Congressional Quarterly, *Congress and the Nation,* vol. 3, pp. 250–251.

30. Sheilah A. Goodman, "Trying to Undo the Damage: The Civil Rights Act of 1990," *Harvard Law Review* 14 (1991), pp. 185–189.

31. Other civil rights cases effectively overturned by Congress include *Alyeska Pipeline Serv. Co. v. Wilderness Soc'y,* 421 U.S. 240 (1975); *General Elec. Co. v. Gilbert,* 429 U.S. 125 (1976), overturned by Pregnancy Discrimination Act, 92 Stat. 2076 (1978); *United Air Lines, Inc. v. McMann,* 434 U.S. 192 (1977), overturned in the Age Discrimination in Employment Act Amendments of 1978, 92 Stat. 189 (1978); *City of Mobile v. Bolden,* 466 U.S. 55 (1980), *Grove City College v. Bell,* 465 U.S. 555 (1984), overturned in the Civil Rights Restoration Act of 1987, 102 Stat. 28; *Smith v. Robinson,* 468 U.S. 992 (1984), overturned in the Handicapped Children's Protection Act of 1986, 100 Stat. 796; *Atascadero State Hosp. v. Scanlon,* 473 U.S. 234 (1985); and *United States Dep't of Transp. v. Paralyzed Veterans of America,* 477 U.S. 597 (1986).

32. 104th Congress, S. 1085.

33. Testimony of Deval L. Patrick, assistant attorney general for civil rights, in testimony provided in a hearing of the Committee on Labor and Human Resources, *Affirmative Action, Preferences, and the Equal Employment Opportunity Act of 1995,* 104th Congress (April 30, 1995), pp. 30–33; Steven A. Holmes, "Veto Threat On Bill to Ban Hiring Rules," *The New York Times* (December 8, 1995), p. A10.

34. Steven A. Holmes, "White House to Suspend a Program for Minorities," *The New York Times* (March 8, 1996), p. A1.

35. Rep. Charles Canady, testimony provided in a hearing of the Committee on Labor and Human Resources, *Affirmative Action, Preferences, and the Equal Employment Opportunity Act of 1995,* 104th Congress (April 30, 1995), p. 9.

36. Barrett and Zachary, "Affirmative Action Foes Advance in California."

37. *Congressional Record* 110 (1964), p. 8921.

38. *Hopwood v. Texas,* 78 F.3d 932, *cert. denied,* 116 S.Ct. 2591 (1996).

39. U.S. Senate, Committee on Labor and Human Resources, *Committee Analysis of Executive Order 12246,* 97th Cong. (Washington, D.C.: U.S. Government Printing Office, 1982).

40. E.O. 9664, 3 C.F.R. 1943; E.O. 10210, 3 C.F.R. 1949; and E.O. 10308, 3 C.F.R. 1949.

41. E.O. 10479, 3 C.F.R. 1953; E.O. 10577, 3 C.F.R. 1954.

42. 3 C.F.R. 1963.

43. E.O. 11375, 32 *Fed. Reg.* 14303.

44. Dom Donafede, "Blacks Await Performance of Promise," *National Journal* (November 30, 1974), p. 1810.

45. See James W. Singer, "A Shake-up May Be in Store for Job Discrimination Efforts," *National Journal* (May 4, 1977), pp. 746–747; Bryner, "Congress, Courts, and Agencies," p. 417.

46. Eric Press and Ann McDaniel, "A Right Turn on Race?" *Newsweek* (June 25, 1984), pp. 29–31.

47. Nicholas Lemann, "Clinton, the Great Communicator," *The New York Times* (January 20, 1997), p. A17.

48. Barrett and Zachary, "Affirmative Action Foes Advance in California."

49. Paul M. Barrett, "Foes of Affirmative Action Target SBA's 8(a) Program," *The Wall Street Journal* (March 18, 1996), p. B2.

50. Steven A. Holmes, "White House to Suspend a Program for Minorities," *The New York Times* (March 8, 1996), p. A1.

51. Paul M. Barrett, "Affirmative Action for U.S. Contracts Is Limited in Rules Using 'Benchmarks,' " *The Wall Street Journal* (May 23, 1996), p. B5.

52. Paul M. Barrett, "White House Memo on Federal Hiring Shows Defense of Affirmative Action," *The Wall Street Journal* (March 4, 1996).

53. U.S. Senate, Committee on Labor and Human Resources, "Committee Analysis of Executive Order 12246," p. 12.

54. 33 *Fed. Reg.* 7804.

55. 41 C.F.R. sec. 60–2.10, 1970.

56. Ibid.

57. *Contractors Association of Eastern Pennsylvania v. Secretary of Labor,* 442 F. 2d 159, 3rd cir. (1971), *cert. denied*, 404 U.S. 854.

58. *The New York Times* (December 21, 1969), p. 39.

59. Congressional Quarterly, *Congress and the Nation,* vol. 3, p. 498.

60. U.S. Civil Rights Commission, "Affirmative Action in the 1980s," p. 2.

61. Congressional Quarterly, *Congress and the Nation,* vol. 2, p. 374.

62. Allan R. Meyerson, "As Federal Bias Cases Drop, Workers Take Up the Fight," *The New York Times* (January 12, 1997), p. A1.

63. Barbara Rosewicz, "EEOC Flexes New Muscles in Mitsubishi Case, But It Lacks the Bulk to Push Business Around," *The Wall Street Journal* (April 29, 1996), p. A24.

64. Kirsten Downey Grimsley, "The Rodney Dangerfield of Agencies," *The Washington Post National Weekly Edition* (February 19–25, 1996), p. 31.

65. Testimony of Shirley J. Wilcher, deputy assistant secretary for federal contract compliance, U.S. Department of Labor, in a hearing before the Committee on Labor and Human Resources, *Affirmative Action and the Office of Federal Contract Compliance* (June 5, 1995), pp. 11–18.

66. Barrett, "Foes of Affirmative Action Target SBA's 8(a) Program."

67. See Rochelle L. Stanfield, "The Black-Jewish Coalition—Shaken but Still Alive After Young Incident," *National Journal* (November 3, 1979), pp. 1849–1852.

68. Tom W. Smith and Paul B. Sheatsley, "American Attitudes Toward Race Relations," *Public Opinion* (October-November 1984), p. 15.

69. Andrew Hacker, "Goodbye to Affirmative Action?" *The New York Review of Books* (July 11, 1996), pp. 21–29, at p. 25.

70. Rochelle L. Stanfield, "The Wedge Issue," *National Journal* (April 1, 1995), pp. 790–93, at 791.

71. Louis Jacobson, "A Speak-No-Evil Veil Lifted," *National Journal* (April 1, 1995), p. 836.

72. Seymour Martin Lipset and William Schneider, "The Bakke Case: How Would It Be Decided at the Bar of Public Opinion?" *Public Opinion* 1 (March-April 1978), pp. 41–42.

73. Anthony Neely, "Government Role in Rooting Out, Remedying Discrimination Is Shifting," *National Journal* (September 22, 1984), p. 15.

74. Douglas Huron, "It's Fashionable to Denigrate Hiring Quotas—but It's Wrong," *Washington Post National Weekly Edition,* (August 27, 1984), p. 23.

75. John David Skrentny, *The Ironies of Affirmative Action: Politics, Culture, and Justice in America* (Chicago: University of Chicago Press, 1996).

76. John Harwood, "Californial Republicans Debate the Pros and Cons of Targeting Immigrants and Preferences in Fall," *The Wall Street Journal* (March 26, 1996), p. A20.

77. Katharine Q. Seelye, "Dole Declares Strong Opposition To Preferences for Sex and Race," *The New York Times* (March 25, 1996), p. A13.

78. "The Jack Kemp Reverse," *The New York Times* (August 15, 1996), p. A20.

3

Death Penalty: Crime Deterrent or Legalized Homicide?

Mary Ann E. Steger and Brent S. Steel

The use of the death penalty in our criminal justice system remains controversial. There are those who argue that putting the convicted criminal to death is justified by the heinous nature of the crime that has been committed and is morally defensible. Opponents will argue with equal force that no crime justifies the taking of a life by the state. The conflict that exists around capital punishment is framed by differing interpretations of the rights that are in question. On the one hand, the interpretation is that society and the victims of crimes have the right to see justice served by a sentence of death in those cases where the legal system has determined that the nature of the crime committed demands the taking of the convicted person's life. On the other hand, others will argue that justice is never served by imposing a sentence of death on persons convicted of serious crimes because the sacredness of human life is a moral principle that cannot be violated by imposing a sentence of death.

The Debate on the Causes of Crime

The debate over the rightness or wrongness of capital punishment is fueled by a profound disagreement about the causes of crime. The "sociogenic" school focuses on the environment and places primary responsibility for crime on society.[1] Poverty, lack of education, high unemployment, unstable homes, the absence of affection, and improper socialization into social norms are cited as causes of crime. The sociogenic approach reflects a liberal political ideology.

The "psychogenic" school is a psychological approach that considers the individual's *propensity* and *inducement* to commit crime.[2] That propensity is determined by the individual's ability to conceptualize right and wrong, to manage impulses, to take risks and anticipate their future consequences. Inducement refers to situational factors, such as access and opportunity, that act as incentives to crime. According to this view, the individual is responsible for his/her behavior because a *choice* is made whether to commit a crime. This view underlies conservative thought and explains why the view's advocates favor severe penalties (such as capital punishment) thought to *deter* individuals from making the *wrong* choices.

A third approach is the "biogenic" or "sociobiological" explanation. This view is less common among criminologists but has been popularized by James Q. Wilson. This school relates criminal behavior to such biological phenomena as brain tumors, endocrine abnormalities, neurological dysfunctions from prenatal and postnatal experiences, and chromosomal abnormalities.[3] Preventive crime policies would entail the development of appropriate screening and other diagnostic tests for persons suspected of such physical or mental disorders.

Those who believe in the sociogenic school are less likely to be supporters of the death penalty than are those who adhere to either the psychogenic or biogenic schools of thought. They do not hold the individual as primarily responsible for his/her criminal behavior and, because of this, do not see a death sentence as an effective deterrent to capital offenses. Instead, they tend to favor a *civil libertarian* approach, which emphasizes the rights of individuals accused of crimes.

In contrast, those who view criminal behavior as a matter of individual choice (the psychogenic school) are likely to see capital punishment as an effective deterrent, because individuals decide whether or not to commit a crime by calculating the amount of risk involved in the commission of the crime and the prospect of punishment. Adherents of this perspective will support policies that take a *law and order* approach, where the emphasis is on protecting the public order by imposing swift and severe punishments on those who commit capital offenses.

Those who adhere to the biogenic school may or may not view capital punishment as a deterrent to crime, but they nonetheless may feel that capital punishment is the appropriate punishment for individuals who cannot be cured of their criminal predispositions. However, the primary emphasis would be on preventive policies that identify those who are biologically predisposed to commit gruesome crimes before they do so.

The Death Penalty in the United States

The death penalty has been used in the United States for a very long time. For example, there were a total of 162 executions performed under local authority in the 1600s, and in the next century the number of executions rose to 1,391. By the late 1800s, the number of executions performed across the United States was quite high, with 1,005 in the decade of the 1880s, 1,280 executions in the decade of the 1900s, and 1,289 in the decade of the 1920s.[4] The number of executions continued to increase in the decade of the 1930s, with a one-year high of 199 executions occurring in 1935. There were over 100 executions a year through the decade of the 1950s.[5] In the decade of the 1960s, the constitutionality of the death penalty became an issue, and most executions stopped after 1967 pending the outcome of various legal challenges to capital punishment. From 1930 to the end of 1970, however, "there were 3,859 executions under state or federal authority (and another few hundred under military authority)," and "forty-two of fifty U.S. states had a death penalty statute at some time and executed at least one offender."[6]

One Supreme Court case that directly affected the nationwide moratorium on the death penalty was the *Furman v. Georgia* (408 U.S. 238) decision in 1972. In this case, the Court ruled that a number of states had capital punishment statutes that were unconstitutional, and the Court's written opinion provided guidelines for revising these statutes. At that time, there were 645 convicted criminals on death row. Just four years later, the Supreme Court cleared the way for the renewal of capital punishment executions in *Gregg v. Georgia,* 428 U.S. 153 (1976) and its companion cases by ruling that the newly revised death penalty statutes reviewed in these cases were now constitutional, since they adhered to the guidelines set down in *Furman*. Executions were resumed in January 1977.

In the period from January 1977 until September 1990 there were 140 individuals executed in the United States. While the number of executions in the thirteen-year period was low, there were still large numbers of convicted felons being sentenced to death. As of September 1990 "there were 2,393 persons on state death rows, ranging from a high of 324 in Texas to two in Connecticut, New Mexico, and Wyoming."[7] In 1996 there were fifty-six murderers executed in the United States, which was the highest national figure since 1957, yet there were still thousands of inmates living on state death rows across the nation.[8]

The striking difference between the number of felons sentenced to death and the number executed is a major issue for individuals and groups supporting and opposing capital punishment. Supporters argue that the number and length of postconviction appeals removes the possibility that capital offenders will be swiftly punished (so that their executions will serve as a deterrent) or punished at all. Opponents, in contrast, see postconviction appeals as important last chances to protect the rights of convicted felons, especially in cases where there is some question about the extent to which constitutional protections were provided for these felons in their trials.

There are several types of appeals available in cases where the death penalty is imposed, including the direct appeal to the state supreme court, the petition for certiorari to the U.S. Supreme Court (a request for the case to be heard by the Supreme Court based on issues raised in the direct appeal), and habeas corpus appeals, where issues are raised that go beyond the trial record and include "newly discovered evidence, fairness of the capital trial, impartiality of the jury, tainted evidence, incompetence of defense counsel, and prosecutorial misconduct."[9] It is very difficult, however, for a prisoner to get a habeas corpus claim considered and even more difficult to secure relief under these appeals. Prisoners must meticulously follow all the procedural barriers that exist to prevent claims from being considered.[10]

The Equal Justice Initiative of Alabama, an organization that argues on behalf of death row prisoners, takes the position that appeals by death row inmates are extremely important mechanisms for protecting the rights of capital offenders. The organization reports that 70 percent of the death sentences imposed between 1976 and 1982 were reversed by federal courts due to "fundamental constitutional violations."[11] In this time period, the federal courts were willing to correct the constitutional errors that were committed in capital cases tried in state courts. In the 1980s, however, the Supreme Court started to restrict postconviction reviews and relieve the federal courts of the necessity to ensure that fairness prevailed in the growing number of state court cases involving the death penalty. This trend led a spokesperson for the Equal Justice Initiative to say:

> In the past ten years the Rehnquist Court has clearly tired of the idealistic expectations raised in the seventies. The decade has seen a strengthening of the inverted notion that due process, equal protection of the law and reliability in criminal case adjudications are not nearly as important as finality when a state wants to execute someone. . . . The consequence of the Court's continuing retreat in capital jurisprudence has been a modern death penalty that is no more predictable, fairly applied or nondiscriminatory than the death penalty the Court stuck down in *Furman* almost twenty-five years ago.[12]

A disturbing fact about the death penalty in the United States is that African-Americans are overrepresented among the inmates on death rows across the nation. Although African-Americans constitute a relatively small percentage of the total population of the United States, 41 percent of the prisoners living under sentences of death in 1993 were listed as black by the Bureau of Justice Statistics and 58 percent were listed as white, with another 1.5 percent self-identified as American Indian, Asian, and Hispanic (the majority of the Hispanic prisoner population is included in the categories "black" and "white"). Of the 226 prisoners who were executed between 1977 and 1993, 53 percent were white, 38 percent were black, 7 percent were Hispanic, and less than 1 percent was listed as "other" (Native American, Alaskan Native, Asian, and Pacific Islander).[13] The implications of these disparities are summarized by the U.S. General Accounting Office: "In 82 percent of the studies [reviewed], race was found to influence the likelihood of being charged with capital murder or receiving the death penalty, i.e., those who murdered whites were found more likely to be sentenced to death than those who murdered blacks."[14]

Public Opinion

The public's opinions on capital punishment are affected by their beliefs about the causes of crime. For law and order proponents, the death penalty has been among the most favored public policies because it is a means to curb the incidence of violent crimes *and* a just punishment (an eye for an eye, a tooth for a tooth) for a grievous offense against society. This emphasis on death as a just punishment is found among those who look to the Bible to justify their position. Their argument is that in the Old Testament death was required as a punishment for a wide range of offenses, including murder, adultery, incest, temple prostitution, bestiality, premarital sex, rape, black magic, kidnaping, cursing parents, careless handling of an animal, blasphemy, perjury, stubbornness, and rebellion. In addition, there are numerous references to death as a punishment for certain offenses in the New Testament. For those individuals who have a law and order perspective, a sentence of death for serious offenses is an appropriate, necessary, and morally justified criminal penalty.

Those who hold civil libertarian beliefs, on the other hand, tend to favor the ideological position that government has the *moral responsibility* to protect human rights. Capital punishment is seen as a violation of these rights. Those who advocate a civil libertarian position are much more likely to favor government policies that extend and protect the rights of those accused of capital offenses, so that, even in states that allow the death penalty for certain crimes, the accused have every opportunity to prove their innocence and escape the death penalty.

Table 3.1

Public Support for the Death Penalty for a Person Convicted of Murder

Year:	% Favor	% Oppose	% Depends/No opinion
1995	77	13	10
1994	80	16	4
1991	76	18	6
1988	79	16	5
1985	72	20	8
1981	66	25	9
1978	62	27	11
1976	66	26	8
1972	57	32	11
1971	49	40	11
1969	51	40	9
1967	54	38	8
1965	45	43	12
1960	53	36	11
1957	47	34	18
1953	68	25	7
1936	61	39	NA

Sources: The Gallup Poll Monthly, no. 357 (June 1995) Princeton, N.J.; *The Gallup Poll: Public Opinion* 1995 (Wilmington, DE: Scholarly Resources Inc., 1996). Question: "Are you in favor of the death penalty for a person convicted of murder?"

Deterrence and Revenge as Justifications for the Death Penalty

There are many forms of criminal behavior in the United States; the categories of crime most commonly referred to include violent crimes against persons (street crime), property crime, white collar crime, victimless crime, and organized crime. The general public seems to pay little attention to most types of crime except for violent street crime and property crime—crimes that tend to be accorded considerable attention by the media. Generally speaking, the more a person is concerned about crime and disorder, the more likely it is that person will support more stringent "punishment" as a "deterrent" against crime. Support for the death penalty for persons convicted of murder is an example of where this logic applies.

There has been substantial support in the United States during the past forty years for the death penalty, and the percentage in favor of capital punishment is currently at its nadir. Statistics on the percentage of Americans favoring and opposing the death penalty since 1936 are reported in Table 3.1. In 1953 just over two-thirds of the American public (68 percent) favored the death penalty for murder, but thirteen years later, in 1966, only 42 percent of the public expressed this same support. Support for the death penalty, however, increased in the 1970s and 1980s, with 72 percent of the Americans surveyed in 1985 saying that they were in favor of the death penalty. In public opinion polls conducted since 1988, over three-fourths of the public expressed support for capital punishment.

Nevertheless, most of the populace believe that the death penalty is unfairly applied. "Two-thirds (64 percent) think poor persons are more likely than average or above-average income people to receive the death penalty for the same crime. And four in ten (39 percent) believe blacks are more likely than whites to be sentenced to death for the same crime."[15] So there is quite strong support for the death penalty even though the public is aware that capital punishment may not be "fairly" applied across social classes and races.

There is evidence that this support would decline dramatically if life imprisonment, without any possibility of parole, were a certainty for murderers.[16] For example, in a Gallup poll conducted in December 1993, the respondents were asked if they thought the penalty for murder should be the death penalty or life imprisonment with no possibility of parole. Only 59 percent of the people surveyed chose the death penalty, and 29 percent chose life imprisonment without parole as the penalty for murder.[17] In addition, support for the death penalty goes down dramatically in cases where the murderers are teenagers. A Gallup poll conducted in September 1994 reported that only 11 percent of the people surveyed thought that a teenager who is convicted of a murder should get the death penalty, and a very large majority of these respondents (71 percent) thought that this teenager should be spared.[18]

When pollsters ask those who favor the death penalty for murder their reasons for supporting the policy, the answer is most commonly revenge—an "eye for an eye" (Table 3.2). In a Gallup poll conducted in 1991, 50 percent of the public said that their reason for supporting the death penalty was revenge. In 1985 only 30 percent of the public gave revenge as a reason. Other reasons given for supporting capital punishment in 1985 and 1991 include deterrence, keeping murderers from killing again, the high costs of incarcerating prisoners for life, and the fact that murderers deserve punishment.

The idea of revenge is given some legitimacy in the Supreme Court's decisions on capital punishment. Justice Potter Stewart, writing on *Gregg v. Georgia,* 428 U.S. 153 (1976), stated that "capital punishment is an expression of society's moral outrage at particularly offensive conduct." Justice Stewart went on to say, "Retribution is no longer the dominant objective of

Table 3.2

Reasons for Favoring the Death Penalty Among the U.S. Public, Gallup Polls 1985 and 1991

	1985	1991
Revenge: an "eye for an eye"	30%	50%
Acts as a deterrent	22%	13%
Murderers deserve punishment	18%	NA
Costly to keep murderers in prison	11%	13%
Keeps murderers from killing again	9%	19%
Removes potential risk to community	7%	NA
Judicial system is too lenient	NA	3%
All others	13%	11%
No opinion	2%	2%

Sources: The Gallup Poll Monthly, no. 357 (June 1995); and *The Gallup Poll: Public Opinion 1995* (Wilmington, DE: Scholarly Resources Inc., 1996). Question asked of those who favored the death penalty: "Why do you favor the death penalty for persons convicted of murder?"

Note: Totals add to more than 100 percent due to multiple responses.

the criminal law . . . but neither is it a forbidden objective nor one inconsistent with our respect for the dignity of men." In this case, Justice Stewart wrote the majority opinion, which condoned the use of capital punishment as retribution when grievous crimes were involved.

Impact of Economics on Opinions Toward Capital Punishment

Opponents of the death penalty may ask the question, "How much is vengeance worth?" It costs several million taxpayer dollars to ensure that those convicted of capital offenses are put to death. Capital trials are more complex and time-consuming and, therefore, more costly than other criminal trials during each stage of the legal process—pretrial, jury selection, trial proceedings, and appeals proceedings. A competently conducted capital trial is preceded by a thorough investigation, and these criminal investigations take three to five times longer than those conducted in noncapital cases. Additional costs are incurred when the investigation uses forensic scientists, polygraphers, mental health professionals, and medical experts. Pretrial motions in capital cases are usually numerous and complex, and these cases typically involve the filing of two to six times as many motions as noncapital cases.[19] There are those among the general public who would prefer to spend the tremendous sums of money needed each year in capital cases on programs designed to prevent or reduce crime. In answer to the support found for the policy among the public, opponents of the death penalty might raise the following question: "By focusing on punishing a few individual offenders, are we merely diverting attention and resources away from fundamental structural reforms that address the causes of violent crime?"[20]

Judiciary

Supreme Court decisions establish policy on capital punishment. For example, in *Furman v. Georgia,* 408 U.S. 238 (1972), guidelines for the creation of state statutes on capital punishment were established. A state statute that imposed the death penalty had to adhere to these guidelines or be declared unconstitutional by the Supreme Court. State statutes were expected to do the following: (1) have the support of a substantial majority of the people in the state; (2) provide statutory guidance and direction so that the decision to use the death penalty will not be made by jury or judge arbitrarily or capriciously; (3) make the new statute applicable only to the most severe crimes and not to those crimes where the sentence of death would be grossly disproportionate and excessive punishment.

In the *Furman* decision, the Court majority held that capital punishment was not "cruel and unusual in and of itself." The arbitrary manner in which it had been implemented by the states did, however, constitute cruel and unusual punishment. *Furman* invalidated the death penalty statutes of the federal government and forty-one states, but most of the states involved rewrote their policy on capital punishment and followed the Supreme Court's direction in doing so. In July 1976 the Court reinstated the constitutionality of the capital punishment statutes it reviewed in the case of *Gregg v. Georgia,* 428 U.S. 153. The majority opinion stated that the new statutes contained "objective standards to guide, regularize, and make rationally reviewable" the process by which the death penalty was imposed, and these state policies became the model for the many states that rewrote and enacted their death penalty statutes.

Procedural Justice for Those Convicted of Capital Offenses

Because the Eighth Amendment to the Constitution forbids "cruel and unusual punishments," capital punishment has been prohibited for some crimes such as rape (*Coker v. Georgia,* 433 U.S. 584 [1977]). Although in several cases the Court has imposed limits on the use of capital punishment, in principle the Supreme Court has upheld the death penalty and has not considered it in violation of the "cruel and unusual punishment" standard. For crimes such as premeditated murder wherein suitable appeal rights have been observed, the Court permits states to administer the death penalty in pursuit of justice (*Gregg v. Georgia*). The Court has further ruled that persons who participate in robberies where a killing occurs may not be put to death if they themselves did not kill or intend to kill the victim of the crime (*Edmund v. Florida*, 458 U.S. 782 [1982]).

The 1986–1987 term of the U.S. Supreme Court represented the inauguration of the Rehnquist era of the high court, with several cases pending for review. One major ruling issued by the Rehnquist Court in 1987 involved a challenge to Georgia's death penalty law on the grounds that statistical evidence showed that killers of white victims received death sentences more frequently than did killers of black victims. In *McCleskey v. Kemp*, 107 S.Ct. 1756 (1987), the Supreme Court turned back that legal challenge in a close 5–4 vote and argued that statistics showing race-related disparities in the imposition of the death penalty were not enough to sustain constitutional challenges to existing capital punishment laws. This decision was a major blow to the opponents of capital punishment and paved the way for the execution of black inmates whose victims were white.

The Supreme Court also has ruled on the constitutionality of imposing the death penalty on juveniles and the mentally retarded. When applying the death penalty to juveniles, the Supreme Court decided that the emotional and mental state of the juvenile offenders must be taken into consideration (*Eddings v. Oklahoma*, 455 U.S. 584 [1977]). In 1989 the Court ruled that the U.S. Constitution permits states to execute the mentally retarded and youth who were sixteen years of age when they committed their crimes. The majority opinion for both cases was based on the reasoning that these factors did not "establish the degree of national consensus that this Court has previously thought sufficient to label a particular punishment cruel and unusual."[21]

In the early 1980s the Supreme Court started to chip away at the number and length of appeals by death row inmates. Prior to this time, lawyers for an inmate on death row might initiate numerous postconviction appeals, and each of these would result in a stay of execution while the petition was pending. Each time an inmate was within hours of being executed, a new appeal would be filed, with the hope that another stay of execution would be granted. The case of Anthony Antone illustrates the delay produced by postconviction appeals. In 1982 this inmate came within twelve hours of being put to death in Florida when a federal court halted his execution after appeals were filed. Two years later the Court refused to block Antone's execution, and he was electrocuted in January 1984.[22]

By the mid-1980s the Supreme Court, under Chief Justice Warren Burger, made a number of decisions on postconviction appeals that signaled that these appeals would no longer routinely produce stays of execution. For example, the Court allowed the state of Florida to execute Robert Sullivan in November 1983 and said, "There must come an end to the process of consideration and reconsideration."[23] In announcing this decision, Chief Justice Burger indicated that the Court's patience with postconviction appeals had run out when he accused Sullivan's lawyer of making "a sporting contest" of the criminal justice system by initiating appeals on his client's behalf.

In 1988 Chief Justice William H. Rehnquist appointed former Supreme Court Justice Lewis F. Powell Jr. to head a committee of judges to study the process by which death penalty sentences were reviewed on appeal. In a speech to the American Bar Association's convention in August 1988, Powell reported that only about a hundred executions had been carried out since the Supreme Court had upheld the constitutionality of the death penalty, and he said that the numerous appeals were the reason that so many death sentences were prevented from being carried out.[24] Postconviction appeals were still contentious eight years later, when the Supreme Court agreed to decide on the constitutionality of the newly enacted Anti-Terrorism and Effective Death Penalty Act of 1996 only nine days after the legislation was signed by President Clinton. This law authorizes significant restrictions on the right of death row inmates to seek review of their convictions in federal courts, and the legislation imposes "new high standards, tight time limits, and stringent restrictions on successive appeals."[25]

Other Supreme Court decisions on the death penalty during 1996 include a ruling that indigent inmates on death row do not have a constitutional right to a lawyer in a second round of appeals in state courts and a ruling upholding the constitutionality of the death penalty in the military. Because of the first ruling, death row inmates who are poor will not be able to effectively challenge their death sentences through multiple appeals. Since the appeals process results in the death sentence being set aside in as many as two-thirds of all of these cases, this ruling may increase the number of executions in the future.[26]

The second ruling upholds the constitutionality of the use of the death penalty by the military. At issue in this case was the separation of powers between the Court and the presidency. In 1984 President Ronald Reagan issued an executive order to bring the death penalty provisions of the Uniform Code of Military Justice into conformance with the Supreme Court's guidelines for capital punishment statutes—guidelines that had been set in the *Furman* case in 1972.[27] In June 1996 the Court validated the constitutionality of this presidential order, which meant that the eight military executions that were pending could go forward.

Federalism

In states with death penalty statutes, state actions have been characterized by a law and order perspective. This conservative perspective is especially apparent since the Supreme Court's *Furman v. Georgia* decision, which has already been mentioned as the case where guidelines for state death penalty statutes were created. As a result of the decision, thirty-five states tightened the statutes under which the death penalty was to be inflicted. Ten states, including North Carolina, Louisiana, and Oklahoma, met the *Furman* objections by requiring mandatory death sentences for specified offenses, while other states, such as Georgia, Florida, and Texas, wrote guided-discretion statutes that allowed the courts to decide whether the death penalty was fair in light of sentences for similar offenses. In both sets of cases, the states were writing laws that reduced the arbitrariness denounced in *Furman*.

In *Gregg v. Georgia* and the companion cases that were decided on July 2, 1976, the Supreme Court of the United States rejected the mandatory death penalty statutes of Louisiana and North Carolina and upheld the guided-discretion statutes of Florida, Georgia, and Texas. The Court also ruled that the death penalty was not inherently cruel and unusual punishment, and the justices in the majority agreed that the Georgia law (and the Texas and Florida laws) did not "wantonly and freakishly impose the death sentence; it is always circumscribed by the legislative guidelines."[28]

The actions of the thirty-five state legislatures in response to the *Furman* decision were of evident concern to the justices; in recording his views on the matter, Justice Stewart referred to "society's endorsement of the death penalty for murder," and he noted further that "a heavy burden rests on those who would attack the judgment of the representatives of the people." In the *Gregg* decision, Stewart went on to argue:

> Retribution is no longer the dominant objective of the criminal law . . . but neither is it a forbidden objective nor one inconsistent with our respect for the dignity of men. Indeed, the decision that capital punishment may be the appropriate sanction in extreme cases is an expression of the community's belief that certain crimes are themselves so grievous an affront to humanity that the only adequate response may be the penalty of death.

Given that the *Gregg* decision was "announced" by Justice Potter Stewart on behalf of himself and Justices Lewis Powell and John Paul Stevens, with the concurrence of Chief Justice Warren Burger and Justices Byron White, Harry Blackmun, and William Rehnquist, it is evident that even members of the high court have viewed the death penalty as a just punishment for grievous offenses against society in certain circumstances.

Governors' Actions

When state governors oppose capital punishment, they can exercise their power to commute the death sentences of inmates in their states who are living on death row. A dramatic example of this occurred in New Mexico in 1986, when the governor at the time, Toney Anaya, commuted the death sentences of all five men awaiting execution in his state. He was reported to say that his reason for doing so was that the penalty was "inhumane, immoral and anti-God."[29] Governor Anaya was at the end of his four-year term, and during his term he had stayed all pending executions. The governor-elect, Garrey Carruthers, had campaigned on the issue and promised to start the paperwork necessary to reinstate the death penalty as soon as he was in office. This is a clear example of the moral debate over capital punishment. The position of Anaya was that the policy was immoral, and, as governor, he could not permit the state to execute an individual. The position of Carruthers was that capital punishment was legal in New Mexico, and, as governor, he was duty-bound to uphold the law. Moreover, Carruthers signaled his approval of the policy by denouncing Anaya's action as bad for the state's criminal justice system.[30]

A similar conflict occurred in the state of New York in 1989, when the state legislature voted to override Governor Mario Cuomo's veto of a bill to reinstate the death penalty. Actually, the state legislature had voted to reinstate capital punishment thirteen times in the years since the nationwide moratorium was lifted, but the state's governors—first Hugh L. Carey and then Mario Cuomo—had always vetoed the bills. In 1989 the state legislators were under pressure from the public and from various groups supporting the death penalty to override the veto. Opponents of capital punishment supported Governor Cuomo's position, which he explained in an opinion piece in the *New York Times* in June 1989, just before the vote to override was expected. He said:

> History teaches us that if New York does so [reinstates the death penalty], two things will ultimately prove true. Men and women—mostly poor men who are minority members—will be put to death. History also teaches that while most will be guilty, at least some of the people executed in the name of the people of New York will turn out to be innocent. We have buried such "mistakes" before. If we go back to death, we will again.[31]

New York did not reinstate the death penalty until September 1996, during the term of Governor George E. Pataki, who strongly supported the policy. In March 1996, Governor Pataki exercised an extraordinary use of his executive power when he removed District Attorney Robert T. Johnson of the Bronx from a murder case against an ex-convict accused of killing a police officer because the prosecutor had previously stated that he was opposed to capital punishment. In the past governors exercised this power of removal only to punish corruption or incompetence or when asked to do so. Pataki believed that Johnson's principles would prevent him from objectively considering a sentence of death in the case, and he explained his extraordinary action in the following way:

> What is in this case clear to me is that the District Attorney, because of his deeply held convictions in this case, was not able to apply the law fairly. . . . The murder of a police officer is an extraordinary act. It threatens the rule of law. It threatens the lives of all of us. It is now subject to the death penalty.[32]

States usually have a well-financed and well-organized bureaucracy on the prosecution's side in capital offense cases. This same bureaucracy, however, does not exist to support the defense in some states, including Florida and Georgia. In 1985, Florida's attorney general, Jim Smith, appeared before the Florida Senate's Judiciary Committee to argue for funding to hire the lawyers that were needed to defend inmates facing execution. Earlier that year, the Florida Supreme Court granted stays of execution to two death row inmates who did not have legal counsel, arguing that an inmate's right to due process was violated if the person was executed without a lawyer. David Von Drehle, in his book on death row inmates in Florida, reported that the state government faced a dilemma, which he described as follows:

> There would be no executions without defense lawyers, and there were no more defense lawyers. Florida voters demanded executions—so Florida politicians were going to have to solve the lawyer shortage. . . . To please pro–death penalty voters, Florida officials were forced to find anti–death penalty lawyers. The death penalty was turning out to be a whole lot more complicated than anyone had anticipated.[33]

Smith's plea was considered legitimate by the senators because he was a strong proponent of capital punishment and was spending "perhaps a million dollars or more a year trying to put men into the chair."[34] Smith asked for and was granted $800,000 to hire full-time lawyers, investigators, and secretarial help so that death row inmates who did not have lawyers for the appeals that were allowed after the state's review could be represented. The bill was quickly passed by the Florida legislature and signed into law in June 1985, and a new state agency was created, the Office of Capital Collateral Representative (CCR).[35]

On first glance, the agency could be considered a due process–civil libertarian action, but this was not the reason that the CCR was funded by the state legislature. The rationale that was used to persuade the legislators to authorize the creation of the CCR was clearly based on law and order thinking. Smith told the senators that if they did not fund the agency and provide lawyers for death row inmates, capital punishment would die out in Florida. He told them that the public would respond to the argument that inmates on death row had to have access to legal counsel if executions were to continue. He referred to the fact that Florida had executed eight men in 1984 and speculated that this figure might double in 1985 if the CCR was in place. His words were, "The people of this state want capital punishment and I think we ought to provide the resources to make it happen."[36] This argument was successful in both houses of the state legislature.

The reasons why Smith's argument was so successful were simple. The public in Florida strongly supported the death penalty and had elected state and local officials who were willing to use capital punishment for serious crimes. In addition, Florida executed John Arthur Spenkelink on May 25, 1979, and became the first state to put an inmate to death after the *Furman* decision in 1972. The state had been one of the national record-holders when both numbers of executions and inmates on death row were counted. It seems clear that many in the state were proud that Florida was leading the nation in implementing the death penalty and wanted the state to continue to take a strong and forceful stand against capital offenses.

Georgia is another state that has executed record numbers of prisoners and has significant numbers of inmates on death row. As was the case with Florida, Georgia amply funds the prosecution in capital cases and underfunds the defense. As recently as 1996, Human Rights Watch reported that there was no statewide, independent public defender system in the state. Providing defense lawyers for defendants who are poor is the responsibility of county government in Georgia, and to defend the poor most county governments simply appoint members of the local bar association who are in private law practice. According to Human Rights Watch, this leads to the following situations:

> The lawyers appointed may not want the cases, may receive little compensation for the time and expense of handling them, may lack any interest in criminal law, and may not have the skill to defend those accused of crime. In contrast to the virtually unlimited access to experts and investigative assistance by the prosecution, the lawyer defending the indigent accused in a capital case may not have any investigative and expert assistance to prepare for trial and present a defense. As a result, the poor are often represented by inexperienced lawyers who view their responsibilities as unwanted burdens,

have no inclination to help their clients, and have no incentive to develop criminal trial skills.[37]

The only action that Georgia has taken to improve the situation for persons accused of capital offenses is the creation of the Multi-County Defender office, which was placed within a unit of the state's bureaucracy, the Georgia Indigent Defense Council. The Multi-County Defender office was to provide specialists to serve as defense counsel in capital cases, but the office has been consistently underfunded. There are "usually over one hundred capital cases pending pretrial in Georgia at any one time," yet the office has not had the resources to hire more than four attorneys.[38] The U.S. Supreme Court's ruling in *Gideon v. Wainwright* (372 U.S. 335 [1963]) requires all states to provide counsel to indigent defendants—including those accused of capital offenses—up through their direct appeal to the state's highest court. There is, however, no constitutional right to legal representation in postconviction cases beyond the appeal to the state's highest court. Georgia provides neither statutory right to counsel in capital postconviction cases nor state compensation for representation. In these cases, poor defendants must rely on volunteer lawyers if they are available.

Comparing the Death Penalty Across States

The nationwide moratorium on executions, which had been imposed in 1967, was not broken for ten years. Actually, only a small number of death row inmates were executed after the death penalty was renewed in certain states, but a substantial number of prisoners lived on death rows under the sentence of death. By 1983 1,050 prisoners were on death row, mostly in Florida, Texas, and Georgia, and more than 40 percent of these felons were black.[39] By 1995 the number of inmates on death row rose to 2,965, according to figures reported by the U.S. Justice Department, and there had been 238 prisoners executed since the nationwide moratorium was lifted in 1976.

In 1995 thirty-seven states had death penalty statutes, but only twenty-two of these states actually executed prisoners in the years from 1976 to 1995. The state of Texas had the most executions by far, with a total of ninety-two during this nineteen-year period. Other states with high numbers of executions were the following: Florida (thirty-three), Virginia (twenty-five), Georgia (thirteen), Louisiana and Missouri (eleven each), and Alabama (ten). Each of the remaining fifteen states executed seven or fewer prisoners during these years, with three states (Idaho, Maryland, and Nebraska) executing only one prisoner each. States use a number of means of execution, including electrocution, the gas chamber, lethal injection, hanging, and a firing squad, and many states include multiple forms of execution in their state statutes.

In recent decades, the role of the federal government in law enforcement has grown, but state and local governments nevertheless continue to carry the major burdens of providing police protection, operating judicial systems, offering probation and parole programs, and maintaining correctional facilities. More than half a million people are employed as state and local government law enforcement personnel, while the federal government employs fewer than fifty thousand persons in all its law enforcement activities. Similarly, state prisons have approximately three hundred thousand inmates, compared with about twenty-five thousand in federal prisons.

Generally speaking, the states tend to pursue a law-and-order high-efficiency direction in their decisions on the punishment of state offenders. Mandatory minimum sentencing laws requiring prison sentences for certain serious offenses are quite common, and a number of states are using determinate sentencing and elimination of parole in order to "toughen up punishments." Such actions proceed from law and order beliefs that the punishment should fit the crime and that persons convicted of serious crimes must not "get off easy" through release on parole. On the efficiency side, however, most states are seeking ways of dealing with offenders other than imprisonment, since imprisonment is an expensive proposition given federal standards for human incarceration. Some states are experimenting with programs such as community-based corrections and expanded work-release opportunities. Not all state-level politicians fit the stereotype of being "unenlightened about justice policy and advocating a narrow law-and-order posture," as indicated by a study of Illinois legislators, which concluded that they were

> quite diverse in their criminal justice ideology . . . They manifested a pronounced conservative strain in their thinking, trumpeting the importance of crime control and advocating stiff prison terms aimed at effecting deterrence, incapacitation, and retribution. Yet they also evidenced an affinity for elements of the traditional liberal agenda. . . . They tended to agree that crime has causes rooted in social inequality . . . that rehabilitation is an important goal . . . that prisons should be reasonably humane, and that community corrections is an idea worth exploring.[40]

American Indians and the Death Penalty

Until 1883 Indians arrested for the murder of another Indian were under the sole jurisdiction of tribal governments if the murder took place in Indian country (the reservation lands under the control of the many American

Indian nations within the boundaries of the United States). American Indian felons were not, at that time, turned over to the jurisdiction of the U.S. federal courts. This principle was affirmed by the U.S. Supreme Court in 1883 in the case *Ex Parte Crow Dog,* 109 U.S. 556, which acknowledged the exclusive criminal jurisdiction of American Indian tribes over Indian people as an integral component of tribal sovereignty.

The *Crow Dog* case involved two members of the same tribe, Crow Dog and Spotted Tail; Crow Dog killed Spotted Tail on reservation land. In keeping with traditional forms of justice among the members of this tribe, Crow Dog and his family apologized and made restitution to Spotted Tail's family. This was the accepted and *respected* method of settling the matter. Non-Indian people, however, were outraged when they found out about this exercise of traditional tribal justice, and Crow Dog was subsequently arrested by federal government authorities and charged with the crime of murder. He was tried in a federal court, convicted, and sentenced to death by hanging. Crow Dog's attorney submitted an appeal to the U.S. Supreme Court for Crow Dog's release on the grounds that the crime had occurred in Indian country, involved two American Indians, and was therefore under the jurisdiction of the tribal government. The Supreme Court agreed and ordered Crow Dog's release.

Two years later the U.S. Congress passed the Major Crimes Act of 1885, which extended federal jurisdiction to cases occurring in Indian country that involved certain major crimes (murder, rape, manslaughter, kidnaping, and assault with a dangerous weapon, for example) and that had American Indians as both the perpetrators and victims. A year later the 1885 act was challenged on the basis that it was an unconstitutional infringement on tribal sovereignty, but the Supreme Court rejected this challenge. Some legal scholars argued that the fact that American Indian felons could be sentenced to death by federal courts was not consistent with the principle that a person has a right to a trial by a jury of one's peers. In addition, they argued that the death penalty is considered repugnant and barbaric by many Indian peoples, which is ironic because the enactment of the Major Crimes Act of 1885 was seen as a tool for bringing the law of "civilized" society to tribal nations, who were assumed to be lacking in both law and governance.[41]

In 1994 there was a further change in the law regarding the death penalty and American Indians. The Crimes and Criminal Procedures title of the U.S. Criminal Code was amended to include the following special provisions for Indian country:

> Notwithstanding sections 1152 and 1153, no person subject to the criminal jurisdiction of an Indian tribal government shall be subject to a capital sen-

tence under this chapter for any offense the Federal jurisdiction for which is predicated solely on Indian country . . . and which has occurred within the boundaries of Indian country, unless the governing body of the tribe has elected that this chapter have effect over land and persons subject to its criminal jurisdiction.[42]

This 1994 provision now allows the tribal governments to determine the criminal jurisdiction in capital cases involving Indian people and committed within lands recognized as Indian country.

Interest Groups

Many organized groups wish to influence public policy in this arena—some because of their moral commitment to justice defined in terms of the rights of those sentenced to death, some because of their moral commitment to justice in terms of the rights of society and the victims of crime, and some because of their professional concerns as members of the law enforcement apparatus of the United States. But these groups have relatively little clout in the national political arena, which led one scholar to conclude that "the fight against crime was mounted by pygmies rather than giants in the world of interest groups."[43]

Those interest groups that are most prominent in trying to influence the major outlines and legal parameters of policy concerning capital punishment, especially as such policy emanates from Supreme Court decisions, can be thought of in two basic categories: (1) *professional groups,* whose members are involved in implementing the policy; and (2) *secondary groups,* whose members are extremely interested in capital punishment because of its moral dimensions but are not directly involved in implementing the policy. Professional groups include such associations as the International Association of Chiefs of Police, the Fraternal Order of Police, the State Patrol and Probation Officers' Association, the National Sheriffs' Association, the National Association of Attorneys General, the National Legal Aid and Defender Association, the American Bar Association, and similar professional associations representing key actors in the criminal justice process.

Secondary groups with memberships that focus on the moral dimensions of capital punishment are more likely to capture the public's attention through their activities than are the professional groups mentioned above. One important way that these interest groups attempt to influence the making of policy concerning capital punishment and its related issues is by means of amicus curiae (friends of the court) briefs, which the groups use to add new points of law, provide expertise, or add important jurisprudential arguments to specific Supreme Court cases. For example, twenty-one of the fifty-two cases involving the rights of the accused and convicted accepted by the Supreme Court in its important 1967–1968 term were brought by the National Association for the Advancement of Colored People, the American Civil Liberties Union, and the American Jewish Congress. Such amicus activity by groups interested in promoting civil liberties and due process led to the formation of an opposing organization—Americans for Effective Enforcement—whose purpose was to provide expert amicus support in favor of capital punishment and strong law enforcement and to provide conservative support for policy issues other than crime.[44]

Professional Groups

The U.S. system of adversary justice gives rise to a tripartite division of labor—prosecutors, defense counsel, and judges—within the criminal justice system, and this specialization of tasks and responsibilities affects the personnel in each of the divisions.[45] Judges bear responsibility for managing conflict and, if they are to be effective, must be impartial, fair, and detached from the issues dividing the defense and the prosecution. In contrast, the professional success and career interests of defense attorneys are tied directly to the interests of the accused. Finally, prosecutors tend to identify closely with law enforcement because their success depends mightily upon the ability of police to secure damning evidence of the commission of a crime.

Consequently, members of these professional associations do not always place themselves similarly on capital punishment issues. Each actor in the criminal justice process has a stake in the maintenance of a legal culture that emphasizes professionalism and appropriate procedures for processing cases. Stuart Scheingold argues that professionals in the criminal justice system divide ideologically along the same lines as do other citizens, but the former's legal training and organizational responsibilities tend to complicate their values.[46] Criminal professionals who think in liberal legal terms (primarily defense attorneys and some judges) will attempt to maximize the rights of defendants in order to protect them from all forms of coercion, and due-process liberals tend to choose the least onerous and most humane sentences and back away from sentences of death.

Moderate conservatives, whom Scheingold expected to find represented among judges and prosecutors, are likely to be comfortable with policies that emphasize either deterrence or retribution. Both are consistent with predetermined sentences based on the seriousness of the crime and the offenders' records. Punitive conservatives who favor heavy sentences that create fear in the hearts of would-be offenders tend to be found in police departments, with some found in the ranks of judges and prosecutors.

All of these professional actors are expected to comply with Supreme Court decisions involving the rights of defendants and those convicted of crimes. State and local criminal justice authorities for the most part have done so, primarily because these authorities are to a considerable degree vulnerable to judicial sanctions if they fail to comply. However, certain professional groups are as intent on blocking or minimizing the implementation of judicial decisions as others may be on implementing them. Interest groups that oppose particular policies often work to minimize the impact of those policies by disseminating information about how the decision might be narrowly applied or interpreted when members carry out their responsibilities in the criminal justice system.

American Bar Association

The American Bar Association (ABA) is the foremost nationwide organization representing attorneys, and it is considered an interest group that has high status, effective organization, and skilled leadership. The ABA is very active concerning issues of crime policy and criminal procedures, and the association often takes public stands on these issues. ABA representatives constitute the key bearers of testimony at congressional hearings on legislative proposals to reform the U.S. Criminal Code. The ABA also is highly influential in the nomination processes that surround the selection of federal judges and is one of the chief proponents of legal reform in states.

The ABA considers itself somewhat above the political fray; hence, the association is not easily placed in either a law and order position or a civil libertarian one. ABA representatives consider themselves to be impartial experts aiding elected decision makers in obtaining worthy goals, and ABA recommendations generally are regarded as nonpartisan and objective. The ABA's underlying foundation is legalism, and such reasoning places the association on the high plane of "a government of laws rather than of men" in the eyes of many governmental officials and much of the U.S. public.

The American Bar Association does not take a position either for or against capital punishment, but in line with its foundation of legalism the ABA does have policies that are related to the due-process rights of felons in death penalty cases. The ABA's policy-making body, the House of Delegates, has longstanding policies supporting the appointment of competent counsel in capital cases; preserving, enhancing, and streamlining the appeals process (habeas corpus review), and eliminating discrimination in capital sentencing on the basis of the race of either the victim or the defendant.[47] In addition, the ABA opposes the execution of mentally retarded persons and those who were eighteen years of age or younger when they committed their crimes. In February 1997 the House of Delegates approved a moratorium on executions that would last until jurisdictions implemented policies to ensure that death penalty cases were administered fairly and according to due-process principles. This is the language used by the ABA policy makers:

> Resolved, That the American Bar Association calls upon each jurisdiction that imposes capital punishment not to carry out the death penalty until the jurisdiction implements policies and procedures that are consistent with . . . longstanding American Bar Association policies intended to (1) ensure that death penalty cases are administered fairly and impartially, in accordance with due process, and (2) minimize the risk that innocent persons may be executed.[48]

Secondary Groups

There are a number of single-issue organizations that focus on abolishing the death penalty. The National Coalition to Abolish the Death Penalty links individuals and organizations at the national, state, and local levels and acts as a clearinghouse for information sharing and the development of campaigns organized to fight the death penalty.[49] Another such organization is the Southern Coalition on Jails and Prisons; this single-issue group wants to initiate a freeze on all executions and proposes life sentences, with felons serving a minimum of twenty years in prison without the possibility of parole, as alternatives to executions.[50]

Some of the organizations organized for the purpose of opposing the death penalty advertise their positions on the World Wide Web sites that they have created and maintain. A sample of the single-issue groups using Web sites includes the following: (1) Murder Victims Families for Reconciliation, a national organization of family members of murder victims who oppose capital punishment; (2) Iowans Against the Death Penalty, which attempts to mobilize people to maintain Iowa's status as a state without capital punishment; (3) Virginians for Alternatives to the Death Penalty, a statewide citizens' organization dedicated to educating the public about alternatives to the death penalty, and (4) a number of state organizations working to abolish capital punishment, including Death Penalty Focus of California, Oklahoma Coalition to Abolish the Death Penalty, Texas Coalition to Abolish the Death Penalty, and the Washington Coalition to Abolish the Death Penalty.

Multi-issue interest groups also get involved in single-issue politics and policy making by forming sections within their organization to deal with these issues. For example, in the 1980s the ACLU had a Capital Punishment Project, whose director was active in a 1988 case involving a teenage girl from Gary, Indiana, under a death sentence for stabbing an elderly woman. The girl was fifteen at the time, and she became a cause célèbr for death penalty opponents. Even the Pope asked for mercy in this instance. What was troubling for many people and constituted the legal challenge to the Indiana capital punishment statute was that Indiana, at that time, had the lowest age threshold for the imposition of the death penalty of any state in the union.

The ACLU maintains the position that capital punishment constitutes cruel and unusual punishment and thereby violates the Eighth Amendment to the U.S. Constitution. Their position is that killing, whether carried out by an individual or the state, is immoral and ought not to be condoned. Execution, according to the ACLU, "is a barbaric anachronism and should be abolished," and this applies to executions of all types—electrocution, lethal injection, the gas chamber, hanging, or firing squad. The organization has an obvious civil libertarian perspective and also objects to the death penalty on moral grounds.

Amnesty International is another very outspoken opponent of capital punishment. This organization is an independent worldwide movement, organized in London in 1961, that works impartially for the release of all prisoners of conscience, fair and prompt trials for political prisoners, and an end to torture, "disappearances," and executions. The organization has always opposed the death penalty and works extensively for the abolishment of this policy in the United States. Amnesty International's position is that the death penalty is a denial of the right to life and the right not to be subjected to cruel, inhuman, or degrading treatment or punishment.

Support for the death penalty comes from those organizations who want the criminal justice system to take a law and order approach. In addition, state or local chapters of professional associations that represent the actors in the criminal justice system will publicly support the death penalty in specific cases. For example, when Governor Mario Cuomo fought the reinstatement of capital punishment in New York in 1989, a number of professional law enforcement groups, including the Patrolmen's Benevolent Association and the Metropolitan Police Conference, led the campaign in favor of the death penalty. Similarly, when New York Governor George Pataki acted to ensure that the death penalty would be considered in a case involving the killing of a police officer by removing the prosecutor who had expressed opposition to capital punishment, his position was supported by the Patrolmen's Benevolent Association. Organizations representing law enforcement officers, who are most in danger of being killed as they perform their duties, may support the death penalty for murders involving the police. Those associations who do support the penalty are expressing the view that capital punishment is necessary as a deterrent for future murders and as retribution for the murders that have occurred.

Congress

The U.S. Congress plays a key role in setting crime policy in response to crime control problems that become national issues. Some of the problems that do reach the national policy-making agenda are gun control, organized crime and drugs, hijacking, terrorism, and bank robbery. In 1970 the Justice Department pressed hard in Congress to gain passage of the Organized Crime Control Act (P.L. 91–452), a statute containing provisions that "severely restricted the use of the Fifth Amendment by grand jury witnesses."[51] In the past government efforts to prosecute syndicate leaders had been hampered by the refusal of major crime figures to testify before grand juries and major crime figures to testify before grand juries and by the invocation of Fifth Amendment rights in doing so.

Congress also has established crime programs that provide for the distribution of funds to state and local governments. A prominent example is the Omnibus Crime Control and Safe Streets Act of 1968. This enactment represented one of the first large-scale attempts to establish a block grant mechanism within the U.S. federal government structure. Block grants provide state and local governments with the direct funds and decisional authority required to accomplish the ends for which the grant program was established. The major portion of the funds expended in the early years of the program was used by police departments to enhance their crime-fighting abilities, although the program supported a variety of rather liberal programs, which often were innovative undertakings that emphasized experimentation in the areas of police–minority community relations and the "diversion of juveniles from the criminal justice system . . . and reforms aimed at more effective policing."[52]

In 1974, one issue that was on the national policy-making agenda was airline hijackings, and in that year Congress authorized the death penalty for hijackings that resulted in death. In the 1980s the nation was very concerned about drug-trafficking homicides, and Congress considered the death penalty for certain drug-related murders in 1988. When this bill was debated in the Senate, senators who supported capital punishment tried to get the measure through as an amendment to the Defense Department's budget.

Senator Alfonse D'Amato (R-NY) sponsored the amendment, and he was not willing to withdraw it and let the Pentagon budget pass until he was assured by the Senate leadership that the death penalty provision would come before the body at a later time for a separate vote. At the same time, opponents of the measure were threatening to filibuster to block a final vote on the budget if the amendment was not removed.[53]

In October 1989 the Senate Judiciary Committee sent a bill to the full Senate that authorized the death penalty for more than twenty federal crimes, including the assassination of the president, murder of a federal official or his family, bank robbery resulting in a death, espionage, murder of a foreign official, murder by a federal prisoner serving a life sentence, killing in the course of hostage taking, kidnaping where death results, and murder for hire.[54] What became problematic was the amendment that the committee added to the legislation to provide safeguards against racially biased applications of the death penalty. The amendment was sponsored by Senator Edward Kennedy (D-MA) who said that the intent of his amendment was to require "prosecutors to show by 'clear and convincing evidence' that racial disparities in sentencing are not the result of discrimination but reflect other non-racial factors." Senator Strom Thurmond (R-SC) opposed the amendment but was the chief sponsor of the original bill; his opinion was that "such a standard would keep prosecutors consumed with trying to develop race-based statistical evidence to prove that the race of the defendant or victim was incidental to the sentence sought."[55] Implicit in these arguments is evidence of the law and order and due process–civil libertarian debates. Kennedy argued that defendants in capital cases must be protected from the possibility that racial discrimination is a factor in court decisions, a civil libertarian argument that is meant to extend protections to defendants. In contrast, Thurmond argued against these protections because they would hamper the ability of prosecutors to argue successfully for death sentences for persons convicted of capital offenses, which is a law and order argument because the intention is to free prosecution lawyers from restrictions that might hamper their ability to enforce the law.

In its debates over capital punishment, Congress focuses on many of the same issues that surface in Supreme Court deliberations, including the imposition of the death penalty on persons under the age of eighteen and on those who are mentally retarded. For example, in the omnibus anticrime bill that the Congress approved in the summer of 1994, capital punishment was prescribed for dozens of federal crimes including treason, genocide, causing a death through a train wreck, lethal drive-by shootings, civil rights murders, and murders committed with a firearm during a federal drug felony.

Yet in order to win the support of critics of capital punishment so that the legislation could pass both houses of Congress, the following provisions were included in the final bill:

> The law barred the federal government from imposing the penalty on persons under eighteen at the time of the offense and on those who are mentally retarded or lack the mental capacity "to understand the death penalty and why it was imposed on that person." They also endorsed the provision barring the execution of pregnant women.[56]

In 1996 Congress debated and eventually passed the Anti-Terrorism and Effective Death Penalty Act. The part of the legislative proposal that dealt with capital punishment was a provision that would sharply restrict the ability of death-row inmates to appeal their sentences after they had exhausted their state-level appeals. Supporters of the provision wanted to limit prisoners to one habeas corpus appeal so that the long delays associated with executions were reduced. In addition, the provision was intended to increase the number of executions that actually took place by lessening the chances that death sentences would be overturned through multiple appeals. A *New York Times* reporter wrote that both supporters and opponents of the legislation agreed that if the measure withstood court challenges, it would "drastically accelerate executions by shaving years off appeals of most capital cases."[57]

Several provisions of the original bill were opposed by a coalition of gun groups, including the NRA. These provisions included the increased wiretap authority for federal agents investigating crimes and lower standards to bring lawsuits against sellers of guns used in crimes. Since these provisions were not included in the final bill, it was supported by the gun lobby's strongest advocate in Congress, Representative Bob Barr (R-GA), who said that he and other conservative members of the House would support it.[58] Civil liberties organizations also opposed the original bill, although for very different reasons. The Washington director of Human Rights Watch, an international human rights organization, was reported as saying the following: "The legislation not only ignores the international trend away from capital punishment, but also violates the spirit of international norms by proposing to make executions more common and errors in capital cases more likely."[59] When the legislation finally passed the Senate in April 1996, it was the fulfillment of efforts by congressional conservatives, which started in Ronald Reagan's presidency, to rewrite the rules governing habeas corpus review, which is the only legal avenue that state death row inmates have to obtain a federal review of their cases.

Presidency

Presidents on occasion have initiated crime policies and created programs that reflect their beliefs about the causes of criminal behavior and the proper anticrime and crime prevention policies to be pursued. President John Kennedy promoted crime policies based upon the notion that the lack of opportunity for youths in urban ghettos was the primary cause of much personal and property crime. But Kennedy's response to organized crime was much different; it reflected more fully the ideas of the law and order school of thought, which held that leaders of organized crime were not "victims" of environmental or socioeconomic factors. The power of government was used to pursue, apprehend, and incarcerate those associated with organized crime.

It was during the Johnson administration that crime emerged as a highly visible political issue. Both the Kennedy administration and urban riots of the late 1960s brought the problem of violence and crime to the attention of the public, and President Johnson was well aware of public sentiment. His approach was similar to Kennedy's and involved a mixture of law and order policies and liberal social programs. Johnson's policy for dealing with criminal behavior was the Great Society program, which included massive expenditures for welfare, education, and training programs intended to alleviate the problem of crime.

The sociogenic view of criminal behavior espoused by Lyndon Johnson took a backseat to the psychogenic/deterrence approach of Richard M. Nixon. Nixon's view of crime policy was, in many respects, a complete repudiation of the sociogenic school of thought. According to his view, drug addicts, thieves, and other lawbreakers were rational persons who chose to violate the roles of society, and as such they should be sternly dealt with by law enforcement agencies. Following this line of thought, President Nixon pushed for stringent punishments: "The death penalty is not a sanction to be employed loosely or considered lightly, but neither is it to be ignored as a fitting penalty, in exceptional circumstances, for the purpose of preventing or deterring."[60]

Gerald Ford was concerned about the fear individuals have of everyday street crime, and during his presidency he favored mandatory incarceration for anyone using a dangerous weapon when committing an offense; for serious crimes such as hijacking, kidnaping, or trafficking in hard drugs; and for repeat offenders. But two aspects of Ford's crime philosophy were not indicative of a law and order approach. These were his preference for rehabilitation of some first-time offenders and the building of humanitarian prisons that minimized the violence prisoners may experience.

With Jimmy Carter, a new emphasis in crime policy became evident. President Carter was very interested in persons of all economic classes having "equal access" to justice. He sought to create an image of U.S. justice as fully representative of the nation's diverse peoples, and Carter stressed "special efforts to identify qualified minority and female candidates for judgeships."[61] As Carter said in 1978, "Too often, the amount of justice that a person gets depends on the amount of money that he or she can pay. Access to justice must not depend on economic status, and it must not be thwarted by arbitrary procedural rules."[62]

Ronald Reagan interpreted his landslide victory in the 1980 presidential election as direct evidence of a "conservative realignment" in U.S. politics. In his first public speech on crime (before the International Association of Chiefs of Police in 1981), Reagan unveiled his ideological attack on the "social thinkers of the 1950s and 1960s who discussed crime only in the context of disadvantaged childhoods and poverty-stricken neighborhoods" and who "thought that massive government spending could wipe away our social ills." He concluded that speech with the call that only appropriate morals "can hold back the jungle and restrain the darker impulses of human nature."[63]

Reagan's tough law and order agenda, with the exception of Nixon's, was unprecedented in recent times. President Reagan sought to appoint federal judges who were inclined to favor the prosecution in criminal cases. Because of the greater use of fixed sentences, tougher penalties, and more flexibility in the hands of prosecutors, during his tenure there were more persons incarcerated in federal prisons with longer sentences. Near the end of his presidency, Reagan signed a bill into law that contained a provision permitting the death penalty for murders committed by people who had participated in at least two criminal operations involving drugs and for those who killed a police officer while committing a crime.[64]

President George Bush continued the Reagan administration's strong law and order tradition and demonstrated his commitment to this tradition by supporting the death penalty. In a campaign speech to the Association for a Better New York, he called for the "swift" application of the death penalty to criminals convicted of drug-related murders and challenged the Democrats running for president to do the same. When reporters questioned him about how executions could be speeded up without violating the due process rights of the convicted, he said, "We've got to find a way. Due process is fine, but we've got to find a way to speed it up."[65] While George Bush was president, he maintained his tough stand by arguing for *mandatory* death sentences for murders in drug-related incidents and by urging that the death penalty be required (rather than just permitted) at the federal level in instances involving the killing of a law enforcement officer in drug cases.

During the Clinton administration, the Alfred P. Murrah Federal Building in Oklahoma City was bombed and 168 men, women, and children were killed. In response to this tragedy, which occurred in April 1995, President Bill Clinton immediately urged the Congress to pass counterterrorism legislation. Congress did pass counterterrorism legislation the following year, but when Clinton signed the Anti-Terrorism and Effective Death Penalty Act into law on April 25, 1996, he authorized legislation that provided *both* new tools and penalties for federal law enforcement officials to use in fighting terrorism *and* a provision that limited habeas corpus appeals by death row inmates to a six-month period after their final state court appeals had been completed. The Clinton administration had not sought the time limit on appeals, which was a prominent part of the final law.[66]

Clinton actually carried out the death penalty when he was the governor of Arkansas, and, as president, he signed a crime bill in 1994 that made dozens of federal crimes subject to the death penalty. Yet capital punishment was one of the issues that former Senator Bob Dole tried to use against Clinton in his campaign for the presidency in 1996. During a tour of California's death chamber, Dole took a strong law and order stand and said that as president he would push for laws to speed up executions of condemned prisoners and appoint conservative judges who would be tough on criminals.[67] In addition, he said that he had tried to speed up executions when he was in the Senate by proposing legislation that limited the time that death row inmates could file appeals to one year. He accused the president of being soft on criminals because Clinton had vetoed limits on the right of appeal a total of three times. Nevertheless, Clinton endorsed the death penalty several times in his official actions as president.

Bureaucracy

Since almost all death sentences are imposed and carried out by the states, there is virtually no substantive policy implementation by federal agencies. Presidents who take a strong stand favoring the death penalty, like any policy issue, may try to symbolically engage the federal bureaucracy to help focus public attention on that issue. Since both Reagan and Bush highlighted their support of the death penalty for drug-related murders, they showcased the Drug Enforcement Administration (DEA) in the national spotlight.

The attorney general and the solicitor general can become highly visible spokespersons for the death penalty. In 1997, as the trial against the "Unabomber" (who for years had sent mail bombs to individuals across the country), Attorney General Janet Reno announced that the government would seek the death penalty against that suspect. Dick Thornburgh, attorney general in Reagan's second term, spoke out in October 1988 and supported Reagan's position on expanding the death penalty for federal crimes, including the assassination of senior government officials. Thornburgh said that he believed the death penalty could serve as a deterrent to capital offenses, and he indicated that he would support efforts to broaden the punishment to cases in which prison guards and senior government officials were killed.[68]

Summary

Though the Supreme Court has ruled that the death penalty as now implemented is not unconstitutional, the manner in which inmates are executed is being questioned. This issue came to a head with the execution in Florida of Pedro L. Medina on March 26, 1997. Medina was executed by electrocution, and when the power was turned on, the leather mask that he was wearing burst into flames, which lasted for several seconds. A reporter wrote that "the unexpected spectacle left many among the two dozen witnesses visibly shaken . . . but the state doctor in attendance said he thought the death had been instantaneous and painless."[69] Lawton Chiles, the governor, said, "I have not thought it was cruel and unusual punishment. . . . If [the state's seventy-four-year-old electric chair is] not working properly or can't work properly we'll have to see what we can do."[70] Death penalty opponents argued that Florida's form of execution violated the prohibition on cruel and unusual punishment, and also maintained that problematic executions were not all that unusual where lethal injection, a supposedly humane method, was used.

When mistakes involving individuals convicted of capital crimes that they did not commit are uncovered, the debate over limiting the federal death penalty appeals process is renewed. This was the case in July 1996 when three Illinois men who had spent eighteen years on death row for a double murder that they did not commit were set free. Now that federal habeas corpus appeals by death row inmates are restricted to a six-month period after final state court appeals have been completed, others who are innocent yet are convicted will not have the time it takes to prove their innocence, assuming that they have the legal, investigative, and monetary resources to do so. In commenting on this case, Richard C. Dieter, director of the Death Penalty Information Center, was reported as saying that "the average length of time between conviction and execution is now about eight years . . . adding that the restrictions probably meant that lengths of appeals would fall well below the average time it takes to discover new evidence of innocence."[71]

One of the innocent men thought that the reason he and his friends were charged, convicted, and sentenced to death for a crime that they did not commit was the racism inherent in the system. Anti-capital-punishment organizations use the issue of race to explain their strong opposition to the policy. One example was this statement issued by the Evangelical Lutheran Church in America in 1991:

> It is because of this Church's commitment to justice that we oppose the death penalty. . . . Despite attempts to provide legal safeguards, the death penalty has not been and cannot be made fair. The race of the victim plays a role in who is sentenced to death and who is sentenced to life imprisonment, as do the gender, race, mental capacity, age, and affluence of the accused. The system cannot be made perfect, for biases, prejudices, and chance affect whom we charge with a capital crime, what verdict we reach, and whether appeals will be successful.[72]

A moral dimension underlies the contemporary debate about capital punishment. Presidents, members of Congress, federal and state judges, interest groups, and state and local criminal justice authorities explain their involvement in terms of very basic assumptions about human nature—about individual responsibility versus social disadvantage, about fear of an oppressive government versus fear of disorder, about the justice of taking human life as a fit punishment for heinous crimes versus the sacredness of human life. The policy debate is about moral principles and constitutional rights and is based on fundamentally different assumptions regarding the causes of crime, the rights of capital offenders, and the legitimacy of government imposing the ultimate punishment. Capital punishment is an issue that will be with us well into the twenty-first century.

Notes

1. For example, see Ramsey Clark, *Crime in America* (New York: Simon and Schuster, 1970).
2. See Edward C. Banfield, *The Unheavenly City Revisited* (Boston: Little, Brown, 1974).
3. Saleem A. Shah and Loren H. Roth, "Biological and Psychophysiological Factors in Criminality," in Daniel Glaser, ed., *Handbook of Criminology* (Chicago: Rand McNally, 1974), pp. 101–173.
4. Raymond Paternoster, *Capital Punishment in America* (New York: Lexington Books, 1991), p. 4.
5. Ibid., p. 10.

6. Ibid., pp. 11, 14.

7. Ibid., p. 21.

8. "56 Executions This Year Were the Most Since 1957," *The New York Times* (December 30, 1995), p. 10.

9. Mark Costanzo and Lawrence T. White, "An Overview of the Death Penalty and Capital Trials: History, Current Status, Legal Procedures, and Cost," *Journal of Social Issues* 50 (1994), p. 8.

10. "Capital Punishment: Is There Any Habeas Left in This Corpus?" *Loyola University Chicago Law Journal* 27 (1996), pp. 523–614.

11. Bryan Stevenson, "The Hanging Judges: Once the Court Said, 'Death Is Different.' Now It Says, 'Let's Get On with It,' " 1996, http://www.thenation.com /issue/961014/1014stev.htm (February 18, 1997).

12. Ibid.

13. As reported by statisticians James Stephan and Peter Brien in "Capital Punishment 1993," *Bureau of Justice Statistics Bulletin* (Washington, DC: U.S. Department of Justice, 1994), pp. 7, 11.

14. United States General Accounting Office, Report to Senate and House Committees on the Judiciary, *Death Penalty Sentencing: Research Indicates Pattern of Racial Disparities* (Washington, DC: General Accounting Office, 1990), p. 5.

15. John Galloway, *Criminal Justice and the Burger Court* (New York: Facts on File, 1978), p. 43.

16. Edmund F. McGarrell and Marla Sandys, "The Misperception of Public Opinion Toward Capital Punishment: Examining the Spuriousness Explanation of Death Penalty Support," *American Behavioral Scientist* 39 (February 1996), pp. 500–513.

17. As reported in a Gallup poll, December 16, 1993.

18. As reported in a Gallup poll, September 28, 1994.

19. Costanzo and White, "An Overview of the Death Penalty and Capital Trials," pp. 10–11.

20. Ibid., p. 12.

21. Linda Greenhouse, "Death Sentences Against Retarded and Young Upheld," *The New York Times* (June 27, 1989), pp. 1, 10.

22. Stephen Wermiel, "Death Penalty Edicts Compound Confusion Say Critics of the Court," *The Wall Street Journal* (May 10, 1984), p. 1.

23. Ibid.

24. An interview with former Supreme Court Justice Lewis F. Powell in E.R. Shipp, "Ex-Justice Powell Says Lawmakers Should Reconsider Capital Punishment," *The New York Times* (August 8, 1988), p. 8.

25. Stephen Labaton, "Bars on Death Row: By Curbing Appeals, Terrorism Bill Shifts Powers to State Court Judges," *The New York Times* (April 19, 1996), p. C19.

26. Linda Greenhouse, "Right to Lawyer Curbed for Death Row Inmates," *The New York Times* (June 24, 1989), p. 7.

27. Linda Greenhouse, "Supreme Court, 9–0, Upholds Death Penalty in the Military," *The New York Times* (June 4, 1996), p. A1.

28. Ibid.

29. Robert Reinhold, "Outgoing Governor in New Mexico Bars the Execution of 5," *The New York Times* (November 27, 1986), p. 1.

30. Ibid.

31. Mario M. Cuomo, "New York State Shouldn't Kill People," *The New York Times* (June 17, 1989), p. 15.

32. Rachel L. Swarns, "In Clash on Death Penalty Case, Pataki Removes Bronx Prosecutor," *The New York Times* (March 22, 1996), p. A16.

33. David Von Drehle, *Among the Lowest of the Dead: The Culture of Death Row* (New York: Times Books, Random House, 1995), p. 279.

34. Ibid.

35. Ibid., pp. 282–283.

36. Ibid., p. 283.

37. Human Rights Watch, *Modern Capital of Human Rights? Abuses in the State of Georgia* (New York: Human Rights Watch, 1996), p. 53.

38. Ibid., p. 57.

39. Michael Engel, *State and Local Politics* (New York: St. Martin's Press, 1985), p. 154.

40. Francis T. Cullen, Timothy S. Bynum, Kim Montgomery Garrett, and Jack R. Greene, "Legislator Ideology and Criminal Justice Policy: Implications from Illinois," in Erika S. Fairchild and Vincent J. Webb, eds., *The Politics of Crime and Criminal Justice* (Beverly Hills, CA: Sage, 1985), p. 69.

41. For additional information on this issue, see David H. Getches, Charles F. Wilkinson, and Robert A. Williams Jr., *Federal Indian Law: Cases and Materials,* 3rd ed. (Washington, DC: Congressional Quarterly Press, 1995).

42. *United States Code* Title 18—Crimes and Criminal Procedure, Section 3598, p. 608.

43. Aaron Epstein, "Burger Court Has Eased Limits on Search and Seizure," *Detroit Free Press* (June 8, 1986), p. 6B.

44. Carol Greenwald, *Group Power: Lobbying and Public Policy* (New York: Praeger, 1977), p. 289.

45. This tripartite division of labor is taken from Stuart Scheingold, *The Politics of Law and Order,* pp. 228–229.

46. Ibid., p. 180.

47. "ABA House of Delegates Approves Call for Halt in U.S. Executions Until Death Penalty Fairness Assured—Press Release," February 3, 1997 http://www.abanet.org/media/feb97/death.html (April 12, 1997).

48. Ibid.

49. "National Coalition to Abolish the Death Penalty," in Shirley Dicks, ed., *Congregation of the Condemned: Voices Against the Death Penalty* (Buffalo, NY: Prometheus Books, 1991), p. 221.

50. "Southern Coalition on Jails and Prisons," in Dicks, *Congregation of the Condemned,* p. 238.

51. Joseph F. Sheley, *America's "Crime Problem": An Introduction to Criminology* (Belmont, CA: Wadsworth, 1985), p. 33.

52. Scheingold, *The Politics of Law and Order,* p. 85.

53. "Death Penalty Amendment Stalls Vote on Pentagon Bill," *The New York Times* (May 19, 1988), p. A13.

54. Joan Biskupic, "Law/Judiciary: Death-Penalty Expansion Bill Is Moved to Senate Floor," *Congressional Quarterly: Social Policy* (October 21, 1989), p. 2805.

55. Ibid.

56. "Death Penalty Debate: Action in Congress," *The CQ Researcher,* 5, no. 9 (March 10, 1995), p. 206.

57. Stephen Labaton, "Bill on Terrorism Gains Momentum in the Congress," *The New York Times (*April 16, 1996), p. A1.

58. Ibid., p. A9.

59. Stephen Labaton, "Stopping Amendments from Democrats, Senate Easily Passes a Counterterrorism Bill," *The New York Times* (April 18, 1996), p. A10.

60. Richard M. Nixon, *Public Papers of the President of the United States* (Washington, DC: U.S. Government Printing Office, 1968), p. 781.

61. Jimmy Carter, *Public Papers of the President of the United States* (Washington, DC: U.S. Government Printing Office, 1978), p. 839.

62. Ibid.

63. Bertram Gross, "Reagan's Criminal 'Anti-crime' Fix," in Alan Gartner, Colin Geer, and Frank Riessman, eds., *What Reagan Is Doing to Us* (New York: Harper and Row, 1982), pp. 87–88.

64. Julie Johnson, "Reagan Signs Bill to Curb Drug Use," *The New York Times* (November 19, 1988), p. A7.

65. Gerald M. Boyd, "Execution Backed in Drug Slayings: Bush Urges Swift Penalties, Citing Murder of Officer," *The New York Times* (April 14, 1988), p. A15.

66. Alison Mitchell, "President Signs Bill on Terrorism and Death Penalty Appeals," *The New York Times* (April 25, 1996), p. A10.

67. Katharine Q. Seelye, "Dole Tours Death Chamber in San Quentin and Calls for Speedier Executions," *The New York Times* (March 24, 1996), p. 14.

68. Philip Shenon, "Wider Death Rule for U.S. Crimes Backed by the Attorney General," *The New York Times* (October 19, 1988), p. 12.

69. Mireya Navarro, "After Fire at Execution, Florida Lawmakers Defend Use of Electric Chair," *The New York Times* (March 27, 1997), p. A10.

70. Ibid.

71. Don Terry, "After 18 Years in Prison, 3 Are Cleared of Murders: Official Apologizes for 'a Terrible Injustice,' " *The New York Times* (July 3, 1996), p. A8.

72. Evangelical Lutheran Church in America, "A Social Statement on the Death Penalty," December 28, 1995, http://www.elca.org/dcs/death.html (April 12, 1997).

4

Gay Rights: Lifestyle or Immorality?

Margaret Ellis

In April 1993 three hundred thousand supporters of the gay and lesbian movement converged on Washington, DC, to protest against oppression based on sexual identity. The political significance of the Washington march was that it signaled the progress this social movement had made since its beginning with the 1969 Stonewall riots in New York City. By the 1990s the gay and lesbian movement has become a formidable policy issue in the political arena. However, despite the increased attention of agenda setters and decision makers, the issue remains more at the margins of the political agenda than a mainstream contender.

For most of those participating in the march, this was a call for the federal government to address the denial of legal protection and rights for homosexuals. For many of those observing this gathering, however, the march represented a collection of misguided moral deviants whose entire agenda was morally repulsive and deserving of condemnation rather than legal protection. Opponents of gay rights have portrayed homosexuals as immoral sinners,[1] have claimed that societal disapproval of homosexuality is justified for the protection of both the traditional family unit and future generations, have blamed homosexuals for the spread of sexually transmitted diseases, especially AIDS, and have asserted that homosexuals are disproportionately likely to be pedophiles.

This dichotomy of views concerning the legitimate standing of the gay community illustrates the chasm that must be bridged in order to understand the nature of the public policy issue surrounding gay rights. This is not simply a constitutional question, but one that involves the moral structure of society and strains the outer limits of tolerance for both those opposing equal protection of the rights of gays and those who feel sexual orientation is not an appropriate basis for the denial of equal protection.

Many Americans recognize that a difference exists between tolerance for a certain lifestyle and mandating legal repercussions for such behavior. If the law of the land reflects the consensus of the majority, then who will be the determinant of the morality of that consensus? Which moral carries the greatest weight—the protection of all citizens, including those who may not constitute a majority, or the moral position of those most strategically placed in the decision-making process, even if that position should result in discrimination? Without abandoning the view that homosexuality represents deviant behavior, most Americans now perceive gay people as a minority group that needs legal protection from discrimination. How far this protection can be extended is the crux of the debate over gay rights.

Advocates of gay and lesbian civil rights stipulate that the immorality in this issue is the discrimination itself. Arguments about the ability to "choose to be homosexual" remain unresolved, and until such time as society can unequivocally prove that such behavior is not due to human nature itself, advocates of gay rights deem differentiation on the basis of sexual orientation to be unjustified and therefore discriminatory, in both intent and outcome. To define constitutional rights as "special rights" on the basis of religious or moral attitudes toward sexual orientation presents numerous questions about equal-protection violations (which supporters of gay rights feel should be answered if the tradition of this constitutional protection is to be upheld). While there are traditional religious arguments that homosexuality is wrong and therefore can be subject to sanction, these arguments are directed at conduct, not at the legality of a certain group of people's enjoying the same benefits of life, liberty, and the pursuit of happiness within the established governmental structure.[2]

The increased success of the gay movement in recent years may be due to the shift in the debate from behavior to identity. This shift forces opponents of gay civil rights into a position of attacking the fundamental rights of citizens themselves, rather than the specific, socially unacceptable behavior of that citizen, a behavior that is unacceptable to most of society. Thus homosexual activists seek to define themselves as a legitimate minority group comparable to other minorities and deserving of the same rights, legal and civil.[3]

Presidency

In large measure, U.S. domestic policies, and most foreign policies, have been developed through cooperation between the executive and legislative branches. The problem most often lies in the president's ability to discern a viable policy that will have the acceptance of the general public.

According to Paul Light, presidential policy making is the product of the input from a stream of people and ideas. At the start of each term, the president is often obligated by a large number of campaign promises and is forced to reduce the policy agenda to a manageable size. By the end of the term, the stream is reduced to a trickle and the president's focus turns to reelection and/or accomplishment of initial programs.[4] The presidential policy stream provides a partial explanation of the role of the president in gay rights policy making and illustrates how the president manipulates social regulatory policy to reflect the values of his constituency and to maintain both his partisan and electoral support. American policy making is normally considered to be rather pragmatic in that policy should be formulated with an eye toward whatever works rather than following one set ideological or philosophical system. Unfortunately, one standard definition of what will work in government is "that which is already working," because this policy has already been given public approval. Policy tends to change slowly and incrementally, and presidents do not tend to attempt implementation of radical changes in policy.

The first time the issue of gay civil rights actually became prominent in a presidential election was in 1980. The campaign, however, did not focus on the pursuit of the votes of gay constituents, but rather found momentum in the denial of votes for those candidates who openly supported gay rights. In the primaries, the Democratic candidates largely supported the homosexual agenda, but the race for the Republican nomination became a contest to see which candidate could be the most staunchly antigay. Reagan positioned himself most advantageously by alluding to the Bible and declaring that "in the eyes of the Lord, homosexuality is an abomination," leaving George Bush and John Connally, a former Texas governor who became a Republican, bickering over which legal rights gays should or should not be allowed to exercise.[5] Reagan interjected the claim that the objection to gay rights was not that American citizens should be deprived of their legal rights, but that this "alternative lifestyle" was not one society could condone.

While the argument centered on gay rights, the underlying purpose of this discussion was not to address this issue, but to create a significant voting cue for the electorate when choosing between the Carter campaign and the Republican candidate. The rise of the conservative right wing of the Republican party and the Moral Majority converged on the issue of gay rights and focused on the Democratic party platform's endorsement of gay rights, depicting Carter as the candidate of homosexuals. Emphasis on the fact that the next president would have the opportunity to make several

Supreme Court appointments translated into the need to protect the country from the formation of an overly liberal Court that would advance the cause of the gay community. The irony in this campaign is that the New Right and the Moral Majority did not have a substantial impact on the way in which most of the country viewed the rights of other minority groups. Support for ERA and women's issues remained strong, while opposition for the gay rights movement increased proportionately. The opposition to gay rights was directed toward morality and the maintenance of appropriate societal values, while support for women's rights was framed by a constitutional equal protection debate.

In 1988 gay rights again had an important function in the presidential campaign, with partisan lines remaining intact. However, the Democratic presidential candidate, Michael Dukakis, refused to pledge to sign an executive order banning discrimination on the basis of sexual orientation in federal jobs and presented a much more moderate position toward gay rights. The Republican nominee, George Bush, deftly took a more moderate position also, answering a questionnaire from the National Gay and Lesbian Task Force with the statement "I believe all Americans have fundamental rights guaranteed in our Constitution."[6] This position, relaxed by comparison with the Reagan agenda, helped to overcome the gay community's fear that the election of yet another Republican president would lead to even greater discrimination. The inability of Dukakis to commit to this challenge, along with other political mistakes by the Democratic candidate, meant that the votes of many white gay males helped to ensure Bush's victory.

The issue of gays in the military captured the national spotlight during the 1992 presidential campaign when candidate Bill Clinton announced his intention, if elected, to overturn the military's existing ban on gays. Consequently, gay rights activists at the 1992 Democratic convention came forward with tremendous support for Clinton. This proved to be a major constituency in that homosexuals numbered more than a hundred delegates. Gay rights groups then donated more than $3 million to the Clinton campaign, putting them among the party's big contributors, along with the Jewish community, the entertainment industry, and environmentalists.

Shortly after his election, word leaked out that President Clinton would remain true to his word and, within days of his inauguration in 1993, would sign an executive order overturning a long-standing military policy. This decision was apparently made completely without any advice from military professionals and sparked a movement to deter the president in his plans. A number of highly respected policy experts—military, civilian, Republican, and Democratic—strongly advised against this move. The American Legion, Veterans of Foreign Wars, and other veterans' groups criticized the plan, and President Clinton eventually agreed to consult with military leaders on how best to make this change. He made it very clear, however, that the change would take place; the only negotiable point was the method by which the change would be effected.

Military policy for homosexuals has had a complex history reflective of a long-standing tradition of discrimination toward minorities in the military, despite the fact that before the armed forces of the United States were formally organized, gays were bearing arms for the nation. The formation of the first formal military unit in this country was accomplished by a known homosexual, Frederich von Steuben, appointed by General George Washington as the first inspector general of the Army. Steuben's contribution to the training and discipline of the troops of the Continental Army was credited as indispensable to the success of the Revolution.[7]

During the Civil War, both Union and Confederate troops employed homosexual soldiers in battle, despite the existence of regulations prohibiting homosexual acts by soldiers. The idea of excluding people for having a homosexual orientation, as opposed to punishing only those who committed homosexual acts, was born during World War I. It was during this time that the military first began to view homosexuals as not only dangerous, but also ineffective as soldiers. The transition from thinking of homosexuality as criminal behavior to seeing it as mental illness occurred during World War II. Psychiatrists helped formulate regulations that banned all those with homosexual tendencies from the military and set forth treatment requirements for those identified as having the "disease" after joining the armed forces. Dishonorable discharges resulted if psychiatric treatment failed.[8]

This policy remained in effect until late 1981, when the Department of Defense instituted a change to military regulations regarding administrative separations for enlisted men. The new policy went into effect in 1982 and voided all clauses in military regulations allowing for the retention of anyone who could be discerned as homosexual, on the grounds that such individuals would "damage the image of the military in the eyes of the American people, our allies, and our potential adversaries and make military service less attractive."[9] This policy replaced psychiatric treatment for homosexuality, was incorporated into the Uniform Code of Military Justice, and remained the formal position of all branches of the military until 1993, when President Clinton partially lifted the ban.

Clinton's proposal to totally lift the ban proved to be impossible, and was quickly characterized as a test of the new president's political power. The polarization of the issue pushed the issue to the top of Clinton's political agenda. By placing gay rights in this highly visible position, Clinton chose one of the most sensitive, value-laden issues of the day. No longer in need of the support of the gay community to ensure electoral success, Clinton was now faced with choosing the solution that would prove most politically beneficial. Without the support of Congress and without a clear mandate from the voting populace, Clinton hesitated to take on the responsibility for this policy modification, and so he sent the proposed change to the Department of Defense for review and recommendation. This lack of decisive leadership led to the observation that Clinton's proposal to lift the ban had been a symbolic gesture, aimed at gaining the support of a crucial voting constituency. In reality, Clinton discovered it was not prudent to make such a decision unilaterally, even though such an action is within the scope of authority of the chief executive. Clinton learned that there are inherent risks in dealing with issues evoking highly controversial moral questions.

In January, shortly after Clinton took office and announced his decision to stand by his campaign pledge, 72 percent of those surveyed in a public opinion poll believed that homosexuals could effectively serve in the armed forces; however, 53 percent did not support Clinton's proposal to lift the ban.[10] By May, 60 percent did not support the president's position,[11] and opposition within the armed forces increased to 74 percent, including 81 percent who believed violent acts against homosexuals would occur.[12] Again, the issue crossed partisan lines. The former senator from Arizona and 1964 Republican presidential nominee, Barry Goldwater, supported Clinton's position: "When you get down to it, no American able to serve should be allowed, much less given an excuse, not to serve his or her country. We need all our talent."[13] Numerous other political leaders, both Republican and Democratic, stepped forward on both sides of the controversy, indicating that the saliency of the issue resulted from more than just political maneuvering: this issue touched the moral fiber of the electorate and escalated the potential impact of policy implementation.

The compromise between President Clinton and military and political leaders was implemented in 1994 as the "don't ask, don't tell" policy. The first version of the plan was actually a "don't ask, don't tell, and don't pursue" policy in which military officials would agree not to actively seek out lesbians and gay men in the armed forces. Senator Nunn and other ban supporters objected to this approach, and the final legislation took out the clause ordering recruiters not to ask recruits if they were gay, leaving this restriction to the discretion of the secretary of defense. The current policy promises not to ask soldiers about their sexual orientation, and to let gays and lesbians serve unless they openly reveal their homosexuality.

In a study of the "don't ask, don't tell" policy, released in February 1996, the Service Members Legal Defense Network (SLDN) reported that the military had discharged 722 service members for homosexuality in fiscal 1995, an increase of 21 percent over 1994. During that period, SLDN reported, the policy was violated at least 363 times.[14] Some argue that this is a violation of human rights and that the issue is not to reduce the influence of sexuality but to provide equal treatment for all citizens. To this group, there is no difference between the struggle of African-American soldiers in the first half of this century and the struggle of homosexual soldiers today.

Returning to the 1993 march on Washington, it is notable that despite the tremendous opportunity for exposure to this constituency, President Clinton and most legislators left town on the weekend of the march. The lack of an official presence was viewed as an attempt to distance the administration from this policy issue. Many senators and representatives closed their offices because of "security concerns," and the march was not reported by any of the nation's three major news magazines, *Time, Newsweek,* or *U.S. News and World Report.*[15] Given the polarization of opinion on gay rights and gays in the military in particular, the march proved to be an unsuitable platform for the official expression of support and/or opposition for proposed resolutions to this problem. President Clinton did, however, issue a statement to the participants in the Gay Rights March, which was read to the march participants on the mall by Representative Nancy Pelosi. In this statement, the president cited what he felt were the administration's accomplishments in addressing gay rights. Among those accomplishments were the pending executive order to lift the ban on gays and lesbians in the military, a budget proposal to increase funding to AIDS research, and the Ryan White Act. The president also pointed out that his meeting with leaders of the gay and lesbian community in the Oval Office at the White House "marks the first time in history that the President of the United States has held such a meeting . . . In addition, members of my staff have been and will continue to be in regular communication with the gay and lesbian community."[16]

Congress

Following the *Bowers v. Hardwick,* 478 U.S. 186 (1986), ruling, which upheld state antisodomy laws, Congress began to pursue an increasingly antigay agenda. In particular, Senator Jesse Helms (R-NC), conservative and stridently antigay, introduced a number of different legislative initiatives to counter what he (and many others) perceived to be inappropriate legal and political gains by this group. These initiatives represented attempts to constrain and control gay rights policies, and a good deal of the legislative action centered on the funding of programs by the federal government. Helms argued that the government has the right not to fund the advancement of a "homosexual lifestyle," grounding the justification for the legislation in the belief that government has a duty to protect the public from the seduction and conversion of heterosexuals to a homosexual lifestyle. The opposition to gay rights legislation worked to repeat what many saw not as a civil rights issue, but as the imposition of an immoral lifestyle. According to Barry Adam, this movement was fueled by the belief that laws protecting gays from discrimination would lead to child molestation, gay recruiting, threats to the traditional family, and an overall national gay conspiracy to destroy the moral fiber of this country.[17]

This argument was manifested in numerous ways during the 1990s and was fueled by the panic generated from the uncontrolled spread of the HIV virus. The failure by Congress to provide funding for AIDS research during the early 1980s was perceived as a partial cause for the spread of this disease, but, at the time, primary responsibility was attributed to the sexual conduct of homosexuals. These factors provided the impetus for Congress to act decisively in addressing gay rights legislation. Three examples of the resultant legislation are: (1) the prohibition on expenditures of public funds on safe-sex education materials, (2) the prohibition of funds to the National Endowment for the Arts (NEA) for "homoerotic" art, and (3) the prohibition of same-sex marriages. All three were part of the ongoing campaign to limit gay civil rights, and both the safe-sex materials and NEA funding amendments were challenged successfully in the courts on the basis that they infringed on the right of free speech.

During the 1990s the spread of the HIV virus and AIDS became a priority issue for most policy makers. In 1985 the American Centers for Disease Control began funding programs aimed at changing sexual behavior, including work undertaken by numerous gay organizations across the nation. These organizations provided education materials and other services to communities, including graphic and explicit descriptions of safe sex practices. Private funds were used to produce the most provocative materials[18] and restrictions were placed on materials that received federal funding and that might "be judged by a reasonable person to be offensive to most educated adults."[19]

In 1987 Senator Helms introduced an amendment to an appropriations bill in Congress to prohibit the provision of federal funds through the Centers for Disease Control (CDC) to either private groups or state and local governments, that would be used "to provide AIDS education, information, or prevention materials and activities that promote or encourage, directly or indirectly, homosexual activities."[20] The focus of the Helms Amendment and the accompanying debate was not simply the provision of these materials to the general public, but more directly the promotion of a homosexual lifestyle. Representative Dannemeyer, a staunch opponent of gay rights, suggested that it would be beneficial to examine how extensive "the movement of homosexuality in America has become in terms of changing the cultural values of our society so that we will accept and equate homosexuality on a par with heterosexual life."[21] Senator Helms offered that "every AIDS case can be traced back to a homosexual act," and that the funding of safe-sex materials contributed to the spread of AIDS because of the contagiousness of homosexuality.[22] Senator Helms stressed as well that the distribution of these materials was ineffective because "the people who are spreading the disease do not pay attention to it anyhow." The literature was also criticized as being pornographic, and legislation was enacted that established an offensiveness standard that was designed to focus on whether AIDS educational materials were designed to encourage sexual activity rather than simple sexual education.

The CDC subsequently set new funding guidelines aimed at eliminating any material which could be considered obscene, and established a peer review panel of ordinary citizens to approve all materials before they were distributed. These guidelines were ultimately challenged in the courts and found to be unconstitutional. The United States District Court of the Southern District of New York found the CDC obscenity standard provided no real guidance to AIDS educators and as such was outside the statutory authority of the CDC. The vagueness and ambiguity of the guidelines were found to have a chilling effect on the expression of sexual identity in public discourse resulting in a form of self-censorship by AIDS educators.[23]

Freedom of speech has provided more consistent support for the protection of lesbian and gay rights than other constitutional doctrines and is an essential tool in balancing the interests of the majority with the protection of minorities. In the restriction on funding of safe-sex educational materials, the decision converged on the morality of the homosexual "lifestyle" rather than the need to uphold constitutional doctrine. The challenge for legislators would be to maintain objectivity in their decision making and to look beyond the current debate, but this is not within the job description of elected representatives. Senators and representatives are elected to represent their constituency; consequently, the constituency that is most adamant in pursuing its agenda provides the greatest electoral benefits to the legislators who set the tone in social regulatory policy.

A second area in which Congress has exercised its authority is through federal funding of the National Endowment for the Arts. The NEA was created in 1965 as a means for public financial support of the arts through an agency with independent grant-making powers. NEA sponsors a diverse representation of artistic and cultural works through grants to individuals of exceptional talent. Funding decisions have always been made by the chairman of the endowment, who is appointed by the president with the advice and consent of the Senate. In 1989 NEA funded an exhibition entitled "Robert Mapplethorpe: The Perfect Moment." The exhibit was scheduled to be shown at the Corcoran Gallery in Washington, DC, but its appearance there was canceled due to political pressures and objections to the nature of the material exhibited in the artist's works. The Mapplethorpe exhibition included two portfolios, one consisting of photographs of sadomasochistic gay male imagery.

The political upheaval and controversy brought about by this exhibition led Senator Helms to propose statutory restrictions on the funding of future NEA projects. The senator justified this restriction on the grounds that the NEA served an additional political function in providing certain groups exposure that otherwise they would have been unable to achieve. Helms pointed out that art critics consider "Mapplethorpe's obscene photographs . . . an effort to gain wider exposure of and acceptance for, homosexuality —which happens to be the stated political goals of all homosexual pressure groups."[24] Some politicians went further and attributed an overwhelming symbolic value to any representation of gay sexuality, finding that NEA funding decisions represented an ongoing battle against "the eroding [of] the moral structure of the country."[25] The restrictions were passed into law and required that funding be awarded only when the material being promoted was deemed not to be obscene according to the categorical definition of obscenity spelled out in the law. Additional congressional action has resulted in the enactment of further restrictions on NEA about the composition of exhibitions and has essentially closed the door to artistic expression regarding homosexuality. It is argued that the funding of representations of lesbian and gay life would violate the rights of practicing Christians not to have their tax dollars spent on promoting a set of sexual practices they view as inherently evil.[26] Thus, these restrictions on government financial support for the arts appear to be grounded in the protection of the values of a religious group, albeit a majority group in the United States. This legislation raises questions as to the appropriateness of basing these restrictions on the moral values of one societal group. Two legal challenges indicative of this concern have been made in response to these restrictions, and in both cases the restrictions have been found to be unduly vague and "inherently subjective."[27]

Due to the state court ruling in Hawaii on same-sex marriage resulting from *Baehr v. Lewin*, the public outcry on all fronts was overwhelming, and

Congress responded quickly and decisively.[28] Bills were introduced into both the House and the Senate that essentially prohibited federal recognition of gay marriages and specified that states need not honor same-sex marriages legally performed in other states. The debate that took place in the House Judiciary Committee concerning approval of the bill, the Defense of Marriage Act of 1996, is indicative of the value-laden content of this policy and the high emotion associated with it.

Barney Frank (D-MA), an avowed homosexual, repeatedly scoffed at the bill and said, "This is not the defense of marriage, but the defense of the Republican ticket." In response, Charles Canady (R-FL) stressed that the federal government should not give an implicit sanction to gay marriage; Canady said, "What is at issue here is whether we choose to give moral equivalency to same-sex marriage." Other arguments along this line came from Sonny Bono (R-CA), who offered Frank an unusual personal apology for not opposing the bill. Bono told Frank, "I simply can't handle this yet. I wish I was ready, but I can't tell my son it's okay," to which Frank replied that he and other gays are seeking tolerance and fair treatment, not approval; "If it bothers people, turn your heads."[29] The polarization of the parties involved, while falling very close to partisan lines, was solidly reflective of whether the member viewed homosexuality as a moral issue.

Supporters of this legislation say the bill accomplishes two important things: First, it restates the long-established understanding that marriage means "a legal union between one man and one woman as husband and wife," and it defines a spouse in the federal law as a "person of the opposite sex." Second, the bill declares that no state will be required to recognize another state's marriage that does not fit within its own definition of marriage. Both the House and the Senate passed the legislation, and President Clinton signed the bill into law on September 22, 1996. Clinton had previously announced he would sign the bill even though he did not support it. The president's spokesman, Michael McCurry, stated, "The President believes the motives behind this bill are dubious and . . . believes the sooner he gets this over with, the better."[30] The American Civil Liberties Union (ACLU), which says the law is unconstitutional, has vowed to challenge it in court.

Each and every session, new legislation is introduced concerning gay rights, both to limit rights and to expand rights. There are currently bills under consideration in both chambers that would amend the Civil Rights Act of 1964, one to prohibit discrimination on the basis of sexual orientation and another to make preferential treatment an unlawful employment practice.[31]

Judiciary

The constitutionality of classifications based upon sexual discrimination is a delicate issue that has garnered most attention in the discourse of civil rights. The question at hand is whether the government can draw distinctions in law between citizens based on "sexual orientation" without violating the equal protection clause. This question remains perplexing and continues to defy full interpretation at all levels of the judiciary. The arguments tend to revolve around the perception that "gay rights" differ from other civil rights in that gay rights are identified by sexual conduct rather than a state of being. This dichotomy between behavior and identity drives the controversy about the legitimacy of gay men and lesbians' seeking civil rights protections. Opponents of gay rights term antidiscrimination laws as "special rights" when addressing this issue, while supporters rationalize that the protection of civil rights for gays is consistent with the fundamental aspects of full, genuine citizenship.

Much of the conflict between homosexual activists and their foes springs from disagreement over the nature of homosexuality. Most gays and lesbians contend that their sexual leaning is either an inborn trait or an immutable and healthy psychological condition developed in early childhood. In contrast, opponents of gay rights feel this behavior is acquired or learned from others and, as such, can be discarded or changed by the individual. This debate has considerable political importance, because if sexual orientation is truly inborn and immutable, the case for broad civil rights protections is valid. If so, then gay men and lesbians might be recognized by the courts as a "suspect class," a discrete and insular minority displaying immutable characteristics and lacking political power. Such a classification would require that any government regulation on gay rights would have to meet "strict scrutiny" of the law and be narrowly tailored to meet a compelling government interest. The application of the strict scrutiny standard in such cases imposes a greater burden of proof on the government and would, in all likelihood, permit a much wider field of civil rights protection. On the other hand, if sexual orientation is viewed as sexual preference, the classification would not be forthcoming, and the provision of strict scrutiny for gay rights would require the involvement of a fundamental right, such as free speech or the right to privacy.

Because this question of sexual orientation versus sexual preference remains unanswered, opponents of gay rights continue to argue that homosexuals are asking for "special rights." The argument surrounding special rights is that gay rights represent the efforts of homosexuals to carve out an entirely new area of civil rights law by basing protections for minorities on behavior rather than on immutable characteristics.[32] This line of thinking holds that since homosexuals already have all the civil rights everyone else has, their claim for protection against discrimination based on sexual orientation is unreasonable.[33] The main thrust of this argument is that private sexual activity between consenting adults is not the basis for governmental regulation, and everyone is governed by the same rules of fairness and protection from discriminatory laws. Supporters of gay rights quickly point out the caveat here that antigay discrimination laws do base their distinction on the private sexual activity between consenting adults and thereby identify certain types of people whom the law will treat differently.

Increasingly, policy makers acknowledge the distinction between special privileges based on sexual orientation and current sexual discrimination laws. Because unjustified differentiation based on sexual orientation is viewed as discrimination, and the American people regard blatant discrimination as reprehensible and in its own way immoral, policy makers are forced to view this question of special rights very precisely. Framing the debate along the lines of the 1964 Civil Rights Act, supporters claim the rights provided are not special rights, and to deny them to gay men and lesbians solely on the basis of sexual orientation is no more legitimate than such discrimination would be on the basis of race, gender, or religious affiliation.

The volume of litigation involving gay rights issues appears to be increasing, partly as a result of more routine and more public involvement of gays in economic, social, and political activities, but also due to the increased salience of the issue to policy makers. Issues that have come to the forefront recently include same-sex marriages, adoption by gay couples, and military service. The federal Defense of Marriage Act of 1996 specifies that states are not required to recognize same-sex unions and bars such couples from receiving federal benefits associated with marriage.[34] This act represents the legislative response to the ruling of the Hawaii Supreme Court in *Baehr v. Lewin* (1993) that prohibition of same-sex marriage was subject to strict scrutiny under that state's equal-protection doctrine. This decision and the subsequent action of Congress have numerous implications for this nation's system of federalism and presents interesting questions in regard to the full-faith-and-credit clause, the Tenth Amendment, and the extent of legislative powers granted Congress under Article I.

Litigation concerning adoptions by gay couples also encompasses the issue of sexual orientation. The courts are being asked to decide whether the best interests of children are interfered with by the sexual orientation of the parent, and many of the same arguments being raised over same-sex marriage appear in the court proceedings of these cases. The majority of these cases involve not only federal law but primarily state laws, and consequently this policy issue also carries a great deal of importance in the interpretation of federalism in regard to gay rights.

Finally, Clinton's "don't ask, don't tell" policy, allowing gays to serve in the military as long as they keep their sexual orientation to themselves, has preoccupied the lower federal courts for the past year. In October 1996 the Supreme Court refused to hear a challenge to this military policy, leaving in place the ruling of the Fourth Circuit Court of Appeals, which emphasized the military's authority to regulate its own affairs.[35] Numerous other cases are pending on the "don't ask, don't tell" policy, but the probability that the Supreme Court will grant a hearing of these cases is considered to be very unlikely. The role of the judiciary in gay rights can be evaluated in terms of three contemporary Supreme Court decisions: *Bowers v. Hardwick*, 478 U.S. 186 (1986); *Hurley v. Irish-American Gay, Lesbian and Bisexual Group*, 115 S.Ct. 2338 (1995); and *Romer v. Evans et al. v. Richard G. Evans et al.*, 116 S.Ct. 1620 (1996).

In *Bowers v. Hardwick*, 478 U.S. 186 (1986) the Supreme Court upheld a Georgia law that made acts of sodomy performed by anyone in any place a crime. The 5–4 decision was one of the most controversial and widely publicized Supreme Court decisions of 1986. The Georgia law had been challenged by Michael Hardwick, a homosexual who had been arrested for acts of sodomy performed in his own home. The Supreme Court refused to find that such acts, even when performed in private places, were protected by the Constitution and ruled that there was no fundamental right to engage in homosexual sodomy. This decision was a considerable blow to the gay rights movement, because it meant that the right of privacy as an argument to protect homosexual activities within one's home was destroyed. In surveys conducted during the 1980s and 1990s, about 75 percent of respondents said they believed sexual relations between two adults of the same sex were wrong.[36] The justices showed less consensus in the *Bowers* decision in that the case was decided by one vote.[37] Because Hardwick had not raised a First Amendment objection to the sodomy laws, the Court ruled solely on the privacy concerns, and because the Court could not identify the involvement of a fundamental right, it used a "rational basis" standard of scrutiny to uphold the governmental regulations. Much speculation has occurred as to the degree to which the Court actually applied constitutional doctrine and the degree to which public opinion played a role in this decision. The dissents in the case admonish the majority for its "almost obsessive focus on homosexual activity" and point out that the decision goes against prior decisions on the right to privacy. The closing lines of the dissent by Justice Blackmun convey a plea for reconsideration of the decision on the grounds that depriving individuals of the right to choose for themselves how to conduct their intimate relationships poses a far greater threat to the values most deeply rooted in our Nation's history than tolerance of nonconformity could ever do.

The level of disagreement and the tone of the dissent in this ruling illustrates the polarization of the issue, even at the highest judicial level. The high court normally asserts its authority to protect individual rights when dealing with social regulations, but in *Bowers* the Court found reason to change direction. The Supreme Court has not addressed the issue of sodomy regarding the right to privacy since that decision.

In *Hurley v. Irish-American Gay, Lesbian, and Bisexual Group of Boston* (1995) the Court considered whether the state of Massachusetts could require the South Boston Allied War Veterans Council, a private group authorized by the city of Boston to organize and conduct the St. Patrick's Day-Evacuation Day Parade to include among the marchers the openly homosexual Irish-American Gay, Lesbian, and Bisexual Group (GLIB). The Court ruled unanimously that the organizers of the parade did not have to include among the marchers a group imparting a message they did not wish to convey. To mandate its inclusion would violate the First Amendment right to freedom of speech. The decision and the opinion did not present new reasoning in regard to First Amendment issues, but it did accentuate the tension between the constitutional doctrines of equality and expression. GLIB contended it had been the object of discrimination due to sexual orientation, in violation of a Massachusetts law prohibiting any distinction or restriction of this nature. The council based its argument on First Amendment freedom-of-expression rights; the Court ruled that a parade could be defined as a group of marchers attempting to make some collective point or expression, and since the message of GLIB did not fit with the message of the organizers, it was left to the discretion of the organizers if they would allow that message to be included.

The importance of this case is that it illustrates the need to frame legal arguments in gay rights cases in line with U.S. constitutional doctrine rather than on state constitutional grounds. Had GLIB framed the argument around its own First Amendment right to freedom of speech, rather than the state constitutional protection against discrimination on the basis of sexual orientation, the Court would have had to balance those interests. Instead, the high court was left with a simple decision between the supremacy clause of Article VI and independent state grounds, and no state constitution would be permitted to enjoy higher legal standing than the fundamental right to freedom of speech. For gay rights activists to change social regulatory policy through the judicial process, litigation must involve federal statutory or constitutional interpretation. While the protection provided by state constitutions is invaluable, to achieve equal protection under federal laws, gays and lesbians must first be recognized by the judiciary as a suspect class or find a violation of a fundamental right in these cases. As the gay community continues to grow in political strength, it is doubtful that they will be ruled a suspect class. Rather, this increased political power, along with growing public recognition of the immorality of all forms of discrimination, has encouraged courts to strike down existing antigay discriminatory regulations.

In *Romer v. Evans* (1996) the Supreme Court decided that specific legislation added to the Colorado state constitution—Amendment 2—violated the equal protection clause of the Constitution because it abridged the right to participate equally in the political process. Amendment 2 had been ratified by Colorado voters in 1992 and precluded all legislative, executive, or judicial action designed to protect the status of individuals based on their homosexual, lesbian, or bisexual orientation or conduct. In a 6–3 decision the Supreme Court ruled this to be a constitutional violation and declared that a state may not "deem a class of persons a stranger to its own laws." Much has been made of the historical significance of the decision.[38] One report went as far as to equate the *Romer* decision with the landmark 1954 desegregation ruling in *Brown v. Board of Education*.[39]

It is normally very difficult to persuade a court that a law or regulation that treats one group differently than another is not an equal-protection violation unless a compelling justification can be found for the differentiation. Since a major defense in gay rights litigation was that upholding traditional moral values was a compelling governmental interest, prior to *Romer* it was difficult for gays and lesbians to persuade the courts that antigay laws were a constitutional violation. For the first time in history the Supreme Court ruled in favor of gay and lesbian civil rights by taking a strong moral stance against discrimination. The majority opinion in *Romer* has a pronounced moral tone but is remarkably short on legal reasoning and analysis. While precedent and doctrine are evoked, the persuasiveness of the argument rests on its moral foundation. Matt Coles of the ACLU said the ruling was the "first time the Supreme Court has said that government cannot justify discrimination simply out of hostility and fear."[40] While failing to recognize gays and lesbians as a suspect class, the court did find that discrimination based on sexual orientation nullifies specific legal protections for this targeted class in all transactions in housing, sale of real estate, insurance, health and welfare services, private education, and employment. Justice Antonin Scalia filed an equally forceful dissent, accusing the majority of taking sides in a "cultural war" through "an act not out of judicial judgment but of political will." Justices Rehnquist and Thomas also dissented, accusing the majority of "inventing a novel and extravagant constitutional doctrine to take the victory away from traditional forces." Rehnquist later said: "The Colorado Amendment was an eminently reasonable means of preventing the piecemeal deterioration of the sexual morality favored by a majority of Coloradans."[41]

Many reasons can be attributed to this judicial shift, but most plausible would be the court's new interpretation of the equal protection clause. In recent years the court has exhibited a tendency toward interpretation that leans heavily in favor of nondiscrimination on any grounds. It would be premature to say social regulatory policy affecting gay men and lesbians will no longer reflect a societal disapproval of homosexual behavior, but given the current interpretation of the equal protection clause, regulations based on sexual orientation may not pass even a "rational basis" standard of scrutiny.

Federalism

Our system of federalism allows policy makers to choose selectively those issues for which the federal government will accept primary responsibility and to leave more controversial, politically sensitive issues for the states to handle. The states have served as the experimental grounds for gay rights policy and, more specifically, local governments have formulated and implemented policy on both same-sex marriage and adoption by gay men and lesbians.

Discrimination in housing, employment, and public accommodations are of grave concern to the gay community. When the 1974 attempt to amend the 1964 Civil Rights Act to include gays and lesbians in the federal ban on discrimination failed, attempts to add sexual orientation to antidiscrimination legislation moved to the state and local level. Elaine Sharp points out that because rights-based federal laws receive minimal attention from the federal government, state and local governments often must implement these policies on their own. Sharp uses the term "culture wars" to describe when implementation of the right to abortion, gay rights, and other highly moralistic issues is forced to the level of local government, thus relieving state governments of policy innovation while maintaining some discretion over the implementation of the policy by city governments.[42]

Opponents of civil rights protections for lesbians and gay men have employed several strategies to attack antidiscrimination statutes that include sexual orientation. The most famous example of this tactic was the successful 1977 campaign led by Anita Bryant, a former Miss America and spokeswoman for Florida orange juice, to persuade voters to repeal a gay rights ordinance in Dade County, Florida. More recently in Colorado, Amendment 2 not only attempted to repeal existing state laws that protect gay people from discrimination but also tried to eliminate the prospect that future laws could recognize claims by this group.

The first gay rights ordinances were adopted in the early 1970s, primarily in university communities such as Berkeley and Palo Alto, California; Boulder, Colorado; Ann Arbor and East Lansing, Michigan; and Austin, Texas. Of the twenty-eight jurisdictions that passed such laws or policies before 1977, eighteen could be classified as college communities.[43] Several cities with sizable and organized gay and lesbian populations, including Detroit, Minneapolis, San Francisco, Seattle, and Washington, were early adopters of legislation, while other large cities such as Atlanta, Chicago, Los Angeles, New York, and Philadelphia considered gay rights ordinances prior to 1975.

As of mid-1996 nine states had statutes that prohibited discrimination on the basis of sexual orientation and an additional seven had executive orders that applied to state government employees.[44] Though estimates differ, approximately 150 city and county governments have now adopted sexual orientation nondiscrimination ordinances, although the nature and scope of those ordinances vary widely.[45]

No state authorizes same-sex marriages, although no constitutional obstacles stand in the way of state legislatures wanting to implement such a reform. Much attention has been given to the difficulty this would raise in regard to the full-faith-and-credit clause of Article IV, but technically there is no constitutional prohibition against states' taking such action. Even though some local jurisdictions in the United States have extended limited recognition and benefits to cohabiting couples, they are in no position to bestow the full rights and responsibilities of marriage, because the law of marriage is made by the states.[46] The issue of same-sex marriages has increased in saliency since the Hawaii Supreme Court ruling in *Baehr v. Lewin* (1993). Although the Hawaii Supreme Court was not the first state court to face this issue, it was the first to rule that the state's refusal to recognize same-sex marriages would be found unconstitutional without a compelling state interest to justify the restriction.[47]

The case was first brought before the court in 1991 by two lesbian couples and one gay male couple after they were denied marriage licenses. The state's high court reasoned that, since the plaintiffs would have been allowed to marry people of the opposite sex, the state's bias against same-sex couples could amount to unconstitutional discrimination based on sex. The Hawaii Supreme Court then returned the case to the trial court to determine whether the state could show a "compelling" reason for denying the three couples their marriage licenses. The circuit court in December of 1996 ruled that the state had failed to present sufficient evidence that the public interest in the well-being of children and families or the optimal development of children would be adversely affected by same-sex marriages, and the couples were allowed to obtain marriage licenses.

In an effort to sidetrack this ruling, in April 1997 the Hawaii legislature introduced and approved a constitutional amendment that does not actually ban same-sex marriages, but would give the state legislature more power to restrict all marriages. It would expand the power of state lawmakers to restrict marriages of opposite-sex couples, while also granting lesbian and gay couples a portion of the benefits available to married couples. If the amendment is ultimately adopted, some believe that in order to ban same-gender unions, the state legislature would have to approve a separate law restricting marriages to opposite-sex couples. The amendment will be put on a statewide ballot, which could be held as early as November 1998.

Thus, the issue arose as to whether other states, under the full-faith-and-credit clause, would be compelled to recognize marriages solemnized in Hawaii. Several policy alternatives were available that could have provided further guidance to the states. Federal courts could intervene and offer interpretations of the clause as it applies to same-sex marriages, or state courts and legislatures could decide whether a compelling public policy justification exists to exempt the state from the otherwise mandatory requirements of the full-faith-and-credit clause.

Whatever means are used to resolve the issue, the outcome would have a significant impact not only on states but on the interpretation of a wide variety of federal laws in which marital status is a factor. Federal laws in which benefits, rights, and privileges are contingent upon marital status include Social Security and related programs; housing; food stamps; veterans' benefits; taxation; federal civilian and military service benefits; employment benefits; immigration, naturalization, and alien laws; trade, commerce, and intellectual property policies; financial disclosure and conflict of interest concerns; crimes and family violence incidents; loans, guarantees, and payments; and federal natural resources and related laws.[48]

The potential impact of such marriages on federal programs and on intergovernmental relations gave a sense of urgency to the need to respond to the Hawaii court decision. At that time only seven other states had statutes that explicitly prohibited same-sex marriages—Indiana, Louisiana, Maryland, New Hampshire, Texas, Utah, and Virginia. Thirty more, however, had statutes that either defined or made explicit references to marriage as a civil contract between a man and a woman. Most states with judicial challenges to same-sex marriages had denied those unions based upon re-

laxed interpretation of equal-protection requirements or traditional defini-
tions of marriage.[49] Although states have retained the sovereign authority to
regulate marriage, this authority is subject to federal exclusion. While
clearly governmental authority to regulate marriage is subject to some constitutional limitations (e.g., miscegenation laws were found to be an unconstitutional violation of the equal protection clause), for the opponents of
same-sex marriages the most expeditious manner to deal with this issue
was, as already noted, congressional action.

A parallel concern for policy makers is the ability of gay and lesbian
couples to adopt children. Adoption is also within the realm of state authority, though it cannot escape the influence of federal regulation. With reference to adoptions by gays and lesbians, the main focus has been on two
statutory requirements: (1) the qualifications of potential adoptive parents,
and (2) legal ramifications of the adoption on the rights of biological or
custodial parents. For gay couples, a question arises where a state statute on
its face limits joint adoptions to "husbands" and "wives" or "married couples." Since no state currently recognizes gay marriages, it can be argued
that adoption in states having this type of statute is virtually impossible.

Given the disintegration of the traditional family structure, through both
divorce and single parenting, the boundaries of a legally sanctioned family
have necessarily been called into question. The U.S. Census Bureau in 1995
reported a growing trend away from households headed by married couples,
as nonmarried families have increased proportionally from 22 percent to 30
percent of all households over the last twenty years. There has been no
accurate count to determine how many of these constitute gay- and lesbian-
headed families, because such parents are often reluctant to reveal their
sexual orientation for fear of losing the child.[50] However, it is estimated
that from two to eight million homosexual parents are currently caring for
as many as fourteen million children.[51] Because the rights of gay and lesbian
individuals to adopt turns primarily on state adoption statutes, and second-
arily on state and federal discrimination laws, it would appear that the
Defense of Marriage Act will affect the ability of gay men and lesbians to
adopt children only in those states stipulating that joint adoptions must be by
"husbands and wives" or by "married couples." Changing the law in these
states may prove difficult, because supporters of this change will be faced with
moral arguments as to the suitability of homosexuals to parent children.

Bureaucracy

The agencies that come to mind with respect to issues of homosexuality are
the National Institutes of Health (NIH) and the Centers for Disease Control

(CDC).[52] The obvious reason is their direct role in dealing with the HIV/AIDS epidemic. Most key health and scientific research agencies fall under the umbrella of the U.S. Public Health Service (PHS), which is directed by the assistant secretary for health of the Department of Health and Human Services. NIH, CDC, and the Food and Drug Administration (FDA) are among the agencies that comprise PHS.

NIH consists of various separate institutes that oversee laboratory research into health matters. Two of the largest institutes at NIH are those involved in AIDS research—the National Cancer Institute (NCI) and the National Institute of Allergy and Infectious Diseases (NIAID). There is abundant literature on the struggle to adequately fund these research efforts, showing how both politics and hysteria played a role in delaying any funding to confront that disease. The federal government viewed this as a budget problem; public health officials saw it as a political problem; gay leaders blamed the delay on lack of access and credibility; and the media regarded it as a homosexual problem that did not interest anyone else. Until it was discovered that HIV/AIDS could be communicated through means other than homosexual behavior, it was considered a "gay disease" and, as such, became a morality politics issue.

Morality politics issues are highly salient, with little need for people to acquire any information (technical or otherwise) to participate in the debate.[53] The saga of the HIV/AIDS epidemic is a classic example of how the lack of information can drive public policy in an inappropriate manner and how, once new information is disseminated, policy innovation can undergo a tremendous transformation.

As was noted before, as early as 1920 congressional investigations were being conducted at naval training bases to determine the extent to which homosexuals were contributing to "immoral conditions" on the base.[54] In the 1950s members of Congress expanded the debate over homosexuality by linking homosexuality to Communism, calling homosexuals a threat to national security. This specter of a security threat was raised in the context of possible Communist infiltration of the government, as alleged by the 1953 McCarthy hearings.[55] Witnesses testifying at the hearings suggested that homosexuals could be blackmailed by Communist spies and that the enemy's knowledge of such immoral behavior could be used as an espionage tool.

The HIV/AIDS epidemic stimulated profound changes in lesbian/gay politics in the 1980s. The various responses, or lack of response, to the epidemic on the part of government, the insurance and medical-scientific industries, the mass media, and religious leaders clearly brought the gay and lesbian community together to form coalitions and a massive grassroots movement to galvanize attention on the issue. During the late 1980s the movement grew dramatically in terms of the numbers of those directly involved, the scope of the agenda, and the political impact on the gay and lesbian community and society as a whole. Through the concerted efforts of the Public Health Service, NIH, and CDC, funding for research to combat this disease was finally procured. Since that time Congress has approved the expenditure of billions of dollars for educational programs, research, and medical care. Between 1987 and 1996 state legislatures also have enacted over two hundred bills addressing HIV/AIDS-related issues such as testing, blood bank screening, confidentiality, housing, insurance, prisons, informed consent, counseling, and medication programs.[56]

Such was not the case with the military. By the early 1990s the debate concerning homosexuals participating in the military began to take a different turn. While the efforts of the bureaucratic agencies began to reap significant rewards in the public sector, the military remained firmly entrenched in its conviction that homosexuals not only presented a threat to national security and adversely affected the troop morale through their immoral behavior, but also presented a medical risk to other military personnel.

Following DOD Directive 1332.14, the military openly and intentionally excluded gays and lesbians from the armed forces in order to "maintain the public acceptability of military service and to prevent breaches of security."[57] The rationale for the military ban against homosexuals rested upon government deference to the judgment of military leaders on the basis of "military necessity." The military's singular mission is, as stated by the secretary of defense on March 26, 1992, to defend America from enemies foreign and domestic, and anything or anyone who interferes with or inhibits the military's ability to accomplish this task threatens America's national security.[58] Therefore the ban remained intact and was widely enforced until its partial removal by President Clinton in 1993.

One recurring argument is that homosexuals present a medical threat to other military personnel. Among the most obvious dangers homosexuals allegedly pose for the military is the threat of AIDS, which would undoubtedly increase for all military members if homosexuals were openly admitted to the services. The argument is that, once relieved of the necessity to restrain their sexual behavior or to hide their homosexual tendencies, homosexual and bisexual service members would be more likely to contract HIV and to spread the virus through peacetime training injuries or through the blood supply during wartime, when there may not be the opportunity to test blood before battlefield transfusions. With an increase in AIDS cases among homosexual members, the military could expect a dramatic increase in personnel costs related to medical care and personnel turnover. Also, in the absence of the ban on homosexuals, there would be solid reasons to anticipate that the military's generous medical benefits would provide an incentive to increase the number of homosexuals entering the military. The crux of this argument is that given all these liabilities, homosexuals present a large and unnecessary medical risk, and there is no military necessity to place American service personnel at risk by lifting the ban against homosexuals serving in the armed forces.

Efforts to reinstate the ban became quite intense, by both private citizens and military personnel, and resulted in legislation being approved in February 1996 that required the mandatory discharge of members of the armed forces who tested positive for the virus that causes AIDS. The legislation was included in a $265 billion military authorization bill and required the Defense Department to begin ousting HIV-infected personnel, regardless of their ability to perform their jobs. The Senate voted to overturn the law one month later, but the House has not responded with similar action. Litigation on this issue has taken place in several circuit courts, but the Supreme Court has refused to take the cases.

The Justice Department, which filed amicus curiae briefs and urged the high court not to take those cases, noted that all the appeals courts that have reviewed the policy have upheld it, so there was no reason for the high court to resolve any split among the lower courts. The Justice Department also emphasized that, to Congress, the statute at issue did not embody "an irrational prejudice against gays and lesbians." Justice officials also noted that past court rulings have said the military "constitutes a specialized community governed by a separate discipline from that of the civilian."[59]

Interest Groups

Members of an interest group, by definition, share some political goals and come together to try to influence the manner in which policy is shaped in regard to those goals. When the issues subject to regulation touch upon fundamental beliefs, the intensity of the commitment to those goals is magnified and group advocacy takes on increased saliency.

Whereas most organizations represent interests of direct, material benefit to their members, members of gay rights pressure groups are also concerned with the principle or moral of the proposed policy. These intangible interests tend to polarize debates in this arena, even though the public debate may appear to concern more tangible benefits. Gay rights are termed by opponents "special rights" to emphasize their view that allowing gay men and lesbians the same treatment as nonhomosexuals serves to legitimate their status. Interest groups that do not wish to have homosexuals recognized as equal participants in the political process regard the protection of individual gay rights as immoral and a threat to society in general. Interest groups that advocate promotion of equal treatment before the law for all individuals, regardless of sexual orientation, believe it is immoral to prohibit citizens from sharing in the benefits of a democratic society based upon private sexual disposition.

While there are interest groups primarily concerned with particular issues, the gay rights organizations are a driving force in the current movement. One of the first organizations to attract national attention was the Mattachine Society, a radical group that favored homosexual rights and Communism. However, from 1953 until the summer of the Stonewall riots, the movement generally had a low-profile, accommodationist stance. Following the Stonewall riots of June 27–28, 1969, triggered by a police raid on the Stonewall Inn, a popular gay bar in the Greenwich Village district of New York City, new organizations were established in most major cities in the United States, sparking a coalition movement that served to unite the gay community. The most popular of the new groups was the Gay Liberation Front (GLF), which experienced phenomenal growth during the 1970s.

During this time the GLF and advocates of radical changes for gays and lesbians worked with groups such as the Black Panthers to gain power and influence. While groups had met informally prior to this time, a bond began to develop after Stonewall and gave substance to the gay rights movement. The Lambda Legal Defense Fund remains among the most active and influential of these groups. Currently, the Human Rights Campaign Foundation is the primary sponsor of several programs nationwide designed to increase activism and to promote the position of gays, lesbians, and bisexuals on campuses, in the workplace, and in private affairs, primarily focusing on issues affecting the health needs and civil rights of lesbians and gay men. State and local groups such as Oregon Right to Pride, the Dallas Gay and Lesbian Alliance, the Massachusetts Gay and Lesbian Political Caucus, and the Southeast Alaska Gay Alliance are also active in large numbers. Since the Stonewall riots, supporters of gay rights have functioned under the interest group model of politics, exhibiting characteristics consistent with group and organizational theory.

Experts have identified two main sources of opposition to gay rights: religious conservatives and certain segments of the business community. Gays are seen as a threat to the social values and cultural dominance of people who are committed to a particular vision of society. The opponents of gay rights frequently refer to homosexuality as a violation of Judeo-Christian tradition, leaving the impression that all such religious communities perceive homosexuality to be sinful. The Christian Coalition, the Eagle Forum, and Concerned Women for America are among the most active religiously based groups that regard homosexual behavior as fundamentally wrong and sinful.[60]

The Christian Right has been the major force behind efforts to enact antigay statewide referenda, notably Colorado's Amendment 2 in 1992 which was orchestrated by Colorado for Family Values (CFV). Other such efforts, however, were not successful. CFV's counterpart in Oregon, Oregon Citizen's Alliance (OCA) twice failed to gain passage of similar antigay initiatives in 1992 (Measure 9) and in 1994 (Measure 13). In 1995 the Idaho Citizen's Alliance narrowly lost its statewide referendum campaign (the same year that Maine's electorate also rejected a similar antigay measure).

The Roman Catholic Church takes a slightly different approach, relying on the distinction between orientation, which is not considered sinful, and behavior, which is not accepted. Unlike Protestant fundamentalists, however, Roman Catholics do not attempt to "convert" homosexuals to heterosexuality, but rather attempt to help them adopt a lifestyle the church finds appropriate.

Although the center of opposition to gay rights is located in traditionalist religious communities, sole reliance on moral and value-laden arguments does not meet well with public opinion. Thus, opponents have learned to state their objections not in terms of religious beliefs but rather in terms of "cultural" or "social" traditions. Claiming to be open-minded and tolerant of societal differences, opponents emphasize that they do not want to "encourage discrimination" but instead want to build a "live-and-let-live atmosphere," meaning that gays can do what they please although the government ought not to give them legal endorsement.

The morality model of politics involves issues that tend to be partisan, focus on deeply held values, and rarely attract compromise solutions.[61] The interest group model of politics, on the other hand, claims interest groups fare best when they limit the scope of the conflict and discreetly lobby policy makers for public policy. In the morality politics model, policy making is a function of religious forces, party competition, partisanship, high salience, and possibly education. In the interest group model, policy making is determined by interest group resources, along with supportive elite attitudes, prior policies, and perhaps education.[62] While interest group politics has been important to the gay rights movement in the last decade, the morality politics model more aptly describes the long-term composition of this issue, even today.

Public Opinion

Judging by public opinion surveys, ordinary citizens do not have a high regard for gay men and lesbians. To summarize a vast array of polling material, gays are perceived as people who have chosen to pursue an un-healthy and immoral lifestyle and whose code of behavior makes them unfit to occupy many important positions in society. For example, one study found that homosexual conduct is regarded as "always wrong" by two-thirds to three-fourths of the adult population, and the prospect of contact with gays inspires discomfort among many heterosexuals. Believing that gays are likely to "recruit" or molest children, the public is decidedly hos-tile to the notion of putting gays in positions of direct contact with children, either as teachers or adoptive parents.[63]

The 1996 Survey of American Political Culture included several ques-tions concerning homosexuals in the rating profile for important issues facing the United States in the 1990s.[64] When asked the question "How wrong do you personally think it is when people engage in the following behavior?" 41 percent responded that marriage between two persons of the same sex is wrong for all persons and should not be legally tolerated, while 33 percent felt sexual relations between two adults of the same sex were always wrong and should not be tolerated. So while nearly half of the respondents apparently felt that marriage between homosexuals is wrong, only one-third believed homosexual relations should not be tolerated. Ho-mosexual behavior is not as strongly opposed as the notion of giving legal sanction to the relationship through marriage. These respondents were also asked to indicate their opinion about allowing gays to serve in the military. Here there seems to be a true split in public opinion: 38 percent favored allowing gays to serve, while 35 percent were opposed. Approximately one-quarter (22 percent) of the respondents remained neutral on this issue.[65]

Despite public antagonism to gays, many Americans recognize that "there is a difference between telling people that an active homosexual life is sinful and telling them that they should support criminal sanctions for that behavior."[66] This is reflected in the growing sentiment that social regulatory policy in regard to gay men and lesbians should not be discriminatory. During the last two decades, research on violence against this group has helped to demonstrate the actual level of discrimination gays and lesbians have en-dured. Since the beginning of the gay rights movement in the late 1960s, a great deal of data has been compiled on antigay violence and victimiza-tion.[67] In a national survey conducted in 1984 of just over two thousand gay men and lesbians, 94 percent reported that they had experienced discrimina-tion at least once in their lives due to their sexual orientation. This discrimi-nation came in the form of verbal abuse, physical assault, abuse by police, assault with a weapon, or vandalized property. Nearly half of those who said that they have been assaulted reported multiple episodes.[68]

Discrimination in employment, housing, and public support payments also has been widespread, causing many homosexuals to hide their sexual orientation to avoid this type of treatment. Between 46 and 80 percent of respondents to the 1992 National Gay and Lesbian Task Force Policy Institute's survey on discrimination against lesbians and gay men claimed they felt compelled to conceal their sexual identity to avoid discrimination in public accommodations. One means of redressing this problem has come in the form of local antidiscrimination ordinances. From 1990 through 1993 at least forty-six cities and counties added sexual orientation to their civil rights codes.[69]

One interesting aspect of public opinion is the changing nature of the support for protecting gay rights. In the 1970s the populations most likely to support gay rights ordinances were either affiliated with universities or university-oriented. By the 1990s, university students accounted for less than half those openly advocating protection for gay rights. In addition, more communities with small gay populations began to adopt regulatory policies favoring gay men and lesbians, as have communities without a substantial number of government employees. The early supporters for gay rights drew heavily from three populations: universities, communities with large gay populations, and communities with many government employees. The political environment surrounding gay and lesbian issues was obviously quite different in 1990 than in 1970.

Numerous reasons are given for this change: increased willingness of homosexuals to openly and actively pursue civil rights, an attitude of increased tolerance for all kinds of people, and a pronounced shift in the public attitudes against governmental discrimination at any level. By 1993, for example, approximately one in five Americans lived in a community that forbade discrimination on the basis of sexual discrimination.

Recent studies indicate that values and perceived morality indeed shape gay rights policy, as many people who value traditional morality regard homosexuality as violating those standards. Nor have the standard-bearers of moral traditionalism been reluctant to emphasize the connection between opposition to the "new morality" and opposition to gay rights policies; they have in fact argued that such policies "condone" or "affirm" homosexuality.[70] Thus moral traditionalism seemingly has a negative effect on support for gay rights policies.

Changes that take place in public opinion do so incrementally. The adoption of antidiscrimination ordinances for gays and lesbians has evolved over the past twenty years. Society still does not give the nod to homosexual behavior, but the current trend toward full protection of the law for all citizens, regardless of classification, mobilizes public opinion to accept fewer restrictions on gay men and lesbians.

Summary

The regulatory policy on homosexuality that emerges from the political system consistently reflects a very conservative, moralistic position—one that is shaped by public opinion and the push and pull of special-interest groups. Public opinion has shifted somewhat in the past decade from total intolerance of homosexuals to one of intolerance of discrimination, particularly discrimination based on an individual's identity. Gay activists have coalesced, as have opponents of the gay rights movement, and both contribute to this debate.

The real controversy over the protection of gay rights centers on a determination of whether the activities of homosexuals reflect an inherent identity/lifestyle or are the result of a conscious choice of sexual preference. When the gay "lifestyle" is interpreted as a product of immutable sexual orientation, there is little argument that the full protection of constitutional and human rights is paramount. However, when homosexual behavior is perceived to be a matter of choice or preference, policy makers follow tradition and label it as immoral. Thus, the degree to which social regulatory policy for gay men and lesbians reflects moral underpinnings is dependent upon the interpretation of the issue by individual legislators, judges, and executives who make policy at the federal and state levels.

Notes

1. Michael Nava and Robert Dawidoff, *Created Equal: Why Gay Rights Matter to America* (New York: St. Martin's Press, 1984), p. 139.

2. For more discussion on this point, see John M. Finnis, "Law, Morality, and Sexual Orientation," *Notre Dame Law Review* (1994), pp. 11–40; Richard F. Duncan, "Who Wants to Stop the Church: Homosexual Rights Legislation, Public Policy, and Religious Freedom," *Notre Dame Law Review* 69 (1994), pp. 393–445; Samuel A. Marcosson, "The 'Special Rights' Canard in the Debate Over Lesbian and Gay Civil Rights," *Notre Dame Journal of Law, Ethics & Public Policy* 9 (1995), pp. 137–183.

3. Dennis Altman, *The Homosexualization of America, The Americanization of the Homosexual* (Boston: Beacon Press, 1983).

4. Paul Light, "The Presidential Policy Stream," in Michael Nelson, ed., *The Presidency and the Political System* (Washington, DC: CQ Press, 1984), pp. 423–448.

5. Randy Shilts, *Conduct Unbecoming: Gays and Lesbians in the U.S. Military* (New York: St. Martin's Press, 1993).

6. Rick Harding, "NGLTF Releases Results of Candidates Survey on Gay AIDS Issues," *The Advocate* (March 1, 1988), p. 14.

7. Shilts, *Conduct Unbecoming: Gays and Lesbians in the U.S. Military,* p. 36.

8. For more discussion of military involvement, see Jeffrey S. Davis, "Military Policy Toward Homosexuals: Scientific, Historical, and Legal Perspectives," *Military Law Review* 131 (1991), pp. 55–108; Jonathan Katz, *Gay American History: Lesbians and Gay Men in the U.S.A.* (New York: Garland Publications, 1990); Allan Berube,

Coming Out Under Fire: The History of Gay Men and Women in World War Two (New York: Free Press, 1990).

9. Department of Defense Directive 1332.14, January 16, 1981.

10. Max Boot, "First Monday in Office: Clinton Picks Take Over," *The Christian Science Monitor* (January 25, 1993), p. 3.

11. Peter Grier, "Key Senators Push Compromise on Issue of Gays in Armed Forces," *The Christian Science Monitor* (May 13, 1993), pp. 1, 4.

12. Melissa Healy, "74% of Military Enlistees Oppose Lifting Gay Ban," *Los Angeles Times* (February 28, 1993), pp. 1A, 23A.

13. Barry M. Goldwater, "The Gay Ban: Just Plain Un-American," *Washington Post* (June 10, 1993), p. A23.

14. Craig Donegan, "New Military Culture," *CQ Researcher* (April 26, 1996), pp. 363–380.

15. David Newton, *Gay and Lesbian Rights: A Reference Handbook* (Santa Barbara, CA: ABC-CLIO, Inc., 1994).

16. William J. Clinton, "Statement to Participants in the Gay Rights March," *Weekly Compilation of Presidential Documents* (May 3, 1993), p. 685.

17. Barry D. Adam, *The Rise of a Gay and Lesbian Movement* (New York: Twayne, 1995).

18. N. Hunter, "Identity, Speech, and Equality," *Virginia Law Review* 79 (1993), pp. 1695–1709.

19. Ibid., p. 1695.

20. *Congressional Record* 133 (October 14, 1987): S14216.

21. *Congressional Record* 133 (October 20, 1987): H8800.

22. *Congressional Record* 133 (October 14, 1987): S14216.

23. *Gay Men's Health Crisis v. Sullivan*, 792 F.Supp. 278 (S.D.N.Y. 1992).

24. *Congressional Record* 135 (October 7, 1989): S12969.

25. *Congressional Record* 135 (September 13, 1989): per Representative Dornan.

26. For further discussion of this topic, see Carl F. Stychin, *Law's Desire: Sexuality and the Limits of Justice* (New York: Routledge, 1995).

27. *Bella Lewitzky Dance Foundation v. Frohnmayer*, 754 F.Supp. 774 (-1991); *Finley v. NEA*, 795 F.Supp. 1457 (1992).

28. 74 Hawaii 530, 825 P.2d 44 (1993).

29. Holly Idelson, "Panel OKs Bill to Undercut Same-Sex Marriages," *CQ Weekly* (June 15, 1996), pp. 1682–1683.

30. Todd Purdum, "Gay Rights Groups Attack Clinton on Midnight Signing," *New York Times* (September 22, 1996), p. L22.

31. *Congressional Bill Summary and Status Report* (May 20, 1996): H.R. 365 (Towns) and S. 46 (Helms).

32. Richard L. Worshop, "Gay Rights," *CQ Researcher* (March 5, 1993), pp. 195–212.

33. For more discussion on this topic, see Suzanne B. Goldberg, "Facing the Challenge: A Lawyer's Response to Anti-Gay Initiatives," *Ohio State Law Journal* 55 (1994), pp. 665–674, and Samuel A. Marcosson, "The 'Special Rights' Canard in the Debate Over Lesbian and Gay Civil Rights."

34. House of Representative Report 104–666, "Report on the Consideration of H.R. 3396, Defense of Marriage Act" (July 10, 1996).

35. Joan Biskupic, "Supreme Court Rejects Challenge to Military Policy on Gays," *The Washington Post*, (October 22, 1996), p. A3.

36. Lee Epstein and Thomas G. Walker, *Constitutional Law for a Changing America: Rights, Liberties, and Justice,* 2nd ed. (Washington, D.C.: CQ Press, 1995), p. 421.

37. Of significance is the fact that since his retirement, Justice Powell has stated that he felt he had made an error in upholding the prohibition and if faced with the decision today, he would rule it an unconstitutional violation to the right to privacy.

38. See Linda Greenhouse, "Speaking for the Majority," *Washington Post* (May 26, 1996), p. E4; Linda Greenhouse, "Gay Rights Laws Can't Be Banned, High Court Rules," *New York Times* (May 21, 1996), p. A1; Joan Biskupic, "Court Strikes Down Colorado's Anti-Gay Amendment," *Washington Post* (May 21, 1996), p. A1; David Savage, "Supreme Court Strikes Down Law Targeting Gays," *Los Angeles Times* (May 21, 1996), p. A1.

39. "Gay Justice: Romer v. Evans," *The Nation* (June 10, 1996), p. 4.

40. David Dunlap, "Recognizing a Ruling, and Battles to Come," *New York Times* (May 21, 1996), p. A1.

41. Greenhouse, "Gay Rights Laws Can't Be Banned, High Court Rules."

42. Elaine B. Sharp, "Culture Wars and City Politics: Local Government's Role in Social Conflict," *Urban Affairs Review* 31, no. 6 (June 1996); Elaine B. Sharp, "Culture Wars and the Study of Urban Politics," *Urban News: Newsletter of the Urban Politics Section/APSA* 10, no. 1 (Spring 1996), pp. 1–10.

43. James Button, Barbara Rienzo, and Kenneth Wald, *Private Lives, Public Conflicts: Battles Over Gay Rights in American Communities* (Washington, DC: CQ Press, 1997), p. 64.

44. The states with such laws are California, Connecticut, Hawaii, Massachusetts, Minnesota, New Jersey, Rhode Island, Vermont, and Wisconsin. The states with executive orders are Colorado, Maryland, New Mexico, New York, Ohio, Pennsylvania, and Washington. See Norman Riccucci and Charles Gossett, "Employment Discrimination in State and Local Government: The Lesbian and Gay Male Experience," *American Review of Public Administration* (June 1996), pp. 175–200.

45. Ken Wald, James Button, and Barbara Rienzo, "Where Local Laws Prohibit Discrimination Based on Sexual Orientation," *PM: Public Management* (April 1995), pp. 9–14.

46. For examples, see Dirk Johnson, "Gay Rights Movement Ventures Beyond Urban America," *New York Times* (January 21, 1996), p. L12; James Brooke, "Denver Breaks New Ground on Gay Rights," *New York Times* (September 18, 1996), p. A15; Tim Golden, "San Francisco Near Domestic-Partner Rule," *New York Times* (November 6, 1996), p. A9; Carey Goldberg, "Virtual Marriages for Same-Sex Couples," *New York Times* (March 26, 1996), p. A8.

47. See *Singer v. Hara,* 11 Wash.App. 247, 522 P.2d 1187 (1974); *Baker v. Nelson,* 291 Minn. 310, 191 N.W.2d 1985 (1971), *appeal dismissed* 309 U.S. 810, 93 S.Ct. 37 (1972).

48. United States General Accounting Office, *Report on Defense of Marriage Act,* GAO/OGC–97–16 (January 31, 1997), p. 3.

49. John Feldmeier, "Federalism and Full Faith and Credit: Must States Recognize Out-of-State Same-Sex Marriages?" *Publius: The Journal of Federalism* 24, no. 4 (Fall 1995), pp. 107–127.

50. Carole Cullum, "Co-Parent Adoptions: Lesbian and Gay Parenting," *Trial* (June 1993), pp. 28–36.

51. C. Patterson, "Adoption of Minor Children by Lesbian and Gay Adults: A Social Science Perspective," *Duke Journal of Gender Law and Policy* 2 (1995), p. 233.

52. Congress, as part of the Preventive Health Amendments of 1992, changed the name of this agency to the Centers for Disease Control and Prevention, but the agency continues to use its original acronym, CDC.

53. Donald P. Haider-Markel and Kenneth J. Meier, "The Politics of Gay and Les-

bian Rights: Expanding the Scope of Conflict," *The Journal of Politics* 58, no. 2 (May 1996), pp. 332–349.

54. John D'Emilio, *Making Trouble: Essays on Gay History, Politics, and the University* (New York: Routledge, 1992).

55. D'Emilio, *Making Trouble: Essays on Gay History, Politics, and the University;* Adam, *The Rise of a Gay and Lesbian Movement.*

56. Gerald Stine, *AIDS Update: 1994–1995* (Englewood Cliffs, NJ: Prentice Hall, 1996), p. 320.

57. Department of Defense Directive 1332.14 (January 16, 1981).

58. Ronald Ray, "A Question of Health," *American Legion Magazine* (June 1993).

59. Biskupic, "Supreme Court Rejects Challenge to Military Policy on Gays," p. A3.

60. Button, Rienzo, and Wald, *Private Lives, Public Conflicts,* p. 178.

61. Randall Ripley and Grace Franklin, *Congress, the Bureaucracy, and Public Policy* (Homewood, IL: Dorsey, 1991).

62. Haider-Markel and Meier, "The Politics of Gay and Lesbian Rights: Expanding the Scope of Conflict," p. 340.

63. Kenneth Sherrill, "The Political Power of Lesbians, Gays, and Bisexuals," *PS: Political Science and Politics* 29 (September 1996), pp. 469–473.

64. This survey was sponsored, designed, and analyzed by the Post-Modernity Project at the University of Virginia. Fieldwork was conducted by the Gallup Organization.

65. Roper Center for Public Opinion Research, *The Public Perspective* 8, no. 2 (February/March 1997), pp. 10–34.

66. Button, Rienzo, and Wald, *Private Lives, Public Conflict,* p. 2.

67. Button, Rienzo, and Wald, *Private Lives, Public Conflicts.*

68. National Gay and Lesbian Task Force, *Anti-Gay/Lesbian Victimization: A Study by the National Gay Task Force in Cooperation with Gay and Lesbian Organization in Eight U.S. Cities* (Washington, DC: National Gay and Lesbian Task Force, 1984).

69. Button, Rienzo, and Wald, *Private Lives, Public Conflict,* p. 74.

70. John Gallagher and Chris Bull, *Perfect Enemies: The Religious Right, the Gay Movement, and the Politics of the 1990s* (New York: Crown, 1996).

5

God or Country: Debating Religion in Public Life

Ted G. Jelen

One of the more salient features of American politics in the post–World War II era is the frequency with which religious beliefs and values have been voiced in the making of public policy. Religiously motivated activists have played key roles in political struggles over civil rights, foreign policy, welfare, abortion, feminism, and gay rights, to name but a few issues. The relevance of religious values to political debate has, of course, been a recurring feature of American politics, but the political articulation of religious values appears to have become more visible in the past two decades.

Not surprisingly, the political expression of religious belief has occasioned opposition and counter mobilization. Obviously, religious activists have been criticized on the basis of the substantive policy positions they have espoused. More generally, the propriety of religious involvement in the political process itself has been questioned. Some observers have raised procedural objections to religiously motivated political activity, arguing that politics and religion should be divided by, in the words of Thomas Jefferson, "a wall of separation."[1]

In this chapter, I hope to illuminate the general issue of church-state relations, and to account for the diverse positions that can be taken on the relationship between the sacred and the secular. I plan to describe the relevance (and irrelevance) of certain political actors and institutions, and to explain the persistence of political controversy in delimiting the province of Caesar from that of God.

The Religion Clauses: Interpretations and Tensions

The source of the persistent conflict over church-state relations in the United States is the fact that the relationship between the sacred and the secular is a matter of constitutional principle. That is, religious freedom is thought to be so fundamental as to be a part of the basic social contract. The constitutional context for church-state relations in the United States has its source in the following clauses in the First Amendment: "Congress shall make no law respecting an establishment of religion, or prohibiting the free exercise thereof." These two clauses, generally termed the "establishment clause" and the "free exercise clause," respectively, have provided the legal setting within which church-state relations have been contested in American politics. Church-state relations become a problem for the American system because there is little agreement on the sparse language of the religion clauses of the First Amendment.

To oversimplify somewhat, there are two general positions which might be taken with respect to the establishment clause. These positions might be termed "accommodationism" and "separationism."[2] An accommodationist might argue that the proper relationship between church and state is one of "benevolent neutrality," in which the establishment clause is taken to mean that government is simply prohibited from extending preferential treatment to any particular religion.[3] However, this stance of "nonpreferentialism" is not thought to proscribe government support to religion in general.[4] Government, from an accommodationist standpoint, is not required to be neutral between religion and irreligion.

Accommodationism appears to be based on two important assumptions. First, accommodationists tend to believe that religion has beneficial consequences for the social order. Religion provides a nonarbitrary basis for moral human behavior and thus limits the scope of political conflict.[5] Second, religion is regarded by accommodationists as a source of social cohesion. That is, differences between religious denominations are considered to be confined to distinctions over doctrine, and do not typically result in different prescriptions or proscriptions for human behavior.[6] In the United States, a "Judeo-Christian tradition" is thought to provide a moral basis for political life, or what some analysts have termed a "sacred canopy" beneath which political affairs can be conducted.[7] Religion is thought to perform a "priestly" function of legitimating political authority.[8] In the nineteenth century, Alexis de Tocqueville (in words that have been quoted with approval by many religious conservatives) noted the consensual nature of American religion as applied to political affairs:

The sects that exist in the United States are innumerable. They all differ in respect to the worship which is due to the Creator, but they all agree in respect to the duties which are due from man to man. . . . Moreover, all the sects of the United States are comprised within *the great unity of Christianity, and Christian morality is everywhere the same*. . . . Christianity, therefore, reigns without obstacle, by universal consent; the consequence is . . . that every principle of the moral world is fixed and determinate, although the political world is abandoned to the debates and experiments of men.[9]

By contrast, separationists have argued that the diversity of American religion makes religion a dangerous stranger in democratic discourse. Religious belief, it is argued, makes absolute truth claims, which are not considered compromisable by believers.[10] James Madison, in "Federalist #10," listed religion as a fertile source of "faction," which he regarded as an important source of political instability.[11] Indeed, many analysts have pointed to the sectarian violence experienced in other nations, and have contrasted that situation with the relative religious harmony experienced in the United States.[12] Given the potential of religious difference as a source of political conflict, separationists tend to regard the purpose of the establishment clause as being the depoliticization (or domestication) of religious belief by confining religion to a "private sphere" of activity.[13]

Separationists tend to view the establishment clause quite broadly, arguing that this portion of the First Amendment prohibits government assistance to religion in any form.[14] As Hugo Black put it in his opinion in *Everson v. Board of Education,* 330 U.S. 1 (1947): "The 'establishment of religion' clause of the First Amendment means at least this: Neither a state nor the Federal government can set up a church. Neither can pass laws which aid one religion, *aid all religions,* or prefer one religion over another." Thus, a separationist view of the establishment clause would prohibit even very general assistance to religion, even if such assistance was favored by a large majority of the population.

It is perhaps not surprising that many accommodationists regard separationism as hostile to religion. For example, a recent collection of essays written from an accommodationist perspective is titled *The Assault on Religion.*[15] While separationism would be consistent with opposition to religion itself, it seems clear that many separationists are quite religious and regard a strict boundary between the sacred and the secular as beneficial to both spheres.[16] Indeed, separationists have argued that the political role of religion is enhanced by strict independence from government assistance. In a religiously pluralistic society, religion is often thought to perform the prophetic role of social critic, by reminding political actors of standards with sources outside the secular realm of politics.[17] Such a critical role might be compromised if religious bodies depend directly or indirectly on government support.[18]

Similarly, there are two general stances that might be taken with respect to the free exercise clause. A. James Reichley has offered a distinction between "communalist" and "libertarian" understandings of religious free exercise.[19] While adherents of both positions would regard religious *beliefs* as inviolate, communalists and libertarians would differ on the extent to which religiously motivated *conduct* should be protected from government regulation.

Essentially, the communalist view of the free exercise clause involves two assumptions: First, that the protection of religious free exercise means that religiously motivated groups can attempt to enact their policy preferences into law. That is, religious motivations are legitimate warrants or justifications for public policy positions.[20] Second, religious *practices* can be regulated to the extent that they violate the moral or religious sensibilities of popular majorities, as embodied in law. From the communalist viewpoint, actions that are otherwise illegal deserve no special protection because they are religiously motivated. The free exercise clause simply means that government may not single out religious practices for special regulation.

To illustrate, consider the recent case of *Church of the Lukumi Babalu Aye v. City of Hialeah,* 113 S.Ct. 2217 (1993). In this case, the U.S. Supreme Court struck down a municipal ordinance banning the Santerian use of animal sacrifice within the city of Hialeah, Florida. A communalist would support this reversal, since it seems clear that the regulation in question was directed at a specifically religious practice. However, a communalist would argue that if Hialeah passed a more general measure banning the slaughter of animals within the city limits for any reason, such a ban would also apply to religiously based animal sacrifice. The right of religious free exercise of the Santerians would not extend to an exemption from a more general restriction on the use of animals.

Of course, the communitarian view of free exercise is quite narrow, and substantially qualifies the idea that free exercise is an inalienable right.[21] However, such a reading of the free exercise clause is quite consistent with the majoritarian, consensual assumptions that underlie an accommodationist reading of the establishment clause. If one important purpose of religion is to promote an ethical consensus on certain fundamental rules of conduct, it follows that religious citizens who fall outside such a consensus will pose problems for the practice of democratic politics.

A "libertarian" view of free exercise, by contrast, would entail the belief that, with certain very narrow exceptions, religious practice would be exempt from government regulation. Unless government could show that a particular religious practice had immediate and severe harmful consequences (e.g., human sacrifice), a libertarian understanding of the free exercise clause would allow religiously motivated exemptions from otherwise valid laws. In the animal sacrifice example cited in the preceding paragraph, for example, libertarians would argue that the Santerians' right to practice their religion freely would supersede the city of Hialeah's right to restrict the killing of animals, regardless of the form such an ordinance would take. Underlying the libertarian view of religious free exercise is the assumption that, under most circumstances, the requirements of citizenship can be trumped by religiously derived obligations. Religion is thought to produce a "higher" obligation, which governments are bound to respect.[22]

Frequently, issues are encountered that involve questions of both religious establishment *and* free exercise. Such issues most typically arise because modern government provides services that were perhaps not contemplated by the framers of the Constitution. In an era of activist government, the question is frequently posed as to whether the granting of a government service to religious groups constitutes unconstitutional "establishment," or whether the withholding of such prerogatives entails a restriction on the free exercise of religion. For example, consider the case of tuition tax credits for nonpublic schools. Many separationists would regard the creation of such credits as a violation of the establishment clause, since religious schools (a large majority of nonpublic schools) would receive the benefit of exemption from a portion of the taxes of the parents of their students. Conversely, accommodationists might regard the denial of tuition tax credits as an infringement on the parents' right of religious free exercise, since the parents of parochial-school students might, in effect, be subjected to "dual taxation." That is, the parents of students at religious institutions are required to pay taxes to support public schools (which their children do not use) and to pay tuition at the private schools their children actually attend. Such a situation might be described as a violation of the free exercise clause, since the taxation/tuition burden renders the exercise of religious belief more costly. Clearly, such a tension between the establishment and free exercise clauses is unlikely to occur if government is in the business of providing public education in the first place.

Further, some free exercise claims ask government to liberate religiously motivated citizens from certain obligations of citizenship. For example, during certain periods of American history, the U.S. government has conscripted young men for military service. In many such periods, the government has granted exemptions or allowed substitute service for people whose religious convictions prohibit participating in warfare. The existence of a legal classification for "conscientious objectors" has typically been justified via reference to the free exercise clause. Arguably, it is unjust (and unconstitutional) for government to require citizens to violate their religious beliefs. However, it has also been argued that making legal provision for conscientious objectors may violate the establishment clause.[23] If religious denominations vary in the extent of their condemnation of warfare (as they clearly do) and if exemption from the risk of military service has value (as it clearly does), the government may well be discriminating in favor of traditional "peace churches" (e.g., Mennonites, Quakers) by allowing adherents of such denominations to avoid conscription. Indeed, access to the status of conscientious objector might be regarded as a governmentally created inducement to join particular churches, which would violate even a very narrow reading of the establishment clause.

The general point here is that there is often a very real tension between the establishment and free exercise clauses. If government is active, in the sense of promoting education or raising armies, simple proscriptions against interference or discrimination will typically be inadequate as guides to the behavior of public authorities.

It should be noted that this view of the tension between the religion clauses of the First Amendment is typically more characteristic of separationists than accommodationists. Accommodationists are generally likely to argue that the free exercise and establishment clauses are consistent and mutually supportive.[24] However, such a reading is contingent on a particular (narrow) reading of the establishment clause, and typically involves granting one clause (typically, the free exercise clause) priority over the other.[25]

A Typology of Church-State Positions

The nature of the competing positions on the religion clauses of the First Amendment suggests that highly religious people can legitimately take a variety of stances on church-state relations. It is simply incorrect to regard accommodationism or libertarianism as "proreligion," or separationism and communalism as the opposite. Moreover, there is no necessary relationship between positions on the establishment and free exercise clauses.

Because there are several possible combinations of stances on the religion clauses, it is possible to construct a typology of possible church-state positions. This typology is displayed in Table 5.1; each cell in the table represents the interaction between positions on religious establishment and free exercise.

Table 5.1

A Typology of Church-State Relations

		Establishment clause	
		Accommodationist	Separationist
	Communalist	Christian preferentialist	Religious minimalist
Free exercise clause	Libertarian	Religious nonpreferentialist	Religious free-marketeer

Source: Ted G. Jelen and Clyde Wilcox, *Public Attitudes Toward Church and State* (Armonk, NY: M.E. Sharpe, 1995), p. 25.

Accommodationists (the first column in Table 5.1) might take either libertarian or communalist positions on the free exercise clause. Accommodationists who are also communalists (the upper left-hand quadrant of Table 5.1) might be termed "Christian preferentialists," because such persons would likely view the establishment clause quite broadly (permitting certain neutral types of government assistance to religion) and would also be willing to restrict the free exercise prerogatives of groups falling outside a presumed cultural consensus. Persons in the quadrant might regard the United States as a "Christian nation," or believe that the United States should adhere to a "Judeo-Christian tradition." Libertarian accommodationists might be termed "religious nonpreferentialists," since people in the lower left-hand quadrant of Table 5.1 might favor neutral government affirmation of religious values and be quite tolerant of the free exercise claims of nonconventional religious groups.

Separationists who take a libertarian view of the free exercise clause might be termed "religious free-marketeers," since they might exhibit strong support for the free exercise claims of all religious groups but oppose government support for or affirmation of religion. Free marketeers might favor confining religion to a private sphere of activity, but permitting maximum religious freedom within that sphere. Finally, separationist communalists might be considered "religious minimalists," since they apparently wish to minimize the role of religion in public life. Such people may regard it as desirable that government restrict the activities of unconventional or unpopular religious groups but may seek to also minimize government support for any religious groups, majority or minority. A minimalist position might entail the belief that religion deserves no special protection and that government should not support religious expression.[26]

Public Opinion

Of course, it is quite unlikely that arcane legal considerations about religious establishment or free exercise often penetrate the consciousness of ordinary citizens. Nevertheless, mass publics do appear to have reasonably coherent, well-formed attitudes about church-state relations.[27] As will be shown below, such attitudes are not necessarily "consistent" in any logical or ideological sense. This is not surprising, since American attitudes about the relationship between God and Caesar are subject to two conflicting forces. First, Americans are a highly religious people.[28] Relative to citizens of other industrialized nations, the extent of religious belief, affiliation, and practice is unusually high. This means that periodically there is a strong temptation on the part of some citizens to translate their religious principles into public policy. Second, and perhaps conversely, the concept of a constitutional "separation of church and state" (a phrase that appears nowhere in the U.S. Constitution) is a powerful positive symbol in American political discourse. While there is little agreement concerning the precise meaning of such separation, the principle itself is not generally contested in American politics.

The content of public attitudes on church-state relations can be summarized rather easily. At the abstract, symbolic level, there exits ample support for separationist views of the establishment clause and libertarian views of the free exercise clause, although such support is by no means unanimous. Recent research has suggested that nearly two-thirds of the American public endorse a "high wall of separation" between church and state, although only about half rejected any government help to religion at all.[29] On free exercise questions, a survey of residents in the District of Columbia area showed near unanimity that "people have the right to practice their religion as they see fit, even if their practices seem strange to most Americans," although support for religious free exercise drops dramatically if the question of lawbreaking is raised. Only 21 percent disagreed that "it is important for people to obey the law, even if it means limiting their religious freedom."[30]

When the question of concrete applications of the religious clauses of the First Amendment is raised, public attitudes become somewhat more complex. With respect to issues of religious establishment, Americans appear to distinguish between public displays of religious symbols (such as Christmas decorations on public property), financial support for religious institutions, and religious socialization in public schools. Free exercise attitudes were similarly structured, with respondents making distinctions between the free exercise rights of those groups they considered dangerous (e.g., "cults," Satanists), the rights of groups considered strange but harmless (e.g., students who seek to wear religious apparel in public schools), and those of immigrants. Thus, attitudes concerning concrete applications of establishment issues were organized around an activity-based heuristic, while free exercise attitudes seemed structured around a group-based belief system. Further, this apparent lack of parsimony does not appear to reflect a lack of sophistication on the part of mass publics, since the attitude structures of a variety of elite populations displayed quite similar multidimensional structures.[31]

Further, there appears to exist a systematic difference in church-state attitudes at various levels of abstraction. Many Americans appear to be abstract separationists but concrete accommodationists. That is, some respondents will endorse the general principle of church-state separation, but will express support for prayer in public schools, tuition tax vouchers, and publicly funded nativity scenes. Similarly, many Americans are abstract libertarians, but concrete communalists with respect to issues involving religious free exercise. That is, there is a tendency to endorse the principle of the free exercise of religion in the abstract, and a willingness to restrict a variety of religiously motivated practices, such as the ritual use of hallucinogenic drugs by Native Americans, religious solicitation at airports, and allowing adherents of minority religions (such as Jews) time off work on religious holidays.

Of course, there is nothing unusual about a disparity between public support for a general principle and public willingness to apply the principle in concrete instances.[32] In this instance, the apparent inconsistency appears to result from a lack of familiarity with the range of possible applications of the First Amendment. Genuine religious diversity is not part of the experience of most Americans. For example, focus group data revealed that some proponents of school prayer changed their views when confronted with the possibility that a contemporary classroom might contain some polytheists (e.g., Hindus). Such respondents conceded the difficulty of composing a nondenominational prayer with such students included, and were not willing to rotate prayers to accommodate members of different religious traditions. As one respondent put it, "I don't want my children praying to Buddha."[33] Generally, when a specific issue involving government support for religion is raised, many members of the mass public are simply not aware that a general constitutional principle may be at stake.

Thus, public opinion on questions of church-state relations is generally coherent, but not necessarily consistent. While the symbols of religious freedom and church-state separation receive high levels of support from mass publics, many Americans are quite accommodationist (on questions of establishment) and communalist (regarding questions involving religious free exercise). This apparent inconsistency across levels of analysis has important implications for the practice of religious politics in the United States.

Interest Groups

A bewildering array of interest groups make demands on the political system that are relevant to the relationship between church and state.[34] Some of these groups are rather ad hoc, and are formed in response to an increase in the salience of particular issues.[35] Other groups combine a narrow issue focus with greater longevity (such as Operation Rescue), while still others have more general issue foci (e.g., Pax Christi, the Christian Coalition).[36]

A few groups have the general relationship between church and state as their primary focus. Several of these, such as the American Civil Liberties Union, People for the American Way, and Americans United for Separation of Church and State, have focused their attention on perceived violations of the establishment clause, and have taken generally separationist positions. These groups have tended to confine their attention to legal work and public education.[37] Such groups have frequently filed amicus briefs in court cases, and monitored legislation and court decisions.

These groups tend to operate at something of a disadvantage, because of the disparity between abstract support for separationism and concrete public support for specific governmental policies that appear to accommodate religious belief. Even direct mail appeals, which are presumably sent to group members or sympathizers, often contain detailed explanations of why apparently innocuous policies are subversive of church-state separation. For example, a recent issue of *Church and State* (the publication of Americans United for Separation of Church and State) contained a long article detailing why a proposed Religious Freedom Amendment to the Constitution would actually be subversive of religious freedom.[38] Given the high level of legitimacy enjoyed by religious belief in the United States, separationist groups seem to have the more difficult case to make. It is perhaps not surprising that such groups have been limited to public education and litigation, given the relative unpopularity of separationism applied to concrete instances.

Conversely, accommodationist groups such as the Moral Majority and (more recently) the Christian Coalition have been able to compete in a wider range of political arenas. While some accommodationist groups, such as the American Center for Law and Justice, have focused on litigation to counteract the activities of separationist groups, organizations such as the

Christian Coalition have been effective in lobbying in legislatures at various levels of government, as well as participating in election campaigns.[39]

The actual effectiveness of religious interest groups is the subject of some dispute. Matthew Moen has argued that, while the Christian Right has fallen short of its earlier goal of transforming the nature of American politics, various Christian Right organizations have become entrenched in state and local party organizations, and have achieved some notable legislative successes.[40] The Christian Coalition, in particular, appears to be quite effective in influencing the actions of local legislatures and school boards, and has generally shifted its focus from national politics to the state and local level.

The political "maturation" of the Christian Right has been accompanied by a shift in interest group rhetoric. Earlier manifestations of the New Christian Right tended to emphasize the language of religious establishment. For example, Jerry Falwell, in his 1980 book, *Listen, America!*, emphasized the extent to which the United States is a Christian nation, and argued that God would hold the nation collectively responsible for the moral corruption that, in Falwell's view, characterized American culture.[41] Falwell also argued that governmental elites had established a belief system, termed "secular humanism," that was the practical equivalent of religious establishment.

By contrast, more recent representatives of the Christian Right have cast their public appeals in the language of religious free exercise. Both Ralph Reed (until recently the executive director of the Christian Coalition)[42] and Stephen Carter[43] have attempted to show how certain government policies have inhibited the free exercise of religious belief and practice in the United States. Many policies, apparently fair and reasonable at first glance, might violate a libertarian understanding of the free exercise clause. For example, it has been suggested that measures that would prohibit discrimination against gays may violate the free exercise clause by forcing Christians into social and business interaction with persons with whom they are religiously forbidden to associate.[44] Similarly, proponents of school prayer now emphasize its "voluntary" nature and argue against allowing school authorities to persecute the expression of religious beliefs.

More generally, accommodationist groups have come to eschew specifically religious considerations, in favor of arguments that emphasize secular individualist values such as fairness, freedom or choice. For example, recent proponents of "creation science" (who argue that the account of creation in Genesis is literally true) have avoided public assertions of the authoritative truth of the biblical account. Rather, such advocates have proposed "equal time" provisions, which would require the teaching of creationism as an alternative to evolution. The different theories of life's beginnings would be placed side by side, with students encouraged to "make up their own minds." Such appeals to "fairness" or "equality" may be more effective than an insistence on the veracity of a particular reading of the scriptures.[45]

Thus, organized groups that seek an accommodationist understanding of the establishment clause have shifted their public arguments to reflect a libertarian understanding of the free exercise clause. While it is difficult to offer a general assessment of such a strategy, it seems fair to assert that the emphasis on free exercise is perhaps more consistent with Lockean individualism, which arguably dominates the American political culture. By focusing on the "rights" of the believer, rather than on the authority or truth of the religious message conveyed, religious groups may have minimized the prospects for separationist countermobilization.

In general, most groups that deal with questions of church-state relations are organized around issues in which the establishment clause is raised by one side or the other. On some occasions, issues of religious free exercise are posed with minimal reference to establishment issues. In such cases, various interest groups might form ad hoc coalitions, which are not necessarily institutionalized or stable. For example, in response to the *Smith* (1990) decision (discussed below), a diverse coalition of Orthodox Jews, mainline Protestants, Southern Baptists, and the American Civil Liberties Union formed in support of the Religious Freedom Restoration Act.[46] In general, "pure" questions of free exercise are generally posed by members of unpopular minority religions, who may lack the resources for sustained political mobilization.[47]

State and Local Government

The late Thomas P. "Tip" O'Neill, Speaker of the House of Representatives, is said to have observed, "All politics is local." Any observer of contemporary church-state relations would discern a good deal of truth in that assertion. In a large majority of cases, controversy over the proper relationship between politics and religion is raised by the actions of government at the state or local level. The arenas in which church-state relations are typically contested initially often involve state legislatures, county boards, city or village councils, or local school boards.

Such a focus on small-scale politics should not be surprising. In several ways, citizens may have more direct contact with local government bodies than with relatively remote federal agencies in Washington. "Retail" religious politics often involves questions of aesthetics, zoning, local taxation, or public education. Indeed, a very high percentage of church-state questions deal with the education of schoolchildren, which has typically been very decentralized.

Such localized concerns have attained the status of constitutional issues, in large part, because of the doctrine of "incorporation."[48] Strictly speaking, the Bill of Rights (including the religion clauses of the First Amendment) is a set of prohibitions on the powers of Congress, or more generally, on the federal government. The strict distinction between restrictions on the federal government and those applied to subnational governments has eroded steadily since the Civil War. Over a period of time, the Bill of Rights has been "incorporated" to include state and local governments. Such incorporation has generally been based on the "due process" clause of the Fourteenth Amendment, which reads, "Nor shall any State deprive any person of life, liberty, or property, without due process of law." This phrase has been interpreted to create national citizenship, and to apply rights of the United States to all levels of government.[49] While the scope of the doctrine of incorporation remains controversial, there is now general agreement that the religion clauses of the First Amendment properly apply to the actions of subnational governments.[50]

The raising of constitutional issues by state and local governments occurs rather frequently in part because of the particular contours of public opinion. Recall that many Americans are abstract separationists but concrete accommodationists. When local governments deal with issues such as Sabbath observances, holiday displays with religious themes, or school curricula, they are operating at an applied level, in which many Americans are simply unaware of the relevance of a more general constitutional principle. Mass publics may seek the presumed benefits of religious accommodation, without considering (or taking seriously) the possible conflicts with the U.S. Constitution. For example, residents of a local school district in which parents are concerned about juvenile delinquency may desire organized public prayer in school, or the posting of the Ten Commandments, as reminders of a shared moral and ethical framework. The pressing goal of reducing antisocial behavior on the part of adolescents may seem much more important than a particular reading of a constitutional provision.

On church-state issues, accommodationist public opinion is likely to be quite formidable at the subnational level. Not only are accommodationist positions generally rather popular,[51] but recent research has shown that churches are important sources of political learning.[52] Further, the socializing effects of religious observance are strongest in precisely the evangelical, pietistic congregations that are most favorable to the teaching of creationism, school prayer, and the like.[53] Citizens who hold separationist viewpoints do not typically receive comparable opportunities for social interaction, and may come to regard themselves as politically isolated on such issues.[54] Thus, even if separationist opinions are relatively widespread, they are less likely to be expressed than more accommodationist perspectives.

To the (considerable) extent that subnational governments are responsive to public opinion, it can be anticipated (and observed) that local officials will often pass and enforce measures that may appear to violate the establishment or free exercise clauses. The electoral incentives to pass popular measures that may involve establishment issues may be quite strong, while there may exist only weak or nonexistent sanctions for having passed legislation that is unconstitutional.[55] Even more typically, issues involving the free exercise clause often involve the religious rights of small, unpopular, and politically impotent minorities. It might take a great deal of political courage (or an electoral death wish) for a state legislator or local official to vote in favor of the rights of Native Americans to ingest peyote, or to advocate publicly the right of some Muslim immigrants to engage in female genital mutilation.[56]

In sum, then, state and local governments have many opportunities to make policies in which the constitutional provisions on religion are relevant. To the extent that subnational governments are responsive to visible public opinion, such governments will have strong incentives to pass measures that are generally accommodationist (on issues involving establishment) and communalist (with respect to questions of religious free exercise). In terms of the typology developed above, state and local policy making in most areas of the United States is likely to take on a Christian preferentialist tone.

The Supreme Court

Because questions of church-state relations involve questions of constitutional importance, the courts (especially the Supreme Court) are the most frequent arenas in which such issues are contested. Typically, the courts become involved when the legality of policies made at the state and local level are disputed. The court has often assumed the role of overruling popular local majorities in favor of the rights of religiously defined minorities.

With respect to the establishment clause, the Supreme Court has typically taken a "separationist" position, beginning perhaps with the Court's opinions in *Everson v. Board of Education* and *Engel v. Vitale,* 370 U.S. 421 (1962).[57] In particular, *Engel* (the Court's first decision banning organized school prayer) has generated a great deal of controversy and congressional reaction (to be discussed below). At this writing, the operative (and controversial) precedent is *Lemon v. Kurtzman,* 403 U.S. 602 (1971), in which Warren Burger proposed a three-pronged test to determine whether the establishment clause has been violated by an act of government. The *Lemon* test would require that a policy be invalidated if that policy has a religious purpose, has a religious effect of either advancing or inhibiting religion, or requires an "excessive entanglement" between government and religion.[58] A government policy is unconstitutional if *any* of these conditions is violated. Further, it should be emphasized that nothing in the *Lemon* test limits its application to specific denominations.

Thus, the Supreme Court has generally held that governmental policies that assist religious institutions, or advance religious beliefs, are unconstitutional. The Court has struck down measures that would require public schools to devote "equal time" to the teaching of creationism and evolution (*Edward v. Aguillard,* 482 U.S. 578 [1987]), as well as several efforts to promote prayer in public schools.[59] Most recently, the court has disallowed an Alabama measure mandating a "moment of silence" in public schools (*Wallace v. Jaffree,* 472 U.S. 38 [1985]), as well as "voluntary" prayer at a high school graduation ceremony (*Lee v. Weisman,* 112 S.Ct. 2649 [1992]).[60] The Court has also held that government assistance to religious schools must be narrowly defined, with a clear secular purpose. Thus it is generally considered constitutional for a state government to provide mathematics textbooks (for example) because the state has a legitimate secular purpose in promoting mathematics instruction. However, general state assistance to parochial schools, or providing instructors, would be unconstitutional (*Abington Township School District v. Schempp,* 374 U.S. 203 [1963]; *Allegheny County v. ACLU,* 492 U.S. 573 [1989]).

Outside the area of public education, the Court has consistently ruled that holiday nativity scenes with religious themes are unconstitutional if created or funded by local government authorities.[61] But in *Schundler v. American Civil Liberties Union* (1997) the Court allowed to stand a lower court ruling that banned (on establishment grounds) a holiday display that contained a nativity scene, a Hanukkah menorah, and a Christmas tree.[62]

More recently, the Court has appeared to relax its strict separationist interpretation of *Lemon.* The Court has permitted state funding for a sign-language interpreter for a deaf student enrolled in a parochial school (*Zobrest v. Catalina Foothills School District,* 113 S.Ct. 2462 [1993]) and has required public schools to permit religious groups to use school facilities after hours if such opportunities are extended to nonreligious groups (*Lamb's Chapel v. Center Moriches Union Free School District,* 113 S.Ct. 2142 [1993]).[63] However, there appears to have been no general movement on the Court toward a more accommodationist reading of the Constitution, nor any serious attempt to overrule or seriously modify *Lemon*.[64]

A ruling at the end of its 1996–97 term indicates that the Supreme Court may be moving in an accommodationist direction on issues involving the establishment clause. On June 23, 1997, the court, in the case of *Agostini v. Felton,* no. 96–552 (1997), overturned on a 5–4 vote a 1985 ruling (*Aguilar v. Felton*) that had prohibited the use of publicly supported instructors for special or remedial education in parochial schools. While some observers have suggested that this case signals a change in the court's approach to establishment issues, it should be noted that the ruling in *Agostini* does not threaten the framework enunciated in *Lemon*. Indeed, Justice O'Connor's majority opinion makes a clear argument that *Aguilar* is being overturned because the Court's majority believed that the *Lemon* test had been misapplied in the 1985 case. At this point, therefore, the potential scope of the Court's apparent accommodationist shift remains unclear.[65]

Until quite recently, the Supreme Court has traditionally taken a libertarian stance toward issues involving the free exercise clause.[66] Although the right to the free exercise of religion has never been absolute,[67] the Court has generally been quite willing to protect the prerogatives of unconventional religious groups. Thomas Robbins has suggested that the Court has historically adopted a three-part test for evaluating the constitutionality of claims involving the free exercise clause. The criteria in question were derived from *Sherbert v. Verner,* 374 U.S. 398 (1963), and *Wisconsin v. Yoder,* 406 U.S. 205 (1972). Under the Sherbert-Yoder test,[68] government must show that "it has a compelling interest which justifies the . . . right to [restrain] free exercise of religion."[69] Such regulations have been subjected to the "strict scrutiny" of the courts, which has required, as a practical matter, the government to show that a particular regulation is *essential* in order to justify the abridgement of religious free exercise. Needless to say, this is quite a formidable hurdle for government policies. Thus, for the first part of Sherbert-Yoder, government bears a substantial burden of proof.

If the centrality of purpose of a particular government regulation of religious practice has been established, the burden of proof under Sherbert-Yoder shifts to the persons or groups who claim that their religious freedom has been violated. Given the established importance of a government regulation, a religious practice must be "central" to the religion under consideration, and the government regulation must involve a "substantial infringement" on that practice.

Finally, courts have generally considered whether a compelling government regulation that restricts religious free exercise is the "least restrictive alternative" available by which the state might achieve its secular goals. A policy might well be deemed unconstitutional if government objectives can be achieved by less intrusive means.[70]

The extent to which the compelling state interest test has been stringently applied can perhaps be seen most clearly in the case of military conscription. The Court has permitted conscientious objection to military service on religious grounds, and has been quite flexible in defining religion for the purpose of draft exemption. The Court has allowed personal codes of morality to serve as the functional equivalent of religion (*U.S. v. Seeger*, 389 U.S. 163 [1965]; *Welsh v. U.S.,* 398 U.S. 333 [1970]), despite the fact that the defense of the nation would surely be considered an "essential" government function.[71]

Under the Rehnquist Court, the Court's traditional deference to free exercise claims appears to be changing. In *Employment Division v. Smith,* 110 S.Ct. 1595 (1990), the Court ruled that Native Americans who used the hallucinogenic drug peyote during a religious ritual were not entitled to legal protection under the free exercise clause. In the Court's majority opinion, Antonin Scalia wrote that actions that would otherwise be prohibited by a state's criminal code are not accorded special protection for religious reasons unless such an exception was made explicit by the legislature.[72] Under the Court's ruling in *Smith,* the criteria appears to have moved away from the compelling state interest standard of Sherbert-Yoder, toward a more communalist understanding of the free exercise clause.[73] In a manner which is consistent with the consensual nature of an accommodationist reading of the establishment clause, the *Smith* decision may signal that the Court will accord legislative acts (and, perhaps by extension, popular majorities) increasing deference. As will be seen below, attention to the implications of *Smith* has occupied the attention of the U.S. Congress in recent years.

Congress enacted the Religious Freedom Restoration Act of 1993 to reverse the *Smith* decision, but the Supreme Court had the last word on this matter. Also coming at the end of its 1996–97 term, the 6–3 decision in *City of Boerne v. Flores* (1997) ruled that Congress's attempt to void the Court's decision in the *Smith* case was not a legitimate application of Congress's enforcement powers under the Fourteenth Amendment. As Justice Kennedy argued in his majority opinion, it is the prerogative of the courts, not Congress, to determine the meaning of a constitutional right. In her dissent, Justice O'Connor explicitly endorsed Kennedy's view of the separation of powers but argued that the high court should have used *Boerne* as the vehicle to overturn the 1990 *Smith* decision, where she had dissented, and to restore the Sherbert-Yoder standard to free exercise jurisprudence.[74]

Thus, the Court has taken a more or less consistently separationist position with respect to the establishment clause, and has shifted from a libertarian to a communalist position on issues involving the free exercise of religion. In terms of the typology developed in Table 5.1, the Court has moved from a religious free-marketeer stance toward one of religious minimalism.

Congress

Perhaps surprisingly, Congress has not typically been proactive in enacting legislation with respect to church-state relations. For the most part, the role of Congress has been to react (usually ineffectually) to the decisions of the Supreme Court. Because Congress is a popularly elected branch of the federal government, members of Congress have frequently sought to respond to accommodationist public opinion. However, due perhaps to the religious diversity represented in Congress, as well as to the extraordinary majorities required to pass constitutional amendments, most congressional efforts to counteract separationist decisions of the Supreme Court have not been successful.

Much congressional attention in the area of church-state relations has been devoted to that hardy perennial, school prayer. Because school prayer is likely an "easy" issue, and because most Americans favor some form of school prayer, members of Congress have frequently sought to pass amendments to bills, House and Senate resolutions, and constitutional amendments which would permit the practice.[75] Since the *Engel* decision in 1962, nearly a hundred such measures have been introduced in the Senate, and several hundred have been introduced in the House.[76] Most of the constitutional amendments in question have used the language of free exercise, emphasizing the voluntary or noncoercive aspects of school prayer. A proposed amendment, introduced by Senators Strom Thurmond (R-SC), Orrin G. Hatch (R-UT), Lawton Chiles (D-FL), James Abdnor (R-SD), Don Nickles (R-OK), and Jesse A. Helms (R-NC), is typical of the genre:

> Nothing in this Constitution shall be construed to prohibit individual or group prayer in public schools or other public institutions. No person shall be required by the United States or any state to participate in prayer. Neither the United States nor any state shall compose the words of any prayer to be said in public schools.[77]

Typically, such measures receive majorities in each house of Congress but fall short of the two-thirds required to pass an amendment to the Constitution. In other cases, members of Congress have attempted to remove issues of school prayer from the Supreme Court's appellate jurisdiction, but these have thus far been unsuccessful.

The pattern of Congress responding to rulings of the federal courts has continued in other areas as well. Early in 1997 House Republicans introduced a "sense of Congress" resolution, backing a judge who had refused (contrary to earlier precedent and a court order) to remove a display of the Ten Commandments from his courtroom.[78] Again, such a resolution is nonbinding, and lacks the force of law, but can be seen as an attempt to acknowledge the accommodationist strand in public opinion.

More generally, Congress in 1993 passed the Religious Freedom Restoration Act (RFRA), which was a legislative attempt to reverse the Supreme Court's ruling in *Smith* and to reinstate the compelling state interest standard in cases involving religious free exercise. As noted, however, in an unexpected legal twist, RFRA was subjected to a court challenge (*City of Bourne v. Flores,* 1997) that allowed the Supreme Court to declare that act of Congress to be unconstitutional.[79]

Finally, Rep. Ernest J. Istook Jr. (R-OK) has proposed a constitutional amendment that would, to a large extent, enact an accommodationist interpretation of the establishment clause. The proposed amendment reads:

> To secure the people's right to acknowledge God according to the dictates of conscience; the people's right to pray and to recognize their religious beliefs, heritage, or traditions on public property, including schools, shall not be infringed. The government shall not require any person to join in prayer or other religious activity, initiate or designate school prayers, discriminate against religion, or deny a benefit to religion.[80]

As is typical, the predominant tone of Istook's amendment is one of free exercise. Nevertheless, the prohibition against discriminating against religion, or denying benefits to religion, is considerably more general in scope than the school prayer amendments that have been offered in the past.

Given the frequency with which local governments attempt to accommodate religious belief in public institutions, as well as the general popularity of an accommodationist reading of the establishment clause (and the highly positive symbol of religious free exercise), it is not clear why congressional attempts to amend the Constitution have not been successful. Most likely, congressional impotence on this set of issues results from a reluctance on the part of some members to revise the Constitution (which, in a civil religion sense, might be regarded as a "sacred" document),[81] as well as the religious diversity represented in the national legislature.[82] Members of mainline Protestant denominations, as well as Catholics, Jews, and non-Christians, have generally been indifferent or hostile to the Christian preferentialist tendencies of some local governments, and the representation of such religious groups in Congress may have been sufficient to prevent the formation of the extraordinary majority needed to amend the Constitution.[83]

Presidency

In contrast to Congress, which has witnessed a great deal of activity on church-state issues, issues involving religious establishment and free exercise have not been high priorities for American presidents.[84] With the exception of Ronald Reagan (to be discussed below), few presidents since *Engel* have made strong pronouncements, or attempted policy initiatives, on the religion clauses of the First Amendment.

Since 1964 (the first presidential election after *Engel*) Republican platforms have routinely offered support for school prayer, while Democratic platforms have generally ignored the issue.[85] Such differences doubtless reflect religious differences in the activist stratum of the two parties which began to emerge as a result of the Goldwater candidacy.[86] However, once elected, presidents of both parties have done little more than offer symbolic support for religion, and have not offered public appeals for specific policies. For example, President Bush invoked religious values that underlay his vision of "a thousand points of light," while President Clinton has publicly praised Stephen Carter's pro–free exercise work, *The Culture of Disbelief.* President Kennedy, when commenting upon the *Engel* decision, used the occasion to urge people to pray privately.[87] Most modern presidents do not appear to have placed a high priority on issues involving church-state separation. Rather, the strategy has typically involved making generally proreligious statements, while avoiding the controversy association with particular church-state issues.

It is perhaps ironic that the most explicit support for religious separationism has come from presidents whose religious identities have been, in some sense, distinctive. President Kennedy, whose Catholicism was something of an electoral liability, did support the *Engel* decision, albeit with a notable lack of enthusiasm.[88] Similarly, Jimmy Carter, whose credentials as a "born-again" Christian constituted a moderately important issue in the presidential campaign of 1976, took an explicitly separationist position on school prayer (which he modified after becoming president).[89] This suggests that Presidents who are identified publicly with a *specific* denomination have been particularly wary of endorsing religious accommodationism, for fear of alienating potential supporters from outside their faith.[90]

One prominent exception to the passive presidential role in church-state relations has been Ronald Reagan. Reagan, elected with the support of several leaders of the Christian Right, invoked religious imagery rather frequently in order to express opposition to abortion and (more directly relevant to present purposes) school prayer. Reagan frequently supported school prayer, and typically invoked his understanding of the intentions of the "Founding Fathers," or spoke of the general desirability of religion: "If we could get government out of the classroom, maybe we could get God back in."[91] In 1982 Reagan did submit a school prayer amendment to Congress, but, again, the amendment was not passed by Congress.[92] Several analysts have suggested that even Reagan, who was perhaps the most publicly proreligion president in modern times, gave only passive and rhetorical support to religious accommodation or free exercise.

Again, it is not entirely clear why there has been so little activity in the area of church-state relations on the part of the chief executive. It may simply be that presidents seek to husband their limited political capital and avoid the controversy active engagement in issues such as school prayer or tuition tax credits might entail. Presidents have had the option of deferring publicly to either state and local governments (where most contemporary church-state issues are contested) or to the Supreme Court. It might also be that demographic groups generally opposed to religious accommodation (members of minority religions, or recent immigrants) tend to be concentrated in large, urban areas rich in electoral votes. The logic of presidential selection may thus operate in favor of a passive presidential role in church-state relations.[93]

Bureaucracy

In general, issues relating to religious establishment or free exercise have received little attention from the federal bureaucracy. Given the preeminence of the courts in such issues and the general unpopularity of the Supreme Court's separationist decisions, there has been little interest in either enforcing or defying the Court's edicts at the level of policy implementation.

One prominent set of exceptions has its source, again, in the Reagan administration. Reagan's solicitor general, Rex Lee, submitted amici briefs in a number of court cases, supporting religious accommodationism in issues involving the constitutionality of state legislative chaplains, publicly sponsored nativity scenes, school prayer, and aid to parochial schools.[94] Cabinet officials from the Departments of Justice and Education testified before Congress in favor of the school prayer amendment submitted by the Reagan administration.[95] Note that even here, the activity of the executive branch is essentially reactive to decisions of the United States Supreme Court.

Occasionally the Internal Revenue Service (IRS) has been active in the area of church-state relations. Traditionally, religious organizations have been held exempt from federal taxes under the free exercise clause. However, in at least one instance, involving Bob Jones University, the IRS revoked a religious tax exemption, because the university had a policy of official racial discrimination.[96] The university argued (unsuccessfully) that the free exercise clause provided an exemption from federally mandated rules proscribing discrimination. Similarly, there are strict limitations on the political activity of tax-exempt organizations. Several religious organizations (including the United States Catholic Conference) appear to have limited their participation in politics as a result of this policy.[97] However, there have been relatively few instances in which a tax exemption has actually been revoked for this reason.

Thus, the involvement of the federal bureaucracy in issues involving church-state relations has been quite limited. Given the limited policy-making powers of the elected branches of government at the federal level, and lacking institutional incentives of their own, agencies of the federal executive branch have not typically been involved in issues of religious free exercise or establishment.

Summary

The conflict over the proper relationship between church and state seems likely to be an enduring feature of American politics. The task of "rendering unto Caesar that which is Caesar's, and to God that which is God's" is not easily accomplished. In particular, two features of religious politics suggest that the general issue will resist stable resolution.

First, church-state relations in the United States largely involve interactions between subnational governments and the federal courts. In some localities, the distribution of religious beliefs and practices (as well as the ethical consequences of religion) may approximate the consensus that Alexis de Tocqueville envisioned a century and a half ago. At the local level, and in some states, an accommodationist reading of the establishment clause seems reasonable, because of a lack of genuine religious and ethical diversity in many states and communities. In such communities, the most publicly expressed portion of public opinion seems likely to desire public accommodation of religious belief and practice. Given the likelihood of local religious hegemony, religiously marginalized citizens typically have recourse only to the courts, since, by definition, minorities tend to fare poorly in the electoral arena. Thus, the area of church-state relations is one in which the classic dilemma between majority rule and minority rights is played out continuously.

An interesting aspect of contemporary church-state relations is the relative ineffectiveness of national elected institutions. Again, it seems likely that the formidable hurdles involved in the constitutional amendment process, as well as the religious diversity of the American people, make congressional efforts in this area ineffectual and deter presidents from expending their prestige on such issues. The fact that presidential identification with a specific religious tradition seems to be a limitation, rather than a resource, attests to the divisive nature of church-state issues.

A second feature of religious politics in the United States is the tension between the two religion clauses of the First Amendment. Unless one is willing to take a very strong accommodationist position on the establishment clause, many government policies can be described as instances of both religious establishment and free exercise. To reiterate, modern governments at all levels provide services to citizens of which the authors of the First Amendment were probably unaware. Given the existence of activist governments, the question is constantly posed as to whether granting a governmentally created benefit (e.g., tax exemptions, school lunches or transportation, access to public facilities) to religious groups or organizations constitutes unconstitutional religious establishment. Conversely, is the withholding of such benefits from religious groups a denial of free exercise? Further, if such benefits are granted to religious organizations, do governmentally imposed requirements (accreditation for private schools, bans on political activity, etc.) also risk interfering with the free exercise of religion? The approach taken in *Lemon v. Kurtzman* (1971) suggests that individual claims and particular government policies will be evaluated on a painstaking, case-by-case basis. The controversy over the precise definition of religious establishment and free exercise, as practiced in the daily lives of Americans, thus seems likely to continue indefinitely.

One possible solution, of course, is to adopt the accommodationist position on the establishment clause, and to suggest that the "establishment of religion" refers only to discrimination in favor of *particular* denominations or traditions. In this viewpoint, neutral, nondiscriminatory assistance to religion poses no constitutional issue at all. While I am not in a position to assess the legal merits of such a position, I would suggest that, as a practical matter, religious accommodation on a national scale may not be politically possible. The earlier discussion of accommodationism suggested that accommodationism assumes, as did Tocqueville, a general religious or ethical consensus. I would suggest that such a consensus does not currently exist in the United States, if indeed it ever did.[98] A large number of Americans profess either very casual or nonexistent religious convictions, and the increasing number of non-European immigrants suggests that Christianity no longer "rules by universal consent." Moreover, the presumed ethical consensus of which Tocqueville wrote does not appear to be viable in the late twentieth century. Issues such as abortion, gay rights, and the social role of women are increasingly debated *within* Christian denominations.[99] Contrary to Tocqueville's analysis, "Christian morality" is *not* everywhere the same.

Given the religious and ethical diversity of the United States, it is difficult to imagine an elected legislature at any level granting government benefits impartially to all active religious groups. Would Congress, or the state legislature of any state, be likely to grant (for example) tuition tax credits, when those credits could be used at religious schools that advocated witchcraft, ritual use of illegal drugs, overt racial discrimination, or aid and comfort to the Sandinista regime in Nicaragua? Inevitably, any attempt to implement a thoroughly accommodationist perspective on the establishment clause would raise the question of what is or is not a bona fide religion.[100] Such legislation would likely raise an enormous number of free exercise claims, and continue the primacy of litigation in religious policy making.

It is thus difficult to imagine how issues of religious freedom and church-state separation can ever be resolved in our current constitutional format. We are, as Justice William O. Douglas argued, "a religious people," with a natural desire to see our most sacred beliefs and values enacted into public policy. We are also a people who value personal and spiritual autonomy, and freedom from government interference. These different national characteristics can be expected to provide a dynamic for conflict over church-state relations for the foreseeable future.

Notes

Thanks are due to Casey Smith, whose research assistance for this piece was invaluable, and to Ray Tatalovich for his insightful comments and guidance.

1. Garry Wills, *Under God: Religion and American Politics* (New York: Simon and Schuster, 1990).

2. Ted G. Jelen and Clyde Wilcox, *Public Attitudes Toward Church and State* (Armonk, NY: M.E. Sharpe, 1995).

3. Kenneth D. Wald, *Religion and Politics in the United States,* 2nd ed. (Washington, DC: CQ Press, 1992).

4. Leonard W. Levy, *The Establishment Clause* (New York: Macmillan, 1986).

5. A. James Reichley, *Religion in American Public Life* (Washington, DC: Brookings Institution, 1985).

6. See especially Russell Kirk, "Introduction," in Russell Kirk, ed., *The Assault on Religion* (New York: University Press of America, 1986); Robert L. Cord, *Separation of Church and State: Historical Fact and Current Fiction* (New York: Lambeth Press, 1982); and Gerard V. Bradley, *Church-State Relationships in America* (Westport, CT: Greenwood, 1987).

7. See Peter Berger, *The Sacred Canopy: Elements of a Sociological Theory of Religion* (New York: Doubleday, 1967), and Richard John Neuhaus, *The Naked Public Square* (Grand Rapids, MI: Eerdmans, 1984).

8. Ted G. Jelen, *The Political Mobilization of Religious Belief* (New York: Praeger, 1991); David C. Leege and Lyman A. Kellstedt, "Religious Worldviews and Political Philosophies: Capturing Theory in the Grand Manner Through Empirical Data," in David C. Leege and Lyman A. Kellstedt, eds., *Rediscovering the Religious Factor in American Politics* (Armonk, NY: M.E. Sharpe, 1993), pp. 216–231.

9. Alexis de Tocqueville, *Democracy in America,* ed. Phillips Bradley, 2 vols. (New York: Vintage Books, 1945), pp. 314–315 (emphasis added).

10. Wald, *Religion and Politics in the United States.*

11. Alexander Hamilton, James Madison, and John Jay, "Federalist No. 10," in *The Federalist* (New York: Modern Library, 1937).

12. Stephen J. Wayne, "Foreword," in Ted G. Jelen and Clyde Wilcox, *Public Attitudes Toward Church and State* (Armonk, NY; M.E. Sharpe, 1995), pp. xi-xii.

13. Levy, *The Establishment Clause;* Leo Pfeffer, *Church, State and Freedom* (Boston: Beacon Press, 1967).

14. Pfeffer, *Church, State and Freedom;* Leonard W. Levy, *Original Intent and the Framers' Constitution* (New York: Macmillan, 1988).

15. Kirk, "Introduction."

16. See, for example, the account of the political thought of Roger Williams, James Madison, and Thomas Jefferson in Wills, *Under God: Religion and American Politics.*

17. See especially Glenn Tinder, *The Political Meaning of Christianity* (Baton Rouge: LSU Press, 1989).

18. For example, some religious bodies risk losing their tax exemptions if their political advocacy becomes too direct.

19. Reichley, *Religion in American Public Life.*

20. See especially Kent Greenawalt, *Religious Convictions and Political Choice* (New York: Oxford University Press, 1988).

21. Richard A. Brisbin, "The Rehnquist Court and the Free Exercise of Religion," *Journal of Church and State* 34 (1992), pp. 57–76.

22. See especially Stephen L. Carter, *The Culture of Disbelief: How American Law and Politics Trivialize Religious Devotion* (New York: Basic Books, 1993).

23. Jesse H. Choper, *Securing Religious Liberty: Principles for the Judicial Interpretation of the Religion Clauses* (Chicago: University of Chicago Press, 1995).

24. Stephen V. Monsma, *Positive Neutrality: Letting Religious Freedom Ring* (Westport, CT: Praeger, 1993).

25. Suzanna Sherry, *"Lee v. Weisman Paradox Redux,"* in Dennis J. Hutchinson, David A. Strauss, and Geoffrey R. Stone, eds., *1992: The Supreme Court Review* (Chica go: University of Chicago Press, 1992), pp. 123–153.

26. Several analysts have offered similar analyses, and have used the term *secularist* to describe the "minimalist" category. See, for example, Jose Casanova, *Public Religions in the Modern World* (Chicago: University of Chicago Press). I prefer the term *minimalist,* since there is no *necessary* connection between taking a communalist-separationist position and hostility or indifference to religion. Indeed, empirical analysis of survey data suggests that many minimalists are quite religious (and religiously orthodox) and reject public involvement of religion for primarily theological reasons. See Ted G. Jelen and Clyde Wilcox, "Conscientious Objectors in the Culture War? A Typology of Church-State Relations," *Sociology of Religion* 58 (1997), pp. 277–288.

27. This section summarizes results reported more fully in Jelen and Wilcox, *Public Attitudes Toward Church and State.*

28. Wald, *Religion and Politics in the United States.*

29. Jelen and Wilcox, *Public Attitudes Toward Church and State,* p. 59.

30. Ibid., p. 115.

31. Phillip E. Converse, "The Nature of Belief Systems in Mass Publics," in David Apter, ed., *Ideology and Discontent* (New York: Free Press), pp. 206–261; James A. Stimson, "Belief Systems: Constraint, Complexity, and the 1972 Election," *American Journal of Political Science* 19 (1975), pp. 383–418.

32. See James Prothro and Charles Grigg, "Fundamental Principles of Democracy: Bases of Agreement and Disagreement," *Journal of Politics* 22 (1960), pp. 276–294; John R. Zaller, *The Nature and Origins of Mass Opinion* (New York: Cambridge University Press, 1992).

33. Jelen and Wilcox, *Public Attitudes Toward Church and State,* p. 152.

34. For overviews, see Allen D. Hertzke, *Representing God in Washington* (Knoxville: University of Tennessee Press, 1988); Clyde Wilcox, *Onward, Christian Soldiers: The Religious Right in American Politics* (Boulder, CO: Westview, 1996); and Robert Zwier, "Coalition Strategies of Religious Interest Groups," in Ted G. Jelen, ed., *Religion and Political Behavior in the United States* (New York: Praeger, 1989), pp. 171–186.

35. John Murley described a number of single-issue groups formed to promote school prayer. See John A. Murley, "School Prayer: Free Exercise of Religion or Establishment of Religion?" in Raymond Tatalovich and Byron W. Daynes, eds., *Social Regulatory Policy: Moral Controversies in American Politics* (Boulder, CO: Westview, 1988), pp. 5–40.

36. Carol J.C. Maxwell, "Introduction: Beyond Polemics and Toward Healing," in Ted G. Jelen, ed., *Perspectives on the Politics of Abortion* (Westport, CT: Praeger, 1995), pp. 1–20.

37. Murley, "School Prayer: Free Exercise of Religion or Establishment of Religion?" p. 7.

38. Rob Boston, "Making Amends," *Church and State* 50 (May 1997), pp. 4–8.

39. See Wilcox, *Onward, Christian Soldiers: The Religious Right in American Politics,* and Matthew C. Moen, *The Christian Right in Congress* (Tuscaloosa: University of Alabama Press, 1989).

40. Matthew C. Moen, *The Transformation of the Christian Right* (Tuscaloosa: University of Alabama Press, 1992).

41. Jerry Falwell, *Listen, America!* (Garden City, New York: Doubleday, 1980).

42. Ralph Reed, *Politically Incorrect: The Emerging Faith Factor in American Politics* (Dallas: Word, 1994).

43. Carter, *The Culture of Disbelief: How American Law and Politics Trivialize Religious Devotion.*

44. Hubert Morken, "Compromise: The Thinking Behind Colorado's Amendment #2 Strategy," paper presented at the annual meeting of the American Political Science Association, New York, September 1994.

45. Alfred R. Martin and Ted G. Jelen, "Knowledge and Attitudes of Catholic College Students Regarding the Creation/Evolution Controversy," in Ted G. Jelen, ed., *Religion and Political Behavior in the United States* (New York: Praeger, 1989), pp. 83–92.

46. Michael Hirsley, "Prisons Fear Law to Restore Religious Rights," *Chicago Tribune* (August 1, 1993), pp. A1, A4.

47. Frank Way and Barbara Burt, "Religious Marginality and the Free Exercise Clause," *American Political Science Review* 77 (1983), pp. 654–665.

48. Levy, *The Establishment Clause;* Fred W. Friendly and Martha J.H. Elliot, *The Constitution: That Delicate Balance* (New York: Random House, 1984).

49. See especially Richard Kluger, *Simple Justice* (New York: Vintage Books, 1977).

50. See, for example, George Anastaplo, "The Religion Clauses of the First Amendment," *Memphis State University Law Review* 11 (1981), pp. 189–190.

51. Murley, "School Prayer: Free Exercise of Religion or Establishment of Religion?" pp. 23–25; Kirk W. Elifson and C. Kirk Hadaway, "Prayer in Public Schools: When Church and State Collide," *Public Opinion Quarterly* 49 (1985), pp. 317–329.

52. Jelen, *The Political Mobilization of Religious Belief;* Kenneth D. Wald, Dennis Owen, and Samuel S. Hill, "Churches as Political Communities," *American Political Science Review* 82 (1988), pp. 531–549.

53. Elifson and Hadaway, "Prayer in Public Schools: When Church and State Collide"; Kenneth D. Wald, Dennis Owen, and Samuel S. Hill, "Political Cohesion in Churches," *Journal of Politics* 52 (1990), pp. 197–212.

54. See Elisabeth Noelle-Nuemann, *The Spiral of Silence: Public Opinion: Our Social Skin* (Chicago: University of Chicago Press, 1984).

55. See Christi Parsons, "Constitution, Shmonstitution," *Chicago Tribune* (June 8, 1997), sec. 2, pp. 1, 7.

56. See Celia W. Dugger, "Tug of Taboos: African Genital Rite vs. U.S. Law," *New York Times* (December 28, 1996), pp. A1, A8.

57. It should be noted that in *Everson* the Court upheld a local ordinance permitting reimbursement of transportation costs to parents whose children attended parochial schools. Nevertheless, Black's opinion contains language that is quite explicitly separationist.

58. Jelen and Wilcox, *Public Attitudes Toward Church and State,* p. 18; Wald, *Religion and Politics in the United States.*

59. See, generally, Murley, "School Prayer: Free Exercise of Religion or Establishment of Religion?"

60. See, generally, Thomas Robbins, "The Intensification of Church-State Conflict in the United States," *Social Compass* 40 (1993), pp. 505–527.

61. Jelen and Wilcox, *Public Attitudes Toward Church and State.*

62. Linda Greenhouse, "Supreme Court Roundup: Court to Decide Whether Harassment Law Applies to People of Same Sex," *New York Times* (June 10, 1997), p. A15.

63. See also James J. Kilpatrick, "One More Look at a Famous Wall," *Indianapolis Star* (July 10, 1993), p. A8.

64. It is perhaps instructive to read Stewart's dissent in *Engel v. Vitale,* as well as Scalia's dissent in *Kiryas Joel Village School District v. Grument.* Both of these opinions defend religious accommodationism from the standpoint of religious free exercise. See Joan Biskupic, "Special School District Ruled Unconstitutional," *Washington Post* (June 28, 1994), pp. A1, A10; Linda Greenhouse, "High Court Bars School District Created to Benefit Hasidic Jews," *New York Times* (June 28, 1994), pp. A1, D21–D22.

65. Linda Greenhouse, "Court Eases Curb on Aid to Schools with Church Ties," *New York Times* (June 24, 1997), pp. A1, A11.

66. Brisbin, "The Rehnquist Court and the Free Exercise of Religion"; Way and Burt, "Religious Marginality and the Free Exercise Clause."

67. See *Reynolds v. U.S.,* 98 U.S. 145 (1879).

68. Robbins, "The Intensification of Church-State Conflict in the United States"; Wald, *Religion and Politics in the United States.*

69. Leo Pfeffer, "The Current State of Law in the United States and the Separationist Agenda," *The Annals* 446 (December 1979), pp. 1–9.

70. See Wald's *Religion and Politics in the United States* for illustrations of the Sherbert-Yoder test.

71. For a more detailed analysis of the religious issues related to conscientious objection, see Choper, *Securing Religious Liberty: Principles for the Judicial Interpretation of the Religion Clauses,* and Leo Pfeffer, *Religious Freedom* (Lincolnwood, IL: National Textbook Company, 1983).

72. David G. Savage, *Turning Right: The Making of the Rehnquist Supreme Court* (New York: Wiley, 1993).

73. Brisbin, "The Rehnquist Court and the Free Exercise of Religion."

74. Linda Greenhouse, "High Court Voids a Law Expanding Religious Rights," *New York Times* (June 26, 1997), pp. 1, C24.

75. Edward G. Carmines and James A. Stimson, "The Two Faces of Issue Voting," *American Political Science Review* 74 (1980), pp. 78–91.

76. Murley, "School Prayer: Free Exercise of Religion or Establishment of Religion?"

77. For a more complete overview of the legislative history of the school prayer issue, see ibid.

78. Katherine Q. Seelye, "House Republicans Back Judge on Display of Ten Commandments," *New York Times* (March 5, 1997), p. A11.

79. David W. Dunlap, "Church v. State: A Landmark Case," *New York Times* (February 2, 1997), p. C24.

80. Boston, "Making Amends," p. 4.

81. Robert Bellah, "Civil Religion in America," *Daedalus* (Winter, 1967), pp. 1–21.

82. Hamilton, Madison, Jay,"Federalist No. 10."

83. Murley, "School Prayer: Free Exercise of Religion or Establishment of Religion?"

84. Ibid.

85. Ibid.

86. James L. Guth and John C. Green, "God and the GOP: Religion Among Republican Activists," in Ted G. Jelen, ed., *Religion and Political Behavior in the United States* (New York: Praeger, 1989), pp. 223–242.

87. Murley, "School Prayer: Free Exercise of Religion or Establishment of Religion?"

88. Phillip E. Converse, "Religion and Politics: The 1960 Election," in Angus Campbell et al., eds., *Elections and the Political Order* (New York: Wiley, 1966).

89. Murley, "School Prayer: Free Exercise of Religion or Establishment of Religion?"

90. Most observers would agree that there were important differences between the levels of personal religiosity of Presidents Kennedy and Carter. Nevertheless, both were publicly identified with particular religious traditions.

91. Matthew C. Moen, "Ronald Reagan and the Social Issues: Rhetorical Support for the Christian Right," *Social Science Journal* 27 (1990), pp. 199–207.

92. Murley, "School Prayer: Free Exercise of Religion or Establishment of Religion?"

93. James MacGregor Burns, *The Deadlock of Democracy: Four Party Politics in America* (Englewood Cliffs, NJ: Prentice-Hall, 1967).

94. Murley, "School Prayer: Free Exercise of Religion or Establishment of Religion?"

95. Ibid.

96. Jelen and Wilcox, *Public Attitudes Toward Church and State.*

97. Patricia Fauser, Jeanne Lewis, Joel A. Setzen, Finian Taylor, and Ted G. Jelen, "Conclusion: Perspectives on the Politics of Abortion," in Ted G. Jelen, ed., *Perspectives on the Politics of Abortion* (Westport, CT: Praeger, 1995), pp. 177–199.

98. See Roger Finke and Rodney Stark, *The Churching of America, 1776–1990* (New Brunswick, NJ: Rutgers University Press, 1992).

99. Ted G. Jelen, *The Political World of the Clergy* (Westport, CT: Praeger, 1993).

100. For an excellent discussion of this issue, see Choper, *Securing Religious Liberty: Principles for the Judicial Interpretation of the Religion Clauses.*

6

Gun Control: Constitutional Mandate or Myth?

Robert J. Spitzer

A well regulated Militia, being necessary to the security of a free state, the right of the people to keep and bear Arms, shall not be infringed.

—Second Amendment, U.S. Constitution

The NRA, the foremost guardian of the traditional right to "keep and bear arms," believes that every law-abiding citizen is entitled to the ownership and legal use of firearms, and that every reputable gun owner should be an NRA member.

—Motto, *The American Rifleman*

A powerful lobby dins into the ears of our citizenry that . . . gun purchases are constitutional rights protected by the Second Amendment. . . . There is under our decisions no reason why stiff state laws governing the purchase and possession of pistols may not be enacted. There is no reason why pistols may not be barred from anyone with a police record. There is no reason why a State may not require a purchaser of a pistol to pass a psychiatric test. There is no reason why all pistols should not be barred to everyone except the police.

—Associate Justice William O. Douglas, *Adams v. Williams* (1972)

The issue of gun control has proven itself one of the most highly charged, and enduringly controversial, in American politics, yet surprisingly little writing has incorporated dispassionate examination of gun control policies and politics. The purposes of this chapter are to inquire whether the state has the authority to regulate guns under the Second Amendment, and if so, how to explain the existing pattern of weak gun control laws. I begin with historical antecedents.

Those who can argue successfully that their contemporary view of the Second Amendment stems from the intent of the framers can claim a certain moral high ground. Early settlers had to rely on their own wits and skills to protect themselves against Native Americans and foreign armies and to keep food on the table. At the same time, the colonists' experiences with regular standing armies generated considerable cause for suspicion. This suspicion partly had its roots in the English Bill of Rights of 1689, which resulted after the Catholic king James II attempted to promote the cause of "papism" by filling the leading ranks of the army with Catholics, to the exclusion of Protestants. King James's oppressive practices eventually led to his overthrow and replacement by William of Orange.

Mistrust of standing armies was a pervasive sentiment during the revolutionary period in America and was related directly to the bearing of arms by citizens. Samuel Adams wrote in 1776, for example, that a "standing army, however necessary it be at some times, is always dangerous to the liberties of the people."[1] Samuel Seabury characterized the standing army as "the MONSTER,"[2] and George Washington observed that mercenary armies . . . have at one time or another subverted the liberties of almost all the Countries they have been raised to defend."[3] Thus, a reliance on the citizen-soldier became synonymous with the revolutionary spirit.

In the Declaration of Independence Thomas Jefferson complained that "he [the king] has kept among us, in Times of Peace, Standing Armies, without the consent of our Legislatures. He has affected to render the Military independent of and superior to the Civil Power." The Declaration of Independence also complained that the British were "quartering large Bodies of Armed Troops among us" and "protecting them, by a mock Trial, from Punishment for any Murders which they should commit on the Inhabitants of these States." The British only compounded these grievances by hiring Hessian mercenaries to fight against colonial troops during the Revolution. The colonists relied on state-based militias to fight the war, rather than risk vesting a national government with a national army that might later pose a threat to the people's liberties. Indeed, even by 1788, the Army of the Confederation consisted of only 697 men and officers.[4]

Yet despite these concerns, the framers recognized that a standing army was a necessity. Article I, Section 8 of the Constitution grants Congress the power "to raise and support armies" (although the fear of standing armies caused the framers to limit appropriations for the military to two years), to "provide for calling forth the militia," and to "provide for organizing, arming, and disciplining, the militia."[5] The modern militia is no longer a citizen army, as it was during the eighteenth century, but now is recognized as the National Guard since passage of the National Defense Act of 1916.

Fears of a standing army also influenced the writing of the Bill of Rights. The congressional committee reviewing proposed amendments reported out this text for what eventually became the Second Amendment: "A well regulated militia, composed of the body of the people, being the best security of a free state, the right of the people to keep and bear arms shall not be infringed; but no person religiously scrupulous shall be compelled to bear arms."[6] The primary change in the final text was the omission of the last phrase; Elbridge Gerry and others felt that the religious exemption could result in numerous citizens exempting themselves from military service, which might necessitate the baneful standing army.[7]

The founders sought in the Second Amendment insurance that states could maintain their militias against a mischievous federal army, or against the encroachments of other states. Absent from these debates was anything resembling an a priori individual "right" to bear arms. The concept of individualism had relevance only insofar as individuals during the early years of the country's history had to supply their own arms while serving in the militia. For example, Congress created uniform state militias through the Militia Law of 1792, which allowed the calling up of "every free, able-bodied, white male citizen of the respective States [between the ages of 18 and 45] in the militia. Each man was to provide his own weapons, two flints, 24 rounds of ammunition for a musket or 20 rounds for a rifle."[8] This kind of armed force was mobilized by President Washington in 1794 to suppress the Whiskey Rebellion.

The debate today about whether the Second Amendment refers to an "individual" or "collective" right to bear arms is directly relevant to the gun control issue. The individual interpretation is championed by the National Rifle Association (NRA). The weight of scholarly opinion argues against the NRA position,[9] but others interpret the Second Amendment as securing an individual right to bear arms.[10]

Interest Groups

The NRA

The National Rifle Association was formed in 1871 by Colonel William C. Church, editor of the *Army and Navy Journal,* and by George W. Wingate, an officer in the New York National Guard. The NRA's beginnings paralleled a rising interest in rifle shooting competitions, which resulted partly from the Union Army's relatively poor marksmanship skills during the Civil War. The organization languished until 1900, when Albert Jones, an officer in the New Jersey National Guard, with the aid of New York governor Theodore Roosevelt, revived interest in forming a group to support marksmanship. The then-forgotten NRA became the vehicle for implementing Jones's plan, and in 1905 the NRA became the primary channel for the sale of government surplus weapons and ammunition to rifle clubs under Public Law 149. In 1921 C.B. Lister, a promotions manager, assumed leadership of the NRA, and due to his efforts, the NRA became affiliated with two thousand local sportsmen's clubs; its membership grew tenfold by 1934. The NRA swiftly became the largest and best organized association of firearms users in the nation.

The NRA is now headquartered in Virginia, where rows of sophisticated computers keep information on the NRA's nearly three million members and on legislators. In a few hours, thousands of letters and mailgrams can be routed to Congress by mobilizing this huge membership. In 1994 the NRA generated revenues of $148 million.[11] Fifty percent of the NRA's revenues come from membership fees and another 15 percent from advertising, mainly by gun manufacturers, in its monthly magazines: *The American Rifleman, The American Hunter,* and *The American Marksman.*[12] In recent years, however, the NRA has accumulated significant debts, and its debt has mounted rapidly, increasing to $45 million by 1996.[13]

With a paid staff of over three hundred, the NRA coordinates a network of fifty-four state groups and about ten thousand local gun clubs. The heart of the NRA organization lies in its mass membership. The NRA fosters this devotion by emphasizing the gun as a cultural phenomenon, not simply a political issue. Beyond this, the NRA has benefited from a kind of quasi-governmental status; federal law for decades stipulated that surplus military arms could be sold only to civilians who belonged to the NRA. This led to an ironic occurrence in 1967 when four hundred members of the Detroit Police Department had to join the NRA in order to obtain surplus army carbines for riot control.[14] A court order ended this special privilege in 1979, the result of a legal challenge by the National Coalition to Ban Handguns (NCBH). The federal government continues to subsidize NRA activities by allowing the organization to hold annual shooting matches at federal military installations at no expense to the NRA, and allowing it the special favor of building target ranges on federal lands.[15]

Institute for Legislative Action (ILA)

This special branch of the NRA coordinates legislative efforts. First formed in 1975, one of ILA's primary responsibilities is to apply political pressure on federal and state elected officials, and to provide the NRA membership with current information and alerts on impending firearms legislation and court rulings. The ILA has become the primary power center within the NRA and its potency has been widely noted. For example, the *Washington Post* observed that "few lobbies have so mastered the marble halls and concrete canyons of Washington."[16] The ILA now consumes over a quarter of the NRA budget. In 1988 the ILA spent $20.2 million on political activities; in 1992 the figure was $28.9 million; in 1994 it was $28.3 million. In addition, the ILA expends considerable resources in communications with NRA members. In 1991, for example, it spent about $10 million on various fund-raising, "alert," and other appeals to members. And in virtually every year since the end of the 1970s, the NRA has spent more money on emotionally charged internal communications than any similar group.[17]

In one very controversial instance, the NRA suffered severe criticism from a fund-raising letter sent out shortly before the bombing of a federal office building in Oklahoma City on April 19, 1995. In the six-page letter, signed by NRA executive vice president Wayne LaPierre, federal government agents were compared to Nazis, in that they were said to wear "Nazi bucket helmets and black storm trooper uniforms," and "harass, intimidate, *even murder* law-abiding citizens." Many expressed outrage at the letter, and former President George Bush publicly resigned his life membership in the organization. He called the NRA letter a "vicious slander on good people."[18] The adverse publicity stemming from the NRA's perceived extremism contributed to the decline in its membership. After reaching a high point of about 3.5 million members in the early 1990s, NRA membership dipped to about 2.8 million by 1997.

NRA PAC

The Institute for Legislative Action also manages the NRA's political action committee (PAC), which is called the Political Victory Fund. Formed in 1976, the NRA PAC has funneled millions of dollars to gun control foes. Throughout the 1980s and 1990s, the NRA has consistently been one of the top-spending political organizations in the country. In 1988, for example, it funneled $1.5 million to George Bush's presidential campaign; four years later, however, it withheld support from Bush because of his support for restrictions on assault weapons imports. It also sat out the 1996 presidential contest, as President Bill Clinton was a supporter of tough gun laws while his opponent, Bob Dole, backed away from his anti–gun control positions of prior years. In the 1994 elections, the NRA PAC spent $5.3 million on direct campaign contributions, making it the biggest-spending PAC in that year's election. The PAC also expends considerable resources on independent expenditures (money spent independent of the campaign of the candidate for whom the money is used); in 1994, it spent $1.5 million on independent expenditures, which accounts for more than a fourth of all the independent money spent by PACs that year. Increasingly, these independent expenditures have been used to attack opponents in Congress and elsewhere through "stealth" tactics; that is, ads that attack opponents on other issues to conceal the fact that the gun issue is the primary motivation.[19]

As is true of most PACs, most of its money goes to incumbents. And although the NRA gives to both political parties, the lion's share goes to Republicans. During the 1985–86 period, for example, the NRA gave $644,000 to 139 congressional Republican candidates and $255,000 to 68 Democrats.[20]

But the NRA does not confine its activities to the legislative branch. Through its Firearms Civil Rights Legal Defense Fund, founded in 1978, the NRA helps to finance legal battles in the courts. This organization is a tax-exempt fund supported by individual and corporate donations and is under the guidance of the Institute for Legislative Action. From 1993 to 1996 the organization provided money to seventy-eight cases. In 1996, for example, the organization gave about $20,000 to aid in the legal defense of Bernhard Goetz, a man who shot four reputed attackers on a New York City subway in the 1980s.[21]

Other Progun Groups

Single-issue progun groups have sprung up mainly because they believe that the NRA is not strident enough in its opposition to gun control legislation.[22] One such group is the Citizens Committee for the Right to Keep and Bear Arms, headquartered in Washington, DC. It includes a research arm, called the Second Amendment Foundation, that publishes gun-related literature.[23] The research arm of the Citizens Committee, the Second Amendment Foundation, publishes progun literature.[24] The Gun Owners of America (GOA) was founded in 1974 by H.L. Richardson, a California state senator and former director of the NRA. The organization is today headed by Larry Pratt, and it claims about 150,000 members.

Progun Arguments

The symbolic importance of the Constitution is evidenced in much NRA literature. One recurring theme in the literature is the argument that the Second Amendment provides absolute protection for any individual's right to own guns. The NRA also argues against waiting periods for gun ownership and for the elimination of gun regulations, stiffer laws, and any restrictions on handguns, including "Saturday night specials."

An analysis of the NRA's rhetorical style was done by Raymond S. Rodgers, who identified five logical and rhetorical fallacies in the NRA's publications.[25] The first was the failure to define terms—for example, the options that are included under the term *gun control*. The second was the use of the "big lie"—that the Second Amendment guarantees an inalienable right to bear arms. The third, the "slippery slope" fallacy, argued that any gun regulation invariably will lead to a total ban on guns and even to authoritarianism.[26] The fourth was the use of "bully tactics" such as name calling, as when gun control advocates were called "gun-grabbers." The fifth was improper appeals to authority, such as using endorsements by John Wayne, Roy Rogers, and Wally Schirra rather than relying on evidence or reasoning.

Gun Control Groups

The ideological antithesis of the NRA is Handgun Control, Inc. (HCI). Based in Washington, DC, Handgun Control is the largest of the antigun groups. Although formed in 1974 by businessman Pete Shields, the organization had few resources or capabilities until the early 1980s, when the murder of ex-Beatle John Lennon spurred interest and fund-raising. By 1981, membership surpassed a hundred thousand. It contributed money to congressional campaigns for the first time in 1980, when it gave $75,000. That year, by comparison, the NRA contributed $1.5 million to campaigns. By the 1991–92 election cycle, HCI had spent $280,000, still a fraction of NRA spending. HCI has sought to copy the NRA's tactical and organizational methods, particularly by building grassroots support among members willing to write letters, make phone calls, vote, and contribute money. By 1990 membership reached 250,000. By 1994 its membership topped 400,000, and it maintained a mailing list of over a million names. Its annual budget is about $7 million.[27]

Handgun Control's original agenda was to restrict, but not ban, the ownership of pistols and revolvers (in particular Saturday night specials). Its focus shifted in the 1980s when Sarah Brady became its chief public advocate (she has headed HCI since 1989). Brady achieved public visibility when her husband, James Brady (press secretary to President Reagan), was seriously injured in the 1981 assassination attempt against the president. Four years later, Brady joined the HCI board in reaction to efforts by gun control opponents in Congress to gut much of the 1968 Gun Control Act (see discussion of the 1986 McClure-Volkmer bill, below). In the late 1980s she and her husband became the chief advocates for enactment of a waiting period for purchase of a handgun, a bill that came to be known as the Brady bill (see subsequent discussion), and which was enacted in 1993.

Another gun control group, the National Coalition to Ban Handguns, was founded in 1974 with a grant from the United Methodist church. The NCBH is composed of a group of national religious, educational, and social organizations. The NCBH was renamed the Coalition to Stop Gun Violence (CSGV) in 1990. The CSGV tends to be more militant and aggressive in its lobbying efforts, but it has been overshadowed by the larger and more visible HCI.

The proponents of stricter regulations, unlike the NRA, have rallied the support of other organizations not exclusively concerned about the gun issue. The U.S. Conference of Mayors in 1972 adopted a strongly worded resolution that "urges national legislation against the manufacture, importation, sale and private possession of handguns" and that "urges its members to extend every effort to educate the American public to the dangerous and appalling realities resulting from the private possession of handguns." The NAACP also has endorsed stricter gun laws, as have elements of the medical profession and the American Bar Association.

Gun Control Advocacy Literature

Such literature emphasizes crime statistics and the "collective" meaning of the Second Amendment as well as supplying anecdotes to buttress arguments for more gun regulations. In recent years HCI literature has adopted a tone reminiscent of NRA literature, as for example when it began a 1993 appeal to members with the bold lettering "WE MUST GET THESE KILLING MACHINES OFF OUR STREETS!"

Each year in the United States, nearly forty thousand people die as a result of the suicidal, criminal, or accidental use of guns. Since 1968, the number of firearms in private ownership has dramatically increased from approximately 60 million to 150 million guns in circulation in 1982, to about 220 million by 1996.[28] Of these, two-thirds are long guns (rifles and shotguns), and a third are handguns. Antigun literature emphasizes that handguns pose a special danger, because they are the weapons used in about 80 percent of gun-related crimes.

Table 6.1

Gallup Polls on Gun Control

Question: "In general do you feel that the laws covering the sale of firearms should be made more strict, less strict, or kept as they are?"

	1975	1980	1981	1983	1986	1990	1991	1993
More strict	69%	59%	65%	59%	60%	78%	68%	70%
Less strict	3	6	3	4	8	2	5	4
Kept as is	24	29	30	31	30	17	25	24

Source: Leslie McAneny, "Americans Tell Congress: Pass Brady Bill, Other Tough Gun Laws," *Gallup Poll Monthly*, March 1993, p. 2.

Historian Richard Hofstadter observed that the United States is the only modern Western nation that clings to the "gun culture."[29] In 1988, for example, America committed 8.4 homicides per 100,000 people. Among the nearest competitors were Sweden at 7.2, Canada at 5.5, Germany at 4.2, France at 3.9, Great Britain at 2, and Japan at 1.2.[30] Thus, despite population size differences, it is obvious that U.S. gun-related deaths are far greater in both proportionate and absolute terms when compared to other industrialized nations. The advocates of stricter gun control legislation claim that other nations' much lower death rates from guns are a consequence of stronger laws.[31]

Public Opinion

As early as 1938, pollsters began measuring public opinion on gun control. The Gallup Poll in that year found that 79 percent of the respondents favored "gun control."[32] Since 1959 Gallup has asked, "Would you favor or oppose a law which would require a person to obtain a police permit before he or she could buy a gun?" The affirmative response rate to that question has fluctuated between 68 and 78 percent.[33]

Gallup also asked whether laws concerning handgun sales should be strengthened, weakened, or kept as they are now. Table 6.1 gives those responses.[34] Women are more likely to favor stricter laws than men, as are young adults (age 18–29), the college-educated, and people living in the East and in urban areas. In addition, the National Opinion Research Center surveyed the public on whether police permits should be required for gun ownership. The responses in Table 6.2 show much public support for that requirement.[35]

A variation of that question was used by researchers Howard Schuman

Table 6.2

NORC Surveys on Permits for Gun Ownership

Question: "Would you favor or oppose a law which would require a person to obtain a police permit before he or she could buy a gun?"

	1972	1977	1985	1996
Favor	70%	72%	72%	81%
Oppose	27%	26%	27%	18%

Sources: National Opinion Research Center, *General Social Surveys* (July 1982), p. 87; *The Public Perspective* (February/March 1997), p. 27.

and Stanley Presser to measure intensity of feelings on both sides of the gun controversy.[36] What these researchers found was that at the purely subjective level, supporters of the permit law responded with slightly more intensity than did the opponents; however, when the respondents were asked whether they ever wrote letters or contributed money to support their position on this issue, the opponents were much more likely to have done so than were the supporters. One reason for this differential, the authors suggested, was the superior organizational effectiveness of anti–gun control forces.

Other gun measures find wide support as well. For example, according to Gallup, 81 percent of Americans reported supporting universal handgun registration in 1993. A 1988 survey found 84 percent favoring laws requiring anyone carrying a gun outside the home to be licensed to do so. Throughout the 1990s over 90 percent of Americans have supported a waiting period for purchase of a handgun, and 66 percent favored banning of semiautomatic assault weapons in 1993.[37]

Despite the wealth of public opinion findings favoring gun control, the opposition can point to survey results indicating support for the use of guns in hypothetical situations of danger or criminal assault. A 1968 Harris survey found that 51 percent would "use your gun to shoot other people in case of a riot."[38] That question probably was triggered by the urban disturbances and rioting that occurred in several U.S. cities during 1968. More recently, a Gallup poll found overwhelming support (72 percent) for using a gun against a likely assailant.[39]

The widespread nature of gun ownership in the United States is reflected in the fact that 59 percent of Americans reported in 1996 having at least one gun in their house, up from 51 percent in 1973.[40] Gun owners are more likely to be men, whites, the less educated, older persons, people with higher incomes, Republicans, Protestants, and manual workers. Two sub-groups reflect the greatest degree of gun ownership: residents of the South, and persons living in towns with populations of less than 2,500 and in rural areas. Fewest guns are owned by easterners and by people living in cities of 1 million or more population.

Federalism

Much of the emotional commitment that feeds the gun culture stems from a long tradition linking guns to the nation's frontier development. Axioms such as "the guns that won the West" and "arm[s] that opened the West and tamed the wild land" underestimate the central role played by home-steaders, ranchers, businesspeople, and the general movement of larger set-tlements across America's western lands.[41] Even after the frontier disappeared, mythic attachments to the gun remained, as reflected in the argument that a boy should be allowed to own a gun because a .22 caliber rifle was a "character builder."[42]

It is difficult to overemphasize the grassroots nature of the gun culture. Obvious regional differences do exist, for example, between Morton Grove, Illinois, where handgun ownership in the home was banned, and Kenesaw County, Georgia, where local leaders passed an admittedly frivolous law making it a crime *not* to own a gun. Thirty-nine states make some mention of a right to bear arms in their constitutions; those that do not are California, Delaware, Iowa, Maryland, Minnesota, Nebraska, New Jersey, New York, North Dakota, West Virginia, and Wisconsin. Except for California, none of these eleven states is located in the South or West, where the gun culture is strongest.

One study devised a measure of the strictness of state handgun laws using seven possible types of regulation. Most states fell in the middle of the distribu-tion, having neither very strict nor very weak gun laws. Generally, the states with stricter handgun control laws tended to have larger populations, were eastern, and committed more resources to criminal justice.[43]

Presidency

The first president to associate himself aggressively with organized gun interests was soldier-hunter-sportsman Theodore Roosevelt. While gover-nor of New York, Roosevelt took an active hand in helping to form an organization to support marksmanship. As president, Roosevelt helped re-vive the National Rifle Association and was himself a member. He also helped to encourage the establishment of firing ranges in public schools.

During the term of President Calvin Coolidge, Congress dealt with several modest but controversial gun control measures, yet Coolidge offered no leadership on the issue. Franklin D. Roosevelt was the first president to actively promote gun-restricting legislation as part of a larger federal assault on crime and gangsterism. The modest gun control legislation that was enacted into law in 1934 and 1938 was the result of this effort.

For most subsequent presidents the gun issue was primarily one more symbolic ribbon to be acquired. Notably, Presidents Dwight Eisenhower, John Kennedy, Richard Nixon, Ronald Reagan, and George Bush were all life members of the NRA. Ironically, it was the Kennedy assassination that prompted renewed interest in stronger gun regulations. President Lyndon B. Johnson stood behind the gun control efforts of the 1960s, but he was not especially successful as compared to his enormous impact on major social welfare legislation.[44]

President Reagan took a consistent and prominent stand against gun control. Even after the assassination attempt on his life in 1981, in a subsequent interview, Reagan said that "if anything, I'm a little disturbed that focusing on gun control as an answer to the crime problem today could very well be diverting us from really paying attention to what needs to be done if we're to solve the crime problem." He also said that existing gun control laws had proven ineffective in regulating guns.[45] After leaving the presidency, however, Reagan reversed himself, endorsing the Brady bill, passed in 1993, and the assault weapons ban, passed in 1994. George Bush similarly opposed gun control efforts during his presidency, and he was endorsed by the NRA in 1988. Four years later, however, the NRA repudiated Bush when he endorsed a ban on the import of assault weapons. After his presidency, as noted before, Bush turned in his life NRA membership because of that organization's strident criticism of agents of the Bureau of Alcohol, Tobacco, and Firearms.

President Bill Clinton has strongly supported gun control efforts, and his efforts were important in the passage of the Brady bill and the assault weapons ban. His role was clearly important; yet the country's increasingly strong support for gun control, coupled with increasing criticism of the NRA, were greater factors in these two efforts.

The national political parties consistently have disagreed with each other on gun control. The Republicans have articulated a long-standing support for gun ownership, and the Democrats exhibit a similar consistency in favor of stronger gun regulations. The issue first appeared in party platforms in 1968, and both political parties have treated the issue in their platforms under the category of crime and criminal justice.[46]

The 1968 Republican party platform urged "control [of] indiscriminate availability of firearms" but also "safeguarding the right of responsible citizens to collect, own and use firearms . . . retaining primary responsibility at the state level." The 1972 Republican platform again endorsed citizen rights to "collect, own and use firearms," but also included "self-defense" as a purpose and emphasized efforts "to prevent criminal access to all weapons," especially cheap handguns, while relying mainly on state enforcement. The 1976 GOP platform was terser; it simply stated, "We support the right of citizens to keep and bear arms." The Republican party also stated its opposition to federal registration of firearms and advocated harsher sentences for crimes committed with guns. The 1976 document conformed fully to NRA policy.

In 1980 the Republican platform wording was the same as in 1976, with an added phrase urging removal of "those provisions of the Control Act of 1968 that do not significantly impact on crime but serve rather to restrain the law-abiding citizen in his legitimate use of firearms." The 1984 platform dropped any reference to the Gun Control Act or to gun registration and said instead that citizens ought not to be blamed for "exercising their constitutional rights" (which presumably meant an "individual" right to bear arms). The 1988 platform supported "the constitutional right to keep and bear arms" and called for "stiff, mandatory penalties" for those who used guns in crime. This wording was kept in 1992 (despite the NRA's refusal to endorse Bush) along with additional wording tying gun ownership to national defense, and criticizing efforts at "blaming firearm manufacturers for street crime." The 1996 platform mentioned the Second Amendment, firearms training, and a plan to conduct instant background checks for gun purchases. It also endorsed mandatory penalties for crimes involving guns.

The 1968 Democratic party platform urged "the passage and enforcement of effective federal, state and local gun control legislation." A specific proposal appeared for the first time in 1972 when, after calling for "laws to control the improper use of hand guns," the Democratic party asked for a ban on Saturday night specials. The 1976 platform again called for strengthening existing handgun controls as well as banning Saturday night specials. But the platform also urged tougher sentencing for crimes committed with guns and, in a partial reversal, affirmed "the right of sportsmen to possess guns for purely hunting and target-shooting purposes." The 1980 platform advocated the same position and reaffirmed that the Democratic party supported the rights of sportsmen to possess guns for sporting purposes. This softening of the Democratic party's stand on gun control probably reflected the caution of its presidential candidate, Jimmy Carter. The 1984 Democratic party platform, reflecting the liberal views of nominee Walter Mondale, made a modest turn to the left by dropping any reference to the sporting use of guns. The platform again called for tough restraints on snub-nosed handguns. The 1988 platform backpedaled on earlier tough language. Its only specific gun regulation proposal was a call for enforcement of the ban on "cop killer" bullets enacted in 1986. It also made a vague reference to the procuring of weapons as an impediment to the jobs performed by police, teachers, and parents. The 1992 platform was stronger and more specific. After asserting that it was "time to shut down the weapons bazaars," it endorsed a waiting period for handgun purchases and a ban on "the most deadly assault weapons." It also called for swift punishment of those who commit gun crimes, shutting down the black market, and stiff penalties for those who sell guns to children. In a bow to hunters (of whom Clinton is one), the platform also said, "We do not support efforts to restrict weapons used for legitimate hunting and sporting purposes." The 1996 platform applauded the enactment of the Brady law and the assault weapons ban, and the protection of legitimate hunting and sporting uses of guns.

Congress

Only eight gun control enactments merit any consideration. The first is the National Firearms Act of 1934. It came as a response to gang violence and the attempted assassination of President Roosevelt the year before. The act's main purpose was to end possession of machine guns, sawed-off shotguns, silencers, and other gangster weapons. Congress went a step further in 1938 by passing the Federal Firearms Act, which tried to regulate the interstate shipment of firearms and ammunition by establishing federal licensing of manufacturers, importers, and dealers of guns and ammunition. The act also prohibited the shipment of firearms to people under indictment, fugitives, and some convicted felons.

Two laws were passed in 1968. One was incorporated in Title IV of the Omnibus Crime Control and Safe Streets Act, which banned the transportation of pistols and revolvers across state lines and forbade the purchase of handguns in stores in a state where the buyer did not reside. The Omnibus Crime Control and Safe Streets Act was passed the day after the assassination of Robert Kennedy and two months after the murder of Martin Luther King Jr.

Gun Control Act of 1968

The key provisions of the Omnibus Act were incorporated into the Gun Control Act of 1968, the second enactment of the year. This statute provides an ideal case study to highlight the political processes affecting a direct effort to regulate firearms. The main arena of conflict was Congress, where numerous efforts were made on the floor to amend this legislation. Lobbying by interest groups was heavy, but the president's influence over the final bill was minimal.[47] The enactment of P.L. 90–618 was spurred by recent assassinations and a wave of public sentiment favoring tougher gun laws. President Johnson had been outspoken in his support for stronger gun laws ever since taking office in 1963, but congressional action was not forthcoming. On June 6, 1968, President Johnson urged Congress "in the name of sanity . . . in the name of safety and in the name of an aroused nation to give America the gun-control law it needs."[48]

The Johnson proposal was introduced into the House on June 10, 1968, as H.R. 17735 by Judiciary Committee chair Emanuel Celler (D-NY), a gun control advocate, and by Senator Thomas Dodd (D-CT), also a champion of gun control, who chaired the Judiciary's Subcommittee on Juvenile Delinquency. The House Judiciary Committee initially voted 16–16 on the bill, thus keeping it in the committee. An agreement was made to reconsider the legislation, however, and it was finally reported out on June 21, after the addition of some qualifying amendments. The House Rules Committee approved a rule for the bill on July 9, after holding the legislation for nearly three weeks. Rules Committee chairman William Colmer (D-MS), a gun control opponent, released the bill only after extracting a promise from Celler that he would oppose any efforts to add registration and licensing provisions to the bill on the floor of the House.

The House of Representatives passed H.R. 17735 on July 24 after four days of vigorous floor consideration characterized by numerous attempts to amend the bill. Forty-five attempts were made to amend this legislation on the floor of the House, including four roll call votes plus one more on final passage. In the more liberal Senate, the gun control bill met with greater support, and more debate centered on whether to strengthen the law or not. Subcommittee hearings began on June 26, and testimony was received from a wide variety of persons including NRA president Harold W. Glassen, who said that the legislation was part of an effort to "foist upon an unsuspecting and aroused public a law that would, through its operation, sound the death knell for the shooting sport and eventually disarm the American public."[49]

The Senate subcommittee approved the measure unanimously and forwarded it to the full committee, where the bill encountered stiff opposition. The bill was delayed and weakened by gun control opponents, including Judiciary Committee chair James Eastland (D-MS). Efforts to push the bill through were hampered by the absence at various times of gun control supporters, including Senator Edward Kennedy (D-MA), who was still mourning the loss of his brother. Finally, the bill was sent by committee to

the Senate floor, where it was debated for five days. The opening salvo
came from Senator Dodd, who accused the NRA of "blackmail, intimidation and unscrupulous propaganda."[50] Seventeen formal motions were
made to amend this bill in the Senate. After the bill's passage on September
18, a conference committee ironed out differences with the House, and
President Johnson signed the bill on October 22.

As enacted, P.L. 90–618 restricted interstate shipment of firearms and
ammunition and prohibited the sale of guns to minors, drug addicts, mental
incompetents, and convicted felons. The act strengthened licensing and
record-keeping requirements for gun dealers and collectors, extended the
tax provisions of the National Firearms Act of 1934 to include destructive
devices not originally covered, and banned the importation of foreign-made
surplus firearms. But the law did not ban the importation of handgun parts,
which effectively allowed for the circumvention of the import ban. One
year later, however, a key provision of the act, requiring sellers of shotgun
and rifle ammunition to register purchasers, was repealed in an amendment
tacked onto a tax bill. This rider was authored by Senator Wallace F. Bennett (R-UT) along with forty-six Senate cosponsors.[51]

Congress enacted a ban on the importation, manufacture, and sale of
KTW ("cop killer") bullets (P.L. 99–408) that was signed into law on
August 20, 1986. Attempts to pass this legislation, which went back four
years, had been opposed by the NRA. The year of the bill's passage, however, the NRA dropped active opposition to the law, a move motivated
partly by the alienating effect the NRA's opposition had on police organizations as well as the NRA's preoccupation with the McClure-Volkmer Bill
under consideration at the same time.[52]

The Firearms Owners Protection Act of 1986

Repeated efforts were made throughout the years to weaken the 1968 gun
law. The most important, and successful, attempt came in 1986, with enactment of the Firearms Owners Protection Act, also known as the McClure-
Volkmer Bill (S. 49, H.R. 4332, P.L. 99–308). This act amended the 1968
Gun Control Act by allowing for the legal interstate sale of rifles and
shotguns as long as the sale is legal in the states of the buyer and seller. The
act also eliminated record-keeping requirements for ammunition dealers,
made it easier for individuals selling guns to do so without a license unless
they did so "regularly," allowed gun dealers to do business at gun shows,
and prohibited the Bureau of Alcohol, Tobacco, and Firearms (ATF) from
issuing regulations requiring centralized records of gun dealers. In addition,
the act limited to one per year the number of unannounced inspections of

gun dealers by the ATF and prohibited the establishment of any system of comprehensive firearms registration. Finally, the act barred future possession or transfer of machine guns and retained existing restrictions (except for transport) on handguns. The passage of this legislation spanned two years and was the culmination of a protracted lobbying effort by the NRA, joined by the Gun Owners of America and the Citizens Committee for the Right to Keep and Bear Arms.

Consideration of S. 49 began first in the Senate, where attempts to weaken the 1968 gun law had been approved by the Judiciary Committee in 1982 and 1984. Floor consideration was not obtained, however, until 1985, the first time the full Senate had considered any gun legislation since 1972. Once on the floor, the bill was subjected to a barrage of amendments designed to strengthen gun controls; none of these amendments, however, was accepted.

The bill's chief Senate sponsors, James A. McClure (R-ID) and Orrin Hatch (R-UT), argued that the proposed restrictions would have no effect on crime fighting but instead represented unjustified limitations on sportsmen, hunters, and dealers. The one significant restriction imposed by the Senate was a ban on the importation of parts for Saturday night specials. The final vote on S. 49 was 79–15, with the strongest support coming from westerners. The relatively speedy passage of this bill was attributed to the pressure of the NRA and its allies and to the fact that the Republican-controlled Senate had a sympathetic Judiciary Committee chairman (Strom Thurmond, R-SC) and majority leader (Robert Dole, R-KS).[53]

In many respects, gun control forces were caught unawares by the speedy Senate action in committee and on the floor. This set the stage for a full-scale fight in the House of Representatives in 1986. Although the gun lobby achieved an important victory, in the process the lobby alienated some key, longtime allies—police groups and organizations. Police dissatisfaction with NRA positions had been growing for some time, and even during Senate consideration of S. 49, Handgun Control had enlisted the support of five national police organizations. In 1986 national law enforcement groups lined up almost unanimously with gun control proponents. Such organizations as the National Sheriffs' Association, the International Association of Chiefs of Police, the National Organization of Black Law Enforcement Executives, the National Troopers Association, the Police Executive Research Forum, the Police Foundation, and the Fraternal Order of Police became increasingly alarmed about the criminal and safety consequences of weak gun regulations. In particular, law enforcement officials were alienated by the NRA's stand against controlling armor-piercing bullets and in favor of legal possession of submachine guns and automatic weapons.[54]

Deliberations on the McClure-Volkmer Bill in the Democratic-controlled House posed a far greater problem for the gun lobby. Judiciary Committee chairman Peter Rodino (D-NJ), a staunch proponent of gun control, had announced that the bill came "DOA—dead on arrival." Many proponents of gun control felt reassured, despite the Senate action, because they had confidence that Rodino would not allow a gun decontrol bill out of his committee. Rodino's comments infuriated the gun lobby, however, and a discharge petition was begun, spearheaded by House bill sponsor Harold L. Volkmer (D-MO). If signed by a majority of the House membership, a discharge petition would force the bill from the committee to the House floor. The opponents of gun control argued that this bill was necessary to eliminate burdensome and unnecessary restrictions on gun dealers and legitimate owners. The ATF countered that, in fact, most of its prosecutions under the gun law involved individuals with prior criminal or felony records.[55]

Despite its well-known support for the NRA, the Reagan administration played a minimal role in these proceedings. Officially, the administration supported S. 49, but the Justice Department offered no testimony at committee hearings. Further, internal ATF memos released to the press revealed doubts about some of the decontrol provisions. Public comments by Attorney General Edwin Meese were similarly equivocal.[56]

Despite the firm opposition of Congressmen Peter Rodino and William J. Hughes (D-NJ, chair of the Subcommittee on Crime), the full Judiciary Committee held a markup session on the bill and reported it to the floor by a unanimous vote. This remarkable turn of events occurred in March as the result of the discharge petition, the first successful petition since 1983. By reporting to the floor first (March 11) before completion and filing of the discharge petition (March 13), gun control forces hoped to salvage some parliamentary flexibility that would allow prior consideration of legislation retaining more gun restrictions. This maneuver failed, however, because Representative Volkmer was able to offer his version of the bill as a substitute for that of the Judiciary Committee.

On April 9 Congressman Hughes offered a package of law enforcement amendments, including a ban on interstate sale and transport of handguns and stricter record-keeping regulations. The package was rejected by a wide margin (176–248). During the vote, police officers stood in full uniform at "parade rest" at the entrance to the House floor. After several other votes on motions to strengthen certain gun control provisions (none was successful), the House adjourned and then reconvened the next day. This time, on the third try, the House approved (233–184) a ban on interstate handgun sales after proponents stressed the difference between sale and transport. A final amendment to bar all future possession and sale of machine guns by private citizens also passed. The bill was approved by a lopsided 292–130 vote on April 10.

Analysis of the voting behavior on the key package of amendments offered by Congressman Hughes revealed that anti–gun control voters were more numerous in the South and border states (83 percent against), followed by the West/Rocky Mountain region (59 percent against), the Midwest (50 percent against), and then the East (38 percent against). Regions with more rural populations and greater gun ownership (and presumably greater NRA influence) provided the strongest support for the progun lobby, but the NRA even did well in some larger states such as Pennsylvania and Texas. In terms of partisanship, House Republicans heavily favored the NRA, with only 40 voting for the Hughes package versus 138 against. The Democrats were less cohesive on this question; they split almost evenly, with 138 for the amendments and 110 against. Thus, the key variables influencing this vote were region, constituency, and attendant ideological disposition toward the gun issue.

NRA applied dual pressure from below (grassroots) and above (lobbying) on the Congress. In all, the NRA devoted $1.6 million to its efforts, compared to the paltry sum of about $15,000 spent by police organizations.[57] The relative inexperience of police lobbying also hurt their cause. As one congressman observed, "The police misunderstood the force of lobbying. Lobbying is not standing in long lines at the door. Lobbying is good information early; it is a presence when minds are being made up."[58]

The House-passed bill, H.R. 4332, differed from the Senate version in a few specifics. They were resolved by the unusual action of enacting a separate bill (S. 2414). Its purpose was to clarify certain sections and to appease police interests, which finally succeeded in persuading Senator Thurmond to take up their appeal. The added provision made clear that guns transported across state lines must be unloaded and locked in an area of the motor vehicle other than the passenger compartment. The clarifying bill also provided for easier government traces of guns and restored certain record-keeping provisions. In this form the bill was signed into law by President Reagan on May 19, 1986.

This legislative case study parallels the experience of the 1968 Gun Control Act in important ways. First, President Reagan's impact was minimal, despite his clear opinions on this subject. Second, the level of political intensity was high, especially in the House. The successful and rare application of a discharge petition coupled with the unusual clarifying bill at final passage illustrate how both conflict and political instability caused these disruptions in legislative routine. The large number of floor amendments revealed the inability of the proponents and opponents of decontrol to resolve their differences within the committees of either house. Third, interest group activity again was abundant and of critical importance to the final outcome.

The Brady Bill

From 1987 to 1993, gun control proponents placed their primary emphasis on the enactment of a national waiting period for handgun purchases in order to, first, provide authorities with the opportunity to conduct a background check on the prospective purchaser in order to void handgun purchases by felons, the mentally incompetent, or others who should not have handguns and, second, provide a cooling-off period for those who seek to buy and perhaps use a handgun in a fit of temper or rage.

The so-called Brady bill (named after James Brady, the former White House press secretary) was first introduced in Congress in early 1987 in the Senate by Howard Metzenbaum (D-OH) and in the House by Rep. Edward F. Feighan (D-OH). It quickly became the top priority of HCI and Sarah Brady, James Brady's wife and HCI leader. The NRA opposed the measure, although as late as the mid-1970s the NRA had supported such a waiting period.[59]

The Brady bill struggle first emerged on the floor of Congress in a House vote in 1988 (the bill was defeated). In 1991 and 1992 both the House and the Senate passed different versions of the bill, but the revised version of the bill stalled in the Senate. The effort climaxed in 1993, when supporters promoted a five-business-day waiting period bill. House Judiciary Committee approval was won on November 4, despite the objections of committee chair and gun control opponent Jack Brooks (D-TX), who also boosted the bill's chances by consenting with reluctance to separate the measure (H.R. 1025) from a new crime bill. Six days later, the full House approved the Brady bill after fending off several amendments (sponsored by Republicans and Rep. Brooks) designed to weaken the bill. One such amendment, to phase out the waiting period after five years, was adopted. The final vote to pass the bill, H.R. 1025, was 238–189.[60]

Following the lead of the House, the Senate separated the Brady bill (S. 414) from the larger crime package. The bill faced a Republican filibuster almost immediately, but this move was forestalled by an agreement between the political party leaders to allow floor consideration of a substitute version that included two NRA-backed provisions. The first called for all state waiting periods to be superseded by the federal five-day waiting period (twenty-four states had waiting periods of varying lengths in 1993; twenty-three also had background checks).[61] This was objectionable to

Brady supporters because many states had waiting periods longer than five days, and the move was seen as a violation of states' rights. This amendment was stricken from the bill by a Senate floor vote. The second measure called for ending the five-day waiting period after five years. It survived a vote to kill it. The Senate then faced another filibuster, which looked as though it would be fatal to the bill. Brady supporters and congressional allies all conceded that the bill was dead for the year. The postmortems proved to be premature, however, as the Republicans decided to end their opposition on November 20, feeling a rising tide of impatience and no sense that they could win further concessions from Democratic leaders. The bill was passed that day by a 63–36 vote.[62]

The bill then went to a contentious House-Senate conference on November 22. The House passed the conference version early in the morning of the twenty-third. Senate Republican leader Robert Dole, however, balked at the compromise, calling it unacceptable. Senate Democratic leader George Mitchell threatened to reconvene the Senate after the Thanksgiving break in order to obtain final action. The two finally reached an accommodation, and the bill was approved in the Senate by voice vote on November 24, with a promise to consider several modifications in early 1994. President Clinton signed the bill into law on November 30.[63]

As enacted, the Brady law codified a five-business-day waiting period for handgun purchases. It also authorized $200 million per year to help states improve and upgrade their computerization of criminal records; increased federal firearms license fees from $30 to $200 for the first three years, and $90 for renewals; made it a federal crime to steal firearms from licensed dealers; barred package labeling for guns being shipped, to deter theft; required state and local police to be told of multiple handgun sales; and said that police must make a "reasonable effort" to check the backgrounds of gun buyers.

In policy terms, the Brady law's consequences were expected to be modest. First, the Brady law does not actually require local police to conduct background checks, and there are wide variations in state record-keeping practices. Second, state experiences with waiting periods showed that about 1 to 2 percent of prospective gun buyers were denied sales as the result of background checks, a figure that may be more significant than this percentage suggests, given that roughly a quarter of state prison inmates reported purchasing their guns legally.[64] The ATF reported that it conducted about ninety thousand Brady background checks each week, using the National Criminal Information Computer system. About 16 percent of those came up with criminal records, and 6 percent as convicted felons.[65] From 1994, when the law went into effect, to the end of 1996 the

Brady law blocked about a hundred thousand gun purchases to felons, illegal aliens, and others.[66]

The political consequences of enacting the Brady bill far outstripped its policy consequences. A crucial swing in favor of the Brady bill occurred in the House between 1988 and 1991, when about thirty-five House members actually switched their votes to support the bill, citing repugnance at the NRA's continued strong-arm tactics. The 1991 House vote thus helped to deflate the NRA's image of invulnerability. According to Rep. Charles E. Schumer (D-NY), a Brady bill supporter, "People realized that there's life after voting against the NRA."[67]

The common partisan pattern observed in other gun bill votes emerged here as well. More Democrats supported the Brady bill than Republicans, but both parties were split. In the House, 184 Democrats supported Brady, with 69 opposed; the Republican split was 54 in favor and 119 opposed.[68] Northern Democrats provided the greatest support for Brady (82 percent); southern Democrats provided the lowest Democratic support (55 percent). As has been true with other gun bill votes, the strongest opposition came from southern, western, and rural representatives regardless of party. Strongest support came from urban representatives.[69]

The election of Bill Clinton put a president in the White House who was much more sympathetic to the aims of gun control proponents. Still, the bill's near-passage in 1992 clearly suggested that the time for its enactment had come, and Clinton's primary focus in his campaign and his first year in office was on a plethora of other domestic policy issues, not including gun control. Indeed, many of Clinton's people were caught by surprise when Clinton began to aggressively promote gun control in late 1993.[70]

The Assault Weapons Ban

In the forefront of the effort to strengthen gun laws in the 1980s and 1990s was the move to regulate or ban various styles of semiautomatic assault weapons. The key event spurring control supporters was a January 1989 schoolyard massacre in Stockton, California, when five children were killed and twenty-nine others were wounded in a shooting spree by a man using a Chinese AK-47 assault rifle. Within weeks, thirty states and many localities were considering bans on these weapons.[71] Two years later, the worst such massacre in American history occurred in Killeen, Texas, when George J. Hennard killed twenty-two people and himself, and wounded twenty-three others, in a cafeteria.

A semiautomatic weapon is one that fires a round with each pull of the trigger, including wooden-stocked hunting rifles. Assault-style semiautomatic weapons have large clips holding twenty to thirty bullets, are more compact in design, have barrels under twenty inches in length, take intermediate-sized cartridges, include extensive use of stampings and plastics, weigh six to ten pounds, and were designed for military use. In addition, they often have pistol grips, grenade launchers, and bayonet fittings.[72]

Responding to advice from within his administration and from the First Lady, George Bush reversed his opposition to assault weapons regulation within the space of a month, announcing a temporary ban on the import of certain assault rifles by executive order in March 1989. The temporary ban was subsequently expanded to include a larger number of weapons, and was then made permanent, earning Bush the ire of the NRA. President Bill Clinton expanded the scope of the import ban in 1993, also by executive order, to include assault-style handguns, like the Uzi.

In November 1993 the Senate passed a ban on the manufacture of nineteen types of assault weapons, but also included a provision allowing gun dealers to sell guns that had already been produced. The measure, added to a crime bill, also exempted 650 types of hunting weapons.[73] That same month, the Senate also passed a measure making it a federal crime to sell handguns to minors.

In the spring of 1994 the House took up the assault weapons ban. From the start, ban supporters shared little optimism that the House would approve the measure. In April, President Clinton weighed in strongly for the ban, enlisting the help of several cabinet secretaries, most notably treasury secretary and gun owner Lloyd Bentsen. Ban supporters received unexpected help from Rep. Henry Hyde (R-IL), a staunch conservative who had opposed gun measures in the past. Thanks in part to Hyde's support, the measure was approved by the Judiciary Committee on April 28, despite the opposition of committee chair Jack Brooks (D-TX).[74]

As the House floor vote approached, bill supporters all but admitted defeat, noting that they were probably fifteen votes shy. Democratic leaders were split on the bill, as House Speaker Tom Foley (D-WA) opposed the measure, while Majority Leader Richard Gephardt (D-MO) favored it. Yet in a stunning finale, the assault weapons ban managed to pass by a two-vote margin, 216–214, on May 5. The drama was heightened when Rep. Andrew Jacobs Jr. (D-IN), at the urging of several colleagues, switched his vote from against to for in the final seconds of the roll call vote. Again more Democrats supported the measure than Republicans, yet party was not the key dividing factor: 177 Democrats were joined by 38 Republicans plus one independent in favor of the bill, with 137 Republicans and 77 Democrats opposed. The bill's strongest opposition came from southern and western representatives.[75]

Because the assault weapons ban was part of a larger crime bill that had passed in different versions in the two houses, a conference committee was called to iron out those differences. Bill supporters initially predicted that the conference committee would complete its work by the end of May. Yet it did not report a bill back to the House and Senate until the end of July. In August opponents actually defeated the bill on the House floor in a procedural vote. Despite this, supporters regrouped and won passage. After similarly tumultuous Senate consideration, the bill, H.R. 3355, was signed by President Clinton on September 13.[76]

In its final form, the assault weapons ban outlawed the sale and possession of nineteen specified types, as well as dozens of other copycat weapons that possessed characteristics similar to the nineteen named types, for ten years. It also specifically exempted over 650 sporting rifles, and limited gun clips to those that could hold no more than ten bullets. Existing assault-style rifles were exempted from the ban, and Congress was given the power to review the inclusion of any additional weapons under the terms of the measure.[77]

Bureaucracy

The Bureau of Alcohol, Tobacco, and Firearms (ATF) was established in 1972 when legal authority related to alcohol, tobacco, firearms, and explosives was transferred from the Internal Revenue Service. Although the bureau's headquarters are located in Washington, DC (under the Treasury Department), its operations are relatively decentralized, as most ATF personnel operate from regional offices around the country. The bureau is organized according to two sections: regulatory enforcement and criminal enforcement. Matters dealing with gun regulations, including licensing, gun tracing, illegal firearms transport and possession, and explosives are handled by the Section on Criminal Enforcement.[78]

During congressional hearings in 1965, for example, Treasury Department officials acknowledged that only five ATF employees were assigned full time to enforce the 1934 and 1938 gun laws. *Congressional Quarterly* reported that in the previous thirty years the Treasury Department had obtained only one conviction involving the improper mailing of firearms to individuals in states that required purchase permits.[79] More recently, government officials from the ATF and elsewhere have admitted that gun smuggling and other illegal gun trafficking have not been high enforcement priorities.[80]

A spokesperson for the ATF reported that during 1980 the bureau conducted only 103 investigations of firearms dealers and that 10 dealer licenses out of the 180,000 nationwide were revoked.[81] In 1985 ATF fielded only 400 inspectors to monitor more than 200,000 gun merchants.[82] In 1994 about 250 agents were responsible for overseeing 280,000 dealers.[83]

Much of ATF's reticence to implement more aggressive gun control enforcement stems from continued NRA harassment. But the ATF also suffered a serious loss of prestige over its handling of a February 1993 raid on the heavily fortified and armed compound of the Branch Davidian cult near Waco, Texas. Four ATF agents were killed and twenty were wounded in an initial assault on the compound, leading to a two-month standoff until ATF and FBI agents stormed the fortress, killing nearly all of those inside. Later in 1993, Vice President Al Gore headed a committee that proposed merging the ATF into the FBI (along with the Drug Enforcement Agency). The plan was dropped, however, and the new ATF director, John Magaw, worked to improve agency morale and effectiveness.[84]

The Clinton administration's support for gun control meant an expanded mission for the ATF. In 1994, for example, ATF extended the prohibition on armor-piercing bullets to certain bullets that formerly could not be fired from handguns. Rapid-fire, "street sweeper" shotguns (developed for military and riot control purposes in South Africa) were subjected to strict ATF regulation on the directive of Treasury Secretary Lloyd Bentsen. Owners of the eighteen thousand such weapons in circulation were required to submit to registration, fingerprinting, and photographing. Dealers of such weapons were also subjected to new fees and regulations.[85]

Judiciary

Gun control does not immediately conjure up an image of judicial activism because the Second Amendment has not been centrally involved in fundamental rights adjudication. This amendment is accorded low status by most legal experts. Irving Brant argued that the Second Amendment "comes to life chiefly on the parade floats of rifle associations and in the propaganda of mail-order houses selling pistols to teenage gangsters."[86] J.W. Peltason wrote that the Second Amendment "was designed to prevent Congress from disarming the state militias, not to prevent it from regulating private ownership of firearms."[87] In state courts, various rulings generally have upheld the power of states to regulate firearms and have associated the right to bear arms with service in a militia.[88]

Supreme Court Cases

There is little constitutional law on gun control, but four Supreme Court cases serve as precedent for interpreting the Second Amendment. The first was *U.S. v. Cruikshank,* 92 U.S. 553 (1876). Cruikshank was charged with thirty-two counts of depriving blacks of their constitutional rights, including two alleging that he had deprived blacks of firearms possession. The Court ruled that the right "of bearing arms for a lawful purpose is not a right granted by the Constitution, nor is it in any manner dependent upon that instrument for its existence." Speaking for the Court, Chief Justice Morrison Waite said that "the Second Amendment declares that it shall not be infringed; but this, as has been seen, means no more than that it shall not be infringed by Congress." At this juncture, the Supreme Court established two principles that it (and lower federal courts) consistently have upheld. First, the Second Amendment does not simply afford any individual the right to bear arms, lawfully or otherwise; second, the Second Amendment is not "incorporated" or applied to the states through the due process and equal protection clauses of the Fourteenth Amendment.

Ten years later, the Supreme Court ruled in *Presser v. Illinois,* 116 U.S. 252 (1886), that an Illinois law that barred paramilitary organizations from drilling or parading in cities or towns without a license from the governor was constitutional. Herman Presser challenged the law after he was arrested for marching his fringe group, Lehr und Wehr Verein, through Chicago streets. In upholding the Illinois statute, the Supreme Court reaffirmed that the Second Amendment did not apply to the states. In his majority opinion Justice William B. Woods discussed the relationship between the citizen, the militia, and the government.

> It is undoubtedly true that all citizens capable of bearing arms constitute the revered reserved military force or reserve militia of the United States as well as the States; and, in view of this prerogative of the General Government, as well as of its general powers, the States cannot, even laying the constitutional provisions in question out of view, prohibit the people from keeping and bearing arms, so as to deprive the United States of their rightful resource for maintaining the public security, and disable the people from performing their duty to the General Government. But, as already stated, we think it clear that sections [of Illinois State law] under consideration do not have this effect.

In 1894 the Supreme Court ruled in *Miller v. Texas,* 153 U.S. 535 (1894), that a Texas law prohibiting the carrying of dangerous weapons did not violate the Second Amendment. Here again the Court said that the right to bear arms did not apply to the states. This reasoning was reaffirmed three years later in the case of *Robertson v. Baldwin,* 165 U.S. 275 (1897).[89]

The final, critical case in this sequence was *U.S. v. Miller,* 307 U.S. 174 (1939). The *Miller* case was founded on a challenge to the National Firearms Act of 1934, which regulated the interstate transport of certain weapons. Jack Miller and Frank Layton, both of whom were convicted of transporting an unregistered 12-gauge sawed-off shotgun (having a barrel less than eighteen inches long) across state lines under the 1934 act, challenged its constitutionality by claiming that the law violated the Second Amendment and also represented an improper use of the commerce power. The Court turned aside those arguments and ruled that the federal taxing power could be used to regulate firearms and that firearms registration was legal. Beyond this, the Supreme Court was unequivocal in saying that the Second Amendment must be interpreted by its "obvious purpose" of ensuring the effectiveness of the militia. Speaking for the Court, Justice James C. McReynolds wrote:

> In the absence of any evidence tending to show that possession or use of a "shotgun having a barrel of less than eighteen inches in length" at this time has some reasonable relationship to the preservation or efficiency of a well regulated militia, we cannot say that the Second Amendment guarantees the right to keep and bear such an instrument. Certainly, it is not within judicial notice that this weapon is any part of the ordinary equipment or that its use could contribute to the common defense.

While the high court's recent decision in *Printz v. United States,* No. 95–1478 (1997), did not involve Second Amendment claims, it was a setback for antigun forces. On a 5–4 vote the ruling, backed by a majority opinion by Justice Scalia and joined by Chief Justice Rehnquist and Justices O'Connor, Kennedy, and Thomas, nullified the background-check provision of the 1993 Brady law because "the very principle of separate state sovereignty" was violated by the requirement that state and local law enforcement officials had to conduct those background checks. The five-day waiting period that the law also imposed on gun sales before they could be completed was not affected, however.[90]

Summary

Since President Johnson's advocacy of gun controls, no president took a leadership role in opposing the NRA until Bill Clinton, with Presidents Reagan and Bush reflecting hostility to gun laws. Congress has enacted only eight gun control laws, which barely addressed the monumental problem of gun ownership, and the Bureau of Alcohol, Tobacco, and Firearms has been a timid enforcer of existing gun control statutes.

The Supreme Court's rulings consistently have paved the way for gun controls by government (with the notable exception of the 1997 decision that struck down mandatory background checks by state authorities), which has caused the NRA to sustain political pressure on Congress, the executive, and state and local officials. The NRA continues to be the pivotal political force in this controversy. The organization's success has come from keeping gun control reforms off the political agenda at both state and national levels. By its very effective use of propaganda and the mythology of the Second Amendment, the NRA has imposed significant political barriers against constitutional arguments favoring gun control. The NRA has held the advantage, even with the passage of the Brady bill and assault weapons ban. If the NRA's financial problems persist, however, its influence is bound to wane.

Notes

My special and most sincere thanks to Grant Podelco, David Solar, and Mark Eichin for their important and valuable assistance. My thanks also to Deborah Dintino, Loretta Padavona, Marcia Carlson, and the Cornell University Law Library.

1. Merrill Jensen, *The New Nation* (New York: Random House, 1962), p. 29.

2. Bernard Bailyn, *The Ideological Origins of the American Revolution* (Cambridge, MA: Belknap Press, 1967), p. 119.

3. Peter B. Feller and Karl L. Gotting, "The Second Amendment: A Second Look," *Northwestern University Law Review* 61 (March-April 1966), p. 51.

4. John Levin, "The Right to Bear Arms: The Development of the American Experience," *Chicago Kent Law Review* 48 (Fall-Winter 1971), p. 155.

5. Harold W. Chase and Craig R. Ducat, eds., *Corwin's The Constitution and What It Means Today* (Princeton, NJ: Princeton University Press, 1973), p. 87.

6. Legislative Reference Service, *The Second Amendment as a Limitation on Federal Firearms Legislation* (Washington, DC: Library of Congress, 1968), p. 6.

7. Ibid., pp. 6–7.

8. John K. Mahon, *The American Militia, Decade of Decisions, 1789–1800,* University of Florida Monographs, Social Science, no. 6 (Gainesville: University of Florida Press, 1960), pp. 20–21.

9. For examples, see Howard I. Bass, "Quilici v. Village of Morton Grove: Ammunition for a National Handgun Ban," *DePaul Law Review* 32 (Winter 1983), pp. 371–398; Lucilius A. Emery, "The Constitutional Right to Keep and Bear Arms," *Harvard Law Review* 28 (1914–1915), pp. 473–477; Eric S. Freibrun, "Banning Handguns: Quilici v. Village of Morton Grove and the Second Amendment," *Washington University Law Quarterly* 60 (Fall 1982), pp. 1087–1118; Ralph J. Rohner, "The Right to Bear Arms: A Phenomenon of Constitutional History," *Catholic University Law Review* 16 (September 1966), pp. 53–80; Roy G. Weatherup, "Standing Armies and Armed Citizens," *Hastings Constitutional Law Quarterly* 2 (1975), pp. 961–1001. For lower federal court rulings, see *American Law Reports, Federal* 37 (Rochester, N.Y.: The Lawyer's Co-Operative Publishing Company, 1978), pp. 706–707.

10. For examples, see David I. Caplan, "Restoring the Balance: The Second Amendment Revisited," *Fordham Urban Law Journal* 5 (Fall 1976), pp. 31–53; David T. Hardy and John Stompoly, "Of Arms and the Law," *Chicago Kent Law Review* 51 (Summer 1974), pp. 62–114.

11. Jill Smolowe, "Go Ahead, Make Our Day," *Time* (May 29, 1995), p. 19.

12. Walter Isaacson, "Leading the Call to Arms," *Time* (April 20, 1981), p. 27.

13. Barbara Vobejda, "NRA Is Said to Lay Off Dozens," *Washington Post* (September 23, 1996); Robert Dreyfuss, "Good Morning, Gun Lobby!" *Mother Jones,* (July/August, 1996), p. 45.

14. Bill Keller, "Powerful Reputation Makes National Rifle Association a Top Gun in Washington," *CQ Weekly Report* (May 9, 1981), p. 799.

15. Spitzer, *The Politics of Gun Control,* pp. 100–103.

16. Quoted in Osha Gray Davidson, *Under Fire: The NRA and the Battle for Gun Control* (New York: Holt, 1993), p. 39.

17. Spitzer, *The Politics of Gun Control,* pp. 105–6.

18. Sam Howe Verhovek, "An Angry Bush Ends His Ties to Rifle Group," *New York Times* (May 11, 1995).

19. Dreyfuss, "Good Morning, Gun Lobby!" pp. 44–45, 47.

20. Spitzer, *The Politics of Gun Control,* p. 106.

21. Jan Hoffman, "Fund Linked to N.R.A. Gave $20,000 for Goetz's Defense," *New York Times* (April 16, 1996).

22. For a survey of various gun groups, see Keller, "Powerful Reputation Makes National Rifle Association a Top Gun in Washington."

23. Walter Isaacson, "Leading the Call to Arms," *Time* (April 20, 1981), p. 27.

24. See, for example, Alan M. Gottlieb, *The Rights of Gun Owners* (Ottawa, IL: Green Hill Publishers, 1981).

25. Raymond S. Rodgers, "The Rhetoric of the NRA," *Vital Speeches of the Day* (October 1, 1983). pp. 758–761.

26. On June 3, 1982, the NRA ran a full-page ad in the *New York Times* in the aftermath of the imposition of martial law in Poland. After noting that all firearms in Poland had been confiscated under the Communist regime, the ad observed that "so long as the Second Amendment is not infringed, what is happening in Poland can never happen in these United States."

27. Wayne King, "Target: The Gun Lobby," *New York Times Magazine* (December 9, 1990), p. 82. The 1994 membership update was obtained from HCI.

28. Tom Goldstein, "Straight Talk About Handguns," *Rolling Stone* (October 28, 1982), p. 23; Spitzer, *The Politics of Gun Control,* pp. 66–69.

29. Richard Hofstadter, "America as a Gun Culture," *American Heritage* (October 1970), p. 4.

30. Fox Butterfield, "Experts Explore Rise in Mass Murder," *New York Times* (October 19, 1991).

31. See Library of Congress, *Gun Control Laws in Foreign Countries* (Washington, DC: Law Library, Library of Congress, 1981).

32. James D. Wright, Peter H. Rossi, and Kathleen Daly, *Under the Gun: Weapons, Crime, and Violence in America* (New York: Aldine, 1983), p. 221.

33. Ibid. Also see Hazel Erskine, "The Polls: Gun Control," *Public Opinion Quarterly* 36 (Fall 1972), pp. 455–469.

34. Leslie McAneny, "Americans tell Congress: Pass Brady Bill, Other Tough Gun Laws," *Gallup Poll Monthly,* March 1993, p.2.

35. NORC, *General Social Surveys* (July 1982), p. 87. The question was, "Would you favor or oppose a law which would require a person to obtain a police permit before he or she could buy a gun?"

36. Howard Schuman and Stanley Presser, "The Attitude-Action Connection and the Issue of Gun Control," in Philip J. Cook, ed., "Gun Control," special issue of *The Annals of the American Academy of Political and Social Science,* vol. 455 (May 1981), pp. 40–47.

37. Spitzer, *The Politics of Gun Control,* p. 119.

38. Wright, Rossi, and Daly, *Under the Gun,* p. 221.

39. *The Gallup Report,* no. 232–233 (January-February 1985), pp. 12–14.

40. *The Public Perspective,* February/March 1997, p. 27.

41. James Wycoff, *Famous Guns that Won the West* (New York: Arco, 1968), pp. 5–6. Also see Harold F. Williamson, *Winchester: The Gun that Won the West* (Washington, DC: Combat Forces Press, 1952).

42. Bob Nichols, "Should a Boy Have a Gun?" *Parents' Magazine* (October 1934), pp. 26, 77.

43. David Lester, *Gun Control: Issues and Answers* (Springfield, IL: Charles C. Thomas, 1984), pp. 98–99, 104. Also see David Lester, "Which States Have Stricter Handgun Control Statutes?" *Psychological Reports* 57 (August 1985), p. 170.

44. Lee Kennett and James L. Anderson, *The Gun in America* (Westport, CT: Greenwood Press, 1975), pp. 197, 204, 211, 227, 238, 243.

45. Steven R. Weisman, "Reagan Tells of Initial Pain and Panic After Being Shot," *New York Times* (April 23, 1981).

46. All references to party platforms are drawn from copies supplied by the national committees.

47. This pattern, as predicted by Lowi's scheme, is observed for the Omnibus Act in Spitzer, *The Presidency and Public Policy,* pp. 65–70.

48. "Gun Controls Extended to Long Guns, Ammunition," *Congressional Quarterly Almanac 1968* (Washington, DC: Congressional Quarterly, 1969), p. 552. The discussion to follow is based on pp. 555–556, 558, 560.

49. Ibid., p. 558.

50. Ibid., p. 560.

51. "Equalization Tax, Ammunition," *Congressional Quarterly Almanac 1969* (Washington, DC: Congressional Quarterly, 1970), pp. 334–336.

52. "Bills on Bullets, 'Designer Drugs' Advance," *Congressional Quarterly Weekly Report* (December 28, 1985), p. 2755.

53. "Federal Gun Law," *Congressional Quarterly Almanac 1985* (Washington, DC: Congressional Quarterly, 1986), pp. 228–230.

54. Also see John Herbers, "Police Groups Reverse Stand and Back Controls on Pistols," *New York Times* (January 31, 1986); Richard Corrigan, "NRA, Using Members, Ads and Money, Hits Police Line in Lobbying Drive," *National Journal* (January 1, 1986), pp. 8–14; Howard Kurtz, "NRA Urging Repeal of Ban on Sale of New Machine Guns," *Washington Post* (August 28, 1986).

55. "NRA, Police Organizations in Tug of War on Gun Bills," *Congressional Quarterly Weekly Report* (March 1, 1986), pp. 502–504.

56. Ibid.; "House Committee Votes 35–0 for Controversial Gun Bill," *Congressional Quarterly Weekly Report* (March 15, 1986), p. 598.

57. Linda Greenhouse, "House Passes Bill Easing Controls on Sale of Guns," *New York Times* (April 11, 1986).

58. "House Votes to Weaken U.S. Gun Control Law," *Congressional Quarterly Weekly Report* (April 12, 1986), p. 783.

59. This change can be taken as evidence of the NRA's increasingly hard line on any and all gun controls. An NRA pamphlet from the time said that a waiting period "could help in reducing crimes of passion and in preventing people with criminal records or dangerous mental illness from acquiring guns." Quoted in Davidson, *Under Fire,* p. 194.

60. Holly Idelson, "Brady Bill Goes to House Floor," *CQ Weekly Report* (November 6, 1993), p. 3048; Holly Idelson, "Congress Responds to Violence; Tackles Guns, Criminals," *CQ Weekly Report* (November 13, 1993), pp. 3127–3130.

61. "Gun Control's Limits," *U.S. News and World Report* (December 6, 1993), p. 25.

62. Clifford Krauss, "Gun Bill Freed From a Logjam; Passage More Likely," *New York Times* (October 28, 1993). The *Times* dubbed the bill's revival "political CPR." Sarah Brady compared it to the Dewey-Truman story, when predictions of Truman's political demise in the 1948 elections proved to be premature. Adam Clymer, "How Jockeying Brought Brady Bill Back to Life," *New York Times* (November 22, 1993); Karen DeWitt, "Five Years Of Struggle By Bradys Pays Off," *New York Times* (November 22, 1993).

63. P.L. 103–159. Phil Kuntz, "Tough-Minded Senate Adopts Crime Crackdown Package," *CQ Weekly Report* (November 20, 1993), pp. 3199–3201; Holly Idelson, "Brady Bill Goes to the Brink, But Senate Finally Clears It," *CQ Weekly Report* (November 27, 1993), pp. 3271–3272.

64. Richard Lacayo, "Beyond the Brady Bill," *Time* (December 20, 1993), p. 29. Data drawn from a 1991 Justice Department survey.

65. "Brady Declares Victory with Namesake Gun-Control Law," *Syracuse Post-Standard* (March 31, 1994).

66. Fox Butterfield, "Maine Case Shows Both Sides of '94 Gun Law," *New York Times* (December 14, 1996).

67. Gwen Ifill, "House Passes Bill to Set 7-Day Wait to Buy Handguns," *New York Times* (May 9, 1991). Prominent defectors from the NRA included Reps. Les AuCoin (D-OR) and Susan Molinari (R-NY). See Steven A. Holmes, "Rifle Lobby Torn by Dissidents and Capitol Defectors," *New York Times* (March 27, 1991).

68. Voting patterns were similar in the Senate, but regional analysis is more statistically variable for Senate votes because of the smaller number of senators. The eleven southern states send only twenty-two senators.

69. Clifford Krauss, "House Votes a 5-Day Pistol Wait but Sets the Measure's Expiration," *New York Times* (November 11, 1993).

70. "President's Jump in Favor of Gun Control Startles Aides," *Syracuse Post-Standard* (December 10, 1993).

71. Robert Reinhold, "Effort to Ban Assault Rifles Gains Momentum," *New York Times* (January 28, 1989); "Bush, a Lifetime NRA Member, Opposes Semiautomatic-Gun Ban," *Syracuse Post-Standard* (February 17, 1989).

72. Nancy Herndon, "Moves to Make Assault Guns Illegal Matched by New Wave of Buying," *Christian Science Monitor* (February 27, 1989); "Deadly Decision on Assault Rifles," *New York Times* (July 26, 1990). The most common of these assault weapons include (in order of popularity) the TEC-9, the AR-15, the Uzi, the MAC-11, the MINI-14, the AK-47, the MAC-10, the SPAS-12, the HK-91, and the HK-93. About fifty types of weapon fall under the assault weapon category, but these ten account for nine-tenths of all assault weapon crime. Jim Stewart and Andrew Alexander, "Assault Weapons Muscling In on the Front Lines of Crime," *Atlanta Journal and Constitution* (May 21, 1989).

73. Clifford Krauss, "Senate Approves Ban on Manufacture of Military-Style Weapons," *New York Times* (November 18, 1993).

74. Katharine Q. Seelye, "In Gun Vote, an Odd Hero for Liberals," *New York Times* (May 7, 1994).

75. Katharine Q. Seelye, "House Approves Bill to Prohibit 19 Assault Arms," *New York Times* (May 6, 1994).

76. For more on the details of this bill, see Spitzer, *The Politics of Gun Control,* pp. 152–57.

77. Neil A. Lewis, "President Foresees Safer U.S.," *New York Times* (August 27, 1994); David Masci, "$30 Billion Anti-Crime Bill Heads to Clinton's Desk," *CQ Weekly Report* (August 27, 1994), p. 2490.

78. *U.S. Government Manual, 1983/84* (Washington, DC: U.S. Government Printing Office, 1983), pp. 437–438; *Federal Regulatory Director, 1981–82* (Washington, DC: Congressional Quarterly Press, 1981), pp. 753–755.

79. "Gun Controls Extended to Long Guns, Ammunition," *Congressional Quarterly Almanac 1968* (Washington, DC: Congressional Quarterly, 1969), p. 552.

80. "U.S. Aides Find Gun Smuggling Is a Low Priority," *New York Times* (September 26, 1985).

81. Keller, "Powerful Reputation Makes National Rifle Association a Top Gun in Washington," p. 801.

82. Mary McGrory, "Pity the Poor, Suffering Gun Owners," *Ithaca Journal* (July 15, 1985).

83. B. Drummond Ayres Jr., "U.S. to Seek Rise in Fee for Gun Dealers," *New York Times* (January 4, 1994).

84. Stephen Labaton, "Firearms Agency Struggles to Rise from the Ashes of the Waco Disaster," *New York Times* (November 5, 1993). The agency was also rocked by repeated charges of sexual harassment and racial discrimination within the agency.

85. "Firearms Agency Bans Armor-Piercing Bullets," *New York Times* (February 6, 1994); Steven A. Holmes, "Treasury Imposes New Regulations on Some Shotguns," *New York Times* (March 1, 1994); "Another Blow to the N.R.A.," *New York Times* (March 2, 1994).

86. Brant, *The Bill of Rights,* p. 486.

87. J.W. Peltason, *Corwin and Peltason's Understanding the Constitution* (Hinsdale, IL.: Dryden Press, 1976), p. 144.

88. National Commission on the Causes and Prevention of Violence, *Firearms and Violence in American Life* (Washington, DC: U.S. Government Printing Office, 1969), pp. 260–262. For a listing of the thirty-five state constitutions that make some mention of a right to bear arms, see Robert Dowlut, "The Right to Bear Arms: Does the Constitution or the Predilection of Judges Reign?" *Oklahoma Law Review* 36 (Winter 1983), pp. 102–105.

89. In *Robertson* the Court said that "the right of the people to keep and bear arms (article 2) is not infringed by laws prohibiting the carrying of concealed weapons."

90. Linda Greenhouse, "Justices Limit Brady Gun Law as Intrusion on States' Rights," *New York Times* (June 28, 1997), pp. 1, 9.

7

Official Language: English-Only versus English-Plus

Raymond Tatalovich

The classic work on nativism in American history, John Higham's *Strangers in the Land,* argues that the movement embodied anti-Catholicism, xenophobia, and a sense that Anglo-Americans were superior.[1] The last period of nativism followed World War I and culminated in passage of the 1924 National Origins Act, which established a quota system that grossly disadvantaged southern European, Asian, and African immigrants to the benefit of northern European immigrants. Today there seems to be another backlash by current residents of the United States—the natives—against the newest wave of immigration from Latin America and especially Mexico. The "official English" movement seeks to gain passage of state and federal laws establishing English as the "official" language of the fifty states and the U.S. Government. Existing reserch[2], however, suggests that apparently a generalized antiforeign sentiment fuels the official English (or "English Only") movement simply because there are so few Spanish-speaking immigrants in the southern states, which account for most of the Official English laws to date.

However, in Arizona, California, Colorado, and Florida perceived grievances against a sizable and growing minority of non-English-speakers gave rise to grassroots movements to enact "official English" measures by popular referenda. By 1985 these four states, which enacted Official English laws by referenda, ranked among the top seven in percentage of Hispanics in the population: New Mexico, 37.8 percent; Texas, 22.8 percent; Califor-

196

nia, 22.1 percent; Arizona, 16.8 percent; Colorado, 11.9 percent; New York, 10.6 percent; Florida, 9.8 percent.[3]

Though Asians were targeted in some localities, the main focus is Spanish-speakers. In no instance, however, did any state adopt Official English legislation for fear that Anglos would be overrun by Spanish-speakers; in 1985 Spanish-speakers represented 7.3 percent of the U.S. population, and the eleven states that adopted Official English statutes during the 1980s are conspicuous for *not* having many Spanish-speaking people or any other linguistic minorities. Less than 1 percent of the population in Alabama, Arkansas, Kentucky, Mississippi, Tennessee, Georgia, North Carolina, South Carolina, and Virginia was Hispanic. In Indiana the figure was below 2 percent, and North Dakota in the mid-1980s had 3,400 Hispanic inhabitants. The statistics are equally low in the four states that acted during the early 1990s. For South Dakota the number of Hispanics was 3,700; there were 5,700 in New Hampshire; the 10,800 figure in Montana represented 1.2 percent of its population, while Louisiana topped this listing with a 1.9 percent Hispanic population in 1985.[4]

Federalism

Before 1980 only three states had adopted official-language laws, and all three were historical curiosities, although like-minded nativist attitudes prompted those enactments: Nebraska (1920), Illinois (in 1923 "American" was codified but changed to "English" in 1969), and Hawaii (1978, when both English and Hawaiian were declared official languages). The Nebraska and Illinois enactments were a backlash from World War I.[5]

Between 1981 and 1990 ten southern and midwestern states established Official English by statute, but politically a more important development was the 1986 referendum in California amending its state constitution for that purpose. Three more referenda in 1988 in Florida, Arizona, and Colorado, along with another in Alabama in 1990, when voters ratified a constitutional amendment proposed by the state legislature, meant that fifteen states had joined the contemporary Official English movement. Since then Louisiana, Montana, South Dakota, New Hampshire, and Wyoming have followed suit, meaning that, by 1997, twenty-three states have official-language laws on the books (Table 7.1). All but a few of these laws are purely symbolic and have no policy implications. For example, section 3–3–31 of the Mississippi code is typical of many language laws: "The English language is the official language of the State of Mississippi."

The enactments of North Carolina, South Carolina, Georgia, Alabama, Mississippi, Arkansas, Kentucky, Tennessee, Indiana, North Dakota, and

Table 7.1

English-Only and English-Plus States

English-Only Enactments*		English-Plus Enactments
Alabama (1990)	Louisiana (1991)	New Mexico (1989)
Arizona (1988)	Mississippi (1987)	Oregon (1989)
Arkansas (1987)	Montana (1995)	Rhode Island (1992)
California (1986)	Nebraska (1920)	Washington (1989)
Colorado (1988)	New Hampshire (1995)	
Florida (1988)	North Carolina (1987)	
Georgia (1996)	North Dakota (1987)	
Hawaii (1978)	South Carolina (1987)	
Illinois (1969)	South Dakota (1995)	
Indiana (1984)	Tennessee (1984)	
Kentucky (1984)	Virginia (1981)	
	Wyoming (1996)	

*The year of enactment (resolution, law, or referendum) is given in parentheses. Georgia in 1986 enacted an Official English resolution but then enacted a law in 1996. The original 1981 law in Virginia was amended in 1986 and again in 1996. In 1991 the Attorney General of Louisiana rendered an interpretation that the state constitution of 1812, when Louisiana entered the Union, contained an Official English provision that its official records reflect the language in use of the United States government.

(to a lesser degree) Virginia were nonissues. Ninety-two percent of senators and 88 percent of representatives in those eleven state legislatures who voted did so in the affirmative, although a detailed analysis showed that in Alabama, Mississippi, North Carolina, and Tennessee white legislators voted in favor, whereas African-Americans voted against or abstained.[6]

The first endorsement of Official English by a locality occurred on November 4, 1980, when 59 percent of Dade County, Florida, voters approved an ordinance whereby "the expenditure of county funds for the purpose of utilizing any language other than English, or promoting any culture other than that of the United States, is prohibited" as well as requiring that "all county governmental meetings, hearings and publications shall be in the English language only."[7] It repealed a 1973 resolution declaring Dade County to be "bilingual and bicultural" and thus established an English-only policy that survived until its repeal by the Dade County Commission on May 18, 1992.

Though San Francisco never adopted an Official English law, what fueled the movement in California was a 1983 battle in that city over the required use of Chinese and Spanish as well as English ballots pursuant to a federal court consent decree. A conservative Democratic member of the San Francisco Board of Supervisors, Quentin Kopp, preferred to urge those voters to learn English, but his colleagues backed down after being lobbied by Chinese activists, whereupon Kopp formed a Committee for Ballots in English to collect signatures to put an advisory question on the ballot. The newly formed organization U.S. English joined forces with Kopp, and on November 8, 1983, Proposition O won 62 percent of the vote in a city known for its social liberalism.[8]

In 1986 language conflict engulfed Monterey Park, just east of Los Angeles, when it passed an Official English ordinance—only the second community in the state (after Fillmore) to do so. It was immediately challenged by the ad hoc Coalition for Harmony in Monterey Park (CHAMP), and the city council rescinded the measure, only to have its supporters turn their energies to enacting an ordinance to require more English on business signs.[9] The next year controversy erupted in Lowell, Massachusetts, because of its growing number of Cambodians (the second largest concentration after Long Beach, California). What precipitated the issue was a state bilingual education law that required Lowell to provide instruction in Spanish, Portuguese, Khmer, Lao, and Vietnamese as well as undertake efforts to integrate the new immigrant students within the school system. In the midst of this turmoil, an Official English referendum was approved by Lowell voters by nearly a three-to-one margin in 1989.[10]

In Suffolk County, a suburban area near New York City, one Official English bill was defeated in 1989, but seven years later the Suffolk County Legislature voted 10–5 (with three abstentions) to so amend the county charter, subject to referendum approval by the voters. (Meanwhile, New York City's Republican mayor, Rudolph W. Giuliani, remained opposed to Official English as was the Republican governor, George E. Pataki. Although Suffolk County is a GOP stronghold, nonetheless its county executive, Robert J. Gaffney (also a Republican), vetoed the measure.11 In Illinois two working-class suburbs of Chicago—Addison in 1986 and Lombard in 1995—passed Official English laws.[12] All told, forty-one counties and fifteen cities so far have passed Official English measures.

On the other hand, English-plus laws, or resolutions codifying official multilingualism, were adopted in 1989 by New Mexico, Washington, and Oregon, and in 1992 by Rhode Island. Major cities such as Atlanta, Cleveland, Dallas, San Antonio, Tucson, and Washington, DC, also adopted English-plus measures.

Judiciary

Going to the courts to challenge Official English is an obvious strategy, since there would seem to be a constitutional clash with First Amendment free speech and civil liberties guarantees. Any long-term societal benefits from an official language are less immediate, and futuristic threats of linguistic separatism akin to the Quebec situation are too remote, when compared to actual episodes of citizens or immigrants being denied a personal liberty. For this reason judges are unlikely to side with Official English movements.

In Huntington Park, California, a rule that municipal court employees speak only English during working hours was overturned by the Ninth Circuit Court in *Gutierrez v. Municipal Court of the Southeast Judicial District,* 838 F.2d 1031, 9th Cir. (1988). A court interpreter filed suit and district court judge Richard A. Gadbois Jr., though a Reagan appointee, issued a preliminary injunction in May of 1985 against the Judicial District of Los Angeles County on the grounds that the work rule likely violated Title VII of the 1964 Civil Rights Act. On appeal, the opinion of the appeals court was authored by Judge Stephen Roy Reinhardt, known to be a liberal Carter appointee. Reinhardt rejected the appellants' arguments that the United States and California were English-speaking jurisdictions, that the rule was needed to prevent the workplace from becoming a "tower of Babel," that it promoted racial harmony, and that supervisors who were not bilingual could not oversee those subordinates who were.

The final defense, that the English-only rule was required by Article III, section 6 of the California Constitution, was rejected on three grounds. First, the provision did not extend to the workplace: "While section 6 may conceivably have some concrete application to official government communications, if and when the measure is appropriately implemented by the state legislature, it appears otherwise to be primarily a symbolic statement concerning the importance of preserving, protecting, and strengthening the English language." Second, the court drew a distinction between official and private uses of language: "Although the precise question of private conversations among public employees was not addressed in the ballot arguments, it appears that the distinction the proponents attempted to draw was between official communications and private affairs. While the initiative addressed . . . the former subject, most if not all of the speech barred here would fall in the latter category." Third, the adoption of a constitutional amendment does not "*ipso facto* create a business necessity. A state enactment cannot constitute a business justification for the adoption of a discriminatory rule unless the state measure itself meets the business necessity test; otherwise employers could justify discriminatory regulations by relying on state laws that encourage or require discriminatory conduct."[13]

When the defendants requested a rehearing of the case by the Ninth Circuit en banc, the refusal by the majority provoked a sharp dissent by circuit judge J. Alex Kozinski, who was joined by David R. Thompson and Diarmuid O'Scannlain. Kozinski charged that "by giving employees the nearly absolute right to speak a language other than English, the panel's opinion will exacerbate ethnic tensions and force employers to establish separate supervisory tracks for employees who choose to speak another language during working hours."[14]

One case that headed to the Supreme Court involved the Arizona referendum. In early 1990 U.S. district judge Paul Rosenblatt, another Reagan appointee, ruled on a lawsuit brought by Maria-Kelly Yniguez, a bilingual employee of the Risk Management Division of the Arizona Department of Administration. Her action came only two days after Election Day in 1988, when the referenda was narrowly passed, and Yniguez asked Rosenblatt to declare Official English unconstitutional and to block its implementation. "I am afraid to speak Spanish at my work place. And I will not do so until I have a court order," said Yniguez, who had actively opposed Proposition 106.[15]

Rosenblatt invalidated the law on free speech grounds. Because the law "is a prohibition on the use of any language other than English by all officers and employees of all political subdivisions in Arizona while performing their official duties," he argued that it could prevent legislators from talking to their constituents or judges from carrying out official duties, such as performing marriages in a language other than English.[16]

On appeal, a perverse series of events caused the Supreme Court to reverse the district court. In *Arizonans for Official English v. Yniguez*, no. 95–974 (1997), the high court did not rule on the merits but rather took issue with procedural issues that the district and appellate courts chose to ignore (agreeing with an amicus brief from U.S. English that the lower court ruling be vacated or reversed). Speaking for a unanimous court, the thirty-five-page opinion by Justice Ginsberg argued that because Ms. Yniguez had resigned before the appeals court ruled in 1994, that court lacked jurisdiction to consider the case. Ginsberg said that the initial mistake was that the lower courts refused a request from the Arizona attorney general to allow the Arizona Supreme Court to interpret the English-only amendment. "Warnings against premature adjudication of constitutional questions bear heightened attention when a Federal court is asked to invalidate a State's law, for the Federal tribunal risks friction-generating error when it endeavors to construe a novel state Act not yet reviewed by the State's highest court," Ginsberg wrote.

That mistake was later compounded by then-governor Rose Mofford, a Democrat who had opposed the Official English referendum, when she refused to appeal the district court ruling, but the Ninth Circuit Court granted Arizonans for Official English, which had spearheaded the voter petition drive, the right to act as appellants in this case. Justice Ginsberg said that the court had "grave doubts" about the "standing" of that private group, but this secondary question was rendered moot because Ms. Yniguez had resigned from her state job on April 25, 1990, the day before the appeals court placed the case on its docket. It took seventeen months before the appeals court learned that Ms. Yniguez had resigned, yet even so, the appellate tribunal proceeded to rule that the amendment was unconstitutional on the theory, which Ginsburg disputed, that Ms. Yniguez still had a claim for damages against Arizona for violating her free speech guarantees.[17] Thus the Supreme Court has yet to decide on the merits of Official English laws and whether their enforcement infringes upon the First Amendment.

Interest Groups

Today there is little doubt that the current activism at the state and federal levels is being orchestrated by a single-issue group—U.S. English. A 1995 issue of its newsletter, which summarized efforts within the states to achieve Official English laws, took credit for the fact that "[i]n just three months, South Dakota, Montana and New Hampshire all enacted U.S. ENGLISH-sponsored legislation" to codify an official language.[18]

U.S. English

Organized in 1983, U.S. English in mid-1995 boasted a membership of 620,000.[19] Its goals statement declares: "A common language benefits a nation and all its people. In the United States, the language bond is more important than in most other nations because Americans are remarkably diverse in origin, race, lifestyle, ethnicity, religion, and culture." Thus its objectives are two: "to make English the official language of the United States Government and to guarantee the right for all our people to learn English."[20] Some quite prominent Americans are listed as members of its advisory board, including novelist Saul Bellow, former senators Barry Goldwater (R-AZ) and Eugene J. McCarthy (D-MN), actors Arnold Schwarzenegger and Charlton Heston, golfer Arnold Palmer, famed heart surgeon Denton Cooley, MD, and former Defense Secretary James Schlesinger.[21] Longtime CBS-TV news anchorman Walter Cronkite also gave his blessings but resigned from the advisory board in 1988 after racist allegations surfaced in the Arizona referendum battle.

In each of the four states where grassroots activists gathered sufficient petition signatures to force a ballot referendum, they created single-issue organizations to promote their agenda: Arizonans for Official English, the California English Committee, the Colorado Official English Committee, and Florida English. Two lesser-known groups with the same legislative agenda are English First and the American Ethnic Coalition (the latter organization's activities are limited to Texas).

The beginnings of U.S. English are traced to Petoskey, Michigan, where John H. Tanton, MD, began an ophthalmology practice in the early 1960s. Tanton had worked with the Planned Parenthood Federation and later with Zero Population Growth (ZPG), having served as its president during 1975–77. When he failed to convince the ZPG board of directors to deal with immigration, he founded another group called Federation for American Immigration Reform (FAIR), which today advocates a moratorium on immigration to the United States. Later he joined Senator S.I. Hayakawa (R-CA) to form U.S. English. An executive director of ZPG said that "there is a path" from organizations like ZPG and Planned Parenthood to concerns about immigration and language.[22]

S.I. Hayakawa was the obscure president of San Francisco State College, but his tough approach to demonstrators during the era of student antiwar protests (1969–1973) catapulted him to political fame. A semanticist by profession, his fears that English was being eroded led Hayakawa to champion the cause of U.S. English. In 1981 he introduced Senate Joint Resolution 72, offering an English Language Amendment (ELA), but no action was taken. Three years later hearings were held on another version, Senate Joint Resolution 167, authored by Senator Walter Huddleston (D-KY), who defended the need for his measure: "For the last fifteen years, we have experienced a growing resistance to the acceptance of our historic language, an antagonistic questioning of the melting pot philosophy that has traditionally helped speed newcomers into the American mainstream."[23]

As to who was undermining Americas' historic commitment to the melting pot, Hayakawa laid the blame squarely on Spanish-speakers—or more precisely, their leadership. He charged that "[t]he ethnic chauvinism of the present Hispanic leadership is an unhealthy trend in present-day America. It threatens a division perhaps more ominous in the long run than the division between blacks and whites." He added: "But the present politically ambitious 'Hispanic Caucus' looks forward to a destiny for Spanish-speaking Americans separate from that of Anglo-, Italian-, Polish-, Greek-, Lebanese-, Chinese-, and Afro-Americans, and all the rest of us who rejoice in our ethnic diversity." The opposition to English, he claimed, consisted solely of Hispanics and misguided teachers of bilingual education: "It is not without significance that pressure against English language legislation does not come from any immigrant group other than the Hispanic. . . . The only people who have any quarrel with the English language are the Hispanics—at least the Hispanic politicians and 'bilingual' teachers and lobbying organizations."[24]

EPIC

Originally the counteroffensive against U.S. English was orchestrated by the English Plus Information Clearinghouse (EPIC), formed in October of 1987 under the auspices of the National Immigration, Refugee, and Citizenship Forum and the Joint National Committee for Languages (JNCL). The National Immigration, Refugee, and Citizenship Forum included more than one hundred national and community groups committed to "democratic pluralism," and JNCL represented thirty-five national language associations dedicated to "the advancement of language study in the United States."[25] Over time its original twenty-seven affiliated groups expanded to fifty-six and then dropped to forty-five.

In addition to the two founding organizations, the forty-five currently enrolled organizations include the ACLU and the leftist National Lawyers Guild, the American Jewish Committee and the American Jewish Congress, the Disciples of Christ, and the National Education Association, plus specialists in language instruction—the National Association for Bilingual Education (NABE), the National Council of Teachers of English (NCTE), the American Council on the Teaching of Foreign Languages, and Teachers of English to Speakers of Other Languages (TESOL). Most prominent are advocacy groups for peoples of Mexican, Puerto Rican, Japanese, Chinese, and Haitian ancestry. Probably eighteen groups may be categorized as ethnic advocacy groups, including the League of United Latin American Citizens, Mexican American Legal Defense and Education Fund (MALDEF), National Association of Latino Elected Officials, National Council of La Raza (NCLR), National Puerto Rican Coalition, Japanese American Citizens League, and Organization of Chinese Americans. Of the remainder, at least four were community-based single-issue groups and two were student advocacy groups, but note that only one union-based organization (IRATE, or the Coalition of Massachusetts Trade Unions for Immigration Rights, Advocacy, Training and Education) joined, and no national or local business or trade associations were members.[26]

The philosophy behind EPIC states that "the core of the strength and vitality of the United States is the diversity of our people, and our constitutional commitment to equal protection under the law," meaning that the national interest requires that all Americans have full "access to effective opportunities to acquire strong English proficiency *plus* mastery of a second or multiple languages." The preamble to the resolution adopted by its founding organizations declares that "English is and will remain the primary language of the United States" but, nonetheless, our "fundamental values and national documents ensure tolerance and respect for diversity and guarantee all persons equal protection under the law." Therefore, "English Only and other restrictionist language legislation have the potential for abridging the citizen's right to vote, eroding other civil rights, fostering governmental interference in private activity and free commerce, and causing social disunity." EPIC is "committed to the principles of democratic and cultural pluralism and encourages respect for the cultural and linguistic heritages of all members of our society."[27]

The organizations aligned with EPIC generally reflect the pattern of ad hoc single-issue coalitions that opposed Official English in the battles over state referenda: Arizona English, Californians United Committee Against Proposition 63, Colorado Unity, and Speak Up Now for Florida. The state interests arrayed against Official English included bilingual educators, the Roman Catholic hierarchy, mainstream Protestant and Jewish churches, the ACLU or its local affiliates, Hispanic leaders and activists, and high-profile Democratic politicians.

State GOP organizations endorsed Official English in Arizona and Texas; 93 percent of the state senators and 96 percent of the state representatives who cosponsored Official English bills in California, Colorado, and Arizona were Republicans.[28] But some Republican politicians went on record as opposing Official English: Governors George Deukmejian (R-CA) and Evan Mecham (R-AZ) and U.S. Senators Bill Armstrong (R-CO) and John McCain (R-AZ). In light of his 1994 gubernatorial reelection campaign, which demonized illegal aliens, it is noteworthy that Pete Wilson (R-CA), as then a U.S. Senator, had endorsed the California Official English referendum in 1986.

The political debate over Official English was subdued or nonexistent in the statutory states (where legislatures passed those laws). But the public rhetoric was explosive during the referenda campaigns, as invariably the charge of racism was hurled against the advocates of English-only. Nowhere else did it reach such a fever pitch as in Arizona. The degree of controversy surrounding its Proposition 106 was due to the punitive nature of the referendum proposal and, more important, to the revelations unearthed in the now-famous Tanton Memo, by the cofounder of U.S. English. The Tanton Memo was inspired to stimulate discussions at the WITAN IV conference on the consequences of immigration to California and the United States. Tanton answered his own rhetorical question—"Is apartheid in southern California's future?"—this way:

> In the California of 2030, the non-Hispanic whites and Asians will own the property, have the good jobs and education, speak one language and be mostly Protestant and "other." The blacks and Hispanics will have the poor jobs, will lack education, own little property, speak another language and will be mainly Catholic. Will there be strength in this diversity? Or will this prove a social and political San Andreas Fault?[29]

Immediately leaders of the anti–Proposition 106 campaign in Arizona labeled the Tanton Memo as "the Nazi memo" and said that its content resembled the discussions held by Adolf Hitler and his advisers as they plotted the rise of Nazism. According to William Meek, a political consultant with the opposition forces: "I think it's clear he's a racist. . . . He's a racist in the pure sense, because he's sitting there looking at demographic information and simply assuming that because there's going to be more of them [minorities] than there are of us, that there's going to be a conflict."[30]

This political bombshell led to the resignation of Walter Cronkite, once the anchorman for the CBS Evening News, from the advisory board of U.S. English and caused its president, Linda Chavez, to resign as well. Chavez viewed the Tanton Memo as "anti-Catholic" and "anti-Hispanic"; her decision also was prompted by information she received from a journalist about financial contributions to U.S. English, FAIR, and Population Environment Balance. When told by reporter James Crawford,[31] who opposes Official English, that those monies came from people who advocated forced sterilization and who subsidized the reprinting of *Camp of the Saints,* which Chavez labeled "a paranoid, racist fantasy" about "Third World people sort of taking over the world," she said, "In a certain point in political life, you realize that perceptions are reality. I just don't want to be in a position to defend those actions."[32] All this ultimately had an effect on Tanton, who stepped down from his position with U.S. English.

Public Opinion

The level of accusations and countercharges in Arizona had an effect on the electorate; its referendum barely passed. But the decisive vote outcomes in California (73 percent voted for Official English), Colorado (64 percent), Florida (84 percent), and Alabama (89 percent) signaled that Official English has substantial public support. County votes in these five Official English referenda were subjected to statistical analysis and the results were consistent if not conclusive: in California, Colorado, and Florida, counties with proportionately larger numbers of Spanish-speakers gave *less* support to the English-only propositions, and residents with a college education also gave less support to those propositions in California and Colorado. The strongest predictor in Alabama, Arizona, and California, however, was a political variable—counties that had voted strongly for President Reagan's reelection in 1984 also gave higher levels of support to Official English. This "Reagan variable" also was second-ranked in importance in Colorado and Florida, which gives support to Jack Citrin's view that "the political right is the core of the 'official language' movement, but the movement attracts support from all along the ideological spectrum."[33]

Dyste examined a California poll three months before the November 1986 referendum and determined that "the strongest supporters of Proposition 63 were Whites, conservatives, and [the] less educated . . . [while the] strongest opponents were Hispanics and Asians, the highly educated . . . and liberals."[34] A multivariate analysis of 1986 California exit polls indicated to Citrin and his associates "widespread support for the English Language Amendment in almost every segment of the electorate. To be sure, Hispanic and Asian voters were less likely to approve Proposition 63 than the other two ethnic groups, but blacks and whites did not differ significantly in their support." Any "cracks in the general consensus about the desirability of 'official English' also were strongly related to party and ideology. Registered Republicans were more likely than registered Democrats to vote for Proposition 63. . . . And this divergence in outlook grows even larger when we compare voters grouped by their evaluation of President Reagan's job performance . . . or other indicators of 'social' liberalism-conservatism."[35]

A bivariate examination of 1988 exit polling on "English as the only official language of the U.S." led Schmid to conclude that "the most striking finding is the marked difference in support for this legislation between Hispanics and Anglos at all educational and income categories in both California and Texas." Moreover, in both states, more than three-fourths of Republicans and conservatives favored Official English, whereas the "only Anglo group [in California] where the majority consistently opposed Official English was among self-reported liberals."[36] Since Proposition 63 had obtained majority approval from whites (72 percent), blacks (67 percent), and Asians (58 percent) but not from most Hispanics,[37] Sonntag revisited this question based on a 1989 California poll and concluded that "the official English issue is not dividing the population along language lines; indeed, there is broad consensus *for* official English legislation."[38] In other words, by 1989 Sonntag found that two-thirds of blacks (66.7 percent) and Asians (67.3 percent) but *also* nearly as many Hispanics (63.9 percent) favored the passage of Proposition 63.

The debate over Official English is likely related to a larger debate over nationalism. What may prove to be seminal research is a study by Citrin and his associates that identified three strains of nationalism in the United States: (1) cosmopolitan liberalism, based on the "melting pot" metaphor, (2) nativism, and (3) multiculturalism. They determined that "cosmopolitan liberalism remains the dominant outlook. The available evidence about the attitudes of blacks and Hispanics indicates somewhat more support for the multicultural perspective, but even among these segments of the general public the symbolic hold of the national creed of individualism and equality of opportunity is impressive." But "[c]oexisting with this general belief in the cosmopolitan liberal virtues . . . is a noticeable acceptance of ideas traditionally associated with nativism, specifically that to be truly American one must speak English and believe in God."[39]

Frendreis and Tatalovich used the same 1992 NES data, but integrated attitudinal questions on nationalism with standard SES and political variables, in order to evaluate whether support is grounded more in consensual values or in conflicting personal attributes.[40] Overall, 65 percent of the NES respondents answered in the affirmative when asked: "Do you favor a law making English the official language of the United States, meaning government business would be conducted in English only, or do you oppose such a law?" But virtually all support for Official English stemmed from cultural attitudes about what makes a good American (speaking English and treating people equally) and support for the melting pot concept. Ideology, party identification, and socioeconomic background had virtually no independent effect on attitudes after taking account of those cultural variables. Frendreis and Tatalovich also tried various techniques to assess if racism (including attitudes toward Hispanics) underlies popular support for Official English, but found absolutely no evidence to support the racism hypothesis, as Tatalovich had argued previously.[41]

Undoubtedly linguistic politics today is intertwined with the immigration issue. Negative attitudes toward the "new" immigrants have been recorded in surveys during the 1990s. In June of 1993 a New York Times/CBS News poll found that 61 percent felt that immigration should be decreased; moreover, the number of respondents saying that "most of the people who have moved to the United States in the last few years are here illegally" rose from 49 percent in 1986 to 68 percent in 1993.[42] A Gallup poll in July 1993 found that 65 percent favored a reduction in immigration, a view expressed by 49 percent in 1986, by 42 percent in 1977, and only 33 percent in 1965. Majorities also believed that immigrants "mostly threaten American culture" or "cost the taxpayers too much by using government services like public education and medical services." Such resentment was targeted at recent immigrants, not older immigrant groups: 62 percent said there are "too many" immigrants from Latin American and Asian countries, whereas 52 percent indicated that the number from Europe was "about right." Those most hostile toward Latin American immigration tended also to disapprove of President Clinton and were conservatives, Republicans, southerners, and whites.[43]

Congress

In July 1992 Senator Robert C. Byrd (D-WV) made the point during floor debate that the United States should stop accepting immigrants who do not speak English. "I pick up the telephone and call the local garage," he said. "I can't understand the person on the other side of the line. I'm not sure he can understand me. They're all over the place, and they don't speak English. We want more of this?" Later Byrd apologized for the remark, saying, "I regret that in the heat of the moment I spoke unwisely."[44] Whether or not Byrd saw the error of his ways, others were not apologetic for insisting that Americans speak English and that English be our official language.

By mid-1995 more than one-third of the House members had signed on as cosponsors of H.R. 123, whose chief sponsors were the late Congressman Bill Emerson (R-MO) and Senator Richard Shelby (R-AL). First introduced on January 5, 1993, this bill stalled in committee because the Democratic Party controlled Congress and the White House. But events soon confirmed my earlier prognosis that Official English would become a partisan issue once it appeared on the national political scene.[45]

H.R. 123, known as the Language of Government Act of 1995, at last count drew cosponsors from among 148 Republicans but only 16 Democrats. Analysis of those backing H.R. 123 (Table 7.2) indicates a linkage between the states that codified English and this effort in Congress to establish an official language.

In 1993 a similar bill was introduced with seventy-seven Republicans and sixteen Democrats as sponsors. Since the partisan makeup among sponsors at that time was 83 percent Republican and 17 percent Democrat, the appeal for this kind of legislation has grown only because the Republicans took control of the 104th Congress.[46] The other constant in the political calculus is the heavy representation of sponsors—three-fifths—from states with existing Official English laws. As with state legislative sponsorship, some bipartisanship exists in the statutory states, but *all* congressional sponsors from the four referendum states are Republicans, which also is consistent with the findings on state legislative sponsorship.[47]

Table 7.2

Sponsorship and Voting on H.R. 123 by the 105th Congress

| | Sponsorship | | Roll Call Vote | | | |
| | Republicans | Democrats | Republicans | | Democrats | |
			Yes	No	Yes	No
Referendum States	34 (100%)	0(0%)	44 (96%)	2 (4%)	0 (0%)	35 (100%)
Statutory States	57 (83%)	12 (17%)	64 (100%)	0 (0%)	12 (24%)	38 (76%)
Other States	57 (93%)	4 (7%)	115 (97%)	6 (3%)	24 (22%)	87 (78%)
Totals	148 (90%)	16 (10%)	223 (97%)	8 (3%)	36 (18%)	160 (82%)

This total does not include one independent, Representative Bernard Sanders of Vermont, although he reliably votes with the Democratic Party; for example, in electing the Speaker he votes for the Democratic candidate. Thus the margin of the final roll call was actually 259–169.

Source: Data on sponsors in *U.S. English Update* 12, no. 2 (Summer 1995), p. 5.

As Quebec voters cast ballots on a 1995 referendum to secede from Canada (it was barely defeated), Speaker Newt Gingrich (R-GA) made his views known. "If we don't insist on renewing our civilization, starting with insisting on English as a common language, we are just going to devour this country. Watch the Canadian results today," he told a business forum in Atlanta. The Quebec referendum was "a serious warning to all Americans that allowing bilingualism to continue to grow is very dangerous and that we should insist on English as a common language," he later told reporters.[48] Gingrich added that a bill would be considered in 1996, which Senate Majority Leader Robert Dole (R-KS) also endorsed, making English the official language of the United States.

Sensing the political momentum behind Official English, in November of 1995 the *New York Times* repeated its opposition because "to require it [English] is blatantly unfriendly, un-American and perhaps an unconstitutional abridgment of free speech." While the paper acknowledged that the Emerson-Shelby bill would allow "common sense" allowances for foreign languages where government provides health and safety services, the editorial was unpersuaded: "But what about tax collectors? How about foreigners seeking help, even seeking asylum?"[49]

Nine months later, on August 1, 1996, the House voted 259–169 to approve H.R. 123 (see Table 7.2). Overall, 82 percent of the Democrats voted nay, whereas 97 percent of Republicans voted yea, and the partisan divide was especially large among the representatives from referendum states. Every voting Democrat from the states where Official English was codified by popular initiative voted against this legislation, whereas the bill won a sizable minority of Democrats in the statutory states and elsewhere. In a rare speech on the floor of the House of Representatives, Speaker Newt Gingrich warned that schools in California teach academic subjects in more than eighty languages and that Chicago schools use one hundred languages. "This isn't bilingualism," he said. "This is a level of confusion, which if it was allowed to develop for another 20 or 30 years would literally lead, I think, to the decay of the core parts of our civilization."[50] Most Democrats believed the bill was unnecessary, unconstitutional, or bigoted, although the legislative sponsors tried to widen its appeal by exempting several documents, including those dealing with national security, international trade, public health and safety, the census, and foreign phrases such as "E Pluribus Unum" on coins and paper money. This bill never reached the Senate in 1996.

Presidency

In the crowded Republican primary field of presidential contenders in 1996, those who supported declaring English the official language of the United States were Governor Pete Wilson (R-CA), Senator Richard Lugar (R-IN), Patrick Buchanan, the columnist and former Nixon speechwriter, and Senate Majority Party Leader Robert Dole (R-KS). Since the Republican primaries attract highly motivated conservatives, and because of the growing importance of the Christian Right to GOP electoral successes in 1994, Dole became outspoken on some "social" issues to solidify his conservative credentials. One was Official English. In September of 1995 he addressed the national convention of the American Legion, telling the veterans that multilingual education should be ended. "Insisting that all our citizens are fluent in English is a welcoming act of inclusion, and insist we must," he declared. "We need the glue of language to help hold us together. We must stop the practice of multilingual education as a means of instilling ethnic pride or as a therapy for low self-esteem or out of elitist guilt over a culture built on the traditions of the West."[51]

What Dole did not mention was the issue that catapulted the language question onto the national political stage: immigration. It takes somebody to dramatize the political power of an issue, and that person was fellow Republican Pete Wilson, governor of California. In his uphill battle for reelection in 1994 Wilson exploited the issue of illegal immigration at a time when a referendum campaign was under way in California to deny undocumented immigrants government benefits. Also heading to the November 1994 ballot in California was a petition drive by Save Our State; this group

red 600,000 signatures for Proposition 187, which would deny
education and nonemergency medical aid to illegal aliens and require
teachers, health care workers, and the police to report any "apparent illegal
immigrants" to federal authorities. Wilson endorsed Proposition 187 (which
passed), and his ploy worked; he soundly defeated his Democratic opponent,
who was against the referendum, and forced incumbent Senator Dianne
Feinstein (D-CA), who expressed concerns about unrestricted immigration
but avoided endorsing Proposition 187, to take a stand. Feinstein narrowly
edged out her GOP rival even though she finally opposed the referendum as
too draconian a measure.

President Clinton was governor when the Arkansas Official English law
was passed, but he disavowed that legislation during his first presidential
campaign. In April 1992 he gave this response to a question via satellite
from a reporter attending the annual meeting of the National Association of
Hispanic Journalists: "I probably shouldn't have signed the one that passed,
but it was passed by a veto-proof majority," Clinton said. "I agreed to sign
it only after we changed the law to make it clearer that it would not affect
bilingual education, something that I have always strongly supported."[52]

Four years later, during Clinton's second presidential campaign, U.S.
English informed its membership about "another" Clinton "flip-flop" on
Official English. Side by side it reprinted two letters. One was an April 10,
1987, letter from Governor Clinton to U.S. English, which stated: "Thank
you for taking the time to express your support for the recent passage of
Arkansas Act 40 which makes English the official language of Arkansas."
It goes on: "I know that Representative Fairchild [a legislative sponsor of
the bill] is pleased, as I am, with the rapid passage of this bill. I agree with
you that facility with English provides a common and necessary bond for
all Americans." But another letter of August 1, 1996, from President Clinton to House Speaker Newt Gingrich, strongly opposed Official English
legislation. It read in part:

> I strongly urge the Congress to reject passage of H.R. 123, the English
> Language Empowerment Act. English is currently acknowledged as the com-
> mon language of the United States throughout the world. There is no need for
> this divisive provision that seeks to require the Federal Government to con-
> duct the vast majority of official business in English only and I intend to veto
> it if passed.[53]

President Clinton objected to Official English on civil liberties and equal
opportunity grounds, but he did not address the issue of overriding importance to its advocates—English as a social glue to avoid societal fragmenta-
tion. It was the GOP contender who preferred to talk about English as

undergirding national unity, and a newsletter from U.S. English took note that "[p]residential candidate Bob Dole endorsed Official English as part of his campaign last year and was a supporter of S. 356 (our Official English bill) while in the Senate."[54]

Bureaucracy

Perhaps the defining moment that polarized the debate over English-only versus English-plus came when Secretary of Education William J. Bennett delivered an attack on bilingual education in New York City on September 26, 1985. Bennett began his statement with the following: "Our common language is, of course, English. And our common task is to ensure that our non-English-speaking children learn this common language." Government has not fulfilled that responsibility, Bennett claimed, and he blamed a 1975 decision by the Department of Health, Education, and Welfare "to require that educational programs for non-English-speaking students be conducted in large part *in the student's native language,* as virtually the only approved method of remedying discrimination." Entrenched bureaucratic interests had caused "this fateful turn" in educational policy, he said as he continued his assault: "We had lost sight of the goal of learning *English* as the key to equal educational opportunity. Indeed, H.E.W. increasingly emphasized bilingual education as a way of enhancing students' knowledge of their native language and culture. Bilingual education was no longer seen so much as a means to ensure that students learned English, or as a transitional method until students learned English. Rather, it became an emblem of cultural pride, a means of producing a positive self-image in the student."[55]

It was shortly thereafter when the Spanish-American League against Discrimination (SALAD), a Miami group, issued a document that "would become a blue-print for the English Plus approach to combating language restrictionism." In part it read:

> We fear that Secretary Bennett has lost sight of the fact that English is a *key* to equal educational opportunity, necessary but not sufficient. English by itself is not enough. Not English Only, English *Plus!* . . .
> Bennett is wrong. We won't accept English Only for our children. We want English plus. English plus math. Plus science. Plus social sciences. Plus equal educational opportunities. English plus competence in the home language. Tell Bennett to enforce bilingual education and civil rights laws you enacted, or tell the President he cannot do his job. English Plus for everyone![56]

Bennett's rhetoric was softened by his successor in the post of education secretary, but it was not until the Clinton administration that this cabinet officer defended bilingual education programs. In the 1996 presidential campaign, when GOP nominee Bob Dole and Speaker Newt Gingrich (R-GA) were advocating Official English legislation, Secretary of Education Richard W. Riley charged that "these efforts to make English the 'official' language and to eliminate programs that teach English are more about politics than improving education."[57]

However, others dissented from the Clinton administration line. One leading proponent of both immigration restrictions and a renewed "Americanization" campaign was Barbara Jordan, an African-American, former congresswoman (D-TX), and faculty member at the University of Texas, whom Clinton appointed to chair the U.S. Commission on Immigration Reform. Created by the Immigration Act of 1990 (P.L. 101–649), the commission produced a two-volume report on immigration that expressed a decidedly conservative viewpoint. In 1994 the commission recommended "that illegal aliens should not be eligible for any publicly-funded services or assistance except those made available on an emergency basis or for similar compelling reasons to protect public health and safety . . . or to conform to constitutional requirements."[58] Prospective employers would be required to verify a job applicant's immigration status through a computer registry based on Social Security and Immigration and Naturalization Service files. And the other recommendations included short-term federal aid to "offset at least a portion of certain identifiable costs to states and localities" from illegal immigration.

In 1995 the commission's second report called for slowly cutting legal immigration by one-third, from a yearly average of 830,000 to 550,000, and favored allowing the immediate relatives of U.S. citizens (parents, spouses, and children under twenty-one) the right to immigrate without a waiting period but eliminated any such preferences for relatives beyond the nuclear family. Nobody from U.S. English was represented on the commission, but its endorsement of Americanization must have been satisfying to them: "The commission supports effective Americanization of new immigrants, that is the cultivation of a shared commitment to the American values of liberty, democracy, and equal opportunity."

Moreover: "Religious and cultural diversity does not pose a threat to the national interest as long as public policies ensure civic unity. Such policies should help newcomers learn to speak, read, and write English effectively." Elsewhere the commission stated that "[i]mmigration carries with it obligations to embrace the common core of the American civic culture, to become able to communicate—to the extent possible—in English with other citizens and residents, and to adapt to fundamental constitutional principles and democratic institutions." While it did not endorse Official English, the commission anticipated that its future work would include considering "other public policies that are believed by some to encourage ethnocentrism in the name of multiculturalism or to promote political separatism in the name of civil rights."[59] President Clinton generally praised the Jordan Commission and endorsed immigration reductions but was mum on specifics other than his position favoring federal aid to help states pay the costs of imprisoning illegal immigrants.[60]

Private sector rules that only English be spoken on the job led to several grievances before the Equal Employment Opportunity Commission (EEOC). By mid-1994 the EEOC had about 120 cases in which 67 different employers were accused of imposing English-only work rules. An appellate court upheld such a requirement at the Spun Steak Company of South San Francisco despite allegations by two Hispanic litigants that English-only work rules violate federal law prohibiting job discrimination based on national origins. In considering their appeal, the Supreme Court invited the Clinton administration to submit an amicus curiae brief. It did, and argued that employers should be prohibited from requiring English on the job unless it is a business necessity, but the appeal died since four justices were not willing to issue a writ of certiorari to hear the legal arguments.[61]

Bureaucratic efforts to force the use of non-English languages are monitored by U.S. English. In late 1995 U.S. English mobilized sixty thousand petitions and protests from Congressmen Bill Emerson (R-MO), Ron Packard (R-CA), and Mel Hancock (R-MO) to force the Internal Revenue Service to rescind its proposal to print Spanish-language 1040 forms and instructions. The previous year the IRS had debuted a test program to distribute half a million Spanish-language forms and instruction booklets at a cost of $113,000, but only 718 were ever returned. In a letter to U.S. English chairman Mauro E. Mujica, IRS tax form director Sheldon Schwartz reportedly said: "We made no plans to continue the test for the 1995 filing season" but indicated that the experience from 1994 would be used to assess future "efforts in the multi-lingual area."[62]

The General Accounting Office (GAO) was asked by Senator Richard Shelby (R-AL), Congressmen Bill Emerson (R-MO), and Congressman William G. Clinger Jr. (R-PA) to investigate, and the GAO reported that the Government Printing Office printed over two hundred documents in languages other than English during the period 1990–1994. That was a very conservative estimate insofar as the GAO indicated that only about half of government documents are printed by the GPO; the others are published by outside vendors or in-house by departments.[63]

Bilingual ballots are required by the 1975 and 1982 amendments to the Voting Rights Act of 1965, which mandate bilingual ballots in 175 counties where at least 5 percent of the population is from an ethnic group deficient in the English language. In 1992 that law was again amended to extend those requirements to thirty-eight more counties in which 5 percent of the voting-age residents or ten thousand residents, whichever is lower, primarily speak a foreign language and are not proficient in English. The bill also stipulated that fifty-eight counties with large Indian reservations must provide bilingual ballots to Indian voters.[64]

On another front, U.S. English raised a protest against the Department of Housing and Urban Development, which had planned to investigate an Official English ordinance in Allentown, Pennsylvania. Its law was passed in 1994, and in early 1995 the mayor was notified that HUD was investigating its ordinance, implying that federal funding could be jeopardized if the ordinance violated federal law. U.S. English chairman Mujica denounced HUD: "This so-called investigation is just a smoke-screen for government. HUD and other government agencies like the EEOC have engaged in a long-running campaign to give government workers the right to speak and write in any foreign language they choose while on the job." According to U.S. English, HUD withdrew its threat of an investigation.[65]

However, in Chicago a group called Latinos United filed a class-action lawsuit against HUD and the Chicago Housing Authority (CHA), alleging that Latinos had been excluded from Section 8 subsidized public housing programs. In agreeing to a consent decree, the CHA admitted that it had purged its Section 8 mailing lists of Latino applicants who failed to respond to letters sent in English without any instructions in Spanish or information on where to ask questions in Spanish. In addition to allocating Section 8 housing to Latinos, the consent degree authorized by the U.S. District Court required the CHA to provide Spanish-language translations of its materials, make recorded telephone messages available in Spanish, have adequate bilingual personnel in emergency and police services, open two bilingually staffed registration offices in Latino communities, and hire a full-time bilingual Latino community liaison person.[66]

Summary

Looking ahead, there may be solace in Sonntag's observation that "language issues are not particularly salient in the United States, as they are in such countries as Belgium where they do indeed function as a powder keg."[67] But Official English carries the potential, given the politics of the moment, to become a highly charged and emotional cause. If anti-immigrant grievances were based on economics alone, the contagion of conflict might not extend beyond a few states with sizable numbers of Spanish-speakers. But symbolic politics are involved here.

Apprehension about immigrants who resist "melting" into American society is not entirely illegitimate as far as most ordinary citizens are concerned. Some conservative intellectuals are very alarmed. For one, Peter Brimelow (editor of *Forbes* and *National Review*) recently labeled the United States an "Alien Nation" because "[t]here is no precedent for a sovereign country undergoing such a rapid and radical transformation of its ethnic character in the entire history of the world."[68] And syndicated columnist Georgia Anne Geyer wrote a book, *Americans No More,* which similarly presents a bleak image of a balkanized America in which immigrants insist on retaining their own cultural lifestyles.[69] So it seems that the message of the purportedly racist Tanton Memo of the 1988 Arizona referendum campaign has resurfaced as mainstream intellectual thought.

The Official English controversy is surrealistic to the degree that popular passions can be inflamed by the accumulation of symbolic indignities to the nation. In 1993 the news stories told us that upwards of a hundred thousand people chanted "Ingles no!" to express opposition to a law making both Spanish and English the official languages of Puerto Rico.[70] Also in 1993 the media reported that federal district judge Alfredo Marquez, a Hispanic, for the first time in the nation's history permitted the oath for naturalized citizenship to be given in Spanish.[71] In 1995 it was the highly publicized account of a child-custody dispute in Texas before state district judge Samuel C. Kiser: the child's Mexican father mainly spoke English but her mother used Spanish at home, prompting Kiser to declare: "Now, get this straight. You start speaking English to this child because if she doesn't do good in school, then I can remove her because it's not in her best interest to be ignorant. The child will only hear English."[72]

This time a liberal columnist, Bob Greene, rose to Kiser's defense, saying that "despite our nation's new devotion to the concept of multi-culturalism, people who do not have a proper command of English are, indeed, at a disadvantage—and children who are not taught English early are at a special disadvantage. So much attention is being given to ethnic pride—so many people seem to be more interested in what country they came from than what country they're living in now—that the basic connective value of a common language has been devalued."[73]

Notes

1. John Higham, *Strangers in the Land: Patterns of American Nativism, 1860–1925* (New York: Atheneum, 1965).
2. Much of the argument that follows is a summarization of the lengthy analysis in Raymond Tatalovich, *Nativism Reborn? The Official English Language Movement and the American States* (Lexington, KY: University Press of Kentucky, 1995).

3. U.S. Department of Commerce, Bureau of the Census, *Population Estimates by Race and Hispanic Origin for States, Metropolitan Areas, and Selected Counties, 1980–1985,* Current Population Reports Series P–25, no. 1040-RD–1 (Washington, DC: GPO, 1989), p. 69.

4. Ibid.

5. Both enactments are discussed in Tatalovich, *Nativism Reborn?* pp. 33–62 and 65–69.

6. Tatalovich, *Nativism Reborn?* pp. 237, 239–241.

7. "Dade County 'Antibilingual' Ordinance," in James Crawford, ed., *Language Loyalties: A Source Book on the Official English Controversy* (Chicago: University of Chicago Press, 1992), p. 131; also see Max J. Castro, "On the Curious Question of Language in Miami," in Crawford, *Language Loyalties,* pp. 178–186.

8. Tatalovich, *Nativism Reborn?* pp. 105–108.

9. John Horton and José Calderon, "Language Struggles in a Changing California Community," in James Crawford, *Language Loyalties: A Source Book on the Official English Controversy* (Chicago: University of Chicago Press, 1992), pp. 186–194.

10. Camilo Perez-Bustillo, "What Happens When English Only Comes to Town?: A Case Study of Lowell, Massachusetts," in James Crawford, *Language Loyalties: A Source Book on the Official English Controversy* (Chicago: University of Chicago Press, 1992), pp. 194–201.

11. Richard Perez-Pena, "English-Only Bill Is Vetoed," *New York Times* (September 14, 1996), p. 16.

12. Lynn Van Matre, "Lombard Adopts English as Its Official Language," *Chicago Tribune* (December 18, 1995), MetroChicago section, pp. 1, 4.

13. *Gutierrez v. Municipal Court of the Southeast Judicial District,* 838 F.2d 1031, 9th Cir. (1988). Also see Laura A. Cordero, "Constitutional Limitations on Official English Declarations," *New Mexico Law Review* 20 (Winter 1990), p. 50.

14. *Gutierrez v. Municipal Court of the Southeast Judicial District,* 861 F.2d 1187, 9th Cir. (1988).

15. Quoted in Russ Hemphill, "Lawsuit Asks Federal Court to Halt Official-English Amendment," *Phoenix Gazette* (November 11, 1988).

16. Felicity Barringer, "Judge Nullifies Law Mandating Use of English," *New York Times* (February 8, 1990), pp. A1, A17.

17. Linda Greenhouse, "Justices Set Aside Reversal of 'English Only' Measure," *New York Times* (March 4, 1997), p. A9.

18. *U.S. English Update* 12, no. 2 (Summer 1995), p. 1.

19. Ibid., p. 8.

20. U.S. English, *U.S. English: Toward a Unified America* (Washington, DC, n.d.). A notation within the text of the pamphlet indicates that other data were current as of March of 1991.

21. *U.S. English Update* 12, no. 3 (Fall 1995), p. 5.

22. William Trombley, "California Elections: Prop. 63 Roots Traced to Small Michigan City; Measure to Make English Official Language of State Sprang from Concern over Immigration, Population," *Los Angeles Times* (October 20, 1986), part 1, p. 3.

23. Remarks by Senator Walter Huddleston, *Congressional Record,* 98th Cong., 1st sess., Sept. 21, 1983, vol. 129, no. 122, pp. S12640–43.

24. S.I. Hayakawa, "The Case for Official English," in James Crawford, ed., *Language Loyalties: A Source Book on the Official English Controversy* (Chicago: University of Chicago Press, 1992), pp. 98–99.

25. *EPIC Events* 4, no. 1 (March-April 1991), p. 3.

26. See listing in Tatalovich, *Nativism Reborn?* appendix A, pp. 261–262.

27. "Statement of Purpose," English Plus Information Clearinghouse, enclosure with form letter to "Dear Friend" from Mary Carol Combs, director, n.d.

28. Tatalovich, *Nativism Reborn?* p. 227, Table 8.1.

29. Andy Hall, " 'English' Advocate Assailed," *Arizona Republic* (October 9, 1988).

30. Ibid.

31. James Crawford, "What's Behind Official English?" in James Crawford, *Language Loyalties: A Source Book on the Official English Controversy* (Chicago: University of Chicago Press, 1992), p. 174.

32. Andy Hall, "2 in U.S. English Quit over Charges of Racism," *Arizona Republic* (October 18, 1988).

33. Jack Citrin, "Language Politics and American Identity," *Public Interest* 99 (Spring 1990), pp. 104–105.

34. Connie Dyste, "The Popularity of California's Proposition 63: An Analysis," in Karen L. Adams and Daniel T. Brink, eds., *Perspectives on Official English* (New York: Mouten de Gruyter, 1990), p. 144.

35. Jack Citrin, Beth Reingold, Evelyn Walters, and Donald P. Green, "The 'Official English' Movement and the Symbolic Politics of Language in the United States," *Western Political Quarterly* 43 (September 1990), p. 544.

36. Carol Schmid, "The English Only Movement: Social Bases of Support and Opposition Among Anglos and Latinos," in James Crawford, ed., *Language Loyalties: A Source Book on the Official English Controversy* (Chicago: University of Chicago Press, 1992), pp. 204–206.

37. Citrin, Reingold, Walters and Green, "The 'Official English' Movement and the Symbolic Politics of Language in the United States," p. 544.

38. Selma K. Sonntag, "Political Saliency of English as Official Language," paper delivered to the annual meeting of the Western Political Science Association, Newport Beach, CA, March 22–24, 1990, p. 2.

39. Jack Citrin, Ernst B. Haas, Christopher Muste, and Beth Reingold, "Is American Nationalism Changing? Implications for Foreign Policy," *International Studies Quarterly* 38 (March 1994), p. 20.

40. John Frendreis and Raymond Tatalovich, "Who Supports English-Only Language Laws? Evidence from the 1992 National Election Study," *Social Science Quarterly* 78 (June 1997), pp. 354–368.

41. See Tatalovich, *Nativism Reborn?* pp. 243–244.

42. Seth Mydans, "A New Tide of Immigration Brings Hostility to the Surface, Poll Finds," *New York Times* (June 27, 1993), pp. 1, 14.

43. David W. Moore, "Americans Feel Threatened by New Immigrants," *Gallup Poll Monthly* 334 (July 1993), pp. 3–5, 13.

44. "Remark on Immigrants Brings Byrd's Apology," *New York Times* (July 27, 1992), p. 8.

45. See Tatalovich, *Nativism Reborn?* pp. 252–257.

46. Tatalovich, *Nativism Reborn?* p. 253.

47. Ibid., p. 227. A comparison of the legislative sponsors in eleven statutory states showed that Democrats predominated among the state senators (65 percent) and state representatives (73 percent), whereas virtually all were Republicans (93 percent and 96 percent, respectively) in three referendum states.

48. "Gingrich Finds Bilingual Moral in Canada's Secession Ballot," *The Washington Post* (October 31, 1995), p. A10.

49. "America Needs No Language Law," *New York Times* (November 25, 1995), p. 14.

50. Eric Schmitt, "House Approves Measure on Official U.S. Language," *New York Times* (August 2, 1996), p. A7.

51. B. Drummond Ayres Jr., "Dole Sounds a Bold Alarm on Education," *New York Times* (September 5, 1995), p. A8.

52. Gwen Ifill, "The 1992 Campaign: Reporter's Notebook; Bush and Clinton Spar, but Out of Arm's Reach," *New York Times* (April 25, 1992), sec. 1, p. 10.

53. *U.S. English Update,* 1996 (special election issue), p. 8.

54. Ibid.

55. William J. Bennett, "The Bilingual Education Act: A Failed Path," in James Crawford, ed., *Language Loyalties: A Source Book on the Official English Controversy* (Chicago: University of Chicago Press, 1992), pp. 358–60.

56. Mary Carol Combs, "English Plus: Responding to English Only," in Crawford, ed., *Language Loyalties: A Source Book on the Official English Controversy* (Chicago: University of Chicago Press, 1992), p. 217.

57. Elizabeth Shogren, "Gingrich Assails American Bilingualism as 'Dangerous,' " *Los Angeles Times* (October 31, 1995), part A, p. 13.

58. U.S. Commission on Immigration Reform, *U.S. Immigration Policy: Restoring Credibility* (Washington, DC: U.S. Government Printing Office, 1994), p. 115.

59. U.S. Commission on Immigration Reform, *Legal Immigration: Setting Priorities, Executive Summary* (Washington, DC: U.S. Government Printing Office, 1995), pp. 30–31.

60. Tim Weiner, "Aid Proposed in Jail Costs for Aliens," *New York Times* (April 23, 1994), p. 10.

61. Richard Carelli, "English-only Jobs at Issue," *Pittsburgh Post-Gazette* (June 4, 1994).

62. "U.S. English Forces IRS to Retreat," *U.S. English Update* 12, no. 2 (Summer 1995), pp. 1, 5.

63. "GAO Study Finds that Hundreds of Multi-Lingual Documents Are Being Printed," *U.S. English Update* 12, no. 3 (Fall 1995), pp. 3, 6.

64. Lindsey Gruson, "Congress Expands the Use of Bilingual Ballots," *New York Times* (August 8, 1992), p. 7.

65. "Allentown: A Case Study in Government Intrusion," *U.S. English* 12, no. 2 (Summer 1995), p. 8.

66. Melita Marie Garza, "CHA Opens Section 8 Lists for Latinos," *Chicago Tribune* (April 23, 1996), pp. 1, 16.

67. Sonntag, "Political Saliency of English as Official Language," p. 2.

68. Peter Brimelow, *Alien Nation: Common Sense About America's Immigration Disaster* (New York: Random House, 1995).

69. Georgia Anne Geyer, *Americans No More* (New York: Grove/Atlantic, 1996).

70. " 'Ingles, No!' Puerto Ricans Shout," *New York Times* (January 25, 1993), p. A9.

71. "New Citizens Take the Oath in Spanish," *New York Times* (July 3, 1993), p. 7 [photo with caption].

72. Sam Howe Verhovek, "Mother Scolded by Judge for Speaking in Spanish," *New York Times* (August 30, 1995), p. A9.

73. Bob Greene, "In Plain English, Not a Bad Idea," *Chicago Tribune* (September 3, 1995), sec. 5, page 1.

8

Pornography: Freedom of Expression or Sexual Degradation?

Byron W. Daynes

Ever since the eighteenth century, government has tried to cope with the problems associated with obscenity and pornography. The first judicial ruling on this issue came in 1815, when a Pennsylvania court held it illegal to exhibit any picture of nude bodies for profit. This was followed in 1821 by the enactment in Vermont of the first state antiobscenity law. But the politicization of the obscenity issue had to await Supreme Court decisions of the 1960s and the outcry that followed a 1970 presidential commission report on this subject. Yet despite the various state and federal laws that punish distributors of pornography, there have been few major inroads into this lucrative market, a market that covers "hard-core videos, peep shows, live sex acts, adult cable programming, sexual devices, computer porn, and sex magazines" and that has been estimated in 1996 to be worth in excess of $8 billion.[1]

One reason for the ineffectiveness of antipornography laws is that demands for their enforcement frequently collide with constitutional guarantees of free expression. Another reason has to do with the decision makers, who often act on their own presumptions as to what is obscene. In his now-famous concurrence in *Jacobellis v. Ohio,* 378 U.S. 476 (1964), the late Supreme Court Justice Potter Stewart, after puzzling over the definition of obscenity, finally said in exasperation: "I shall not today attempt further to define the kinds of material I understand to be embraced within that shorthand description [hardcore pornography], and perhaps I could never succeed in intelligently doing so. But I know it when I see it, and the motion picture involved in this case is not that."

Judiciary

The Warren Court (1953–1969), which was dedicated to free expression, saw obscenity as a barrier to protected expression under the First Amendment and wanted to minimize its impact on free expression. It was not until *Butler v. Michigan,* 352 U.S. 380 (1957), that the Warren Court first broached the problem of definition. In this case, older standards of judgment were rejected, including the "isolated passages" test (which judged the obscenity of a work on the basis of isolated parts of that work without assessing its overall worth or objective) and the "most susceptible persons" test (which considered the concerns of individuals most responsive to the objectionable material).

Although the Warren Court was unable to define what obscenity was, it decided what obscenity was *not.* The criteria used by the Warren Court to define the obscene became so broad and unmanageable that the term *obscene* all but disappeared. This development began in 1957 with *Roth v. U.S.,* 354 U.S. 476 (1957). The Court decided that a work could be considered obscene if it appealed "to the average person, applying contemporary community standards, [and where] the dominant theme of the material taken as a whole appealed to prurient interests."

The Warren Court continued to broaden its standards in subsequent cases. In *Manual Enterprises v. Day,* 370 U.S. 478 (1962), Justice John Harlan said that for a work to be obscene it should have "prurient interest" as well as being "patently offensive." Furthermore, a work had to fail all the *Roth* tests individually and be "utterly without redeeming social value." This "social value" test, viewed by civil libertarians as the most important criterion, all but eliminated any possibility that a work might be considered obscene, because virtually every work, it could be argued, has at least a modicum of social value and importance.

In at least two respects the approach to obscenity taken by the Burger Court (1969–1986) was identical to that of the Warren Court. First, the new Court insisted on viewing the movies and reading the books firsthand; second, it was just as reluctant to define obscenity. In the important case of *Miller v. California,* 413 U.S. 15 (1973), the Burger Court decided against the use of expert testimony to aid in defining obscenity because "hard core pornography . . . can and does speak for itself." But the Court moved toward specifying more restrictive standards in making those judgments when five justices, for the first time in many years, agreed on what standards ought to prevail, namely, whether the average person, applying community standards, would find that the work, taken as a whole, appeals to prurient interest; whether the work depicts or describes, in a patently offensive way, sexual conduct specifically defined by the applicable state law; and whether the work, taken as a whole, lacks serious literary, artistic, political, or scientific value. *Miller* thus substituted a more restrictive "serious value" test for the open-ended "utterly without redeeming social value" test, thereby expanding obscenity as a category of unprotected expression.

The Burger Court also moved close to defining obscenity when, in *Miller,* it articulated specific acts and words that might be labeled obscene: patently offensive representations or descriptions of ultimate sexual acts, normal or perverted, actual or simulated; and patently offensive representations or descriptions of masturbation, excretory functions, and lewd exhibitions of the genitals.

The Burger Court in the *Miller* decision seemed committed to the need for state and local involvement in determining what standards for judging obscenity should prevail in a particular community. Yet at the same time, the Court determined there were certain universally obscene acts that in fact might contradict some community standards. This became a fundamental contradiction of the Burger Court approach, since the discretion of juries, legislatures, and judges in determining the nature of community standards was to extend no further than the "universal" list of obscene acts established by the Court.

The Burger Court also was concerned with child pornography, but the Court found a major problem in this area, since child pornography did not fit any of the categories previously established nor did it fall under the *Miller* standards of obscenity. By 1981 thirty-five states and Congress had prohibited the distribution of child pornography, while twenty of those states restricted such material without reliance on any specific obscenity standard.[2]

Such broad restrictions on free expression collided with the First Amendment. Some legal questions were answered by the Supreme Court in the 1982 case of *New York v. Ferber,* 458 U.S. 747 (1982). Following the lead of Congress and the state legislatures, the Supreme Court determined that stricter standards should govern when children were the objects of obscenity. Whether the material was obscene or not was of less importance than whether children were being victimized through sexual exploitation. Child pornography was not to be judged "as a whole" but could be banned based on "isolated passages." Thus the Burger Court began judging child pornography by the very standard that the Warren Court had discarded years before.

The focus of the Rehnquist years has been on pornography's intrusion into communications and on "child pornography." Instruments of communication that have drawn the Court's attention have included cable television, the telephone, and the Internet. In the *Denver Area Consortium v. FCC,* 116 S.Ct. 471 (1996), a case dealing with cable television, the Court supported cable TV providers by protecting them from stringent statutory restrictions, suggesting that Congress had gone too far in trying to police cable television programming, and that the FCC had been "overly restrictive." Regarding the telephone, the Court held firm to government restrictions in *Sable Communications of California v. FCC,* 492 U.S. 115 (1989), indicating that statutory law could restrict "dial-a-porn" broadcasts to protect minors without undercutting the protections of the First Amendment. The Court did refuse to totally ban "dial-a-porn" as a form of communication for adults; instead, the Court stressed the reasonableness of using the "least restrictive" means to oversee the broadcasts.

The most important challenges facing the Court in the 1990s has been indecency of communications in cyberspace, defined as "the nonphysical 'place' where electronic communications happen and digital data are located."[3] Attention has centered on the Internet, an international network of networks connecting more than 9,400,000 host computers worldwide, 60 percent of which are located in the United States. Standards of decency imposed by other countries on the United States have raised constitutional questions, as happened in 1995 when CompuServe, a U.S. Internet service provider, decided it would restrict its approximately 4 million subscribers from gaining access to explicit sexual discussion groups and pictures, because a Munich federal prosecutor and the Bavarian police complained that this material violated pornography laws in Germany, and they wanted the service to stop carrying it.[4] CompuServe complied, but in so doing raised questions in this country of individual privacy and First Amendment freedoms.

The Supreme Court, on June 26, 1997, ruled in *Reno v. American Civil Liberties Union,* no. 96–511 (1997), that parts of the 1996 Communications Decency Act that shielded minors from "indecent" and "patently offensive" materials on the Internet were unconstitutional violations of free speech. The 7–2 majority included both ideologically liberal and conservative justices: Souter, Stevens, Ginsburg, Breyer, Kennedy, Scalia, and Thomas.[5]

The most productive area of focus among obscenity cases for the Rehnquist Court has been the area of child pornography, in both its distribution and production. While the Court has been protective of minors, it has also been careful to make sure that any child pornography law has not been too all-encompassing. In *Virginia v. American Booksellers Association,* 484 U.S. 383 (1988), for example, the Court rejected, as too all-enveloping, an amendment to a Virginia law that would have allowed the state to restrict any or all visual and written sexual or sadomasochistic material thought harmful to juveniles.

Knowledge and a proper interpretation of what obscenity is seemed to be important to the Rehnquist Court when in *U.S. v. X-Citement Video,* 513 U.S. 804 (1994), the Court determined that Rubin Gottesman, owner of the X-Citement Video store, was selling videos featuring an actress who was well under eighteen years of age. The Court felt that the owner may not have really known this to be the case and thus should not be held accountable for it. In *Knox v. U.S.,* 510 U.S. 939 (1993), however, lack of knowledge about what is obscene, and a presidential intervention, did not protect Stephen A. Knox, a Pennsylvania State graduate student, who was in possession of three videotapes featuring young girls fully clothed, but in provocative poses. Knox thought that the girls in the video could not be considered to be exhibiting "sexually explicit conduct," since such conduct had always been defined as the "lascivious exhibition of the genitals or pubic area." These girls were all fully clothed and not engaged in sexual conduct; yet Knox was arrested in 1991 and later, after many court appeals, ordered to go to prison on March 9, 1995, to serve a five-year sentence. The Clinton Justice Department told the high court that the term "lascivious" actually meant children engaged in sexual conduct, and urged that the conviction be overturned. The request by Attorney General Janet Reno, however, was greeted with charges made by 125 Republicans joined by some Democrats in the House as well as some conservative interest groups, that the Clinton administration was "soft" on child pornography.[6] As a result of the criticism, Reno reversed direction and supported the conviction on January 17, 1995. The Supreme Court let the conviction stand.

What of the future actions by the judiciary in handling pornography? A potentially new tactic involved *American Booksellers Association v. Hudnut,* 475 U.S. 1001 (1986), that defined pornography as "sexual discrimination" against women, but U.S. district judge Sarah Evans Barker ruled that the Indianapolis ordinance, which prohibited "all discriminatory practices of sexual subordination or inequality through pornography" (defined as "the graphic depiction of the sexually explicit subordination of women"), was unconstitutionally vague and therefore unconstitutional. Justices Warren Burger, William Rehnquist, and Sandra Day O'Connor dissented on the grounds that the case should have included detailed briefings and oral arguments.

Congress

Restrictions on obscenity first came in the mid-1800s, with the enactment of the Tariff Act of 1842, which prohibited obscene prints and visual depictions. Since the 1950s, Congress has legislated in several important areas (Table 8.1) with particular interest in (1) distribution of obscenity through the U.S. mails, (2) the restrictions on child pornography, and (3) the more recent concern for the victims of pornography.

Unlike the judiciary, Congress has been guided by an explicit working definition of obscenity.[7] However, when Congress confronted the problem of child pornography, the working definition proved no more useful than had the presumptions maintained by the Court. Nonetheless, in 1984 Congress strengthened previous legislation aimed at protecting minors by significantly raising the penalties against pornographers, increasing the penalty against first offenders from $10,000 to a maximum of $100,000; second offenders' fines were raised from $15,000 to $200,000. Child pornography now commands a place in the federal budget, as a portion of the 1996 budget funded the Child Pornography Prevention Act of 1996, which expanded the definition of what child pornography would consist of to "any visual depiction, including any photograph, film, video image or picture" wherein "such visual depiction is, or appears to be, of a minor engaging in sexually explicit conduct."[8]

On April 20, 1994, the House of Representatives voted on a "sense of Congress" amendment to the Equal Justice Act of 1994, stating that the House recognized child pornography as "a serious national problem" and that the Congress has a "compelling interest in the protection of children from sexual abuse with exploitation by pornography." Passage of the amendment was overwhelming, with a vote of 425 yeas to 3 nays with 9 not voting.[9]

The response of the Congress to child pornography has taken various forms. In 1985 it was the Computer Pornography and Child Exploitation Act of 1985; the next year, Congress passed the Child Abuse Victims' Rights act; in 1987 it was the Child Pornography Act; in 1987 and 1988 two laws referred to as the Child Protection and Obscenity Enforcement Acts of 1987 and 1988 were passed. By 1988 there were some thirty-two federal laws dealing with child pornography.[10] By the 1990s Congress shifted its attention to the victims of pornography. In 1992 Congress passed the Pornography Victims' Compensation Act and in 1994 approved the Child Sexual Abuse Prevention Act. In 1995 there were two child pornography enactments—the Protection of Children from Computer Pornography Act of 1995 and the Child Pornography Prevention Act of 1995.

Table 8.1

Legislation on Obscenity Introduced in Congress, 1956–1997

	Years									
	1956–1960	1961–1965	1966–1970	1971–1975	1976–1980	1981–1985	1986–1990	1991–1995	1996–1997[1]	Total
Mail/postal service	7	3	6				1	1		18
Protection from obscenity	1									1
State control over obscenity	1		2							3
Transportation of obscenity	1							3		4
Study of obscenity	3	2	4							9
Sale of obscenity		1						2		3
Obscenity and subversion	1									1
Criminal Code and obscenity					3	2				5
DC bill on obscenity		1	1							2
Obscene communications			1			1	9	2	1	14
Children and obscenity			2	1	9	5	17	7	3	44
Advertising of obscenity			4				1			5
Definition of obscenity			2	1	2					5
Victims of obscenity						2	5	3		10
Importation of obscenity						1	1			2
Education							1			1
Arts and obscenity							1	1		2
Internet								4		4
Enforcement of laws								1		1
Total by year	14	7	22	2	14	11	36	24	4	134

Source: Congressional Records and Congressional Quarterly Weekly Reports for each yearly period.
[1] Includes only the first four months of 1997.

Perhaps the most controversial of all recent pornography-related acts passed was the Communications Decency Act, which was overwhelmingly passed in 1996 by the Senate by a vote of 84–16.[11] The bipartisan nature of the bill and its overwhelming approval may mask its controversial aspects, however. After all, who could vote against "decency"? What politician wants to have to explain a vote against it? The act has one major failing: it does not define what is meant by "filthy," "lewd," "indecent," or "obscene." Presumably "community standards" are to guide the decision makers in their interpretation of these words.

Congress in the 1990s also questioned the funding of the arts. The controversy broke out in 1990 when the National Endowment for the Arts (NEA) funded the "Robert Mapplethorpe: The Perfect Moment" exhibition in Cincinnati. Seven photographs among the 175 in the exhibition displayed homosexual lovers, and it was these photographs that were considered obscene. Chief among the critics of the NEA was Senator Jesse Helms (R-NC), who charged that the NEA was giving taxpayer money to "sleazeballs . . . under the pretext of having produced something that they call art. And I submit to you that that is a farce. But it's worse than a farce; it's a fraud on the taxpayers of America."[12] Some members of Congress supported Helms's position that decency standards should first be established before money could be granted through the NEA, but the U.S. Court of Appeals for the Ninth Circuit ruled in 1996 against establishing such criteria, fearing that any criteria would be too restrictive.[13]

Congress, during the past decade, has also attempted to monitor sexually explicit messages over the telephone. Its primary concern has been the children that might be exposed to the "dial-a-porn" services intended for adults. In response to this problem, Congress passed the Telephone Privacy Act of 1990, the Telephone Decency Act of 1987, the Telephone Privacy Acts of 1990 and 1995, the Consumer Protection Act of 1991 (regulating 900 services), as well as the Telephone Consumer Assistance Act of 1991.

Cable television also came under some scrutiny by the Congress when in 1985 it passed a Cable-Porn and Dial-a-Porn Control Act to limit the broadcasting of obscene language. In 1992 Congress passed the Helms Amendment, designed particularly to protect children from indecency on cable television by allowing cable operators to control indecency over both the public-access channels and commercial channels. A 1996 Supreme Court case passing judgment on this statute indicated that operators ought to have the right to determine whether to allow indecent material over the commercial channels, but restricted cable operators from banning such programs coming from public-access channels.[14]

Also of some interest was Congress's attempt to eliminate so-called soft porn from military base stores. Concerned Women for America, an interest group that has devoted its attention to overseeing governmental activities in this area, determined that as a result of the military allowing the sales of *Playboy, Penthouse,* and *Hustler* magazines and adult videos, the U.S. government was "the largest seller of pornography in the world," generating "$4.3 million a year in earnings for the government and tens of millions in sales for pornographers."[15] In light of these charges, members of Congress sympathetic to this argument passed the Military Honor and Decency Act of 1996, which became part of an appropriations bill signed by President Clinton. Almost immediately the American Civil Liberties Union and Bob Guccione, publisher of *Penthouse,* filed a district court suit against the law, and U.S. district court judge Shira A. Scheindlin, a Clinton appointee, declared the act to be unconstitutional.

Few members of Congress could hope to win reelection by campaigning in support of expanding access to pornography. In fact, Congress has long looked for a structural means of restricting pornography, and such thinking led Congress to propose, beginning in 1960, a commission to study obscenity. The commission proposal did not pass in 1960 but was reintroduced in 1963, 1965, and 1966 before finally winning approval in 1967.

While the repeated introductions of a commission bill might suggest Congress's eagerness to establish the commission, Congress was not so interested to receive the commission's final report in 1970. The Senate and President Richard Nixon were both upset when the commission report was leaked to the press, and on October 13, 1970, the Senate rejected the commission's findings and its recommendations by a 60–5 vote (with 34 abstentions). In particular, the Senate rejected the following findings and recommendations:

1. That there is "no evidence to date that exposure to explicit sexual materials plays a significant role in the causation of delinquent or criminal behavior among youths or adults";
2. That "a majority of American adults believe that adults should be allowed to read or see any sexual materials they wish";
3. That "there is no reason to suppose that elimination of governmental prohibitions upon the sexual materials which may be made available to adults would adversely affect the availability to the public of other books, magazines, or films";
4. That there is no "evidence that exposure to explicit sexual materials adversely affects character or moral attitudes regarding sex and sexual conduct";
5. That "Federal, State, and Local legislation prohibiting the sale, exhibi-

tion, or distribution of sexual materials to consenting adults should be repealed."[16]

There were also attempts in the House during the 91st and 92nd Congresses to reject the majority report of the Presidential Commission on Obscenity and Pornography and to adopt a minority report expressing more concern about the negative properties of pornography and the damage it may do.[17]

Presidency

Early presidents did not devote too much attention to the concerns of pornography beyond their desire to protect the postal system. Typically the early presidents pardoned many of those who had been convicted of transmitting pornographic materials though the mails, commuted the sentences of others, and granted clemency to still others who had been incarcerated.[18] Those most active in using this authority included Presidents Cleveland, McKinley, Theodore Roosevelt, and Woodrow Wilson. Only a select few contemporary presidents could be called major advocates of antipornography campaigns. Democrats John F. Kennedy and Lyndon B. Johnson gave support to existing laws protecting free expression, as did Dwight Eisenhower, but Eisenhower would not protect the free flow of information in the mail system if "indecency" was an issue. "The other limit I draw is decency. We have certain books we bar from the mails and all that sort of thing; I think that is perfectly proper, and I would do it now."[19] Republicans Richard Nixon and Ronald Reagan made obscenity and pornography campaign issues and spoke out forcefully against its spread.

At a news conference on August 29, 1962, John F. Kennedy was asked to comment on a Supreme Court decision that prevented the postmaster general from restricting pornographic matter in the mails. He responded that existing laws already governed such distribution and that he believed the Post Office's main responsibility was not to make judgments about the nature of pornography but, rather, to carry out the law. Lyndon Johnson's first reaction to obscenity legislation came in the context of the 1966 District of Columbia crime bill, which he vetoed on November 13 of that year. Two years later, at the request of Congress, President Johnson appointed the well-known, eighteen-member Presidential Commission on Obscenity and Pornography to make a thorough study of obscenity and its effects on society.

Nixon was particularly interested in pornography as a public issue. Much of his concern grew from his attempt to blame the Democrats in Congress for inaction on his legislative agenda, which included measures opposing obscenity. In a May 1969 message to Congress he emphasized the need to halt the traffic in unsolicited sex-oriented material and mentioned how many complaints had been received by the White House and Congress on this matter. Nixon understood that no solution would be easy, given the First Amendment protection of expression, but he proceeded to sponsor various measures. Nixon also understood that statutory law would not be enough to make major advances against obscenity. In addition, Nixon appealed for grassroots opposition to pornography, maintaining that "when indecent books no longer find a market, when pornographic films can no longer draw an audience, when obscene plays open to empty houses, then the tide will turn. Government can maintain the dikes against obscenity, but only people can turn the tide."[20]

In a September 1969 speech to the National Governors' Conference, President Nixon again said that antipornography legislation was one of his twenty-four high-priority issues for congressional action. In his State of the Union message on January 22, 1970, he echoed a theme that he would carry into the congressional districts as he campaigned for Republicans in the midterm elections: that government has a special responsibility to bring a halt to pornography. But no legislative action was forthcoming in 1970.

The issue was further galvanized by the 1970 report of the President's Commission on Obscenity and Pornography, a commission that Lyndon Johnson had staffed two years earlier. Its majority report had been rejected by the Senate one week before being publicly repudiated by President Nixon, who declared in one of his most pointed attacks against the commission report that

> so long as I am in the White House, there will be no relaxation of the national effort to control and eliminate smut from our national life. . . . The warped and brutal portrayal of sex in books, magazines, and movies, if not halted and reversed could poison the wellsprings of American and western culture and civilization.[21]

Although it appears that Richard Nixon failed to get most of his program enacted, Congress did enact limited prohibitions against obscenity during this period. In 1968 P.L. 90–299 made it a federal crime for anyone to place obscene or abusive telephone calls from the District of Columbia across state lines or to foreign countries. Congress also amended the Postal Reform Act of 1970 (P.L. 91–375) on August 12, 1970, to include a prohibition against mailing sexually oriented commercial advertisements to reluctant adults as well as a prohibition against mailing obscene matter that might appear on envelopes or wrappers.

In 1984 the Republican Party made clear its opposition to pornography;

the party platform stated that "the Republican Party has deep concern about gratuitous sex and violence in the entertainment media, both of which contribute to the problem of crime against children and women. To the victims of such crimes who need protection we gladly offer it."[22] President Reagan gave full support to this platform statement by focusing considerable attention on the problem. A year earlier he had been persuaded by Morality in Media to take on the entire sex-related market by putting a "torpedo into the whole sex industry."[23] In his 1984 State of the Union message, however, President Reagan spoke of the needs of parents and children, rather than responding to a more broadly undefined segment of the market, suggesting that parents needed reassurance that their children would not be abducted or become objects of child pornography.

By May 1984 Congress had enacted the Child Protection Act of 1984 (P.L. 98–292), and at the bill-signing ceremony President Reagan expressed his disgust for those who abuse children "whether by using them in pornographic material or by encouraging sexual abuse by distributing this material." He added that, despite what the 1967 presidential commission had concluded, there was a link "between child molesting and pornography" as well as one between "pornography and sexual violence."[24]

In a May 1984 speech given by Reagan, the president announced that the attorney general, at the president's request, would establish a new president's commission to investigate the effects of obscenity on society. In May 1985 Attorney General Edwin Meese named an eleven-member commission to recommend measures, where appropriate, to control the distribution and production of obscene material. This commission was quite different from the one created by Lyndon Johnson and dramatically illustrates how fundamentally different a liberal Democratic approach can be from a more conservative Republican approach. The 1967 Commission on Obscenity and Pornography was controversial because its recommendations diverged sharply from the general public's beliefs and the politicians' views of those beliefs.

The 1967 commission had been staffed with social scientists, criminologists, attorneys, and other professionals who had some experience with obscenity law and its effects on people. By contrast, the 1985 Attorney General's Commission on Pornography was more heavily staffed by law enforcement persons.[25]

The 1985 commission, in contrast to the earlier commission, worked from an agreed-upon definition of pornography as material that is "predominantly sexually explicit and intended primarily for the purpose of sexual arousal."[26] Budgetary and time constraints were also a factor and concern of the 1985 commission. This commission was limited to a one-year time period and to budgetary constraints of $500,000.[27] This commission at times used heavy-handed methods to procure information and establish itself. It sent, for example, some eight thousand letters to retail chain stores warning them that they were guilty of displaying popular soft pornography if they sold magazines such as *Playboy* and *Penthouse,* and therefore might be identified as distributors of pornography. Findings of the 1985 commission focused on two main areas, child pornography and the pornography of sexual violence—areas that some commissioners on the 1967 commission thought had been ignored. In the area of sex and violence, the commission drew one of the sharpest distinctions from its 1967 counterpart when concluding that "the available evidence strongly supports the hypothesis that substantial exposure to sexually violent materials . . . bears a causal relationship to antisocial acts of sexual violence and, for some subgroups, possibly to unlawful acts of sexual violence."[28] In all, there were ninety-two commission recommendations for dealing with pornography. A number of the recommendations encouraged stern enforcement of obscenity laws already a part of state and federal legal codes.

Two of the eleven members, Ellen Levine and Judith Becker, while indicating that much of the report could be considered intelligent and reasonable, asserted in a twenty-page written statement that the evidence examined by the commission had been "skewed to the very violent and extremely degrading" and that the limited budget and examination period had proven to be impossible barriers to the proper assessment of commission findings.[29]

George Bush did not see a need for further commission studies, nor did he believe it necessary to spend a lot of time worrying about pornography. Where he did choose to focus his energy was child pornography. That seemed a safe, uncontroversial area for the president. To the members of the Religious Alliance Against Pornography on October 10, 1991, he suggested that the administration's efforts to eliminate mail-order pornography via its Project Postporn had been successful. His primary concern seemed to be the effect unsolicited mail would have on children. Bush did not always stay with this uncontroversial area, however; instead he got mired down in the quicksand of funding for the National Endowment for the Arts (NEA), trying to balance funding for art with a refusal to fund what Bush called "filth." The president encouraged the chair of the NEA, John Frohnmayer, to in some way avoid funding the "excessive cases."[30] The dilemma was not resolved under Bush and was inherited by Bill Clinton.

Clinton attempted to limit his involvement with pornography to looking at the evils of child pornography. Yet for Clinton, this focus was not free of controversy, since he became the first president to be charged by critics in

Congress with being "soft" on child pornography. Twenty-two senators and eighty-two representatives bitterly complained to the attorney general that Clinton and the administration had reversed direction regarding the previously mentioned Court decision involving Stephen A. Knox and his possession of the videotapes of fully clothed young girls in sexually provocative positions. Previously the Bush administration had supported the Knox prosecution, but Solicitor General Drew S. Days III, a Clinton appointee, had asked the Court to lay aside the Knox judgment on the grounds that the federal appeals court had given too broad an interpretation of the law in upholding the Knox conviction. In prior cases, persons convicted of similar violations had to possess pictures of nude persons.[31]

This change of direction by the Clinton administration was what precipitated the charge from angry critics in Congress. The Senate passed a unanimous, nonbinding resolution to the effect that nudity and "lascivious exhibition" should both be considered violations of the law, and that this law, as applied to children, needed to be applied broadly. With this, Clinton fired off a letter to the attorney general, Janet Reno, stating:

> I find all forms of child pornography offensive and harmful, as I know you do, and I want the federal government to lead aggressively in the attack against the scourge of child pornography. It represents an unacceptable exploitation of children and contributes to the degradation of our national life and to a societal climate that appears to condone child abuse.[32]

Clinton indicated that he agreed with those incensed senators regarding the intended scope of the child pornography law and ordered attorneys in the Justice Department to "promptly prepare any necessary legislation" making sure that the federal laws would apply to all aspects of child pornography and child exploitation.[33]

This tougher stance by Clinton conveniently fit in with his emphasis, since 1996, on strengthening family values and protecting children in and out of the home. This is what may have led him to sign the Telecommunications Act of 1996, which had as a part of the statute the Communications Decency Act, which dealt with obscenity, sexual harassment, and misuse of telecommunications.

Bureaucracy

The key agencies that have been involved with pornography over the years have included the Federal Communications Commission (FCC), the Federal Bureau of Investigation (FBI), the U.S. Postal Service (as both a cabinet department and an independent agency), and the U.S. Customs Service.

Federal Communications Commission (FCC)

Although the Federal Communications Act forbids the FCC from censoring questionable material, the U.S. Code (18 USC K 1464) prohibits obscene and profane language in broadcasting. In most cases, the FCC supports station management's control over content. In the July 9, 1981, memorandum opinion on cable television channel capacity, the FCC ruled that a cable system operation should not be allowed to censor programming "on a channel set aside as a public forum, to which the programmer has a right of access by virtue of local, state or federal law" because this would "impose a system of prior restraint."[34]

In 1986 a New York station received a letter from the FCC in regard to complaints the FCC had received about the insults and blue humor of Howard Stern, an announcer who is a frequent object of such investigations. These were only three of some twenty thousand complaints that the FCC received that year, doubling the number they had received in 1985.[35] Fines imposed by the FCC can be brutal, as seen in 1993 when Infinity Broadcasting Corporation, the home base for Howard Stern, was fined $600,000 for some of his on-air remarks with guests. Despite this, and possibly because of this, Stern's radio program in 1993 was the top-rated program in New York City, Philadelphia, Los Angeles, and Washington, DC, with an audience estimated to be more than 3.5 million people.[36]

The Telecommunications Act of 1992 gave the FCC still another responsibility in reducing the decency violations on the airwaves between the hours of 10 P.M. and 6 A.M. on both commercial and public radio stations that broadcast during those hours.[37] This will be even more time-consuming, since it is during these hours when more of the violations probably occur. Concern about the Internet could give the FCC an even broader reach and authority if computer networks are put under the jurisdiction of the FCC, as some in Congress wish to see.

The FBI

Prior to 1955 the FBI could arrest individuals carrying obscene materials only if those materials were transported on common carriers. In 1955 Congress passed a law that made any interstate transportation of pornography illegal, whether it was by common carrier or by private automobile. The potential for FBI involvement was illustrated in 1996 when it helped to break up an organized pornography ring. In July a Federal grand jury charged sixteen persons who were a part of a pedophilia club, sharing original pictures on-line and recounting their pedophilic experiences to those connected on the system.[38]

The FBI has also become involved in pornography investigations, using the Mann Act (18 U.S.C. Sec. 2423), to indict violators of pornography. At one time, this act was concerned only with the transportation of females across state lines for illicit purposes; in recent years, the act has been broadened to include the transportation of males as well as females across state lines for purposes of prostitution and the transportation of minors for the purpose of engaging in sexual conduct for commercial reasons.[39]

The FBI has also been involved in widespread nationwide dragnets. One operation in 1988 consisted of a thirty-month investigation in which sixty different raids took place at the same time on warehouses where pornographic materials were presumably stored. Nothing tangible came of these 1988 raids, however.[40]

As more direct measures have begun to be taken against pornographers, the FBI has been asked to conduct "computer stings," as in December of 1996 when some twenty cities were searched to find which computer services and Internet services were soliciting children for illicit sex. Most of the FBI's field offices were involved, with fifty-one of fifty-six of them participating along with local and state police from Virginia, Maryland, Florida, and the District of Columbia. Over a three-year period on this operation, a total of eighty arrests were made and sixty-six felony convictions were handed down.[41]

U.S. Customs

The U.S. Customs Service and the U.S. Postal Service are also agencies that monitor the flow of pornography. Although U.S. Customs has no official authority to make judgments about what is or what is not obscene, the nature of the agency's work puts it in a position to determine what books, magazines, devices, and films enter the country. Most foreign films, in fact, have been given a Customs review before entering the United States. Customs also spot-checks suspicious packages and, in conjunction with the Postal Service, on occasion withholds first-class mail. Customs does have the authority to prohibit the mailing of sexually oriented advertisements; to prohibit any "office of the United States" from aiding in the importation of obscene or "treasonous" books or articles;[42] and to prohibit the actual "importation or transportation into the United States" of any obscene material.[43]

Critics of Customs have suggested that agents, in effect, can censor, because the importer or producer of the material must spend precious time and money in courts to reacquire the material that has been seized by Customs. Furthermore, the limited route of appeals works in the Customs Service's favor. As James Paul and Murray Schwartz contended, "The absence of administrative formality makes it easier for the government official to decide against the contesting citizen in a borderline case. Precisely because there is not the check of a formal adversary hearing nor easy review in the courts, Customs procedure delegates considerable power to the few who decide what publications shall be suppressed."[44] Much of the focus of the Customs Service since 1983 has been directed to child pornography; it was Customs that developed a Child Pornography Protection Unit to respond to these requests made of them.

Customs agents frequently work with postal inspectors, the FBI, and local police departments. In 1986 the Customs Service was instrumental in intercepting pornographic materials from Europe coming to Dr. Charles M. Barry, a sixty-six-year-old psychiatrist. He was a child molester who represented himself as a Christian counselor and volunteer worker in orphanages. Customs intercepted the material and traced it to Barry as well as securing search warrants that led to his eventual arrest. Indeed, child pornography cases involving Customs personnel rose from 12 in 1983 to 220 in 1986 and have continued to increase as the U.S. government becomes more involved in this area.[45]

Although Customs appears to have been fairly active in combating the traffic in pornography, seizures have varied according to the nature of the statutes in force, the supply of agents qualified for this sort of work, and how enterprising the pornographers happen to be. The General Accounting Office (GAO) Report for April 20, 1982, indicated that pornography seizures in New York decreased from 15,020 in 1975 to 1,580 in 1980. The change was attributed to an increase in federal statutes against pornography as well as to a reduction in the number of Customs agents serving this area. In addition, the report indicated that the reduction also may have been because pornographers were using other techniques, such as domestic reproduction of pornographic foreign films.[46]

U.S. Postal Service

The U.S. Postal Service has caused more concern for civil libertarians than Customs, because Congress has provided the Postal Service with sufficient leverage through statutory authority to detain and restrain the mail, as well as broadening the Postal Service's authority into such areas as fraud and false advertising that helped in the investigations of "900 number" cases where the mail is used to deliver products once ordered.[47] It has resorted to seizure, exclusion, branding certain publications as unmailable, blocking the mail sent to certain persons through the use of mail covers, and revoking mailing privileges.

At times postal inspectors have operated independently in their prosecutions, as they did in 1996 when, in a two-year operation centered in New Jersey, postal inspectors broke up a child pornography ring that led to the arrest of forty-five persons. It was so lucrative that it netted the operators some $10,000 a week.[48] Success in this endeavor led in August of 1996 to the disclosure of the closing of a $500,000-a-year child pornography ring headed by three Americans who were operating from Acapulco; this turned out to be the largest child pornography distribution ring U.S. law enforcement had seen up to this time. Seized were thousands of videos and still photographs involving some three hundred Mexican boys as young as seven years old. As a result, some fifty-six individuals were arrested throughout the United States for having received the material by mail order.[49]

It is clear that it is illegal to send any depiction of sexual activity or "overtly sexual poses involving children," whether they have been found obscene or not.[50] The mailing need not be obscene if children are involved, according to the Child Protection Act of 1984. Any depiction of abuse or exploitation of a child—a person under eighteen—that is sent through the mails is sufficient to violate the law.

The Postal Service also has worked in conjunction with state and local police, the FBI, the Customs Service, and U.S. attorneys to combat the spread of pornography. Because sex crimes and distribution of pornography so frequently overlap jurisdictions, often involve more than one city, town, and county, and may even involve international contacts, this cooperative effort is probably the most common pattern of activity for the Postal Service. Inspectors have also been part of coordinated sting operations, as in Operation Borderline and Project Looking Glass in 1986 and 1987. In these two operations some 338 search warrants were obtained, leading to 207 indictments. Thirty-five child molesters were discovered through these operations.

As the Internet has become an important means of communication, postal inspectors have become involved with overseeing communication via the computer. The Postal Service has discovered that the computer has been particularly important for pedophiles as they communicate with each other. As a result of such laws as the 1978 Protection of Children Against Sexual Exploitation Act and the Child Protection Act of 1984, the Postal Service has been given the authority to trace computer messages of suspected pornographers, well before the transmission of pornographic material takes place through the mails.[51]

Interest Groups

Amicus curiae (friend of the court) briefs filed before the Supreme Court and public testimony before Congress suggest which groups most actively

Table 8.2

Amicus Curiae Briefs to the Supreme Court on Obscenity Cases[1]

| | Classification of interest groups filing briefs | | | |
| | To restrict access | | To expand access | |
	1957–1984[2]	1985–1997[3]	1957–1984	1985–1997
Interest Group	(N)	(N)	(N)	(N)
Parent/child	2	24		17
Single-issue	2	83		59
Law-related		73	2	31
Religious	1	45	2	35
Museums/libraries			2	1
Multi-issue		86	9	44
Arts			5	
Authors/press			23	47
Total	5	311	43	234

[1]Includes the first four months of 1997.
[2]Included in this period are forty-two obscenity cases.
[3]Included in this period are twenty-one obscenity cases.

try to influence obscenity policy making. I classified the types of interest groups that filed amicus briefs in major Supreme Court obscenity cases from 1957 to 1984 and from 1985 to 1997 (Table 8.2). As becomes quite evident, there has been much more interest-group involvement with the courts since 1985. There is a greater number of interest groups today than there was decades ago, as the Supreme Court in the 1990s has become increasingly involved in a broader range of these concerns.

The overwhelming number of interest groups submitting friend-of-the-court briefs did so in only a limited number of cases (Table 8.3). The exceptional pattern was that followed by the ACLU, which repeatedly petitioned the Supreme Court. Interest groups seeking to expand public access to pornography and free expression were far more likely to look to the Court to find resolution in the first period (1957–1984) than in the second period (1985–1997). Since 1985 the groups favoring restricted access have appeared before the Court in larger numbers.

Groups in the earlier period that repeatedly filed briefs argued for expanded access whereas in the recent period groups filing at least four amicus briefs were about evenly divided between those supporting and those opposing restriction of information. One commonality exhibited across the entire period is that the ACLU remained the most active group in support-

Table 8.3

Most Active Interest Groups Filing Amicus Curiae Briefs[1]

Most active restrictive interest groups, with number of briefs filed	Number of Briefs	Most active expansive interest groups, with number of briefs filed	Number of Briefs
(1957–1984)		**(1957–1984)**	
Citizens for Decency Through Law	8	American Civil Liberties Union and affiliates	22
		Council for Periodical Distributors Assoc.	6
		Assoc. of American Publishers	6
		Authors League of America	5
		American Library Association and affiliates	4
		International Periodical Distributors Assoc.	5
		American Book Publishers Council	4
		American Booksellers Assoc.	4
(1985–1997)		**(1985–1997)**	
National League of Cities	5	American Civil Liberties Union	16
National Governors Assoc.	5	NAACP	6
National Assoc. of Counties	5	Anti-Defamation League of B'nai B'rith	4
Council of State Governors	5	American Jewish Congress	5

(continued)

Table 8.3 *(continued)*

International City Management Assoc.	5	PHE[2]	4
U.S. Conference of Mayors	5	American Booksellers Assoc.	6
National Institute of Municipal Law Officers	5	American Jewish Committee	4
Center of Missing/Exploited Children	4	Association of American Publishers	6
Concerned Women for America	4	Council for Periodical Distributors	6
Nat'l. Assoc. of Criminal Defense Lawyers	4	Int'l. Periodical Distributors Assoc.	6
Nat'l. Coalition Against Pornography	4	Assoc. of College Stores	4
Rutherford Institute	7	Freedom to Read Foundation	6

[1]Only those interest groups that filed four or more briefs are listed, due to the high volume of briefs.
[2]PHE is a North Carolina–based distributor of films, magazines and books.

Table 8.4

Interest Group Testimony to Congress on Obscenity[1]

| | Classification of interest groups giving testimony or giving written statements | | | |
| | To restrict access | | To expand access | |
Interest Group	1957–1984[2] Number of statements	1985–1997[3] Number of statements	1957–1984 Number of statements	1985–1997 Number of statements
Government	8	29	4	
Parent/child	1	3		
Single-issue	14	14		
Law-related	1	2	4	
Religious	38	8	2	
Health-related	11		1	
Education	3	1	1	
Multi-Issue	10	4	2	6
Arts	3		2	
Authors/press	7		13	9
Fraternal/ethnic	3			
Labor/business	4		1	2
Women's groups	4			
Museums/libraries			1	2
Computer				8
Media		1		1
Victims		1		
Total	107	63	31	28

[1]Included the first four months of 1997.
[2]Included in this period are thirty-seven congressional hearings.
[3]Included in this period are fifteen congressional hearings.

ing expansive access, while Citizens for Decency Through Law dominated the earlier period by working to restrict access to information as well as by testifying before Congress (see Table 8.4). However, Citizens for Decency Through Law ceased judicial lobbying after 1985.

Most organizations petitioning the Supreme Court are motivated by self-interest and principle. These include organizations of authors, presses, and distributors. Civil libertarians, libraries, museums, artists, presses, and minority interests have all favored freer access to expression except where minors and nonconsenting adults were involved. Among those groups representing the press, the more established groups tended to file amicus briefs in support of media access. Because the Supreme Court has long been supportive of a free press and freedom of expression, in the earlier period many antipornography watchdog groups instead concentrated their efforts on the legislative branch. The changed strategy since 1985 would seem to reflect the increased number of child pornography cases to reach the Court and the perception that the Rehnquist Court may be more sympathetic to antiobscenity arguments.

A similar examination of groups that testified before the Congress indicates which groups either testified or submitted written statements to congressional committees on pornography from 1957 to 1997 (Table 8.4). Many more groups favoring restrictions on access to information testified before Congress than did organizations in favor of expanding public access in both periods of time. Among the 107 groups that testified against obscenity in the earlier period, religious organizations predominated. The major exceptions to this pattern were the American Lutheran Church and the Methodist TV, Radio, and Film Committee, both of which favored greater public access.

However, religious bodies, notably Catholic and Protestant groups, generally were not as strident in their advocacy as the single-issue group Citizens for Decency Through Law (see Table 8.5). This group, a legally oriented antiobscenity organization, has been involved for years in filing amicus briefs and in staging grassroots campaigns against pornography. A large number of the single-issue groups to petition the Congress, in fact, were affiliates of the Citizens for Decency Through Law, except for testimony received from Eradication of Smut and Morality in Media. As expected, Postal Service representatives tended to be sympathetic to restrictions on indecency, although the Postal Service did testify on behalf of expanded access to information in a few of the hearings. Groups of physicians, hospitals, and psychiatrists also were supportive of restricting access.

In the later period (1985–1997) it was governmental groups and single-issue groups that dominated the testimony. Because it was often before the Court, the ACLU again was the most active group advocating expansion of expression; booksellers and publishers repeatedly urged the Congress to limit restrictions on free expression. Citizens for Decency Through Law, on the other hand, was the most active group supporting restrictions, followed by the Department of Justice and the U.S. Postal Service. There were many groups more selective in focusing on one or two hearings to give testimony. The American Library Association, arts groups, and associations of authors and press associations testified in favor of expanding public access to information, just as they had done before the Supreme Court.

One curious omission from these data is feminist groups, which by and large have been extremely critical of pornography. Yet the only women's

Table 8.5

Most Active Interest Groups Testifying to Congress on Obscenity[1]

Most active interest groups to restrict access	Number of statements	Most active interest groups to expand access	Number of statements
(1957–1984)[2]		(1957–1984)	
Citizens for Decency		American Civil Liberties	
Through Law	18	Union and affiliates	13
U.S. Postal Service	16	American Book	
		Publishers Council	6
National Assoc. of		Authors League of	
Evangelicals	3	America	4
Methodist Church—Bd. of		U.S. Postal Service	
Temperance	3		4
National Council of Catholic		Assoc. of American	
Men	3	Publishers	3
National Assoc. of Letter			
Carriers	3		
(1985–1997)[3]		(1985–1997)	
American Civil Liberties		American Civil Liberties	
Union	3	Union	6
U.S. Dept. of		Council for Periodical	
Justice	9	Distributors Assoc.	3
Citizens for Decency		American Booksellers	
Through Law	10	Assoc.	3
Christian Life Comm.:			
Southern Baptist Conv.	3		
U.S. Postal Service	7		

[1]Only those interest groups that testified three or more times are included on this list.

[2]Included are thirty-seven congressional hearings.

[3]Included are fifteen congressional hearings. The year 1997 included only the first four months.

groups to offer testimony before Congress were the more traditional organizations, such as the Federation of Women's Clubs, the National Women's Christian Temperance Union, and the Women's Democratic Club of Philadelphia. Newer feminist groups such as Women Against Pornography, Take Back the Night, Women Against Sexual Harassment, Women Against Violence in Pornography, the Feminist Anti-Censorship Task Force, and Women Against Violence Against Women chose not to express their views in this way.

How effective are the antipornography groups at the grassroots level?

One study of censorship campaigns in eighteen communities found that most ended in failure in terms of any long-run suppression, because the booksellers successfully appealed to the courts and local officials failed to back the censorship campaigns. Rodgers concluded that because anti-pornography groups were unable to rally public opinion, "those who attempted to censor basically had to do so alone," and they had to settle for limited, short-term, or symbolic successes.[52]

Morality in Media focused its efforts in 1984 on Buffalo, New York, desiring to remove nudity and sex from the Playboy TV cable channel there, but Morality in Media's protests were not persuasive with the Buffalo City Council because cable TV still was a personal option paid for by the subscriber. In 1986 the National Federation for Decency, a Christian group with central headquarters in Mississippi, did picket convenience stores to get them to remove their adult magazines. It, along with a strong letter from the 1985 Attorney General's Pornography Commission telling drugstore and convenience store chains that they had been identified as being involved in "the sale or distribution of pornography" and would be so named in the commission report, encouraged more than eight thousand of them to remove the publications. The National Federation for Decency claimed that the number of outlets selling the magazines had fallen by twenty thousand over a three-year period, due in part to their constant picketing.[53]

An increase in interest in child pornography laws, the presence of the Internet, and the use of government money for the arts have all in the last few years encouraged greater activity on the part of antipornography interest groups. Such groups as the American Family Association, Pat Robertson's *700 Club,* and the Christian Action Network have been active in opposing funding for the National Endowment for the Arts, whereas the American Arts Alliance, the American Council for the Arts, and the Arts Coalition for Freedom of Expression, along with many individual artists, have been equally active in supporting government funding.[54] The Religious Alliance Against Pornography served as a sympathetic audience for George Bush, who spoke to them in October 1991, talking of the horrors of pornography and encouraging this group not to give up in what they were doing.[55]

The Internet has become a modern-day target of conservative anti-pornography groups such as the Family Research Council, whose spokespersons have accused the information network of allowing young people to have easy access to pornographic material. The Internet has been defended by such groups as the Electronic Frontier Foundation, a Washington-based group supporting civil liberties on computer networks.[56]

The National Law Center for Children and Families, a Virginia-based group, has been very vocal in arguing the importance of funding measures to protect against child pornography. Most interest groups have advocated stringent laws such as the Child Pornography Prevention Act of 1996. The ACLU, of course, has worked just as hard to dissuade policy makers from shifting their focus from actual abuse of children to a "concern about images and fantasies." The ACLU position is that "people's thoughts are their private thoughts."[57]

Federalism

The 1985 Attorney General's Pornography Commission saw a need for state legislatures to update their obscenity statutes and to make them consistent with standards in the landmark 1973 obscenity case of *Miller v. California* (1973). Implementation at first was uncertain in many states, but many have since complied (see Table 8.6). Private possession of pornography is not thought, in general, to be a serious violation unless it is the possession of child pornography.

Cities and counties have written some unusual ordinances to try to combat pornography, but many of these raise important constitutional questions. On November 23, 1983, an ordinance introduced in the Minneapolis City Council held that pornography discriminated against women. The ordinance defined pornography as "the sexually explicit subordination of women; graphically depicted, whether in pictures or words" and categorized it as one type of discrimination based on gender.[58] By defining pornography in this way, individuals could bring lawsuits based on the city's civil rights ordinance. The antipornography ordinance was supported by the Minneapolis City Council, but Mayor Donald Fraser vetoed it on the grounds that it was ambiguous and vague.

Although this approach failed in Minneapolis, its effect was felt in other communities throughout the United States. One direct consequence of the Minneapolis experiment was the enactment of a similar antipornography ordinance in Indianapolis, which was adopted by the Indianapolis City and County Council in May 1984. The ordinance would have allowed city residents who believed their rights were violated by obscene material to file complaints with the city Office of Equal Opportunity, which could issue, subject to court review, a cease-and-desist order against the distributor.

Localities have allowed and, in some instances, encouraged restrictive antiobscenity campaigns in their communities, but most have not been too successful, even in conservative areas. A number of states and local areas have been frustrated in their attempts to monitor pornographic materials. While Albany, New York was successful in 1985 in passing a law against the display of "offensive sexual material" in public areas,[59] the next year Maine

Table 8.6

State Laws on Possession of Obscene Materials, 1997

Alabama	——	Montana	——
Alaska	——	Nebraska	——
Arizona	——	Nevada	——
Arkansas	Felony; $2,000 fine	New Hampshire	——
California	——	New Jersey	——
Colorado	6 or more, class I misdemeanor	New Mexico	——
Connecticut	——	New York	6 or more, class A misdemeanor
Delaware	——	North Carolina	——
Florida	3 or more, first degree misdemeanor	North Dakota	——
Georgia	——	Ohio	——
Hawaii	——	Oklahoma	Felony; 5 yrs prison, $5,000 fine
Idaho	——	Oregon	——
Illinois	——	Pennsylvania	——
Indiana	——	Rhode Island	——
Iowa	——	South Carolina	——
Kansas	——	South Dakota	——
Kentucky	——	Tennessee	——
Louisiana	——	Texas	6 or more, class A misdemeanor
Maine	——	Utah	——
Maryland	not illegal	Vermont	——
Massachusetts	——	Virginia	——
Michigan	——	West Virginia	——
Minnesota	——	Washington	llegal
Mississippi	——	Wisconsin	——
Missouri	——	Wyoming	——

Note: In most states possession of obscene materials is permitted as long as they are not to be distributed. In those states with limits on the number of obscene items any person can possess, it is assumed that a person who possesses that many obscene articles does so with the intent to distribute the same.

voters turned back an attempt to make it a crime to sell or in any way promote pornographic materials. The Christian Civil League of Maine was the principal interest group behind the referendum attempt, but opponents managed to convince voters that the issue was really one of censorship.[60]

By 1990 the Supreme Court did allow Ohio (in *Osborne v. Ohio,* 1990)[61] to ban the private possession of pornography, although in the same year it refused to allow the city of Dallas, Texas to license "adult" businesses (in *FW/PBS v. Dallas,* 1990).[62] In 1994 eighty thousand Colorado citizens signed a petition to amend the Colorado constitution to remove what many have considered to be a liberal free-speech clause. Supporters of the amendment felt that this clause made the Colorado document more liberal than the U.S. Constitution in its interpretation of what obscenity is.[63] Unfortunately for those voters, the measure lost.

One policy on which state, local, and federal governments agree is firm opposition to child pornography (Tables 8.7 and 8.8). All but a few states have enacted strong prohibitions against child pornography. The fines and penalties are all strong, and severe in many cases, with states generally requiring felony penalties for violating child antipornography laws. Many of these states restrict child pornography whether or not it has been found to be obscene.[64]

Even had the Supreme Court supported local standards in obscenity cases, it is doubtful whether there would be sufficient consensus among local decision makers on what community standard would prevail. In a study of Detroit, for example, Douglas H. Wallace found that "there was no uniform standard or criterion being used by these subjects [those being tested] as they evaluated the stimulus items. The variability of their responses . . . in their mean ratings of the pictures, and the differences between the 'sexual liberals' and 'sexual conservatives' do not support the *single contemporary community standard* hypothesis."[65] Even in an Idaho town of forty-three thousand, where one might expect more homogeneous views, a 1978 study found that "pornography was dichotomized differently by different individuals."[66] Thus not even in this medium-sized city did an obvious community standard emerge.

The Internet has posed some difficult problems for states. Ann Beason of the ACLU claims that few states have understood the Internet in the sort of restrictive laws they have passed. The Georgia legislature even tried in 1996 to outlaw pictures of marijuana on the Internet, and in 1995 the same legislature attempted to bar the transmission of "fighting words" or vulgar expressions to minors on the Internet. A number of states have incorporated on-line communication into their child pornography laws, including Illinois, Kansas, Maryland, and Montana. Illinois even prohibits solicitation of a minor by computer.[67] What state legislators don't always consider in their zeal to protect children from Internet transmissions is that when children are restricted, adults are also frequently limited in their freedoms.

Public Opinion

Is pornography a salient issue for most citizens? There is enough opinion research on this topic to draw some conclusions about how the public assesses this problem. At the outset, one thing is certain: Pornography is pervasive in almost all communities. A 1977 Gallup poll found that X-rated

Table 8.7

State Laws on Possession of Child Pornography, 1997

State	Law	State	Law
Alabama	3 or more items, Class B felony	Montana	10 yrs prison, $10,000 fine
Alaska	Class A misdemeanor	Nebraska	Class II misdemeanor
Arizona	Class 2 felony	Nevada	Category B felony
Arkansas	Class C felony	New Hampshire	Misdemeanor
California	Felony; $2,000 fine	New Jersey	Crime of fourth degree
Colorado	Class 1 misdemeanor	New Mexico	————
Connecticut	2 or more, Class C felony	New York	Class E felony
Delaware	Class A misdemeanor	North Carolina	Class I felony
Florida	Third degree felony	North Dakota	Class A misdemeanor
Georgia	Misdemeanor	Ohio	Fifth degree felony
Hawaii	————	Oklahoma	Felony; 20 yrs prison, $25,000 fine
Idaho	3 or more, felony; 15 yrs prison, $25,000 fine	Oregon	Class C felony
Illinois	Class 4 felony	Pennsylvania	Third degree felony
Indiana	Class A misdemeanor	Rhode Island	————
Iowa	Serious misdemeanor	South Carolina	Felony; 5 yrs prison
Kansas	Severity level 5 person felony	South Dakota	Misdemeanor
Kentucky	Class A misdemeanor	Tennessee	Class E felony
Louisiana	3 or more, min. 2 yrs prison, $10,000 fine	Texas	Third degree felony
Maine	3 or more, 2 yrs prison, $10,000 fine	Utah	Second degree felony
Maryland	Misdemeanor; 1 yr prison, $2,500 fine	Vermont	————
Massachusetts	————	Virginia	Class 3 misdemeanor
Michigan	Misdemeanor	Washington	Class C felony
Minnesota	Gross misdemeanor	West Virginia	Felony; 2 yrs prison, $2,000 fine
Mississippi	Felony	Wisconsin	Class E felony
Missouri	Class A misdemeanor	Wyoming	————

movies, adult bookstores, and even massage parlors existed in communities of all sizes, ranging from those with more than 1 million people to towns with populations of 2,500. Only in rural areas, in towns with fewer than 2,500 inhabitants, were movie theaters not showing X-rated films.[68]

Despite the 1967 president's commission, which suggested that there was no evidence linking pornography to social deviancy, most citizens believe there is such a relationship. The link for some people is articulated by one researcher when he indicated that "pornography is the theory, and rape the practice."[69]

The latest poll shows a plurality of Americans still believe that there is a

Table 8.8

State Laws on Importing or Promoting Child Pornography, 1997

Alabama	Class B felony
Alaska	Class C felony
Arizona	Class 3 felony
Arkansas	Class C felony
California	Felony; fine and imprisonment
Colorado	Class 3 felony
Connecticut	Class C felony
Delaware	Class D felony
Florida	Second degree felony
Georgia	Felony; 5 to 20 yrs prison, $100,000 fine
Hawaii	Class A felony
Idaho	Felony; 15 yrs prison, $25,000 fine
Illinois	Class A felony
Indiana	Class D felony
Iowa	Class D felony
Kansas	Severity level 5 person felony
Kentucky	Class C or B felony
Louisiana	2 to 10 yrs prison, $10,000 fine
Maine	Class C crime
Maryland	Felony; 10 yrs prison, $25,000 fine
Massachusetts	10 to 20 yrs prison, $10,000 to $50,000 fine
Michigan	7 yrs prison, $50,000 fine
Minnesota	Felony; 5 yrs prison, $10,000 fine
Mississippi	Felony; $25,000 to $100,000 fine
Missouri	Class B felony
Montana	100 yrs prison, $10,000 fine
Nebraska	Class IV felony
Nevada	Class A or B felony
New Hampshire	Class B felony
New Jersey	Crime of second degree
New Mexico	Third degree felony
New York	Class D felony
North Carolina	Class F felony
North Dakota	Class B felony
Ohio	Second degree felony
Oklahoma	Felony; 20 yrs prison, $25,000 fine
Oregon	Class B felony
Pennsylvania	Second degree felony
Rhode Island	10 yrs prison, $10,000 fine
South Carolina	Class C felony; 3 to 10 yrs prison
South Dakota	Felony
Tennessee	Class B felony
Texas	Third degree felony
Utah	Second degree felony
Vermont	10 yrs prison, $20,000 fine
Virginia	Class 5 felony
West Virginia	Felony; 10 yrs prison, $10,000 fine
Washington	Class C felony
Wisconsin	Class C felony
Wyoming	———

Table 8.9

Public Views on Link Between Pornography and Rape

Question: "The next questions are about pornography—books, movies, magazines, and photographs that show or describe sex activities. I'm going to read some opinions about the effects of looking at or reading such sexual materials. As I read each one, please tell me if you think sexual materials do or do not have that effect. Sexual materials lead people to commit rape: yes; no; don't know/no answer."

	1988	1991	1993	1994
Yes	56%	53%	56%	48%
No	35	37	33	41
Don't Know/No Answer	9	10	11	11

Source: National Opinion Research Center (NORC) polls for the designated years.

Table 8.10

Public Views on Link Between Pornography and Morals

Question: "The next questions are about pornography—books, movies, magazines, and photographs that show or describe sex activities. I'm going to read some opinions about the effects of looking at or reading such sexual materials. As I read each one, please tell me if you think sexual materials do or do not have that effect. Sexual materials lead to breakdown of morals: yes; no; don't know/no answer."

	1988	1991	1993	1994
Yes	62%	60%	63%	57%
No	32	34	30	36
Don't Know/No Answer	6	6	7	7

Source: National Opinion Research Center (NORC) polls for the designated years.

link between exposure to sexual materials and committing rape, though apparently fewer people today are convinced of that relationship than before (Table 8.9). However, a much larger majority do express the opinion that exposure to sexual materials leads to a breakdown of morals in society, a sentiment that has persisted since the late 1980s (Table 8.10).

While most people in the country (92 percent in 1986) have confidence in their innate ability to determine what pornography is, agreement on what to do about it is less obvious, though in most cases a majority favored restrictions.[70] Most commonly branded as pornographic by the public are depictions of sexual intercourse in magazines (84 percent), X-rated movies (77 percent), and depictions of homosexual sex acts (86 percent).[71] Also, nine times as many people favor making community standards on pornographic

Table 8.11

Public Views on Strictness of Pornography Laws

Question: "Do you think the standards in your [1977: this] community regarding the sale of sexually explicit material should be stricter than they are now, not as strict, or kept as they are now?" As printed in Tom W. Smith, "The Polls—A Report: The Sexual Revolution," *Public Opinion Quarterly* 54, no. 3 (Fall 1990), p. 427.

	1977	1985	1986
Stricter	45%	43%	45%
Less Strict	6	4	5
Kept as Now	35	48	43
No Opinion	14	7	5

Source: Gallup polls for these years.

Table 8.12

Public Views on Access to Pornography by Adults and Minors

Question: "Which of these statements comes closest to your feelings about pornography laws?"

	1988	1990	1993	1994
There should be laws against the distribution of pornography whatever the age	43%	41%	41%	37%
There should be laws against the distribution of pornography to persons under age	18	50	52	54
There should be no laws forbidding the distribution of pornography	5	6	3	3
Don't know/no answer	2	1	2	1

Source: National Opinion Research Center (NORC) polls for the designated years.

sales "stricter" as compared to the minority (5 percent in 1986) who would allow "less strict" criteria (Table 8.11). Furthermore, surveys indicate that a majority of the public wants more protective standards for children under eighteen years of age, to prevent their exposure to pornography.[72] In 1994 slightly more than one-third of Americans would support a similar ban for all persons regardless of age (Table 8.12).[73]

Summary

Obscenity is a classic example of the fundamental conflict between the constitutional guarantees of free expression and the collective goal that society represents some kind of moral order. An activist Warren Court refused to ban publications on the same grounds that Congress and the states had used. This gave the Supreme Court exclusive authority to define obscenity on a case-by-case basis.

Given the constitutional obstacles to limiting the spread of obscenity among adults, the states and Congress turned to child pornography as their overriding concern. Various enactments since the late 1970s began regulating child pornography without bothering, in many cases, to prove whether the materials were "obscene" or not. This approach has since been upheld by the Burger Court in its *Ferber* ruling.

Although the nation's citizens generally oppose rigid censorship of books and films, there exists a consensus against absolute free expression. Most people want some type of obscenity standard regarding the materials available for public distribution, and recent legislation to curb child pornography finds a sympathetic public opinion. Even groups representing authors, presses, and distributors reluctantly testify before Congress in favor of limiting obscene materials to adults only. Child pornography is still present with us in the 1990s. There are signs, therefore, that the 1985 commission report may have more impact on sympathetic policy makers than the 1967 commission study had on the political leadership.

The conflict between free expression and pornography in our democratic system has been heightened in this age of the Internet, an unregulated communication system that seems a perfect forum for the exchange of ideas—some of which have been considered lewd, if not pornographic. Decision makers will need to come up with more effective policy guidelines balancing free expression and restriction of that expression for the twenty-first century. "Knowing it" on sight, as did Justice Potter Stewart, may not be good enough for the future of expression on the Web.

Notes

A special thanks is due my research assistant, Ms. Suzanne McConkie, for all the help she provided on the tables in this chapter.

1. In this chapter the terms *pornography* and *obscenity* will be used interchangeably to refer to material that is sexually explicit and is designed to cause sexual arousal. This description of the pornography/obscenity market is found in Eric Schlosser, "The Business of Porn," *U.S. News and World Report* (February 10, 1997), p. 44.

2. The twenty states are Arizona, Colorado, Delaware, Florida, Hawaii, Kentucky, Louisiana, Massachusetts, Michigan, Montana, Mississippi, New York, New Jersey, Oklahoma, Pennsylvania, Rhode Island, Texas, Utah, West Virginia, and Wisconsin. See Daniel S. Moretti, *Obscenity and Pornography: The Law Under the First Amendment* (New York: Oceana, 1984), appendix E, p. 127.

3. See Michael Adler, "Cyberspace, General Searches, and Digital Contraband: The Fourth Amendment and the Net-wide Search," *Yale Law Journal* 105 (January 1996), pp. 1093–1120.

4. John Markoff, "The Media Business: On-Line Service Blocks Access to Topics Called Pornographic," *New York Times* (December 29, 1995), p. 1; "Bavarian Police Probe Sparked CompuServe's On-line Censorship," *San Francisco Examiner* (December 30, 1995), p. A12.

5. Linda Greenhouse, "Court, 9–0, Upholds State Laws Prohibiting Assisted Suicide; Protects Speech on Internet," *New York Times* (June 27, 1997), pp. A1, A16.

6. Linda Greenhouse, "Supreme Court Roundup: Child Smut Conviction Vacated After U.S. Shift," *New York Times* (November 2, 1993), p. B7.

7. For example, a 1973 statute gave a very specific definition of obscenity as "an explicit representation, or detailed written or verbal description of an act of sexual intercourse, including genital-genital, anal-genital, or oral-genital intercourse, whether between human beings or between a human being and an animal, or of flagellation, torture, or other violence indicating a sado-masochistic sexual relationship." See S. 1400, 93rd Cong., 1st sess., section 1851(b)(2) (1973).

8. Pamela Mendels, "Child Pornography Issue Raised in Budget," *New York Times* (October 3, 1996), p. A11.

9. "Amendment Offered by Mr. Smith of New Jersey," *Congressional Record* (House), April 20, 1994, pp. H2536–H2539.

10. See "One 'Porn' Law Too Many," *Washington Post* (May 23, 1989), p. A14.

11. Telecommunications Act, U.S. Code, vol. 104, sec. 501–561 (Title V) (1996).

12. Louise Sweeney, "11th-Hour Arts Funding: Congressional Compromise Gives NEA Three Years of Life But Doesn't Lay Obscenity Issue to Rest,"*Christian Science Monitor*, November 2, 1990, p. 13.

13. Tim Golden, "Court Bars Decency Standards in Awarding of U.S. Arts Grants," *New York Times* (November 6, 1996), p. A10.

14. See "The Cable Indecency Decision," *New York Times* (July 1, 1996), p. A12.

15. Concerned Women for America newsletter, March 1997.

16. "Resolution Declaring that the Senate Reject the Findings and Recommendations of the Commission on Obscenity and Pornography," *Congressional Record,* 91st Cong., 2nd sess., December 17, 1970, p. 42318.

17. *Congressional Record,* 92nd Cong., 1st sess., January 25, 1971, p. 460.

18. This examination of the earlier presidents and pornography comes from *CIS Index to Presidential Executive Orders and Proclamations,* part I: April 30, 1789 to March 4, 1921, "George Washington to Woodrow Wilson. Obscenity and Pornography," 1910–44–165 (Bethesda, MD: Congressional Information Service, 1987).

19. "The President's News Conference, June 17, 1953," *The Public Papers of the Presidents, Dwight D. Eisenhower, 1953* (Washington, DC: U.S. Government Printing Office, 1954), p. 431.

20. "Text of President's Message on Obscenity," *Congressional Quarterly Weekly Report* (May 9, 1969), p. 702.

21. "Statement About the Report of the Commission on Obscenity and Pornography," October 24, 1970, *Public Papers of the Presidents of the United States* (Washington, DC: U.S. Government Printing Office, 1971), p. 940.

22. *Congressional Quarterly Almanac, 1984,* vol. 49 (Washington, DC: Congressional Quarterly, 1985), p. 51B.

23. "Reagan Is Urged To 'Torpedo' Pornography Industry," *Boston Globe* (29 March 1983). Online. Retrieved from DIALOG File 631.

24. "Child Protection Act of 1984: Remarks on Signing H.R. 3635 Into Law," May

21, 1984, *Public Papers of the Presidents of the United States: Ronald Reagan,* book 2 (Washington, DC: U.S. Government Printing Office, 1986), pp. 721–722.

25. Its membership included Henry Hudson, chairman, U.S. attorney for the Eastern District of Virginia; Judith V. Becker, associate professor of clinical psychology, Columbia University; Diana D. Cusack, former vice mayor of Scottsdale, Arizona; Park E. Dietz, professor of law, behavioral medicine, and psychiatry, University of Virginia; James C. Dobson, president, *Focus on Family,* a syndicated radio program; Edward J. Garcia, federal judge, U.S. Court for Eastern District of California; Ellen Levine, editor, *Woman's Day*; Tex Lezar, counselor to former attorney general William French Smith; Rev. Bruce Ritter, president, Covenant House (a child care crisis center); Frederick Schauer, professor of law, University of Michigan; Deanne Tilton, president, California Consortium of Child Abuse Councils.

26. Attorney General's Commission on Pornography, *Final Report,* vol. 1 (Washington, DC: U.S. Government Printing Office, 1986), p. 229.

27. Robert Pear, "Panel Calls on Citizens to Wage National Assault on Pornography," *New York Times* (July 10, 1986), p. 10.

28. Attorney General's Commission on Pornography, *Final Report,* vol. 1, p. 326.

29. Ibid., p. 199.

30. Jacqueline Trescott, "Bush on Art vs. 'Filth,' " *Washington Post* (June 7, 1993), p. D4.

31. David Johnston, "Clinton Calls for Expansion of Child Pornography Laws," *New York Times* (November 12, 1993), p. A14.

32. "Letter to Attorney General Janet Reno on Child Pornography," November 10, 1993, *Public Papers of the Presidents of the United States: William J. Clinton,* book 2 (Washington, DC: U.S. Government Printing Office, 1994), p. 1952.

33. Johnston, "Clinton Calls for Expansion of Child Pornography Laws."

34. *In the Matter of Amendment of Part 76 of the Commission's Rules and Regulations Concerning the Cable Television Channel Capacity and Access Channel Requirements of Section 76.251,* 87 FCC 2d 42 (1981).

35. See Alex S. Jones, "F.C.C. Acts on the Complaints of 'Indecency' on Radio," *New York Times* (November 22, 1986), p. 11.

36. David Holmstrom, "FCC and Courts Grapple with Public Complaints over Radio's 'Shock Jocks,' " *Christian Science Monitor,* February 4, 1993, pp. 1, 4.

37. See "Enforcement of Prohibitions Against Broadcast Indecency" in 18 U.S.C., sec. 1464 (1993).

38. Tim Golden, "16 Indicted on Charges of Internet Pornography: Allegations of Molestation Are Also Filed," *New York Times* (July 17, 1996), p. A8.

39. Howard A. Davidson, "Sexual Exploitation of Children," *F.B.I. Law Enforcement Bulletin* (February 1984), p. 28.

40. Lawrence A. Stanley, "The Child-pornography Myth," *Playboy* (September 1988), p. 41.

41. "Child Porn Crackdown," *USA Today* (December 12, 1996), p. 3A.

42. See 18 U.S.C. Sec. 552.

43. See 18 U.S.C. Secs. 1462, 1465; 19 U.S.C. Sec. 1305; 18 U.S.C. Sec. 1699.

44. James C.N. Paul and Murray L. Schwartz, *Federal Censorship: Obscenity in the Mail* (Glencoe, IL: Free Press, 1961), pp. 90–91. It was found that during 1946–1956, rarely did any importer protest seizure by U.S. Customs. Ibid., p. 90.

45. See Mary Thornton, "Customs Service Leads War on Child Pornography: Publications from Abroad, Sexual Exploitation in U.S. Are Inspectors' Targets," *Washington Post* (August 9, 1986), p. A8.

46. GAO Report, *Sexual Exploitation of Children—A Problem of Unknown Magni-*

tude, Report to Chairman, Subcommittee on Select Education, House Committee on Education and Labor, April 20, 1982, General Accounting Report, B–207117, p. 50.

47. See 18 U.S.C. Sec. 1341.

48. David Stout, "Child Pornography Mailing List Leads to 45 Arrests Nationwide," *New York Times* (May 10, 1996), p. A13.

49. Julia Preston, "Acapulco's Smut Ring: The Children Remember," *New York Times* (August 9, 1996), p. A1.

50. "Mailing of Child Pornography," United States Postal Inspection Service http://www.usps.gov/websites/depart/inspect/kid-porn.htm.

51. 18 USC 2251–2253.

52. Harrell R. Rodgers Jr., "Censorship Campaigns in Eighteen Cities: An Impact Analysis," *American Politics Quarterly* 2 (October 1974), especially pp. 375, 380–381, and 389.

53. Matthew L. Wald, "'Adult' Magazines Lose Sales as 8,000 Stores Forbid Them," *New York Times* (June 16, 1986), p. 1.

54. Louise Sweeney, "The Arts and U.S. Tax Dollars: Federal Endowment for Arts Shaky," *Christian Science Monitor,* April 23, 1990, p. 8; Sam Walker, "Arts Agency Still in the Hot Seat: The National Endowment for the Arts Struggles to Reclaim Its Stature and Quiet Critics," *Christian Science Monitor,* August 6, 1993, pp. 12–13.

55. See "Bush Hits 'Horror' of Pornography," *Boston Globe* (October 11, 1991). OnLine. Retrieved from DIALOG File 631.

56. Rory J. O'Connor, "Debate Continues to Heat Up Over Sex on the Net," *Mercury Center/San Jose Mercury News,* July 3, 1996, http://www.sjmercury.com/netmyth.htm.

57. Pamela Mendels, "Child Pornography Issue Raised in Budget," *New York Times* (October 3, 1996), p. A11.

58. This definition of pornography was later expanded in the Model Antipornography Law to include "the graphic sexually explicit subordination of women through pictures and/or words that also includes one or more of the following: (i) women are presented dehumanized as sexual objects, things, or commodities; or (ii) women are presented as sexual objects who enjoy pain or humiliation; or (iii) women are presented as sexual objects who experience sexual pleasure in being raped; or (iv) women are presented as sexual objects tied up or cut up or mutilated or bruised or physically hurt; or (v) women are presented in postures or positions of sexual submission, servility, or display; or (vi) women's body parts—including but not limited to vaginas, breasts, or buttocks—are exhibited such that women are reduced to those parts; or (vii) women are presented being penetrated by objects or animals; or (ix) women are presented in scenarios of degradation, injury, torture, shown as filthy or inferior, bleeding, bruised, or hurt in a context that makes these conditions sexual." See "Model Antipornography Law," *Ms.* (April 1985), p. 46.

59. "Pornography Limit Voted in Albany," *New York Times* (June 2, 1985), p. 23.

60. Matthew L. Wald, "In Maine, Obscenity Vote Brings Warnings of Purges and Plans for Prayer," *New York Times* (June 10, 1986), p. 8; Matthew L. Wald, "Maine's Anti-Obscenity Plan Is Soundly Defeated," *New York Times* (June 12, 1986), p. 27.

61. 495 U.S. 103 (1990).

62. 493 U.S. 215 (1990).

63. Dirk Johnson, "Colorado Vote Will Test Law on Obscenity," *New York Times* (October 9, 1994), p. 12.

64. See UT 1994 Utah Laws, Chapter 131, http://www.ncsl.org.

65. Douglas H. Wallace, "Obscenity and Contemporary Community Standards: A Survey," *Journal of Social Issues* 29 (November 3, 1973), p. 66.

66. Coke Brown, Joan Anderson, Linda Burggraf, and Neal Thompson, "Commu-

nity Standards, Conservatism, and Judgments of Pornography," *Journal of Sex and Research* 14 (May 1978), p. 94.

67. See Senate Bill 747, enacted July 1995; sponsor, Sen. Dudycz.

68. "Public Concerned About Porn, but Divided over Court Decision," *Gallup Opinion Index* 142 (May 1977), pp. 5–6.

69. R. Morgan, "Theory and Practice: Pornography and Rape," in L. Lederer, ed., *Take Back the Night* (New York: William Morrow, 1980), pp. 134–140.

70. "Opinion Roundup: A Pornography Report," *Public Opinion,* September/October 1986, p. 31.

71. *Time*/Yankelovich Clancy Shulman poll, July 7–9, 1986, in "Opinion Roundup," Ibid.

72. Both the 1970 pornography commission report and a 1985 Canadian survey found that adolescents were more often exposed to pornography than adults. Attorney General's Commission on Pornography, *Final Report,* vol. 1, pp. 916 and 921.

73. "Opinion Roundup: A Pornography Report," *Public Opinion,* September/October 1986, p. 33.

Conclusion

The Social Regulatory Policy Process

Raymond Tatalovich and Byron W. Daynes

In our previous edition we summarized the attributes of social regulatory policy making as fourteen propositions. Since the theoretical rationale for those hypotheses was established there, we will limit this discussion to these eight case studies.[1] Abortion, pornography, affirmative action, and gun control appeared in the first edition; a previous chapter on school prayer was broadened to the entire policy debate over church and state, while an earlier case study on crime was narrowed to focus on the death penalty. The chapters on Official English and homosexuality are new contributions to this volume.

There are two interrelated ideological dynamics in social regulatory policy. First, "moral" conservatives (which Lowi distinguishes from "fiscal" conservatives) defend the normative status quo, whereas liberals willingly accommodate changes in societal values.[2] Second, moralists want individual freedoms subordinated to community norms, whereas liberals defend personal liberties from government regulation. The former applies to all eight case studies; the latter also applies, with two exceptions. Where liberals are apt to curb governmental infringements respecting homosexuality, abortion, bilingualism, affirmative action, and even pornography (for adults) and would abolish the death penalty, they are not supportive of an individual's right to bear arms or to display his/her religiosity in the public sphere. In certain respects the debate over gun control is a deviant case from the typical course of social regulatory policy making.

Proposition 1a: Single-issue groups are the lobbies that most increase public awareness and the political significance of social regulatory policy.

Groups that Theodore J. Lowi expects to become mobilized over distributive policy ("beneficiaries"), economic regulations (trade associations), and redistributive policy ("peak" associations) would typically not be engaged in contentious social regulations, because most interest groups are created to defend the economic interests of their memberships, not to champion moral crusades. In none of our cases was the U.S. Chamber of Commerce or the AFL-CIO (both "peak" associations) involved; indeed, rarely were any unions or business groups mentioned.

More often "principle" or "altruism" are the motivating forces behind moral conflicts, though "interest" may come into play.[3] Rallying around prochoice issues is primarily symbolic since only a fraction of the women who support legalized abortion have had or will ever have an abortion. Opponents of capital punishment do not reside on death row, just as advocates of strong gun controls are no more likely to be the victims of crime than other people. Nor do supporters of English-only live alongside huge concentrations of Hispanics. While pornographers have a pecuniary motive, those mainstream publishers, librarians, and authors who rail against censorship are defending free speech and press more than any profits derived from obscenity.

Grassroots activism is linked to single-issue advocacy—National Right to Life Committee vs. National Abortion Rights Action League, National Rifle Association vs. Handgun Control, Inc., U.S. English vs. English Plus Information Clearinghouse—especially by people who defend the status quo. Because the established interests that take sides in moral conflicts tend to favor social change, single-issue groups are the preferred organizational strategy for defenders of the normative order. Single-issue groups have been organized to promote censorship of pornography and support for school prayer, but they were not as instrumental in rallying the opposition forces. However, some church-state "separationists" have utilized such organizations to monitor litigation and legislation.

Proposition 1b: Single-issue groups promote absolutist positions on social regulatory policy that polarize the debate as one of nonnegotiable, moral alternatives.

Writing in 1958, longshoreman-turned-philosopher Eric Hoffer characterized the "true believer" as a zealot who is committed to one cause.[4] This attribute of single-issue membership brings a disruptive influence to normal political discourse and consensus building. Social regulatory policy making at the national level is analogous to episodes of community conflict at the local level.[5] Gun owners are more passionate about gun control than citizens without weapons; prolifers who resort to civil disobedience believe that God is on their side, as do Christian conservatives who oppose homosexuality. The foreword, by Theodore J. Lowi, argues that moral discourse is polarizing. True, values and religion are sources of moralizing, but political ideology and "rights" rhetoric can have similar effects. Demanding "my rights"—real or imagined—is *the* rationale for abortion, homosexuality, free expression, and racial preference.

Proposition 2a: Courts promote legal change in social regulatory policy by asserting individual rights and liberties against traditional social values.

Courts historically have made policy that "legitimates" certain private behaviors. The degree to which personal behavior ought to be regulated is a public consideration that is weighed against the individual's desire to be free from government interference. How society defines this balance is the essence of social regulatory policy.

Judicial activism regarding social regulations commenced with the school desegregation ruling in *Brown v. Board of Education,* 347 U.S. 483 (1954), and the trend has accelerated. Every issue discussed in this volume eventually reached the Supreme Court, and questions involving abortion, church-state relations, death row appeals, affirmative action, and now child pornography have jammed the federal dockets. The high court's concern for civil liberties and minority rights has displaced its earlier focus on economic disputes.[6]

With a 1957 ruling the Court began viewing antipornography laws as infringements on free press; rulings in the early 1960s declared school prayer a violation of the establishment clause; in 1973 the Court constitutionalized a right to abortion. But there are notable exceptions to this pattern. The Court has refused to extend the "cruel and unusual punishment" prohibition to capital punishment, has held that explicit racial quotas by public agencies violate the equal protection clause (although affirmative action programs have been upheld), and has not ever acknowledged an individualistic right to bear arms. Gay rights is a mixed case, since the high court in 1986 upheld state antisodomy laws but, most recently, invalidated state enactments that deny civil rights coverage to homosexuals. So far the high court has not ruled on the merits of Official English laws.

Proposition 2b: Federal courts have expanded the opportunities for using litigation to change social regulatory policy outside the normal political process.

The debate over judicial activism and judicial restraint gained new prominence as a result of the judiciary's intervention in sensitive moral disputes. Moral conflicts invariably involve questions of civil liberties and rights, which makes litigation strategy a primary means for promoting legal changes *outside* the normal political process. The abortion ruling, in particular, revived a lively debate about "fundamental rights" adjudication.[7] The legal dilemma is that litigants who petition the courts argue that certain persons are being denied liberties in real situations, while the state tries to argue that long-term, indirect dangers will confront society if deviant social behavior is permitted. Given this choice, judges would tend to side with the plaintiffs.

The Supreme Court's *Roe v. Wade* (1973) decision nullifying the anti-abortion laws of forty-six states and the District of Columbia as infringing upon inherent privacy rights in the Bill of Rights was, according to some prolife scholars, "the most radical decision ever issued by the Supreme Court."[8] This doctrine of "incorporating"—or applying—the Bill of Rights to the state governments is not found in the first ten amendments or elsewhere in the Constitution, nor was incorporation the original intent of the framers who designed the Constitution. Rather, this jurisprudence evolved after the Supreme Court began to broadly interpret the Fourteenth Amendment, which prohibits any state from denying its citizens their "life, *liberty,* or property" (emphasis added) without "due process of law." Because incorporation doctrine is judge-made law that is not grounded in the language of the Constitution, this activist jurisprudence has inspired a strong dissent among conservatives.[9] Whether the conservative critique is valid or not, the mere allegation that incorporation is an illegitimate doctrine intensifies the political controversy surrounding judicial activism.

Proposition 3a: Presidents generally do not exert decisive leadership to change social regulatory policy, although they may make symbolic gestures.

We hypothesize only modest—and mainly symbolic—leadership from the White House, mainly because the states and the federal courts are the primary social regulatory policy makers. Thus presidential leadership would be rhetorical, though the political constraints seem obvious. How aggressively would any president promote legalized abortions, pornography, or racial quotas? How often would a president disparage religion, oppose the death penalty, or glorify homosexual relations? What is suggested by these illustrations is that presidents usually do not champion the liberal agenda of changes in social regulations, though they may publicly defend the popular (read conservative) positions on those issues. However, when presidents rhetorically enter the social regulatory arena to politicize moral disputes, their activities are notably colored by partisanship.

Proposition 3b: Republicans exploit social regulatory policy to mobilize conservative voters, whereas Democrats are constrained not to abandon liberalism.

The optimal strategy for a Democrat is to equivocate and say little in order not to offend conservative public opinion or to alienate that party's liberal wing. Both Kennedy and Johnson sidestepped the pornography issue, and Jimmy Carter tried to muddle his way around the abortion debate. If any Democrat seemed to act in a contrary way, it was Clinton. President Clinton is a "new" Democrat who supports capital punishment and opposes child pornography, but he too flip-flopped elsewhere. Clinton advocated "mending, not ending" affirmative action programs (although he never explicitly defended quotas or preferential treatment). He also tried to redeem a campaign pledge to gays by lifting the ban on homosexuals in the military, but backed down, and eventually signed legislation prohibiting same-sex marriages. Yet Clinton retained his liberal credentials by opposing English-only, the ban on "partial birth" abortions, or any school prayer amendment (though the Clinton administration issued guidelines on religious-oriented activities that were deemed constitutional).

Republicans can be outspoken on social regulations because the preferences of their party's rank-and-file and those of the general electorate are compatible. The beginning of the political backlash was the 1968 presidential campaign by Richard Nixon, who attacked crime, drugs, and pornography, but President Reagan elevated the "social agenda" to embrace prolife issues, school prayer, and the death penalty while opposing child pornography, racial preferences, and gun control.

Proposition 4a: Congress usually opposes the federal judiciary and aligns itself with the state legislatures on social regulatory policy.

Conflict between the high court and the popular branches of government is not uncommon, and sometimes the Supreme Court is forced to yield to democratic pressures. According to Walter Murphy, there is no serious tension between the judicial and legislative branches until the high court renders a controversial ruling.[10] When that happens, in the face of a prolonged and intense outcry from public opinion and Congress, "judicial retreat" is the usual Supreme Court response. The best example of this was the shift on capital punishment during the 1970s.[11] In *Furman v. Georgia* (1972) the Supreme Court came close to declaring the death penalty a "cruel and unusual" punishment in violation of the Eighth Amendment. But after revisiting that question in *Gregg v. Georgia* (1976), the Court has upheld capital punishment as constitutional, and today has taken steps to shorten the appeal process of death row inmates.

On abortion, while the Supreme Court has not disavowed its precedent in *Roe v. Wade* (1973), nonetheless its ruling in *Webster v. Reproductive Health Services* (1989) has opened the door to more state abortion regulations. Essentially abortion has been transformed from an absolute right to a qualified right. On child pornography, *New York v. Ferber* (1982) was a departure from the high court's deference to free expression in obscenity cases. Rather, it followed the lead of Congress by upholding as constitutional new federal child pornography legislation. But looking ahead, a new clash between the legislative and judicial branches may be provoked by the 1997 *Boerne v. Flores* decision invalidating the Religious Freedom Restoration Act of 1993. Since that law passed the House and Senate with more than two-thirds of the vote, showing bipartisan as well as liberal and conservative support, it would not be unexpected to find the new GOP-controlled 105th Congress trying to reassert the legislative position through a proposed constitutional amendment.

The fundamental reason why Congress opposes the judiciary but sides with state legislatures on social regulatory policy is that political forces constrain the popularly elected branches to affirm community norms.

Proposition 4b: Electoral pressures encourage Congress to represent traditional values in social regulatory policy.

T. Alexander Smith noted that, though elected officials would not ordinarily take positions on "emotive symbolic" policies, public opinion would "insist on getting its own way," and thus legislators would have to address those demands.[12] Whenever the citizenry is aroused by moral conflicts, public opinion weighs heavily in congressional deliberations. The best evidence from the past is drawn from legislative voting behavior on civil rights, but this proposition comports with our case studies as well.[13]

In the 1980s Congress approved tough restrictions on child pornography and in the 1990s extended capital punishment to a range of federal crimes.

Congress passed a law to undermine same-sex marriages, regularly promotes the prolife agenda (including its latest attempt to ban "partial birth" abortions), and provoked the latest round of church-state litigation by its recent efforts to strengthen religious liberty via the Religious Freedom Restoration Act. On affirmative action, Congress originally disavowed racial quotas but abdicated its responsibilities to the judiciary and the bureaucracy to define guidelines for affirmative action. We have federal gun control statutes, but they are few in number and far between, and Congress even softened some gun control provisions during the Reagan era. The House approved an English-only bill, and the Senate, which so far has not acted, probably has enough votes to approve that measure.

Proposition 5a: Public opinion is often conservative, sometimes moderate, and rarely liberal, but always less intense with respect to social regulations as compared to the ideology of those who favor social change.

Our case studies show that public opinion is conservative insofar as the majority favors school prayer, capital punishment, Official English, and bans on child pornography and access to obscene materials by minors, as well as being opposed to same-sex marriages, racial quotas or preferential treatment, and abortion on demand. Again gun control is the exception, since a virtual consensus exists on regulating gun possession even though people may believe that they have a right to bear arms.

Since we have argued that moral conflicts are grounded in status politics, a reverse class dynamic operates. Sociologist Seymour Martin Lipset observed in the 1960s that elites are more tolerant than the masses, and he attributed this to "working-class authoritarianism": "The poorer strata everywhere are more liberal or leftist on economic issues. . . . But when liberalism is defined in non-economic terms . . . the correlation is reversed. The more well-to-do are more liberal, the poorer are more intolerant."[14]

Similarly, psychologist A.H. Maslow defined a hierarchy of needs: (1) physical, (2) safety, (3) love, (4) self-esteem, and (5) self-actualization.[15] Only after the physical requirements for survival are met can people be motivated to satisfy the next level of need. If episodes of status politics increase during times of economic prosperity, it suggests that moral conflicts will increase as we proceed into the postmaterialist era.

On social regulations, though the potential for conflict is greater than with other types of policies, the degree of popular zeal is not very intense unless awakened by mobilizing forces. Public disinterest may explain why the final outcome of moral conflicts depends less on the force of public opinion than on single-issue groups and their ability to manipulate the passive majority. Even where the public is receptive to legal change, as with gun control, responses to surveys about gun control are no gauge of the intensity of public opinion. Thus, for a long time members of Congress could disregard the majority sentiment and not suffer politically so long as they did not offend the NRA. Public opinion was not a reliable ally for the antigun lobby.

Proposition 5b: Legal changes in social regulations that make major revisions in community norms will be resisted by the public, especially any "target" populations.

Opinion polls cited in the case studies indicate that public attitudes toward social regulations are generally stable, showing only gradual change over many years. Longitudinal data show that popular opinions on abortion, gun control, the death penalty, and school prayer have resisted major fluctuations since Gallup or NORC began surveying those topics.[16] And when major revisions in community norms are mandated by law, notably the judiciary, public opinion will not readily accept them. The majority still favors school prayer despite the Supreme Court's ruling, and a rise in acceptance of legal abortions preceded, rather than followed, the *Roe* decision.

The perceived legitimacy of official acts has implications for the consensus-building process and compliance with the law. Subgroups in society that have intense feelings about social regulations that appear to "target" that group will probably resist having to comply. And sometimes the cooperation of those population subgroups is needed for effective implementation. How willing are Catholic hospitals and physicians to perform abortions? What are the odds that gun owners (let alone criminals) will register their firearms voluntarily? How likely is it that every teacher in the Bible belt will refrain from religious activities in schools?

Proposition 6a: Agencies of the federal government usually have limited jurisdiction over social regulatory policy.

Although the enactment of civil rights laws increased the federal role in social regulatory policy, in other areas the impact of the federal bureaucracy on policy implementation will be marginal compared to that of states and localities.

There is no national agency charged with enforcing church-state separation, though the solicitor general as amicus could support those private litigants who ask the federal judiciary to enforce the Supreme Court's church-state decrees. The abortion controversy potentially affects many federal agencies, but mostly in minor ways, and there is always the possibility that Congress will micromanage the implementation of abortion policy (as with Medicaid funding). The Bureau of Alcohol, Tobacco, and Firearms is supposed to enforce the federal gun laws, while antipornography legislation delegated regulatory authority to the FCC, FBI, the U.S. Customs Service, and the U.S. Postal Service. All four—but mainly Customs and the Postal Service—give some attention to antipornography enforcement, though more could be done with additional personnel and money.

The weakly enforced federal gun laws stem largely from ATF's reliance on voluntary compliance, since a relatively small number of agents have to monitor 280,000 gun dealers. And federal authorities have not executed anyone in decades. As with antipornography enforcement, an ongoing administrative problem with the Equal Employment Opportunity Commission is that its budget and personnel have not kept pace with the growing numbers of claims filed by women and minorities who allege employment discrimination. The EEOC, and the Office of Federal Contracts Compliance, are supposed to oversee affirmative action policies that can impact thousands of public and private organizations.

Apart from the modest role given to federal agencies, compared to the scope of these problems, the vigilance with which federal agencies discharge their duties depends upon external political constraints. The administrative arena is a microcosm of the legislative arena of power.

Proposition 6b: The ability of federal agencies to implement social regulations depends on the liberal vs. conservative pressures exerted by the Congress, presidency, judiciary, supportive groups, and regulated interests.

The administrative arena is circumscribed by these institutional actors, notably the courts, since beneficiary groups often petition the courts to ensure rigorous enforcement of statutory law and judicial decrees.[17] The interplay of the left and right political forces defines the vigor with which social regulations are enforced by the bureaucracy. The lackluster enforcement record of the Bureau of Alcohol, Tobacco, and Firearms is explained by its concern for survival in a hostile political environment. ATF lacks the necessary personnel, and historically the antigun lobby has been no match for the NRA, its allies in Congress, and progun presidents such as Ronald Reagan, who even wanted to abolish ATF.

Four decades ago the enforcement of laws against adult pornography was stalled by an overly vigilant judiciary's defense of free expression. Today, however, with Congress enacting new child pornography laws that were upheld by the Supreme Court, and with Presidents Reagan, Bush, and Clinton promising a renewed battle against child porn, a new policy consensus has been forged behind aggressive law enforcement by the FCC, FBI, Customs, and the Postal Service.

A backlash in Congress fueled by prolife legislators resulted in curbs on the U.S. Civil Rights Commission and the Legal Services Corporation while, on abortion funding, Congress has micromanaged the use of Medicaid funds ever since passing the Hyde Amendment in 1976. Though Congress never mandated racial quotas in hiring and actually disavowed "reverse discrimination" in one amendment to the 1964 Civil Rights Act, the use of numerical quotas resulted because agencies, in league with the courts, assumed that no other approach would achieve an integrated workforce. No president until Reagan meddled with this policy strategy, which shows the political clout generated when supportive groups (minorities), an Equal Employment Opportunity Commission controlled by civil rights advocates, and a sympathetic federal judiciary join forces. For the Office of Federal Contracts Compliance (OFCC)—at least before the high court nullified some federal set-asides—its administration of minority set-aside programs in federal contracts seemed to accommodate all parties. Executive orders began those initiatives; they were willingly implemented by OFCC, backed by supportive "beneficiary" groups (minority contractors), and tolerated by other nonminority businesses.

Proposition 7a: Federalism is important to social regulatory policy because historically the states had jurisdiction over most of these issues.

The movement toward economic regulation of capitalism by the federal government did not displace the state governments, because previously the states had intervened little in the marketplace.[18] But social regulations involved a pervasive role by state governments, and localities, long before federal intervention began. Even now, state "police powers" ensure that subnational governments will be more than equal partners in this federal relationship.

Antiabortion, antipornography, antisodomy, and death penalty statutes date back to the nineteenth century, whereas the movement to allow school prayer began in the early decades of the 1900s. Only four states codified English as the official language before 1980, although today twenty-three have done so. Over most of our history, gun control by state governments has been deliberately weak or nonexistent. In numerous other ways the states safeguard public order, safety, health, and moral character. Whether gambling is a vice to be discouraged or a virtue to be exploited through state lotteries, and how the age of adulthood is defined for the purposes of alcoholic consumption, driving, or reading sexual materials, varies by state. Most states enacted "blue laws" to regulate Sunday sales, and the majority still refuse to legalize marijuana use, prostitution, or homosexual relations. Imposition of capital punishment varies widely by state and region as well.

Proposition 7b: The enforcement of social regulatory policy often depends on the compliance of state and local officials as well as on decision makers in the private sector.

No federal law is easy to implement, but there are unique problems with social regulations. One, already noted, is that federal agencies may lack sufficient personnel, or social regulatory enforcement may not be their top priority. Another complication is the sheer number of persons "targeted" by social regulations. The ban on school prayer involved tens of thousands of local school districts; affirmative action guidelines affect hundreds of thousands of employers; gun control affects millions of U.S. citizens. Given the magnitude of the implementation problem, compliance may depend wholly on voluntarism by the "target" populations, on state and local authorities, or even on private legal actions.

Ensuring compliance with judicial decisions on church-state violations or discrimination against non-English-speakers regularly involves private parties (and their interest-group allies) who file lawsuits against recalcitrant public authorities and private organizations. The history of the Supreme Court's church-state litigation is a history of "separationists" who bring suit against governmental authorities. And normally, notwithstanding the denial of tax exemption to Bob Jones University because of discriminatory behavior, the IRS grants legitimate church-related institutions immunity from federal taxation. With abortion, on the other hand, state governments and Congress have enacted "right of conscience" laws to allow noncompliance by hospitals, physicians, and health care personnel whose religious values or moral convictions disavow that practice.

The ultimate problem with social regulatory policy is that consensus building is more difficult to achieve compared to other policy types. There is no easy way to mute moral disagreements at either the policy-making or implementation stages, because the antagonists view these disagreements as nonnegotiable. The fact that the Supreme Court promulgates law does not automatically bring the matter to a close; even a constitutional amendment is no assurance that controversy will end.

The classic example of social regulatory policy at the federal level was the ratification of the Eighteenth Amendment in 1920—Prohibition—although the illegal manufacture, sale, and consumption of alcoholic beverages was not halted. In 1933, on the eve of the New Deal, three-fourths of the states ratified the Twenty-First Amendment to repeal Prohibition and to refederalize policy on alcoholic consumption by allowing the states to regain their authority to legalize as well as regulate and tax the consumption of alcoholic beverages. According to policy analyst Kenneth J. Meier, what began as a "two-sided" morality policy (the "drys," who abstained, versus the "wets," who drank) evolved, following the Twenty-First Amendment, into a "one-sided" morality policy where, today, "only one 'acceptable' position" predominates among policy elites and the citizenry.[19]

Thus, our eight case studies of social regulatory policy are "two-sided" moral conflicts that seemingly will persist until they simply become irrelevant with the passage of time. Only at that juncture will a de facto settlement in public opinion be achieved—when the normative order, law, and social regulatory policy are once again mutually reinforcing.

Notes

1. Raymond Tatalovich and Byron W. Daynes, *Social Regulatory Policy: Moral Controversies in American Politics* (Boulder, CO: Westview Press, 1988), pp. 210–225.

2. Theodore J. Lowi, *The End of the Republican Era* (Norman, OK: University of Oklahoma Press, 1995), chapters 4 and 5.

3. On this issue, scholars are beginning to take issue with the pluralist assumptions of "economic" motivation and argue that altruism plays a role in political behavior. See Kristen R. Monroe, Michael C. Barton, and Ute Klingemann, "Altruism and the Theory of Rational Action," in Kristen Renwick Monroe, ed., *The Economic Approach to Politics* (New York: HarperCollins, 1991), pp. 317–352.

4. Eric Hoffer, *The True Believer* (New York: New American Library, 1958).

5. See James Coleman, *Community Conflict* (Glencoe, IL: Free Press, 1957).

6. See Glendon Schubert, *Judicial Policy-Making* (Glenview, IL: Scott, Foresman and Company, 1965), chapter 6.

7. Paul Brest, "The Fundamental Rights Controversy: The Essential Contradictions of Normative Constitutional Scholarship," *Yale Law Journal* 90 (1981), pp. 1063–1109.

8. John T. Noonan Jr., "Raw Judicial Power," *National Review* (March 2, 1973), p. 261.

9. See Raoul Berger, *Government by Judiciary: The Transformation of the Fourteenth Amendment* (Cambridge, MA: Harvard University Press, 1977).

10. Walter F. Murphy, *Congress and the Court* (Chicago: University of Chicago Press, 1962), pp. 246–247.

11. See Lee Epstein and Joseph F. Kobylka, *The Supreme Court and Legal Change: Abortion and the Death Penalty* (Chapel Hill, NC: University of North Carolina Press, 1992).

12. T. Alexander Smith, *The Comparative Policy Process* (Santa Barbara, CA: CLIO Press, 1975), p. 91.

13. Warren E. Miller and Donald E. Stokes, "Constituency Influence in Congress," *American Political Science Review* 57 (1963), pp. 45–56; Aage R. Clausen, *How Congressmen Decide* (New York: St. Martin's Press, 1973).

14. Seymour Martin Lipset, *Political Man: The Social Bases of Politics* (Garden City, NY: Anchor Books, 1963), p. 92.

15. Abraham H. Maslow, "A Theory of Human Motivation," *Psychological Review* 50 (July 1943), pp. 370–396.

16. Trend data on attitudes toward school prayer were reported in John A. Murley, "School Prayer: Free Exercise of Religion or Establishment of Religion," in Raymond Tatalovich and Byron W. Daynes, eds., *Social Regulatory Policy: Moral Controversies in American Politics* (Boulder, CO: Westview Press), pp. 23–25.

17. This formulation is a slight modification of James Anderson's conceptualization of the administrative decision-making process. See James E. Anderson, *Public Policymaking,* 3rd ed. (Boston: Houghton Mifflin Company, 1997), p. 233.

18. See Richard Hofstadter, *The Age of Reform* (Cambridge, MA: Harvard University Press, 1955).

19. Kenneth J. Meier, *The Politics of Sin: Drugs, Alcohol, and Public Policy* (Armonk, NY: M.E. Sharpe, 1994), p. xiv.

Case Index

General Index

AND BRIAN JONES

TEST

TURE

The balloonists' own
epic tale of their
round-the-world voyage

HEADLINE

First published in 1999
by HEADLINE BOOK PUBLISHING

10 9 8 7 6 5 4 3 2 1

British Library Cataloguing in Publication Data

Jones, Brian
     The Greatest Adventure: the round-the-world
     balloon voyage of the Breitling Orbiter 3
     1.Jones, Brian 2.Piccard, Bertrand
     3.Breitling Orbiter 3 4.Ballooning
     5.Flights around the world
     I.Title II.Piccard, Bertrand
     910.4'1

Hardback ISBN 0 7472 7128 3
Trade paperback ISBN 0 7472 7129 1

Typeset by
Letterpart Limited, Reigate, Surrey

Map illustrations by Paul A. Duffy
Letterpart Limited, Reigate, Surrey

Printed and bound in Great Britain by
Butler & Tanner Ltd, Frome and London

HEADLINE BOOK PUBLISHING
A division of the Hodder Headline Group
338 Euston Road
London NW1 3BH

www.headline.co.uk
www.hodderheadline.com

CONTENTS

DEDICATION

This book is dedicated to the team whose combined skills designed and built *Breitling Orbiter 3* and guided the balloon around the world. To commemorate their achievement, we quote from the fax which we sent to Control when we crossed the finishing line over Africa on 20 March 1999:

Hello to all our friends,
We can hardly believe our dream has finally come true. We almost got lost in political problems, in the slow winds of the Pacific, the bad headings over the Gulf of Mexico. But each time, with God's help and great teamwork, the balloon got back on course to succeed.

We are the privileged two of a wonderful and efficient team that we would like to thank from the bottom of our hearts, now that we are sharing with Breitling the results of five years' work.

ACKNOWLEDGEMENTS

So many people were involved in the round-the-world attempt that we cannot thank everyone individually. But we are grateful above all to Theodore (Thedy) Schneider, head of Breitling SA, whose unfailing generosity and enthusiasm sustained the project from first to last.

We should also like to thank Duff Hart-Davis for his help in preparing the text of this book.

Bertrand Piccard
Brian Jones

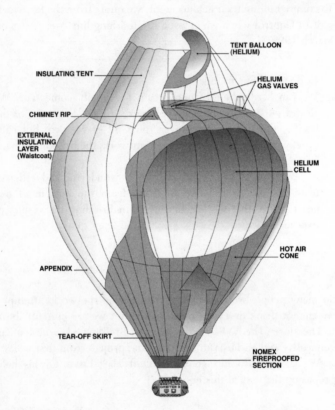

TENT BALLOON
(HELIUM)

INSULATING TENT

HELIUM
GAS VALVES

CHIMNEY RIP

EXTERNAL
INSULATING
LAYER
(Waistcoat)

HELIUM
CELL

HOT AIR
CONE

APPENDIX

TEAR-OFF SKIRT

NOMEX
FIREPROOFED
SECTION

© Breitling

A Rozier balloon works on a combination of gas and hot air, a principle invented by the eighteenth-century aviator Jean-François Pilâtre de Rozier. For take-off, the gas cell is partially filled with helium. As the balloon climbs, the heat of the sun and diminishing atmospheric pressure together make the helium expand. If the pilots want to level off or descend, they vent helium through valves in the top of the gas cell. At night, for extra lift, they burn propane or kerosene in short bursts, warming the air in the hot-air cone, which transmits heat to the helium. The two appendices, coming down either side of the envelope, are safety valves. If the balloon goes through its natural ceiling, either because it has ascended too fast, or because the pilots have pushed it up by burning, excess helium is forced out down the appendices, which are open at the bottom. The purpose of the relatively small tent balloon – also full of helium – is to hold the insulating tent clear of the top of the gas cell, and so minimize the transfer of heat into the balloon during the day, and out of it at night. The only way balloon pilots can steer is by climbing or descending in search of winds blowing in the direction they want. During their round-the-world flight Bertrand Piccard and Brian Jones depended heavily on the skilled predictions of their two weather experts in Geneva, who were constantly telling them the best height at which to fly in order to find the winds they needed.

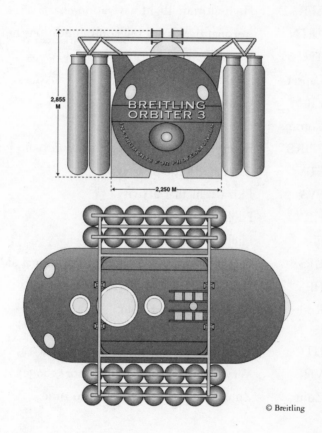

© Breitling

TECHNICAL TERMS

AERAD	High-altitude flight navigation chart
AFTN	Aeronautical fixed telecommunications network
ATC	Air traffic control
Capsat	Satellite telefax system
CB	Cumulo-nimbus cloud
Comms	Communications
EPIRB	Emergency personal identification radio beacon
ETA	Estimated time of arrival
EVA	Extra-vehicular activity
FIR	Flight information region
FL	Flight level
GPS	Global positioning system (navigational aid)
HF	High-frequency radio (long range)
Knot	Nautical mile per hour. One knot = 1.16 miles per hour
UTC	Universal time code – same as Zulu
VHF	Very high frequency radio (short range)
Zulu	Zulu time = Greenwich mean time

CHAPTER ONE

TAKE-OFF

BERTRAND

For everyone involved in the preparation of the *Breitling Orbiter 3* balloon, the winter of 1998–9 was a time of high anxiety and tension. My two earlier attempts to fly round the world had failed, one after six hours, the other after nine days; and our sponsors, the Breitling watch company, had made it clear that our third balloon would be the last: there would be no *Orbiter 4*. The race was on, as five other teams were making ready to launch in various parts of the globe. A round-the-world balloon flight was generally accepted as the last great challenge in aviation, maybe even the greatest, because it had to combine the power of technology with the unpredictability of nature.

We had little information about the Remax team, who were proposing to take off from Australia and fly a colossal balloon at extreme height in the stratosphere, but all the other starters were well known to us. In the United States Jacques Soukup and Kevin Uliassi each had a balloon under construction. Andy Elson, a former colleague of ours, was preparing the Cable & Wireless balloon for a launch in Spain; but our most dangerous competitor was the tycoon Richard Branson, whose *ICO Global Challenger* was nearing completion in Morocco.

After working on the *Orbiter* project for five years, I think I had become slightly obsessed with its importance. Hoping all the time that I might manage a tremendous achievement, I was driven on by a feeling of relentless pressure: even when I was cutting the lawn at home, I was thinking, 'Maybe it's foolish to be doing this rather than devoting more time and thought to some detail I may have forgotten.' Whenever I turned my attention to anything not connected with the balloon, I felt like a naughty child who had abandoned his homework to play in the garden.

After two failures I was well aware that the people around me didn't know whether to trust me or not. Scepticism increased still further when, in November 1998, I decided to change my co-pilot, asking Tony Brown, who had been going to fly with me, to stand down, and appointing in his place Brian Jones, the project manager.

Under Brian's calm and able direction, construction of the envelope and gondola had proceeded well at the Bristol firm Cameron Balloons. In purely technical terms we were well advanced: on 16 November the gondola, envelope and associated gear were loaded on to two forty-foot lorries and began the journey to our launch site at Château d'Oex, the ski village and ballooning centre 3,000 feet up in the Swiss Alps. We were ready to go at any time from early December – but we were held up by factors outside our control: the war in Iraq, which meant it was unsafe to fly over that country; the restrictions for overflying China; and – most important of all – the weather.

For the all-important task of finding and predicting wind patterns that would carry us round the globe, we had retained the services of two outstanding meteorologists, Luc Trullemans, a Belgian, and Pierre Eckert, a Swiss, who soon proved themselves absolute magicians. At first, though, we were all frustrated. Several times the met men telephoned to say that they saw a good weather slot coming up but that the winds would carry the balloon to Iraq or to prohibited parts of China – and so we had to pass up the chance of launching.

BRIAN

On 18 December tension increased dramatically when Richard Branson took off from Marrakesh. On this, his third round-the-world attempt, he was accompanied by the two other veteran balloonists, Per

Lindstrand and Steve Fossett – a formidably experienced team – and his equipment was as high-tech as money could buy. The chances of his succeeding seemed all too good. 'I know it's not a normal race,' my wife Jo wrote in her diary, 'but we felt as if we'd been left behind.'

The next week was tough going. We tried to concentrate on our own preparations, but one eye was inevitably on Branson's progress – and he did us no good when, without permission, he entered Tibetan air space and flew up over central China, explaining that it was impossible to comply with the authorities' instructions to land because of the vertiginous mountain terrain. Earlier in the year Bertrand had led a delegation to China, where he negotiated permission for balloons to cross the country using a precisely specified corridor; now it looked as though Branson had finished our chances, for the Chinese immediately banned all further balloon flights for the duration.

Then, on Christmas Day, we heard that Branson had been carried southwards by a low-pressure system over the Pacific, and forced to ditch in the sea near Hawaii. When his balloon landed in the water, the mechanism that was supposed to release the flying cables and separate the envelope from the gondola failed to operate, so the capsule was dragged along the surface by the wind at 20 mph. Fortunately the crew managed to escape and were rescued none the worse, but the gondola and envelope were lost to the sea.

Our feelings were mixed, to say the least. We regarded Branson as a friendly rival, but now he had increased our difficulties enormously, and it took nearly six weeks of intensive negotiation with the Chinese to win back the permission we had taken such trouble to gain. Not until the beginning of February 1999 did they agree to let us overfly the country, and even then they would only allow us to cross the southern part, below the 26th parallel. This meant that our weather men had a tiny target, 6,000 miles away, at which to aim.

Working from forecasts and computer models, Luc Trullemans and Pierre Eckert searched ceaselessly for a weather window that would give us the necessary track. What they had to do was predict, from existing patterns, the connections and interactions between different systems of wind that would give us the trajectory we needed – a task of astonishing complexity.

At last on Tuesday, 9 February, Luc spotted a possible slot for the following Sunday and Monday. On Friday the Breitling plane flew to Bristol to bring out the launch crew, and on Saturday, amid growing excitement, the gondola was fuelled up, the envelope was laid out on the launch field at Château d'Oex, and a tanker bringing the liquid helium set out from Paris on its eight-hour drive. (Because commercial vehicles are not allowed to drive in France at weekends, special dispensation had to be obtained for this journey.) But then, on Sunday, Luc and Pierre saw conditions worsening on the first part of the route, to North Africa, and to everyone's immense disappointment the attempt had to be called off. From that moment, the press and public stopped believing we had any chance of success.

It may be that in the long run Branson did us a service, for the Chinese ban made both Kevin Uliassi and Jacques Soukup abandon their attempts. This left only one immediate competitor, Andy Elson, who had flown with Bertrand in *Orbiter 2*. On the following Wednesday, 17 February, Andy and Colin Prescott took off in the Cable & Wireless balloon from Almería, in southeast Spain.

This created still greater stress in our camp. With another capable crew on its way and reports of good progress coming back, time seemed to slow to a snail's pace: every day that passed reduced our hopes of catching up, until finally our chance of winning the race appeared to have gone.

BERTRAND

A few months earlier, I had had a very strong intuition that this attempt was going to succeed, but now I was perplexed by all the problems confronting us. The weather was terrible, with a lot of unseasonable rain and avalanches claiming lives all over the Alps. February was drawing to a close – and normally the end of the month marked the end of the season for round-the-world ballooning attempts because thereafter wind patterns were not usually so favourable. Convinced that the weather window had closed, our team dispersed from the launch site at Château d'Oex, and I took my family to ski at Les Diablerets. Stefano Albinati called me from Breitling to suggest that we find a day for a press conference at which we would announce that our plans for the year were cancelled. We set the date as 8 March.

I was in despair. The next day my wife Michèle and I invited some friends to dinner in our rented chalet. To cheer me up they brought along some bottles of fine wine, and we had a happy evening. That was a decisive moment for me because it was a reminder that, whatever might happen, the most important thing was not to win success and glory but to have true friendship. Surrounded by close friends, it would be easier to cope with all the people who were sure to criticize yet another failure.

But, early next morning, the telephone rang. It was Luc, full of excitement. 'Bertrand!' he exclaimed. 'Listen. There's a really good slot coming up on the first of March.'

'You're joking,' I told him.

'Not at all,' he said, and he described what he and Pierre were seeing on their computers: over the western Mediterranean a big depression was forming, and they felt sure they could swing the balloon round the edge of it, anti-clockwise, so that after flying down over France and Spain we would be carried eastwards over Africa on just the trajectory they had been seeking.

I was amazed, because I thought our chance had already gone. Andy Elson was already seven days out, over the Sudan and heading for Saudi Arabia. But now Luc's call gave me a tremendously strong feeling that we were faced with a serious possibility. Before earlier flights we had established a system of alerts. If things were looking good, the first warning to stand by went out four days in advance. At launch minus three, the alert would be confirmed, and the launch team of eight would be called out from Bristol to join the pilots at Château d'Oex. At launch minus two the rest of the team would assemble. And so, on 25 February, our first warning went out.

BRIAN

My wife Jo and I had been in Château d'Oex since the middle of November, so when the team decided to disband it was a major undertaking, as well as a major disappointment, to pack everything up and head for home. The car was full to the gunwales, and we had just crossed the border into France when Bertrand came through on our mobile phone and said, 'Brian — drive slowly! There's just a chance we may go.' Surprised and a little doubtful, we stopped near Mâcon, where we had something to eat.

Then Alan Noble, the flight director, phoned through and said, 'Maybe you'd better turn round.' Bertrand rang again, more cautious. 'Better *not* turn round yet,' he said, 'because then we won't be tempting fate.' After some debate Jo and I decided to carry on: the idea of unloading all our gear again in Château d'Oex was awful. We felt it would be better to drive home even if we had to fly back to Switzerland the next day. If we could touch base in Wiltshire, unpack everything and reload with clean clothes, we could somehow close a chapter and make a fresh start. We had this feeling, almost superstitious, that we should make a clean break. So we abandoned plans for a night stop in France and headed back to England as fast as possible.

We reached home at midnight – and in the event we had to turn straight round. By 10 o'clock next morning, Friday, we were boarding an aircraft at Heathrow, bound for Geneva, along with three members of the technical team – Kieran Sturrock, Pete Johnson and Bill Sly. Also on its way was the eight-man launch team from Cameron Balloons, driving a van from Bristol because they had to bring specialist tools with them.

On the plane the cabin crew were in such high spirits that one of them gave his entire briefing as a take-off of Sean Connery – doing it so well that you could easily imagine it was James Bond in charge of the public address system. Some of the passengers didn't realize what was going on, but others enjoyed it immensely.

Also with us was Brian Smith, one of the controllers who were going to monitor the flight from Geneva. Now he made the most of his status as a former British Airways skipper by sending a note up to the captain to inform him he had part of the *Breitling Orbiter 3* team on board. The response was immediate. We were all moved up from our economy seats in the back of the aircraft to Club Class, where we were plied with champagne. When the captain briefed the passengers, he said how pleased he was to welcome us on board. Later the cabin service director presented me with a teddy bear and asked me to take him round the world, suggesting that if the bear completed the circuit he might raise a lot of money at auction for a children's charity. I took the little brown creature, wearing his Union Jack T-shirt, and stuffed him in my bag. For obvious reasons we called him Sean.

Back in Château d'Oex, I called Alan, who was on his way out. I found him in a negative frame of mind. He was convinced that Bertrand and I were not really trying to go round the world. Rather, he thought, we were desperate to get the balloon into the air, just to make a flight of some kind. His sceptical attitude spread to the launch team, and I tried to gee the crew up by saying, 'Look – this is for real. Bertrand and I have been talking to our met people, and there's absolutely no way we're going to call a flight unless there's a significant chance of going all the way round.'

BERTRAND

It was strange to realize that maybe only five people were taking the alert seriously. Everyone else thought we were simply out to make advertising for Breitling by getting the balloon into the air for a few days. Brian and I, on the other hand, were perfectly clear that we would take off only if we had a really good chance. Luc and Pierre, our met men, were still insisting that the weather window was the best we'd had all year.

Alan remained cynical. 'If you'd had this slot at the beginning of the season, you'd never have taken it,' he told them.

'Of course we would!' they replied.

His expression softened slightly as he said, 'So you're really serious?'

'*Absolument!*' cried Luc. 'We're convinced.'

Preparations went ahead at a brisker rate. The gondola was sitting on its trolley on the floor of the workshop in Château d'Oex. Above it on one side was a gallery full of armchairs and tables, together with a kettle and a coffee machine. It was there, during the past three months, that we had held all our discussions and brainstorming sessions about how to solve technical problems and evolve the best possible systems. Now the place came alive again, and the atmosphere grew tense, as we analysed the weather patterns and debated whether to go or not.

By Sunday, 28 February, the gondola was out on the launch field, with the envelope of the balloon stretched out, but still wrapped, in a long sausage beyond it. Inside the workshop we all sat around and struggled to take the crucial decision. Some of us were sunk in the armchairs – which were covered in brown Dralon and had no castors, so that they were very low – and some were perched on higher seats, giving the whole gathering a slightly ridiculous appearance.

Should we carry on or not? I was completely *tiraillé* – torn apart inside. My longing to go was dragging me forward, but my fear of failure was pulling me back.

Brian and I both knew this was our last chance for 1999. We could cancel the launch and keep our balloon for next year – with the risk that somebody else would succeed during the summer in the southern hemisphere. On the other hand, we could take a chance and go. If we succeeded, we would become the first; but if the weather turned out less than perfect, we would fail, and have no balloon to make another attempt later.

So – at one moment I was saying to myself, 'It's too late in the season. Let's stop. Let's keep the balloon for next year.' A second later I was thinking, 'No, we can't do that. We *have* to take the risk and go. But only if the weather is going to be perfect – and how do we know that it will be?' Before the balloon had any chance to go round in circles, my mind was doing just that.

Alan and Don Cameron, head of the firm that built the balloon, were still far from positive. 'From the weather maps we've got,' they said, 'We just don't see how you can get round the world.'

'Of course you can't do it by looking at maps,' retorted Luc. 'You can only do it by working out trajectory calculations, because when the balloon is moving the weather will be moving as well. The high and low pressures are shifting all the time. It's not a static situation – it's dynamic.' He looked at Alan and said, 'You get them up there, and I'll get them round.'

The pressure on Brian and me seemed even heavier, and we knew we could not control fate, or the future. I said that when the time for a final discussion came, I would not push in any direction, but rather listen to everyone else's arguments. I strongly felt that if I kept quiet, fate would have a chance to declare itself and bring us all to the right decision.

At the crucial meeting we two hardly spoke. Luc and Pierre held the floor, confirming that the window still looked excellent. Even then Alan was doubtful, and he asked, 'How long do you think the flight will take?'

After a short conference the met men replied, 'Sixteen days.' Most of us had been thinking of a figure more like eighteen or nineteen, and for the first time Alan smiled, for sixteen was the figure he had been holding in his mind. 'If you say sixteen days, I say yes for the take-off. Any more, and you might not have enough fuel for safety.'

'I don't want you to fall out of the sky in the middle of the Pacific or the Atlantic,' he added. 'But now I think we can go.'

'All right,' I said. 'Everybody has to vote individually – because if we fail, I don't want anyone to start saying, "I was against it all along". And if we succeed, I don't want the ones who were against it claiming, "I was for it all the time".'

It was exactly 1 p.m. when we held a show of hands. The decision was unanimous: to take off. 'OK,' said Alan. 'Now we need to tell the technicians to go ahead immediately' – and he phoned them out on the launch field. After the severe disappointment of the cancelled take-off two weeks earlier, they had been awaiting our decision with some anxiety.

Earlier in the day Luc and Pierre had assured us that it was not going to rain in the immediate future, and the technical team had begun to assemble the envelope, attaching the Velcro and seventy-odd karabiners to cobble together the outer layer, which consisted of the top tent, the waistcoat and the hot-air cone. Then it started to drizzle, putting them in a dilemma.

During the winter a tremendous amount of snow had fallen and we had used a piste-basher to compact the covering on the launch field. On top of the snow the team had laid out immense square sheets of black polythene, meant for covering silage pits, to stop the balloon freezing to the ground. But heavy rain would be disastrous: if the envelope got soaked and the temperature fell below zero during the night, the fabric would freeze to the groundsheets and might have torn when the envelope started to inflate. Another problem was that Velcro does not seal properly when wet – a failing which had already been responsible for the deaths of two balloonists.

BRIAN

On the last day before take-off Bertrand and I kept away from the launch site as much as possible. We stayed together all the time, going shopping, walking about, sitting and talking over a coffee, all the while building our relationship. We wanted to escape from the pressure of the media and the public, and to be more relaxed for the take-off than Bertrand had been for *Orbiter 1* and *2*.

The gondola was already loaded, but in the supermarket we bought a few items of fresh food – bread, cheese, margarine and fruit. From the Hôtel de Ville, where we were staying, we got meals pre-cooked and vacuum-packed: salmon, chicken, emu steak and vegetarian burgers. The fresh food would last only a few days, but already on board were nineteen days' worth of dehydrated rations, as well as 150 litre-and-a-half bottles of water, stowed beneath the floor. Although Bertrand would have preferred carbonated water, we decided it was potentially dangerous as the escaping bubbles might produce more carbon dioxide than our breathing and saturate the filters in the cabin. In a last-minute drive to save weight we discarded some tins of mousse-type puddings, deciding we could do without them. We took no alcohol – not even a bottle of champagne to celebrate with, if celebration were called for. Our only luxury was two small tins of *pâté truffé*.

One factor to our advantage was that no other launches were in prospect. Earlier in the season, when several teams were preparing for take-off, Camerons had had to provide launch crews for all their balloons. Now that we were outside the normal weather window and everyone else had given up, there was no competition: we got the pick of the bunch, and the crew who came out from Bristol were the ones who had designed and built the envelope. Among them was Don Cameron himself, a canny Scot nearing sixty, founder and owner of the firm; with him came Dave Boxall, Gavin Hailes and Andy Booth, all of whom we particularly wanted to have at the launch.

On Sunday evening we had supper in the Hôtel de Ville, our last meal on earth – well, for some time at least. To put it like that sounds as if we were going to the guillotine – and that was almost how it felt. It was a strange time altogether. Then we went to bed for a short rest before the big day.

BERTRAND

According to the weather forecast, the morning of 1 March 1999 should have been fine. But before dawn the valley which cradles Château d'Oex was full of mist, and the sky was overcast. In the Hôtel de Ville Brian and I were both wide awake by 5 a.m., well aware that for the past twenty hours technicians had been working out on the launch field, a few hundred yards away, getting the balloon ready for take-off. After five years of preparation, of false starts and dashed hopes, the moment of truth was upon us.

I woke with a start, adrenaline already pumping, and immediately thought, 'What's happening on the field?' I grabbed the phone, called Alan Noble on his mobile, and asked, 'How's it going?'

'Bertrand,' he replied, 'you should be asleep.'

WHAT? Was everything over? Had they failed to inflate the balloon?

'You ought to be sleeping,' he repeated. 'We don't need you for two hours at least.'

'What's happening in two hours?'

'You're going. Everything's perfect. The balloon's standing up, almost fully inflated. There's no wind.'

'Alan!' I cried. 'I can't possibly sleep any more. I'm coming now.'

Immediately I felt a complete change in the physiology of my body. No more relaxation or trying to rest. I was one hundred per cent alert, ready to go. It was still dark, and when I went downstairs there was nobody in the restaurant except Brian, Jo, myself and one waitress, who had got up early to look after us. Brian ate a croissant, but I couldn't manage one because my mouth was too dry. Instead I had some muesli cereal and tea, but I was in such a state of nerves that when I went back to my room to brush my teeth and pick up my bag, I started to get stomach contractions and threw up. 'That's incredible,' I thought. 'Such a thing has never happened before. I've never been so afraid.' It made me realize that I was facing the most important moment of my life.

It so happened that 1 March was my forty-first birthday. The year before, I had taken off in *Breitling Orbiter 2* on my grandfather's birthday, and I had felt then that it was a sign of fate, that I was going to succeed. The intuition proved false: we failed. So now, on my own birthday, I thought, 'Maybe this is something I have to do myself, and not count on family fortune.'

BRIAN

I hardly slept at all. Jo and I were together, and there were a thousand things I wanted to say, but I just didn't feel like talking. I lay there wondering if she was asleep, and Jo – she told me later – did the same.

I felt just as nervous as Bertrand.

At 6 a.m. we drove the short distance to the launch field, passing quickly through the deserted streets of the village. The temperature was a couple of degrees below zero, and because of the mist we could see neither the stars nor the tops of the surrounding mountains, which rose three or four thousand feet above us. Then, as we turned on to the main road, our balloon came into view.

The sight stopped us dead. This was the moment about which we had been talking and dreaming for months – and now the reality came as a shock. In a blaze of arc lights the slender, towering envelope was gleaming brilliant silver against the black sky. One hundred and seventy feet high – tall as the leaning Tower of Pisa, not far short of Nelson on his column in Trafalgar Square, more than half the height of the Statue of Liberty – it rose like a colossal exclamation mark, emphasizing the vast scale of our undertaking. Escaping helium eddied round it in white clouds, like dry ice. At its base the chunky horizontal cylinder of the gondola, painted fluorescent red, was partially hidden by the double row of titanium fuel tanks ranged along each side. Men were swarming round it, some holding ropes, others manipulating hoses. The size of it was awe-inspiring. The volume of the envelope – the balloon itself – was 650,000 cubic feet, and the whole assembly, including the gondola and fuel, weighed 9.2 tons. This was the majestic giant in which we were going to commit ourselves to the sky.

'Can you believe it!' Bertrand exclaimed. 'That's ours!'

As we drove slowly towards it, with the balloon growing bigger and bigger in our eyes, my mind flew back thirty years to the launch of the Apollo 11 mission to the moon. In 1969 I had watched enthralled on television as the crew went aboard, and now I felt we were re-enacting the scene. I knew Bertrand had seen the Apollo launch live at Cape Kennedy, but now he was feeling such strong emotion that he didn't mention it. We were both wearing navy blue flying suits made of a soft, fireproof fabric, with the jackets which Breitling had specially created for us over the top. Our names and blood-groups were inscribed on chest-badges, and we carried survival knives strapped to the trousers of our suits. 'I think we look quite professional,' said Bertrand quietly as we approached the waiting crowd. 'If only these people knew how frightened we are inside!'

We parked our Chrysler Voyager next to the team's vehicles. The moment we got out, we were swallowed by the crowd, and to escape from all the people we had to run to the press conference in a building immediately beside the field. Word had gone round that the flight was on, and the room was full – but still there were only about a third as many people as at the launch of *Orbiter 2*. Then, there had been reporters standing on chairs and tables, trying to get a view. Now, after twenty-odd failures, very few people still believed that it was possible for a balloon to fly round the world, and it was difficult to find anything new to say. Alan made a brief speech. Then Luc and Pierre gave a meteorological briefing to the cameras. Bertrand was eager to get into the gondola and concentrate on our pre-flight checks, so he kept his remarks uncharacteristically short.

I had already noticed that when he and I appeared together he always spoke of flying with far greater eloquence than I could muster. Now I thought that something flippant would be best. 'Because this is Bertrand's birthday,' I said, 'we made a collection. Everyone was incredibly generous, Breitling particularly, but our difficulty was that we didn't know what to give him. We couldn't decide between a flight in a balloon and a round-the-world holiday trip – so, as a compromise, we thought we'd give him both.'

The Breitling publicity girls came up on to the platform, gave him a croissant with a single candle stuck in it (to represent a cake) and everyone sang 'Happy Birthday.'

Outside, the technicians were continuing their preparations. The tanker truck full of liquid helium, at minus 200°C, had arrived from Paris, and as the eighteen-man crew from Carbagas continued to inflate the balloon, under the orders of Roland Wicki, helium pouring through the vaporizers was making a continuous loud whistle. Firemen from Château d'Oex were helping to hold the envelope in position with ropes. Inside the cramped gondola Kieran Sturrock, our electronics specialist and master technician, was going through a long list of checks. The only fault he found was a slight leak from the cylinder of pressurized nitrogen which powered the valves used to release surplus helium from the top of the envelope. He tightened the connection as much as he could, though without quite managing to close the seal fully.

BERTRAND

The launch teams had started inflation at 3 a.m., and throughout the second half of the night everything went well. Then, as dawn broke, the wind began to blow. Gentle at first, it started to gust through the valley – the last thing any of us wanted. The balloon was already at its full height and beginning to sway about: any strong wind would be dangerous, as it might damage the envelope and dash the gondola against the ground. In the worst possible scenario, one of the tanks of liquid propane might split, explode and engulf the whole contraption in flames. It was clear that we had to take off as soon as possible.

The time came to say goodbye to our families – a moment we had both been dreading. Every time I set eyes on Michèle and our three daughters – Estelle (eight), Oriane (six) and Solange (four) – I wondered, 'Can it be right, risking so much in trying to go round the world?' I felt my conviction steadily diminishing.

At my earlier attempts the girls had started off full of confidence, but as more and more journalists asked them, 'Aren't you afraid something might happen to your daddy?' they began to be fearful. Then, after I had twice returned from failure not only alive but in good shape, they became confident again, and positively looked forward to further take-offs. So now they were happy enough. I took them in my arms and said, 'You see how wonderful this balloon is. This time we're really going.' That made them a little sad, especially Estelle, but none of them seemed really worried. More important to them was the fact that this was a Monday, and they were missing school.

For Michèle it was harder. But when I thanked her for backing me up so nobly through five years of struggle, she remained absolutely steady and only said, 'Be careful. I trust you not to take risks in an attempt to bring off something if it's impossible.'

Next I went to my father Jacques and thanked him for passing down such a great taste for adventure, for enabling me to meet all the fabulous people, astronauts and explorers with whom he had come into contact through all his underwater expeditions. Those men were the heroes of my childhood – giants who had come to our house for lunch or dinner and shown me how beautiful life could be if you explored the world and human nature. I thanked my father for giving me the energy with which to prepare for our journey round the earth. A telling photograph taken by Bill Sly, a member of the balloon team, shows both of us with tears in our eyes. We were not overcome or hysterical – just deeply moved; and although we were surrounded by cameramen taking pictures, both of us drew strength from those moments of intimacy, a private island in the middle of the throng.

I also went up to Thedy Schneider, head of Breitling; but, knowing that he doesn't like to talk a lot in emotional circumstances, I simply said, 'Thank you for trusting me.'

BRIAN

I, too, found the moment of parting incredibly difficult. I was anxious that I might break down in front of the cameras: I thought that if Jo could hold herself together, I would be all right, but if she began to cry, I would have a problem because I might not be able to speak. When I went up to her, in the middle of a mass of people, she was absolutely stoical: she stood there looking supremely confident. I felt very proud of her. When I gave her a kiss, she just said, 'Go do it' – and that was it. I thought, 'Thank God,' and turned away. Not until I saw a video film of the parting, months later, did I realize that as I moved off tears were streaming down her face.

BERTRAND

At 8 a.m. Brian and I climbed into the gondola, going in head-first through the rear hatch. We had made it an absolute rule that nobody would enter the capsule wearing outdoor shoes – a precaution designed to keep out any moisture that might condense on the portholes and obscure our vision as we climbed. So we approached in spare pairs of boots, and left them outside. The press had insisted that we stick our heads out of the hatch, and this we did, one at a time, while they took pictures. Then we took particular care to prepare the hatch correctly, so that we would not lose pressure as we climbed. My father came with a handkerchief to clean the seal minutely before we closed the clamp, as he had done so often before diving in his submarines.

BRIAN

All the time the wind was becoming more boisterous. High above us
the silvery Mylar envelope was crackling and crisping, as if someone
was wrapping a gigantic turkey in tinfoil. Hair-raising noises started to
emanate from the gondola itself. Lashed beneath it was a raft of
polystyrene blocks a foot thick to elevate the gondola and so hold the
fuel tanks clear of the ground. As the balloon heaved and tugged, the
smooth underbelly of the capsule started to rub on the polystyrene,
and the screeching, creaking sounds were appalling. When the whole
package began to lift clear of the ground and was jerked five or six
feet into the air before being smashed down again, the onlookers
thought the gondola itself was cracking and coming apart. The
movement became so violent that the fire crew decided to lash our
tether to their five-ton truck rather than risk the main strongpoint
pulling out of the ground.

Inside, we were getting thrown about as we struggled to complete
our pre-flight checks:

'VHF radios.'
'On.'
'Frequency one one nine decimal one seven.'
'Correct.'
'Altimeter pressure.'
'Set.'
'Fire extinguisher safety pins.'
'Removed.'
'Life-support system.'
'On.'
'Gas valve.'
'Open for check.'
'Two red lights.'
'OK.'

And so on for more than fifty items.

Concentration was difficult because of the noise and because stores
and equipment kept tumbling out of the bunks on to the floor,
blocking the narrow corridor along the middle of the capsule. Yet even

when we were ready we had to stay anchored for a few more minutes: with the weight of us two on board the balloon needed more helium for lift-off, and the gas crew continued to pump. Bertrand was talking to Alan Noble on his mobile phone, but for the moment we had handed over control to the ground crew and there was nothing we could do to help them.

My first tasks after take-off lay outside the gondola, so I climbed out through the top hatch and sat aloft, holding tight as we were thrown about. There was no danger of falling off because round the roof of the capsule ran the load frame, a heavy, double-decker rail about knee-high, which supported the load of the gondola and fuel tanks. We called this ring of stainless steel 'the playpen' because it gave a feeling of security, and beyond it were the titanium outriggers that carried the propane cylinders.

All round us spectators were crowding close, shouting with excitement, unaware of the danger they were in. If the balloon had split or been blown over, several of them might have been injured as the heavy fabric collapsed on them. Any one of our thirty-two propane tanks could have ruptured and exploded. If it had, there would have been an instant, devastating fireball. As it was, with the gondola being jerked around, one of the tanks got caught up on a cable: its lower end was dragged out of vertical alignment, and when it came free again it swung violently against the side of the hull. What with the wind, the shouts, the clashing of the tanks and the screeching of the polystyrene, direct voice communication was impossible.

BERTRAND

A hundred yards away across the packed snow, members of the Balloon Club of Château d'Oex had been preparing a hot-air balloon for take-off, with an experienced pilot in charge. Its aim was to ascend ahead of us and find out the state of the wind layers in the valley, as well as taking up journalists and photographers. The crew got it more or less inflated, but then, to our dismay, we watched them pulling it down again because the gusts had become too strong. When I saw that I thought, 'Now our problems are starting.' Brian's face turned paler and paler until it was white as a sheet.

In spite of the difficulties, neither of us considered calling off our own launch. I felt fatalistic. I knew the balloon could easily be ruined taking off in these conditions. If we sustained damage as we left the ground, we might have to come down again almost immediately – and a forced landing in the mountains would be extremely dangerous. First, we would have to find somewhere relatively flat, and then there would be a high risk of the propane cylinders exploding on impact. Nevertheless, we both felt there was no way back: we had to carry on. During an interview the day before I had said that if we didn't go, everybody would think us idiots; if we went, and failed, everyone would dismiss us as incompetent; and if we went and succeeded, everybody would say, 'Well, of course, it was perfectly simple.' So there was nothing for it but to take off and do what we thought was right.

For a while I too went up on top of the capsule. By then it was full daylight, and although the sky was still grey, the sun came burning through the mist and caught the top of the envelope. In the nick of time Luc and Pierre's prediction was proving right: the departure window they had forecast was above us, and the next front was already moving down from the north.

Three professional air traffic controllers from Geneva had volunteered their services for our flight, and two of them – Greg Moegli and Patrick Schelling – had established a control post in Château d'Oex itself. Their immediate task was to keep other aircraft away from the balloon's initial flight path, and Greg later described the operation as one of the craziest he had ever known. There were five helicopters, two airships and two fixed-wing aircraft circling the launch site; all the pilots were demanding permission to come as close as possible, and all were in a state of over-excitement.

On the ground the crowd had become enormous. At the last minute word had gone out that we really were on our way, and several thousand people had assembled. To one of them it seemed that the balloon had taken on a life of its own. 'It was like an animal,' she said, 'roaring to go.' Along with many others, she thought the fire engine was about to go round the world as well.

The plan had been that the ground crew would weigh us off, tell us when they were ready to cut the tether, and give us a countdown from ten to one. In the event none of that happened. Unable to risk disaster any longer, Alan simply waited for one more big bounce and at 9.09 a.m. local time – 08:09 Zulu time – at a moment when the balloon was rising, severed the rope with his Swiss army knife. Sky News later described the take-off as 'not so much a launch – more of an escape'. (Zulu time, designated by the letter 'Z', is the international term for Greenwich mean time. We remained on Zulu time throughout the flight.)

Just after we had lifted free, I climbed down into the cabin again and stood with my head out of the upper hatch, while Brian remained squatting on the roof. As we lifted away the noise was incredible. People were screaming at the tops of their voices to wish us good luck. They had waited months for this moment, and now they really let go. The intensity of their feeling brought tears to our eyes. The radio commentator was yelling so loud that he nearly swallowed his microphone, as if at the finish of some race. The bells of both churches, Protestant and Catholic, were ringing wildly. The fire engine's siren was wailing. The pent-up tension and excitement seemed to propel us into the sky.

BRIAN

We took off with a fair old jerk, and I had to cling tight to the rail of the playpen. For several hundred feet the babel of voices came with us, but Bertrand, sitting in the right-hand pilot's seat, shut the clamour from his mind as he began to monitor his instruments. From the view through the porthole in front of his head he could see that we were ascending, but only the instruments gave him our rate of climb.

We were both amazed by the speed at which we were rising. We seemed to be going up like a rocket. My first job was to cut free the polystyrene blocks, but when I looked down over the edge of the gondola we were already 500 feet off the ground, and I thought, 'There's no way I can ditch the blocks now, because on their way down they may plane away and kill somebody.' So the blocks stayed in place and came round the world with us. Abandoning that task, I lowered the antenna trays, the long trailing antenna unit for the satellite telephone – with its attached red anti-collision light and white strobe light – and the array of solar panels.

Very soon, only a thousand feet up, we hit the first inversion layer –
a level at which cold air close to the snowy ground meets warmer air
above. The balloon came up against the invisible barrier and stopped
climbing. In open country that would not have mattered: the envelope
would gradually have heated in the sun and we would have started
upwards again. But the process might have taken some time, and here
in the Alps delay was potentially dangerous because if we'd remained at
the same height we would have started to drift sideways and might
have been carried into the mountains. One early attempt to fly round
the world, by Larry Newman in the *Earthwind 1* balloon, in 1993,
failed after only an hour for that very reason. The crew could not
manoeuvre fast enough and hit a hillside.

The way to restart a climb is to shed weight or use the burners, so
Bertrand called out, 'One bag of sand!' and I started pouring the first
fifteen kilos (33 lb) of ballast down through a light fabric tube designed
to send the sand clear of the capsule and disperse it safely. A moment
later he reached up through the hatch, grabbed me by one ankle and
shouted, 'Look out – I'm going to burn!', warning me to keep clear of
the propane jets. Blue flames roared six feet up into the hot-air cone,
warming the helium in the gas cell above, and we started to climb once
more.

Once through the inversion layer we accelerated again and I had to
hurry through my tasks. We needed to shut the hatch and pressurize
the gondola at around 6,000 feet above sea level – and we were going
to reach that height in just a few minutes. As soon as I'd done
everything, and double-checked that everything *looked* all right, I
scrambled back in, and we both cleaned the seal, lifted the heavy
ring-clamp into place and snapped it tight. Abruptly we were in
complete silence.

We stood and waited anxiously. When Bertrand first shut the hatch
after take-off in *Orbiter 2*, within twenty seconds he heard a whistling
hiss which showed that the seal was not airtight and that he was losing
pressure. The result was that for the first few days of the flight he was
obliged to stay at relatively low altitude. So we listened again for any
abnormal sound – but there was nothing: only beautiful silence. We
looked at each other and grinned. The hatch was airtight. The balloon
was climbing. We were on our way.

BERTRAND

After such a protracted build-up, it was wonderful to be airborne at last. But as we climbed away from Château d'Oex, among the snow-laden mountains, we paused briefly at a third and last inversion layer. Then the balloon suddenly seemed to shoot skywards. We'd been aiming for 200 feet per minute, but the variometer showed that our rate of climb was six times as fast – which was positively dangerous. An ascent as rapid as that could cause the envelope to burst as the helium in the gas cell expanded with heat from the sun and diminishing atmospheric pressure. In theory, the excess helium should be forced out down the appendices – two tubes of material three feet in diameter that ran from the gas cell down either side of the envelope to within a few feet of the bottom – but it was possible that the expansion of the gas was becoming too rapid for the tubes to discharge it fast enough. Even if the appendices were working normally, the balloon might eject a massive amount of helium through them, obliging us to compensate for the loss of lift by burning large quantities of propane.

'We need to vent,' I said. Swivelling the right-hand pilot's seat half round, I reached down behind me to operate the pneumatic system that controlled the valves in the top of the envelope. When I opened the knob of the nitrogen bottle and operated the pneumatic switches, the compressed gas went *whissshhh*, forcing its way up the narrow pipe that reached from the gondola right to the top of the envelope, where it pushed open the valves. Our natural inclination was to retain as much helium as possible because we had no reserve supply. But we soon found that one discharge was not enough: we had to vent again and again before we brought our climb under control.

By the time we finally got the balloon stabilized, we had already used up a third of the nitrogen that powered the pneumatic valve-opening system because of the leak that Kieran Sturrock had observed before take-off. That was alarming because it looked as though we would soon have to go on to the manual system, which consisted of a hand-pull on the end of a long wire; so we tried to economize by closing the nitrogen bottle off after every shot rather than leaving the pneumatic system live and the tube full, thus cutting the leak to a minimum.

We both kept thinking uneasily of other balloons that had burst in similar circumstances. The most recent was the *Global Hilton* balloon in January 1998, from which Dick Rutan and Dave Melton had managed to escape by parachute. Two weeks before that, *J-Renée* had split its envelope an hour after take-off in December 1997 because the pilot, Kevin Uliassi, had also been unable to vent helium quickly enough. At least he managed to fly the balloon down – which was more than could be said of Jean-François Pilâtre de Rozier 200 years earlier: rapidly expanding hydrogen burst his envelope, came in contact with smouldering straw in the burner, blew up and killed the inventor.

My mind was also on my grandfather, Auguste, and his first flight into the stratosphere in 1931. The similarities between that take-off and ours were uncanny. The balloon he built was enormous – nearly as big as ours – and he too was in a pressurized gondola. All his equipment was new and, like us, he had too much wind for safety. Before launch a rope became tangled in the winch that opened the gas valve, but nobody noticed it. The ground crew were supposed to wait until he gave them word to cast off, but the wind was so strong that they let go before he issued any command. His assistant suddenly said: 'That's odd – I'm seeing a chimney through the hatch.'

'Which part of the chimney?' my grandfather asked. 'Top or bottom?'

'Top,' came the answer.

To which the inventor replied, 'Obviously we're in the air!'

When he tried to slow their ascent by opening the gas valve, he couldn't do it because of the tangled rope, and his balloon hurtled upwards at a dangerous speed, climbing more than 50,000 feet in half an hour. When he closed his hatch he heard a tell-tale whistle – as we had in *Orbiter 2* – but he managed to seal the leak with a mixture of vaseline and hemp fibre.

As this memory flashed through my head I thought, I hope there are *some* similarities in each generation of our family but not that we turn out to be the same in everything!

Gradually our climb steadied. Pressurization was perfect, and at 08.28 Zulu we sent our first radio message to air traffic control in Geneva:

Geneva Delta. This is Hotel Bravo – Bravo Romeo Alpha. Good

morning. Overhead Château d'Oex. Passing 10,000 feet. Climbing to flight level two two zero. Heading one eight three degrees. Everything on board OK.

Back came the answer:

Good morning, *Breitling Orbiter 3*. I read you loud and clear. Report flight level two two zero. Good luck.

BRIAN

Our control centre had been set up in the comfortable, ultra-modern VIP lounge on the ground floor of the main terminal building at Geneva Airport. Led by Alan Noble, our controllers were working in pairs, each pair doing an eight-hour shift. Alan's assistant Sue Tatford was a formidable organizer, who made it one of her duties to confine the media to the press room next door and stop them bursting in. The second pair consisted of John Albury and Debbie Clarke (often known as 'Debs'), balloonists of wide experience, and among my closest friends. The third were Brian Smith (better known as 'Smiffy'), an airline pilot and, like myself, a balloon examiner, and his wife Cecilia ('C') – collectively 'the Smiffs', and again, good friends.

Alan and Sue were Cameron staff, but the others had volunteered their services free of charge. As a back-up – and a very efficient one, because she had worked as a controller for *Orbiter 2* – there was my wife Jo, who was not officially a member of the team now that I was flying, but nevertheless spent much of her time in the control centre, putting in a stint whenever there was a crisis or one of the regulars needed a break. The fact that everyone knew each other well was a great help, and meant that whenever a crisis blew up, the atmosphere remained that much calmer. Nevertheless, later in the flight when the balloon encountered difficulties members of the team sometimes stayed on long after their own shifts had finished. They could get meals in the airport's excellent restaurant, and when they needed to sleep they had rooms in the Holiday Inn, a two-minute drive away.

Smiffy and C found their initiation fairly traumatic. When I recruited them, they imagined that Jo and I would be working with them and would give them a hand. As things turned out, they were thrown in at the deep end. When they reached the control room after the launch they were, in C's own words, 'barely computer-literate', and they found themselves having to master complicated procedures at high speed. Alan and Sue instructed them but had no time to linger or repeat things – and after two days Smiffy felt so stressed that he was on the verge of quitting. His particular worry was that he and Cecilia were simply not competent enough to be left in charge at night. But soon his experience of airline flying and ballooning came together with his knowledge of meteorology and air control, and quite suddenly he found he was in his element.

From the balloon, soon after 10:00 Zulu, we reported to Control: 'We are heading for the Matterhorn. It would be a gorgeous picture if a plane could hurry up and make it there.' Alan, who had been taken by helicopter down to Geneva from the launch site, replied:

> Receiving your messages OK. Have spoken with Luc and passed position, speed, altitude. They will come back soonest with best cruise altitude. Was slightly alarmed that you had climbed 20,000 feet in little more than an hour. However, giving the Matterhorn good clearance sounds sensible.

The weather had turned out perfect, and our views over the Alps were dazzling. We sailed smoothly over the 14,000-foot peak of the Matterhorn and, next to it, Monte Rosa, with Italy beyond. On our other side we had Mont Blanc and all the French Alps. We flew straight over Les Diablerets, where Bertrand had skied so often, and the mountains, known to him by heart, in which he had done much of his hang-gliding.

Once we had crossed the Italian border, we felt comfortable enough to send a fax message – ostensibly from both of us, but in fact composed by Bertrand:

> It is now time for a tea-break to relax in front of an absolutely wonderful view of the Alps. Overflew Matterhorn, entering Italy five minutes ago. The take-off was a stressful moment with all that wind, and it is now so calm. Even for the third time, it is always the same emotion, to see the family and friends waving. We are specially thankful to all the people who allowed us to

jump into this incredible adventure. In this new world of our narrow gondola, we have the impression time has stopped.

BERTRAND

By the middle of the day Brian was worn out: weeks of ever-increasing stress and an almost sleepless night had drained him, so at 13:30 Zulu he turned into the bunk for a nap. With myself at the controls, *Orbiter 3* flew on southwards, slowly but smoothly, over Italy and France. In complete silence I watched the mountains file past the portholes. I knew I was taking the biggest gamble of my life, but for the first time in months, maybe even years, I was feeling fabulously well and confident. All our team had done their very best, and now, alone in the cockpit, I had no option but to trust the wind and the unknown.

CHAPTER TWO

ORIGINS

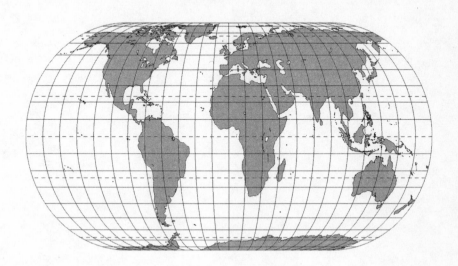

BERTRAND

To find the origins of the Breitling *Orbiter* project I have to reach back more than half a century, through two generations of my family, for both my father Jacques and my grandfather Auguste were pioneering scientists with a strong taste for exploration. Each was much honoured not just in his native Switzerland but throughout the world, and it was their challenging outlook on life, as much as their achievements, that gave me my taste for adventure.

My grandfather, a physicist, was a professor at the University of Brussels. Because he wanted to study cosmic rays, he invented the principle of the pressurized capsule and built a balloon that would carry him into the stratosphere, where the rays are not absorbed by the atmosphere as much as they are lower down. In 1931 he reached a height of 16,000 metres and a year later over 17,000 metres – almost 60,000 feet – becoming the first man to enter the stratosphere and, by the way, also the first to see the curvature of the earth with his own eyes. More than that, however, he proved that it was possible to fly at extreme altitude, above clouds, wind and bad weather, where planes would burn far less fuel in the thinner atmosphere. The principle of his invention was later used for pressurized aircraft and space capsules. In

their day his flights were astounding achievements, and he returned to earth a hero, greeted like the latter-day astronauts when they came back from the moon.

Next he invented a submarine called the bathyscaphe, or deep diver, in which the principle of the stratospherical balloon was applied to ocean exploration. He made his first descent, to just over 10,000 feet, in company with my father. Then, on 23 January 1960, my father, together with Don Walsh, a US Navy officer, dived to the deepest part of the ocean – 11,000 metres, or seven miles down – in the Mariana Trench in the Pacific Ocean.

My father continued with the development of submersibles, building the world's first tourist submarine, with room for forty passengers. Next came a submarine designed to drift in the Gulf Stream, going with the current for 3,000 miles from Florida to Nova Scotia, rather as a balloon is carried by the wind. His aim was not that the craft should make rapid headway but that it should stay under water for a month at a time, keeping pace with the fish and other sea creatures borne by the stream.

This expedition was organized jointly with the Grumman Aerospace Corporation, which was opening an oceanographic department. In 1968, when I was ten, our family went to live at West Palm Beach in Florida for two years. Grumman was also building the lunar modules for the Apollo space missions, so that in Cape Kennedy we became good friends with several of the astronauts, as well as with Wernher von Braun, the head of the American space programme.

At a highly impressionable age, from ten to twelve, I witnessed every launch from Apollo 7 to Apollo 12, often watching alongside the astronauts who had manned previous missions. Better still, these heroic figures came for drinks and meals at our house, talked about their flights and gave me signed photographs. Seeing them not only on television and in the newspapers but also in the flesh, I felt I was at the heart of a pioneering movement that had caught the imagination of the entire world. Fired by the excitement of exploration, of breaking barriers and above all of witnessing a tremendous undertaking from the inside, I got such a taste for adventure that all the flying I myself did later seemed a natural consequence.

At the age of sixteen I became disheartened by the thought that mankind's last great adventure – the journey to the moon – had been completed and there was nothing left to do. Then in 1974 I saw a hang-glider, one of the first in Europe. Immediately I spotted a new opportunity and learned to fly. The physical challenge of hang-gliding thrilled me, especially when I started doing aerobatics; but soon I realized that the sport gave me something far more important than pure excitement in that it raised my level of awareness. The inherent danger forced me to concentrate absolutely, and that in turn enabled me to live intensely in the present moment, setting aside all thoughts of past and future and connecting me to myself. When I started doing aerobatics I found I scored much higher in exams, both at school and at university, because not only my mind but also my intuition and my confidence were functioning more efficiently. I flew not because I wanted to outstrip all rivals or emulate my illustrious forebears: it was more a matter of getting to know myself better. My most important discovery was that, once I was properly connected to my own inner resources, and really feeling inside my body that I was alive, I could achieve much more, not just in hang-gliding but in life also.

On my way home after a day in the air, every second of the flight, every thought and every emotion would live again in my memory, and the rest of the day seemed mundane in comparison. I saw that in normal life most people are on automatic pilot, using only part of their capabilities, but that if they could deepen contact with themselves they would become far more effective and efficient.

At that time there were no instruments to give a hang-glider pilot his speed. When I wanted to do a loop, I had only my own feeling to tell me precisely when to push on the control bar. If I pushed too early, without enough speed, the glider would stall as it came over and then tumble; if too late, the glider would stay in the dive, become too stressed and break. There was only one correct instant for starting a perfect loop, and the choice of it became obvious when my awareness was higher.

Many of the sports that became popular in the 1970s – wind-surfing, free-fall parachuting, snow-boarding, roller-skating – were of the same kind: because they made practitioners use their bodies as instruments, they gave people not only exercise and excitement but, more importantly, a means of getting back to themselves through intuition and true emotion.

I owed much to my father, the scientist in the family, but I was also strongly influenced by my mother, the daughter of a Protestant priest, who studied music, psychology, oriental religion and philosophy. From early childhood I endlessly discussed ideas with her as we went for walks in the country. When I started flying, I was able to try out my new theories of self-awareness on her.

It was my exploration of human psychology, through hang-gliding, that brought me to medicine and led me to become a doctor. I saw that the people who feel bad in life are the ones who are not connected to themselves in the present moment: their connections are either to the past – in which case they tend to be depressives, always worrying about things that did not happen as they wanted – or to the future, in which case they often exhibit anxious behaviour. I realized that the present moment is the only one in which you can change something in your life, and is therefore all-important. I wanted to make use of the insights I had gained from hang-gliding by applying them as therapy in psychiatric medicine – not, of course, by pushing my patients to fly, but by teaching them to connect themselves to their inner resources and capabilities.

After five years' medical training at the University of Lausanne, I decided to take three years off to travel and try other forms of flying, including motorized hang-gliders and microlights. I then returned to Lausanne to complete my studies and went on to do eight years of postgraduate practice in psychiatry and psychotherapy. Throughout that period I kept up my aerobatic flying and began to specialize in a particular type of hang-gliding. During demonstrations at air shows a balloonist would take me up, dangling beneath the gondola, and launch me from a height of 6,000 or 7,000 feet. While I performed loops and spins and wing-overs, laying sky-trails with smoke boxes, loudspeakers on the ground would play the music of Jonathan Livingstone, sung by Neil Diamond. In due course I became European aerobatics champion.

During my postgraduate phase I learned hypnosis and realized that this was the medical equivalent of what I had been doing in the air. I was delighted to have found a link that enabled me to deepen my understanding of flight and medicine at the same time.

In all this flying I never felt I had to prove anything to my father or grandfather. Andy Elson, who became a rival balloonist in the race to be first round the world, often said that my only goal was to make myself as famous as them – but in fact it was much more than that. My profession was not to build submarines or balloons, as they had done: it was to be a doctor, and to explore the human condition – the mind and the soul – rather than the physical world. But it was true that I had harboured a spirit of adventure since childhood: I liked the style in which my heroes lived and worked, and the taste for exploration they had given me remained very strong.

By the age of thirty I had lost count of the number of times I had gone aloft under a balloon, pulled my release mechanism and glided down, making loops and spins. Yet I never considered flying a balloon myself, because the idea of allowing myself to be pushed by the wind, not knowing where I might land, seemed ridiculous. With my hang-glider I could control my descent precisely and land back on the spot from which I had taken off. Often the pilot of the balloon had to wait for two or three hours in the mountains before his team could rescue him, and I decided I would never go in for such an absurd sport.

Then, one evening in Château d'Oex at the end of January 1992, I was invited to a big dinner for balloon teams, and because I had been delayed by an interview I arrived late. When I came into the enormous room, I found hundreds of people starting to eat and only one seat unoccupied. I had no choice but to take it, and so found myself next to Wim Verstraeten, a friendly, round-faced Belgian, always smiling, who had dropped me from his balloon a couple of times.

Wim told me he had been invited as a pilot to take part in the first transatlantic balloon race, the Chrysler Challenge, due to be held in the autumn; he suggested that I, with my medical knowledge and wide experience of flying, would make a useful co-pilot and bring new skills to the enterprise. I scented a fabulous adventure, remembering how, in Cape Kennedy, I had met Charles Lindbergh, who in 1927 made the first solo crossing of the Atlantic in his single-engined *Spirit of St Louis*, and I accepted the offer immediately.

I realized that to go with the wind would be a fundamentally new experience and would call for a major mental adjustment on my part. Until then, in the air, I had always had the wind in my face: I had habitually fought it to overcome turbulence and control my progress. Now I would have to do the opposite and go wherever the wind took me. The idea seemed very strange. Nevertheless, I learned to fly a balloon and looked forward to the challenge – and before it came, fate seemed to send me a message.

That summer I flew to China with a party of doctors to study aspects of traditional Chinese medicine. Finding I had a moment of free time in Shanghai, I went into an antique shop, where I spotted a bowl of what looked like bronze medallions. One in particular took my fancy, and I asked the proprietor of the shop what the characters on it signified. He told me they were an ancient proverb meaning, 'When the wind blows in the same direction as your path, it brings you great happiness.' Fascinated, I bought the medallion immediately. Just as I was trying to accept the idea of flying with the wind, along came this mysterious sign, at precisely the right moment.

In August, when the crews gathered in New England for the start of the Chrysler race, I took the medallion with me, and at the press conferences Wim joked that we would win because his co-pilot had this magic talisman. In fact, we did win – not, of course, because the medal itself was magical, but because the ideograms on it had a magical significance. The teams who tried to fight against the elements ditched in the ocean but luckily were rescued. After five days and nights in a tiny, unpressurized gondola, Wim and I crossed the coast of Portugal and landed in Spain.

From that flight I gained not only a taste for ballooning but also an invaluable new friend. Because the forecasts from the official weather bureau proved hopelessly inaccurate, Wim made contact in mid-ocean with an expert working at the Royal Institute of Meteorology in Brussels, Luc Trullemans. He at once told us what to do to escape from the storms that had been dogging us. 'Climb above the bad weather,' he told us – and so we did. By going high, we harnessed some of the energy of the depression that had been making life so miserable and accelerated away ahead of it.

I came home thrilled by the experience, and found it amusing to tell people that Wim and I had won the race by trusting the winds rather than struggling to impose our will on the elements. We had gone with the wind and the weather, becoming friends of the Atlantic. All we could do to change direction was to fly higher or lower. At our ceiling altitude of 20,000 feet the winds carried us southeast, and when we went very low, only a hundred feet above the sea, they turned northeast.

Back in Europe, people asked us what we planned to do next. Almost as a joke we said we were going to fly round the world. When King Baudouin – then the ruler of Belgium – invited Wim and me to the Royal Palace to hear the story of the flight, he asked about future plans. I mentioned the idea of a round-the-world flight, and as soon as we left the palace I said to Wim, 'I have to tell you a story.'

During the 1930s my grandfather was invited by King Leopold (Baudoin's father) to talk about his flight into the stratosphere. After Auguste had described it the King asked what he would like to do next. The professor outlined his plans for a bathyscaphe, to which Leopold's response was, 'Well, that's really interesting. If you need any help raising funds, just ask me.' Back at the university, my grandfather related details of his audience with the monarch and said, 'Now that I've told the King about the bathyscaphe, I've got to go ahead with it.'

I turned to Wim and said, 'OK – so now we have to go round the world.'

CHAPTER THREE

ENTER BREITLING

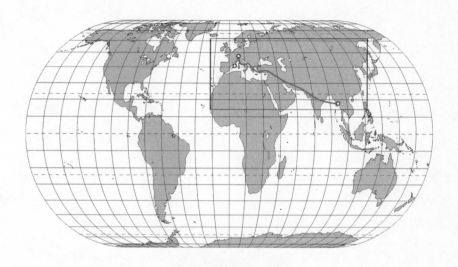

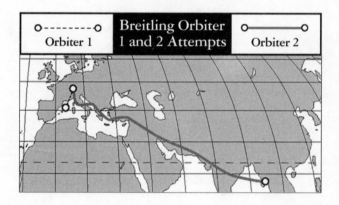

BERTRAND

Who would finance our round-the-world attempt? Only a company passionately interested in aviation history, whose products were so good that I would be proud to advertise them.

The main sponsor of the transatlantic race had been Chrysler, the car manufacturer, but competitors had also been allowed to find personal sponsors for their own equipment. I happened to know Theodore (Thedy) Schneider, owner and chief executive of Breitling, the private company that makes high-quality aviation chronometers in Grenschen, in the German-speaking part of Switzerland.

From its start the firm had been associated with aircraft instruments, and its sponsorship of projects was directed towards powered flying machines. But when I approached Thedy, he responded immediately and gave Wim Verstraeten and me some help. I posted the Breitling logo in prominent places, and when we won the race the publicity was tremendous, with Breitling up alongside Chrysler in hundreds of photographs. Having asked for nothing, the watchmakers reaped a handsome reward.

At the beginning of 1993 I went back to the firm with an outline of my ambitious idea for a round-the-world attempt. Thedy's response was positive: if such a flight proved technically feasible, he would be part of it. I then approached the Swiss Institute of Meteorology (generally known as Météo Suisse), a weather office with experience of routeing ocean-going yachts around the world. At my request, thousands of computer simulations were performed to calculate the chances of balloons launched from different latitudes in Europe and North Africa at various seasons. The best advice was that we should launch in winter from somewhere 40 degrees north and fly at 10,000 metres. The computers reckoned the trip might take twenty days.

Armed with this information I went to the Bristol firm Cameron Balloons, who had built the entrants for the transatlantic race – and indeed made almost all the balloons that later attempted to fly round the world. After some study Camerons replied that they could have a pressurized gondola constructed out of carbon fibre and Kevlar, a combination which is lighter and stronger than steel, and that they themselves could make a really large envelope capable of lifting the capsule, its crew and enough fuel to keep the craft aloft for a three-week flight.

Actual construction of the gondola would be left to specialist manufacturers, but the general concept was mine, and I asked Camerons to use the system that had served my grandfather and father so well. The capsule would be a horizontal, pressure-tight cylinder, very similar to my father's last submarine. Inside would be a tank of liquid oxygen which would evaporate gradually, allowing the crew to breathe, along with lithium hydroxide filters to absorb the exhaled carbon dioxide.

Everyone agreed that the balloon should be a Rozier type, named after its inventor, the eighteenth-century aviator Jean-François Pilâtre de Rozier (see diagram on page viii). This type of balloon functions on a combination of hot air and gas. The main lift is provided by a large volume of helium in a gas cell. During the day, the heat of the sun causes the gas to expand and keeps the balloon aloft. At night the pilots burn propane or kerosene to heat the air in the hot-air cone, which in turn heats the helium, and so increases lift. Camerons saw that in a long-range balloon, insulation of the envelope would be all-important. The transatlantic balloons, being white, had heated up a lot during the day and cooled quickly at night; by giving the new envelope a waistcoat of aluminium-coated Mylar, the manufacturers would be able to slow these processes beneficially.

Probably one of my best ideas was to ask Camerons not only to construct our balloon – they were building for our rivals as well – but also to become fully involved in the flight itself. I wanted Alan Noble, one of their managers, to act as our flight director, as he had done during the Chrysler Challenge. Soon Alan became not just my privileged link with the factory but a good friend whom I could trust fully.

With a realistic proposal in front of them, the people at Breitling were keen to back the attempt whole-heartedly. And when they saw there was a chance of writing a new chapter in aviation history, they decided – if they could afford it – to be the sole sponsor and to make this the company's big project for the next few years.

As soon as Alan had come up with a costing, I went to see Thedy Schneider again. The moment the boss saw the figure, he said, 'Well, that's possible for us. Where do I send the money?'

'Thedy!' I said, slightly taken aback. 'I have no idea.'

'You must know,' came the answer. 'Now we've decided to go for it, we've got to move fast because there are others in the race. Where do you want the money sent?'

'Well,' I stalled. 'I can call Alan Noble.'

'Go ahead, then.'

Thedy handed me the phone. I dialled Camerons and explained the position. Alan, after a couple of double-takes, gave me an account number – whereupon Thedy wrote out a cheque for the first tranche. Within three days the money was at the factory in Bristol.

'We've got the cash,' said Don Cameron, 'but no contract. What do we do?'

'We have to work even harder, because these people are incredible,' Alan replied.

So the project got off the ground in the best possible spirit. Throughout the enterprise nobody ever considered Breitling to be mere sponsors: we saw them more as partners, members of the team, closely involved with every development. On my side, I never wanted money to come through me because I thought it was better that each partner should be responsible for his own speciality. Funds went straight to Alan at Camerons.

After leaving Thedy's office I drove for an hour towards home, but then stopped at a restaurant to recover from the intense emotion I was experiencing. I felt I had just been given the green light to start building my life's dream, and that in future nothing would be the same. The next years would be both very exciting and very difficult. I picked up the telephone and rang Wim. I explained that the project was on, and said I wanted to invite him officially to be my co-pilot on this incredible adventure. I told him how happy I was at the prospect of resuming the friendship we had built over the Atlantic.

That was in June 1995. For our weather team, I approached Météo Suisse, who produced Pierre Eckert, an expert on routeing yachts. To work with him I asked for the help of Luc Trullemans, from the Royal Institute of Meteorology in Brussels, who had given us such invaluable advice during the Chrysler race. The two are physically quite different – Luc tall, extrovert, smiling, enthusiastic and always eager to explain what he is doing; Pierre smaller, quieter, more serious in manner, not displaying his considerable ability, a keen cyclist and an ecological officer in local government. But when, at my invitation, they met for the first time in Château d'Oex they struck up an immediate rapport that demonstrated the international brotherhood of weathermen; and this pair, whom we came to know as 'the met men', proved out-and-out winners. Putting them together was a gamble that paid off magnificently. None of the other teams employed two weathermen: either they thought one was enough, or they feared that two would battle for supremacy. Our two, far from doing that, praised and complemented each other, so that the value of the pair became incalculable.

Luc had begun studying meteorology as a hobby, and only later made it his profession. He was never a pilot himself, but balloons entered his life when one landed in his back yard in Belgium: the pilot invited him to make the forecast for a meeting, and there he met Wim Verstraeten. Wim asked Luc to be his weatherman for his forthcoming flight over Mount Kilimanjaro in Tanzania, during the late 1980s, and that turned out a big success. Wim then sought Luc's help during the Atlantic flight of 1992 – and so it was that I met him after we had won the race.

For the Breitling flights Luc and Pierre had two principal sources of information. Pierre used ECMWF, the European Centre for Medium-Range Weather Forecasting, in Reading, England, and Luc got forecasts via the Internet from NOAA, the American National Oceanographic and Atmospheric Administration. These two organizations process observations from all over the world – from satellites, radio-balloons, aircraft, ships – and produce computer models that give forecasts for the next fourteen days. Much of the information comes from geostationary satellites, 23,500 miles out in space, which can observe the movement of clouds and so gauge the speed and direction of wind; also, by measuring infra-red radiation, they can give temperature profiles. Polar orbiter satellites, flying lower, analyse temperatures more precisely.

In planning our balloon flights the met men's main interest was in the wind forecasts, and from these – always moving ahead in space and time – they computed likely wind trajectories. The model that Luc used was particularly interesting because it derived from observations of the spread of fallout over Europe after the nuclear accident at Chernobyl. Working backwards, an expert deduced what the weather patterns must have been at the time to spread the radioactive particles as they did. The model was developed for use in forecasting should another nuclear accident happen, and it was used during the Chrysler Atlantic race. The balloon was taken as the equivalent of a single particle, blowing with the wind in different layers at various altitudes, and the model proved incredibly effective. All the other teams competing in the round-the-world race had access to the model, but we had an invaluable advantage in the form of two high-class brains working in synergy.

In Bristol, at a brainstorming session in the Princess of Wales pub close to the Cameron factory, someone suggested that our balloon be called the *Breitling Orbiter*, and everyone concerned adopted the name enthusiastically. Wim knew an Englishman called Andy Elson – a powerfully built fellow in his early forties, made rather dishevelled-looking by a straggling beard and the absence of one front tooth, but a skilled technician who had made the first balloon flight over Everest. Wim was convinced that Andy was the best engineer for high-altitude flight, so Alan commissioned him to take charge of the construction of our capsule on the general lines we asked.

It was Andy who introduced the idea of using kerosene fuel rather than propane. The great advantage of kerosene is that it is much lighter to transport. To carry enough propane on the first *Orbiter*, we would have needed a ton of titanium tanks. The synthetic rubber bags containing the equivalent amount of kerosene weighed only 100 lb.

Already I knew we were in a race. During the winter of 1995–6, while the *Breitling Orbiter* was still being built, Richard Branson and Per Lindstrand were in Morocco with their team, waiting for a favourable weather slot to take off in the *Virgin Global Challenger*. As it turned out they never got one, and they waited the whole winter without being able to launch. The only man who did get airborne was the American Steve Fossett, who took off from St Louis in America and flew alone in his unpressurized gondola for some 2,000 miles before coming down in Canada.

Now, in the winter of 1996–7, we had the same two competitors. Steve Fossett was making ready a new *Solo Spirit* near St Louis, and Branson was again preparing to take off from Morocco. To me, the strangest feature of Branson's gondola was its shape: a vertical cylinder, which would be very bad in the waves if he had to ditch in the sea, and with a sleeping space at the bottom – the coldest part. A further curiosity was that the atmosphere in his capsule was maintained by compressors, which were heavy and noisy and would use a lot of fuel.

Camerons had subcontracted the construction of our gondola shell to another company, Tods, but the first model did not survive the test process. When over-pressure was established inside, the capsule leaked badly at the points from which it was suspended, air forcing its way out. Tods immediately agreed to build another, but it was not ready until September 1996. This made the fitting of the equipment a rush, and when the gondola reached Switzerland it was still almost empty. Together with other technicians, Andy Elson had to kit it out at top speed, working under difficult conditions in a small hut at Château d'Oex.

We were eager to fly in December, but as the year drew to a close our craft was still not ready. On 7 January 1997, while we were still working, Branson took off from Morocco. This produced an atmosphere of desperation in the Breitling camp – but then came a big surprise. Next morning Alan rang me and said, 'If you switch on your

TV, you can watch Mr Branson's landing.'

I was astonished to hear that during the night the Branson team had hit some severe problem. This forced them to drop all their food and water and most of their fuel to avoid crashing before they came down in Algeria. The nature of the problem was never disclosed, but rumour had it that the balloon climbed too fast, went through its ceiling and lost so much helium that it could not stay airborne once the heat of the sun faded.

Once again the race was open, and when Luc and Pierre gave *Orbiter* a green light for the following Sunday, 12 January 1997, we took off from Château d'Oex. In retrospect I have to admit that the balloon was probably not ready. During the night before take-off we couldn't even load our food because the gondola was full of technicians: wires trailed everywhere and altogether the final hour before departure was a nightmare. Yet all the other omens seemed good. Thousands of people turned out to witness the take-off and the atmosphere was magical. In a short speech to the crowd I recited lines from a Belgian poet, saying that if the world is spherical, it is made that way so that love and friendship and peace can go round it. Because I had secured the support of the International Olympic Committee, our balloon was emblazoned with the five Olympic rings and the burners were ignited with the Olympic flame, brought specially from the Olympic museum. Our balloon was planned to be a symbol of peace linking all the countries of the world for two or three weeks. The weather was perfect, with not a cloud in the sky, and the wind at high altitude was ideal as it would carry the balloon at a good speed straight towards the jet stream.

Alas, all these hopeful auguries proved false. After only half an hour in the air one of the fuel tanks overflowed dramatically, sending a flood of kerosene across the floor of the gondola and contaminating our water reserve. By then the balloon was at 27,000 feet and flying beautifully at 60 mph, but Wim and I knew at once we could not stand the vapour, and we started to descend. Having taken off at 9 a.m., we ditched at 3 p.m. in the Mediterranean south of Marseilles. The disappointment was crushing, the frustration immense. As the capsule took salt water on board and we sat miserably on it in our survival suits and life jackets, a coastguard plane roared low over our heads, indicating that rescue boats were on their way; but our personal safety seemed relatively unimportant. We felt we had destroyed our dream. Although the gondola was towed ashore, everything in it was ruined. The envelope could not be recovered for two months, and by the time fishing boats brought it ashore it was smothered with algae and barnacles.

We flew home by private jet, with feet bare, clothes still wet, and carrying one square metre of the envelope which we had cut away for a souvenir. That same night I was back in my own bed, my dream shattered. But then in the morning Thedy Schneider rang and said, 'Cheer up! The world wasn't made in a day. Probably we'll need more than one attempt to go round it.' We agreed that there is only one certain way of never failing in life – and that is never to try.

At the debriefing in Geneva three days after the disaster, Alan Noble asked, 'Well – what's the form? Do we try again?'

'Of course!' Thedy told him.

'When can we start on a new balloon?'

'Ten seconds after you tell me how much it will cost.'

At the next meeting Alan came armed with a figure, and when he named it, within barely ten seconds Thedy said, 'OK, then. So we go!'

There were no recriminations about the failure of the fuel system, and we again commissioned Andy Elson to build a capsule. This time I was determined to be more closely involved in its construction, and I asked Wim, together with Breitling, to make a greater commitment – to come to Bristol more often to keep an eye on progress, and to take a more detailed interest so that both of us would be able to put right any defect that might manifest itself in flight.

During the year of *Breitling Orbiter 2*'s construction, our rivals were again hard at work. Steve Fossett, who had made a beautiful flight from St Louis to India, was building a new balloon. So was Branson. Two further challengers were the Americans Dick Rutan and Dave Melton, who were planning to take off from Albuquerque in New Mexico, and Kevin Uliassi, who was aiming to make a solo flight. But at Camerons it gradually became clear that Wim had too much work to do running his own balloon company in Belgium. Worried that he was not devoting enough time to our project and that he would never learn the gondola's systems thoroughly enough, Alan and I decided to take a third pilot – a partner who would be fully competent to fly the balloon while I was asleep and a technician able to carry out repairs if things went wrong. So it was that, in the summer of 1997, Andy Elson joined the flight team, and the gondola was modified to carry an extra crew member.

Then, in May, a new man appeared on the scene. He was a friend of Andy's and a highly experienced balloonist in his own right: Brian Jones.

BRIAN

My background was utterly different from Bertrand's. I was born in Bristol, where my father worked as a legal executive in a solicitor's office, specializing in matrimonial cases. My mother, who came from Wick, in the far north of Scotland, worked as a school secretary.

At home I was happy as could be, but by nature I was quiet and self-effacing, and this led to my being bullied at school, where rough treatment undermined my self-confidence and made me play truant. After doing that several times I felt dreadful shame hanging over me, and when I learned that the authorities had written to my parents, I was so scared that I ran away. Somehow I had formed the idea of walking to Scotland, and at the age of thirteen I set off northwards through Bristol. After seven hours, not far clear of the city, I went to sleep in a barn. There I was found by the farmer, who handed me over to the police.

As a member of the Boy Scouts I had very much enjoyed outdoor life, and in the Air Training Corps I developed a passion for flying; but, loathing school, I made a complete mess of my exams and left with only one O-level, in English. I took a job as a clerk with British Aerospace at Filton, in the northwest suburbs of Bristol. Soon, however, I realized that was a dead end, and I applied to join the Royal Air Force.

With a single O-level I had no chance of becoming a pilot – a minimum of five was needed – and the RAF offered me work as an administrative apprentice. I took the job and put myself into the force's equivalent of night school – the RAF Education Section. A year later, having passed the necessary extra four O-levels, I applied again for pilot training – only to be refused once more. Instead, I became a loadmaster, first on Hercules C-130 transports, later on Puma helicopters.

In seven years on Hercs I went all over the world and had numerous lively assignments, among them a mission to rescue the British Embassy staff from Phnom Penh during the Vietnam War. The Viet Cong were so close to the airfield that crew members were issued with bullet-proof flak jackets, and our pilot did what the Americans called a Ke Sanh approach, coming in high, at about 1,200 feet, until he was almost over the airfield, then tilting the nose steeply down, aiming for the piano-key markings on the end of the runway, with full flaps and gear down, to land with an almighty bang.

Twice, on separate training flights, we went round the world west-about, taking fifteen days to complete each circuit. On those trips the same aircraft and crew went the whole way: we would fly for eight or ten hours, then have a sixteen-hour break, with a longer stop-off in Hawaii.

During my helicopter service I did three tours in Northern Ireland, where we flew many sorties into the border areas known as bandit country – so dangerous that everything and everybody had to be moved by air. We would drop off army patrols and special forces, pick up prisoners and deliver food to outposts. On such missions the crew were always armed – the pilot with a rifle and pistol, and myself, alone in the back, with a machine gun and side arm. We never knew when the weapons might be needed.

When I left the RAF in 1977, at the age of thirty, I worked as a salesman and then as a sales trainer in the pharmaceutical industry before setting up my own wholesale catering equipment firm, Crocks, in Frome, Somerset, with the help of my sister Pauline. For a while the business did fairly well, and I also had two retail shops. But by far my greatest stroke of luck during those years was that I met my wife, Jo, who was a partner in a catering business – supplying food, rather than equipment – also in Frome.

Then in 1986 I was invited to fly in a hot-air balloon at a festival in Bristol, and immediately became hooked. I sold the shops, and with some of the capital bought a balloon of my own. By 1989 a major economic recession had set in. It hit the catering industry particularly hard, and because Crocks clearly could not provide a living for both of us, I left the business temporarily in my sister's hands.

Providentially, in that same year there was a major development in

British ballooning regulations. Until 1989 anyone holding a private pilot's licence had been allowed to fly a balloon, and there was no such thing as a commercial licence. Then the Civil Aviation Authority issued the first commercial licences, which meant that pilots could fly passengers for money. The result was that ballooning business took off.

Seeing a new opportunity, I began to fly commercially and also worked as a consultant for balloonists who wanted to carry passengers. I was already an instructor, and when I became a flight examiner and the National Training Officer for British instructors, my objective was to encourage higher professionalism in the sport. In 1994, together with Andy Elson and Dave Seager-Thomas, I set up a partnership, High Profile Balloons, which operated balloons for companies like the Royal Mail and Mitsubishi Motors. So, by the time I joined the Breitling project in May 1997, I had a good ballooning pedigree.

It was Andy Elson who invited me to take charge of planning for *Orbiter 2*. Things were not going well at Camerons, largely because Andy – though a competent technician – was not a great organizer, often promising to get something done but sometimes not quite managing it. Besides, he could become angry, and was liable to storm out of the workshop, slamming the door, after a setback. Being naturally calm, I found I could exercise a stabilizing influence, and saw many ways of improving procedures. Also, because I had done survival training in the RAF, I organized the training for the balloon pilots – and it was during one of the sessions at Camerons that I met Bertrand Piccard.

At first I was slightly in awe of this slender, intense-looking man, with his receding hair, high, intelligent forehead and penetrating blue-grey eyes, because it was he who had initiated the whole *Orbiter* project. However, I soon formed a favourable impression, noticing that he had time for everyone he met. If he came into a room full of people and two of them were important, he would shake hands with everybody else as well, whether they were secretaries or just someone holding the door open. Another great advantage for me, with my non-existent French, was that Bertrand spoke excellent English with a full command of technical terms.

It had already been agreed that during *Orbiter 2*'s flight I and Jo would act as the second pair on the control team in Geneva. When the workshop moved to Switzerland I became more and more closely involved in the preparations. During the build-up to launch I got to know Bertrand better, and I generally acted as a soothing agent whenever Andy flew off the handle. I became known as 'Andy's user-friendly interface'.

BERTRAND

As with the first *Orbiter*, the project fell behind schedule. One deadline after another came and went. Andy had every technical detail of the capsule in his head but none of it was written down, and whenever I asked him if he was sure something or other would really work, he replied, 'Bertrand – trust me. I'm not a doctor!' The rest of us accepted his shortcomings because we were afraid that if we put too much pressure on him, he would walk out for good. Eventually we saw it was too late to call his bluff: we should have stood up to him earlier, but now all we could do was go with him.

Personal frictions exacerbated the technical problems. Andy began to say that Wim was not showing sufficient commitment, that he had not trained enough, and spent too much time talking on the telephone. At one point he said, 'If Wim flies, I don't.'

Because I was still indebted to Wim, I could not possibly stand him down. I told Andy that if I succeeded without Wim, I might well see my face in the newspapers but I would never again be able to look at myself in the mirror. Andy eventually agreed that he would take off with both of us, but only on condition that he and I alone flew the balloon. Wim, he said, could deal with communications and naviga-tion.

In the extremely narrow confines of the gondola such bickering would be intolerable; we knew of many other crews who had come to grief through friction at close quarters. And so, to defuse the tension, I brought my psychological training to bear. All three of us talked through our lives and discussed our characters, deliberately highlight-ing our differences and finding ways to respect each other's peculiari-ties. By thus getting to know each other better, we built a good team spirit before take-off.

Once again our main competitor seemed to be Richard Branson, and we were constantly looking over our shoulders in the direction of

Morocco. Time and again we received messages saying he was not ready to launch – but we were never quite sure how to take these. There was always a suspicion that he was playing for time. One day in October 1997 his project manager, Mike Kendrick, rang Alan and asked us not to take off for the time being because Branson was about to go to China to negotiate rights of passage and did not want anything to prejudice his chances of gaining general permission for balloon overflights. Mike also suggested that Alan call Steve Fossett with the same message.

But Branson did not go to China, nor did we hear any more until a couple of months later when he inflated his balloon and prepared to take off. Unfortunately, because his weather slot was so small, he had to inflate during the day – a dangerous procedure in the desert, where violent, gusting winds almost always get up as hot air rises from the sand. The envelope took off without the gondola and flew on its own to Algeria, where it ruined itself on landing.

As for us . . . Andy, perennially optimistic and disorganized, kept telling people we were ready when in fact we were not. 'Just a few bits and pieces to tidy up,' he would say, but the bits and pieces took two months to sort out. The result was that during all those weeks Branson was afraid we would go, and in the end this pushed him into attempting a premature take-off.

At last, in January 1998, our balloon really *was* ready – but when the gondola was lifted by a crane at the Château d'Oex launch field, some of the fittings which attached the main cables from the capsule to the load frame pulled out. The gondola fell back on the trailer and was damaged; the load frame, the burners and some of the pipes were bent, so take-off had to be postponed while repairs were made. After ditching in the Mediterranean in *Orbiter 1* I thought I could never feel more humiliated; but now, after this idiotic accident, our team looked even more ridiculous in front of the 270 journalists who had come to Château d'Oex.

Eventually, after our weathermen had found a good-looking slot, *Breitling Orbiter 2* took off on 28 January. As that was my grandfather's birthday, I thought it must be a lucky day for me. Little did I know that I would have to wait for my own birthday to take off on a successful flight. As soon as we reached 6,000 feet and closed the top hatch, we heard a hissing, whistling sound from the rear hatch. It was leaking. A combination of haste, bitter cold and exhaustion had led to the hatch being fitted incorrectly – and this meant that until we could get it properly sealed we would have to fly low, missing the fastest winds.

For me, history seemed to be repeating itself once too often: exactly the same problem had afflicted my grandfather when he took off for the stratosphere. However, he managed to seal the crack with a mixture of hemp and vaseline, while we tried in vain with a plastic bag and silicon sealant. So the first day of the flight was spoiled by anxiety – and on the second morning there was another shock when we found that we had somehow lost a third of our entire fuel supply. We never discovered quite what happened, but two of the six tanks, each containing 500 litres of kerosene, had emptied during the night. I felt really fed up with kerosene leaks, but I decided it would not be a good idea to express my disgust to Andy and kept to myself a promise that I would never fly again with that fuel system.

Only very fast and direct winds would carry us round the world with the fuel we had left. But because of the weather patterns we had to fly the balloon relatively low and slow for four days, during which Andy, accepting responsibility, went outside the gondola, hung below it on a rope above a 5,000-foot drop, removed the rear hatch and reset it correctly – after which it gave no more trouble.

By then I knew there was no chance of the flight succeeding, because the only strong winds were crossing the middle of China, and the Chinese were refusing all balloons permission to overfly their country. After more than a year of negotiations, to be baulked by sheer bureaucracy was infuriating, because as we approached the border we knew that up ahead of us there was a jet stream travelling at 160 mph, which would have swept us across the Pacific to California in only four days. But the Chinese remained adamant. There are international agreements allowing a civilian aircraft making an occasional flight to cross any country, but the small print says that every country is allowed, for safety reasons, to impose restrictions – and China imposed restrictions on the whole country for the entire year.

It so happened that the Vice-Prime Minister of China was in Switzerland during our flight, and every time he looked at television or a newspaper all he saw was 'CHINA REFUSES PERMISSION'. He felt

In 1931 and 1932 Professor Auguste Piccard, inventor of the pressurized capsule, made the first two flights into the stratosphere (*Piccard Archives*).

In 1998 *Breitling Orbiter 2*, a similar shape and size to the stratospheric balloon, landed in Burma after a record flight of 9 days, 17 hours and 55 minutes (*Breitling*).

Brian Jones (*left*) and Bertrand Piccard during the construction of the *Breitling Orbiter 3* capsule, seen through the back hatch. On the far left is the liquid oxygen tank (*Gamma*).

Breitling clock/stop watch

Warning light panel

External lighting

External video monitor

Flytec variometer

Carbon monoxide detector

Oxygen monitor

Carbon dioxide/ propane/sulphur dioxide monitor

The central part of the instrument panel in the cockpit. To the left are the electrical systems, heating and life support controls and electrical fuses; to the right are the GPS, satellite telephone, remote camera controls, emergency systems and the gas valves (*Bill Sly*).

Some of the team during the assembly of the gondola in the workshop at Château d'Oex. From left to right: Brian Jones, Bertrand Piccard, Stefano Albinati, Thedy Schneider, Alan Noble, Pete Johnson, Kieran Sturrock, Joanna Jones and Roland Wicki (*Breitling*).

Final preparation of the equipment, before loading. Brian and Bertrand with Pierre Blanchoud (*Bill Sly*).

After three months of doubt and false alarms, the *Breitling Orbiter 3* capsule is finally brought on to the launch field (*Bill Sly*).

Like a ghost in the middle of the night, the silver-coated mylar of the *Breitling Orbiter 3* reflects the arc lights of the launch field, while the vapour of the liquid helium shrouds it in mist. An absolutely calm night was needed for this very difficult operation (above – *Annie Clement*; below left – *Edipresse – S. Féval*; below right – *Edipresse – P. Martin*).

The worst moment of the take-off: saying goodbye to loved ones. (Above left) Brian and his wife, Jo, in front of the cameras (*Yvain Genevay*).

(Above right) Bertrand and his father, Jacques, cannot hide the tears in their eyes as the moment of truth comes with the take-off (*Bill Sly*).

Bertrand, on his birthday, with Michèle and their three daughters, Estelle, Oriane and Solange (*Yvain Genevay*).

When the sun rises over Château d'Oex, the people can see the balloon for the first time. The envelope was so fragile it could not be inflated for tests; it could only be inflated once for the flight itself (*Breitling*).

Friendly rivals: (Above left) Steve Fossett takes off from the Busch Stadium in St Louis in *Solo Spirit* at the beginning of his round-the-world attempt (*Associated Press/St Louis Dispatch*); (above right) Richard Branson's *ICO Global Challenger* flying high above Mount Fuji on 24 December 1998; (left) Andy Elson's Cable & Wireless balloon ditches in the Pacific on 7 March 1999 – suddenly the route was clear for the Breitling team (both *PA*).

In the dangerously gusting wind, the *Breitling Orbiter 3* finally lifts off. After three months of waiting and doubt nobody believed it would, so the emotion is even greater on the launch field where thousands of people are waving and cheering (*Chas Breton*).

Still at a low altitude, the balloon will eventually climb to the same altitude as the jet plane flying above, at 30–35,000 feet (*Chas Breton*).

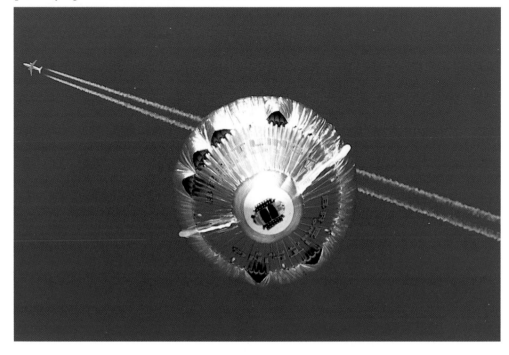

he must do something, so he started faxing Beijing, but it was Chinese New Year and permission did not come through until we were over Burma (now called Myanmar) and almost out of fuel.

Without a full load of fuel *Orbiter 2* lacked the endurance to skirt China, and our mission was therefore doomed. Nevertheless, we pushed on – but at very low altitude to avoid being carried into the prohibited region – because we wanted to acquit ourselves as well as we could.

After the technical setbacks nothing further went wrong, and crew relationships turned out easier than they had been on the ground. However, Wim's lack of training on high-tech equipment meant that he could never be left alone in the cockpit, so Andy and I had to work alternate shifts. In that situation it was clearly useless to have a three-man team, and while the balloon was still airborne I privately made a second promise: that if ever a third *Orbiter* took off, I would have to change the crew.

Throughout the flight our morale was frequently bolstered by the messages that Brian Jones was sending up from the control centre. Always calm and good-natured, often witty, he kept everyone amused, and he did so much to lighten the atmosphere on board that I felt that in spirit he was with us in the gondola. One of his more memorable communications reached us over Afghanistan. 'Watch out,' he warned, 'because the people down there have very strange habits. At weddings the men dance round the tables firing weapons into the air. If you receive any invitations, please refuse and keep going.'

Because the higher winds would still have pushed us towards China, we flew extremely low – between 1,000 and 3,000 feet – for one day over Pakistan, three over India and one above the Bay of Bengal. As we sat out on top of the gondola, cruising at between 20 and 30 mph in complete silence, spices from cooking and incense from temples came wafting up, along with the faint shouts of children. This was emphatically *not* what we were meant to be doing: we were supposed to be flying fast and high, inside a pressurized cabin, in pursuit of our dream – and here we were, flying slow and low in the warm air, going nowhere.

But it was a magical experience. Having no goal any more we felt no stress, and once again I realized how important it is to accept whatever life brings. If we had fought against our situation, we would have suffered a lot: we might even have landed and gone home angry and despairing, blaming the entire world – especially China; but, by making the best of what had happened to us, we were choosing not to suffer. It almost seemed to me then that suffering involves an active decision: if you refuse to accept what life brings, you suffer, but if you accept your fate, you feel less pain.

Wim agreed with me, but Andy became irritated and wanted to land: he had had enough of Breitling and its balloons, and he almost seemed bored with our enterprise. He had already found another sponsor for future projects in the form of the Scottish property magnate James Manclark, President of the Elephant Polo Association, who had promised to finance him a new balloon. Andy, in other words, was already a potential competitor of ours. If we came down early and Breitling did not commission a third balloon, that would be one more rival out of his way.

In faxes from the control centre Alan Noble urged him to keep going. He saw that a premature landing would bring ridicule on the whole enterprise and might put Breitling off a third attempt. Then, in a cleverly worded message he told us that the record we had to beat was the one set by the *Voyager* aircraft flown by Dick Rutan, who had circumnavigated the globe in nine days and one hour. A new endurance record was in our reach, and it was something really worth going for.

The idea put Andy in good humour. He settled down again with his pencils and ruler and returned to navigational calculations. When we landed in Burma we had indeed established a new duration record for any form of aircraft, un-refuelled and non-stop, of nine days and eighteen hours – or, to be precise, 233.55 hours. We had flown 5,266 miles. Even if we had failed in our ultimate objective and our success was more philosophical than technical, I felt happy and proud.

BRIAN

When we knew the balloon was going to land in Burma, a party of us set out from Switzerland to help recover the crew and equipment. Because there were no direct flights to Rangoon (renamed Yangon), Breitling hired a private jet, a Falcon 2000, and off we went, stopping in Bahrain to refuel. The party included Stefano Albinati (a professional jet pilot, who was flying the aircraft), Monika Pieren (the Breitling project manager), Alan Noble, myself and several members of the press.

We reached Rangoon before the balloon landed, but when we tried to organize a recovery helicopter, the Burmese military demanded £6,000 an hour to provide one. After prolonged negotiations we secured a better deal – Monika, a formidable negotiator, really came into her own, deciding what was a reasonable amount and offering only that. But the argument took so long that we only caught up with the balloon just as it was coming down safely to land in a dry paddy field some sixty miles north of the city. Immediately after touch-down it was surrounded by an enormous crowd of people who flocked to the scene from the nearby villages. Some of them, it was said, had gone down on their knees to pray to the huge silver shape as it floated over them.

When Bertrand and I met as he walked away from the gondola in high spirits, one of the first things he said was, 'I've made two promises – and if I don't keep them, you must remind me. I'm not flying again with kerosene, and I'm not flying again with the same crew. The spirit on board was good, but next time I want to get round the world.'

We had trouble hauling the envelope down because there was no way of releasing helium from the tent balloon in the top except by puncturing it – and it was floating way out of our reach. Resorting to military methods, we asked a soldier to fire a few rifle shots through it: he loosed off several rounds, but they seemed to make no difference. In the end we asked the locals to help us pull the balloon down – and they went berserk, ripping at the fabric, hacking at it with knives, until they effectively destroyed it. There was quite a wind blowing, and some hilarious scenes ensued when a bicycle got caught up in the cables and was dragged aloft, to the great consternation of its owner.

When the giant at last collapsed, the military carried off the trail rope, which you lower as the balloon is coming in to land to steady its approach, and much of the envelope. The crew and all the spectators disappeared, leaving me in charge. To my relief, a huge recovery truck soon appeared, and its crane lifted the gondola on to the back with no difficulty. It was during our drive into Rangoon that we ran into problems, for in the villages the top of the gondola kept catching on electric cables slung low over the road. By then I was feeling quite ill, having got a touch of sunstroke from working against time in a temperature of 110 degrees, so I slumped in the front seat while an intrepid local stood on the back of the truck and used a long bamboo with a fork on the end to hoist each wire clear of the burners. Again and again, as he let a cable go it hit a propane tank lashed across the back and there was a brilliant blue flash, causing one blackout after another. Especially when it grew dark our progress was spectacular. The sixty-mile journey back to the city took fourteen hours. Our local liaison man had to return to the villages next day with enormous handfuls of paper *kyats*, to pay for the damage we had caused.

At that time the Burmese authorities were very nervous about communications. No citizen was allowed to use the Internet, and every foreign telephone call, incoming or outgoing, was logged. The military were keen to get their hands on our gondola so that they could extract our communications gear, but we managed to spirit the whole thing away and hide it in the grounds of a factory until it could be crated and shipped off to Singapore.

THIRD TIME LUCKY

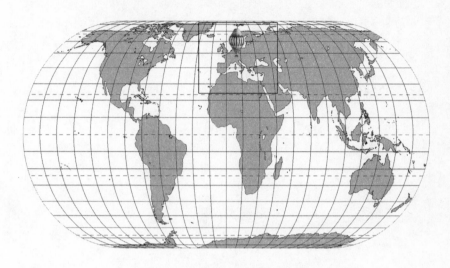

*Château d'Oex,
Switzerland*

BERTRAND

Back in Switzerland we were greeted as heroes, and within a couple of days Thedy Schneider had authorized the team to proceed with *Orbiter 3*. This time he appointed Stefano Albinati, who had flown the *Orbiter 2* recovery team out to Burma, to coordinate the project from Breitling's side. For this third attempt I decided on a two-man crew because I knew we could manage with two; carrying a third man would mean forgoing a lot of fuel as each man, his food, water, oxygen and personal equipment amounted to a burden of nearly 900 lb. I felt very sorry for Wim Verstraeten, but clearly a good friendship — even an important one — was not a sufficient basis on which to fly round the world.

Looking for a new co-pilot, we wanted someone who could devote at least half his time to the project over a period of a year. Our first choice was Tony Brown, a flight engineer on the supersonic Concorde. Tony, a stocky man in his fifties with a bushy moustache, managed to obtain leave of absence from his job, and with more than 5,500 flying hours to his credit he clearly had strong credentials. Yet all too soon I realized that he and I were going to have trouble working together.

When Tony joined us, everything was running smoothly and to schedule. But he seemed to feel he had to fight his way into the team.

It seemed to me that he thought I was playing the role of the chief too much; I wasn't giving him enough room, I was arrogant, and not taking enough care of him. For my part, I found that he brought with him some fairly rigid ideas. Although he was a good balloon pilot, he had never flown big distances; even so, he started explaining to me how to fly round the world. To come along, as we say in French, 'with your big shoes on', is not really the way to set about joining this kind of team project. But at least Tony and I could discuss our characters quite freely and acknowledge the fact that we had difficulty coping with each other, and we agreed we would have a go. That was between August and November 1998. But when we began technical training, my disillusion with him increased as it became clear that we could never combine our talents profitably.

I began to look with more and more interest at Brian Jones. I had seen how hard he worked and admired the ingenuity and constructive approach he brought to solving problems. His excellent aeronautical knowledge was enhanced by a strong sense of humour – and he was a very likeable person.

At the beginning of March 1998, immediately after his return from Burma, we appointed Brian project manager of *Orbiter 3*, in charge of the capsule's construction. Sometimes you feel a natural empathy for people even if you don't know them well. I felt drawn to Brian and saw that, besides having a calm temperament, he was extremely efficient. One thing I liked about him was the way he got things done. If we saw something going wrong with the preparation of the gondola, he would immediately write on the board, 'CHANGE THAT' – and he would follow up the instruction, which was directed partly at himself as an *aide-mémoire*, and partly at the technicians. He never prevaricated, but followed everything through from beginning to end. I myself tended to confuse people by putting up too many suggestions at once, and Brian always brought order into my rather haphazard creativity.

It was his idea that he should become our reserve pilot. At one of the first *Orbiter 3* meetings he said, 'You need a back-up, because there are only going to be two of you this time.' When everyone agreed enthusiastically, he suggested he should start to train with us on the gondola's systems – which he did. Later he made a tentative inquiry as to whether he too could have a flying jacket, like mine and Tony's. He never asked for one straight out, but I sensed that he was hankering after one. So I phoned Breitling and asked them to make another, explaining that once the project was over it would be Brian's only memento, the only thing to remind him that he had been reserve pilot. The firm responded quickly, and when Brian got his jacket he was delighted. Our relationship was starting to build, and I began to regret that he would not be on board when we took off.

On 16 November the gondola, envelope and associated gear were loaded on to two forty-foot lorries and set off for Château d'Oex. The crew went after them, settled in Switzerland and continued to prepare for the launch, which might take place at any time from the beginning of December to the end of February – the period during which global wind patterns are most favourable.

I started to look even harder at Brian and wondered why on earth I hadn't invited him to be my co-pilot in the first place. Later I realized I was not the only one feeling the strain. In her diary, Brian's wife Joanna wrote:

> The pilots seem very aggressive. It affects everybody. Living in Château d'Oex is not much fun any more. No one is clear what the problem is. It just becomes very tense.

On 23 November the tension between Tony and me finally erupted. We were doing technical training inside the gondola, and nothing was going right between us. Already, weeks earlier, Tony had said that if, once we were airborne, I did not let him take a big enough part in decision-making, he would find it a problem. Now I realized that what was proving an interesting psychological exercise on the ground could well become a dangerous antagonism during the stress of the flight and that we needed to resolve the problem quickly. So I deliberately increased the pressure of the training – and that night, during dinner at the Hôtel de Ville, the friction between us finally burst into flames.

When a heated argument broke out, and I insisted that I was not going to change good elements in the project just to please Tony, he snapped back with, 'All right, then. I won't fly. Fly with Brian.'

In my head I was saying, 'Oh yes! Oh yes!'

Tony turned to Brian and said, 'Brian – take my place.'

Brian, being a wise fellow, replied quietly, 'Don't bring me into this.'

After dinner I knew what I wanted, but not how best to achieve it. Pierre Blanchoud, our aeronautical adviser, urged me to take the decision. 'It's your project,' he said. 'You went to Breitling. You're the one who must decide.'

'Yes,' I replied, 'but that's why it's so difficult. If I make a mistake, the consequences could be disastrous.'

'All right,' he said, 'just go to sleep and see what the night tells you.'

Next morning I saw everything crystal clear: I wasn't going to fly with Tony, and I explained my decision to him. After breakfast we drove together to the workshop and shook hands, both feeling strong emotion. He told me he thought I had the ability to fly round the world, said how sorry he was we could not do it together and wished me good luck. I admired his stoicism and self-control. When I phoned Thedy to tell him about the change, he immediately asked why I hadn't chosen Brian in the first place. 'I'm sorry,' I said, 'but he didn't fly on Concorde – and the Concorde connection seemed to be interesting for the project.'

The newspapers made quite a meal of the switch – which was certainly a drastic move as it came so late in the project: if a suitable weather window appeared, we might need to take off within days. Journalists quoted Wim Verstraeten as saying that I could not sustain a friendship, was jealous of rivals and kicked out anyone who criticized me. People started attacking me for ditching pilots and for some of the technical decisions I had taken. I was also criticized for choosing to launch from Château d'Oex, where the weather was still bad. Switzerland was a good starting-point for anyone who had permission to fly straight across China, but because we now had permission only to cross the extreme south of the country, the choice no longer looked a wise one.

Andy Elson also weighed into the controversy. His plan to fly with James Manclark had not lasted long, but by then he was lining up to take off with another sponsor, Cable & Wireless, and he was preparing to launch from Spain as soon as possible. *Orbiter 3*, he said, had absolutely no chance of going round the world because it did not carry enough fuel. The auxiliary tanks on his own balloon, he boasted, contained more than our entire supply.

My only way of answering the critics was to complete a round-the-world flight. Appointing Brian in place of Tony gave me a feeling of tremendous liberation. I just hoped that I wasn't, once again, being blind. I had been blind about my first choice. Was I about to make another mistake?

BRIAN

When Alan Noble asked me to manage the *Orbiter 3* project soon after I had returned from Burma in February 1998, I lost no time in putting together a new team, and took an early opportunity to make an announcement in the workshop. Remembering how Andy's temper had unsettled other members of the technical team – sometimes to the extent that they too would walk out – I told everyone, 'We're not accepting tantrums because they're so detrimental to morale. Nobody walks out on this team. If anybody does walk out, you keep walking.'

Having known Tony for years, I could see from the start that he and Bertrand would have problems getting on with each other. One day as I was going through some paperwork in the office, I saw that Tony had insisted on having the term 'co-pilot' precisely defined. What did it mean, exactly? And why would Bertrand be captain, above him? All this was spelled out. I looked at Bertrand and said, 'This is complete bullshit!'

But my suggestion that the two pilots should have a back-up was a purely practical idea. My point was that either Bertrand or Tony could easily have an accident, right up to the moment of take-off, and if that happened there would be somebody ready to step in. At the launch of *Orbiter 2* the temperature was minus 16°C, and the field and gondola were covered with ice. Anyone could have slipped and broken an ankle.

Because I'm not a particularly pushy person, I was hesitant in inquiring about the flying jacket. I knew a third jacket hadn't been planned – nobody had thought about it – and I didn't *ask* for one. I just mentioned it to Bertrand and said, 'I'm a little disappointed that nobody seems to be taking me seriously as a reserve.' The jacket was just one example of this – but I didn't need to mention it again. He picked up on the idea immediately and, without saying anything more, went ahead. When a pilot's jacket appeared with my name on it, I thought, once again, 'Well — what a nice guy he is! He cares.'

At Camerons we had learned many lessons from the designs of the first two *Orbiters* and made whatever improvements we could devise. The gondola, though similar to its predecessors, incorporated a few such changes. It was made from two skins of woven Kevlar and carbon fibre, with a gel coating and foam insulation between them, like a bullet-proof waistcoat. One important innovation was the introduction of double-glazed, twelve-inch portholes, one on each side of the pilots' desk. The earlier gondolas had no portholes, and when the single-glazed hatches froze up the pilots couldn't see out at all.

We also had to design a new burner system because Bertrand stuck to his decision to switch from kerosene to propane fuel. For this we borrowed Pete Johnson, one of Camerons' best burner engineers, who joined the project full time. In other areas our star performer was Kieran Sturrock, first and foremost an electronics specialist but with a very good background in physics. Pete and Kieran made as highly efficient a pair as the met 'brothers' Luc and Pierre did.

As for the envelope, at 650,000 cubic feet its volume was fifteen per cent greater that that of the *Orbiter 2* balloon, and its shape was modified in an attempt to give it better insulation. In designing it we received much help from the École Polytechnique Fédérale de Lausanne, which ran numerous computer simulations on our behalf, investigating ways of reducing fuel consumption. Their conclusion was that to save fuel, the most important thing was to keep the balloon cool during the day.

So, on the shoulders, around the top of the gas cell, some of the Mylar was backed by a thin layer of high-density foam. The envelope was so large that more than twenty people were involved in its construction, which was highly complex. The outer skin was made of aluminized Mylar, a very light fabric strengthened with a mesh. Inside that was a second skin, and the two together gave the balloon a form of double-glazing and air conditioning. The aim was to stabilize the temperature inside the envelope as far as possible by controlling heat exchange, the idea being that during the day the envelope would reflect solar heat away, and at night the air gap between the skins would help conserve heat generated internally by the burners.

In daytime some solar heat would still penetrate the skins, which would make the balloon climb when warmth reached the gas cell and hot-air cone. To help get rid of excessive heat, Camerons placed small electric fans round the top of the hot-air cone. Each had its own solar panel, so that when the sun shone the fans would receive power and suck out the warm air. At night, when the balloon needed to retain heat, the fans would shut down because they no longer had any current.

The gas cell itself was made of nylon proofed with a laminated helium barrier. In putting the cell together, Camerons worked on a belt-and-braces philosophy: they punched thousands of holes in the expensive fabric and sewed the pieces together, then took other pieces of fabric and welded them over the seams. It was strange to reflect that *Orbiter 3* was the most sophisticated balloon ever built, yet it could never be fully tested on the ground. The envelope was so huge that it had to be made in pieces and, although Camerons ran computer simulations, until the whole contraption took to the sky nobody knew exactly how it would perform.

In a burst of unashamed nepotism I brought in Jo as project secretary, to do all the buying and back-up administration in the office. Once again I organized survival training for the pilots, and we majored on survival at sea because coming down in the ocean was obviously the likeliest danger the crew faced. Our equipment was geared to landing in water and included a survival suit and life jacket. The jacket had a personal survival pack attached to its base, containing a life raft, flares, water bags and energy sweets. We also had location aids – a heliograph, rocket flares and an EPIRB (emergency personal identification and rescue beacon), which talks direct to satellites. The idea was that a satellite would spot us, pin-point our position and start relaying messages to rescue-coordination centres. If all else failed – or if we had to bale out and parachute wearing only pyjamas – we would still be wearing Breitling emergency watches, which contain radio beacons capable of transmitting signals on the international distress frequency 121.5 MHz. Through that means alone, a passing aircraft or satellite should be able to locate us.

Bertrand had learned the drills the year before, so I took Tony

Brown to the RAF test pilot school at Boscombe Down, and to the swimming pool at the Oasis leisure centre in Swindon. In the decompression chamber at Boscombe Down we went through drills for dealing with hypoxia, or shortage of oxygen, learning how to recognize oxygen deficiency, which reduces the victim's mental powers without him being aware of it.

In the presence of a doctor, with everyone wearing oxygen masks, the pressure in the chamber was reduced to the equivalent of 30,000 feet. One guinea pig would then remove his mask, and the rest would watch for tell-tale signs of oxygen starvation – bluing of the lips and finger nails – while he began trying to do simple sums or just write down his address. Although he did not realize it, his faculties would quickly start to fail. At one point Tony was concentrating so hard on counting backwards that he ignored the doctor ordering him to replace his mask. In tests the previous year Bertrand had gone quiet and confused, tending to look around with a vacant expression on his face. As for myself, having been in the chamber several times, I didn't take my mask off; but on earlier occasions I had started giggling, as if slightly drunk.

In the water the instructors made conditions as unpleasant as they could. The swimming pool was equipped with a wave machine and a water cannon which, together, could simulate moderate seas and heavy, cold rain. With water blasting at us, it was no easy task to remove our parachute harnesses, deploy the one-man life rafts, struggle into them and make them secure. We also went to Bristol Airport, where a box had been fitted out to resemble the inside of the gondola. The fire crew put us in and filled it with smoke, and we then had to rescue a dummy – an unnerving experience.

As I had done some parachuting in the RAF, I knew what it was like to be frightened jumping out of aeroplanes, and I abstained from further parachute training. Bertrand, of course, had done plenty of parachuting, but before *Orbiter 1* he did some free-falling to learn how to turn and stabilize descents.

In the team we put a lot of emphasis on crew relationships. 'Crew resource management', or the handling of human factors on the flight deck, has become an important subject in the airline industry. In the old days the captain ruled absolutely, and nobody would dream of criticizing him or questioning his decisions; but in the past ten years all that has been swept away, and it is now the duty of even the most junior person on a flight to speak up if he or she has something on their mind. The whole crew has to work as a team. On the *Orbiter 3* project we brought in a specialist to talk about the subject.

As the weeks went by, I could not help but be aware of the ever-increasing tension between Bertrand and Tony. I did what I could to smooth things over, keeping myself in the background, not letting my hopes of flying rise too high. I was in a bit of a dilemma. On the one hand, as manager of the project, I was trying to calm things down; on the other, as reserve pilot, I couldn't say too much in case the others felt I was trying to ease my way into the cockpit. Then the boil burst, and for a few days chaos prevailed.

When Tony left and Bertrand asked me if I would fly instead, I said, 'Of course.' Suddenly I realized why he had been staring at me so often during the previous few days. From the way he'd been looking at me I thought I must have had something hanging out of my nose! When I went back to our apartment at one in the morning, apprehensive about Jo's reaction to the news, she came out with a brilliant remark. 'There's only one thing that *really* worries me,' she said. 'What happens if the world really is flat?'

'The reserve is in the hot seat,' she noted, after that explosive dinner – and in fact, although nothing had been said to the media, I knew I was going to fly in Tony's place. That weekend we flew back to England so that we could break the news and say goodbye to our families.

My appointment as the second pilot was finally announced at a press conference in Château d'Oex on 9 December 1998. The fact that I was going to be in the air meant that Jo would have no one to partner her in the control centre, so John Albury and Debbie Clarke moved up into our place and Jo became first reserve. Bertrand and I pressed ahead with our training, and once again there was laughter in the workshop, which had become a very dour place.

When Branson took off on 18 December and ditched in the ocean six days later, for us the most fascinating thing about his debacle was that we knew it was coming thirty-six hours before he did. Luc and Pierre saw that he was in a very strong jet stream over the Pacific heading for America, but they felt sure from their computer models that a branch of the jet would take him to Hawaii. We could not understand why his advisers didn't tell him to fly lower to escape from the trap. If he'd come down from 11,000 metres to 6,000 or even 8,000 metres, he would have picked up a slower wind going in the right direction – but it seems that nobody passed him this vital information. But then if their computer projections suggested they were on the right path, they would not have realized the problem.

Branson's failure gave us confirmation that a jet stream is far from continuous. It consists of air that has been compressed between a cold front, a warm front and the tropopause – the layer of the atmosphere immediately below the stratosphere. If it has little space in which to move, it travels very fast; but when it has more space, it spreads out, slows down and splits. Branson inadvertently went out on a branch of the jet. Few people outside our team knew that he had tried to obtain Luc's services for his flight, offering the Royal Belgian Meteorological Service a year's salary for a month's work. Luc replied that he was working for us out of friendship and because it was his passion.

BERTRAND

In spite of all our setbacks during the winter – the bad weather, our aborted take-off in mid-February, the Chinese block, Andy Elson's launch on 17 February, the lack of suitable weather windows – I never gave up hope. Always, in the background, there were dozens of matters to be arranged besides the actual preparation of the balloon. Luckily, our relationship with the International Olympic Committee had remained perfect: we planned to carry a message of peace to all the countries we passed over, and the IOC warned their national Olympic committees that we were coming. The IOC also gave us much help in trying to obtain permissions – from China, from Iraq and from Iran. This last alone took two weeks' solid work because at first the Iranians said no, and we had to explain how important clearance was for us.

For everyone concerned, the time before take-off was immensely hectic. For me, it was the culmination of five years of hard work, of involvement and of hope. For five years I had nursed this dream in my heart and my head, and it was intensely painful to see hope nearly dying.

Through all our last-minute difficulties and doubts, my confidence was bolstered by the fact that I knew I had a first-class co-pilot, a partner with very high human qualities. Brian and I had talked together a great deal. We realized that we were very different kinds of people: our characters, backgrounds and families, our jobs, our experiences in life, our country and our language — all could hardly have been more different.

Yet in some things we were alike: we were both completely honest, with flexible characters, and we set a high store on good human relations. Neither of us would cheat. Neither of us would lie. This helped us to build a good relationship quickly, sometimes just by discussing our differences and joking about them. If we were both exactly the same, I said, it would be pointless having both of us on board. By cultivating our differences, we would be able to build a strong complementary partnership. The condition was that we had to accept and respect each other's idiosyncrasies — and that was how we founded a very strong friendship and respect for each other. By talking together constantly we got rid of the need to have one chief and one person obeying orders.

In the end, I think, we were three. There was Brian, there was myself, and there was Both-of-Us — and Both-of-Us was the one who always did the right thing at the right moment.

CHAPTER FIVE

HEADING SOUTH

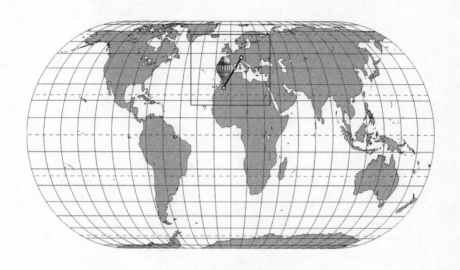

1–3 March
Switzerland to Morocco

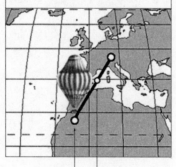

Southern Morocco
08:00 Z
FL 173
32 knots

Balearics
08:00 Z
FL 196
32 knots

BERTRAND

During the first afternoon of the flight I kept the balloon between 20,000 and 22,000 feet. The sun was not heating the helium very much because the envelope's insulation was so good. To maintain altitude I had to burn propane quite often – and that wasn't a nice discovery. We had known from the start that we would have to burn at night, but if we had to burn during the day as well we would go through our fuel at an unacceptable rate. In time I realized that in fact it was better to have things this way round: with less efficient insulation, in daylight the balloon would have heated up more, climbed faster, and vented more helium through the appendices. That might have saved us a bit of propane, but at night we would have lost far more heat, radiated out through the fabric of the envelope into the darkness, and our overall consumption of fuel would have been far greater.

Brian slept for an hour and a half, from 13:30 to 15:00. He woke up with a headache, so I gave him some Ponstan, a relatively powerful, prescription-only analgesic, and at 17:00 he went back to bed for another ninety minutes. That was almost the only time we had recourse to the comprehensive first-aid kit, which I had stocked with every drug we could conceivably need, including morphine. I must have spent £500 on medicines – for the lungs, for the kidneys, for the blood, for haemorrhoids, for diarrhoea, for constipation. In the event, none of them was needed.

At sunset, when we were both again in the cockpit, our first real problems set in. For some reason the fax had gone out of action, and the antenna for the satellite telephone had frozen, so we could not use that either. But the worst worry was that we were using far too much propane. To maintain height, we had to increase our burning time even before dark fell because, as the sun went down towards the horizon, its power diminished. And now, at dusk, we hit another snag. The pilot lights – small, high-pressure flames that ignited the burners on top of the gondola – began to function erratically. They should have stayed alight all the time and ignited the burners automatically, governed by timers on the instrument panel. But they kept extinguishing themselves, and we had to use an electronic sparker to re-ignite them. This was exceedingly tiresome because one of us had to stand up repeatedly, go back a couple of steps and reach upwards to press the button on the burner control panel, mounted on the wall next to the fuel control unit in the ceiling of the central corridor.

In my little green notebook I recorded that we were having to burn for sixty per cent of the time: every ten seconds, a blast of six seconds from one of our double burners. We looked at each other and thought, 'We're really in the shit!'

No doubt the fax could be got going and the telephone would unfreeze. However, the fuel consumption was something else. If we had to rely on manual ignition, that in itself would be a nightmare. But the prospect of running out of fuel in a few days was infinitely worse. Calculations of consumption made on the ground had varied wildly: some had given us a maximum duration of twelve days, while others had put the figure at twenty-four. Now it looked as though our chances of making a full circuit were perilously slim. At the rate we were burning, we would run out of propane in less than a week.

So, after a period of calm, our workload exploded. We had to keep relighting the burners to control the balloon's height, while at the same time trying to reactivate the fax and talking on the radio to the air traffic controllers on the Côte d'Azur – a very busy area. We were in frequent contact with the control tower at Marseilles to tell them what we were doing: they, naturally, wanted us to maintain an even height, and there we were swooping up and down as much as 3,000 feet because the burners kept blowing out. We explained that we were having problems, and asked for a blocked flight level so that we could flop through the middle of it dolphin-wise until we could get the balloon stable.

I went to bed at 19:45, but it took me a long time to go to sleep because I was so used to the continuous, soft snoring of the kerosene burners which had been the hallmark of *Orbiter 2*. The sound was exactly like the steady roar of a commercial aircraft, and just as soothing. Now I had to get used to the intermittent, sharper roar of the propane burners. I seemed to doze off and wake up about two hundred times before I resorted to ear-plugs. Even then I remained uneasy, thinking about the dreadful amount of fuel we were getting through. At one point in the night I imagined I felt the balloon dropping, and I convinced myself that Brian had suddenly had to switch to the second pair of tanks, having exhausted the first. If we'd gone through one whole pair before half the first night was through, our chances were as good as finished. Everything had started so well, and now this first night was turning into catastrophe.

BRIAN

We originally planned to take twenty-eight tanks of fuel, arranged in fourteen pairs, with seven pairs on each side of the gondola. The right side was designated 'green' and the left side 'yellow'. But, midway through the project, Bertrand had the idea of adding four auxiliary cylinders, one at each corner, to give us extra range in case we had to sweep down over Africa at the start of the flight. That was exactly what we were doing now.

Every tank contained 250 lb of liquid propane mixed with ethane, a more volatile gas, to increase fuel pressure at high altitudes. Propane stays liquid at temperatures below minus 40°C. Above that, it turns into gas, which produces pressure to push the liquid out of the tank and to the burners. But at minus 50°C or lower – the sort of temperatures that prevail at high altitudes – the propane would not vaporize, and we needed the ethane, which does not liquefy until minus 89°C, to produce enough pressure.

Each pair of tanks was suspended on a strain gauge — a weighing device — so that at any time we should have had a good idea of how much propane was left in them. That was the theory. What we hadn't realized before we took off was that the strain gauges were highly susceptible to changes in temperature, and in the air, with the temperature varying widely, they became useless. At one stage a gauge would show minus forty kilogrammes, and at another moment it would shoot up to 200 — a complete nonsense.

Above us, on either side of the roof of the gondola, there were three burners, each regulated from its own control panel, and we had various options for bringing them into action. The No. 1 burner on each side could be used on its own; Nos 2 and 3 could be burned as a pair; or we could use all three together — and in an emergency we could use both sides simultaneously, with six burners running at once.

The prolonged burning on the first night made us fear that our stock of fuel was critically small. But because the strain gauges quickly proved unreliable, we had no way of calculating how much we were using, and all we could do was wait until the first pair of auxiliary tanks ran out. From their performance, we would be able to plot a rough graph and work out how far all sixteen pairs would be likely to take us. On the first and second *Orbiters* Andy Elson had been convinced that kerosene was the only fuel to use, but after the earlier disasters Bertrand had felt we must switch to propane because its technology was well known and it produced heat more efficiently than kerosene. So we had never been certain how long our tanks would last — and now suddenly we found that the bloody fuel gauges weren't working. The whole thing was turning into a fiasco.

At least the fax was back in action. During my stint at the controls I exchanged messages with Kieran Sturrock and Pete Johnson, the Cameron engineer who designed the burners. Both were still at the Hôtel de Ville in Château d'Oex, and they sent back minutely detailed instructions:

If you want to try adjusting the manual valve to give a small residual flame, here is how you do it. There is a cap head bolt in the end of the toggle lever. Find the right Allen key — it will be metric — and undo the bolt two or three turns (anti-clockwise).

Operate the toggle until it clicks to On, then adjust the screw until you get the small flame you want. Running on autopilot with a small residual flame like this may cause an alarm to go off.

Such thoroughness was typical. Kieran and Pete had been our star technicians throughout, involved in every aspect of the gondola's construction, and tremendously knowledgeable about its systems, as well as being enthusiastic about the enterprise in general. Now they were ready to field questions from us in the middle of the night and work on them immediately.

On the other hand, Kieran sometimes felt he was not getting the back-up he needed, and when he found that Alan had not responded to his instructions about repairing the fax, he fired off a blistering message to Geneva – although he did warn the startled recipients by telephone that his anger was directed at Alan rather than the team in general:

What the fuck are you playing at in the Control Room? You are supposed to be responsible for the lives of two men in an experimental balloon, not running a social club. If we are only able to achieve the current level of service – two several-hour blackouts in thirty-six hours – you should be considering whether you need to abandon the flight before the balloon enters more unforgiving territory. If we are having problems, we should be looking for causes and solutions, not assuming they will go away.

Investigation revealed that the trouble was due to overloading at the earth station through which our messages were being routed and to a difference in the speed of the various modems being used. Once the problem had been identified, it was promptly sorted out.

At 22:20 I faxed Control:

Hello whoever is down there. Brian in the seat. The launch was more than a little exciting. It was amazing the amount of valving we had to do to prevent the balloon climbing above FL 220. Both gas valves were open for over a minute at a time. Anyway, we are up here now, Lord knows for how long. We'll get an opportunity for some calculations when the first pair of tanks are empty – please God not tonight. We're both a bit tired, but, as they say, if you can't take a joke, you shouldn't have joined. If Jo is there, lots of love.

In a few minutes I got a reply:

Hello, Brian, Wife here. Your message was perfectly timed. I have just entered the Control Room with John and Debs. I can't sleep, so will spend a couple of hours here and then disappear to the Holiday Inn. Back again tomorrow after breakfast. Your launch was a little more exciting than advertised! I think I have calmed down now.

What I hadn't mentioned was that, as a joke birthday present, I had given Bertrand a tiny black-and-white toy football, which I presented to him, carefully gift-wrapped, as soon as we were clear of the mountains. When anyone tapped the wretched thing, it played that awful song '*Olé! Olé! Olé! Olé! We are the champs! We are the champs!*' four times over – and when Bertrand first heard it, he laughed, 'Oh no! It's too early! We mustn't tempt fate.' Nevertheless, we hung the ball on its string from one of the lights in the cockpit, and occasionally, when we bumped into it or touched it by mistake, it started to sing – whereupon we would cry, 'Not yet! Wait!' Once it had started its routine there was no way of stopping it except by removing its batteries.

BERTRAND

When Brian shook me awake at 01:45 on the morning of 2 March, my first words were, 'Did you really switch to the second pair of tanks?' 'No, no,' he reassured me, 'we're still on the first.' Immediately I felt hopeful again, and I was further cheered by the fact that our progress precisely matched the met men's forecast. We were flying at 22,000 feet, on a heading of 210 degrees, and making 25 knots – exactly what Luc and Pierre had specified. Soon we turned even more to the west, on 222 degrees, but again it was according to plan.

Brian went to sleep, and I flew for the rest of the night. In the early hours of the morning I found I needed to burn for only twenty-five per cent of the time, with the burners coming on in four-second bursts every sixteen seconds. At first light, even after our very heavy consumption during the first hours of darkness, the first tanks were still not empty, and I thought, 'This is fantastic. We probably have at least sixteen days of flying after all.'

Before dawn broke we were over the Balearic Islands – Mallorca and Menorca – off the east coast of Spain. It was a beautiful moment, with no clouds anywhere, a full moon reflected in the sea and lights shining from the black islands far below.

I realized how different this flight was from the previous attempts. On *Orbiter 2* I had felt much more philosophical. At an early stage, when we knew we would not be able to go round the world and the flight had become aimless, I accepted the feeling of being carried by the winds, of not having any goal. Now that I saw our ultimate target was within reach, I became much more tense, concentrating hard on every aspect of the balloon and its performance. It was strange to reflect that *Orbiter 3* was the most sophisticated balloon ever built, yet this was its maiden flight. Camerons had run through computer simulations of how it would perform, but it could never be fully tested on the ground, and nobody had known how it would behave when it took to the sky.

The telephone was still not working, but at 06:15 the sun came over the horizon behind us on our left, and I shut the burners down. I carried out the sunrise checks, switched on the solar array and cut the strobe and the red navigation light. Then at 08:00 Brian woke up, made himself breakfast and came into the cockpit, where we spent the whole day together.

BRIAN

Anyone with a tendency to claustrophobia would have been horrified by the dimensions of the capsule in which we had sealed ourselves for the duration. The gondola was in essence a short tube with rounded ends, sixteen feet from nose to tail, and seven feet in diameter. To cut down noise and condensation, all its inside surfaces were padded with knobbly white fireproof foam insulating material. The biggest single space was the cockpit at the front, where there was just room for both pilots to sit side by side on comfortable, high-backed rally-type seats taken from a car. In front of these was a desk with a straight inner edge and a curved outer rim to fit the half-dome of the nose. The surface of the desk was cut from a sheet of transparent acrylic, so that we could see down through it and out through the forward hatch in the lower part of the nose. Facing each seat, at head height, was a twelve-inch porthole for forward vision, and the black instrument panel was mounted across the nose above the table, between the pilots.

Immediately behind the right-hand seat, partitioned off, was a tiny kitchen shelf, no more than two feet square, with a wash-basin set in its working surface and a little water heater in the form of a rectangular metal box mounted on the bulkhead. Apart from two miniature kettles, designed for use in cars, the water heater was our only cooking apparatus. For the first few days of the flight, while our fresh food lasted, we would switch it on, let it warm up for half an hour, and then lower one of the bags containing pre-cooked meat or fish into the water.

Behind the kitchen area was the starboard bunk, with storage spaces above and below. Because we had decided in advance to use only the bunk opposite for sleeping, this one was permanently covered by our survival kit — parachutes, life rafts, immersion suits and so on — which was laid out for immediate use in the event of an emergency. The central corridor, about two feet wide, was just high enough to allow us to stand upright. We are both of medium height — Bertrand 5 ft 10 in, myself one inch shorter — but anyone taller would have had to stoop. The sleeping bunk on the port side of the corridor was seven feet long but only two feet wide, with less than that from the bunk to the rack above. When the curtain was drawn across the inner side to shut the bunk off from the passage, the occupant was enclosed in a space not much bigger than a coffin.

Each bunk had a foam-rubber mattress and a built-in harness — an extra safety feature which we incorporated after Steve Fossett's spectacular crash in the Coral Sea the previous summer. In the middle of the night, at around 28,000 feet, his balloon was ruptured by violent winds and slashed by hail in a storm cloud. Finding himself hurtling downwards, he turned his propane burners on at full power and lay flat on his back in his bunk to minimize damage from the impact on hitting the sea. This almost certainly saved his life, but by the time he emerged from the floating gondola the envelope had caught fire, and he was almost asphyxiated by toxic fumes when the blazing remains of the balloon collapsed on top of him. By then he was holding his life raft in one hand and his emergency beacon in the other, but he was in such trouble that, instead of switching the beacon on, he pressed the test button by mistake. This meant that it gave out only two or three bleeps – but, by a miracle, he was directly underneath a satellite, which picked up the transmission, and he was rescued.

We decided that, if we found ourselves descending out of control, we would do the same as Steve had, and strap ourselves in as well. All the storage spaces were packed tight with food, clothes and equipment; the only other open area was at the back, where a small toilet was tucked into one corner and, on the other side of the rear hatch, stainless-steel cylinders of liquid oxygen and nitrogen were secured to the wall. (The nitrogen was for re-pressurizing the gondola and fuel tanks – operations that might have become necessary at high altitude.) In such cramped quarters there was almost no possibility of taking physical exercise – but the view from the toilet was spectacular.

A breathable atmosphere was maintained by the life-support system, which drew oxygen from the tank and circulated it round the gondola, while lithium hydroxide filters absorbed the carbon dioxide given off by our breathing. A tube carrying air enriched with oxygen passed along the upper wall of the sleeping bunk on its way to the cockpit, and the person in the bunk could get more fresh air by opening a hole in the tube, which sent a gentle breeze over one's face.

We had three oxygen systems. The main cabin system produced a constant flow, taking oxygen from the liquid oxygen (lox) tank and injecting it into the air to produce a breathable atmosphere. (It was also possible to connect a mask to this system.) Then we had a system which delivered 100 per cent oxygen (under pressure if needed) through masks connected to our flying helmets, which we would don if the cabin pressure failed. Finally, we had oxygen on our parachutes – because if you bail out at 30,000 feet without special breathing apparatus you are liable to suffer brain damage.

Detectors showed the percentage of oxygen in the air, which we could adjust via the normal lox system, and other monitors continuously measured levels of carbon dioxide, sulphur dioxide and propane in the cabin. A series of warning lights came on if pressure inside the gondola rose too high, as well as showing if the gas valves at the top of the envelope were open or closed, and if the burner pilot lights were working normally. If our living conditions were fairly basic, our equipment was as high-tech as money could buy. Electric power came from twenty solar panels, each three feet wide and eighteen inches tall, which trailed below us on a long line in an array like a four-sided kite so that, no matter what heading the balloon was on, some of them were always facing the sun. The moment the sun came over the horizon every morning, *bang!* – they sprang to life instantly, and we could see the charge coming through on the instruments.

Electric power was stored in five car batteries under the floor of the cockpit. In case they failed, we also had dry lithium batteries designed to last seventeen days. In fact the power system proved highly efficient: the only time the panels failed to charge the batteries fully was late in the flight when, in the jet stream, we were surrounded by cirrus cloud which partially obscured the sun, and in the second half of the night we had to switch to the lithium battery supply.

Our most valuable single instrument was the global positioning system (GPS), which continuously showed the position of the balloon on a small moving map, and gave us our heading and our speed. The instrument's black-and-white screen was only three inches by two and a half, and often it covered the whole of the country below us; but it had a zoom facility to enlarge details. When we saw from our maps that an airfield or a navigation beacon was coming up ahead of us, we could dial in and get an instant reading, telling us that beacon X, for example, was 255 miles away on a bearing of 085 degrees. The GPS display also had a line showing what our trajectory would be if we held our present heading: as we climbed and descended, heading east, we could see the line changing direction, a little to the north or a little to the south. This made it possible to aim directly at chosen targets. At the bottom of the screen was a digital read-out of speed, direction, altitude and position. As back-ups, we had two more GPS in our main and spare laptop computers, and we could call up the figures on the computer screens if necessary. There was also a hand-held GPS in our survival pack.

Two radar transponders automatically gave out our identity, altitude and position to air traffic control centres along our route. The controllers would ask us to 'squawk' a number – say 5555 – and when we punched that in it told them who we were. An orange light flashed on our transponder unit whenever a radar station was interrogating it to check our identity. For voice communication we had VHF (short-range) and HF (long-range) radio and a satellite telephone. Bertrand often used the satphone to talk to Luc and Pierre in French, so that he knew exactly what our weathermen were thinking. But most exchanges with the control centre went via one or other of our two Capsat fax transmitters. We would tap messages into a laptop computer (provided by Devillard in Geneva) and transmit them through satellites; replies from Control came up on our screen, and although we could not print the messages because we had no printer on board, every one was retained on the computer. Bertrand, being no sort of a typist, tended to send very short messages, whereas I went in for longer missives.

Alan Noble had insisted on this system because it reduced the possibility of error. Radio or telephone messages could be garbled or misheard, but with the fax everything was clear. On the whole it was extremely efficient, but sometimes, when we were directly beneath a satellite, the balloon would create its own cone of silence, blocking the antenna and cutting transmission. Whenever a message came up an orange light would flash, and – especially when we had sent down an important question – we were like children eagerly waiting for the answer in the post. In case of failures, almost all our equipment was duplicated or triplicated.

Our instruments included two altimeters – one standard, with revolving hands like a clock, and the other electronic, which gave a read-out in red digits. There was also a radio altimeter, which worked only at 2,500 feet or below by sending a beam straight down, and was for landing in low visibility. A variometer gave us our rate of climb and descent. To make a complete record of the flight, a barograph was automatically taking a reading of altitude every few seconds. This instrument was sealed by an official observer before take-off, and we had no access to it while we were in the air.

We also had four video cameras, two mounted outside the gondola, one mounted inside, and another inside which could be either mounted or hand-held. By putting digital video recordings on to our laptops with a digital Logitech camera we could send clips by satellite telephone back to Control.

BERTRAND

We relied heavily on all this sophisticated equipment; but even more we depended on the expertise of the team supporting us from the ground – not least our met men. I don't think Brian or I realized how hard those two were labouring on our behalf. They were supposed to be alternating in twelve-hour shifts, but frequently they overlapped each other. Luc never went to bed before one o'clock in the morning because he had to wait for the latest weather model, which came in over the Internet at midnight; and he was always up again at six or seven, back in the control centre, to analyse the night's models. Because there was no spare desk space, he worked throughout the flight with his laptop perched on a little round coffee table which he had commandeered from the restaurant – and whenever there was the slightest chance of a celebration, he nipped next door for a glass of champagne with the girls in the press room.

Another vital element of support came from the three air traffic controllers who had volunteered their services for the duration of our flight: Greg Moegli, Patrick Schelling and Niklaus Gerber – known collectively as 'the balloon Mafia'. All had full-time jobs at Swiss Control, the official air traffic control organization at Geneva Airport, but they were working on flexible timetables and arranged to cover for us whenever they could take time off. Their role was to obtain clearance for the balloon from air traffic control centres round the world. Every centre had to be alerted to our approach either so that other aircraft could be directed to keep clear of our likely track, or so that we could change height to avoid busy flight paths.

Every commercial pilot has to file a flight plan before take-off, giving the route he is proposing to fly, but ours was extremely unusual in that we did not know exactly where we would be going. The plan filed by Greg – who incidentally bears a startling resemblance to Luciano Pavarotti – gave a grandiose outline of our route:

> Château d'Oex, Switzerland – crossing the Alps – Nice – the Balearic Islands – Morocco – Mauritania – Mali – Niger – Chad – Sudan – Saudi Arabia – Oman – India – Burma – South of China – Pacific Ocean – California – crossing USA – crossing Atlantic Ocean – Canaries – intended landing in North Africa east of 10 degrees lat.

In the box for 'Estimated duration of flight' he had put '20 days' and under 'Aircraft colour and markings' he had entered 'Envelope silver grey, capsule red, name *Breitling Orbiter 3*'. Normally each country updates the plan and hands it on to the next as an aircraft leaves its FIR, or flight information region, but because the track of the balloon could not be forecast exactly, Greg and his two colleagues sent out their own updates. These they passed to the communications centre at Swiss Control, where a team of more than thirty people put them in the correct form and sent them out over AFTN – the Aeronautical Fixed Telecommunications Network.

Our trio also made hundreds of telephone calls to clear the way for us and smooth our path. For twenty-four hours every day during the mission they were receiving coordinates of the balloon's position and passing them to the relevant centre. Every day, on a spread-out map of the world, they put in markers with details of our latest track, height, speed and position. One of their main objectives was always to reserve a block of vertical air space around the balloon so that there would never be any danger of collision with commercial traffic. Often they had a hard time explaining to local controllers that the balloon was sixty metres high, weighed nine tons, and was not flying level like an airliner but going up and down. Normally, they asked for a separation of at least 2,000 feet.

The prime aim of Luc and Pierre's strategy was to send our balloon out on a trajectory which, after maybe ten days and 6,000 miles, would bring it to precisely the right spot on the southwestern border of China. An inexperienced observer might well have questioned the wisdom of their tactics at the very start of our journey as, instead of launching us eastwards, they had sent us southwest, down across the Mediterranean and on over North Africa. We appeared to be heading in the wrong direction – but the met men knew exactly what they were doing.

Satellite imagery had shown them a big depression centred over the western end of the Mediterranean. Because the winds around an area of low pressure always blow in an anti-clockwise direction, they knew that the balloon would swing round the periphery of the depression, heading (in succession) southwest, south, southeast and finally east as the winds ejected us from the low and took us away over the Sahara.

The only way we could alter course was by changing altitude – by going up or down in search of winds that would push us in the direction we wanted. We could climb by burning propane, and descend by venting helium or by letting the balloon cool and sink on its own. To help us maintain the track we needed, Luc and Pierre were constantly advising us on the height at which we should fly, and we kept telling them what winds we were actually finding. Hundreds of routine messages passed back and forth in standard aviation terminology. 'Flight level two three zero' meant 23,000 feet, 'flight level two eight zero' 28,000 feet, and so on. Thus at 10:25 on the first day, as we were still climbing after the launch, I had reported on height, wind direction and speed:

> FL [flight level] 214 has a track 171 [degrees] m [magnetic] at 20 knots. FL 240 has a track 180 at 18 knots.

Back came the answer from Control:

> Have spoken with Pierre. He says FL 210 is good for daylight hours but will probably advise FL 180 for tonight.

Twenty knots is about 23 mph. With some 25,000 miles ahead of us, that seemed a painfully slow rate of progress.

The balloon tended to revolve slowly as it flew. As far as we could tell, the gentle rotation was caused by the variation in wind pressure on the upper and lower sections of the 160-foot-high envelope: the currents hitting the top of it were often different from those striking the bottom. Sometimes, having turned clockwise for a few hours, it would suddenly start going the other way. But the movement was never fast enough to be disconcerting: on the contrary, it meant that different views kept coming past the portholes.

Already, on the morning of Day Two, Control was passing up requests from journalists for telephone interviews, and we told them we would be happy to comply whenever we were not too busy. At 10:17 I reported that we were burning slowly to try to rise above a layer of mist and get out into true sun. Three minutes later, when I saw we were doing 43 knots on flight level 232, I asked, 'Is it too fast for Luc?', and something of the extent of the met men's knowledge is revealed in their reply:

> Try to stay at FL 240, which should have a track of 235 magnetic, until 12 Zulu, and 225 magnetic between 12 Zulu and 18 Zulu. The speed should vary between 40 and 50 knots. We will run a longer forecast in the beginning of the afternoon to evaluate the possibility to overfly more exotic regions (we suppose you know Mallorca already). There are no weather hazards on your track. We just see some clouds over the northern coast of Algeria with tops at FL 150. Stay at FL 240 – no higher. Best regards – Luc and Pierre.

BRIAN

Throughout Day Two the burners continued to give problems, but by trial and error we more or less mastered them, setting the timers so that the residual flame from one burn ignited the next, and our consumption of fuel came down to a reasonable level. A greater worry was the build-up of ice on the fuel-control unit, in the ceiling next to the top hatch. Round the upper hatch, set into the shell of the gondola, was a penetration plate – a wide metal ring with connectors in it, through which passed the control taps that activated the fuel system. The metal conducted cold from the atmosphere, so that during the night moisture from our breath in the cabin air froze on to the unit, and to get at the controls we had to scrape it away. In one fax we described it as 'a horrible job, worse than painting a ceiling'. Ice had also formed in thin sheets on the envelope of the balloon – probably inside the hot-air cone – because propane gives off a large volume of water when it burns. Later I complained to Alan:

> We're getting little showers of ice onto the gondola, very disconcerting. It's like someone trying to get in. Did you notice anybody caught in the rigging when we took off?

From the start Bertrand and I had a marvellously open relationship. He had always insisted on complete candour, and early in the flight he insisted once again, 'Brian – if I do anything you don't like, you must say so. Or if I start to smell and have bad breath, for goodness' sake tell me.' It was the same with our sleeping arrangements. We agreed that whenever either of us felt seriously tired, we would talk about it frankly, decide who was the more exhausted, and that person would go to bed while the other remained on duty. But an open system like this works only if nobody cheats – and in our case, it was out of the question to cheat, as it was not in our characters, and in any case we were both striving to reach the same goal.

In normal flight during the day the balloon was absolutely steady – so much so that often we had no sensation of moving. If the life-support fans were running, circulating air, they made a noticeable hum, but at other times there was complete silence. After our first rather disturbed twenty-four hours it was easy to sleep, and on the foam rubber mattress we both slept really well. I found it more comfortable to sleep naked, but Bertrand wore pyjamas with short legs and sleeves. Some people thought we were crazy to undress at all: if anything suddenly went wrong with the balloon, the person in bed might be at a severe disadvantage. But if something had gone wrong at altitude, we couldn't have baled out in our day-clothes any more than if we were naked or wearing pyjamas. We would have had to dress up in survival suits. The point was, we hoped we were in for a three-week marathon, and the best way of getting through it was to make life as natural as possible. So we undressed and cleaned our teeth and behaved as much as possible as if we were at home.

Although we shared a duvet, each of us had his own sleeping bag made from a sheet. Bertrand also had a special pillow which came from the Town and Country Hotel in Bristol, where he had often stayed. He had been so comfortable there that he asked Sue Tatford to go and get one of the pillows for him. She felt ridiculous making such a peculiar request, but the hotel gave her a pillow with good grace – and here it was now, trying to get round the world in a balloon.

In our domestic habits we were very gentlemanly: whenever I got up, I would clear the bed and leave it ready for Bertrand, and he did the same for me. On one occasion he even left a chocolate on my pillow. In matters of personal hygiene we took equal care. There was no question of having a shower, but when we got up or went to bed we would generally have a complete rub-down with wet wipes (the kind you use for washing babies) and neither ever complained that the other was becoming smelly. In fact there was practically no dust or dirt in the gondola: the few clothes we had remained remarkably clean, and we wore the same things for four or five days.

A regular pattern of life quickly developed. We each wanted eight hours' rest, and Bertrand, who preferred to sleep while it was dark, would turn in during the early evening and sleep through the first part of the night. I would wake him a few hours before sunrise, and then go to sleep myself until about the middle of the day. This suited me, as I didn't have to get up and dress in the coldness of the night. Usually when I woke Bertrand I made him a cup of tea while he made the bed for me; he would drink the tea and some orange juice as he flew the balloon while it was still dark. Then, as dawn broke two or three hours later, he would get his breakfast.

When I woke up in the middle of the day, I got my own breakfast, and at the end of the afternoon Bertrand made his dinner. We tended to spend the afternoons together, until sunset – and Bertrand was kind enough to describe those as 'really nice moments'. If we were flying slowly, they seemed really long, but if we were travelling fast they passed all too quickly.

As for food – for the first few days we lived like lords. We would put the water heater on for half an hour, drop a bag in for twenty minutes, and then eat hot fillet steak, emu meat, chicken or salmon with knives and forks off plastic plates. We also had apples, bananas and nuts, and water or orange juice to drink. We kept no fixed meal times, but ate whenever we felt like it. Because the kettle took twenty-eight minutes to boil for a hot drink, and because there was only room in the heater for one portion of food, we had to plan meals well in advance, and usually we ate at different times. This was not only because one of us was always on a working shift: separate meals had another advantage in that if there had been anything wrong with the food, only one of us would have been affected. Also, we tended to want different things.

Food was stored in spaces under the bunks. Bertrand had found some very light but strong boxes made of corrugated plastic which we modified so that they would slip perfectly into racks. There was another space under the floor at the rear which we used as a fridge, keeping the butter, cheese and orange juice down there because the temperature was about zero, even when the cabin was warm. Slim as he is, Bertrand has a much bigger appetite than I have, and he seemed to eat twice as much. But food never bothered me. I had to eat to stay healthy, but I never felt particularly hungry. I tended to have breakfast when I woke up – muesli at first, later *panettone* – and after that I would eat once in every twenty-four hours. Bertrand always gave himself a tremendous breakfast: a large beaker of muesli-type cereal with powdered milk, orange juice and sometimes *panettone*.

Although the main role of the water heater was to warm up our packets of pre-cooked food, it also provided hot water for washing. We could move the drain tube about over the tiny sink to rinse our hands. From the sink the water drained into plastic bottles, and whenever one was full we would empty it down the toilet. Under the sink was a space in which we stored our plates, cups, tins of powdered milk and so on.

The toilet was a pan with an airtight cover on top and a valve at the bottom, and when we had something to dispose of, we would drop it in the bowl, seal the lid, close the cover and open the valve. The pressure trapped in the toilet blew the contents downwards and out of the gondola. The bowl was coated with Teflon so that nothing would stick to it, but Bertrand had learned from previous experience that the most efficient method of disposal was to line the bowl with a plastic bag. Having found some French supermarket bags which were a perfect fit, he bought several rolls, and whenever we needed to answer a major call of nature we used a new bag. We didn't seal the bags – just folded the top over. Then, as we opened the valve, they'd go out *bang!*, very fast, and we imagined that most of the contents would vaporize.

We were concerned that every time we emptied the loo we would be using up some of our pressure, so when we just wanted to pass water we used red plastic pee-bottles, and it was the duty of anyone who had a bowel movement to empty the full bottles into the bag before discharging it.

The performance was something to which I hadn't much looked forward, but when the time came I found I was taking a close, clinical interest. 'Bertrand,' I said, 'your pee's too dark. You're not drinking enough' – and he was delighted I was looking out for him so well. Our garbage went into dark grey plastic bags, which were stored near the toilet. We were fairly careful about where we dropped anything – but it was with some reluctance that we rejected the idea of attaching to each offering a label saying 'Virgin Atlantic Airline'.

BERTRAND

Life was altogether very comfortable. The gondola was warm during the day, and we had wonderful, constantly changing views. Between 20,000 and 24,000 feet the outside temperature was minus 35°C, and the moisture from our breath condensed on the hatches. At night it froze, but then in the day, when the sun came on it, it melted again.

For as long as we were heading south we had twenty-four hours between sunsets; but when we turned east and eventually started travelling at 100 knots, there were only twenty hours between one sunset and the next – so, with eight hours' sleep apiece, we had only four hours together, and it seemed a very short time. We got the impression we weren't seeing enough of each other.

We were very careful to record as much information as possible. The previous two flights had produced almost no data, and when we were planning the third trip Brian had insisted that as much technical data as possible should be preserved. Not only had Kieran Sturrock designed automatic data-logging sensors, but we also had special technical log books, which were supposed to be filled in every hour or two, giving fuel state, readings from the life-support system monitors, outside temperatures and so on. Not being much of a typist – using three fingers only, increasing by one in each successive Breitling balloon – I recorded personal impressions in longhand in a green notebook, but Brian preferred to tap his thoughts into the laptop.

Many people who have never flown a high-tech balloon imagine that the pilots have little to do. In fact we were almost always busy or asleep – and although we both took a book along, neither of us opened it throughout the twenty days of our flight.

We were carrying, as a talisman, a copy of Guy de Maupassant's novel *Une Vie* (A Life), which he had given to Jules Verne, author of *Around the World in Eighty Days*. Verne was so fond of the book that he had it finely bound in leather, with his initials inscribed on the cover in gold, and the copy had been lent us as a good-luck token by the original owner's great-grandson, Jean-Jules, who works full time to promote the spirit of his ancestor. As he said, he felt we were the only balloon team who embodied the true love of adventure that characterized his great-grandfather: seeing that we were neither money-grubbers nor record-hunters, he was keen that something which had belonged to Jules Verne should go round the world with us.

It so happened that he had made the presentation at a moment when I was racked by doubts – about my previous co-pilot, about the flight, about the wisdom of the whole enterprise. The ceremony was held in the Jules Verne restaurant in the Eiffel Tower in Paris; and when I opened my heart to Jean-Christophe Jeauffre, founder and organizer of the Jules Verne Adventure Association, asking whether he thought I was right to risk so much – my family, my job, my nice life – he gave a robust answer. 'It's not a question of whether or not you have a *right* to fly,' he said. 'You have a *duty*. Mankind needs people to do things like this. People are going to dream with you. The fact we're giving you this unique book shows how much we trust you.' I found his words very moving, and returned to Switzerland with my energy restored, suddenly seeing everything clearly. In other words, that book was one of the crucial factors that got *Orbiter 3* into the air and me out of the ocean of doubt in which I had been drowning.

During the afternoon of Day Two we reached a speed of 49 knots – our fastest yet – and we eagerly watched the GPS in the hope that we would hit 50. Then Alan phoned to say, 'Slow down! Slow down!', and we descended gently from 24,000 feet to 16,000. There our speed fell to 31 knots, and when we entered Moroccan air space we were doing only 25. Our controllers knew that it was psychologically difficult for us to reduce the pace, but the met men could see from their weather patterns that it was the only thing to do. Alan kept saying, 'Don't worry. If you go any faster, you'll head up to the Black Sea, and you'll never reach China at the right point.'

The only real frustration for us was when we got orders we could not understand. If any puzzling instruction came up, we would fax back asking for a report on the general situation so that we could appreciate all the factors involved. We hated the idea of the balloon being remote-controlled. Quite soon Geneva realized it was best to give us several different indications. The first was the general weather pattern, with the forecast track, and the second the track that, ideally, they would like us to achieve. Sometimes the two matched, sometimes they didn't. The best occasions were those when we could even improve on what the met men were forecasting by finding a wind heading a few more degrees in the direction they wanted us to fly – in which case we would call Control and ask, 'Shall we take it?' To which they would reply, 'That's great! That's perfect! Go for it!'

Then we would work to hold the ideal track, going up and down as necessary. If we started to lose our heading, we would try to work out why, and maybe climb or descend a little. The clouds rarely gave any indication of direction or speed because generally they just sat there outside the portholes, coming with us. The only way to fly the balloon accurately was to keep an eye on the GPS, which gave us our track degree by degree and our speed knot by knot. By logging our heading, speed and altitude, we created a wind profile, and our log accumulated dozens of entries indicating fine changes: 'Flight level 157, 185 degrees, 24 knots. Flight level 160, 180 degrees, 23 knots.' In only 300 feet of height variation the wind could change by five degrees – an enormous difference considering the distance that lay ahead of us.

On the evening of Day Two we were still making only 25 knots, and we passed slowly over Almería, where Andy Elson had taken off twelve days before us. Before our own launch Luc and Pierre studied his track closely, comparing it with their computer models. Again and again they said, 'We think he's going to do this' or 'We think he's going to do that' – and their predictions were proving extremely accurate. Already he was over India, thousands of miles ahead of us.

Yet since our own departure I had ceased to worry about him. I thought it was better to concentrate on our own flight. We were doing our best, and things were going well; we could not influence what Andy was doing, and so could not influence the outcome of the race. That would be left to fate. It seemed quite likely that if we got all the way round the world, we would come second. I'd always told myself that I wanted to make the round trip even if I turned out not to be the first; so if I *was* second, I would at least have done everything correctly, made my best effort and lived through a phenomenal experience.

We left the Mediterranean a little east of Gibraltar, and entered Moroccan air space as the sun went down in a blaze of glory to the right of our track. As usual, the balloon was revolving slowly, once every two or three minutes, so the spectacular red sunset came past one porthole after the other. Evidently we flew over a prohibited area, for later we heard that Control had received a mild complaint from the Moroccan authorities. The message ended: 'It's OK this time, but please don't do it again.'

During the afternoon Brian had slept for two hours, again suffering from a headache, and I continued flying for the first hours of darkness. Then at 20:00 I went to bed and Brian took over. In my diary I noted that I slept deeply for five hours, and then spent two hours relaxing and dozing.

BRIAN

I spent much of the night grappling with an intermittent electrical problem with the burner override control. The system was supposed to cut the burners automatically if propane failed to ignite and spurted up into the envelope unburnt, or if the burners became too hot – indicating that a tank was almost empty – resulting in vapour rather than liquid propane coming out of the nozzles. When the burners kept flaming out, the only thing I could do was to isolate the safety systems – which meant that if the burners received gas but failed to ignite it, a cloud of vaporized, unburnt fuel would go up into the hot-air cone. When it did light, there was a loud *ba-boom!* and the whole balloon shook, sending a shower of ice rattling down on top of the gondola.

The situation became fairly fraught, especially when there were two or three consecutive detonations. Sitting in my seat trying to regulate the burners, I would suddenly realize that they had failed to ignite – whereupon I would have to leap up and hit the sparker button before a second charge of unburnt fuel went up into the envelope. (Bertrand, when he was in the hot seat, was so delighted to have efficient burners for the first time that he would have flown right round the world by manual control if necessary: the failure of the automatic systems irritated him far less than me.)

That night we also had the first problems with our variometer, officially known as the Flytec. Most of our other instruments were duplicated, but we only had one variometer to measure our rate of climb and descent, and now it went berserk, telling us that we were descending or ascending at high speed when in fact the balloon was flying level. We relied on the Flytec so heavily that its erratic behaviour caused us serious concern, so I faxed the control room and asked them to contact the manufacturers, describe the fault and request advice. Fortunately, during a pressure test before launch, Bertrand had investigated a hissing sound and identified its source as the Flytec coupling among the mass of wires and plastic pipes behind the instrument panel. So now he knew straightaway how to locate and un-couple the variometer and send some shots of pressurized cabin air down the static tube that connected it with the outside atmosphere. The trouble lay not in the instrument itself, which was of very high quality; the problem seemed to be that water condensed in the extension pipe which we had added. Although we cleared it for the time being, the malfunction recurred every couple of days, and the instrument continued to behave erratically every now and then.

Every couple of days we had to change the carbon dioxide filters, which were called 'scrubbers' because they cleaned the air. I explained to Bertrand that 'scrubber' is slang for prostitute, and we began to include the word in our messages: 'Bertrand says he's just changed the scrubber because it was dirty,' or, as Bertrand himself faxed, 'I've changed the scrubber because I wanted somebody new to talk to.'

On the evening of Day Two several Swissair pilots called us to wish us well, and the sound of friendly voices coming out of the night was immensely cheering. Then at 20:00 the first pair of fuel tanks finally gave out. They had lasted two days and a night, exceeding our expectations, and their performance was a great encouragement.

BERTRAND

We changed shifts at midnight. Brian went to sleep, and after a few hours over Morocco I was rewarded by one of the most magnificent sights I had ever seen. 'Absolutely incredible view of the Atlas mountains, with a full moon,' I faxed at 04:48.

> Everything is black, except patches of snow that are gleaming white. The effect is to emphasize the relief, as if in an extra three-dimensional picture. It's like looking at a daylight scene through very strong sunglasses. Except for the white areas, the landscape is entirely black: the brilliance of the moonlight makes the peaks seem much closer to us than they really are. Far in the distance the lights of Marrakesh are glittering.

We were still heading southwest, away from the direction we ultimately wanted – but that remained the met men's strategy. The balloon was flying well, and I was having to burn for less than a quarter of the time: three and a half seconds every sixteen seconds. I had shut down all the automatic alarms and was monitoring all the burners very carefully.

That morning, while I was still on duty, a big event occurred: my first visit to the toilet. As I have said, the view from the seat was fantastic, and as nobody was flying close to us we didn't need curtains over the window. Unfortunately my session ended in fiasco as the lavatory became jammed, and I had to go through the elaborate flushing routine two or three times, closing the lid with the rubber seal and then opening the valve at the bottom. I was really embarrassed: the last thing I wanted to do was to block the system, specially the first time I used it – and there I was, rushing back to the cockpit to make sure our altitude was stable before returning to try the procedure again. At last it went *tsssschhh,* and everything was gone.

Sunrise over the Atlas was superb. The mountains were mostly dark red, with no snow any more, because we were farther south – though white summits still showed on the northern horizon. It was rather alarming to find that during the night large icicles had formed around the bottom of the envelope and the cables were sheathed in ice. When the sun came up the ice began to melt, so that water dripped on to the gondola, only to freeze again immediately, hazing over our view through the portholes.

On the whole the portholes stood up to the harsh conditions extremely well: they were double-glazed and had silica-gel crystals in the space between the two pieces of acrylic to mop up any moisture that might creep in. The hatch covers, on the other hand, were only single-glazed, so they attracted moisture, which froze solid every night. They were our simple dehumidifying system, drying the air in the cabin. Two or three times a day we would sponge up whatever water had collected and squeeze it into the sink, and thence into a storage bottle. (Somebody calculated that in three weeks two pilots would breathe out a total of forty litres of water.)

My report of the glorious sunrise evidently put Alan in a good mood, and he faxed from Control: 'Bertrand: Good Morning. Aren't these Cameron balloons good? The IOC has asked you to start sending out the Peace message.'

I replied:

Dear Alan, Sorry if you are jealous, but I think I have a date with a nice air traffic control Moroccan woman who keeps on calling me with a sweet voice. She loves to have me loud and clear, and always asks me about my position.

For the IOC peace messages (the ones signed by the pilots), please wait until we have passed Libya, because I don't want that country to believe it's a provocation. We could start to send them from Egypt. But the message signed by Mr Samaranch can be sent already now to the countries we have over-flown and will overfly in the next few days. Please call the IOC to explain that.

Later Alan became slightly alarmed by my report of ice because of the extra weight the balloon might be carrying, and wondered if we could fly lower for a while to get rid of it:

We are suggesting you might like to descend tomorrow to perhaps 10,000 feet to let the ice melt and dry the balloon. You will also be able to go for a walk and get some fresh air. If you agree, it would be good to let the balloon go down naturally shortly before dawn. Then spend a couple of hours at low level before returning to altitude. The meteo gurus say this will not affect your track, and the loss of speed is expected to be small.

BRIAN

For most of Day Three we continued to head southwards at what seemed a desperately low speed. We had to be very patient because everything seemed to be taking such a long time. When we had the problem with the Flytec, for instance, we struggled with it for hours. If we faxed Control, it might be twenty minutes before a reply came because the messages had to pass through a ground station which was often busy.

Naturally we were itching to turn east and accelerate, and at last, in the evening, we began to swing round, degree by degree, as Luc and Pierre had predicted. At 22:30 we were at 17,700 feet on a heading of 115 degrees, though making only 22 knots. Every hour the fax automatically sent down details of our position, and on the half hours in between we reported manually to indicate to Control that we were still alive. We did this because in theory the balloon could fly for the rest of the day with both pilots dead and the automatic system functioning before it sank slowly towards the ground for lack of heat from either sun or burners.

It did not help to know that Andy's balloon was so far ahead – but it seemed to us that he was advancing even more slowly than we were. Control had started passing us reports on his progress, and that night – the fourteenth of his flight – he was somewhere north of Bangkok. 'When Luc comes in, please ask him for an update and opinion on Andy's balloon,' I faxed. 'Seems to me that Bangkok is a pretty good position for avoiding China completely.' Until then we had thought that our only chance of winning the race would come if Andy was carried up against the closed Chinese border. In fact, although it took him a long time, he managed to avoid China altogether.

Minor technical problems continued to plague us. The system that monitored the air in the cabin set off an alarm when it began to show a sulphur dioxide content of 0.4 parts per million. I thought the gas might have been given off by the lithium batteries, but because I wasn't sure, I consulted Control. The query was passed to Kieran, who suggested taking out the battery packs and passing our hand-held warning unit over them one by one. 'Once you have isolated the culprit, it needs to be bagged and sealed until it can be dumped. The alarm is set at a low level, so no cause for concern at the moment.'

That encouraged me to turn off the alarm system for the time being, but I must have been feeling combative, because I reported, 'If the second-stage alarm activates, the only way to deal with the ear-piercing noise is to put the fire axe through the speaker.' In the end the episode degenerated into farce: we took the instrument out, reset it, waved it around over the batteries and couldn't find anything – yet over the top of the bunk it started registering again. We began to think that something in human wind might be setting it off – so we faxed down and asked, 'Could it be the fact that we were farting in bed that set it off?' The answer came back: 'Possibly'. In self-defence I felt bound to point out that 'it was Bertrand in the bunk at the time of the alarm. Mine are distinctly Eau de Givenchy.'

Another annoyance was that the plug on one of our kettles, which fitted into a 12-volt socket designed for a car cigar-lighter, had overheated and melted, and later in the night I contacted Kieran to discuss the feasibility of rewiring the kettle through the switch for the water heater. In the end this was what I did, causing Bertrand to admire my skill with a soldering iron, and surprising myself when it worked first time.

BERTRAND

When I went to bed that night the noise of the burners was absolutely regular, like somebody snoring. Every sixteen seconds there was a four-second burn – a soothing rhythm. But whenever the balloon started to climb too much, Brian had to cut the burners for one or two firings – and that moment was always uncomfortable because it broke the pattern. I kept waking up and thinking, 'No burners! Has Brian gone to sleep in the cockpit? Have we got a problem?' Then the sound would start again and I knew everything was all right. The noise became so deeply engrained in my subconscious that when we were back on earth after our landing, for two weeks I would often wake up in the middle of the night with a feeling of terror, thinking the burners had shut down. When I switched on the light, I realized I was in my own room and went back to sleep with a smile.

BRIAN

Soon after midnight I got a fax from Pierre Eckert – still at work in the Swiss Météo office – that banished all small irritations: a marvellous confirmation that he and Luc had us where they wanted us:

The turn to eastern direction happened quicker than expected, but in accord with the latest version of the numerical model. We also reached the latitude we were looking for with exactly the timing we discussed last Sunday, before your take-off.

Starting from now, you should have headings between 90 magnetic and 100 magnetic at all levels above FL 180 – I suggest that you stay at FL 180 (or below if you do not lose too much speed) until you go down for de-icing and your jug of fresh air. Anyhow, the later perspectives are good. I think we will bring you to FL 240 as soon as the ice has melted. Your trajectory then is to the east and stays at around 25 [degrees of latitude] north to the Red Sea. Oman should be reached by Saturday.

I am presently on a night shift and start to be pretty tired. The weather over Geneva is active. I just gave a storm warning. On your track I see no problem. By the way, how many camels did you see for the moment? Best regards, Pierre.

CHAPTER SIX

FRESH AIR OVER AFRICA

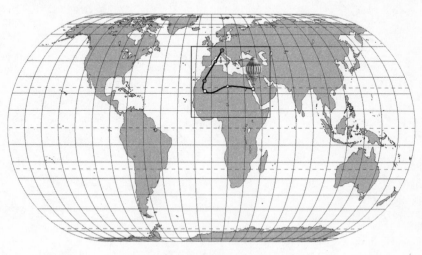

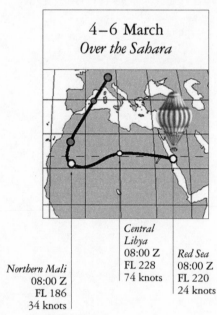

4–6 March
Over the Sahara

Northern Mali
08:00 Z
FL 186
34 knots

Central
Libya
08:00 Z
FL 228
74 knots

Red Sea
08:00 Z
FL 220
24 knots

BRIAN

At 01:44 on the morning of 4 March I faxed John Albury at Control to make quite certain there would be no misunderstanding about the manoeuvres ahead:

> I must talk to Bertrand when he wakes up, but I have the following thoughts. Towards the end of darkness tonight we descend to low level to lose the ice. Then let the sun get to work and climb to 24,000 feet. I'm inclined to retain the polystyrene blocks under the gondola for some protection in case we have to land with tanks still fitted, but probably to get rid of the yellow-side auxiliary tanks. The ice is quite amazing – large icicles all around the base of the skirt (reminds me of a lady I once knew). Most of the time there are small showers of it falling on the gondola, I assume because the envelope is flexing—
>
> Have you given Debs one on that very comfortable couch yet? Or shouldn't I ask?
>
> I think I'll sign this Bertrand in case I'm in trouble.
>
> Love, Bertrand (don't we all?).

BERTRAND

When I took over from Brian before dawn, the view was fantastic, with the moon shining on the Sahara and a million stars glittering above. Several times I doused the cockpit lights so that the stars would show up more brightly. I realized we were following the old route of the Aéro-Postale – the first commercial airline to deliver mail – which used to fly from Paris, via Toulouse, to Dakar in Senegal, and on across the South Atlantic to Brazil. Those pilots – Jean Mermoz, Henri Guillaumet and above all, Antoine de Saint-Exupéry – were the real pioneers of commercial flying. In *The Little Prince* Saint-Exupéry wrote about the very places we were passing over, so I couldn't help wondering which of all those million stars was the star of the little prince.

Back in the right-hand pilot's seat, I read through the messages which had come in while I was asleep. Essential technical information from the ground was spiced with jokes, especially now that our first video report had gone out on Swiss television, CNN and other stations, and friends were sending personal messages. I was much moved to find that Michèle had sent this fax:

Je suis maintenant au centre de contrôle avec les enfants, et nous sommes très heureuses de nous sentir ainsi plus près de toi et de te suivre mieux des yeux – sur les cartes et du coeur – en pensées et informations partagées avec toute l'équipe d'ici. Nous sommes ravies de savoir que tout continue de bien se passer pour vous. Transmets à Brian toutes nos amitiés et dis-lui qu'il est très photogénique with his American hair cut. *Les enfants sont très confiantes dans votre vol et leurs prières vont aux vents pour la réussite de votre projet et l'aboutissement de votre rêve. 'Bonjour Papa' de Solange – 'J'espère que tu réussiras' d'Estelle, baisers – 'J'aimerais que tu réussisses ton tour du monde et je te donne trois baisers' – tapes avec l'index d'Oriane. Salutations de Sandro Haroutounian qui nous prépare notre dîner ce soir au restaurant de l'aéroport. Nous vous embrassons tous les deux. Michèle & Co.*

I am now in the control centre with the children, and we're very happy to feel closer to you, following your progress better with our own eyes on the maps, as well as with our hearts, sharing all the thoughts and information of the team here. We're thrilled to know that everything is still going well for you. Give Brian our best love, and tell him he is very photogenic with his American haircut. The children are very confident about your flight and say their prayers to the winds for the success of your project and the fulfilment of your dream. 'Good morning, Papa,' from Solange – 'I hope you'll succeed,' from Estelle, kisses – 'I would love you to succeed in going round the world, and I give you three kisses' – taps with her forefinger from Oriane. Greetings from Sandro Haroutounian, who is preparing dinner for us at the airport restaurant this evening. We embrace you both. Michèle & Co.

It was wonderful for me to know that my family had seen what a fantastic job the team in the control centre was doing. But to hear from Michèle like that was also a good way of discharging emotion. When Brian and I were alone together, our emotions remained perfectly stable; but when a loving message came straight from my wife and children, it went like an arrow to the heart.

Michèle had bought a big map of the world with the idea that she would stick a pin into it to mark each day of our progress – exactly as my mother had done for my brother Thierry, my sister Marie-Laure and me when our father was drifting for a month in the Gulf Stream. But the spread-out globe looked so vast that she was afraid that a few pins over Europe and Africa, each an inch apart, would worry the children. So she put the map back in the cupboard and waited until we were nearly across the Pacific; then she fixed it on the wall in the corridor at home, with all the retrospective pins in position, and said to the girls, 'Look – there's the world, and this is where Brian and *Papa* have got to already. There's only Central America and the Atlantic to go.'

As the sun came up on Day Four, it shone through the frozen porthole, creating an extraordinary effect. With one hand I held the video camera to film it and with the other I scratched away the ice, making strange patterns, until at one point the shapes on the glass looked exactly like the earth seen from space.

Light revealed the spectacular, dark red colours of the desert.

Somebody had warned us how boring it would be to fly over the Sahara, with nothing to see for days on end, but the reality was quite the opposite. The views that unfolded below us were absolutely fabulous. Every hundred kilometres there was something new – different colours, different shapes, different sand, different rock. For me, the desert was alive: I suddenly realized that the mineral part of the earth is just as alive as humans, animals, trees and plants. The light was alive, the sand was alive; far from being empty, the desert was full of potential. Most landscapes have already been shaped and finished by a combination of natural forces and man, so there is little scope for change. The desert, in contrast, is right at the beginning of evolution, full of the possibility of life.

It struck me that all normal life derives from a thin layer of humus formed on desert. If you have water, you can make trees grow, and the falling leaves make humus. We tend to think that the earth itself is humus, but that is completely wrong. Humus is a miracle – a thin layer spread over the surface of the desert. On that brilliant morning I saw that all life is a miracle – and that the whole planet could be a desert, like Mars. Flying over the Sahara, we could almost have been above another planet.

That first day over the desert was a completely new experience. I opened my notebook, picked up my pen and wrote:

> The desert below looks like the bottom of the sea, with the same kind of shapes. Now and then we see incredible reliefs formed by rocks sticking out of the sand, some like the spines of gigantic dinosaurs, which stretch for kilometres. So much variation of shape and colour, between yellow and black, with every shade of red, and one area of bright, coppery blue, which looks almost as if it still contains water.
>
> In front of such an immense void, such an amount of nothing, I can imagine that people would be moved to write. I think of Saint-Exupéry, running the sand through his fingers beside his aircraft after he had been forced down by engine failure, and writing great books. It is very arrogant to think that there is nothing here. It's only our human mentality which makes us suppose that, because there are no men, there is nothing. If we

really think, we realize the desert's full – full of sand, full of air, full of dryness, full of colour, full of light, full of dunes – and that's why it's full of potential. It's full of emptiness – and to see emptiness for once is wonderful.

I spent hours staring at the desert, writing, feeling its strangeness. For me, that was one of the most beautiful passages of the flight.

BRIAN

The desert had the same effect on me – and there was the surprise factor as well. We expected the Caribbean to look like a picture postcard, and we knew how dramatic northern India might be, but we never dreamed that the desert would be the most spectacular sight of all. Because it was so unexpected, its beauty came as all the more of a revelation.

Still in the early hours of the morning, we swung back on to a southerly heading, and asked Control for reassurance. Shouldn't we be turning east and climbing to catch the jet stream, rather than going down to de-ice? In his first message of 4 March Alan confirmed:

We don't have a met man here yet, but my understanding of the situation is that height, speed and track are not critical at this time, but will become more critical within the next few days. Therefore now is a good time to de-ice, sinking naturally with the dawn. While you are at low level and with a good view of the ground [it] might be a good time to drop the empty cylinders.

Unlike the main battery of twenty-eight propane cylinders, our four auxiliary tanks had no automatic release mechanism, and the only way to drop them was to go outside the gondola and cut them free. Hence the need for an EVA, or extra-vehicular activity. In our planning we had hoped that only one EVA would be needed – and clearly, it had to take place over a totally remote area, where the falling tanks couldn't do any damage, and at a moment when there were no clouds below us to obscure our view of the ground. Ideally, we needed to make the drop at a time when we weren't travelling too fast, because to go down low and then come up again could lose us several hours of valuable progress. If we'd descended at a time when we were doing 100 knots, we would have lost a lot of time. Apart from dropping the tanks, we wanted to get rid of as much ice as we could – most of all the coating that was partially obscuring the portholes.

The idea of an EVA was exciting, and as we prepared for it, letting the balloon descend gently to 10,000 feet, our adrenaline was flowing; but when we opened the top hatch and climbed out, we found it was lovely just to sit out in the fresh air on top of the gondola and enjoy the feeling of being completely still. Anyone susceptible to vertigo would have been in severe trouble, for one looked straight down through two miles of air to the sandy wilderness below. Luckily we both have a good head for heights, and although there was a safety harness, neither of us felt any need to put it on.

The ice was prodigious. Some of it was already melting and water was pouring down off the envelope, though any drips that fell on to the propane tanks froze again immediately. Stalactites ten feet long dangled from the skirt, joining it to the gondola. In theory there was a small risk of being hit by falling lumps, but the accretion of ice inside the envelope seemed to consist of only very thin sheets, which were melting before they fell.

Kieran had suggested that our ignition problems on one side of the burner system were due to an electrical short on one of the detectors. It turned out that he was correct in his diagnosis, and I set to work fixing the fault, while Bertrand attacked the icicles with a fire axe and knocked the coating off the cables. As he laid about him he felt like a boy again, smashing the icicles around the eaves of the family chalet. Then his parents used to say it was a shame to break such beautiful things, but now he hit out with abandon, sending ice cascading downwards. As he said, it was probably the first time that ice had rained on the Sahara in several thousand years.

We were travelling at only 25 knots and seemed not to be moving at all. It was very warm, and just to breathe fresh air was a delight. Above us the sky was cloudless, and below us an infinity of sand and rock stretched away as far as the eye could see. With the burners shut down, there was not the slightest sound to spoil the silence. On the rugged bars of the load frame and its outriggers we felt perfectly comfortable.

When I lay on my front and reached out over the back right corner to cut the white nylon tape to free one of the auxiliary tanks, Bertrand did hold me by the ankle – but that was the extent of our security precautions.

Having set up our cameras to record the event, we did a countdown and I tried to cut the tape with a knife. When it proved too tough, I resorted to a pair of powerful bolt-croppers – and away the tank went, tumbling end over end, glinting in the sun. We watched it all the way to the ground, and in the final few seconds of its descent we saw its black shadow hurtling to meet it at the point of impact. A puff of sand showed where it slammed into the desert. We speculated about what might happen to it, deciding that if it remained on the surface it would probably crumble away in time, after years of bombardment by sandstorms; but if it buried itself in the sand it might lie there for a couple of millennia before some archaeologist dug up the mysterious object.

With the four tanks gone, there remained a good deal of pipework – flexible hoses with couplings on them. Our advice had been to save as much weight as possible by slinging them away as well, but they were expensive gear, and we looked at each other and thought, 'These are too good to jettison. You never know – they might come in handy.' So we kept them – and thank God we did, because later in the flight we had a fuel problem and found we needed them.

There were a couple more constructive jobs to be done outside. Having repaired the burners, I fitted a second aerial for our telephone, while Bertrand cleaned the outside of the portholes. He made up a window-cleaning kit by taping together a telescopic boat hook and a radio antenna with a sponge on the end. And there he sat, 10,000 feet up in the air, applying his Heath Robinson window-cleaner with immense pride.

In our high spirits we were just like two schoolboys. As I filmed my partner at work, I commentated, 'I'm now filming Bertrand trying to clean some bird doo-doo off the window with his special chamois leather,' to which he responded, 'Not *trying* to clean. Cleaning!' (When the film was shown in Switzerland after the flight, people failed to realize that the reference to bird doo-doo was a British joke and started speculating on how the stuff could have got there.)

Much as we enjoyed our time outside, we wanted to get on. Everything seemed to be going well and we felt in control, but we were both keenly aware that a tremendous effort had been made by dozens of people to create the balloon and send us on our way, and we felt almost guilty about playing around outside.

During the EVA the balloon slowly gained height as the sun heated it, and by the time we finished our various tasks we had climbed to 12,500 feet. Rather than descend to a really low level to trap the atmospheric pressure there, we opted to repressurize the gondola from our cryogenic tanks of liquid nitrogen and oxygen. Once again, we took particular care to clean the seal before closing the hatch. Then we inserted the ring-clamp and listened. There was perfect silence.

Our enjoyment of the excursion comes through in an ebullient fax which I sent Control at 11:13. After listing the tasks carried out, I ended:

Gave the Touareg tribesmen a gift of a lithium filter, several empty water bottles and a waste bag. Hope they can make good use of it. I suppose Alan will write it off on the books as a charity donation. Took several photos. Couldn't get the cat back in, so the damn thing will just have to stay out all night. Look forward to the next EVA. The desert is an amazing sight – saw the tanks hit the sand, so don't entertain any claim for personal injury.

Sue Tatford faxed back:

Good morning, boys. Sue here. Latest news on Andy: flight time 15 days 22 hrs 44 mins so far. Alt. 18,000 feet, 19.06 N 112.12, east of Hainan, over South China Sea.

Your ideal flight level for next 24 hours will be FL 220. The jet stream is around FL 260. Luc insists that at the moment its speed is too high and its trajectory too far north for the next two days, and would position you wrongly for later on. From now on our target is the triple point between Saudi Arabia, Yemen and Oman for Saturday evening.

Just received a letter, via the IOC, from Uday Saddam Hussein, son of the Iraqi leader. He says, 'It is with great pleasure that we can take part in the success of this peaceful flight.' He doesn't say you can't cross his country. But he adds, 'Sorry we can't ensure the safety of the balloonists.'

BERTRAND

People sometimes ask why we didn't start from North Africa, rather than spend the first three days of the flight slowly making our way southwards. The answer is that in most other countries there were too many difficulties. We would have had to transport the gondola on a big truck with a crane. People might have said at the last moment, 'I'm sorry, we're on strike,' or 'It's my sister's wedding – I can't come.' I wanted to take off from a country where we had everything under control. America would have been another possibility. There, everything is efficient and the jet streams are close overhead, especially in the south. But then we would have been faced with the Pacific for the last stage of our flight, and we thought that vast expanse of ocean was something to tackle early on. Also, an American launch would have made it extraordinarily difficult to aim for South China. All in all, we decided Château d'Oex was a good compromise. To launch from there was not, as some people thought, a marketing decision by Breitling. But the enthusiasm and friendship of the villagers helped us choose Château d'Oex in preference to any other Alpine valley.

Now at last we were heading due east. We didn't care much about Saddam Hussein, but we did want to make contact with Andy Elson and Colin Prescott in the Cable & Wireless balloon. The fact that they were over the South China Sea meant that they had somehow managed to get round the Chinese mainland. That seemed an amazing feat, and we were full of admiration, so, after repeated attempts to fax the balloon directly, we asked Control to pass on a joint message which we had written at dawn:

Dear Andy,
The sun is now rising on the desert of Mali, and it must soon be sunset for you. That's the disadvantage of being so far in front. It's strange to talk to you by fax during a round-the-world attempt, because I was used until now to be with you in the same balloon.

I hope your control centre sent you my congratulations when you got the duration record. Thank you for having brought Brian into the Breitling project – although I think he still doesn't realize he's now IN the balloon. Actually, I don't realize it either, after all this waiting. Please give my best regards to Colin. Take care. Best wishes, Bertrand.

Hi, guys, Brian here. Flew over your launch site two days ago. Seems I'm always having to clear up behind you. Hope you received my e-mails – otherwise I have to throw the insults all over again. Heard last night you were over Thailand. I can't believe that you're going to overfly all those lovely girls without stopping. After all the things I've done for you, surely you're going to slow down and wait for us?? Good luck, chaps – and stay safe. Don't go upsetting any farmers on the way. Remember we have to come after you.

I was also trying to make contact with *Mata Rangi,* the papyrus boat in which Kittin Munos was attempting to cross the Pacific from South America to Japan. The project was also sponsored by Breitling, and the aim was to check theories of migration, rather as Thor Heyerdahl had done with his raft, *Kon-Tiki,* in the 1940s. In 1997, when the first *Orbiter* ditched in the Mediterranean, Kittin was caught in a terrible storm off Easter Island. His boat was destroyed, and he survived only because he was wearing his Breitling watch, with its emergency beacon. He pulled up the antenna, attracted attention and was rescued. Now I felt a great sense of solidarity with him: we were exploring together, he on the sea, Brian and I in the air. When we tried to phone him that day we couldn't get through, but we did establish contact three days later and found he was doing as well as we were.

At 13:15 I reported that we were 'trying to stabilize our monster' at around 22,000 feet. Our track was perfect – 085 degrees, almost due east – and we were doing 40 knots. Twenty minutes later we were 600 feet lower and the wind had backed slightly to the north, to 078 degrees, but we were making 48 knots. From the control centre Sue Tatford reassured me, 'Your track is excellent, and from now on you can go up to FL 230 but no higher. Your speed will increase at around

18:00 to 50–60 knots. This is OK.'

At 15:19 Zulu we passed through the Greenwich meridian, which made us feel we were well and truly on our way. 'This time we really have the impression of having started the round-the-world flight,' I told Control. 'We have made the 180-degree turn according to our two angels' predictions and are finally flying east, with our full initial fuel reserve. Speed 55 knots. We are still eating the delicious meals prepared by the Hôtel de Ville. We'll go for the dehydrated Nestlé food in a few days, when the fresh food is finished.'

My last remark proved optimistic. That same day our menus took a downward turn because, even inside its vacuum wrapping, our remaining fresh meat had started to smell. After a careful inspection, we decided not to risk eating it, sealed it in double plastic bags and stowed it under the floor. The chicken lasted another couple of days, and after that we turned to vegetarian meat substitute with dried mashed potatoes, which proved to be excellent when reconstituted with hot water. To spice our food we had salt, pepper, tomato ketchup and mango chutney.

I made a note in my diary that it seemed extraordinary to be suspended *in* the air *by* air. The principle of having warm air and gas trapped in an envelope was absolutely simple, yet to make the balloon fly correctly was extremely complicated. As if to confound me, however, when Brian went for a nap that afternoon the balloon flew itself so perfectly and was so stable that I felt relaxed enough to listen to a CD for the first time. I chose a disc by a group called Era, who play a mythical kind of music – half religious, half mysterious – which had a marvellously soothing effect as I listened through headphones and gazed down at the desert.

In the evening our weathermen urged us to keep on the most southerly track we could find. Having swung round on the outside of the depression, the winds had begun to back north again, between 72 and 78 degrees. Our speed increased to 65 knots – the fastest so far – and Luc came on the phone in a state of some excitement. 'Bertrand,' he said, 'I'm so happy I have tears in my eyes. I really think this time you're going to hit the south of China, and that you'll make it.' Even though they weren't in the balloon, Luc and his colleague, like everyone in the control centre, were feeling just as emotional and excited as we were.

BRIAN

Day Four was also the day when Sean the bear came out into the open. I had forgotten all about him until I found him in my bag and put him on the pilots' desk. When we sent down a picture of him flying the balloon, John Albury was delighted and faxed, 'Hope he does not suffer from air sickness and likes your terrible jokes.' The people at Breitling, though, weren't very happy: they thought it a little unprofessional of us to be fooling around with a toy and didn't push for the photograph to be issued to the media. But this in no way dampened our own high spirits; at that stage of the flight we were in a state of euphoria, and everything seemed to be fun. With our good track, reasonable speed and low consumption of fuel, we even dared to start thinking that we had a unique chance of making a historic flight. Both of us were driven on by a colossal charge of hope, which sometimes became so strong that we had to take deep breaths and physically choke it down.

A lot of our pleasure derived from the fact that we were feeling more confident and were fairly sure we were not going to make idiots of ourselves. If, after all that build-up, we had landed only a few hours into the flight we'd have looked really stupid. The important thing now was to concentrate and not make any mistakes.

Sometimes we found that a layer of wind was thinner than the height of the balloon. Then it was essential for the pilot to work almost all the time just to keep the balloon stable. Also, if left to itself, it would usually start to sink gently, so even during the day it needed one push of propane every three or four minutes. We could never take our eye off the ball for long.

Another element in our enjoyment was the fact that we were getting quite good at flying our giant and were gaining confidence in our ability. Every balloon handles differently, and I'd never flown one with anything like *Orbiter 3*'s dimensions. In a hot-air balloon, a good pilot is at one with his craft: he flies it by feel, sensing what it is doing, and makes it react as he wants rather than letting it fly him. Now that was starting to happen on a big scale with Bertrand and me, giving us a sense of pride combined with one of relief at the realization that we were in control.

BERTRAND

Yet I was by no means complacent. I felt a special responsibility towards all the people on the ground who had backed me through three attempts: Breitling, the staff at Camerons who built the balloon, the IOC (godfather of the *Orbiters*), the control team, the air traffic controllers, the weathermen. They continued to give me their trust, and I could not let them down. I felt specially indebted to the Swiss Foreign Ministry and its diplomats in China, who had made such efforts to secure permission to fly over the southern part of the country. After all the work and worry I had given them, it would be horrible to have to land before we even reached the Chinese border.

The evening of Day Four brought another phenomenal sunset over the desert. After dark Luc sent a weather update and urged us to keep to 22,000 feet, predicting that during the night our track would turn south, from 080 to 115, and that our speed would vary between 55 and 68 knots. That all sounded ideal, so I went to bed happy.

BRIAN

So far our flight path had not been likely to cause any political difficulties. But now we were heading for Libya, and beyond it Egypt and other Middle Eastern countries, any of which could cause problems. We had asked them all for permission through the normal channels, and it had been granted immediately; but one had to remember that the last Allied aircraft to fly in Libyan air space were the F-111s that dropped bombs in a botched attempt to eliminate Gaddafi. The result was that American and British balloons were unpopular, to say the least, and Branson and Fossett had both been harassed. At least our balloon was Swiss – but there was a tinge of anxiety behind the joky fax I sent Control at 20:35:

> Do you think the good Colonel is going to let us through without any hassle? We could save one of our special green bags in case we see his tent. Please ensure the Swiss are not about to declare war on any Arab state.

At that stage we were still over Algeria, about 120 miles north of the town of Tamanrasset. A message from our air traffic controllers told me to call the tower there, giving a telephone number and two radio frequencies. I tried the phone but got only a continuous tone, indicating that the number was invalid. The radios were no better. Not wanting to arrive in Libyan air space without warning, I relayed my position to a passing aircraft and asked the pilot to hand it on. John, on duty in Control, gave me the radio frequencies again, and at 23:37 I got through on one of them, but the reception was so bad that I didn't feel confident the Libyans knew we were coming.

For a few minutes the atmosphere was tense, and messages passed back and forth between balloon and Control in quick succession:

Control

Brian – Confirm receipt of met [report] from Pierre and Luc a few minutes ago. Air traffic control are happy with you, and Algiers will pass you on to Libya in the normal way on the usual frequency, which Greg [Moegli] will inform me of shortly. Be assured all is OK. John.

Control

Brian – Just had call from Greg. You will be passed when the time comes to Tripoli by Algiers. It apparently has to go via Tunis to Tripoli. Tripoli apparently are reluctant to give out the frequency to Algiers at this stage, but Greg does not see a problem. I have to fax ATC when you are twenty minutes from the Libyan border, so I will be watching you! John.

Balloon

John – Met received. Thanks. Now climbing to find more speed. Suspect track will back a bit and we will enter Libya at about 25.5 N around 02:10 Z. Now passing FL 191. 086M[agnetic]. 49 kts. Brian.

Control

Brian – Are you happy with my last message, ref. Tripoli via Algiers? Little Friend.

Balloon

John – Nag, nag, nag, nag, nag. Yes, I got your messages. Now FL 220. Have sacrificed about six degrees of easterly for the extra speed of 64 knots. Assume this is acceptable. Brian.

Our increased speed brought the balloon to the Libyan frontier earlier than I had forecast, and we flew over the border at 01:57. Algiers said they had handed me over to Tripoli on HF radio, but reception was still so bad that there seemed no chance of getting through. 'No contact with Tripoli Control on VHF either,' I reported, 'so go ahead and talk to Greg, please.' A few minutes later John faxed, 'Brian, Greg is trying Tripoli for us, so bear with me and I will let you know.'

On the ground, our control centre had woken Greg at 2.30 a.m. to seek his help. Tripoli had refused to give any radio frequencies – he never found out why – and somehow he had to clear our path. As he said, 'It was like a miracle. I called Algiers. They were very helpful. They gave me a phone number, and at three in the morning I rang Tripoli. That guy also was very helpful. He said, "The balloon's too far to the south. We cannot reach them. But there are some control towers down there, and here are the radio frequencies . . ." '

Radio communication remained difficult all night – but at least nobody was ordering us to land.

BERTRAND

I slept exceptionally well, and when Brian woke me with a cup of tea at 07:00 I felt thoroughly refreshed – except that, as usual, I had butterflies in my stomach. I was excited at the thought of going back to the cockpit and eager to hear what had happened during the night, as well as to read the messages.

We were still over the desert – 'Even more sand than on the previous days,' I noted – but soon I had reason to send Control a jubilant fax:

Hallo, Sue – I'm just back in the cockpit after a long sleep. FL 228, track 086 at 74 knots. Position N 26.29 E 16.43. If we admit the definition of the jet stream to be a wind over 70 knots, then you can announce to the press room that we have just entered into the jet for the first time.

Naturally I felt triumphant – and what was the reaction from the ground? Our weathermen immediately told us to slow down! 'Thank you for your message,' Control answered, 'but you were asked NOT to go faster than 70 knots. However, Luc says your present speed and altitude are probably OK. He is checking.'

The temptation to carry on as we were was very strong. I faxed at 08:36:

> The balloon is flying perfectly stable without burning or valving, but above speed advised: 75–76 knots. If Pierre and Luc want us to slow down, I can valve a little, but experience shows that it will then be hard to find a new equilibrium lower. And the track is closer to 80 than 86.

Luc and Pierre were resolute, and their strategy remained the same. We were still being carried along on the fringes of the big Mediterranean depression around which they had slung us at the outset. If we went too fast, we would get ahead of the weather system and be sent north. Our correct option was to move east at the same speed as the low pressure, keeping as far south as possible. So we had to go down – but only a few hundred feet. I opened the gas valves three times, for twenty seconds at a time, and lost 1,400 feet. I reported to Sue:

> Following your request I went lower and found 63 knots and 91 degrees at FL 214. It seems we can play with track and speed by changing little altitude, so please tell what would be the ideal track and speed, and I'll play to try to find it.

Alan replied that our present track was adequate, and we continued steadily on our way with the balloon stabilized at 21,400 feet. But its insulation was so good that we were flying far below its ceiling – the height to which expanding helium would lift it in the heat of the day before excess pressure started to force gas out through the appendices.

We discovered that by lying on our backs with our heads in the bulge of the rear hatch, one at a time, we could look right up and see the appendix tube on that side of the envelope. It was the same at the other end: we could squint up through one of the pilots' portholes and keep an eye on the other tube – so whenever we saw that the gas cell was very tight, we started monitoring the appendices. As the balloon approached its ceiling, we would watch as helium was forced down the tubes from the top: we could see them bulging as it was pushed progressively lower. As long as there were still five or six feet of floppy, uninflated tube at the bottom, we knew we were not losing any gas.

BRIAN

During the afternoon I'd become considerably irritated by the continued erratic behaviour of the Flytec variometer, and by the apparent failure of our control centre to get to the bottom of the problem. My faxes to Alan took on an edgy note: 'It's grouchy Brian here – Bertrand is setting up the Logitech camera for a video clip, if you're interested in having that before you return to the hotel and the comfort of a Teacher's.'

Alan bristled up suitably:

Dear Brian, I don't mind you getting grouchy, but you know the rules. There are people down here who want to know you are OK! Yes – I would like to download everything and anything in the next hour, so I can get back to my comfortable king-size bed with down-filled quilt and adjacent mini-bar. Flytec: between the two of you you couldn't accurately describe the difference between night and day.

Not to be put off, I persisted in trying to explain the problem and asked Alan to call Peter Joder, of Flytec, and get some advice 'before we go to Plan B and take it out. Plan C of course involves the fire axe.'

Alan did call Flytec, but while he was grappling with the problem on the ground, we had more urgent matters to attend to – not least, making contact with Cairo air control. We eventually managed this by means of a relay through an Egyptair aircraft. At 18:30 we gave a live interview on Sky Television.

BERTRAND

Later that day, still over southern Libya, I got a telephone call from the IOC, during which I asked them to send out the peace message signed by Brian and myself to all the national Olympic committees of the world, along with a note asking them to pass on the text to governments, the press and so on. We had hoped to transmit the message direct from the gondola, but it would have taken hours – and all our electricity – to send off 190-odd faxes, so we asked the headquarters to put them out on our behalf.

The message read:

Our balloon has just taken off from Switzerland, location of the headquarters of the International Olympic Committee, which is sponsoring our attempt at a non-stop balloon journey round the world. Or rather our planet, as, seen from the sky, the forms and colours traced by plains, mountains, rivers and oceans inspire one's respect.

We have no engine on board, and it is the breath of the wind alone which is pushing us towards your country. Perhaps we shall fly over it, or perhaps the air currents will carry us in another direction. Whatever happens, the wind allows our balloon to become, for a few days, a link among all the countries of the world as well as an ambassador of the Olympic ideal based on peace, mutual understanding and solidarity. But above all, we are motivated by the desire to enter into contact with the inhabitants of all countries to express to them what we see from the sky.

When we contemplate the immensity of the firmament from which our balloon is suspended, we cannot but admire with humility and modesty this immeasurable whole to which mankind belongs. In a little corner of the universe, our planet is located, and we can look down affectionately on Nature, a kind of cradle in which human beings are born, grow up and die. We cannot help thinking of man's great good fortune in being able to live there, or rather the good fortune he would have if he could live there in harmony with his environment, his neighbours and himself.

Seen from the sky, no two mountains are alike, no river draws the same line as any other, and we well know that no human being resembles his neighbours. It is this diversity that constitutes the wondrous richness of our planet that, at the same time, sometimes gives rise to the most terrible conflicts. And yet, all men have their feet on the ground and their heads in the sky, just as every river has its source in the mountains. As it flows towards the sea, so human beings follow their destinies. They live their lives as best they can. They may do so in war and blood or in the wellbeing that arises from tolerance, sport or the innocent smile of a child. Everyone has the power to choose his way and to aspire to the height necessary to better understand the meaning of his or her life.

Today, our path has crossed yours and, tomorrow, the wind will push us towards another country. We shall continue our flight and you will continue your life, which is also a great adventure. In the final analysis, we are perhaps in search of something to guide our steps.

Already, we are saying goodbye. But above all, we ask you please to help us to spread this message of peace around our planet, which needs it so badly.

It was a great relief that we were crossing Libya without trouble. Ahead lay Egypt, but that seemed to present no difficulties, and at 19:00 I went to bed without any worries, little thinking that Brian was in for an exciting night.

BRIAN

More difficulties were looming: it looked as though our track was going to take us over the northeastern corner of Sudan, and we had been hoping to avoid the country altogether. Its rules stated that all pilots must give seventy-two hours' notice of any approach and, as far as we knew, nobody had done that on our behalf. Nevertheless, for the time being everything seemed to be going well, and at 21:00 I fired off a sparky fax:

My dear friends John and Debbie,
Hope I haven't made things awkward re Sudan. We have made it

our target to clip it, which shows that we have maintained the best southerly track, and it is another country to add to the list – Gosh, did you just see that flying pig go by? Bertrand tucked up in bed now. We had to fight over the teddy bear. FL 230, 114 degrees, 52 knots. I am determined to send just one nice letter to my friends which contains no insult at all – you may want to frame it. Lots of love, Brian.

Half an hour later things were looking less rosy. Belatedly, I saw from the map of Egypt that we were heading for a danger area. The wind was taking us just to the south of the High Dam at Aswan, around which was an exclusion zone that extended out to a thirty-five mile radius. One could understand the Egyptians' sensitivity, because if anyone managed to bomb the dam and breach it, they would probably release a flood big enough to destroy most of the country. But surely no one could imagine that our balloon posed a serious threat.

The air controller in Cairo began asking tiresome questions. What was our route? How long would we be in his zone?

'I've done the usual Arabic shrug of the shoulders,' I faxed John, 'but they don't like it from an infidel.'

At that moment the burners went out. The balloon began to lose height rapidly. I realized that our latest pair of tanks had run out and had to switch to a new pair. Then I found that a crucial valve had frozen solid and the pilot light would not ignite. Trying to deal with the radio and attend to the burners simultaneously was a nightmare because the radio headset had a lead only three feet long, and I had to pull it off every time I needed to stand up and move back to grapple with the burner control panel. So much unburnt propane was spurting up into the hot-air cone that, when it did finally light, there was a tremendous *whumph* of an explosion.

In the middle of all this Cairo came through demanding to know our exact position, and I couldn't give it because for the past ten minutes I had been struggling with the burners. When the Egyptian started ordering me to change course and avoid the restricted area, I grabbed the telephone, called up John and asked him to get our own air traffic controllers in Geneva to sort the fellow out.

Luckily for my peace of mind, it was only later that I found out how the exchanges went. Normally, in air traffic control work, everything is cut and dried. The controllers give headings and keep aircraft well apart, and the pilots do what they ask, without question, all in English, and all in standard air control jargon. But here, as Greg Moegli put it later, 'the mentality was improvisation. We had to adapt, be prepared to start arguing and haggle like in a bazaar.'

Once again Greg was woken in the middle of the night. He immediately phoned Cairo and told them the balloon was on its way. The reaction was immediate and apparently final. 'You can NOT overfly the dam,' his counterpart told him. 'It's absolutely definite. You have to pass thirty-five miles north or south – otherwise we'll launch fighters.'

Greg took a deep breath and 'tried the honey', saying, 'Look – I understand your problem. We've got a problem, too, because they can't steer the balloon. You understand? It can only go with the wind. But by the way, I'm a controller, like you, and perhaps you can help us.'

That brought an instant response. 'Oh!' said the Egyptian. 'You're a controller too? Fantastic! Where are you working?'

'Geneva,' Greg told him. 'We have a lot of traffic here as well.'

'OK,' he cried, 'for you, I give twenty miles. I give fifteen miles!'

In the event, we passed twenty miles south of what John, by then, was calling 'the damn dam', and there was no further trouble on that score. In fact, Greg had made such a brilliant job of charming Cairo that the controller there kept trying to chat me up. 'Don't worry, don't worry,' he called over the radio. 'We've got you on radar now. You're OK.' But at 22:32 I sent off a fax to Brian Smith which showed how hectic things had been aloft:

Brian, hello! Welcome to Dante's inferno. Well – it was until the pilot lights went out. Why is it so damn typical that a pair of tanks that last in excess of thirty-six hours run out when Cairo control are telling me I have to change course to miss the damn dam? 650 feet per minute down, desperately trying to turn on the completely frozen valve, then the pilot light won't go. Then I have to switch to double burners, damn nearly blow the gas cell out through the top tent. Ah well – that's ballooning, as they say . . .

What's the good news? Well, the cameras weren't running, and Bertrand slept through it. Thanks for the assistance from down there. Headless chickens rule OK. What on earth do we do for fun when this is all over? FL now stable at 217, having recently visited several others.

We'd made a rule that the pilot on duty would never wake his partner except in a dire emergency, and I was glad I had stuck to it through that minor crisis. The balloon had never been in danger, but our temporary rate of descent had been very disconcerting because our clearance was for a protected flight level of 3,000 feet – and even if we'd been flying in the middle of that when the burners failed, we must have gone through the bottom of it and into illegal air space within a couple of minutes. In the event, we probably went a thousand feet lower than we should have, but there was no point in telling air traffic control; the only thing to do was to climb back out as fast as possible.

Next, Sudan. When I tried to contact Khartoum air traffic control on HF radio, there was no response. 'Can't we just sneak through Sudan?' I asked Control. 'I did a relief operation there once with the RAF. Please call them and say that Jumima from Juba says it will be OK.' Smiffy, who had recently come on duty, had other ideas. 'Just becos you relieved yourself in Sudan, cuts no ice now, Lootenant,' he replied. 'Just sneak through? Not British, old chap. Go through all burners blazing.'

We followed his advice and never heard a word. Our transponder was continuously giving out our position and details, so the Sudanese must have known where we were, but they never so much as came on the air.

Just before midnight I got a pleasant surprise: a message from the Cable & Wireless balloon, typed in Andy Elson's inimitable style:

Hello brian and bertie
Congratulations on joining us in the air, We heard your inflation was a bit iffy? What do you expect if I'm not there?

Now we hear you are having trouble with ice. What's the problem not enough gin?

So you've decided to follow us and be second well done, lets all have a party at the end? I think cameron's should pay they have made most money from these adventures.

Sorry you missed your jet stream due to Iraq. What will you do now? We anticipate our flight lasting 26 to 28 days depending on how long we have to wait for the pacific and Atlantic weather systems. Currently waiting at Taiwan for 48 hours for the pacific route to open for us.

Very best wishes from both of us for a safe and enjoyable flight.

Colin and Andy

Sorry lost your number then been too knackered swimming the formosa straight towing a balloon is bloody hard nothing like training at Swindon pool loads of hugs andy.

That message made my spine tingle. Andy was stuck over Taiwan, forced to loiter for a couple of days for fear that the wind would sweep him south and dump him near Hawaii, as it had dumped Branson. In a couple of days we should reach China, and we might not be all that far behind. We were catching up fast . . .

The best feature of that night was the performance of our main-line fuel tanks. The first auxiliary pair had lasted thirty-six hours and the second thirty-three; but our first regular pair, desig-nated Tank Pair 8, had held out for a record forty-one – a huge encouragement. By the time I turned in at 03:30 on 6 March, I'd had enough for one night, and told Smiffy, 'Oi, I'm off to bed now to dream of air traffic controllers falling off a dam because their engines won't fire.'

BERTRAND

When I took over from Brian before dawn on Day Six we were still over Sudan. I was at the controls when the sun rose – another beautiful dawn – and I wrote:

I will soon be a great expert on deserts, because this one, the Nubian desert, is different yet again. The mountains are very dark, with light grey sand in the valley-bottoms. It looks as though there is heavy rain at times, and all the sand is washed down. Nature is beautiful even when it is entirely mineral. This is how the whole earth must have been in the beginning. When I flew the Atlantic in 1992 we spent five days above water. This time on *Orbiter 3* we've had five days over sand. But this crossing of the desert gives much more motivation than the three last months, which were a cruel desert to cross.

One mountain stood much higher than all the rest, with cloud on the summit, and in an early fax I reported that I had just seen 'the local Fujiyama, except that the snow was replaced by a cap of cloud. He is alone in the Sudanese desert.' Then at 06:00 we passed over the coast of the Red Sea, and I could see that the desert ran right to the edge of the water – a wonderful sight. 'I'm so happy to see all these beautiful places on our planet,' I wrote. 'Brian and I are privileged indeed to have such impressive sights all round us.'

By then we were rapidly approaching Saudi Arabia – or, if we were unlucky, Yemen. A telephone call from our control centre warned us not to go too far south, towards Eritrea and Ethiopia, because a small war was going on there. When I heard that, I felt that *any* war is horrible: it seemed impossible, inexplicable, that men could be killing each other down below while we floated by above them in a kind of paradise.

'People are fighting and dying without even knowing why,' I wrote, and I reflected on how ephemeral our own interest in war normally is. We read briefly in a newspaper that a war is going on and then turn the page. We see people dying on the television news and zap to another channel. But the people caught up in the conflict may be handicapped or suffer for the rest of their lives, especially if they have lost loved ones. We don't understand how terrible it is to be left with permanent scars. How few people, I thought, have the good fortune that Brian and I have had. Why were we so lucky? Why did we come from backgrounds so affluent that we could devote our energy to going round the globe in a balloon while other people were fighting to survive, to run faster than the enemies trying to kill them? I found no answers to these questions but started to feel more and more concerned for the life of our world.

In his first message of the morning Alan faxed:

Experience suggests that Saudi ATC will be more alert and helpful than Sudan. When you make contact with Jeddah please advise frequency and station in a routine message so we can keep Swiss Control happy.

Have there been any further sightings of the flying insect Kieran says was in the gondola at launch? Did it escape when you did your EVA? The media are very interested.

My wife said she heard Brian last night. She says she gets more information from the TV than from me. Was sorry to hear you had run out of fresh food. Of course, you could always eat the fly!

For once Alan had missed something. 'If you were a more attentive listener to *Suisse Romande* radio,' I told him, 'you would know that the little mosquito who tried to escape by going south with our balloon stopped living a few hours after take-off. I bit him before he bit me.'

As we approached the Saudi coast directly opposite Mecca the air was hazy, so we could not see the buildings. However, we were in contact with the air traffic controller at Jeddah, close to the holy city, and I wrote, 'This makes one respect God, whatever one's religion, and whatever name one gives Him.'

When Brian got up at midday he was full of indignation, and he lost no time in telling Control why:

The blinking bed is wet. Bertrand and I have given each other some stern looks, and even Sean has been interrogated. Upon careful investigation, we found that the internal insulation only comes to the level of the top of the mattress, so there is a lot of condensation building on the gondola internal wall next to the mattress. The bedding is now hanging around in the gondola – it's like a Chinese laundry in here.

The temperature in the capsule was still comfortable, but I noticed that Brian seemed to need fewer clothes than I did. We both wore blue Karrimor trousers, but whereas Brian was happy in a shirt, I usually wore a blue Breitling sweatshirt and maybe a fleece on top. It had been the same with Andy in *Orbiter 2*: I always had four or five layers on, while he was practically naked.

That afternoon was one of the most pleasant of the flight. We spent it together in the cockpit, and because there was little radio traffic our workload was light. We had time to watch big cumulus clouds float around the balloon, drink tea and talk about our lives. Brian told me about the places he had lived in and what had been important to him, and I spoke of my own experiences. Everything was extraordinarily peaceful and relaxed.

Sometimes, during a lull in the conversation, we would put in a burn to lift ourselves over a big cumulus ahead. The clouds weren't dangerous, but often we were travelling faster than they were, and if we had gone through one the balloon would have collected a lot of moisture or ice, so it was better to avoid them. We felt as if we were playing with the huge, fluffy white masses, hoisting ourselves smoothly over them, then coming down again.

As the sun was setting we spotted some small villages in the valleys – the first human habitations we had seen for five days. We were doing 46 knots at 18,000 feet, and anyone looking up would certainly have been able to make out that the silvery object high in the sky was a balloon. I remembered Per Lindstrand saying that when *he* was flying at around 40 knots, he felt sure it was far too slow to make it round the world. Now, our average speed since launch was exactly that – and still we reckoned we had enough fuel to keep going all the way. For us it was becoming clear that the right way to get round the world was not to fly fast at high level all the time but to play with different layers of wind, even if some were slow.

Yet fuel and the wind were not the only limiting factors: political constraints were threatening to play a part. Up came another message from Alan:

> Warning. Your present track will take you across a large danger area in Yemen. We are calculating a new track that should miss most of Yemen. We want to reduce south track to a minimum until clear. So no lower than 220 and no higher than 240 for the moment. Further meteo in thirty minutes.

I answered, 'Warning received. Climbing to 220–230 and will give you the new track. I am a little worried because we are slower than the forecast received on 4 March. Is it a problem or an advantage?' Soon Alan was reassuring us – 'Luc says slow is good' – and giving details of the tracks and speeds we could expect at various heights. But ahead of us lay a prohibited zone over which, according to our aeronautical charts, intruders would be fired upon without warning.

CHAPTER SEVEN

TROUBLE AHEAD

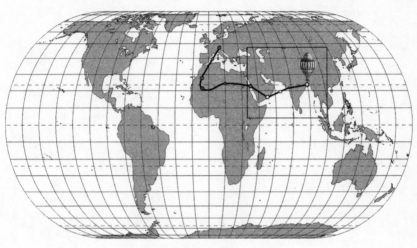

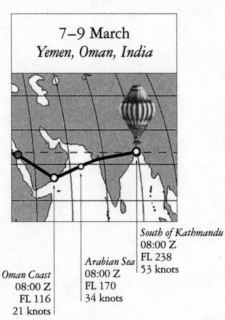

7–9 March
Yemen, Oman, India

South of Kathmandu
08:00 Z
FL 238
53 knots

Arabian Sea
08:00 Z
FL 170
34 knots

Oman Coast
08:00 Z
FL 116
21 knots

BRIAN

The danger zone – edged in red on the map – lay across our front in a broad band running from southwest to northeast, almost cutting Yemen in two. Our support team could see that we had little chance of circumnavigating it, and although Luc and Pierre did their best to steer us round the edge by telling us to fly higher and sending us more to the north, the wind would barely allow a big enough deviation.

None of us knew why the Yemenis had declared the area prohibited, and we could only suppose it was used for military training. But Bertrand was fairly cynical about the locals' ability to take out high-flying aircraft, reckoning that their heaviest armament would be a few shotguns normally used for riot control. So, as we were at 21,000 feet, we did not feel too vulnerable.

Nevertheless, even though we were going to pass over the red zone at night, anxiety ran high among our air traffic controllers in Geneva. As one of them – Patrick Schelling – said, you never knew what sort of fanatics might be loose in such wild country, and anyone might start firing at a strange target overhead. His mind went back to the dreadful incident over Belarus in 1995 during the Gordon Bennett balloon race, which started from Switzerland. The organizers had obtained clearance, but the local civilian authorities failed to inform the army, who scrambled a helicopter, forced one balloon to land and shot down another, killing the two pilots. Now he decided that if the Yemenis would not give us clearance, or at least reasonable assurance that we would not be fired on, he would have to bring us down.

He could see we were heading for trouble as soon as we came over the Red Sea, only 150 miles from the Yemeni coast, and he spent the whole of that Saturday afternoon battling with the problem. At least communications proved reasonably good, but the Yemenis' English was limited, and Patrick was never certain about the mentality or real intentions of the people with whom he was dealing. There was always the risk that they would agree to his request and then take hostile action anyway.

It had never been part of our plan to fly over Yemen, and so we had no diplomatic clearance. This meant that Patrick had to negotiate from scratch. His first call was to Sanaa Airport, but he had some difficulty getting through to the tower because the Yemenis rated it a secure area, and for a while refused to give him the number. In contact at last with the local controller, he launched into the first of many discussions. The man in charge asked him to send a fax to the Yemeni civil aviation authority requesting permission for an overflight. This he did immediately; but no answer came back, so he kept calling the Sanaa control tower, asking for clearance.

It took him some time to explain what was happening because the man on duty had only broken English and kept asking, 'What is the balloon's destination?' When Patrick said, 'It's going round the world,' he repeated 'What is its destination? If you have flight plan, you must have departure point and destination.' The Yemeni insisted that he himself could not give clearance because he lacked the authority to do so. All Patrick could do was keep talking to him until he felt fairly sure that nobody was going to do the balloon any harm. All the while he was trying to gauge the man's mentality: was he really trying to help, or was he just giving worthless assurances and absolving himself of responsibility? Patrick realized that, although he was talking to a fellow controller whose job was to provide safe skies for aircraft, his opposite number belonged to an alien culture and might take an entirely different view of round-the-world balloon flights. He might not give a damn about what happened to *Orbiter 3*.

In the end Patrick was reasonably sure that everything would be all right. He felt he had won a psychological victory by making direct contact with the person in charge of operations, rather than with some distant superior. But the controller never said, 'You're cleared.' He just talked round and round the subject. If the balloon had penetrated the closed zone by only fifty metres, it might have been enough for some idiot to make trouble. As Patrick drove home, having done his utmost, he was still haunted by memories of the Belarussian disaster. What went through the minds of people who could do something as barbaric as that?

If Patrick *had* decided to bring us down, we would have had to ditch in the Red Sea – but our own control centre never let on to us how close we came to being halted in full flight. One message from John Albury did give a hint that there was some difficulty on the ground: 'Ref Yemen. We have had no official reply but Patrick has spoken to Sanaa ATC and he gets the impression it will be no problem.' He also gave us a telephone number and radio frequency for the supervisor in charge, and said that if all else failed, he would call Alan in to speak to diplomats. We realized that Patrick must be negotiating on our behalf, but we had no idea how long and difficult his conversations were proving.

I reported my efforts to find a more northerly track and skirt the top edge of the danger zone:

John – Been up to 21,000 feet. Track between 099 and 104 all the way. Descending to FL 198, where I had 098 or 099. Best I can do, I'm afraid – My arithmetic says we will be at the area in 5.5 hours from now, so plenty of time for track to change maybe. Could you tell Nik, Patrick and Greg that we appreciate their efforts very much, and I will let them buy me another lunch when it's all over. Jeddah has us on radar and seems happy.

Bertrand and I were irritated by having to divert northwards after making such efforts to keep south over the past few days, but Luc, when pressed by Patrick, was implacable. Twice in one message he urged us to stay as close to track 090 as we could and then, after we had passed the restricted zone, to descend to around 13,000 feet to find a track of 100:

> We have confirmation of no problem with the zone in Yemen but it is suggested that you telephone the number given previously – I think this is really a courtesy call, but they have coordinated matters for your overflight. YOU may want to offer ME lunch, because I have been running around like a . . . on your behalf!

We never got through to the number John gave us, and at 19:15 I told him that although I'd 'been up and down like a whore's drawers' looking for 090, the best I could find was 093. 'So we go through the north end of the restricted zone, by the looks of things. My estimate is that we will fly out of the zone at 01:00 Z.'

In the control centre the atmosphere remained electric, but at 20:34, not realizing how difficult the Yemenis had been, I reported: 'Had powdered mash and veggie burger for supper. My, how the mighty have fallen.' John kept my mind off potential disaster by passing up the most important item of terrestrial news – that Dusty Springfield had died – and asked if I wanted to be informed of the result of tomorrow's Grand Prix. Later Jo chipped in with a message telling me that Andy and Colin, in the Cable & Wireless balloon, were now south of Osaka and expected to start crossing the Pacific in a couple of days. When Luc asked if we needed to go low, to shed ice, I replied, 'No, we do not need to go down. We are happy to keep our garbage on board if we can get to faster winds sooner. No ice that we are aware of.'

From 19,000 feet we were getting tremendous views of yet another type of desert. The small bumps all over it reminded Bertrand of chicken pox.

By 23:15 I reckoned we were over the northern edge of the prohibited zone and told Smiffy, 'It may be my imagination, but it appears that according to the topo chart we are in the area – What say you, Gunga Din?' Smiffy came back with, 'We reckon you're just in it, mate. Story of your life. Just skimming the top edge, but it depends on the thickness of your felt-tip pen.'

While Patrick fenced with the Yemenis, Luc and Pierre had been doing intricate calculations for the next leg of our flight, and just before I went to bed they came through with their master plan:

> Our computations for the next two days drive us to northern India between FL 180 and FL 240. The most northerly point of the trajectories is at around 90 E of longitude, and is a little bit too much in the north to avoid high ground over the Himalayas and to fulfil the Chinese requirements.
>
> Thus we have to gain a piece of south now! At the time which is best convenient to you, you should come down to between FL 100 and FL 130. Speeds have to stay between 20 and 25 knots. The goal is to reach a latitude of 17 N before crossing the Arabian Sea. This means you must stay at a lower altitude for about twelve hours.

Although we ourselves never spoke to Yemen, we knew from the orange light flashing on our transponder that we were interrogated by their radar as we went over – and we took the fact that they were watching us as a good sign.

BERTRAND
At 02:30 Zulu Brian went to bed, and after a couple of hours I was rewarded by the sight of a magnificent sunrise breaking over yet another desert. But before I had time to marvel at it, an astonishing message came in from Jo:

> I've just had a telephone call from Alan, who has been contacted by the Cable & Wireless Control Room to say that their balloon is landing seventy miles off the coast of Japan. The reason given is that the balloon is 'iced up'. They plan to land in the sea, and search-and-rescue are with them now. We are checking the web site and watching CNN on television, but as yet we have no further information. Will keep you posted.

My reply now seems rather flat – but perhaps I was in shock when I sent it:

> This is unbelievable news. I take no pleasure out of it, as it must

be very frustrating for them. But of course it gives us more chance to be the first around. It also brings fear that the same problem could happen to us.

I could hardly believe it. I was afraid for the two crew men – both good friends of ours – but at the same time I couldn't help thinking, 'If we do get round, we're not going to be second.' I felt immediately that the world's attention was focused on us because now we were the only ones left in the race. But I said to myself, 'If Andy's ditched, maybe we're also going to ditch if there's really bad weather ahead.' Altogether I went through a tremendous mixture of conflicting emotions.

Two hours later a fax from Smiffy confirmed that the Cable & Wireless balloon had come down in the sea and that the crew had been rescued. Of course I was desperate to pass on the news to Brian, but I kept to our agreement that neither of us would wake the other unnecessarily, and when eventually he stuck his head out of the bunk I said, 'Brian, I've got the most incredible news. What d'you think it is?'

Instantly he said, 'Andy's down.'

Maybe some telepathy was involved. Like me, Brian was surprised and shocked, but also hugely relieved. We had caught up a good deal on Andy, but when he went down we were still four days behind him, and we would have been inhuman if we hadn't felt excited by our new opportunity. We guessed that Alan, too, must be feeling pulled in all directions because the Cable & Wireless balloon had also been built by Camerons. Later that day he told us he had spoken with the Cable & Wireless Control:

> The official story is that the balloon flew into snow squalls, but this was not the only reason for landing. They say the main reason was lack of electrical power – some problems with solar panels – possibly lack of sunlight in poor weather conditions.

On the ground the news evidently had a wide impact. Alan told us the media would want to talk to us, and that we had better work out what we planned to say. He asked us to make a short video clip with a commentary in English: 'This would probably be used around the world if we receive it soon enough.' He also said that an aircraft would be coming up to film us the next day for an interview – 'they appear to be very interested in the icicles'.

Later, when we met Andy in Bristol, he gave a more detailed account. He said that, together with Siemens, he had devised some highly efficient solar panels, and he was so convinced by their perform-ance that he took no back-up lithium batteries. When he found himself in cloud over the Sea of Japan, he had the choice of going up – which would have sent him in a dangerous direction, towards Hawaii, where big thunderstorms were raging – or of staying low and flying in the right direction, but under the clouds. Down there, the solar panels could not recharge his batteries, and after one day he ran out of electricity. Without power he could not pump kerosene from the tanks to the burners, and he could not talk to his control centre. The balloon just died and he was forced to ditch.

Meanwhile, we had to continue on our own track. Fax and tele-phone communication was becoming patchy because we had reached the very limit of the area covered by the East Atlantic satellite and were trying to switch to the Indian Ocean satellite, in geostationary orbit 23,500 miles out in space. The trouble was that, with the satellite almost directly overhead, our antennae were often in the radio shadow of the balloon. As always, Control was anxious that we should not go off the air for any length of time and, still early in the morning of 7 March, Alan urged us to maintain contact by any method we could, even if it was only by HF radio.

As we approached Oman, Smiffy tried to telephone Muscat air traffic control to update them on our progress, only to be told that the man in charge was out saying his prayers. When he called half an hour later and received the same reply, Smiffy, without thinking, told the Arab, 'He must have been very naughty, then.' At 04:54 I reported, 'Somebody called me on 121.5, might have been Salalah Control, but he was unable to hear my answer.' It was nearly 07:00 when I at last made proper contact with the Salalah tower, and I told Smiffy, 'I guess he and I can't have had the same praying time up to now, but we finally managed to meet.'

Just after that I found that, by lying flat on the floor with my head in the dome of the rear hatch, I could get a contact through

Brian's mobile phone using Oman's network; so I rang our control centre and found myself talking to Thedy Schneider. I knew that our flight had placed a huge weight of responsibility on him, and that if anything happened to us he would never forgive himself. So it was good to have a chat, and even though he was his usual gruff self, between the words I could feel how strongly he was wishing us well. I also spoke to Luc and Pierre, who confirmed that our position was perfect for entering China at the right point.

Stefano Albinati was also in the control room that morning, and he sent a long fax saying, 'Dear Pilots, Everything goes so well that I really feel useless . . .' But he gave us detailed results of the Australian Formula One Grand Prix, which had been won by the Ulsterman Eddie Irvine, and ended, 'The next Grand Prix is in only five weeks. You may have landed just before in Malaga! Big kisses, Stefano.' These were the only items of news we wanted to hear: we were happy to be protected from all the rest – wars, murders, catastrophes and political scandals.

Following the instructions of the weathermen, we had come down to relatively low levels – 10,000 or 11,000 feet – and with the heat reflected off the desert hitting us from below the gondola became uncomfortably hot, with a temperature of 28°C (82°F) and 76 per cent humidity. There was nothing we could do to improve matters, and Brian told John and Debbie, 'Every time I opened the window, blinking Bertrand closed it again. I'm fed up with that. When I grow up I'm going to be captain of a round-the-world balloon, and then I can have all the windows open.'

After a long spell over the pock-marked desert, we flew above the extraordinarily flat plateau of Oman until it plunged abruptly to the coast of the Arabian Sea.

My own thoughts often took a philosophical turn. I found the balloon an ideal place in which to think and write, and in my little green notebook I recorded:

This planet is beautiful. We have to make people aware of its beauty and its open spaces – not so that they believe it is paradise, but so that everyone can seek paradise together. I devoutly hope that it is not necessary to go through hell on earth to gain access to paradise. We can look for paradise also through harmony and wisdom.

BRIAN

My latest worry was that much of the Velcro round the outer skin at the base of the gas cell was hanging open. Peering up the sides of the envelope, we could see big gaps. The lower section of the outer skin could not separate from the top section because the two were held together by a large number of karabiners, but the failure of the Velcro seal looked alarming.

'Are we going to lose a lot of the heat we put into the hot-air cone straight up through the outside of the envelope?' I asked.

Alan's reply was reassuring:

It may in fact improve duration, as we want to ventilate the space between the two skins. If hot air gets between them at night, I think it will give up its heat to the gas cell before exiting at the top. Some loose Velcro was noted when the balloon was inflated. This was due to the rain that fell on the balloon when it was laid out. Velcro loses fifty per cent of its strength when wet.

I told him that we too had noticed that part of the Velcro sealing ring round the bottom of the waistcoat was open after take-off, but that much more of it had come undone since: 'It shows daylight in four segments, which amounts to approx fifty per cent of the equator.'

As soon as we were well out over the sea and had made sure there were no ships below us, we dropped three empty fuel tanks using the automatic release gear. This was operated by electricity: when we switched on the circuit, it heated an element which gradually melted through the nylon tape holding each cylinder in position. 'Some good news for you,' I told Control:

The tank disconnects worked perfectly. We have jettisoned tanks 7A and 7B, plus 8A. It was a bit disconcerting that the weight of Pair 7, before dropping, showed as 20 kilos, and that they took sixty-two and sixty seconds to release. Pair 8 showed a weight of 150, so we tried burning with them, and confirmed there was in fact no fuel left before releasing 8A, which took forty-four seconds to melt tape.

I was disappointed to find that the shedding of 200-odd pounds seemed to make little difference to the balloon's performance: our rate of climb remained practically the same. Fuel was so vital to us that Alan asked if the tanks we had dropped could have contained propane but no pressure, and, if the same thing happened again with an apparently empty pair, could we try pressurizing them with nitrogen? I replied, 'In answer to your questions, No, No, No, as Margaret Thatcher would say.' I pointed out that tank 8A had run out in the middle of the night, and that, together with its partner, it had given us 41 hours of burning. According to the computer at Control, each pair should give us 33 hours 15 minutes of heat, but so far we had averaged 35 hours 30 minutes – an important gain.

Now our target was India, and during the evening of 7 March John briefed me with details of how to contact Bombay air traffic control. 'Your first good move would be to address them as MUMBAI, as that is what the locals now like to call themselves,' he advised. 'Good luck and goodness gracious me in an Indian takeaway accent!' Soon after that he confirmed that Greg Moegli had already spoken to the Indian controllers, and that they appeared to be 'helpful and friendly . . . Mumbai know you are coming and where you are now'.

At 17:32 John surprised me by sending up congratulations on passing the 10,000 kilometre mark. It was good to realize we'd beaten the record of 8,700 kilometres set by Bertrand in *Orbiter 2* – although in fact we had done it quite a few hours earlier – but galling to hear that champagne had been broken out in the press office. Bertrand was firmly asleep. We were making only 31 knots and seemed to be crawling towards the Indian subcontinent; at 10,000 kilometres a week it could take us a month to complete a circumnavigation. But Luc and Pierre insisted that we had to remain low and slow. In a met update at midnight they faxed:

We have to keep you at FL 180 for the next forty-eight hours in order to arrive over China at 26 N. Higher altitudes are faster, but lead more to the north . . . Overnight, look for a mean track of 070. Target on coast of India will be close to Porbandar [on the Gujarat coast] early afternoon 8 March. The entry into China is expected the 10th at 00 Zulu. We can then climb to get higher speeds and stay below 26 N. The entry over the Pacific will need some adjustment in order to get the jet stream at the right moment. Early simulations show an arrival over Morocco the 19th.

Arrival over Morocco! What a thought! The precision of our weather wizards was inspirational – but we were going to need quite some patience to keep going for another ten or eleven days. Meanwhile, seeing that Jo had been doing several stints in the control room, I gave her the time of night:

Hello the wife. Are you a glutton for punishment, or what? Another night shift? Not carrying on a secret liaison with Bertrand by Capsat, are you?

Can't believe it's a week now. When I get back I'm going to give the travel agent what for. I have video pictures of tiny rooms, having to share bed with another holiday-maker, damp bedding, appalling breakfast buffet. Not even a minibar. I suppose the only good news is that there appears to be no building going on around. Of course I get to sit at the Captain's table every night. I'll be here till about midnight. Strange feeling the way the nights sneak up every day. Give a bob or two for a shower. Suspect Bertrand would pay more – for me to have one, that is. Found crooks and nannies that wet-wipes have never seen before.

Celebrated Andy's landing by putting on clean underwear. If we fly too much longer, when I change my undies, it will be with Bertrand's. Have a nice evening – see if you can get a pay rise out of Alan. That should take at least all night. Lots of love – Brian at FL 156.

BERTRAND

When I awoke early on the morning of 8 March, I was thrilled to learn that we had beaten my own distance record. At least we had achieved *something*. Again I was bewitched by the beauty of the dawn. When the sun came up out of the ocean there was a lot of little cumulus below us, and for the first and only time in our circuit of the globe, I saw a ship – a tanker. An hour later, with Elton John on the CD player, I told Jo at Control that 'I would accept to change the *musique* for a good bottle of Bordeaux wine, but not the blue sky'. By constant experimentation I discovered that the layer of wind carrying us along on the 70 degree track we needed was only 300 feet from top to bottom.

In a telephone call Luc told me he reckoned we should be back over Morocco on 18 March – a day earlier than he had advised Brian. The news brought on a tremendous surge of hope and emotion. 'We haven't even reached India yet,' I thought, 'and yet he's confident we're going to succeed.' All the more reason to concentrate and make no mistakes. The distance ahead of us still seemed so colossal that the idea of finishing the course was almost impossible to grasp – but Luc was so calm and logical that he inspired me with enormous confidence.

During the next hour I composed a long fax, in French, and asked Control to pass it to Gérard Sermier, the Breitling press attaché in the press room. The dispatch included my outstanding memories from the first week of the flight, and I set them down (I wrote) because 'what interests me most is to retain the impressions, rather than just the facts, of this unimaginable experience'.

I rhapsodized about the variety of deserts we had flown over, 'the immense spaces without a single human trace', and recalled how Saint-Exupéry had sat writing beside his downed aeroplane 'facing the desert, facing himself'. Even inside our capsule I seemed to smell the odour of hot sand that burns in the pages of his book *Terre des Hommes* (Land of Men). I described how I had imagined that, like Saint-Exupéry, I was letting the sand run through my fingers, to gain closer physical contact with the earth, but decided that I preferred to stay far up in the sky for as long as God, the wind and chance allowed. I concluded with a brief sketch:

When the full moon had risen over the snowy peaks of the Atlas, the stars came out one after another above the Mauritanian desert, and a light, white mist enveloped the balloon. Now the regular snoring of the burners makes me think the balloon itself is breathing. Everything is calm. I'm still looking for the star of the little prince.

After the demise of Andy's balloon we had started getting numerous requests for media interviews. Every day messages were passed up by Control from journalists seeking appointments, and we did our best to fit them all in – but they all asked the same questions, making us wish that inquiries could be pooled.

My shift in the cockpit seemed to pass slowly, not least because our pace was so leisurely. 'Thirty-three knots is a lot of wind speed when you want to take off or land with a hot air balloon,' I faxed, 'but here I promise you it gives the impression not to move. Planes relaying our position to Mumbai every now and then.' The track I was holding averaged 70 degrees, and this obviously pleased Luc and Pierre because when they came into the control centre they were reported to be smiling, and they passed me a number of small adjustments to height and direction 'to make you arrive at exactly 26 N over China'.

Obviously they were excited that they had managed to line us up so that we would head straight for the magic point. After leaving the low pressure over the Mediterranean, we had been picked up by a high-pressure system centred over India. Because this was turning clockwise, it would first take us a little to the north and then eject us to the east. It seemed a miracle that the high was in just the right place at just the right moment to push us out due east, at 90 degrees, precisely between the 25th and 26th parallels – exactly where we wanted to be.

BRIAN

At 22:00 on the night of 8 March I woke in high spirits. 'Hello and top of the morning to you. Who are you, anyway?' I blasted off at Control when I took over in the pilot's seat. 'Brian here well rested and out of the communal damp bed. Twice round the block, bit of Tai Chi, dropped Tank 8B (on purpose), and now feeling full of the joys of winter.' Smiffy and Cecilia hit back with, 'Glad you're feeling full of beans – good way to dry the bed, too. I have faxed your position and flight level to air traffic control. Better polish up your best Bombay/Welsh accent for Mumbai.'

Rising to the bait, I faxed back:

My best Indian accent (head movements to suit): Greetings to my most honourable friend Brian and his most beautiful wife. We are being over the sea, and not being to see much of anything. I am forward looking to speak to my verly dear friends in the beautiful city of Mumbai (frantic head shaking here). Our track is most very confusing to our simple selves, so we are exploring varying altitudes to come to the number 065 (chapati and pilau rice). With very best wishes, Sahib, your humble servant Brian at FL 210 and climbing slowly.

Alas for our jokes! Little did we realize that in Geneva our people had suddenly seen a major obstacle looming ahead. Nik Gerber was on duty at Swiss Control at 11 a.m. local time when he got a call from our team, who told him they had a problem with India. He was surprised, because flight plans had already been forwarded to the Indian stations on our route, and no query had come back. Now Bombay was claiming that we did not have diplomatic clearance. Because no papers could be found, they said, the balloon could not fly over India.

At first Nik did not take the threat too seriously, thinking it could be easily sorted out. He told Control he would come in soon after 1 p.m. and help untie the knot. But when he arrived he found everyone in a panic. Sue Tatford was uttering curses as she searched furiously through a file of documents. After a desperate hunt, she had to admit that no permission existed. Alan had applied for diplomatic clearance back in August and asked for it again by fax and teleprinter, but it seemed that no document had ever arrived, and in the rush to get the balloon ready the matter had been overlooked.

Now what? There was no way the balloon could fly round India – and no time to obtain clearance through the normal channels. Disaster threatened. At 14:54 a message came from Bombay saying, 'No authority available with DECA [the aviation authority]. Advise Hotel Bravo – Bravo Romeo Alpha to avoid Indian territory.'

That was a totally unrealistic request. To us approaching in the balloon India offered a front 2,000 miles wide, and we were heading right for the middle of it.

Nik rang the air traffic controller in Bombay and urgently tried to make him see reason, but all the man would say was, 'Listen, we have no secondary radar, so we can't pick them up. There is great danger. They're about 400 kilometres off the coast. It is a waypoint for airliners. We can't see them, and we have no radio contact. It's impossible for us to get them through the Bombay approach area.'

When Nik continued to reason, the controller asked, 'What *is* this balloon, anyway? How does it steer? How many engines has it got?'

'No engines,' Nik told him. 'It can't steer except a little bit by going up and down.'

'All right,' said the Indian. 'I give you the phone number of Mr Saran, Deputy Director General of Civil Aviation.'

In Delhi it was already 6.30 p.m. but, with everyone in the control room on edge, Nik put in a call, reached the Deputy Director, and spent the next fifty minutes on the phone. Mr Saran, hull-down in his bureaucratic bunker, could not understand why the balloon had no clearance. Nik explained that repeated applications had gone unanswered. The Deputy Director then demanded an exact route and precise estimates for the overflight. He insisted that the balloon maintain an altitude between 20,000 and 22,000 feet. Pierre immediately said that would be possible from the met point of view. After nearly an hour of discussion and argument, Mr Saran at last gave permission, and issued instructions to his controllers to let the balloon through. But, he said, Nik must telephone Mr Wasir, his Number Two, and explain everything to him because he did not have time to do it himself.

Fortunately, hardly any of this reached me in the balloon. One message from John did say, 'Chaos here ref India, but Nik is doing a great job sorting it out.' He told me I would need to give him a position report with flight level 'at least every hour without fail' – but we never realized that our flight was threatened with sudden, premature termination, and only when we were half way across the subcontinent did Control let on that the Indian authorities had demanded that we ditch in the Arabian Sea.

BERTRAND
When later on I heard about all that fuss, I couldn't help thinking of Jules Verne's novel *Around the World in Eighty Days*, first published in 1873. The central character, Phileas Fogg, is confident that he can cross

India swiftly on the new railway, but when he reaches a hamlet called Kholby the train stops and he finds that the line goes no farther, leaving him with a gap of fifty miles to cover to Allahabad. His response is to buy an elephant and cross the gap on that. Latter-day bureaucracy had almost proved our own undoing, but skilful advocacy by Nik – the modern equivalent of the elephant – had kept us going.

We came over the coast in the dark, so all we saw were the lights of Porbandar, 250 miles northwest of Bombay. That night our fuel consumption was the lowest ever: one second of burning every twenty-eight seconds – an insignificant amount. Part of the gain seemed to come from being at relatively low level – we were at 15,000 feet – although nobody could explain why altitude made so much difference. Later in the night, to find the track of 73 degrees that the met men wanted, we went up to 25,000 feet, and our speed picked up from 35 to 50 knots.

At sunrise we were between Porbandar and Bhopal, and to celebrate the fact that we were back over inhabited territory I changed into clean clothes. I was happy to be flying over India again: a year ago we had glided over the subcontinent at low level in *Orbiter 2*, sitting on top of the gondola as though on a magic carpet, and now, as we passed on a far higher trajectory, I enjoyed remembering how the smells of cooking and incense had wafted up to us, along with children's voices.

That day, our ninth in the air, was a crucial one because it was the last on which we could adjust our approach to China. As I concentrated on holding the course dictated by Luc and Pierre, I suddenly heard an aeroplane calling me. 'Hotel Bravo – Bravo Romeo Alpha,' said the pilot, 'I have a surprise for you.'

'I love surprises,' I replied. 'What is it?'

'Just a second,' – and then in my headphones, speaking French, I heard the voice of a good friend, Charles-André Ramseyer, one of a delegation from the Swiss Tourist Office, flying out for a conference. He told me that another of the passengers had seen us and started to shout: 'Look! There's the Breitling balloon!'

It was Charles-André who first introduced me to the world of ballooning: in 1978, when he was director of the tourist office in Château d'Oex, he phoned to say that he was organizing the first ballooning week in the village and that he would like me to go up with

Flying over the Alps was the moment of truth. In complete silence, Bertrand and Brian were able to observe the perfect functioning of their new balloon (*Edipresse – S. Féval*).

As they were carried south by slow winds, they got a great view of the Matterhorn through the left porthole (*Bertrand Piccard and Brian Jones*).

Meanwhile, in the Geneva control centre, there was plenty for all the team to do: (Above left) Luc Trullemans explains to the press the forecasted trajectories (*Keystone*). (Above right) Greg Moegli and Niklaus Gerber cleared the way for the balloon through all the air traffic during its long journey (*Edipresse – Di Nolfi*). (Below left) Pierre Eckert calculated the trajectories of the wind from the computer. (Below right) Patrick Schelling, the third air traffic controller at Swiss Control (both *Patrick Schelling*).

During the first EVA, Brian concentrates on dropping one of the empty auxiliary fuel tanks. Bertrand washes the outside of the portholes with a sponge tied to an HF radio antenna and a boat hook (*Bertrand Piccard and Brian Jones*).

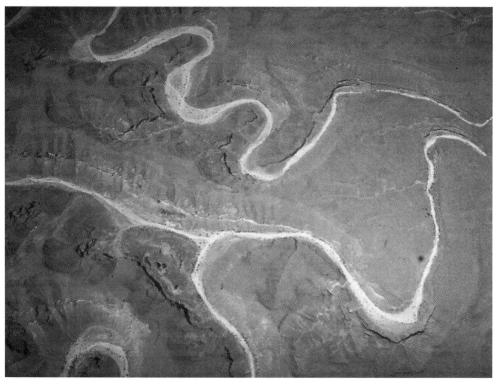

Flying for a week above the North African desert created a lasting memory of its different shapes and colours. Observing the desert and its emptiness shows how miraculous and fragile life is on this planet (*Bertrand Piccard and Brian Jones*).

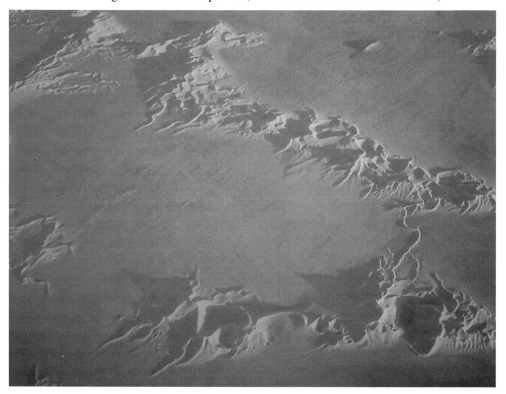

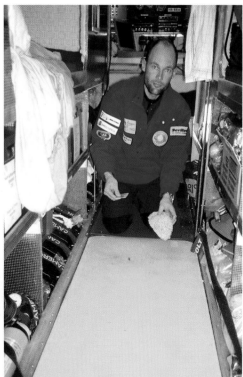

Brian installed in the cockpit in front of the instrument panels. Under his left hand is the laptop computer used to send and receive the faxes. Inside the main corridor of the gondola, Bertrand mops the floor of all the water and ice chipped from the fuel control unit on the ceiling (*Bertrand Piccard and Brian Jones*).

Bertrand showing that, even when Mum and Dad are not there, you have to brush your teeth! (*Bertrand Piccard and Brian Jones*).

Brian and Bertrand celebrate their successful crossing of China by making Chinese hats out of their navigation maps (*Bertrand Piccard and Brian Jones*).

Trying to keep the right altitude in order to maintain a good trajectory, the balloon was sometimes only a few hundred feet above the top of the clouds (*Bertrand Piccard and Brian Jones*).

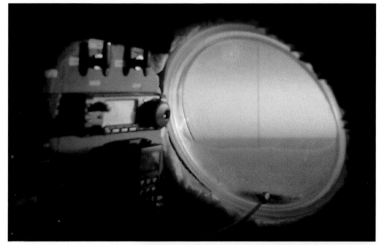

As the sun rose over China, the entire country was covered by clouds (*Bertrand Piccard and Brian Jones*).

Travelling for five days at slow speed and low altitude above the Pacific, with thunderstorm clouds in the distance that could tear the balloon apart, the ocean became a mirror in which Bertrand and Brian confronted their emotions, doubts and anxiety (*Bertrand Piccard and Brian Jones*).

On the sixth day of the Pacific crossing, the balloon finally entered the jet stream south of Hawaii and was surrounded by typical cirrus clouds coloured by the sunset (*Bertrand Piccard and Brian Jones*).

The crossing of the Gulf of Mexico was the worst period of the flight. The balloon began to head for Venezuela instead of Africa at low speed, consuming far too much propane. Inside the gondola, Brian and Bertrand were out of breath with suspected pulmonary pre-oedema. When Brian woke up, both of them realized they needed to wear oxygen masks to get their breath back (*Bertrand Piccard and Brian Jones*).

one of the balloons, be dropped and give a hang-gliding demonstra-
tion. I accepted immediately – and that was how I entered the world of
ballooning. So now it was fantastic to have this man suddenly come past
in a plane over India, and to hear his voice. He told me he had tears
pouring from his eyes, and that the whole of the Swiss delegation was
crammed into the cockpit, all crying, such was the emotional shock of
seeing our beautiful balloon, alone in the sky, riding the winds of
heaven 10,000 kilometres from home.

That encounter was one of the little signs of fate that seemed to mark
our enterprise. As I said, *Orbiter 2* took off on my grandfather's birthday,
and *Orbiter 3* on my own. Luc Trullemans came from the very institute of
meteorology that had guided my grandfather to the stratosphere in 1931.
Later, over the Pacific, we flew close to the Mariana Trench, where my
father made his dive to the deepest part of the ocean.

Also over India, the film producer Garfield Kennedy sent up a chase
plane to film the balloon in flight. After several delays, including one
caused by an intake of the wrong fuel, the turbo-prop aircraft flew past
us three or four hundred metres away and took some reasonable
footage. Unfortunately, all it showed was the balloon flying in the sky,
and we could have been anywhere in the world. Another problem was
that the microwave link between our cameras and theirs did not work,
and the film crew had to wait until after we landed to get shots inside
the gondola.

That afternoon brought one of the most memorable moments of the
flight: Brian and I were together in the cockpit, and we suddenly
realized we could see the peaks of the Himalayas, poking up through
the clouds away to our left. They were probably 300 miles off, but we
were so high that they made a stunning array along the northern
horizon. One mountain stood out taller than all the rest, so we thought
it must be Everest. I had always been envious of Branson because he
had phenomenal views of Everest when he crossed the prohibited part
of China: the shots taken from a chase plane of the *ICO Global
Challenger* among the 8,000-metre peaks are the most fabulous pictures
I have ever seen of a balloon in the air. Now, even though the Himalayas
were far away, seeing them for ourselves we felt we had to some extent
caught up with him.

I had already begun faxing ahead, once a day, to the Chinese to say that we were on our way and were going to be able to fulfil the conditions they had imposed. I also gave them our estimated time of arrival over the southwestern border. They never answered, but because I had had some experience of dealing with them I didn't really expect to hear much and took no news to be good news.

I felt more and more grateful to the three stalwart air controllers in Geneva who were smoothing our path around the world with such efficiency and good humour. At 11:34 on the morning of 9 March I faxed our own people:

> Hello. Would you please pass on this fax to Swiss Control. We specially want to thank Patrick, Greg and Nik for all the work they do for our expedition, and all the help they bring us. It is so comfortable and safe to know that local air traffic controllers are also informed by Swiss Control. Many thanks and best regards to all of you. Brian and Bertrand.

BRIAN

India went to our heads. The jokes passing between capsule and Control became more and more ridiculous. Because I had mis-typed my name on a previous fax, I continued with variations and took to signing faxes 'Banir', 'Bnria' and 'Biriani'. Brian Smith signed himself 'Nairb', and made remarks like 'Sikh and ye shall find'. All this was brought on by the inefficiency of Indian communications, which drove us nearly demented. Radio contact was almost always difficult, and we relied a lot on relays via passing aircraft. Pilots were helpful about passing on messages, but it was annoying that local air controllers kept demanding to know our position – often every ten minutes.

On the night of 8–9 March our burners had started faltering again, and at midday on the 9th I faxed down:

> Having thought we had fixed the burner autopilot trip-out last night, Captain B took control and the thing tripped again. One really does have to talk to it in English, and especially if one gets serious then it is *très important* that it is a genuine English lump hammer . . . Calcutta handed us on (or is it off?) to Dacca. 'Radar service terminated' – he could have fooled me. Bertrand

going to bed soon, so hopefully the burners will settle down too. If Mr Singh calls thanking you for the little green bags coming down from the heavens, deny all knowledge, or tell him it's an Italian take-away. Nairb.

Soon we were over Bangladesh, and the controllers there proved thoroughly hospitable, the tone being set by the first message we got from Dacca:

Hotel Bravo – Bravo Romeo Alpha. This is Dacca Control. On behalf of the authorities and the people of my country, I wish you the best of luck and a very good flight around the world.

Our passage over that friendly country was brief. Soon we were over Indian territory again and heading for Burma, now known as Myanmar. Although we were heading almost due east, we were gradually edging to the north, creeping up towards the critical 26th parallel – and this kept us on tenterhooks. Back in Geneva our weathermen were absolutely steadfast, telling us we had to go right up, almost to the limit, where the wind would take us dead east at 090 degrees. Our air controllers were also working with their usual tenacity. 'ATC in Myanmar are aware of your position and are happy,' John Albury told me on the evening of 9 March:

Greg is looking after Myanmar and Patrick is on the case with China. There is no traffic in the area, so that is one thing less to worry about. Be sure that you have the mountain heights absolutely correct. I have the highest peak at 14,000 feet at a place called DALI, by a large lake approx 30 km from the large town XIAGUAN. Peak is at 25.42 N 100.04 E. If you miss that, you are OK. Please confirm receipt for sure.

The Myanmar air controllers obviously knew about us, but they had trouble grasping the idea of a round-the-world flight, and we had a splendid exchange:

Air traffic control: Hotel Bravo – Bravo Romeo Alpha, what is your departure point and destination?

Myself: Departure point, Château d'Oex, Switzerland. Destination, somewhere in northern Africa.

Air traffic control, after several seconds' silence: If you're going from Switzerland to northern Africa, what in *hell* are you doing in Myanmar?

In Geneva Greg was having similar conversations. His contacts were quite helpful but intensely bureaucratic. 'We need a clearance number,' one of them insisted. 'We cannot give you permission without.' As lengthy discussions proceeded, the balloon was speeding across the northern part of the country, and when, after about four hours, the controller phoned Geneva with the great news that he had finally obtained a clearance number, Greg was able to tell him, 'Thank you very much. The balloon's already over China!'

We seemed to flash across Myanmar. We were making nearly 80 knots, and in any case we went over a narrow part of the country. For the first time we encountered the particular kind of turbulence – in the form of waves – that is caused among mountains by wind hitting steep faces and becoming unstable. As I watched my instruments I suddenly noticed the variometer shooting downwards. The balloon was dropping at the rate of 600 feet a minute. For a few moments I thought there was something wrong and that we were falling out of the sky. The movement was nothing like as sudden and violent as when an airliner hits turbulence, but it was alarming to see from the variometer that we were changing height so rapidly. Instinctively I started burning, but found I couldn't stop the descent – and then I realized what was happening. When I took my hands off everything we started climbing again, just as fast. I reported to Control:

I think we must be in mountain waves. Balloon going up 600 feet per minute and the same down, track varying widely. Think I'll just let it do its own thing for a while and see what happens. No point in fighting it. Flight level varying between 240 and 255.

Keeping to our normal schedule, Bertrand had gone to bed. Before he did, we had held a discussion about how we should enter China. Should we both be in the cockpit when we crossed the border? After all, it was going to be a momentous occasion – one towards which we had worked all out for more than two years. In the end we decided that it wasn't worth breaking the sleep patterns which we had established so successfully: we would both be tired the next day, and nothing much would be gained. So Bertrand went to sleep, feeling slightly sad to miss what he felt would be a 'fabulous moment'.

The Chinese had seen us coming, and their first reaction was entirely characteristic. They called Control and said, 'Your balloon's heading for the prohibited zone. It must land.' Luc and Pierre told them not to worry, assuring them that the wind would keep us south of the 26th parallel and that we would not break the magic barrier. Control faxed us:

> When you get a minute it might be prudent to try to raise the Chinese on HF. They have requested we contact them by radio. Please try Kunming Control . . . just so they know you are kunming.

The day before, using a special number which he had obtained from the Swiss Embassy, Bertrand had tried to call the head of the air traffic control at Beijing. He got through all right but found that nobody there spoke English. When he said, 'This is the Breitling Orbiter balloon', only Chinese came back, and when he asked for an English speaker there was no further reply. After a baffled silence, the man had hung up on him.

A few minutes later I reported:

> John – Thanks for the concern. I have spoken to Yangon [formerly Rangoon] on HF with difficulty but OK. I have tried Kunming Control, without success so far. Re 'No traffic to worry about': there was an aircraft at similar level, probably no more than five miles away, crossed in front. I put out a call on 121.5 to draw his attention to me, but no response. Tricky so-and-sos, these Chinese. I think I can choose a track now. Do you want

090 or 085? I know I want to stay south of 25.5 N.

John confirmed that our best track was 090, 'so stay with that if you can'. He said he would bring the other air traffic to Greg's attention, and suggested that we were probably still too far from Kunming to make radio contact, as well as being shielded by mountains. When I did eventually get through to a Chinese controller, his immediate response was none too welcoming. 'You are not allowed to cross 26 degrees north,' he said. To which I replied, 'Yes, we're aware of that.' John – about to go off duty in the control centre and never one to miss the chance of a pun – sent a fax saying, 'Nice doing business with you. By the way, we reckon it is now 5 a.m. where you are, so you should see a chink of light on the horizon.'

Shortly before dawn on the morning of 10 March we were speeding towards the Chinese border at 84 knots and a height of 26,000 feet, within half a degree, or thirty miles, of our permitted limit. I faxed exultantly:

Step right up for the main attraction, boys and girls. Ninety degrees you have. China here we come.

CHAPTER EIGHT

CHINESE PUZZLES

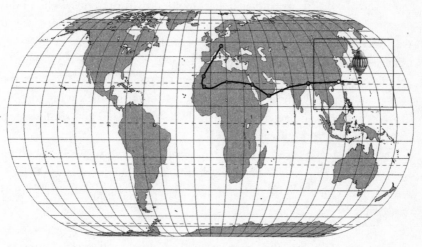

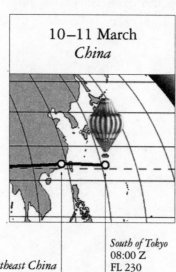

10–11 March
China

South of Tokyo
08:00 Z
FL 230
38 knots

Southeast China
08:00 Z
FL 180
70 knots

BERTRAND

I don't think Brian would ever have been in a position to utter those words had it not been for the intensive diplomatic manoeuvring that took place in the months leading up to our launch. Before the flight of *Orbiter 2* the Swiss Embassy in Beijing had been extremely active on my behalf, working to negotiate permission for an overflight. Arthur Mattli, the *Chargé d'Affaires*, and his wife Florence had even spent hours standing in the snow in front of the closed door of the Ministry of Foreign Affairs trying to deliver a diplomatic note. After our attempt had ended in Burma, they told me they were prepared to try again, but this time they reckoned there would be no chance of success unless I myself came out to China. The Chinese, they said, always preferred to meet the people they were negotiating with to make sure they were serious.

So it was that in August 1998 we went out. The party consisted of Alan Noble, Tony Brown, myself and Michèle, and Pierre Blanchoud, the team's aeronautical adviser. We flew Swissair from Zurich to Beijing, where we were delighted to meet our diplomats. Although we had talked to them for hours on the telephone and exchanged innumerable faxes, we had never met them in person. They arranged for us to visit the National Sports Commission, the Ministry of Foreign Affairs and the Civil Aviation Authority, where we met the deputy director of all the country's air controllers. Discussions were conducted through an interpreter, though the Swiss ambassador, Dominique Dreyer, spoke excellent Chinese and was often able to clarify important points.

At the Ministry of Foreign Affairs we had a formal meeting, sitting in big armchairs ranged round the sides of the room, with nothing in the middle. The first words of our hosts, translated by interpreters, were:

> We are grateful to you for coming to see us, because we think we can solve the problems together. But you have to realize that by heading straight for China last year in your other balloon, and asking for permission to enter only the day before, you caused us enormous difficulties. We worked very hard to arrange clearance, and you had it two days later. But unfortunately, due to other problems, by then you had had to land in Burma.

This was not correct. We had applied for clearance more than a year before that take-off, and the Chinese knew it perfectly well. But all I said was, 'I'm really sorry we caused so much trouble last year, and that's why we've come now, with an important part of our team, so that the same problem doesn't happen again.' So our discussions got off to a good start, and after we left the meeting I asked the Swiss ambassador, 'Was I right to answer like that?'

'Absolutely,' he said quietly.

'Well!' I said indignantly, 'I really wanted to tell him that what he was saying was wrong.'

'He knows!' the ambassador exclaimed with a smile. 'He knows perfectly well. There's no need to tell him. By being polite you saved the situation. Now we're talking about the future, so don't worry about anything said about the past.'

On our way out, the man from the Ministry of Foreign Affairs said quietly, 'I hope you win this race round the world. You're a good team, and we thank you for building good relations with China.'

At another meeting our hosts assured us that they were sympathetic to our project, not least because ours was the only team that had taken the trouble to travel out and meet them. Nevertheless, they explained that to have balloons flying over China would cause them serious problems. One difficulty was that in most places they had no radar, and civilian traffic was controlled by telephone. When a pilot wanted to fly from A to B, he had to call air traffic control and ask for clearance. He might easily be told to wait for ten or twenty minutes because another aircraft was already using that route. If a balloon came across the country, the authorities would have to cancel all flights for the duration of its passage. There would be no difficulty if, two months in advance, we could send precise details of where, when, at what height and speed and on what heading the balloon would cross the border.

That was impossible, of course, and we said so.

Then, through the interpreter, the deputy director said, 'I have an idea. Could you fly above the traffic?'

'We *could*,' I told him, 'but at that altitude there would probably be hardly any wind, so it might take us a month to cross the country.'

He laughed and said, 'We don't want that. So you'd better stay at 30,000.' He emphasized that he did *not* want us flying over northern areas, and least of all over Tibet. He was afraid that we might be forced down in some place so remote or mountainous that the Chinese would not be able to rescue us. They would then lose face by appearing to be incompetent.

The best I could promise was that we would let the Chinese know three days before take-off that we were about to start, and we would warn them when we were twenty-four hours away from the border. We could then tell them our entry and exit points, and once we were in their air space we would send a satellite fax every ten minutes giving our exact position to within twenty metres.

This satisfied them. On those conditions, they said, they would allow us to fly, but only along a precisely defined corridor, which would be specified three days before we arrived. If the wind brought us to the border at a different point, they would move the corridor to accommodate us.

At the end of the week we went home happy, with the feeling that the Chinese liked and trusted us. Three months later we received our permission. So did all the other teams – although in their case they were required to keep their flight path either below the 26th parallel or above the 43rd. As I mentioned earlier, when Richard Branson made his flight in December 1998, we passed up one favourable weather window because we could see that the wind would probably push us over the areas that we knew were out of bounds. Sure enough, as Branson flew southwards over Nepal, the wind changed suddenly and sent him far to the north, across the prohibited parts of China.

The reaction was predictable: through their embassies the Chinese immediately sent faxes to all the other balloon teams saying that permissions were cancelled until the situation had been re-evaluated. I quickly responded with a message saying, 'I accept your decision. We're not at all happy, but we will not take off until new permission is forthcoming.'

We then began intensive discussions, pointing out that we had taken the trouble to visit China and had promised to respect whatever conditions were imposed on us. In reply, the Chinese said they had supposed a pilot would have better control of his balloon. According to the letter we received from them, Branson had been unable to steer accurately and had not spoken to any air traffic controllers; nobody knew where he was (they wrote) and the authorities had had to cancel ten commercial flights.

Now, they said, we must give an absolute guarantee that if we wanted to overfly China we would keep south of 26 degrees latitude or north of 43. As far as we were concerned, north of 43 was impossible because it lay along the border with Russia and was the most dangerous air space imaginable: any aircraft passing through it was liable to be shot at by both the Russians and the Chinese. The southern alternative was possible, and the Chinese favoured it because in those areas – the main commercial air corridors – they did have radar, and all the air traffic controllers spoke English.

But what had happened to the earlier promise of a special corridor? The answer was that the military authorities, infuriated by Branson's flight, had clamped down and refused to allow it. After a while we began to feel that we were dealing with two different groups – one that wanted to help us, the other opposed to all balloons – and it seemed that there was a good deal of argument between the two.

Our exchanges were conducted partly through the Swiss Embassy in Beijing and partly through the Chinese Embassy in Bern, and with the latter I had a stroke of luck. One of the diplomats in Switzerland had translated some of the *Tin-Tin* stories – Hergé's wonderful cartoon series about a boy adventurer – into Chinese, and when he realized that Hergé's model for Professeur Tournesol (better known to English readers as Professor Calculus) had been my grandfather, he was thrilled. Although he had no power to influence decisions, he was immensely helpful, preparing all transmissions and forwarding them promptly. He also came to see our balloon in Château d'Oex, where he was able to test the quality of our communications equipment for himself by calling Beijing from the gondola.

Even with his help, the process of negotiation was extremely wearing, mainly because of the time difference: 8 a.m. Chinese time, when the working day began in Beijing, was 1 a.m. our time, and often we would get a telephone call between two and four in the morning saying that our latest fax had been received but that extra documents were needed. At our home in Lausanne Michèle would often be up half the night, typing, printing and faxing the documents which I was dictating from the Hôtel de Ville in Château d'Oex.

We tried every possible channel: people who had contacts in the Chinese press, people who knew the Chinese President, people who knew the air traffic controllers, people with friends working for Chinese commercial airlines. Other balloon teams were badgering away as well, all of which must have produced an incredible amount of work for the Chinese.

Many factors swayed things in our favour. Chief among them was the deep involvement of the Swiss Ministry of Foreign Affairs and the Ministry of Defence and Sport, whose representatives put our project at a level of national interest in their discussions with China. Then there was the fact that we had a Swiss-registered balloon, and the Chinese were angry with British balloonists. In the past I had taken the trouble to obtain a certificate of airworthiness from the Swiss Federal Organisation of Civil Aviation, and this appeared to be helpful. Finally, there was our behaviour: we never criticized any Chinese reaction.

For two months, every time we saw a good weather slot coming up, I faxed the Chinese to say that we had a chance to launch but that we were not going to take it because we respected their decision. Finally, I think, we won their confidence, and they granted us permission on three conditions. First, we had to guarantee that we would fly below 26 degrees north; second, that if we strayed north of the limit, we would land; and third, that if we found ourselves approaching China on a trajectory that would bring us to the border at an inappropriate point, we would come down in India, Pakistan or Iran.

Brian and I went to the Chinese Embassy to give the necessary guarantees. The papers were in both languages, and when the First Secretary asked me, 'Are you willing to sign?' I said, 'Do you think I have any choice?' That made him laugh, and he replied, 'Well – it's the only way you can do it.'

In one way we had achieved an important victory, but at the same time we had signed what might turn out to be an official death warrant for our flight, for we had put our names to an agreement that would force us down if the wind sent us only slightly off course. Our target was minute, amounting to only about five per cent of the country and offering a very narrow front to anyone approaching from the west.

At one stage the Chinese attempted to add one more condition: the Swiss government had to guarantee that I would keep my promises. Naturally the government said it could not give guarantees on behalf of one of its citizens – to do so would be illegal. I phoned the Chinese Embassy.

'Can *your* government give a guarantee that none of your diplomats will exceed the speed limit on Swiss highways?' I asked.

'Of course not,' came the answer, 'but we don't care. Just get a guarantee from your government and we'll give permission.'

The exchanges went on and on. It was terrible – a real dialogue of the deaf. But at last we managed to find a formula which the Chinese could accept: our side guaranteed that M. Bertrand Piccard and Mr

Brian Jones committed themselves to land if they were pushed out of the correct approach corridor.

All this made me realize that if we wanted to go round the world, we also had to make a tour of all the countries, mentalities and personalities involved. We would not just be dealing with wind and weather: we would have to accommodate the whims of a huge number of human beings.

When I woke up at 23:00 Zulu on 10 March 1999, the first light of dawn was breaking. I stuck my head through the curtain and asked, 'Where are we?'

'We're in CHINA!' Brian replied.

That was an incredible moment – *so* nice! We could feel that everyone at Control was tremendously excited. Our weathermen had sent us on a swirling trajectory of 13,000 kilometres and threaded us through the eye of a needle. Their feat was a masterpiece of planning, and quite rightly they were proud of it.

Excitement was also running high at the Swiss Embassy in Beijing. The diplomats there had become real friends, and when at last they heard my voice emanating from Chinese air space they came through on the satellite telephone, describing how they too had burst into tears of sheer delight. Florence and Arthur Mattli faxed to Geneva a cartoon of a decidedly Chinese-looking balloon bearing the hand-written message, '*Chers Bertrand et Brian, Bienvenue en Chine!*' and embellished with the signatures of all their colleagues, including the ambassador, Dominique Dreyer. Control described the cartoon to us as they had no means of faxing pictures.

Cecilia Smith was on duty and told us that everybody at the control centre was thrilled by our progress. 'Sometimes we feel as if we are living in a dream,' she faxed:

Jo is writing her diary, and has just mentioned that while she slept today you left India, flew over Bangladesh, over Burma and approached the Chinese border. And she wasn't asleep that long! Well, these are extraordinary times.

Feeling very emotional, I replied:

Hallo, my friends. Thank you very much for your nice fax. I think one of our greatest strokes of luck is to have such a wonderful team. It's fabulous here to feel how much you are behind us and with us. Warmest regards, Bertrand. PS FL between 240 and 250, with constant track 88 at 79 knots.

The weather did not match the occasion. Rain was falling on China. Almost the entire country was covered by bad weather, and the only hole we found in the clouds was over Kunming. There we saw the airport runways and planes on the tarmac. I called the air traffic controller and said, 'If you look up now, you'll see our balloon. We're exactly overhead.' He replied, 'I have no window. I cannot look outside.' Then another voice broke in, saying, '*I* can see you. It's beautiful!' The speaker never identified himself, but we thought he must have been a pilot, sitting in his cockpit on the runway. Then and later we found the Chinese air traffic controllers extremely professional. Their English was adequate provided that we stuck to the limited vocabulary of international air-control jargon. Talking to each other in Chinese, they passed on our position from one controller to the next.

We had about 1,500 miles to go to cross China, but already our met men had almost put that huge country from their minds. They knew we were going to skim across it, straight as an arrow, on our 90-degree heading, with the 26th parallel no more than thirty miles to our left, and their minds were already ranging far ahead:

We are very happy that we could drive you into China within half a degree latitude of the target. This is the result of eight days of sweating for you and us. From now on it is important to stay on a northerly track in order to attack the Pacific. If we stay at the present altitude we risk to drift towards the equator in the medium range.

So we propose that you come down to FL 180 after 04:00 Zulu . . . The track should evolve to 095 magnetic during the next twenty-four hours. It should not exceed 100. The speed should evolve to 60 knots first, below 50 knots later. The weather will become cloudy, but the top will not exceed FL 120.

We will leave China at around 15:00 Zulu. The track should then slowly bend northwards. We will stay at this altitude for forty-eight to sixty hours. We can then catch a good jet stream at higher levels, leading into the middle of the Atlantic in nine days. Best regards, Luc and Pierre.

There we were, sweeping on at 80 knots, and they were telling us to slow down! That was a really difficult moment for me because I loved the feeling of going fast on that easterly track – and now, without really understanding why, we had to vent helium, lose height and slow down. The clouds were starting to build, and some were right beside the balloon, with their tops above us. They did not look really dangerous, but they could have created serious turbulence. Also, we didn't want the envelope to get soaked by their condensation. I felt very tense. The balloon was moving like a porpoise, dropping 900 feet, climbing 900 feet, and the clouds were boiling all round us – a fascinating but most unnerving combination.

As always, our air controllers were smoothing a path ahead of us. For Patrick Schelling, Taiwan was 'an easy one', because he had personal contacts in the tower there and had arranged everything in advance. Also, our steady track and speed enabled him to predict exactly when we would enter Taiwanese air space. As we approached, a peculiar fax reached Swiss Control from Vietnam, addressed to British Airways:

Vould you plese lett us hev the balon campton present position and ETA over Ho Chi Minh FIR.

Greg replied that he was at Swiss Control, not British Airways, and that the balloon had already passed Vietnam – whereupon a second fax arrived:

We are received message of you. Your reply is highly appreciated.

BRIAN

When I joined Bertrand in the cockpit he craftily turned on the video camera and caught me preparing my breakfast. As I started spreading butter he said, 'That's wonderful *panettone*. I'll zoom in on it – it will give everyone an appetite.'

'This is breakfast on 11 March at 8 a.m. Zulu,' I commentated.

'If you're already making your *panettone* for tomorrow,' Bertrand told me, 'it may be a little dry, because today's the tenth. I have to check with your beard. Yes – it's a beard of ten days, not eleven!'

After that burst of high spirits he became preoccupied because we had lost our track and he was having to burn repeatedly in an effort to jump over clouds. He phoned the weathermen and said that conditions were lousy. 'Why do we have to fly so low?' he demanded. 'Well,' they said, 'we've done a re-evaluation, and you can go back to your original flight level of 270.' Back we went, with the impression that in the past three or four hours we'd lost helium, burnt propane and wasted time – all for nothing.

After such a build-up, China was a bit of a non-event. We could hardly believe that we would keep going fast and straight across the entire country – but that was what happened. With minimal steering by us, the balloon held its 90-degree track with an almost uncanny accuracy. As somebody remarked, it was like walking a 1,500-mile tightrope. Because of the bad weather, we saw nothing until we approached the east coast. There the clouds began to break up, but the air was hazy and the visibility still poor. My main feeling was one of relief that we had gone through the eye of the needle with no difficulty. Until that moment China had been the great bogey looming ahead – the one place where our flight might be brought to a sudden halt by sheer human obstinacy. Now that the danger was past, we both felt buoyant.

Just before we left Chinese air space at 12:04 I faxed, 'Got the next map out – it's all blue.' For the second time in the flight we were at a point of no return. The first had been at take-off, and now the biggest obstacle of all lay ahead of us: the Pacific. Just to raise Bertrand's morale, I said, 'D'you realize that the Pacific is wider than the distance we've done from Château d'Oex to here?'

As if to show that he knew what we were feeling at that moment, Stefano Albinati, a very straight guy not given to displays of emotion, sent us this fax:

I just wanted to tell you that although I'm comfortably seated in the Control Centre, my heart is beating at 200 knots per second. The Pacific in front of you is big, but not as big as my admiration for what you are doing. I wish you all the best for the crossing.

CHAPTER NINE

PACIFIC BLUES

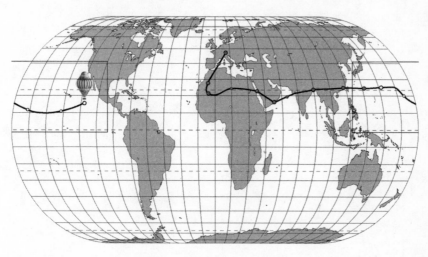

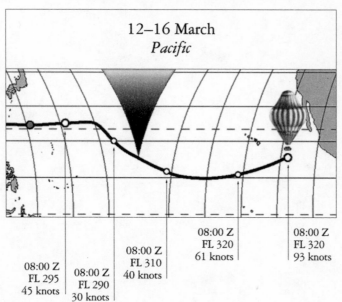

12–16 March
Pacific

08:00 Z
FL 295
45 knots

08:00 Z
FL 290
30 knots

08:00 Z
FL 310
40 knots

08:00 Z
FL 320
61 knots

08:00 Z
FL 320
93 knots

BERTRAND

Faced by 8,000 miles of water, I picked up my pen and wrote:

> This is exactly my definition of adventure. Adventure is some-
> thing out of the usual pattern, a point at which you cannot avoid
> confronting the unknown, so that you have to dig inside yourself
> to find the courage and resources to deal with what may lie
> ahead, and to succeed.

Many major human achievements are not real adventures because
although they may be very dangerous, the people involved know
exactly what is going to happen. For us, the ocean ahead was a
complete unknown: facing it was a difficult moment – but a fabulous
one. I love dealing with that kind of situation, because I find that having
to tackle the unknown helps me to deal with life when I come back.
Life itself is a big unknown and a big adventure. But many people never
realize how interesting the adventure of life can be. So when we were
confronted by the Pacific, I found it a beautiful metaphor of life itself.

Yet if I was excited, I was also frightened. As the sun went down,
while we were between China and Taiwan, the electrically operated

valves on one side of the burner array jammed open. Huge flames roared up into the hot-air cone, and to stop them burning a hole in the envelope we hastily shut off the fuel. Switching to the three burners on the other side, we had to reset the timers on the instrument panel and stabilize the balloon. We wondered if dirt had got into the system, but technicians on the ground thought that the cause of the trouble was probably cold, and that the valves were becoming iced up. We could well have done without such problems at this point: now that we were approaching the colossal expanse of the Pacific, the possibility of total burner failure was infinitely more alarming than when we had been over land. I had only to think of Richard Branson and Andy Elson, both of whom had gone down in the ocean.

To make matters worse, our heading had swung down to 101 degrees and the wind seemed to be taking us much too far south. At that stage our plan was to cross the Pacific in a straight line – but already were losing the track we wanted. It was a southward deviation that had ended Branson's latest attempt.

For the first time I wondered if our valiant met men were fully confident about the next move. They had worked incredibly hard to steer us safely to China and across it, and perhaps because all their energy had been focused on the mainland, they seemed unsure what strategy to adopt for the Pacific. Certainly they were hampered by a shortage of information – there was very little weather information coming from those vast wastes – and while one of their models showed that we should take a northern route, the other showed the opposite – that a southern route was our best bet. All they could suggest for the moment was that we dawdle while they calculated new trajectories.

'These problems shatter the fragile confidence that we've built up,' I wrote. All our high technology had been working so well that the sudden malfunction of the burners gave us quite a shock. When I went to bed I felt really scared, and to get to sleep I resorted to self-hypnosis.

To disconnect from the concentration of flying the balloon, and to stop doing fuel calculations in my head or worrying about the noise of the burners, I employed a favourite technique. Lying on my back, I closed my right fist and squeezed hard, with my curled-up forefinger and thumb facing me, imagining that I was crushing all the stress and tension inside my hand. Then I inhaled deeply and held my breath, exerting as much force as I could in blocking my breathing and clenching my fist while gazing hard at a point on my hand. When I could not hold out any more, I breathed out and let my fist open of its own accord. Already I could feel the tension transforming into relaxation, and in my head I recited a slow account of how the lassitude was spreading to my wrist, to my forearm, to my upper arm, to my shoulder, to the other arm, to my head, to the back, the abdomen, the stomach and the feet – until I felt completely relaxed.

Then I told myself a story about how I had gone outside the gondola and was lying on a very warm and comfortable cloud, looking at the balloon, which was drifting gently away from me and being flown by Brian, so that I didn't have to take care of it.

Relaxing on my cloud, I visualized the balloon flying through a gigantic rainbow and passing through all its colours. First came red, the colour of excitement and stress; next, orange (a bit softer); then yellow (like a wonderful field of oilseed rape, very restful to the eyes and spirit); then green (like the prairies of the American Mid-West, with a gentle breeze moving the grass in soft waves). Then came blue (even more relaxing, because it is the sky and the sea together, with no horizon between). Finally the balloon went into indigo, the deep shade of the night, with practically no colour any more, everything almost black. When I could scarcely make out the balloon any longer, I turned on my side and fell into a deep sleep.

BRIAN

Like Bertrand, I was thoroughly on edge. We never became the slightest bit irritated with each other, but as the night wore on I did get more and more ratty with the control centre. We had signed a written agreement with Oakland Oceanic Control, the organization near San Francisco responsible for air traffic in the area ahead of us, and just before 09:00 Zulu I faxed our own team saying:

Well, it looks like the decision has been made to have a go at this large puddle in front of us. Please confirm that you have a copy of the Oceanic airspace reporting contract available for all teams to read. We assume you will take care of initial notification. Good morning from Brian. FL 180, climbing to FL 260 with permission.

I followed that a few minutes later with, 'Lock Luc's skis in the cupboard until this flight is over. By order. Captains Piccard and Jones.' The message continued:

These problems have put Bertrand completely off his dinner. I find it very hard to believe the trouble with the valves is a temperature problem. We had a lower ambient temperature over Burma last night and they worked perfectly. Anyway, it's only minus 23 degrees. What will happen if it goes to minus 56?

Minutes later, up came another message, this time from Alan. Evidently he felt we weren't doing enough to let other people know where we were, and his patronising tone did nothing to soothe my feelings:

The Pacific Ocean is a large and reasonably empty place. And I don't want to alarm you, but . . . the air lanes between Taiwan and Honolulu, and Japan and the Americas, are quite busy. There is no radar control and possibly nobody looking out of the front windows of passing jet airliners. Aircraft will be flying assigned flight levels, and it is important that you advise the controlling authority on HF, and the Control Centre by Inmarsat, before – that is BEFORE – commencing any altitude excursions. Technically, I think you should have permission before executing any change.

If you change flight level by mistake, or in an emergency, you should broadcast on 121.5 your position and details of your old/present flight level and intended new flight level. Then advise ATC and Control . . . suggest you leave a transponder squawking, as some modern aircraft have anti-collision radars that will pick up your signal.

Some new video/digital pics would be welcome celebrating your passage across China. Tomorrow it won't be news.

It seemed to me that almost everything Alan said was perfectly obvious. Talk about teaching grandmothers to suck eggs! My answer, partly ironic, showed distinct signs of irritation:

Thank you for that confidence booster. I read the Oceanic agreement a couple of hours ago. Three hundred feet margin is very difficult to keep to, but I'm sure we'll do our best. Transponder has been permanently on for fixed-wing collision-avoidance systems. Bertrand Spielberg is in bed now, so no piccys for a while. We were too busy over China to play with the cameras.

By midday I had more to worry about than the erratic valves. 'Track seems to be veering slowly but steadily,' I reported. 'On this track we will be a long, long way south. Would like some reassurance please that all is OK, and an idea of what is likely to happen track and speed wise.' For the first time in the flight I felt that the people on the ground weren't really responding to our needs.

On top of worries about our heading, I saw that dead ahead of us on the map lay two danger areas, designated W 172 and W 184, about which we had no information. Perhaps it was just as well that I did not know that, at Swiss Control, Patrick Schelling was already grappling with a sudden and potentially explosive problem. The first time he heard the name Naha, he was unaware that any such place existed; it turned out to be the main city on the island of Okinawa, and above it was an air-training area. When Patrick called the Naha control tower, the supervisor, who had only limited English, kept saying in a high voice, 'Danger area! Very hot! Very hot!' The man seemed extremely nervous, crying, 'Circumnavigate!' But our air controllers could see that if we kept going we were going to penetrate area W 184, and once more their only option was to negotiate. As on previous occasions, they were dealing with people from another culture and had to be extremely careful not to give offence.

Patrick tried every conceivable way of getting his opposite number to give us clearance: he soft-soaped him with his spiel about all being brothers in air traffic control, but he never succeeded in making him utter the magic word. The supervisor told him that Japanese aircraft were flying and that he could not ground them. Several times he repeated his warning cry, 'Very hot! Very hot!' Eventually, after protracted discussion, Patrick confronted him with a radical question: 'Can you ensure the safety of the balloon?' The sudden answer was, 'Yes, yes' – and that was the end of the argument.

Up in the gondola I was unaware of these exchanges, but I was nervous about the danger zone and agitated by the lack of information coming from Geneva. My deteriorating temper showed clearly in successive messages:

John – Looks like the Breitling bus is going to blunder on through the danger area W 172. Has anybody said anything about it in Swiss Control? FL 250, track 097, 84 knots. So fast in fact that my hair (what little I have – lots compared to some, though) is blown back. We have built-in showers here. One can stand under the top dome or the fuel control unit most of the day and get lots of cold water falling. Course it's all frozen at the moment, saving itself for when Bertrand steps out of the bunk right below it.

John – I don't mean to get a strop on, but . . . Have you stopped putting our questions on a board? Last few messages have asked if all the teams are *au fait* with the procedures over the Pacific as per the contract we signed with the Americans, HF frequencies, reassurance from Luc/Pierre that we are going the right way, any progress on setting up the satellite phone for Pacific on rod antenna, and comments on the danger area coming up . . .

This last brought a sharp retort from Alan:

Listen, Testy Face. We thought you were joking. Have you read the contract? It doesn't affect you for several days crossing the Pacific, until you come under the control of Oakland, California . . . At the moment you are under the control of the Japanese, with whom we do not have a contract . . . Luc says track 094 is the perfect track, but your last reported 092 will be OK if you can't do better . . .

Danger Area W 172 is permanent and unlimited. ATC will

normally tell you if you can't go through, in which case you must turn round and go back. Seriously, you've been through quite a few danger and restricted areas – you can't balloon around the world without doing this – and if any are active, it would be normal for Swiss Control to be notified when the flight plan is filed, and then advise the aircraft before penetration. We are checking W 172 and W 184 with the Japanese by phone and will get back to you.

Danger area W 184: coordinated with the supervisor at Naha for clearance, but they have a big air-warfare exercise there tonight at 22:00 Z, with fighters, bombers, missiles, submarines, so better get a move on and don't worry if the bangs and flashes rock the gondola a bit. The Japanese self-defence force is aware that you are in the region and that you will probably cross the area. So don't worry . . . too much.

I thought this must be at least partly a joke, but it didn't strike me as very funny. 'OK, Buggery Bollocks,' I exploded. 'You said you were going to look in the book re Satphone. We know you of old – you probably have the procedures in your head and in your Burgundy bag, neither of which the team can get to.' Presently I realized that the exchanges were getting overheated: after receiving a hesitant and sweet note from Debbie asking for our flight level I felt a little guilty and calmed down:

I'm not really miffed at anybody down there. It's just that our dearly beloved Flight Director is more efficient at winding up than the chain on a cuckoo clock.

John replied:

You upset us so much that everyone has gone back to the hotel for nosh and wine, and I have been given the duty of turning the lights off before I join them! Joking really. No – we still all love you dearly . . . I thought you would have enough entertainment watching the forthcoming air display around you. Can you let me know if the Japanese air force are using F-16Js or the older version of F-16Gs with the earlier radio antennae and extra wing stores and older leading-edge flaps (serial nos would be appreciated).

Tense as things were in the capsule, we heard later that the atmosphere in the control centre had become far from comfortable. I was so preoccupied with my own difficulties that it did not occur to me that our teams in Geneva were also working under considerable stress. Their hotel accommodation was comfortable enough, and they were getting good meals whenever they wanted them, but at work the pressure was steadily building. Paradoxically, the farther we flew and the greater our chance of success, the higher the tension mounted. My own close friends – John and Debbie, Smiffy and C – made my and Bertrand's safety their paramount concern, and they were on tenter-hooks for every minute of every shift, fearing that something could go wrong. As Smiffy remarked when the flight was over, 'It was like holding our breath for three weeks on end'.

After those barbed exchanges, he took Alan aside and asked him to ease off. Then Jo – who, according to the others, had been exhibiting heroic self-control for days on end – had a fit of hysterics, screamed at Alan that he was going to wreck our chances by being so unsympathetic, burst into tears, ran out of the room and locked herself in the loo.

The remarks about a major military exercise, which we thought were jokes, turned out to be absolutely true. We passed straight through danger area W 184 without seeing a thing – but we might have given ourselves a fright if we had had our noses glued to the portholes because a good many aircraft were flying that night.

Bad radio communications were yet another annoyance. 'No contact with Naha on this awful HF set,' I told John. 'Have had two aircraft call me on 121.5 to tell me to call Naha, but I can't hear a damned thing.' Just as I handed over to Bertrand, with the sun coming up, we got some reassurance in the form of a friendly fax from Oceanic Control at Oakland, California, promising us every assistance – but by then I'd had enough for one night.

BERTRAND

'Hello to all of you,' I faxed when I took over. 'I'm letting the balloon stabilize with no burning. It stays around FL 271 at track 092 and 74 knots. No HF contact with anybody except VHF on 121.5 with planes relaying to Naha or Tokyo. Time for my morning cup of Earl Grey tea.'

Later that morning we went over the island of Iwo Jima, which American forces captured from the Japanese after desperate battles in February 1945. A hat of cloud sat on top of its single volcanic peak, and on another little island nearby I could see an airfield, so I called the controller and said we were passing. He wasn't the slightest bit interested, but an American pilot picked up our conversation and came so close that I heard his engines.

'Who's flying near the balloon?' I called.

'US Navy Gulfstream 4,' he answered cheerfully, and asked a lot of questions about what we were doing. I reported to Control:

Flew overhead Iwo Jima. They didn't even bother looking up to see the balloon. Probably the last time something strange appeared in their sky it was some US Air Force bombers, fifty years ago. Maybe this time they were all in the shelters, but I promise you, I didn't use the toilet at that moment . . .

A reassuring message came from Control, settling the points that Brian had raised earlier: our teams in Geneva were all briefed on Pacific and Atlantic procedures, Luc and Pierre were confident we were going the right way, and the satellite telephone was now working. That same day – a big moment for me – we flew past the Mariana Trench. I was delighted to find that the line of my horizontal adventure was crossing the site of my father's great vertical endeavour, and I phoned him there and then to tell him.

At the end of the 1950s deep-sea diving had developed into a race rather like ours. On one side was the bathyscaphe *Trieste*, invented and built by my grandfather and father; on the other was a copy of their submersible built by the French Navy. I had read newspaper articles describing how keen the competition had become to reach the deepest point of the ocean, and I was very proud that my father had won the race. Now, overflying the Mariana Trench, I was taking part in another international contest of the same kind, against very rich and well-equipped competitors. Could I add one more victory to my family's tally? At some moments I was confident it would be my fate to succeed, but at others I began to think it impossible that my generation could continue this success story. As in the preparation of the project and the flight, I was oscillating between hope and anxiety. To have lived in that state for five years had been a most exhausting experience – but at least I was now close to the moment of truth.

BRIAN

People were now watching our progress from all over the world, and excited e-mail messages of encouragement had started to pour into the Breitling website. We learnt later from Alan Kirby – a retired British nuclear physicist who cheerfully described himself as 'a balloonatic' – that he downloaded nearly 5,000 e-mails from well-wishers, and altogether, during our flight, between 8,000 and 9,000 flooded in. They came from every corner of the earth – from Australia, New Zealand, Dubai, Malaysia and Brazil, as well as from Europe – but the majority were from North America, and it was clear that thousands of enthusiasts there were hoping we would overfly their country.

'Good evening, Bertrand and Brian,' wrote Ralph R. Davis of Walnut Creek, California. 'You may not be Americans, but you sure have some fans here in the States.' Jane Matheson, a former classmate of Bertrand's at North Palm Beach in Florida, sent fond remembrances and asked if he still had scars on his knees where she kicked him. A man who styled himself 'Montgolfier' was planning to put up 'a small armada of balloons' to meet us as we hit the West Coast. 'Would like if possible for you to drop altitude, to meet us,' he wrote. 'Will let you know well in advance if armada is in position or has been aborted.'

All at once, however, our circumstances changed, and our chances of a flight across North America vanished. At Control Luc announced a drastic change of plan. Rather than keeping us to the north, he and Pierre had decided to send us southwards, far down over the Pacific, to pick up a jet stream that was forecast to form there in three days' time. The proposal was so startling that Brian Smith took Luc aside and asked to see this new jet stream on his laptop. When Luc said, 'Oh – you don't understand: it doesn't exist yet. It'll be born three days from now,' Smiffy turned pale.

The decision to go south threw all our air controllers' forward planning into chaos. They had expected the balloon to fly over North

America, but now they had to file a plan for a flight via Mexico and Cuba, and the communications centre at Geneva Airport hastily had to look out the relevant new addresses: Miami Oceanic, New York Oceanic, Honolulu, Oakland Oceanic, Havana, Kingston (Jamaica), Curaçao, Santo Domingo – all had to be alerted.

Evidently realizing that their new plan would alarm us, Luc and Pierre broke the news by sending us a detailed analysis of the latest weather situation:

Dear Brian and Bertrand,
After a lot of discussion with Alan, we decide to take the southerly route over the ocean. Luc will phone to explain. The required flight level will be between 260 and 280, with tracks between 093 and 098, and speed around 35 knots until 00:00 Z. Afterwards you may climb to the ceiling. I think it is 295 for this period. Track will go from 095 to 150 in twenty-four hours, with speeds between 25 and 30 knots. The day after, you will descend in latitudes between 13 and 15 north, with speeds between 20 and 25 knots.

This very special manoeuvre is necessary to catch the very fast sub-tropical jet stream that we observe now, starting southwest of Hawaii through Central America going to North West Africa.

This major departure from earlier strategy made us all the more anxious because we had the impression that the weathermen themselves were confused. In fact, after trying the northern route for twenty-four hours, they had seen that it would give a bad result. After re-running all their calculations, they had discovered that if we went north the distance would of course be shorter and our speed would be greater, but – fatal flaw – bad weather coming along behind would catch up with us, and we would risk being brought down in the sea by thunderstorms, as Steve Fossett had been. The southern route, towards the equator, would mean three or four days at low level and low speed – a depressing trajectory, but one that would bring us to a jet stream which would start to build south of Hawaii in a few days' time. So far, the jet stream they were talking about existed only on their computer models, three days in the future.

The prospect of going south was horrific – not least because Richard Branson had come to grief doing that very thing. After setting out on the northern route he had diverted southwards, and disaster followed. Now our own team was telling us to follow the same course. Instead of heading straight east across the Pacific and hitting the coast of North America somewhere in California between Los Angeles and San Francisco, we were going even farther south than he had – a thousand miles south of Hawaii, passing at one stage closer to Australia than to any point in the northern hemisphere, and adding a couple of thousand miles to our journey.

BERTRAND

Brian and I both formed the impression that our met men, with no really good weather pattern available, were choosing the worse of two poor options. I had serious doubts, and felt so depressed that I telephoned Michèle and told her I thought we were going to fail because we didn't have enough fuel to fly so far and so slowly.

'Bertrand,' she said, 'I don't understand. An hour ago Luc and Pierre were completely confident. You only have to do three or four days at low speed, and then you'll get the jet stream. What are you afraid of?'

'Well,' I told her, 'I don't see how we can rely on a jet stream that doesn't exist yet.'

She called the met men again, told them how apprehensive we were, and asked what they really thought. 'They've no reason to be depressed!' Luc cried. Immediately he phoned me back and we talked in French. When I asked if he was truly confident about sending us south, he said, 'Bertrand, do you trust me? Yes or No?'

In that situation I felt it was better to say yes.

'Yes,' I said.

'OK – so just do it! The situation's under control.'

That was the defining moment of the flight. If we'd kept to the northern route we would have failed because it was leading to violent thunderstorms that could have torn the balloon apart and sent us hurtling to the sea. In any case, it would not have brought us to the jet stream. At the time, though, we could not tell what lay ahead, and I said to Brian, 'I have to admit, I feel a little afraid.'

'Thank God!' he replied. 'I've been wanting to tell you – I'm shit scared too!'

That was a wonderful moment. The confession that we were both so frightened brought us closer together than ever, and gave us strength to face whatever lay ahead.

BRIAN

I'd always had this fear of the unknown – and it was certainly a comfort to know that Bertrand was scared as well. But just admitting it didn't make me feel better for long. I continued to feel really frightened, not least because I kept remembering Steve Fossett's terrifying crash – the worst thing for me was thinking about what would happen if we ditched.

Before the flight of *Orbiter 2* Camerons had tested the gondola, and we knew it floated very well because the kerosene tanks were relatively light and the capsule had keels that were designed to fill with water and stabilize it. *Orbiter 3*'s gondola was far more top-heavy. What with the weight of the load-frame and outriggers round the top of the capsule, plus the titanium propane tanks, I thought it would almost certainly turn over if we came down in the sea, and we might never be able to escape from the capsule through either of the hatches.

If we found ourselves upside-down in the ocean, our only chance would be to pile all loose equipment at the front and hope that the gondola would tilt nose-down at a steep enough angle to bring the rear hatch clear of the water. Even then, we might easily drown trying to escape: with a hatch open, the gondola could fill with water and sink, taking us to the bottom with it. If we had to parachute from a height – forget it. We were six, seven, eight days away from rescue: the chances of anyone finding us in time to save our lives were extremely remote, and even if an aircraft managed to locate us and drop a large life raft, there was no guarantee we would survive until a ship arrived.

At sunset I looked out of the porthole and saw these whacking great cumulo-nimbus clouds (known in the trade as CBs), any of which might contain wind-shear and hail violent enough to destroy our envelope by ripping it to shreds. It was vast clouds of exactly this kind – bigger than any that form over land – that had nearly killed Steve

Fossett the previous summer. As dark came down I wondered, 'Am I going to fly into one of them during the night?' There was no way of telling if one lay in our path.

The only sure way to avoid the clouds was to fly above them, but at dusk they might easily be two or three hundred miles away, sitting on the horizon, and it was impossible to tell how high they reached or where they might move to during the night. It was the prospect of feeling the balloon suddenly start to shake about in the dark that haunted me most. I became a little paranoid, and every few minutes I would dim the lights in the cabin and peer out to see if the stars were in view. If they were, I knew we couldn't be in cloud.

BERTRAND

Generally the clouds would form in the morning from moisture rising off the warm sea and condensing in the cooler air above; in the middle of the day they grew huge, and by evening some would start to dissolve.

We were trying to hold a track of 123 degrees, but we were surrounded by these CBs, whose tops reached to 28,000 feet. Our ceiling was 30,000 feet, so we generally had 2,000 feet of clearance above them. But luckily, whenever we came close to one of the really enormous clouds, our track diverged a little from the direction of the wind which was moving it. As we wove in and out of the threatening monsters, we had the feeling that the balloon was being guided from above by a benevolent, unseen hand. The sky was full of dangerous clouds, yet in some miraculous way we never ran into one.

Often we found that the lower part of a cloud was travelling in the same direction as us, but more slowly. Far above, one saw that the wind had sliced off its top and thrown it hundreds of miles away, turning it into cirrus clouds – masses of tiny ice crystals, shining in the sun. In some places we would see a whole flotilla of smaller clouds clustered in a circle round a single big one, and we thought such formations must be caused by local depressions.

'Over the Pacific the clouds are alive,' I wrote in my journal. 'They grow as much horizontally as they do vertically, and by good luck all the tallest ones – the dangerous cumulo-nimbus thunder clouds – are to the south of our track.' In one of his faxes Luc told us there were gigantic storms to the south, and said, 'Maybe you can see them?' We could, and very menacing they were – tremendous masses of cloud on the horizon.

Communications became extremely difficult. Our fax and telephone both went dead because we were right beneath the Pacific satellite: with the shadow of the balloon blocking the antennae, we floated on for two days out of direct contact with Geneva. At one point Jo noted in her diary, 'We've been out of communication with them for almost twenty-four hours, and everybody in the Control Room is quiet.'

The fact that the telephone and fax were dead inevitably increased our sense of isolation. It was an extraordinary feeling, to be drifting in silence over the middle of an ocean 8,000 miles wide. The Pacific became like a vast mirror in which Brian and I could see our emotions nakedly reflected. It was impossible to cheat or fool ourselves: we really were afraid. Brian quoted lines from *The Rime of the Ancient Mariner*:

> *Alone, alone, all, all alone,*
> *Alone on a wide wide sea!*

Our only contact was with the air traffic controllers at Oakland, outside San Francisco, whom we could reach on HF radio. As we drifted on in the middle of nowhere, I smiled to myself when I remembered how, when we were planning the gondola, I had told Alan I didn't want any HF radio on board: I said it was too expensive and heavy, and didn't work anyway. Satellite devices, I assured him, were much better. Fortunately the HF was still a legal requirement for this kind of flight.

Now we were entirely dependent on HF – and when I asked San Francisco if they could patch me through to Luc on their telephone line, a minor miracle occurred. The man in Oakland said, 'Of course – just tell us who we have to charge,' and put me through. At that very moment Luc was hurrying into the control centre saying, 'They're only 130 miles away from storms. I *have* to get a message to them somehow.' The words were hardly out of his mouth when the phone rang, and there was San Francisco with: 'We have a radio relay call for you.' Luc stared at our people and said, 'That's incredible! He's here! God's here!' Over the link he warned me of the CBs ahead, and told us to climb as high as we could to avoid them. So for the first time in ages I was able to talk to Luc, and I vowed that I would never make bad jokes about HF radio again. Once more, some outside force seemed to be directing events on our behalf.

BRIAN

Inside the gondola it was so cold, and so many things were going wrong, that it only needed a little spark to put me in a bad temper. Control didn't seem to understand what we were going through: they obviously didn't appreciate how tired we were or how demoralizing it was to be so cold. Angered by their failure to put themselves in our place, I really snapped back at upcoming messages from Alan. It was mainly my fault that the atmosphere became antagonistic – but at the time I did feel there was a certain lack of sensitivity on the ground.

When the weather guys changed their minds, for the first time I was tempted to think, 'Well – it's easy enough for *them*. They're not thousands of miles away from the nearest land.' After what they had already achieved I could not doubt their ability – but what they were now proposing seemed crazy. Did they know what they were doing? Doubt made it impossible to keep my own fears at bay.

It so happened that, in the moments of worst anxiety, technical problems multiplied. For the first time in the flight we were struggling to get as high as possible to keep above the clouds, and the higher we went, the lower the temperature fell. The cabin heaters, which ran on propane, were hardly working; and the pilot lights were failing because they were getting clogged with ice, so at night the gondola became miserably cold – only a degree or two above freezing. I had taken to wearing three pairs of survival-type, fleece-lined trousers, as many layers as I could manage on top, and a huge blue duvet jacket which had been supplied for Wim Verstraeten, with my feet wrapped in the detachable hood. Bertrand and I shared the jacket, because it was always warm and comforting to the pilot coming on duty. The difference was Bertrand wore the hood on his head.

We could live with it – but cold definitely saps the spirit. In the first fax of my stint on 11 March I complained that it had taken me half an hour to de-ice the fuel control unit in the ceiling of the central passage. Before, we had been able to clear it by scraping with a credit card, but now I had to nip away with pliers at the great chunks of ice which had built up on the burner valves. No. 3 electric valve was still jammed in the full open position, and No. 4 was jammed slightly open, so that the whole right side of that burner system had to be shut down. No. 1, on the left side, had jammed open twice in the previous two hours. I was scared that all the burners would soon be out of action and that our flight would come to an abrupt end. 'It would be really nice to know what is happening,' I faxed:

> The learning curve for juggling is quite steep up here. We will now make a video clip, assuming we can force a smile.

Alan's reply was by no means sympathetic:

> Brian: I go off duty at night to the sound of your moans. I come back on . . . to be faced by yet another bleating fax complaining that some bit of kit isn't working . . . Reading your messages has become so depressing that we have had to start a Real Message file and a Message No One Can Read Without Worrying file. We prefer the nice cheery messages that Bertie sends.

For all his sarcasm, he had to admit that nobody could yet explain what was wrong with the fuel system, and I became still more apprehensive when tank pair No. 6 ran out after only twenty-four hours and fifty minutes of use – which showed how much we had been having to burn. Then Alan made things still worse by telling me that Luc expected our speed to decay even further, from our present 45 knots to 35 or even 30. This, he assured me, was 'part of his game plan', and he was still estimating our total round-the-world time at twenty days. 'At your present rate of use,' he said, 'you should have enough propane to keep going past the necessary line of longitude in Morocco as far as Egypt.'

Was that estimate realistic? Or was he just saying this to cheer us up? It was all too easy to feel cynical.

To raise my own morale, I began composing limericks and faxing them down. By no means all were printable, or even very good, but one or two caught the prevailing atmosphere:

Of a hairy-faced pilot called Jones
'Twas said that he frequently moans
Of the burners all night,
With no pilot light.
The boss — he just sits there and groans.

Alan hit back with:

One of those chaps flying Breitling
Was dyslexic when it came to his pilotling.
He went on to say
That flying this way
Over the Pacific was really quite frightening.

The exchange of verse lifted my spirits. By then we had swung on to a heading of 155 — steeply southeast — and our speed was down to 35 knots. Even so, my next message to control was much more cheerful. 'Hello John, Old Bean,' it began:

The moon appears in my porthole about every five minutes. Are you sure we are not flying in circles? The bed's wet again. So the sheet is hanging up to dry. Doesn't help much when it falls in the puddle on the floor. Come on, then — who wrote the ditty for Alan? It was far too clever for a Cameron executive.

Another boost came in the form of a fax from the indomitable Steve Fossett, who wrote, 'Dear Bertrand and Brian, Your flight is truly impressive. Your patience with the launch and slow trajectory are paying off. I hope you will enjoy a safe flight to Mexico.' Typical Steve, we thought — implying we would get no farther than Mexico. Our reaction was to phone Control immediately and say, '*We're* not stopping in Mexico!' Alan laughed and said, 'It's precisely because of faxes like this that you have to succeed.'

Our team on the ground had been consulting the makers of the valves for clues about how to get them functioning properly, and Kieran Sturrock suggested several ingenious possible methods for making the burners work better. In the end, however, he agreed that they must be frozen up, and the only way of sorting them out properly was for us to go down to low level, where the ice would melt, and make another EVA, during which we could thaw the valves out with hot water if necessary. 'When you EVA,' Alan wrote, 'throw out everything you don't need. Height will mean speed within the next few days.'

BERTRAND

The EVA was an extraordinary experience. We brought the balloon down to 6,000 feet, and below us the Pacific lay totally calm – absolutely no waves of any kind. Once again we were in the middle of nowhere. We looked at each other, and I said, 'Well, the last time we went outside, we were over a desert of sand. This time it's a desert of water – but this one's really frightening.'

It was early on a glorious sunny morning when we climbed out through the top hatch, and for a few moments we sat there awestruck by the utter silence – no cry of a bird, not the slightest sound of wind or sea. This time there were no icicles round the skirt of the balloon, but water soon started to pour down on us as sheet-ice melted from the inner surface of the envelope. As we had no hammer, Brian took the T-piece junction from the pipes of the auxiliary tanks and hit the ice coating from the solenoid switches on the defective burners. In our survival packs we had some chemical hand-warmers, so we squashed the gel contents around to start the reaction and tied the packs around the electronic valves.

We then discovered that the valve for the No. 9 tank pair was leaking and decided to bypass it by changing the hoses round, substituting the ones which had originally been on the auxiliary tanks – and which we had almost jettisoned during our first EVA, over North Africa. We must have been quite severely stressed, because we both had difficulty trying to think through the fuel system. We'd had so many confusing problems that we had to talk everything through, and we spent some time sitting out in the sun, saying, 'If we close this valve, how will the fuel transfer? If we've got a leak here, how can we bypass it?' We made no mistakes in effecting the repairs, but we erred on the side of caution.

We also threw overboard everything we didn't need, including used scrubbers (the lithium hydroxide filters for the cabin air system) and any unused ones we knew we could do without. Over went all the remaining sand ballast, the fresh food that had gone off – the meat in an advanced state of decomposition – and accumulated garbage. Altogether we shed 128 kilos of weight. Once again I cleaned the portholes with my Heath Robinson apparatus, and we moved one of the external video cameras so that it would film the front of the capsule and the bottom of the envelope. The whole exercise cost us about six hours.

Inside the gondola again, Brian sent down a report on what we had done, and ended:

> Laying along the outriggers to get to tank valve 14 A from the outboard side, because of the antenna tray, with Bertrand holding my foot, was not much fun. Anyway, we are very pleased with ourselves, and the gondola smells much nicer after some ten days or whatever inside. Now you are going to lock us up for another eleven days – bloody sadists.
>
> Totally alone and very surreal, sitting on top of the gondola 6,000 feet above blue, blue and more blue.

By now time and date had become thoroughly confusing. In the gondola we were still at 18:00 Zulu on 11 March, but dawn was already breaking, and if there had been anyone below, it would have been the morning of 12 March. In the centre of the instrument panel was a Breitling clock – a collector's item, borrowed from the company museum and at least fifty years old – with hands, showing only twelve hours. To keep us straight on Zulu time, behind the clock I fixed a long, slim piece of paper, with 'AM' on one side and 'PM' on the other, which we could slide back and forth to show whether it was morning or evening.

After the EVA Brian went to bed, leaving me in charge. Soon we were heading southeast at the highest flight level we had achieved so far

– 30,500 feet. I had expected the balloon to go higher, but that seemed to be its ceiling for the time being. In three days' time, our met men told us, we would need to go to 33,000 feet. On our maps the expanse of the Pacific looked terrifying. The first map showed one tiny strip of land on the left, and the rest was blue. The next map was blue from edge to edge. The third map was blue except for a small strip on the right – and as we were making only 35 knots it seemed we would take for ever to cross that vast expanse.

Our control team, obviously realizing we were not happy about our new track, sent reassuring messages, saying that they had spoken again to Oakland and Tokyo, and that Tokyo air traffic control had wished us good luck. Smiffy and C faxed:

Just to let you know – we know how you feel about the change of the met plan, but we are getting very good vibes from Luc and Pierre. Have every confidence in their forecast. The fast winds will be worth waiting for.

When I spoke to Smiffy and told him how daunting our surroundings seemed, he passed on a fascinating e-mail message from Jan Abbott, an astrologer in Devon, who said that for the past two years she had been charting the attempts at round-the-world flights:

Over the last six days I have been following your flight progress against the astrological chart cast for your take-off on 1 March. As the relevant planets on that day align with your own birth charts and the chart of the first-ever manned balloon flight, in 1783, the possibility of your success is great, and may be destined. I send my very best wishes. Safe journey, and hope your landing by the pyramids in Egypt brings you back to earth gently.

'Isn't that incredible?' Cecilia faxed. 'And to receive it just at this point in time!' Incredible indeed it was to get such a message at the moment of greatest doubt. Then came a fax to say that we had passed the 20,000 kilometre mark, and for a while my spirits went up again.

Not for long. Soon Alan was telling me that, although we had just

completed one EVA, he might want us to do another almost immediately:

> It seems that you are still carrying some pieces of equipment
> that are of doubtful use. We may need to plan another EVA to
> get rid of those and absolutely everything you don't need –
> spare water, dirty clothes, excess filters. We have to get you to
> 36,000 feet if you want to be in North Africa on
> 22–23 March. Suggest you start planning now what you will
> be able to drop at next EVA . . . Sorry to nag, but it's a
> priority to get your weight reduced.

He also repeated that the Americans needed to be told our flight level
every hour, but after I had told him that I could not get through to
anyone on the radio, and that it was difficult to write faxes because I
had no pilot light and had to keep standing up every few seconds to
re-ignite the burners by hand, his tone softened:

> Bertrand: I am sorry you have to deal with some technical
> problems, and that the Pacific is so wide and the winds slow, but
> Dr Noble – the well-known psychiatrist who will shortly be
> opening an office in Lausanne – warns against allowing depres-
> sion and tiredness to set in.
>
> I know we are sitting in comfort, and well fed, but the feeling
> here is very positive. Luc is close to betting a year's salary that he
> will get you to North Africa, but we will have these slow winds
> while we move you towards the tropical jet. I have seen the
> forecasts from the US computer, and they are brilliant – and you
> know I wouldn't lie to you.

After six years of collaboration, I knew I could trust Alan completely
and was confident he would never hide the truth from me. We had
gone through so many experiences together – and this adventure, if it
came off, would be an extraordinary victory for him as well.

In spite of our uncertainties, I was able to enjoy the beauty of our
surroundings. We had a wonderful, radiant sunset, and with the
repositioned camera I was able to film it igniting the bottom of the

envelope with fiery light. We noticed that when the burners lit, the air went up in one side of the hot-air cone, and we could see vapour from the burnt propane escaping from the mouth of the balloon on the other side.

That night I slept very well – despite dreaming that I was in a commercial airliner which had to ditch in the ocean. I remember the plane going down, and when I woke up I just hoped that the dream hadn't been a premonition.

Alan urged us to get the HF radio working, and suggested we try contacting the airfield on Wake Island, 600 nautical miles to the south-southeast, or any aircraft that might be flying from it. 'Don't worry about the press office or anything that is non-essential,' he wrote – and twice more he emphasized, 'Please remember to include flight levels with every message.'

BRIAN

The twelfth of March was one of my worst days. After the EVA I developed a ferocious headache, and in my diary I scribbled, 'Was completely useless and had to go to bed. Fitful sleep and had to get up to take Ponstan.' My first message to Control said, 'Alan – Just up from feeling absolutely terrible – much better now. Give me twenty minutes or so to get my head round the situation, and I'll come back to you.'

When I did fax again it was with a dire list of deficiencies. We couldn't raise anybody on the HF radio, I told him; the satphone wasn't working on either antenna; it was taking an age to stabilize the burners; our track was all over the place, and too much to the north. Nor, I wrote, was there much future in trying to shed more weight:

The only significant weight left is the fuel – before we get to desperation stakes like getting rid of the high-pressure nitrogen tank. By my calcs, our ceiling should be in the order of FL 320, but obviously I'm about 3,000 feet out. In order to get to 360 we would need to lose another 1,500 kg – almost ten full tanks.

Whilst you may seem confident down there, up here things are quite different. We are having to give ourselves a good talking-to in order to keep it all together. The positive thing is that we definitely complement and support each other – so 100 per cent for CRM [crew resource management].

Then Alan sent a fax which really got my goat:

> You have been in the Oakland FIR since 155 degrees east. Aren't you reading your Aerad chart FEP 3? This FIR covers ten per cent of the surface of the globe. Don't you remember our exchange of messages about the Memorandum of Understanding? You wanted our assurance that we had read it. We had. Had you? The MOU refers to Oakland. So you're in the hands of the Yanks. Regards Alan.

That was too much. The atmosphere was getting nasty, and I hit back:

> Alan, my sense of humour failure warning light is flashing. I don't need lectures or criticism – just advice. OK? There are so many confusing things going on up here, and I'm freezing cold. I have good comms with Tokyo. Can't get Oakland. So I'm staying put. FL 263, 100 degrees magnetic, 31 knots. Brian.

Alan's reply was uncompromising:

> Brian – when I criticise you, you will be in no doubt. I pointed out – quite humorously, I thought – that you are strolling through air space that belongs to one air traffic unit, and have been doing so for many hours, and are not aware of it. You could have endangered your safety, and the safety of others. Not something to keep quiet about to preserve your sense of humour – unless you want to die laughing.
>
> Better keep yourself warm and check the oxygen levels. Could you be hypoxic?

He went on to a detailed discussion of what could be wrong with the valves, the autopilots and the linkage of the tanks. His message ended, 'Friends again?' But I was in no mood to be conciliatory:

> Alan – let me summarize things for you. I came on duty from a

fitful sleep with a headache. Bertrand was in a bit of a state, rather like me the day before yesterday. We were unable to relax and rationally discuss the problems at that time – mainly due to tiredness and stress over quite a few days. It was important for him to go to bed.

The phone doesn't work. The HF wasn't working. The pilot lights don't work. The fuel control unit is just one big lump of ice. We can't run the kettle and the HF together, so we are keeping warm the best we can. I have to leave the desk every two minutes or so to relight the burners and try to stabilize them, whilst trying to keep the balloon level.

I'm sure when the sun is up our spirits will rise, and hopefully our efficiency along with them. Until then we need all the help and advice you can give.

Never not friends. You just piss me off sometimes . . . Brian

Alan, realizing what a state we were in, came back with a much gentler message addressed to 'Brian, my old mucker, my old friend,' and saying: 'Sorry to have given you a hard time earlier. I wasn't fully *au fait* with the health problems.' He ran through various possible solutions for our burner problems, said he was consulting Pete Johnson and Kieran Sturrock, and suggested that we should go for another EVA to reconnect tank pairs 2 and 9 in their original coupling.

BERTRAND
Before the flight we had held many discussions with Alan about how relations between air crew and ground control tend to deteriorate after a few days' flight. The balloonists start to think that the control centre is not pulling on the same rope as they are, and both sides become angry with each other. We knew this had happened before, and within a few hours Brian and I realized that we were falling into a similar pattern. Alan, too, saw that the tension was the product of normal stress and nervousness, and tried to smooth things down.

I said to Brian, 'You know, it's good that Alan is able to play the role of the bastard, because he's got broad enough shoulders to take what we throw at him – and that's fine.' Brian laughed, and recovered his sense of humour – but in the preceding hours, for the first time during the flight, he really had lost it. We realized that his aggressive exchanges with Alan were a good way of discharging some of the anxiety that we had on board – a method of transferring some pressure from ourselves to him on the ground.

I wrote in my journal:

> March 13 is an important day. The news is good. We still have to do forty-eight hours at low speed before picking up the jet which should bring us to Mauritania on the morning of the 19th – forty-eight hours crawling across the biggest desert in the world, the Pacific. I have to suppress every desire except to follow the path of the winds. But hope is coming back. Brian and I are making plans and dreams again. Maybe the most difficult thing is to control our impatience, and our tremendous desire to succeed.

Thinking of the immense distance of sea that we had to cross, and the two coasts so far apart, I felt highly emotional, and I remembered the Chinese ideograms used in the ancient *I-Ching* book which I had studied in February, before we took off. My teacher had explained to me one special paragraph about how one can learn to go through fear, to jump over the abyss. The Samurai, for instance, are taught to go beyond fear in order to become stronger and better connected to themselves; the hexagram of the Samurai shows a baby bird being pushed out of the nest, so that it has to learn to fly before it hits the ground. That hexagram is a very difficult one to master, but it is the one that produces the best results if you manage to go with it. Now, over the ocean, I had to go through my own fear and learn to fly: I had to dominate my own feeling of vertigo as I walked on the edge of the abyss.

Usually, in normal life, it is possible to avoid fear. Man does this by changing his activities or by taking medication or drugs. But here in mid-Pacific there was no escape, and this new experience was full of rich lessons. If you accept fear or anxiety instead of fighting it, you can learn to go through it and connect yourself to inner resources that will bring you a new confidence in life.

BRIAN

Added to everything else, I had always had a great fear of water. When I was a kid, I was a complete wimp when it came to water, and that was why I took to flying so well. I felt an affinity with the air, and from the start loved flying.

Still the e-mails were piling into the Breitling website:

Looking up to the sky, I wish you a good journey. And a safe return towards the earth, but not too soon. (Jonathan Adriaens, Belgium)

Hold on. The world is not too big. Just wind must be your friend. FLY FLY FLY FLY FLY FLY FLY FLY FLY FLY to finish. (Pavol Kvackay, Slovakia)

Congratulations gentlemen on your continuing success and good fortune as Zephyrus's sweet breath carries you gently around our beautiful earth – May a huge bottle of champagne and a hot shower await you – God bless. (Greg Eastlund, Minnesota, USA)

I am curious what are the toilet arrangement on board? (Dodo, t.a.)

Congratulations, you are now in one row with the Wright bros, Amelia Earhart etc. Maybe you can go non-stop to the moon by a balloon next time. See ya. (Hooly, Rotterdam)

One of the most stirring messages came from Neil Armstrong, who wished us good luck, and another memorable one, published on the Internet, reached us on 13 March:

Dear Bertrand and Brian, All of us at Virgin take our hats off to you for an incredibly bold flight. It really does look like you could do it this time. Look forward to greeting you back in Europe. Have a safe and very uneventful journey across the Pacific. May the winds be kind to you. Kind regards, Richard Branson.

BERTRAND

The message set me thinking about Branson. He is someone I admire, because he puts a lot of energy into everything he does, and he has done very well. Of course, when it comes to flying, he is more interested in breaking records than we are because we fly more for the fun of it. During the race to be first round the world, we were in an interesting relationship, each of us saying nice things about the other. Every time Richard was asked about me during interviews, he described me as a friend, said how much he liked me, and remarked on what a pity it was that he had not got to know me earlier as he would have asked me to fly with him.

In my own interviews I spoke of my admiration for him and said how friendly I found him. In winter 1997–8, when his envelope flew off on its own and the gondola of *Orbiter 2* fell from the crane, I got him on the phone and said, 'We should really fly together. You bring your gondola, I'll bring my envelope, and we'll make a balloon.' Only a joke perhaps, but it gives an idea of the good atmosphere that existed between us.

Hope came in the form of yet another forecast from Luc and Pierre. On Saturday 13 March they said our track would continue to be southeasterly and that we would see no improvement in speed above our miserable 35 knots. But then on Sunday, as the track backed from 145 degrees to 105, our speed would begin to pick up. By Monday we would be travelling due east at 100 knots, and on Tuesday our speed would increase to 120. At that rate it would be 'Saturday into Mauritania for dawn landing at 0 knots'.

'The other good news,' Pierre told us, 'is that in these equatorial latitudes the air is less dense, and you are higher than you think you are with an altimeter setting of 1013. Luc says that in real terms you have to add 3,000 feet to the height shown on the altimeter.'

Yet again Alan reminded us to 'REMEMBER FLIGHT LEVELS', and sought to encourage us by writing, 'Luc wants me to tell you that the met is getting better and better. He now predicts North Africa 19 March.'

In my journal, on 14 March, I wrote:

I believe that by surviving these days above the Pacific, sur-rounded by doubt, veering from hope to anxiety, we will be able to do a lot when we get back to normal life. At least we have discovered that inside ourselves we have resources to cope with many difficulties.

I was thinking of Peter Bird, a man of superhuman endurance, who rowed across the Pacific. His first two attempts failed, but on the third he rowed from San Francisco to Australia in four months, making an amazing film of himself on the way, talking to his camera. Then he tried to cross in the opposite direction, and disappeared in the ocean. After his death a friend of his in Dijon commissioned a trophy, in the form of a flight of titanium steps, to commemorate his extraordinary perseverance, and began awarding it annually to people who had made exceptional efforts. The first four recipients – Peter and three friends – all died trying to row the Pacific. Next Peter's friend gave it to someone who successfully crossed Antarctica on foot – and then, after the flight of *Orbiter 2*, he awarded it to me. I was really impressed by the knowledge that at some point we would cross Peter's track. I felt humble when I reflected that he had performed such incredible feats not with an agreeable companion, but alone. I wrote:

I want to remember what I am feeling right now for the rest of my life. We are crossing a desert of water, but I would not like to stay in it for forty days. In any case, it would take me more than forty days to learn to have more inner freedom, to let go more, to be less tense, to trust life, and trust the winds.

BRIAN

Early on 14 March Bertrand woke me so that we could make our third and final EVA. Kieran agreed with our theory that the link-up of fuel pipes which we had improvised during our second excursion had actually made things worse: as the balloon rotated slowly, the sun would strike the tanks on one side, warming them up, so that fuel automatically transferred itself from that side straight across to its cold partners opposite, and the burners would not work properly because they kept getting vapour instead of propane liquid. Our mission, now, was to re-establish the original connections and deal with the leak in another way.

We knew we would lose communications as we went down to low level, so before we started we told San Francisco what we were doing. Then, to save time and fuel, we descended only to 15,000 feet, and put on oxygen masks, connected by long tubes to our tank, before opening the top hatch. It took just a few minutes to rearrange the hose connections and jettison as much weight as we could. We kept only the food that we needed for five more days of flight and dropped everything else, including a lot of water and even most of our spare filters. Alan wanted us to throw out spare clothes as well, but that would have improved our ceiling by only five or ten feet. Because a great deal of water was falling from the envelope, we stayed at low level for a while to get rid of most of the ice.

What we could not know was that Oakland had become so worried by our silence that they had declared an air–sea rescue alert. Strict international rules govern such situations. Normally, if any aircraft is thirty minutes overdue, air controllers automatically progress to what they call the Distress Phase, and launch a rescue sortie. Especially in the Pacific, every minute is critical because the distances are so great. Oakland, telephoning Geneva, said that because they had lost all contact with the balloon they were preparing to move into the Distress Phase. Alan asked them to wait, explaining that we had merely gone down to do the EVA and that he felt sure we were not in trouble. But, to his dismay, when he asked if Oakland had any aircraft flying that might be able to get in touch with us, the controller answered, 'We have no plane in that region, sir. Nobody ever goes there.' Alan was horrified. 'Nobody ever goes there?' he echoed. Not the least of his anxieties was the colossal bill which would land on Breitling if rescue aircraft did take off from the Marshall or Midway Islands: he knew it would run into hundreds of thousands of dollars.

Luckily, before that happened we re-established contact. At 19:52 Zulu, as we were climbing again, I faxed Control to say 'EVA success-fully completed' and gave a few details of what we had done. A message from Jo warned us that Alan was 'heading for some supper with steam coming out of his ears, so he might slap your wrists later'. I replied:

Reference Alan's smoking ears – we're not monkeys up here. We told San Francisco exactly what we were doing. We spoke to them during the descent, and then called them all the way up on the climb. Eventually got them at around flight level 200. We had also agreed with the Control Centre that during communications loss, as long as our EPIRB [emergency beacon] was not transmitting, we were OK.

I was annoyed that our professionalism had been criticized when the loss of communication was really not our fault. Later I reported to John:

> Threw out most of our food this morning, so not much choice now. Bertrand won't open the *pâté truffé* until we're over USA – I told him I'm not going round again. So it's pasta with cheese sauce once more. Burners are huffing and puffing a bit, have to keep getting out of the seat to re-light them. Kieran should know there's a design flaw here: we should either have sparkers on the front panel, or an electric chair-lift to get me to the burner control panel – but a sports model, because it doesn't half go *whumph* when a couple of shots of unburned propane go up there.

In an attempt to solve that problem, during one of his shifts on duty Bertrand built an ingenious connection made of wire and string that allowed us to open the manual valve from our seats. I, too, made a small innovation designed to ease our life. I took a mirror and lashed it in position on the instrument panel, angled up so that I could see through the top hatch whether or not the burners were working without turning round. This was particularly useful at night – and during the day, by repositioning the mirror, I could keep an eye on the bottom of one appendix, also without getting up.

BERTRAND

While our telephone and fax were out of action, I suddenly heard an Air France pilot talking on the radio to Tahiti in French. So I put in a call, got Tahiti first, then the pilot, and we spoke in French. I asked if he would call a friend of mine, Gérard Feldzer, President of the French Aero Club and a captain on Airbus. 'Oh,' said the pilot, 'I know him very well. I'll give him a message.' As soon as he got to Tahiti he sent off an e-mail, so that Gérard received greetings from the middle of the Pacific.

After the EVA the wind swung us to the east and our speed increased to 60 knots. A form of countdown had begun, because on the GPS the degrees of longitude – which had been increasing steadily with our easterly progress until we reached the international date line – were now decreasing, from 180 west towards the distant and magical figure of 9 west, which marked the finishing line over Mauritania.

By 02:00 Zulu on 15 March we were doing 70 knots, and our speed kept creeping up: 73, 74, 76. We were finally entering the jet stream, and all round us were gorgeous colours. The balloon was flying so high, at 32,000 feet, that we seemed to be enveloped in pink veils of cirrus. My notebook records that we were surrounded by cirrus clouds and residual CB heads, cut off from the main clouds by the wind. Up there, at our ceiling, the balloon formed a cloud of its own consisting of very small crystals; and as this kept direct sunlight off the envelope, I had to burn repeatedly. With every push of propane moisture condensed outside the envelope, so that a dark cloud, like smoke, formed around the balloon and came along with us. It was rather unpleasant, and to get rid of it I went down slightly.

Worries about fuel grew ever more insistent. In my journal I wrote, 'I feel the kind of tension I would if I were spending money borrowed from the bank, without any hope of being able to pay it back. Every push of propane is something we're losing for ever.' Our reserves seemed perilously small – we were down to six pairs of full tanks – and we had thousands of miles to go. We had burnt two-thirds of our propane in covering only half our course. And the higher we flew, the shorter the time each pair lasted: from the record duration of 41 hours, we were down in the twenties. Everything now depended on the weathermen: if they were right, we still had a chance; if they were wrong, we were doomed to fail. We just had to believe them and their computerized models.

BRIAN

The fifteenth of March, our fifteenth day in the air, was a more cheerful day altogether – partly because Bertrand chose to believe that one of the air controllers at Oakland was in love with him. As a joke, Bertrand had more or less made it a rule that we would never talk about women because, cooped up as we were in the gondola, it would be too cruel. But suddenly we were in touch with this girl, who had an incredibly sweet voice. When she kept calling, hour after hour, to ask our position, I reported to Control: 'Good comms with San Francisco. One of the controllers is a lady, and Bertrand is sure she fancies him.' Her presence certainly stimulated us to put in positional reports more often, in the hope that we would hear her voice again.

The downside of the day was that, from some inexplicable source, I caught a cold and a sore throat, and also got a mysterious soft swelling on the back of one hand. At least the minor ailments gave us another chance to open Bertrand's expensive medical kit, which had scarcely been touched. A dose of paracetamol reduced the cold symptoms, but the swelling presented more of a problem. Fearing that it might have been caused by an infection, Bertrand said that if it didn't go down in a couple of days, he would prescribe antibiotics. But I – thinking of all the champagne that would be flowing if we got round – resisted the idea, as being on antibiotics would deny me my share. Instead, I rubbed emu oil on the swelling and waited to see what would happen.

On the ground, our controllers were on a bit of a high. 'Things really ARE looking up,' faxed Smiffy and C. 'Pierre has told us it's such a good jet track he's making plans for you to continue round again. What a scoop!' Limericks came back into fashion and flew in both directions. I was pleased with one I sent down:

> Wiv Smiffy and C in control
> My mate said, 'They're out on parole
> From the Betty Ford clinic.'
> I fink it's a gimmick:
> Next week they'll be back on the dole.

The Smiths lost no time in returning the ball:

> There was a young girl from Madras
> Who had the most beautiful ass –
> Not round and pink,
> As you might think:
> It was grey, had long ears and ate grass.

For as long as everything was going well, our messages remained on a high level of facetiousness and ribaldry. At that moment my only real problem was the temperature. 'I'm at flight level 310,' I told John at 06:50:

> It's jolly dark and jolly cold. I've got three pairs of trousers on, a pair of Jo's knickers (so she's probably not wearing any), and a rather large jacket that Wim had last year. I'm just considering whether to eat or put my balaclava on. Can't do both, of course. Wondering whether I can put the hand-warmers in my boots, or should I keep them in case the burner valves freeze again?

Lucky for me that I did not know what was happening in Geneva. At Swiss Control Greg Moegli was on duty and trying to make contact with his opposite numbers in Mexico. As he said afterwards, 'The guy didn't speak English well, and when he couldn't understand what I was saying, he started to sound aggressive. So I said, "Stand by. I'll call you back in twenty minutes." '

Greg rushed home and woke up his wife, Claudia, who is from Colombia. 'Speak to this guy,' he said, and she talked to him in Spanish. The Mexicans then became very helpful, but they pointed out that the balloon had no clearance to cross their country; so at 3 a.m. Claudia had to sit down and type a letter in Spanish, which Greg immediately faxed to Mexico City and Cuba. Greg feared that Cuba might present a big problem, but Claudia managed to charm the Commandant General of the civil aviation authority and, four hours later, clearances came through from both places.

BERTRAND

By the end of Sunday, 15 March, we were heading for Mexico at 73 knots, exactly as Luc and Pierre had predicted we would. Our confidence in them was fully justified, and hope ran high again. 'We are very happy to be here,' I faxed Control, 'even if it is sometimes difficult.' I had been listening to a CD of the Eagles, and the words of the song 'Hotel California' – 'We're prisoners here of our own devices' – seemed to apply perfectly to Brian and myself.

Then Luc advised us to gain one more degree southwards to pick up speed by positioning ourselves in the centre of the jet. We did move south, but, as it turned out, slightly too much: the jet was probably spreading, and we strayed towards the outside of it. When we were above the clouds, we had the impression we were being pushed northeast, but below the clouds we went the opposite way — illustrating again that a jet stream is not a single, unified mass of wind, but probably includes a variety of air currents that wind round its core in a spiral.

None of us could know it at the time, but that was the only mistake Luc or Pierre ever made, and it was the beginning of our worst problem.

CHAPTER TEN

CAST ADRIFT

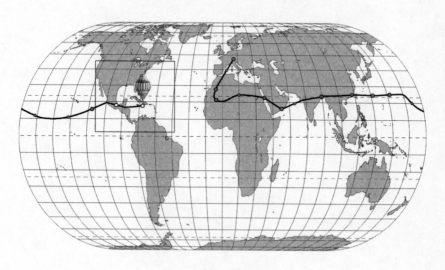

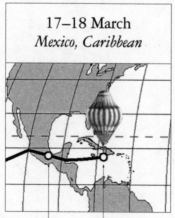

17–18 March
Mexico, Caribbean

Southern Mexico
08:00 Z
FL 340
54 knots

Jamaica
08:00 Z
FL 350
56 knots

BERTRAND

On 16 March I went to bed just after sunset, but I was cold in the bunk, and it seemed to take me hours to get to sleep. Then I had a very strange dream: Brian and I had got round the world but were the only people who knew we had done it. We had to avoid everybody until the official ceremony – I wasn't even been able to say hello to anyone.

As usual, Brian woke me a few hours before dawn. He was holding a torch to his mouth, as if it were a microphone, and said, 'Hello, Dr Piccard. How do you feel about being the long-distance record holder for ballooning?' I played my part, as if in an interview, and said, 'Well – the distance record will only be a consolation prize if we don't make the whole circuit. So I really hope we'll get round.' Then I added, 'Wasn't that a good answer for someone who has just got out of bed?' 'Yes,' he said, 'it was a brilliant answer – and this is Brian Jones, speaking in *Breitling Orbiter 3* for Radio X.' What I didn't realize was that he had set up the video camera and was filming the whole performance.

During the night we had beaten Steve Fossett's distance record of 14,236 miles, made before he came down in the Coral Sea in August 1998 – although in a balloon you don't really *beat* anything or anybody.

Your passage is too gentle for such a term. Rather, I think of every record as a gift of the wind. Anyway, a lot depends on how the calculation is done. In terms of sheer distance we had outstripped the record long before, but the FAI (Fédération Aéronautique Internationale) had decreed that, in determining total distance, flights must be broken up into segments and that a segment only counted if its length was at least half the earth's radius – that is, 3,000 kilometres (or 2,000 miles). Our initial passage down to Morocco was too short to count as a segment, so our distance was measured directly from Château d'Oex to Egypt, losing us 6,000 kilometres.

During the night the balloon had exceeded 100 knots for the first time, and in the middle of the day I reported a 'personal speed record in a balloon' of 102 knots. Luc and Pierre were in ecstasies: they had brought off their incredible gamble of sending us so far south and were confident we would remain in the jet all the way to Africa. Brian and I really thought we were going to make it, and in all media interviews everyone sounded euphoric. Everything suggested that we would come hurtling home, and the press started to say that we were on our way to success as we 'just had the Atlantic left'. In fact we still had 8,000 miles to go.

BRIAN
The faxes show how spirits picked up all round, and Sue caught the general tone with her umpteenth limerick:

> There were two balloon pilots over the Pacific
> Who said, 'Now we must be specific.
> With a record to break,
> We could do with a cake –
> And a glass of champagne would be t'riffic.

I'd never dreamt that we would get all the way round, but I had been praying inwardly that we would at least reach the USA. If we conquered the Pacific, we would automatically have the distance record – and probably the duration record – which in itself would be a triumph. Already we had accomplished an unbelievable flight, and even if it ended west of the Atlantic we would still be fêted. Realizing that we couldn't now fail altogether was a tremendous relief to me.

One result of crossing the Pacific was that the Atlantic suddenly seemed far less daunting. In fact, ridiculous as it sounds, it seemed such a small challenge as to be almost insignificant.

BERTRAND

All through 16 March we continued eastwards at high speed, flying at our ceiling of 34,000 feet. But one major disadvantage of travelling in the jet stream is that cirrus clouds come with you, shading out direct sunlight. And because we were in cirrus and the balloon was forming its own cloud around the envelope, we had to keep burning a lot to maintain altitude even in daylight. The result was that we were getting through an awful amount of fuel, and for the first time we had to start using our lithium batteries at night because the sun wasn't charging the main batteries enough during the day. To save power, we sent messages to Geneva by fax (which uses very little current) and asked them to inform Oceanic Control in Oakland about our position. So I lost contact with the amazingly beautiful woman – as I'm sure she was – who had been fancying me.

Geneva was getting position reports automatically every hour from our Capsat system, and once we had established the relay procedure, all we had to do was to fax them on the half hour with our flight level and a confirmation of our position. They would then pass on details to Oakland, telling them precisely where we were. The system was a great boon to us because it meant we didn't have to monitor the HF radio continuously and could listen to music on CD. To be constantly tied to the radio was frustrating because whenever one of us was asleep, the other had to switch off the loudspeaker and listen through headphones, and the leads were so short that we couldn't reach either the kettle or the burner controls with the headset on.

Then came the first hint of trouble. Having pushed us farther to the south to stay in the centre of the jet, Luc and Pierre suddenly told us we were going *too* far south: we needed to pull our heading back from 84 to 80 degrees.

In the afternoon Oakland Oceanic Control handed us over to the Mexican control centre at Mazatlán. 'Mexican ATC is happy,' Alan told us. 'So are the Cubans. And New York is orgasmic at the thought of having you in their airspace over the Atlantic.' The media were behaving as if we had already completed our mission. 'Garfield Kennedy, ITN and NBC are planning to put chase planes in the air over Mexico,' Alan faxed. He continued:

> Unfortunately, you will arrive over Mexico at dusk and be out over the Caribbean before daylight. Garfield will want to attempt to download the good video footage again. Last time they got no pictures, only sound. Could you please follow the wiring round and make sure that all connections are good. They can't say what is wrong – only that we should check everything and make certain the green light is on on the transmitter under the desk. Many thanks.

Later that day I encountered another problem. Luc wanted us to climb still higher, so I tried to shed weight by dropping two empty tanks – 10A and 10B. I saw 10A fall away all right, but I never saw 10B go, though it made the normal noise of a tank being released, and in some alarm I reported to Control that it might be stuck.

Our method of ditching the tanks was to pass an electrical current through the bit of a soldering iron. The nylon tape holding the tank in place was wound round the bit of the iron and held fast by a spring. When the bit became hot it melted through the tape, releasing the tank. But when this one failed to drop off, I couldn't tell what had happened. Through the dome of the top hatch I could see that the retaining strap was still tight, but not why.

When Alan heard about the situation, he too became worried. 'Maybe when Brian is awake you should both jump up and down to shake the gondola,' he advised, and went on:

> I am serious about this suggestion, because it would be terrible if the tank was to drop over Mexico. Also suggest when you talk with Garfield in the chase plane that you ask him to count the number of tanks on each side – but don't tell him why! If the tank is stuck, you will need to go down and outside to see if you can release it manually while still over water.

BRIAN

We didn't have long to deal with the problem because we were only a few hours from the Mexican coast. The idea of another EVA seemed outrageous. We were flying at 34,000 feet and 105 knots: if we went down, we would lose the jet stream – and probably our whole flight. At the very least, a four- or five-hour delay would cost us 500 or 600 miles and a big expenditure of fuel. But we were prepared to make the sacrifice, and fail in our mission, to avoid injuring or killing anybody on the ground. The dilemma was torture for us.

We talked to the technicians at the control centre, but nobody could throw much light on what the cause of the problem might be. Because there had been so much ice around the cylinders, we first thought that the rogue tank must be frozen into place. If so, there should be no problem because we were going to pass over Mexico at night, when the temperature would be well below zero, and there would be no chance of the ice melting and the tank falling away.

All the same, following Alan's instructions, we tried to dislodge the tank by jumping from side to side in unison, one of us at the front of the capsule, the other at the back. We certainly got the gondola rocking, and we could hear the full cylinders clanking against its sides – which suggested that they were loose, and not iced up. But nothing fell. Through the outrigger bars we could see that the strap that held 10B in place was still under tension, so we assumed the tank was well secured. Concluding that the straps must have been routed wrongly and that there was no chance of the cylinder falling on its own, we felt very relieved that we didn't have to go out again and could carry on safely. In fact (as we discovered just before landing) heat had welded the burnt edge of tape into a hard lump, which was too thick to pull through the eye of the weighing mechanism, making it jam.

But Alan was still not satisfied. He advised us to try various other moves, suspecting that the cylinder had become wedged between its neighbours. If that was so, he faxed, we might have to consider an early EVA, possibly on oxygen at high level. 'Warning:' he added, 'very soon you will have an island below, or almost below. Check the position carefully on your charts before any drop.' After all our efforts, the strap still appeared to be tight.

In spite of the problem, and the major anxiety it was causing us, there was great excitement in the control centre. 'Hi, guys,' Cecilia faxed. 'Enthusiasm and spirits are running high throughout the world in support of your flight! Thought I'd share a few of the messages that have come through on the Internet:

Go on! Do it! (Karl, Bulach, Switzerland)

You guys are a great source of encouragement for people with dreams. PLEASE LAND IN EGYPT, by the Giza Pyramids. You can make it! God bless all your excellent team. (Nabil Mikhail, Cairo, Egypt)

Beware, free-range chicken farm by the Pyramids. (Tom Holt Wilson)

Hello, this is Apron Control Crew from Zurich airport. All the best. You will make it!'

The mention of the chicken farm was a reference to the occasion when, during a festival at Northampton, with eighty-odd balloons taking part, I inadvertently flew over a chicken house and was banned for the rest of the event – no mean humiliation for the chief flying instructor. The incident has pursued me ever since.

That night, after seven days over water, we at last made landfall by crossing the coast of Mexico. From 34,500 feet I could see nothing below us, but I was elated and sent down my latest offering:

> *The girls in Mexico City*
> *I'm told are incredibly pretty.*
> *But we're just passing by*
> *In the Mexican sky.*
> *Dammit – it seems such a pity.*

In the early hours of 17 March I reported:

Contact with Mexico City on VHF. Huh – so that little puddle was what they call the Pacific. Thanks for the Internet messages. It's really nice to know that so many folks are following our little jaunt.

Soon, however, trouble set in. To maintain our extreme altitude I was having to burn constantly, and our latest pair of tanks were about to go dry after only sixteen and a half hours. If the remaining four pairs did no better, clearly we were not going to make the Atlantic. 'Could be ice, or just the burners at this altitude,' I faxed. 'We need to ask Luc if there is any chance of achieving this speed at a lower level, otherwise we could be in the dwang.'

Then came the worst shock. We were already well inland when I felt the gondola twitch and heard a faint noise. 'I'm pretty sure we just lost the tank that was hung up,' I reported — and I gave our precise position in case someone should later find the tank, or, worse, the damage it had caused. Bertrand — in bed at the time — also heard the noise, felt a flush of adrenaline course through his entire body and pulled the pillow over his head. Later he told me he could not go back to sleep because of the terrible visions racing through his mind.

It was a dreadful moment. If we'd killed somebody, the whole flight would be ruined and our dream destroyed. After that, the night was full of worries — about the tank, our fuel, our speed, our heading. At 05:10 I reported:

At FL 335 track is 095 — too far to the south, I fear. This is a really tricky one. Tank pair 3 is still going, but I'm sure it's running on vapour. With the size of these tanks there seems to be an enormous amount of vapour. Therefore difficult to assess fuel usage until I go on to a new pair. I am already south of Luc's target for 06:00 Zulu by about half a degree, so I assume too far south is bad.

I think I'm most concerned about the fuel situation, though, if the Atlantic crossing needs to be high. Will let you know what transpires. Hope we don't get our collar felt by Mexican police-man for hostile acts from the air with regard to that tank. It looks as if it fell over the lower part of the mountains, according to the map. Fingers crossed.

Messages flashed up and down as I urgently sought advice on what compromise to make between height, speed and direction. At 06:10 I sent down my latest assessment:

> Pair 3 lasted nineteen hours to absolutely empty. They started in the middle of last night at 10:30 Zulu. Sunrise was at 14:00 Zulu. They have lasted until 05:30 Zulu. We did quite a lot of burning during the day. It seems that when we are in the jet there is often stratus/cirro stratus above us. There is no doubt, I think, that we do have to burn more fuel above, say, 30,000 feet. So if the last four pairs give similar performance, they will last until 12:00 Zulu on Saturday – that is, completely out of fuel, with no landing reserve, of course.
>
> I think we would use less fuel if we managed to stay clear of cloud, and/or could fly at around FL 300. I don't know how much, so the trade-off between speed and altitude is a difficult one . . . Down to Luc's and Pierre's calculations now, I suppose. But the gut says we have to go for it.

Along with all the other irritations, the alarm on the burner control monitor had started going off every minute even though nothing was wrong, and I faxed for immediate instructions from Kieran on how to disable it without damaging anything else. In due course he faxed back, and I managed to quell the noise by delving into the mass of wires in the burner control panel – though not before it had started going off every twenty seconds. In spite of the difficulties, I was enjoying things and told John and Debbie, 'Never a dull moment, is there? We're certainly having to fight for it.' I was becoming more and more preoccupied with the question of whether or not we had the resources to tackle the Atlantic, but still I felt fairly buoyant. At 09:34 I told Alan, who had just returned to the control centre:

> Tank Pair 9 [which we had reckoned to be empty] still going after four hours. Every little helps. Assuming we are going for the Atlantic, would like to be kept abreast of current thinking and be part of the decision-making process, please. Unfortunately we can't see the tank which was hanging on. The dome is just not tall

enough, even trying to use a mirror. I'm pretty sure I felt it go, though . . . One of the webbing straps is gone, whereas before we could see it . . . Hope to God we didn't hit anything.

Alan, trying to analyse why we were using so much fuel, reckoned that at some time during the past twenty-four hours we must have accidentally pushed the balloon through its ceiling and caused it to vent helium, thus reducing its lift and forcing us to burn more often. Ice on the envelope would not make much difference, he assured us – but he was very concerned about fuel. Advising us to come down from 34,000 to 33,000 feet, he added:

It is VITAL that you do not push the ceiling. You need to squeeze every last gasp of propane from each tank, and monitor fuel use constantly. Our [computer] programme still says you can complete the circumnavigation with a little to spare, but we need good wind speeds and no further increase in fuel consumption.

By 10:00 Zulu I was exhausted, and faxed, 'Bertrand up now, so both active for a while. I think I'm going to let him put me under a spell tonight. If I don't sleep soon, my skin is going to be terrible for the homecoming.' Then, as an ominous last thought, I added, 'FL 335, but we've lost 10 knots and gained five degrees right.'

BERTRAND

It was so cold in the bunk that even with two sleeping bags together, one inside the other, I was still shivering and only dozed lightly. When Brian woke me, he told me the balloon had burnt a tremendous amount of propane and that our chances of reaching Africa seemed poor. Soon he went to bed and left me alone in the cockpit, with my stomach full of butterflies.

I think I had been undermined by the cold. Whatever the cause, my morale hit rock bottom that morning and I saw no beauty in the dawn as the sun rose over the wooded mountains of Mexico. Our speed dropped dramatically and our track veered from due east to nearly 110 degrees: we were no longer heading for Africa but for Venezuela, and final disaster threatened. Even when Luc came on the phone and said,

'Don't worry – your trajectory will swing to the left, and in eighteen hours you'll pick up the jet stream again', I found it very hard to believe him.

A temporary lift arrived in the form of a message from Buckingham Palace, relayed by Alan, who added 'I'm not joking' at the end of it:

> His Royal Highness the Duke of Edinburgh requests the company of Dr Bertrand Piccard and Mr Brian Jones when he visits Cameron Balloons in Bristol on 1 April 1999.
>
> If Dr Piccard and Mr Jones are successful in completing their round-the-world balloon flight, the Duke will be accompanied by Her Majesty the Queen.

'Wonderful to see the Queen if we succeed,' I replied, 'but even more wonderful to succeed.' Not being in a good mood, I added over the phone, 'I like people who believe in us whether we succeed or not. So if the Queen is waiting to see what happens before she decides whether or not to visit us, she'd better not come!' Alan laughed and said, 'Bertrand, generally speaking, you're right, but the Queen is an exception.'

By then I was direly worried by our speed, which had fallen to 42 knots, and by our track of 100 degrees, which had swung back a little but was still too much south. 'When is the jet going to help us again?' I wanted to know. To take my mind off our present anxieties, I asked about the new duration record claimed by Andy Elson before he came down in the Sea of Japan, and whether we stood to beat it. John answered:

> Andy's record claim is seventeen days, eighteen hours and thirty-five minutes. Per Lindstrand has claimed an altitude record of 11,095 metres (we think you have probably exceeded that!). Dick Rutan's round-the-world flight [in the powered *Voyager* aircraft] was 41,000 kilometres.
>
> Luc is happy with your track, but has warned that speed will not pick up for twenty-four hours. However, this has been accounted for in his plan, and he is still expecting the round-the-world to be OK for Saturday.

At that very moment, a ceremony to celebrate Colin and Andy's flight was being held at Camerons in Bristol. When Don Cameron congratulated the crew on their new absolute duration record, Andy responded with a wry smile, 'Until bloody tomorrow!'

In spite of these various encouragements my spirits remained low, not least because I had begun to feel very strange. For some reason I couldn't explain I was completely out of breath, panting even when I had made no physical effort. As time went on I became more and more uncomfortable – and then, well before his rest period was up, Brian emerged from the bunk looking white and unsteady.

'I can't breathe,' he said.

'I can't either,' I told him. We were both shaken by our sudden disability. Soon I felt so ill that I called Control on the satellite phone and, hearing that Michèle was there, asked to speak to her. That was probably a mistake, for at the sound of her voice I broke down and burst into tears.

'Can you imagine,' I sobbed, 'it looks as though we're going to fail *now*, so close to our goal. After all this effort . . . We're going more and more to the south and we're running out of fuel. We can't see any way out of this problem. We're never going to make it.'

Michèle was very sympathetic, but she remained perfectly calm. 'I don't understand,' she said. 'The weathermen are confident you're going to get back to the jet.' She was certain everything would work out all right. Her good sense steadied me a little, but still I felt very ill.

That was also my first chance in ten days of speaking to Swiss Radio, which had been broadcasting my father live from the studio every afternoon. So I phoned them and gave a short commentary: 'I am in the cockpit. Brian is trying to sleep. We're both out of breath and it's really not the best of days.' When they heard me gasping and hardly able to talk, everyone on the ground became extremely anxious and started to call doctors and specialists for advice. It was all too easy for them to visualize horrific scenarios: the two pilots falling unconscious and silent as the balloon drifted away southwards, out of control, to vanish for ever in the wastes of the ocean.

Brian and I, though uncomfortable, were quite clear-headed. We knew where we were and what we were doing. We could calculate perfectly well. But Control, not being sure of that, started asking obvious questions to test us. At first Brian didn't realize what they were doing and became angry. When Alan asked him, 'When's your birthday?' he burst out with, 'For Christ's sake! We've got enough fucking trouble up here without you worrying about when my birthday is!' Alan persisted, and Brian said, 'Well, it's the twenty-seventh of March.'

'OK. What's your phone number?'

'For fuck's sake, Alan . . . ' And then he suddenly realized that they were trying to check whether we were hypoxic – short of oxygen – whereupon he laughed and calmed down.

Our symptoms were not those of hypoxia. Nor did it seem we were suffering from another possible problem – a build-up of carbon dioxide in the atmosphere of the gondola. The digital read-outs of the CO_2 monitors had not moved at all, and neither of us had a headache. One sensor, on top of the bunk, had been covered with clothes and so may not have been working; but the other was right at the front of the capsule, behind the instrument panel, and was probably functioning properly. In spite of the reassuring readings, we felt we were slowly being asphyxiated.

BRIAN

While in bed I had been finding it hard to breathe, but it wasn't until I got up that I realized something was seriously wrong. As I looked out through the curtain I saw Bertrand sitting in the right-hand pilot's seat, slumped against the bulkhead, gasping like a fish.

When he started talking to Michèle in French, I couldn't follow what they were saying, but clearly he was distraught and in a hell of a state. I realized we were both suffering from accumulated stress, though luckily I had slept reasonably well and wasn't feeling too bad at that moment. 'Look,' I said, 'it's all right. You're knackered, so get yourself into bed.'

Off he went, burying himself in three sleeping bags, with all his clothes on and wearing an oxygen mask connected by tube to our central supply. Every five or ten minutes, wearing my own oxygen mask, I went to look at him to make sure he hadn't died in the bunk.

On the ground, people were telephoning doctors and specialists in a frantic search for clues as to what could be wrong. Alan faxed:

Brian, I am talking with the top professor in Switzerland. He wants to know if you have the drug Nifedipine on board. This is used to help prevent something called pre-oedema. He is concerned that your symptoms may be those of early pulmonary oedema [an accumulation of fluid in the lungs], which could be serious.

We recommend you descend to FL 250, or less, until we have further medical discussions. You should also increase oxygen content of atmosphere – but be careful not to make it explosive. Can also use bottled oxygen for direct delivery. Please report results. Back soon, Alan.

As I sat at the pilot's desk, I kept thinking, 'I *don't* feel at all well, but it's hardly surprising after what we've been through,' and I tried to accept the breathlessness as just another discomfort. Then, with the benefit of the oxygen, I gradually began to feel better.

As my head cleared, I thought, 'Well – screw the instruments. They may not be working. I'm going to change the filters and see what happens.' So I changed both the CO_2 and the carbon filters, and in a few minutes things started to improve.

Through all this I was still having to fly. We had been at 34,400 feet, but I kept finding that the balloon wanted to go down and was having to burn every twenty seconds to maintain altitude. So I settled at 32,000 feet and, after consulting Alan about other possible flight levels, I added:

If Michèle is there, please tell her Bertrand is OK. He is still in bed and is on oxygen. He was a little emotional on the phone.

Got your message re oedema. I'll ask Bertrand when he wakes. But we have both been on constant-flow oxygen for half an hour, and I feel much better. Cabin oxygen level now 18.9 per cent – equivalent to 26.9 per cent at sea level. I will be careful, but we don't want to jeopardize the flight unnecessarily.

The balloon has stabilized reasonably well around FL 320. I am certainly using a lot less fuel at this level, and have 100 degrees, 38 knots.

Alan replied:

Luc is happy with your float altitude of around 320. If we lose a little speed but save a lot of fuel, it's a good strategy. Track is also OK.

We are considering whether you might be suffering from long exposure to styrene [in the glue used to bind the shell of the gondola]. To clear that, you could de-pressurize at altitude, and re-pressurize using nitrogen and lox. However, this might be a wild goose chase.

Please ask Bertrand to stop calling radio and TV stations. His breathing problem is now the talk of Switzerland, and we are telling the media that you are both too busy and tired to talk to them.

To re-pressurize, we would have released oxygen for one second and nitrogen for four seconds, and repeated the process until correct pressure was obtained, creating a mixture of 20 per cent oxygen and 80 per cent nitrogen. In the end, though, we had no need to do this.

The one positive result of our discomfort was that everyone on the ground at last realized we were not having a picnic but were engaged in a difficult and dangerous endeavour. To the public, everything had perhaps seemed too easy until that moment.

Control had phoned the manufacturers and discovered that styrene can in certain unusual situations act as a depressant and can also cause difficulty in breathing. For a few moments this seemed to fit the bill. Although not exactly depressed, we were tired, frightened and sad-dened by forebodings of failure – and we were certainly having trouble with our respiration. But when we looked back on our mysterious affliction, we decided that the Swiss professor's diagnosis had probably been correct and that we were suffering from a pre-oedema of the lungs brought on by breathing exceptionally dry air for days on end. It was so cold inside the gondola that all moisture was condensing on the hatches, and the moisture content of the air was very low – only about

29 per cent. Breathing air like that when we were tired and cold could have caused the condition. When we put on masks, the oxygen helped, obviously, but the masks also trapped moisture, which gave further relief. Bertrand had included drugs for oedema in his medicine chest, but we didn't take anything because we were so uncertain.

After checking Bertrand again and finding that he was still comfortable, I called Michèle myself. I didn't know what had passed between them, but I wanted to reassure her. 'Don't worry,' I told her. 'Bertrand's OK. He's gone to bed, he's on oxygen, and whatever this crisis is, we'll get through it.'

'Thank you, Brian,' she said. 'You're a very nice man.'

I also spoke to Jo, who came up with a wonderfully moving remark: 'If love and best wishes could be your fuel, you'd now be on your second lap.'

I asked Jo to contact the head of the RAF Aeromedical Centre at Boscombe Down, who had put us through our hypoxia drills in training. He thought our symptoms pointed to carbon dioxide poisoning – except that neither of us had a headache, normally the first sign of excessive CO_2 in the atmosphere.

BERTRAND

In spite of the cold and the bulky mask, I fell into a deep sleep and woke two hours later much refreshed. Physically, things were better, but we were in a dilemma. I still wasn't sure what was for the best. Should we fly high to achieve a better speed and track? Or should we fly low in order to use less fuel and have more time to think? The weathermen wanted us to go high, but Alan was insistent that we burn less fuel.

While I was asleep Brian had brought the balloon lower, but our speed had fallen drastically. He had done exactly what Control had instructed, yet we felt powerless as we headed more and more to the south, being pushed further away from the jet.

A friend of mine, Pierre Steiner, a doctor who practises hypnosis, had heard me panting during the radio interview and had an intuition that he must help me; so at 10 p.m. local time in Geneva he went to the control room and asked to see Pierre Eckert. The met man was a bit surprised, as were the controllers, who thought this stranger might be some sort of freak. But Pierre Eckert came through on the satellite phone and asked, 'Do you want to speak to him?'

'Of course!' I exclaimed. 'Immediately!'

So the second Pierre came through and gave me a hypnosis session over the phone. He knew me very well because we had conducted some workshops and training sessions together, and he knew my 'safe places' – a technical term that means the thought, feeling, image or memory in which you feel safe and comfortable. Once a hypnotist establishes what a person's particular refuges are, he can always lead him or her back to a state of calm.

Pierre said, 'Let your safe places come back into your memory' – and at once I started to feel better. Then he went on, always speaking when he heard me breathe out:

> You know, you and Brian are doing the most difficult thing in the world. It's absolutely normal that you're anxious. Before every great success, there's bound to be a phase of anxiety. Without that, there's no big achievement. If you felt comfortable above the Gulf of Mexico, it would probably mean that twenty people had gone round the world before you. In fact, the more anxious you are, the better it is, because it means you're that much closer to success. You and Brian have already flown farther than anyone in history. Don't give a damn about being anxious! It's great to be anxious! Enjoy it! When you land in Africa, you'll look back on your anxiety as the first sign of your triumph.

In professional terms, he had 'reframed' our situation: he had described what was happening but had put a completely different interpretation on the facts. The result was wonderful: I felt infinitely better. When Pierre Eckert came back on the line, I thanked him for putting the other Pierre through; I said I felt much better and would like to try something new. What should we go for in terms of heading and altitude?

'Go as high as the balloon can fly,' he told me. 'Go to the extreme limit. I think you'll find the wind a little more to the left, and you'll escape from Venezuela. As high as you can – that's the last chance of saving the flight.'

So I switched on the burners and went up and up, regardless of fuel consumption. Then I phoned Michèle again. I told her I'd had two hours of good sleep, and that after the hypnosis session with Pierre I felt a new man. 'Brian's now in bed,' I said, 'and I'm trying the last possible manoeuvre to save the flight.'

Being in contact with her made me feel better still; but as we talked I was burning, burning propane like there was no tomorrow – and still we were heading disastrously for Venezuela. Then suddenly I said, 'Michèle! Something's happening. Wait . . . Yes! The wind's changing. The GPS is showing one degree more to the north. Now it's two degrees! Now it's three! This is *fabulous*.'

I was so excited that I kept up a running commentary. 'I've only a hundred metres left before we hit the ceiling . . . But look! Incredible! Now we're really turning . . . We've gone round *ten* degrees! Can you believe it, Michèle? Twelve degrees!'

'No!' she exclaimed. 'How strange we should be talking at this very moment!'

'Even better,' I told her. 'From a hundred, the track's gone to eighty-five. Amazing! Now, really, I think we're going to do it!'

It did seem extraordinary that Michèle was live on the phone when the miracle occurred, and that she was able to share my excitement. By the time she rang off we were at 35,000 feet, and all at once we were no longer heading for Venezuela but for Jamaica. Our speed was still only 41 knots, but our track was 82 degrees and exactly what we wanted. In a few minutes our prospects had been transformed.

When Brian took over again after a two-hour rest, I was thrilled to tell him about the momentous change in our fortunes. I then went back to bed and, keeping Pierre's words in mind, used self-hypnosis to bring on sleep. The safe place I chose was a scene from my childhood. Every evening when I went to bed as a boy, a turboprop plane used to come droning over Lausanne on some regular flight, and I would always listen for the comforting sound of its engines coming through my window as I was falling asleep. Now, imagining that the roar of the burners was the sound of the plane, I quickly fell into a deep sleep.

BRIAN

Back in the cockpit, with hope rising, I found that our drift to the north kept increasing. I faxed the Smiths, on duty in the control centre:

It's been quite a day – as if we hadn't had enough of those already. Need to ask a question at this critical stage. We've been given a set of targets, but already we're tracking to the north of them. Is this OK? Is it an advantage to encourage more north?

Cecilia replied:

In answer to your questions, I wish you could see the map we have here that shows the jet stream lying just to the north of you. It extends right across the Atlantic. Luc is not here now, but before he left I asked him if your track is good, and he said it was. Luccing at the map, the jet lies just northeast of Cuba, and it shows a steady increase in speed as you progress east . . . Jamaica know you're coming: 124.0 or 128.1 [MHz] when you get in range.

I realized our people on the ground were doing everything they could to keep our spirits up – and we were both heartened by a message from Bertrand's father, passed on by the press centre at Geneva:

Mes chers Bertrand et Brian,

Vous avez presque la victoire. Vous êtes fatigués, tendus, impatients d'atteindre le but. Qui ne le serait pas dans ces conditions? Tout le monde vous soutient de toutes les forces possibles.

Tout en étant prudents, ayez encore le courage d'aider, en réussissant, tous ceux qui vous aident ici de toutes leurs forces, de tout leur cœur, et de toute leur capacité. Il ne vous reste guère à faire que le millième de ce que vous avez fait en comptant les années que vous avez passées sur ce projet. Moins de trois jours pour arriver à 'votre Méridien' – avec un vent qui va encore accélérer pendant ce temps.

Courage. Tout le monde vous aime et vous embrasse.

Papa, Mercredi soir, 17 Mars.

PS. Peut-être qu'un peu d'exercice physique vous ferait du bien? (Je juge de loin.) Pourrait-on envisager une descente à 2,500 m et une bonne aération de quelques heures au hublot avant la traversée de l'Atlantique? (De nouveau, je parle de loin!) Pardon pour les conseils. C'est seulement pour vous dire combien on pense à vous.

My dear Bertrand and Brian,

You have victory in your grasp. You are tired, stressed out, impatient to reach the end. Who wouldn't be in these conditions? The whole world is backing you with every possible kind of support.

While remaining prudent, in the midst of your success, have the courage to help all those who are helping you here with all their strength, with all their heart, and with all their might. If you take into account the years you have devoted to this project, you only have to accomplish a thousandth of what you have achieved already.

Less than three days to go before you arrive at your meridian – with a wind that's going to keep accelerating all the way.

Courage. Everyone loves you and embraces you.

Papa, Wednesday evening, 17 March.

PS. Maybe a little physical exercise would do you good? (I'm judging from afar.) What about a descent to 2,500 metres and a good airing for a few hours with the hatch open, before the Atlantic crossing? (Again, I'm speaking from a distance!) Forgive me for offering advice. It's just to tell you how much everyone is thinking of you.

Bertrand was much moved by his father's solicitous good wishes, but there was no realistic chance of another low-level EVA, pleasant though that would have been. Our only option was to stay high. And just when we needed it, another psychological boost arrived from the air controller on duty at Kingston, Jamaica. When I came on the air with 'Hotel Bravo – Bravo Romeo Alpha: flight level three-five-zero, tracking zero-eight-one,' a delicious woman's voice answered.

'OK,' she said. 'What you doin', man?'

'We took off from Switzerland,' I answered. 'We're hoping to get round the world and aiming for Africa.'

'Hoowhee!' she cried. 'You guys sure am takin de chance!' Then she asked, 'Where are you anyway?'

'Overhead Kingston.'

'Stand by.'

Everything went quiet for a couple of minutes. Then she was

back, sounding a little disappointed. 'Bin outside,' she reported, 'but I can't see ya!'

Afterwards Bertrand claimed that I'd fallen in love with her – just as he had with the lady from Oakland, California – and when I'd gone off duty he called her up to say goodbye on my behalf. But even if the romance was short-lived, it came at just the right moment to raise morale. I took to signing myself 'Brian de honky man', and after some exchanges about cumulo-nimbus clouds ahead of us over the Caribbean, Smiffy came back with:

> Well, hello, Man. Hoowhee – sounds like de pinkies up dere am makin a hit wid de locals. Good news for de price of bananas. Pull down de blinds – don't want dem limbo dancers getting in for free agin. Can't see no more weather on de chart . . . You agree with your flight conditions?

I answered:

> Hey, Man, don' gimme no jibe. You done teke dem damn CBs, and you done shove 'em.
>
> I think that in deference to our position Pierre should give the next met brief in rap style.
>
> It be a little up and down. Is it possible we could be having some down-draughts – light ones? The balloon occasionally takes it into its head to do a dive. Takes a lot of burning to get it back up.

As our speed wound up to 60 knots, everyone started piling on the jokes, saying they would see us in the bar at the weekend, and so on. But our people on the ground knew as well as we did that our fuel was critically short, and nobody was sure whether we had enough to cross the Atlantic. 'Most important,' Debbie faxed me at 10:30 Zulu, 'can you please give us exact status of fuel situation, tanks in use now, and for how long, and tanks remaining full. Alan suggests we take the yes/no-go decision for the Atlantic over Puerto Rico.'

There were too many unknown variables for anyone to make an exact computation of how long our propane would last. One was the temperature at high altitude over the Atlantic: how often, and for how long, would we need to burn in order to stay above 35,000 feet? But the most important factor was the speed of the jet stream. If it picked up to 100 knots or more, as we hoped, we would be home and dry.

BERTRAND

When I got up and came into the cockpit, I asked Brian where we were. He swivelled round in his chair and said, with a huge smile on his face, 'Bertrand – we're already past Jamaica and on our way to Haiti.' By then our speed was 65 knots – a fifty per cent increase over the 45 knots which had been predicted – and the miracle had begun. From that moment we were always faster than the forecast.

Flying over the Gulf of Mexico we had seen beautiful islands, and when we passed along the north coast of Honduras, many different countries were in sight: Mexico, Guatemala, Belize. But we had ceased to care about the scenery. The important thing was to have islands beneath us, and if we decided we had to ditch rather than tackle the Atlantic, it was here – before we passed Puerto Rico – that we would have to do it.

By the time dawn broke on 18 March, we had overflown Haiti and were overhead Santo Domingo. Our team at Swiss Control could not get through to Haiti, but the Puerto Rican air controller was a ball of fire. 'Don't worry,' he said, 'I'll tell them what you want.' Obviously he enjoyed acting as a relay. His counterpart in Santo Domingo was just as lively, and after talking to me exclusively in specialist jargon for a few minutes, he asked eagerly, 'What's it like up there?' When I tried to explain, he said, 'That sounds great! If you do it again, please give me a call, and I'll come with you.'

In the control centre eyes were starting to focus on Africa, and Alan reported:

> Everything is looking good at this end, but we should talk in around three hours when you are over Puerto Rico, just to check numbers and confirm the Atlantic crossing is feasible.

The balloon was at its ceiling. Heading and speed were perfect. Then suddenly we started drifting south again. When I called Luc and Pierre, they said, 'Don't vent any more helium than you have to, but your heading *is* bad: you have to lose height.'

What had happened was that we'd again been flying in cirrus cloud but, strangely enough, this time it had the effect of keeping solar heat trapped around the balloon so that the envelope became hotter and hotter and started to shed surplus helium through the appendices. I could see the tubes bulging full, right down to their lower ends.

It was a horrible dilemma. What was I to do? Every instinct told me to stay high. If we descended, we would have to burn more to gain height again later. In a game of poker it would have been a case of double or bust. But there was no point in having a bad track and enough fuel; we would be better off with a good track and dwindling propane. So I chose to double and took the terrible decision to open the valve at the top of the envelope and vent precious helium to make us descend.

Swivelling my seat round, I turned on the nitrogen tank and twisted the knob. *Psssshh* went the gas, forcing its way up the tube. Red lights came up on the instrument panel, showing that the valve was open. I vented five times, for twenty seconds each time, keeping my finger on the button. (We had made this a rule so that the valve wouldn't be left open by mistake.) After a while we started to lose altitude, and the descent seemed to do the trick, putting us back on the right heading; but for the whole of the rest of the day I had to compensate for the lost gas by burning precious propane.

Our remaining stock of fuel was pathetically small. We had one pair of tanks still full and one half-full – at most, forty hours of burning time. But as we headed towards Puerto Rico there was another favourable omen. We were shaping up to take the critical go/no-go decision when I noticed that the transponder code which Puerto Rico had given Brian to punch in was 5555. My lucky number, my favourite number, has always been five because for all the luckiest, happiest parts of my childhood, before my mother died, we were always five in the family. Fives had already appeared at particularly important moments in my life, and when I saw them again now, I couldn't believe they had come purely by chance. When I noticed the figures on the screen I stared at Brian and said, 'This is incredible! I don't know where this comes from, but surely it's a sign that we have to go, and that we'll do it.'

On the ground the media were becoming frantic. After the high drama of our falling ill, which went out live on radio and TV, everyone was hanging on one big question: were we going for the Atlantic or not? So many journalists were converging on the press room, which was separated from the control centre only by a partition, that the place was becoming seriously overcrowded. Some of the horde were forced to squat in the restaurant, and every time one of our team moved anywhere a dozen reporters pounced. 'It's just like a zoo here with journalists,' Alan told us. 'Pierre even gave an interview while he was having a piss! But I guess it's what Breitling invested in, so we're doing our best to keep everybody happy.'

It was during the afternoon of 18 March — already evening at the control centre — that we had to take the official go/no-go decision. Alan was proposing that we should do it live, in the middle of a staged press conference, so he faxed some instructions:

The conversation will be short and in English, because most of the crews here at the moment are British or from America — every big network. I will ask you about fuel tanks, number left; check life support; will advise brief met; ask how you feel about continuing on across; say it's OK by me, but final decision is yours.

Please do not prolong the call by asking to talk to Luc. We want to clear the Control Centre as quickly as possible, and then we can get Luc/Pierre to call you for any further briefing you need.

At the appointed hour, with television cameras from all over the world focused on him, Alan came on the phone and asked formally for our speed, our heading, our height and our fuel state. In the cockpit, with the loudspeaker switched on so that we could both hear, I held the receiver while Brian sat beside me with the necessary papers.

When we had run through the agreed formalities, Alan said, 'I think you can go for it.'

'Bertrand!' cried Brian. 'Tell him we're going anyway!'

Into my head came a marvellous remark made by Dick Rutan in a message which he sent me before the launch of the first *Orbiter*. Describing his own flight round the world in the *Voyager* aircraft, he told me how, for the last two days, he was convinced he had too little fuel to make it and how, when he landed, there was just half a gallon left. In conclusion he said, 'Bertrand, you always have to remember, the only way to fail is to quit.'

At that critical moment of our own flight, I quoted Dick's words. 'The only way to fail is to quit,' I said, '*and we're not going to quit*. Even if we have to ditch in mid-Atlantic, we go for it.'

Brian was one hundred per cent with me. We both had the feeling we could do it, that this was our last chance, that we had to go. To ditch in the big waves of the Atlantic would be dangerous and unpleasant, but not nearly as bad as going down in the Pacific. The odds were that rescue aircraft or ships would reach us fairly quickly. Yet our decision to carry on was not made in a fit of madness or despair: there was humour in it too. With our camera running, I consulted Sean the bear, who was sitting on the pilots' desk as usual. 'Sean,' I said, 'if you *don't* want us to do it, make a sign.'

Of course he did not move – but just in case, Brian addressed him sternly: 'Sean,' he said, 'before you answer, remember something. If you don't want to face the Atlantic, we have to ditch off Puerto Rico. And in Puerto Rico they *eat* bears.'

When the little fellow still made no move, we thanked him formally for being so helpful and said, 'Let's go!'

Emotion welled up again when a fax arrived from our three faithful colleagues at Swiss Control:

Cher Bertrand, Dear Brian,
Just to tell you how we three controllers, along with all our colleagues at Swiss Control, are gripped by your voyage round the world. All of us are living through highly charged moments. We're being constantly interrogated at meals, and people are trooping around the big display board with its map of the world to check up on your progress.
We all wish you good health and the form, both physical and psychological, to attack this grand finale. And even if you decide to stop, you can be assured that you have given us the

chance to take part in a huge, passionate and extraordinary adventure.

All courage – and our best wishes. Niklaus, Greg and Patrick.

As always, they were negotiating hard on our behalf. As we were leaving the Caribbean, the New York Oceanic controller told Niklaus that he had heavy traffic outbound from the area and asked him to bring the balloon down from its altitude of 35,000 feet. When Nik made a counter-suggestion – that the aircraft should fly lower – he was amazed when the American promptly agreed, saying, 'That's a good idea.'

But things soon became more difficult. At that time of the evening the area we were going to pass through next was heavily used by commercial aircraft, flying north and south, and New York told Nik that it was impossible for the balloon to continue eastwards at 35,000 feet. He was surprised because he had never expected to have any problem with the Americans. Now he said that he could not stop the balloon and that it had to stay at its present flight level because that was its most economic height.

New York Oceanic quoted a letter of agreement, which it had received from Breitling in advance of the flight, saying that we would be travelling between 31,000 and 33,000 feet. 'Stick to the agreement,' said the controller – and hung up. Nik waited a few minutes, called again and said, 'Listen – we have to talk about this a bit more.' He explained that the letter had been written two months earlier and that the jet stream had turned out to be higher than expected.

'Yes,' said the American, 'but what about all these other pilots? They can't stop their climb at 290 – it's not economic.'

'Surely you can discuss it with them?' Nik persisted. 'Ask them to stay at 290, or go up to 390, just for one night. Why not?'

'Well, we'll see. Maybe we'll try.'

'You do realize,' Nik added, 'that if our guys have to descend to 310, they won't make it. They'll ditch in the Atlantic – and you know who'll have to get them out? That's you, because they'll be in your control region.'

After a full thirty seconds' silence, the American said, 'Listen – I'll call you back.' Half an hour later he gave us clearance.

BRIAN

In going for the Atlantic we knew we were taking a calculated risk. Even if we failed make the coast of Africa, we would get more than three-quarters of the way across the ocean and would then be in fairly easy reach of rescue helicopters based at the American airfields on the Azores. If we ditched the chances of dying were quite small.

Down in the control room Alan was thinking ahead:

> Our best guess at the moment is a landing in Mali on Sunday at sunrise, but that might change. Mali is mainly desert and has lions, leopards etc . . . Getting to you could be a problem. We are going to fly in by private jet, but we might then have to get four-wheel-drive vehicles and drive across the desert because there do not seem to be any helicopters in Mali . . . If we miss Mali, the Nigerians are not being particularly helpful, and we can't get any aircraft into Libya. If you have the fuel, Egypt is still the best bet.
>
> James Manclark has been on the phone. So has Kevin Uliassi. Both offered congratulations on the flight so far and wished you success.

Acknowledging his fax, I returned to my facetious mode:

> Thanks for your thoughts on landing in Mali. You keep adding another twelve hours on to our journey.
>
> One thought which may help us get to Egypt, and might save your bottom in the rear of a four-wheel drive: do you think there would be any chance of pre-positioning a couple of *Orbiter 2*'s fuel tanks along our route – after the finish meridian, of course? We could simply tape them on and continue out of trouble.

To speed us on our way we got a wonderful message from Pierre Blanchoud, our aeronautical advisor, addressed to both of us:

> Luckily we have the prospect of a fast, high-altitude flight, in a

blue sky, without fear of CBs, because in winds of this speed CBs cannot form, and if one does climb almost to your height, it will soon disperse. Our maps show us a jet stream which will take you to Egypt without any problem.

Brian – Your dream has become a reality, and you may well land in the vicinity of the Pyramids.

Bertrand – Profit from these unforgettable moments of the flight. You should talk to the wind, your ally, and thank it, just as the sailor thanked the dolphin which saved his life. Observe how the clouds scatter from your route to let you pass, and how the cirrus above you shows you the route to follow, the jet stream . . .

You must remain concentrated and vigilant, both confident and receptive of what your intuition tells you. Visualize your landing in the sand – and until we meet again, may God hold you in the palm of His hand.

CHAPTER ELEVEN

LAST LAP

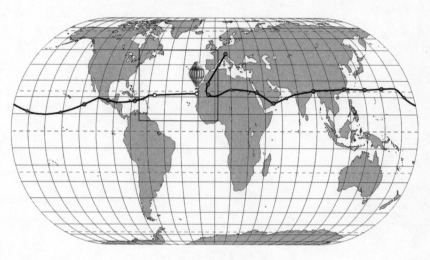

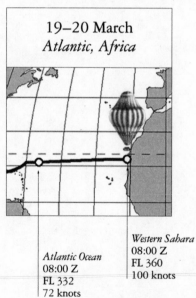

19–20 March
Atlantic, Africa

Western Sahara
08:00 Z
FL 360
100 knots

Atlantic Ocean
08:00 Z
FL 332
72 knots

BERTRAND

We went out over the Atlantic like a rocket. At 05:00 Zulu on 19 March – still for us the middle of the night – we were doing 80 knots, on a true track of 078, heading for Africa but also edging towards the centre of the jet stream. Dreadful as it had been to be ejected from the jet over the Gulf of Mexico, it was fantastic to be pulled back into it now. The cold was intense: outside the capsule the temperature was 50 below, and inside it was minus 2°C. One of our heaters had failed completely and the pilot light on the other had been reduced by ice to a pathetic flame an inch high. If I put a hand in front of the fans that were supposed to circulate warm air from the heating units, I felt only a cold draught.

When Brian woke me and I went back to the cockpit, it was still completely dark; and when the sun came up I saw that we were surrounded by cloud – a thick layer, probably alto-stratus, moving at the same speed as us. Inside the layer there was no sunlight, bringing the danger of condensation freezing on to the envelope and icing it up. To climb above the cloud I had to burn what seemed an appalling amount of propane, aware that every push was one less in the tanks. I forced myself to stop calculating precisely how much fuel might be left. Then at last we came out into full sunlight and our speed went up to 85 knots.

With frozen fingers I added a few words to my diary: 'I'm praying that the jet stream keeps us in its centre and doesn't eject us.' Every time I spoke to Pierre or Luc on the phone, I asked the same question: 'Are you sure we're not going to be ejected again? We just can't afford that.' And every time they answered, 'Don't worry. You're right in the centre. But if you could fly even higher, you'd go even quicker because the core is still above you.'

When I heard that the control centre had become a forest of parabolic antennae and that the media were going crazy with excitement, I noted:

I just cannot allow myself to think about things like that — because if I did, I would start to believe we'd already succeeded. I'm just not allowing myself to think of all the hopes of our team and our families and friends. I'm really starting to think we're going to do it, but I'm not allowing myself to believe it. And I think that even if we do succeed, I still won't be able to believe we've done it.

Everything had become unreal. For the past two days we'd been experiencing the extraordinary sensation of knowing that we were on the point of pulling off one of the greatest achievements imaginable and yet not being able to believe it. It hardly seemed possible that all those people in the control centre could be working on our behalf, and ' it seemed equally incredible that hundreds of journalists had become obsessed by what we were doing. We felt that suddenly the eyes of the entire planet were on us.

Time seemed to have stopped. There was no time any more. The beginning of the flight was both yesterday and an eternity ago. We had to count on our fingers to decide what day it was and enter the date in our log book.

In those moments of suspension I made a couple of promises to myself. One was that, if we succeeded, I would not take revenge on anyone who disparaged us during the project. I would not even hit back at critics like the self-styled aeronautical expert who had been briefly involved in another round-the-world balloon attempt that never got off the ground. The man appeared on Swiss German television saying that Breitling was mad to send off these two pilots, who were bound to fail. The balloon was too small, he claimed; it did not carry enough fuel, its crew was not properly trained, and it had taken off only for publicity purposes. Now I thought, let him and a few others eat their words.

During that afternoon the flight was smooth, the balloon was well balanced at 35,300 feet – just below the ceiling – and was making from 84 to 90 knots. Everything looked so promising that after Brian took over from me I was too excited to sleep. All the same, as I lay in the bunk listening to the burners, I was completely at ease. My body was so relaxed that I felt I was outside it: I had the impression that although my mind was awake, my body was asleep and refreshing itself.

That night was in any case made shorter by the fact that we were speeding eastwards and would cross the finishing line next day. Also, we were cutting down on our rest periods because we wanted to be in the cockpit together when that great moment came.

BRIAN

I couldn't believe how cold I was when trying to sleep. I was inside my sleeping bag, which was supposed to be effective down to Arctic temperatures – minus 35°C – but I never did get my feet warm. When I took over from Bertrand in the cockpit I was wearing every garment I had, including three pairs of trousers and several tops, with the whole lot inside the sleeping bag. Part of the trouble was that it was almost impossible to get one's circulation going by taking exercise. After the advice from Bertrand's father, I did try some press-ups – just possible in the central corridor if you kept your elbows in; but after getting out of bed one morning and doing thirty or forty squats, I found I could hardly move – so after that I gave exercise a miss.

The tension was affecting everybody. Having sent Control several messages and got no answer, I found that in my anxiety I'd been using the wrong fax. 'Sorry, must be the excitement,' I wrote. 'Am now on Capsat 2. No wonder you weren't talking to me.' Twenty minutes later I faxed:

Flight level 360, with 95 knots. Desperate to see 100 knots, but don't worry – I'm not desperate enough to go through the ceiling – unless there's a lady's boudoir above. We did flight level 365 earlier. How close is that to Per's record?

Control replied that, according to Alan, our pressure altitude must be about 38,000 feet, 'so all that noise must be these records breaking'. By then, after some jokes about how much alcohol was being consumed on the ground, I was addressing Smiffy as 'Squiffy':

Hello, Squiffy and C, How are you? Looks as if it may be the last night I sit here and freeze me diddlies in this seat. I suspect that if we're still flying tomorrow night, we'll both be at the helm. Another degree west, and I'll be able to fold the map so I can see land ahead. The back of my hand has swollen up, for some strange reason. Thought I must have knocked it, but it's starting to look like an infection. Won't it be absolutely typical that I'll be on antibiotics and therefore not able to drink anything for a week. You'll have to drink it for me. There – have you just seen his eyes light up, C?

Little did I realize what a huge web of people was helping us. When I asked Smiffy if he could find out the sea state in the Atlantic, he called his friend Mickey Dawson at New York Oceanic. After a chat, Mickey asked how he could help, and when he heard the request he exclaimed, 'Holy cow! Is he going to ditch?'

'No, no,' said Smiffy. 'He's just a Brit, and a bit cautious.'

'OK,' said Mickey. 'Give me ten minutes.'

When he called back, he said, 'Now! I've been talking to this really nice lady of the San Juan coastguard in Puerto Rico, and here's the weather at the surface: wind 310 at ten knots, one metre waves . . . '

Messages from our met men were consistently reassuring. 'Congratulations – you are in the middle of the jet stream,' Pierre faxed at midnight Zulu. 'However, the higher, the faster.' Urging us not to fly below 34,000 feet, he predicted a steady increase in our speed to 120 knots and concluded:

This leads to an entry into Egypt at 03:00 Zulu [on 21 March]. If you fly higher, it will be even faster. Flight level 380 gives 01:00 Zulu, for example. But save your fuel.

On the ground things really were going crazy. Control started to send us more of the Internet messages that were coming in from all over the world, especially America. 'Incredible!!! Keep it up and land safe,' wrote one man in Seattle. From California came, 'Go, cats, go', and from New Jersey, 'Doing a great job, guys. You're almost home.' What we did not know at the time was that Andy Elson had gone on television in the UK and claimed that, having done all the fuel calculations, he knew we were not going to make the coast of Africa.

BERTRAND

When Brian went to bed, I promised to wake him an hour before we reached the finishing line. As we sped towards Africa it was still fully dark. At that moment we were on tank pair No. 5 – a good omen for me. When I pressed the button on the instrument panel to see what sort of crazy figure the weighing mechanism would give, it read: 55 kilos. I remained completely still, overcome by an immense feeling of thankfulness. The sight of those magic figures made me cry and pray, both together. Afterwards I noted in my journal:

I love those signs. I don't know where they come from – but I'm happy to accept them as one of the mysteries of life. Many people don't even recognize such signs, and I am sure I myself miss a lot of them. The best moments are those at which you recognize a sign as it appears. Such coincidences cannot happen by chance. Once again I really have the impression we're being guided.

In a later entry I continued:

During our three-week flight in our own magical world of the gondola, there has been no let-up in the suffering of the people on the planet on which we've been looking down with so much admiration. There must be something we can do to alleviate all this suffering, using the celebrity that we are bound to get. It

would be nice to start a foundation of our own, which could give
help every year to some charity that promotes greater respect,
tolerance and harmony between people, and between people and
nature. We don't understand why we have so much luck up here.
But let's do everything we can to spread it around us.

That led me to think about the prize of one million dollars which the
American brewing company Budweiser had offered to the first crew
round the world. The company had stipulated that half the money
should go to a charity, and during the flight Brian and I had often
thought how nice it would be, when the time came, to choose a
recipient.

In the control centre the Smiths were on duty. 'Hello, my friends,' I
faxed. 'When we cross the finish line, you will all be in the gondola
with us. It will be the victory of passion, of friendship and of
endurance – that's why it will be the victory of all of us.'

'Thank you for your message,' the Smiths answered. 'We've been
with you all the way along, and we're not going to let you cross the
finishing line without us. You may be in range of Canaries Control:
124.7, 119.3 or 126.5.' A few minutes later Cecilia came through
again:

Dear Bertrand,
This will probably be my last message. It now feels like the lull
before the storm in here! I don't suppose I'll be able to get to the
keyboard after this.

Just wanted to say what a great honour it has been working
with you both on this very special project. Smiffy and I have both
said from the start how much we hoped the good guys would
win. We felt it was so important that, as Jo has said so often, the
prize must surely – HOPEFULLY – go to two balloonists who
feel passionately about ballooning. Now it seems that dream must
come true.

Much love from us both – Cecilia and Brian.

At 05:56 I faxed Control again to say, 'Hello, approaching the coast' –
but there was absolutely nothing to see. The GPS indicated we were

After nearly three weeks of flight, the *Breitling Orbiter 3* crosses the deserts of North Africa for the second time. Inside the balloon nothing has changed, the same concentration is still required, but on the ground champagne is overflowing in the control centre (*Bertrand Piccard and Brian Jones*).

Half an hour before landing in the Egyptian desert, the ice falling from the balloon envelope has collected on the red capsule as it flies low over the eroded terrain (*Bertrand Piccard and Brian Jones*).

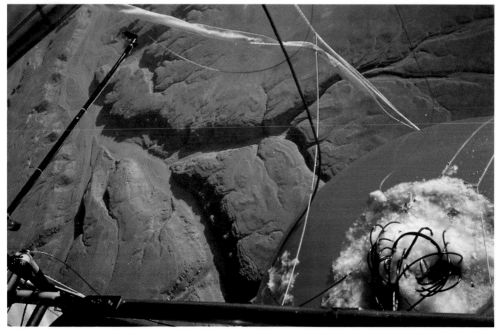

The first encounter with the Breitling aeroplane, taking pictures and filming as the balloon comes in to land in the Egyptian desert (*Popperfoto/Reuter*).

Seen from the Breitling jet plane, Brian and Bertrand try desperately to deflate their balloon as it turns into a vast sail which drags the capsule across the sand (*Sygma*).

Waving and cheering at the aeroplane: having landed safely in Egypt in the middle of nowhere, Brian and Bertrand start to realize that their dream has come true (*Martin Rütschi*).

As three hundred journalists desperately tried to get transport to the landing site, the only way to take a celebration picture was with a remote control camera. Note the ice on the tanks which shows how little fuel was left (*Bertrand Piccard and Brian Jones*).

Brian washing his hair with the only warm bottle of water (*Bertrand Piccard and Brian Jones*).

After seven hours in the desert, an Egyptian rescue helicopter finally arrives (*Bertrand Piccard and Brian Jones*).

As the news of the successful landing reaches the control centre, Alan Noble, flight director, sprays the rest of the team with champagne (*Associated Press*).

The two weather gurus, Pierre Eckert and Luc Trullemans, worked in synergy during the whole project. Together they were greater than the sum of their parts (*F. Wichser*).

The ground control team were almost as excited as the pilots after the success of the mission. Left to right (back): John Albury, Debbie Clarke, Brian Smith, Sue Tatford, Cecilia Smith. Front row: Joanna Jones and Alan Noble (*Cecilia Smith*).

The real moment when Brian and Bertrand could express their pleasure and their joy was when they were able to share their triumph with the rest of the team, with their families and with the thousands of people who had come to Geneva to welcome them as heroes (above – *Edipresse – Di Nolfi*; left – *Sygma*; below – *Popperfoto*).

Bertrand and Brian receiving the Olympic Order from Juan Antonio Samaranch, president of the IOC, beside the Olympic flame in Lausanne (*IOC Olympic Museum – Maeder*).

Her Majesty Queen Elizabeth II gave Bertrand and Brian the Charles Green salver at Cameron Balloons in Bristol, where the Queen also met the other team members (*PA*).

Bertrand and Brian at the monument erected in Château d'Oex to celebrate their successful flight (*Yvain Genevay*).

Back to Paris, where the book belonging to Jules Verne is returned to Jean-Jules Verne, the great-grandson of the famous writer (*Sygma*).

'We took off as pilots, flew as friends, and landed as brothers' (*Keystone*).

Symbolized by this frozen hatch in front of the rising sun, the greatest adventure of all is probably life itself (*Bertrand Piccard and Brian Jones*).

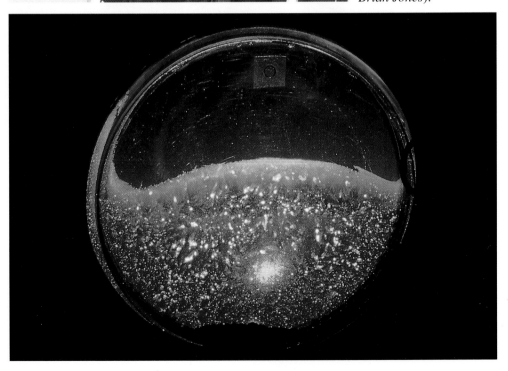

about to make landfall, but I had no visual evidence of it. That part of Africa was uninhabited and there was not a light to be seen – a big difference even from the west coast of India, where we had spotted Porbandar from miles away. From Geneva Jo answered:

> Good morning, Bertrand and Brian. According to our calculations, you should be crossing the coast now. Welcome to Africa! I hope you will have a beautiful sunrise and a glorious day. Much love – and we are thinking of you both.

I replied:

> Dear Jo, Your calculations are right. We are just coming back now to the Western Sahara after almost three weeks around the world. The hours before the finish are probably the longest of my life. First light of day just coming now. Best XXX – Bertrand.

Dawn was fabulous. At 06:15 the sun came over the horizon dead ahead, and I saw again the desert I had loved so much twenty days earlier. The finishing line was still 500 kilometres away, but, at the rate we were travelling, we would take only three hours to reach it. I wondered what could still stop us, when suddenly both burners blew out. I tried to re-ignite them without success. I whispered to myself, 'This is unbelievable, we are going to fail by just a few kilometres.' I took a deep breath to relax and finally managed to re-ignite the flame. A moment later I got a call to say that a chase plane with Terry Lloyd of ITN on board was coming up to film the balloon and conduct interviews.

The sun was barely up when I saw the small private jet come past. We were so high up that the pilot could not use his flaps and gear to slow down but had to keep going at high speed, leaving a huge white trail of condensation around us. As he went screaming past, Terry came on the radio, demanding that I wake Brian for an interview.

'Terry,' I said, 'throughout the flight we've kept our rule of never waking the other unless there's an emergency.'

'*Please*, Bertrand,' he pleaded. 'I absolutely need Brian for British TV.'

'All right,' I said. 'All I can do is talk loud enough over the radio so that, if Brian happens to be awake, he'll hear me and get up.'

'Talk louder, Bertrand! Shout!'

'Don't worry – I'm shouting.'

My raised voice soon took effect. Brian stuck his head out through the curtain of the bunk and staggered into the cockpit practically naked.

BRIAN

As the balloon sprinted towards the finishing line, we both put on our Breitling fleeces for the benefit of the video we planned to make and sat in the cockpit, counting the degrees of longitude downwards. Our speed was creeping up above the 100-knot mark.

But the flight was not over yet. As ever, our ground team were working away on our behalf. In the control room Brian Smith was exhorting everyone not to get carried away but to keep their eyes on the ball. Patrick Schelling faxed to say, 'We're almost there, but we still need to coordinate with air traffic control.' When he spoke to the tower at Dakar, which controlled Mauritanian air space, the man on duty said, 'Oh – so you're coming round again!' He said he would rather we flew at 35,000 feet but would accept our level of 36,000. Clearance had already been arranged for Libya and Egypt.

We knew that the main problem now confronting the control centre was that of recovering us when we came down. They didn't want us to land in Mauritania or Mali: apart from the leopards that Alan had mentioned, there were apparently mines scattered all over the place; and there were no helicopters. The next available country was Algeria, but the Algerians weren't very keen to have us and would not guarantee our safety. After that came Libya: Bertrand really wanted to land there because he'd heard that Gaddafi has a 200-strong, all-female bodyguard. But even if the good Colonel had given us a friendly welcome, he wouldn't have let the press planes in – and he might even have denied access to Breitling's private aircraft, which was bringing the recovery team.

That left Egypt – and towards the end of the flight the advice from Control was simply to stay as high as we could and keep going as fast as we could for as long as possible. I began to feel a bit stupid, because ever since Puerto Rico I'd been saying in faxes and interviews that I wasn't sure we had enough fuel to reach the African coast – and suddenly here we were proposing to carry on for several thousand kilometres. The reason was that our speed had tripled over the last leg – something we could not have foreseen.

Both of us had a feeling of invincibility, that we could do whatever we damn well pleased. Go to the Red Sea? Carry on to Saudi Arabia? All sorts of silly notions flashed through our heads. Yet one idea loomed large for me.

At the first press conference I faced after Bertrand invited me to fly with him, somebody asked me where I hoped to land if we made it round the world. Off the cuff I answered, 'By the Great Pyramids in Egypt.' Now that this seemed a real possibility, the press latched on to it and turned it into a major theme. As it turned out, however, we had to fight to keep ourselves away from Cairo because the wind there was too strong for a safe landing. We didn't want any more than four or five knots of wind at ground level, but around the Pyramids the wind was blowing at twenty knots; to attempt a landing in that would have been almost suicidal.

As we drew near the finishing line at 9 degrees 27 minutes West, Alan – ever the practical organizer – rose to unprecedented heights of politeness and emotion. He faxed:

Gentlemen: What you are going to achieve today is an historic event of world proportions. Consequently it has to be stage-managed.

I propose the following, which has been agreed by Breitling:

1. When you have crossed the line, you phone the usual number at the control centre to confirm time of crossing. I will briefly congratulate you (and probably burst into tears). That conversation will be covered by a single live TV camera crew that will send the image world-wide.

2. When that conversation ends, please wait two or three minutes while I fight my way into the press centre. Then please call 717 7999. This conversation, which I will conduct, will be live before a huge crowd of journalists. I would like both of you to speak and say what you feel. (Bertrand – please persuade

Brian: the media say they have not heard enough from him.) I will then pass just a few questions to you from journalists. To save time, I propose Bertrand answers them in French, Brian in English – but please be brief. After a few minutes please say that for reasons of power you cannot continue, but that you hope to see them all when you return to Geneva.

3. Then please call back on the control centre number to talk with Michèle, Jo and Thedy in private.

We expect you to cross the line at approx 10:30 Zulu. I will come back to you later to discuss landing, but at the moment we are assuming Egypt. I'm proud of you both. Alan.

BERTRAND

As we were coming up to the finishing line the phone went dead. The antenna had frozen again, so we could not call Control, and nobody could call us. We crossed the line without knowing the precise moment because we were travelling so fast that when we looked at the GPS we found we were already past the mark.

We stood up and embraced, shaking hands, slapping each other on the back, and shouting, 'It's incredible. We've done it! We've done it!' We gave the little football a push, and off it went: *'Olé! Olé! Olé! Olé!'* For the first time its parrot cry of 'We are the champs! We are the champs!' was appropriate. Nineteen days had passed since Brian had given it to me a few thousand feet above the Alps.

In the control room the assembled throng was waiting desperately for news. When no call came through, Alan faxed:

According to our poll report you crossed the line at 09:54 Zulu. Congratulations, guys. You did it. Well done from everybody here at Geneva. Love you both. Alan.

Brian and I had been discussing how we could describe the feeling that we had been helped on our way by some higher force, and now we hit on the idea of calling this agency – which had guided us through so many obstacles – an 'invisible hand'. Without wanting to appear naively religious, we were keen to float an idea that people could interpret in any way they liked. And so we formulated a joint message:

Hello to all our friends in Geneva.

We can hardly believe our dream has finally come true. We almost got lost in political problems, in the slow winds of the Pacific, the bad headings over the Gulf of Mexico. But each time, with God's help and great teamwork, the balloon got back on course to succeed.

We are the privileged two of a wonderful and efficient team that we would like to thank from the bottom of our hearts, now that we are sharing with Breitling the results of five years' work. We are eternally grateful to the invisible hand that has guided us through all the obstacles of this fantastic voyage.

Soon after we had sent our fax the satphone came alive again, and we had our pre-arranged press conferences, with Alan holding the fort at the other end. We could hear, live, the fantastic scenes taking place in Geneva. Champagne was flooding and being squirted everywhere. People were laughing, crying, cheering, embracing. All the journalists were so swept up in the emotion, so conscious that they were witnessing a great event, that they could not stop talking. Many of the world's leading networks continued transmitting the proceedings live not for five or ten minutes, but for a whole hour.

Among the crowd in the control room was my father. I knew quite well that he would not be able to relax until the flight was over. Instead of giving vent to his delight like everybody else, he remained very rational and kept his emotions hidden. 'Bertrand,' he said quietly over the telephone, 'it's fabulous, what you've done. But you still have to land, and I want to remind you of something very important. Probably you've thought of this, but in case you haven't, when you land, *you must bend your knees.*'

As a teenager it had sometimes hurt me to be treated as a little boy, but now I knew how important it was for my father to give any advice that would help to keep me safe. It was also a way for him to cope with his emotions. I myself find it so much easier, so much more natural, to let feeling show, to let it out. But that is not my father's style. He had broadcast live on Swiss radio every day and made frequent visits to the control centre, but although he had been terribly afraid for us all through the flight, all he did was to reassure others, saying there was nothing to worry about. For three weeks he slept badly and probably suffered more stress than Brian or me.

Others were less restrained. Stefano Albinati and I had a wonderful conversation, but then he was so overcome that he plunged the top half of his body into an open cupboard and stood there, with his head in his hands, back to the room, convulsed by sobs.

BRIAN

In the balloon we soon felt a sense of anticlimax. We were still flying. The same desert was still below us. And the gondola was just as cold. When a journalist asked me over the satphone, 'What are you going to do now?' I answered, 'When I can get through to my wife on the phone, I'm going to tell her I love her, and then I'm going to have a cup of tea.'

The great British reaction! But we did bring out our precious *pâté truffé* – the only tinned food on board. We had meant to eat it to celebrate crossing America, but things had gone so badly between Mexico and Honduras that we hadn't felt like it then. Instead, we attacked it over Mauritania. The cans were of the old-fashioned type, which you open by peeling off a strip round the walls with a slotted key. One of the keys was missing, so Bertrand set about the can with his yellow Swiss Army knife, specially made for Breitling. (It is a tradition in the Piccard family that its male members have a Swiss Army knife in their pockets at all times: Bertrand's father and grand-father both kept the knives which they had taken with them into the stratosphere and to the bottom of the ocean, and Bertrand had brought three knives of his own on the flight.) The tin resisted his efforts so strongly that he had to give up, and we opened the other can instead. We spread the *pâté* on some digestive biscuits which had originally been provided – irony of ironies – by Tony Brown.

Our ridiculous wrestle with the *pâté* tins made us laugh, and that broke the feeling of anticlimax. Thereafter, we just got on with the flight. The cold was worse than ever because we had accidentally blown the element of our second kettle by switching it on with no water in, leaving us no means of heating water. For food we were down to a few biscuits and *panettone*, some smoked emu, Etivaz Gruyère cheese, pumpernickel and margarine. In the storage space beneath the floor our bottles of water had frozen solid: to get a drink, we had to bring up a bottle at a time, crack the plastic and melt lumps of ice by putting them into cups and cradling the cups in our hands.

Another empty fuel tank hung up, and then a third. I thought the rogues might be held on by large accumulations of ice, and that we were going to have to be careful when we descended to lower altitudes as they would probably start to drop off when we reached warmer air at about 10,000 feet.

On the ground, the Breitling reception committee was about to set out for Egypt: Alan faxed to say that he would be leaving in two hours' time with Thedy Schneider and a rescue team. Meanwhile he gave us some instructions and advice:

I propose a high-speed, high-level flight over Libya. Once well across the border into Egypt, commence a gradual descent down to, say, 5,000 feet, keeping air traffic control advised of your intentions. As you go down, your track will change from 92 to 98 degrees true. We are looking to land you 26 to 28 North, 29 East, but the exact position is beyond our abilities to predict at this time. There are some large open areas and a few ranges of hills which appear to be no higher than 1,200 feet.

Suggest you have items ready for immediate use as ballast, with the usual provisos about not killing anybody below. You will need to decide how you are going to deal with the hung-up tanks. If they fall off as you touch down, the loss of weight will send you up again. It might be better to go outside and cut them free before you stabilize at low level.

Despite the fact that we will reach Cairo late tonight, and have helicopters that are supposed to be able to take off at first light, I think it unlikely we will be with you for the landing. Don't be tempted to leave the balloon inflated for too long – we don't want a repeat of the problems we had in Burma.

BERTRAND

We spent the whole of 20 March crossing the desert at very high speed. Three weeks earlier we had flown slowly over these huge expanses, full of hope that we might succeed. Now we were above them again, with success behind us, and I found that immensely satisfying. For safety reasons we were covering an extra 4,000 kilometres, yet that seemed nothing but a pleasure. The balloon was going easily and, apart from the cold, everything was fine.

Inevitably, before take-off, we had sometimes talked about the possibility of establishing new records — for distance, duration and altitude. Every time we started on that tack, one of us said '*Shhhh!*' because we didn't want to tempt fate. After bagging the absolute distance record we had also broken the absolute duration record during our crossing of the Atlantic: in the whole history of aviation nothing had flown longer or farther than we had without refuelling.

But still, out there, was the altitude record. Until the last lap we had never thought seriously about going for it, because an attempt on it would be a huge extravagance: we would burn a lot of propane and risk venting helium if we pushed the balloon through the ceiling. But now that we were in sight of touchdown, it was a different matter.

BRIAN

I said nothing about records to Bertrand when he went to bed, but at 16:05 I faxed John at Control to say:

> I hope the barograph is working. This is our last chance to get altitude for very little fuel, so we are going close to the ceiling to see if we can put the altitude record in the bag. FL 371, 113 knots.

That brought a sharp retort:

> You arrogant little git! More records indeed! If you go for altitude, do NOT lose your track, as you need to stay as far south as possible, due to possible 18-knot winds at the surface near Cairo tomorrow a.m. Also, do not lose helium.
>
> Alan reminds you that you have a radio altimeter, which will help your descent to low level.

His last sentence was too much: the radio altimeter was our largest instrument, right in the middle of the panel. We'd been sitting looking at it for nearly three weeks, and it was hardly possible for us to forget it. I couldn't let the remark go without a sarcastic riposte:

> Thank Alan very much for the flying lessons. The radio altimeter – is that the one with the three little white hands, or the sexy yellow one with the orange button? Would he like to be Training Officer next year?

With short burns I pushed the balloon gingerly upwards, and for two or three minutes I scanned the bottom of the gas cell constantly with a big torch. When I saw it go really tight, I decided, 'Right – that's it.' In due course Control confirmed that we'd taken the record with a corrected altitude of 38,500 feet. When Bertrand woke up, he emerged from the bunk saying, 'Brian! You know, it's a pity we didn't go for the altitude record, and this was our last chance.' I gave him a big smile and said, 'Don't worry. I did it while you were asleep.'

Next on the fax was Jo, addressing us lavishly as 'my heroes!' and saying she had given a bag of my clothes and shaving equipment to Alan, *en route* to Cairo. She sent love and congratulations from the family, then handed over to John, who added:

> The Queen (yes, the proper one) and Tony Blair, as well as Jacques Chirac, have sent congrats. Juan-Antonio Samaranch has announced you will both receive the Olympic Order. Will you still speak to me?!

I replied:

> Hi, Sweetheart (not you, Albury),
> Did the Queen give the message over the phone? I hope the old git didn't try to sell her a balloon. I've got to bring the beard back to Geneva, so Bertrand doesn't look too grubby. I assume the plan is to bring us straight back? Nobody tells us anything. Do you think they will let us stop at a hotel to clean up? They should insist on it, otherwise it'll take a week to get rid of the smell. Tell John he can still use my Christian name when we are on our own. FL 365 and doing 130 knots.

BERTRAND

My last night at the controls was the most wonderful of the flight. A slender crescent of new moon rose ahead of us, born of the desert. Once more I was living the intimate and loving relationship that we had established with our planet, but this time I was totally relaxed, thanks to the feeling of success. I had the impression that I had left the cockpit and was flying among the stars, which had swallowed our balloon. I felt so privileged that I wanted to enjoy every second of that world of the air.

Soon after daybreak *Breitling Orbiter 3* would have to land in the Egyptian sand. Brian and I would be lifted away from the desert by helicopter, and we would immediately have to find words to satisfy the curiosity of the public; but at that moment, as I sat muffled in the down jacket, the bite of the cold brought home to me that I was living one of the best moments of my life. 'The only way I can make this instant last,' I wrote, 'is to share it with others. We'll have to write a book, and we'll sign it together, Brian and I, as a reflection of the wonderful spirit of this flight.'

My mind was ranging ahead, thinking of what would happen in the next days and weeks and years. Every now and then the intensity of the cold brought me sharply back to the present, but for the first time in twenty days I had no fear of failure and I found it a huge pleasure to fly the balloon without worrying about what would happen if I made a mistake or if we were on the wrong track.

Watching the stars, I thought about the invisible hand and found myself wondering about God. Neither Brian nor I are conventionally religious, but we both believe there is a God. I believe in the God that has created human beings, but not at all in the God that humans have created.

It seems to me that most religions have created the God that they would like to have − a human projection, not a mystical reality. Officially I am a Protestant, but I hate to say I'm either Protestant or Catholic − or anything else. Rather than belonging to any one denomination, I am Christian, because I find that Christianity is a good way to explain life and to find a path to God. In its original form Christianity is a completely tolerant religion, and the same is true of Islam or Judaism or Buddhism or Hinduism: all these religions originally allowed people to open their hearts to others, and to God, and to make a space for divinity inside themselves.

But instead of speaking about 'religion,' I prefer to speak of 'spirituality' – a means of admitting God to our hearts, rather than a system of ideas worked out to prove that one god is better than another. My most important quest is for a sense of the essential. I do sometimes go to a place of worship, but it may be to a mosque or a Buddhist temple as often as to a Christian church, depending on where I am. I remembered intently how, during my last trip to China, I got down on my knees in a Buddhist lama temple to pray for the success of my flight. The guardian obviously found it a little strange to find a foreigner kneeling in his temple, but then I saw in his eyes that he realized how important this moment was for me.

Very often we are lost in life, swept up in automatic thoughts and reactions, and lose sight of the essential: most of the things we pursue are trivial – we cannot take them with us when we die. I think it important to have moments in which we perceive the essential, deep inside our hearts. Sometimes I find such moments in churches, but I have also found them in meditation and in flight: my hang-glider or my balloon has sometimes been my church.

There were many such moments during the flight of *Orbiter 3* – and not only when things were going well. Often they came when things were going badly – for instance, when we were over the Pacific, flying slowly, frightened and racked by doubts; for me those were fabulous moments, when I felt the essential of life, of just being alive and aware, and seeing what really matters. Confronted by the Pacific, by water, air and light, I sensed that the earth is alive in a mineral sense (as I had over the desert), and I knew I had to accept things as they were. Once I did that, I found great serenity and confidence.

This is not a fatalistic outlook; rather, it is a philosophy of acceptance. Many elements in life can be controlled, but some cannot. One is the direction of the wind; others are death, disability, accidents and illnesses. You cannot change them – you simply have to accept them. Acceptance is very important – and ballooning is a philosophy of acceptance which helps one go through life.

Late in the night I discovered that the jet stream contained many layers of wind, each separated from the other. The layers were so

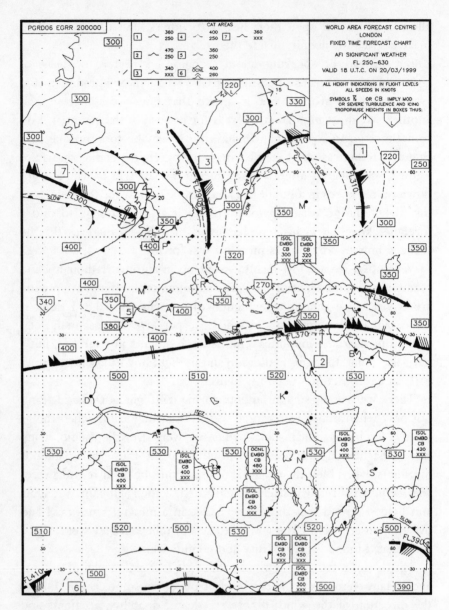

Weather chart for Africa on 20 March 1999, the final day of our flight. The thick black lines show the jet streams. It was the beautifully straight one across Africa that carried us to Egypt; those over northern Europe were fragmented, and would not have brought us across the Atlantic. Each thick arrow indicates 50 knots of wind, each slanting line 10 knots.

sharply defined that, every time we moved up or down, or from one to the other, the envelope changed shape, billowing out at one side like the sail of a boat and tucking in at the other. By watching the compass and the GPS, and glancing up to see which side of the balloon was being inflated or deflated by the gradients of the wind, I could tell if the new layer we had entered was better or worse than the one we had just moved out of. Our aim was to keep as far south as possible; so when the left side of the envelope bulged, I knew the wind was pushing us to the right and tried to keep in that layer. Physically as well as visually, flying the balloon became just like sailing a yacht – for I could hear the Mylar fabric of the envelope slapping in the wind and see its shivering silver in the light of the burner flames.

Sometime that day Don Cameron had flown over from Bristol to stand in for Alan at the control centre. Now he sent a message congratulating us on our 'magnificent achievement' and giving us advice for the morning: we were to begin our descent as we crossed the Egyptian border and should aim to land near a village called Mut soon after sunrise. I responded:

> Thanks for your landing suggestions – and also a lot of congratu-
> lations to you and your factory for having built such a wonderful
> balloon. It was (and still is) a real pleasure to fly it through the
> skies of this planet.

Soon, more emphatic orders came up from John: 'DO NOT LAND IN THE GREAT SAND SEA, as you will be there for weeks. It is not good at all, and even helicopters do not go there.' I replied that I understood the problem, but asked why, in that case, we couldn't carry on for 150 miles beyond Mut and get close to the Nile valley? John's answer was that we should not fly for more than a couple of hours after sunrise because the wind always gets up in the desert as the sun climbs and hot air starts to rise off the sand.

Don could well have given the press more information about what was happening. Three hundred reporters and cameramen had massed in Cairo, where they were waiting for us in the middle of a sandstorm. Everyone at Control knew we were going to land a long way to the south, where conditions were much calmer, yet there was no contact between those who knew where we were heading and the press.

In the small hours of the morning, exhaustion overcame me before the end of my stint and I asked Brian if I could have two more hours' sleep. He kindly got up – and it was this changeover that messed up our plans for landing.

BRIAN

Once again our controllers in Geneva were talking their way through a problem. The Egyptians had given us permission to overfly the country but not to land. Our team argued over the telephone: 'Listen – the balloon is running out of fuel. If the pilot doesn't have permission to land, he'll have to declare a full emergency, and you'll be obliged by the international rules to deal with it' – whereupon the Egyptian controller said, 'OK. In that case, I give you permission.'

Our maps, which seemed very accurate, showed a green area that looked like a river valley or oasis near the place formerly called Mut, now Dakhla. We thought the green could be cultivated fields, and a better bet for landing than the desert, so we decided to go for that. Soon after I had taken over for my final stint, I faxed Control:

> Hello boys and girls. Brian back in the driver's seat for a while so that Bertrand can put on a face pack and get his rollers in. If you could send up a cup of tea, it would be preferable to even one of Smiffy's jokes now.
>
> If it's going to be a Jones landing, then it will probably be one bounce in each of the villages/towns mentioned. Tell Alan we don't need advice about checklist items, how to fly the thing or what lines to pull. Leave us a little pride. However, all other assistance regarding landing strategy, balloon performance and forecasted winds is gratefully accepted.

Then at 02:23 I faxed:

> Fuel state (and what a state). Both pairs 5 and 11 showing 26 [kilos] on contents gauge. What this means, I don't know, but it should equate to about six hours' burn time, so should be OK.
>
> If calculations are wrong, we have been told not to land in the

Great Sand Sea, but not why. Is there a chicken farm, or is it a quicksand-type surface? What we don't want to have to do is descend to a level with too little wind, and have to use fuel to climb back up to find the winds again. So an educated guess at a wind profile from Luc would be nice.

Switching back to tank pair 5 now. They are on the leading edge, and will probably be dropped before landing. Isn't it exciting!

John swiftly put me right:

The Great Sand Sea is not to be landed in because it is deep sand, you daft old fool. It will be days before they get you out. There are airfields at ASYUT, NEW VALLEY (AL KHARIJAH) AND DAKHLA (MUT), and roads that look OK. Alan is heading for Mut, so see what you can do.

I faxed back:

There's so much ice in here that when we start our descent it's going to be like the Nile in the gondola, rather than the other way round. We just may lose comms. If so, assume we are OK unless we really cock it up, in which case we will start up the EPIRB [emergency beacon]. Otherwise we will avoid using distress comms equipment and try hand-held Icoms for comms with rescue craft and ground.

Thanks for the message [about the sand]. Hasn't anybody got shovels down there? I really don't think we are going to make Mut . . . Anyway, according to my map there is rising ground immediately after the road, which could make life difficult on an overshoot, and winds unpredictable. Al Kharijah is a good place for Alan *et al.* to start, but don't put your dosh on Mut.

Later still I added:

Typical balloon pilot – can't make a decision. I think we may now do better to consider a possible approach on the road to the northwest of Mut. Next road could be 180 nautical miles on, and would put us well into the morning sun. So considering initiating descent at 26.45 East. What do you think?

That message crossed an up-coming one from the met men, which suggested the same thing: that we should begin our descent at sunrise and aim for Mut 'or track leading from it to northwest'.

'Everyone here is very concerned for your success and safe landing,' Luc continued. 'Please make every effort to report your safe landing to us as soon as it has happened.' Still on a high, I responded: 'Don't worry. If at all possible, you'll be the first to know we're down safely. Then I'll tell Bertrand.'

CHAPTER TWELVE

HARD LANDING

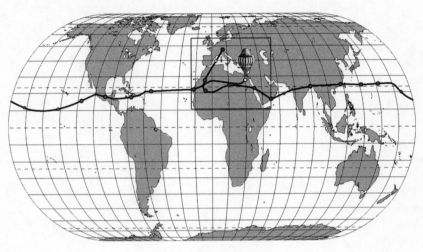

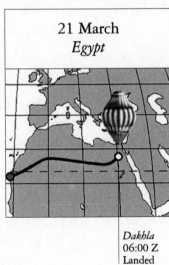

21 March
Egypt

Dakhla
06:00 Z
Landed

BERTRAND

We had trained for the landing on the supposition that I would be flying the balloon as we came back to earth and that Brian would carry out all the tasks that needed to be done outside. This made sense, as I had landed a big Rozier balloon twice before, and he had specialized in the external systems, practising on the release mechanisms that needed to be operated in sequence from on top of the gondola. But when he woke me for the last time he had already started the descent and was in full control of the balloon's flight, speed and direction.

He wasn't having an easy time, but he'd got the feel of it, so there seemed no point in taking over from him. We therefore switched jobs, and when the time came I was the one who went outside. It wasn't the most sensible arrangement because we kept having to give each other advice about what to do next, but at the time it seemed the sensible option.

BRIAN

We started our descent from 32,000 feet as we crossed the border from Libya into Egypt, our plan being to come gently down at about 300 feet a minute, progressively losing speed. By then we were doing

130 knots, and we had worked out what our trajectory should be from the winds that the met men had predicted for various levels. But it turned out that Luc and Pierre's forecast was quite wrong, and we continued to travel much too fast. Nor could we bring the balloon down at the rate we wanted. At first I found I could lose height simply by keeping the burners switched off; but the heat of the sun rapidly intensified, and at around 20,000 feet the sheets of ice that had formed on the inside of the hot-air cone started to melt and smash down on the gondola.

The noise inside the capsule was tremendous – thumps and bangs and slithering crashes – and the envelope was shedding so much weight that the balloon no longer wanted to descend. The only way we could continue down was by venting helium. I opened one gas valve and kept it open for what seemed ages, but still we were not descending. From his position under the hatch Bertrand called, 'Open the other!' I did so, and suddenly we found ourselves dropping out of the sky at 800 feet a minute – far too fast. Then another load of ice fell off, and we started up again.

BERTRAND

On our way down, while Brian was at the controls, I saw an opportunity for a fabulous photograph. The red, rising sun was glowing through the frozen porthole, and the effect was so striking that I simply had to take a picture. 'Brian,' I said, 'I'm sorry. I know it's not really the moment, but could you just move out of the way . . .'

Because of the bombardment by falling ice, I had to wait some time before I could open the top hatch – and when I did, sheets of ice and gouts of water cascaded in. Until that moment, for twenty days the gondola had remained dry and in good order; now suddenly it was awash, an absolute mess, with water and ice everywhere.

When I climbed out on top of the gondola I was suddenly in the sun. The air was warm, and ahead of us lay dark, rocky hills eroded into deep gullies. I shovelled masses of ice overboard with my hands and prepared the fifty-metre-long guide rope, setting it in position for deployment. The rope was made of hemp and weighed nearly 100 kilos; the idea was that in the moments before touchdown it would drag along the ground and keep the gondola side-on to our line of advance. Then I took out the safety pins from the release mechanism at each corner of the load-frame so that we could fire off pneumatic charges to separate the envelope from the gondola if we had to. I also filmed everything – the envelope, the ice, Brian in the cockpit. I felt it was important to record everything. But when I tried to pull up the dangling solar panels, I found that after three weeks' inaction I had become incredibly weak, and the array felt so heavy that I had to call on Brian for assistance. With him standing under the hatch, holding the end of the rope, and me calling out, 'One, two, three – pull!' we heaved in unison. Another job was to release all the lines connecting the gondola to the envelope and cut the thermocouple wires with bolt-croppers – altogether a lot of work.

BRIAN

There was no way we were going to land in the river valley: we missed it because we simply couldn't get the balloon down fast enough. At 3,000 feet, instead of the fifteen knots predicted, we still had twenty-eight, and not until we were down to 1,000 feet did we at last slow down.

The Breitling party which had flown out to meet us was already in the area and had been trying to call us on the emergency frequency, 121.5, from their Canadair jet. After a fruitless search for the balloon, the pilot was on a final approach to Dakhla airfield when suddenly, ten seconds from touchdown, he heard my voice in his headphones calling, 'Any station – this is *Breitling Orbiter* balloon. Do you read us?' Instantly he shoved the throttles forward, overshot the runway and climbed away. Stefano Albinati rushed up to the cockpit, and once the aircraft had gained height found he could talk to us easily. I gave him our GPS coordinates and he headed in our direction.

Dakhla was less than a hundred kilometres away, so we knew the aircraft would be with us in a few minutes. Bertrand took his camera on to the roof to film it coming – and a tremendous moment it was when we saw it. As the white jet began to circle us, low over the desert, rocking its wings as a sign of victory, Alan Noble came on the radio. I told him we'd missed the river valley but that we would try to land close to a road marked on our maps some eighty kilometres ahead.

'OK, then,' he said. 'Why don't we go and spot it for you?'

'Fine,' I agreed, and the plane disappeared ahead of us. Within minutes it was back and Alan was saying, 'Believe me, there is no road out there. You might as well land as soon as you can.'

Bertrand, back inside, started to stow all the loose equipment. We needed to keep the laptop out for communication with the control centre, so we left it on the desk. I was still struggling to steady our descent, standing in the corridor for quick access to the burner control panel and peering out through the portholes, which gave very poor downward visibility – particularly as at that moment the gondola happened to be flying backwards. Ridiculous as it must sound, we failed to use the famous radio altimeter about which Alan had pestered us the day before.

Just as I was thinking, 'We must still be about 150 feet up,' I glanced down through the curved glass of the front hatch and saw stones. They looked extremely close. I was wondering whether convex glass could have a magnifying effect when Bertrand, who was watching through the rear hatch and therefore looking forward, shouted, 'Brian – look out! We're not even ten metres up! Hold tight! We're going to hit!' Immediately I switched on full burners. We both stood clutching the top rail of the bunk with our knees bent to absorb impact. Seconds later there was an almighty *BANG!* as we hit the ground.

We were down for no more than a second. With the weight momentarily taken off it, the balloon snatched us back into the air. Up we went again, bouncing straight to 300 feet, where another blast from the burners stabilized us and stopped us coming down.

Looking out, we realized it was the most horrendous place in which to try to put down a balloon. We were approaching a plateau of sand, but beneath us, running up to the edge of the flat ground, was a steeply sloping mass of eroded rocks – and it was these we had struck. Fortunately the polystyrene blocks which I had failed to cut away after the launch took the brunt of the impact and saved the capsule from significant damage. More important, they prevented our remaining four fuel tanks from striking the rocks: had one split, the consequence might have been a catastrophic fireball. Fate had played its hand once again.

Over the radio came Alan's cynical voice, awarding us five out of ten for our attempt at touchdown. Bertrand went back on the roof and saw, a mile or two ahead, a flat plateau that looked perfect for landing. 'Give it five minutes,' he advised. 'Then we'll be over a suitable area.'

We were travelling at five or ten knots, with the Canadair plane still circling. Members of the party were filming us – among them the official observer from the Fédération Aéronautique Internationale, Jakob Burkard, whose job was to record the precise moment of our touchdown.

When we reached the level stretch of ground, Alan called, 'It looks good. Take it.' Bertrand, inside again, apparently told me to put my helmet on, but I was so busy I never heard him. He pulled on his own helmet and, seeing a single red light on the instrument panel showing that only one of the gas valves was open, he suggested I open the other as well, and leave them both open, to vent a substantial amount of the helium. This is the way to land a Rozier, as it effectively transforms the balloon from a gas balloon into a hot-air balloon.

Now at last *I* was flying *it*, rather than having it fly me, and I brought us in with a few careful final burns. At the last moment we again both clutched the rail, but there was hardly any impact, and after one more tiny bounce we finally came to earth, with the capsule travelling lengthways. The gondola slid along on its belly for a few yards, then stopped. For a moment we looked at each other, speechless with the realization that we were safe. The flight was over, and we were surrounded by utter silence.

Then Bertrand cried, 'Check the time! Check the time!' I did so. It was a few seconds after 06:00 Zulu on Sunday, 21 March. Quickly I retrieved the laptop, which had shot off the desk and flown across the cabin, giving me a hefty clout on the side of the thigh, and at 06:01, seeing that we still had a signal on the Capsat, I hurriedly faxed to Control: 'The Eagle has landed. All OK. Bloody good. B.'

With hindsight, I feel slightly embarrassed to have used what seemed a rather unoriginal phrase, but it was completely spontaneous: the sight of the desert must have triggered a subconscious memory of the moon landing. I wanted Control to know we were safely down, but I didn't have time to type anything longer or more poetic.

In fact Control knew we were down, for three successive sets of figures from our GPS had been the same. Quickly Sue came back: 'Is the plane with you? Or anyone on the ground with you? Please advise status.'

BERTRAND

My ears were hurting because in the rush of preparing to land I had dragged my helmet on in a hurry and nearly ripped my ears off. As soon as the gondola settled, we both pulled the red rope of the rip panel through the top hatch to release the main body of helium, but the envelope stayed up, held aloft by the gas in the little tent balloon at the top.

Imagine the scene. The sun was fully up. We were absolutely in the middle of nowhere: the fluorescent red gondola on the ground, the silver envelope overhead, and a white three-engined jet plane circling us only forty or fifty feet off the ground. We learned later that in the plane's cockpit the automatic ground-proximity warning was screaming, 'PULL UP! PULL UP!', but the pilot was on such a high that he ignored it.

Grabbing still and video cameras, I opened the rear hatch and scrambled outside to film the scene before the balloon collapsed. As I put my left foot down on the sand it left a print, and I had the same thought as Brian when he faxed that echo of Neil Armstrong's famous message from the moon. Like the lunar surface, the desert was unmarked, and when I saw my own footprint, I thought, 'Well, for Armstrong and Aldrin, it was wonderful to set foot on land so far *from* the earth – but for me, now, it's a thrill to stand *on* the earth again.'

As I went out I was almost overcome by emotion. Determined to film the balloon while it was still inflated, I ran away from the gondola and immediately found I was out of breath from the unaccustomed exercise. The envelope was leaning at an angle of maybe forty-five degrees, with wind already blowing into its mouth and making the Mylar billow. While I filmed I kept talking – to no one in particular – to heaven, perhaps – saying, 'This is fabulous! Thank you! Thank you!' Then the Breitling plane came by on a really low pass, and I filmed that too, holding the camera in my right hand and waving with my left.

Over the radio Stefano told Brian that he had to go back to Dakhla to refuel, but that they would send people to rescue us. Now that I had at least some pictures in the can, I asked Brian to pass out the first-aid box. I put it down on the sand, stood the video camera on it, set it up and left it running. Then I went back into the gondola, closed the rear hatch and said to Brian, 'OK – now we can make the official exit!' So we emerged again and had ourselves filmed as if by an invisible cameraman. The relief and joy of getting down safely made us turn the whole thing into a celebration.

We stood there, alone in the silent desert. I was still wearing my flying suit, with three layers of fleece beneath it, and soon began to sweat – but there was so much to take in and film that for the moment I didn't bother to strip off. Into my head there came again that strange dream from a couple of nights before – about how Brian and I had completed our journey round the world but hadn't been able to tell anybody about it. Now, in a curious way, the dream had become reality: we had made our circumnavigation, but there was nobody on the scene with whom we could share our joy.

BRIAN

When we scrambled out through the rear hatch, we realized how lucky we had been. The plan had been to jettison the remaining fuel tanks on one side of the gondola while we were still well off the ground and to come in to land with the denuded flank of the capsule leading. With the high workload, we simply hadn't had time to cut away the tanks; the trail rope slid ineffectively over the sand, but by a miracle we had landed end-on, so that the presence of the tanks made no difference.

Now we could see all too clearly how little fuel we had left. The remining liquid propane was so cold that even on the ground in the desert ice was forming on the outside of the cylinders and showed the level in each plainly. We reckoned that if we had put all our remaining stock together, it would have filled one tank less than a third full and given us only a few more hours of burning. That was how close we had run things.

The Canadair jet circled overhead for about ten minutes before it flew away. On the emergency radio frequency Alan told us he was going to try to reach us overland with four-wheel-drive vehicles. That made us both furious. We thought that in a last-minute burst of meanness he was trying to save money by not hiring a helicopter, and the last thing we wanted was a five-hour wait, followed by a five-hour drive through the desert, before we got to a hotel where we could have a shower and a meal. In fact the trouble was not cheese-paring on Alan's part: there was another reason altogether.

At Control in Geneva a call came in from some sort of agent in Cairo whose name sounded like 'Zigzag'. Mr Zigzag – as he instantly became known – was demanding double the amount budgeted by Breitling for a rescue helicopter: he wanted 30,000 dollars, or else the helicopter already on its way would be ordered back. This threw the controllers into a panic because all the main decision-makers had gone off to Egypt; but after some debate, they resorted to their list of confidential telephone numbers, and Brian Smith called the private number of the Swiss Foreign Minister. The response was instantaneous – so quick that it took Brian by surprise. The Minister listened courteously and said he would see what he could do. No one in the control centre is sure what happened next, but four hours later Mr Zigzag rang back to say that the problem had been resolved: two helicopters and a C-130 Hercules transport plane were on their way. Furthermore, there would be no charge.

Back inside the gondola, we activated the satellite telephone and called Control to confirm that we were down in one piece. But after thirty seconds communication was cut, and we couldn't get through again. Instead we sent a fax:

06:39 – We are absolutely in the middle of nowhere. Possible five-hour wait now for pick-up. Kept the envelope, but next time, Don, let's have a method of ripping out the top tent balloon. Anybody want to buy some sand? Thanks, gang: see you soon. Bertrand and Brian.

Sue replied:

Please keep this on so that we can communicate. Someone will be here until your rescuers get to you. However, we have all been up all night, and have now had champagne for breakfast . . . Don't build too many sandcastles.

We could have built any number – and they would have given a bit of variety to the scene. The desert around us was totally flat, as flat as anything could possibly be, in every direction. The surface was of soft, yellow-brown sand with a scattering of pebbles, and there was no vegetation, no insect life, no birds or animals – nothing. Apart from the envelope shifting in the wind, the only thing moving was the heat haze round the horizon. It was as if we had landed on another planet, and somehow it felt entirely appropriate that after such a marathon flight we were alone in a world of our own, instead of landing live in front of CNN cameras.

Soon, though, we heard engines again, and another plane appeared – a turboprop Pilatus PC 12, which some journalists had rented and brought over from Switzerland. This one flew desperately low – no more than fifteen or twenty feet up on its last pass – as we stood waving and holding our arms aloft in a victory sign. Then a third visitor came into view – a tiny red-and-white four-seater plane, whose pilot announced himself by radio as Peter Blaser, a Swiss balloon pilot and a friend of Bertrand's. Deciding he wanted to witness our landing, he had flown all the way from Switzerland with his wife and a friend, stopping in Malta, Cyprus and Cairo – and even if they missed the landing itself, they had beaten all the 300 journalists still stranded in the Egyptian capital to the site of our touchdown.

The little plane flew off, and again we were alone – except for a couple of swallows and dragonflies which materialized out of the desert, appearing from nowhere, and skimmed round and round the silver fabric of the envelope. Thinking they might be thirsty, we put out some water – but of course they paid no attention.

Because we'd been hoping for a quick airlift out, we had already started unloading essential equipment that we wanted to take with us: survival packs, first-aid kit, radios, computers and so on. Bertrand was responsible for the films and I took charge of the data-logging units and the barograph. We piled this stuff outside.

We also brought out some bottles of water, not only to drink, but to enjoy a treat which I'd been looking forward to for days – washing our hair. The bottle we'd been drinking from during the night had only a little ice in it, but the rest were frozen solid, so we laid them in the hot sand to thaw and carried on with other tasks. When the great moment for a shampoo came, I stripped to the waist, selected the bottle I knew to be the warmest and handed it to Bertrand so that he could pour its contents over my head while I soaped and rinsed. Then we changed places and, with the warm water gone, I doused his head with water so icy that he yelled in protest.

'Don't be such a cissy!' I told him.

'But it's freezing,' he protested – and I chuckled, because I knew he wasn't exaggerating.

BERTRAND

With the planes gone, we were left in silence, except for the sound of the Mylar envelope rustling in the breeze. Then, as the surface of the desert warmed up, the wind began to rise and the balloon became fully inflated by air blowing into its mouth. Not wanting to lose the envelope – now an important piece of history – we decided to try bringing it down; so we put the safety pins back into the release mechanism and blew open one corner after another to release the flying cables one by one. The balloon leant over more and more, but it was still exerting such a pull that it tugged the gondola over on its side and dragged it across the sand for about ten metres, breaking the communications antennae.

A minor panic set in. A moment earlier, we'd felt perfectly safe – and both our control centre and the Breitling party thought we *were* safe. But, suddenly, we had no contact with anyone. It was extremely hot and, with both of us on the verge of exhaustion, we now faced the possibility that the envelope might drag the gondola not for a few metres but for hundreds. If the fuel tanks struck a rock, the whole thing could explode in an instant. Disaster threatened.

'For Christ's sake, let's cut away the envelope completely,' said Brian – but I was determined to keep it. So we attacked it with our survival knives, running round it, waiting till a gust forced it down towards us, then slashing at it and twisting the blade sideways in an attempt to puncture the gas cell. Besides billowing up and down, the envelope was rolling sideways, and we kept having to jump out of the way as it bore down on us. The rubbery membrane of the gas cell proved incredibly tough: we were stabbing with all our strength, but our knives seemed to make little impression on it, and Brian's only reward for his efforts was a sprained wrist.

BRIAN

We didn't seem to have got anywhere with our knives, so I suggested we try firing emergency flares at the gas cell. We had a pack of mini-flares, with a pen-type gun, powerful enough to go up two or three hundred feet before they burst in stars. We fired three, but they simply bounced off the thick skin.

Then I said, 'I know what'll do it – our distress rocket.' Designed for use in the jungle, it was supposed to penetrate the tree canopy and climb to 1,500 feet – a fairly major firework, and we had only one. So I stood in the mouth of the balloon, holding the tube in my hand, and aimed the rocket straight upwards. I suddenly wondered if this was such a good idea, and glanced at Bertrand for reassurance. The recoil was so powerful that it pushed me back a couple of metres. A ball of fire burst into the mouth of the balloon, shooting up to hit the gas cell – and bounced off, then ricocheted around the inside of the balloon until it fell and burnt its way through the side of the hot-air cone, setting fire to the Mylar. Bertrand was holding a bottle of water and rushed to pour it over the flames, while I made a dive back into the gondola for a fire-extinguisher.

Between us we put out the blaze, but the struggle left us feeling shattered. We were standing there defeated, not knowing what to try next, when natural forces again came to our aid. Up swept a huge gust of wind, which twisted the balloon sideways and brought to the top all the cuts we had made in the gas cell. To our intense relief the envelope collapsed of its own accord – so fast that it caught Bertrand by surprise and came down on top of him. Suddenly he found himself forced to the ground, half smothered by heavy fabric. The weight of it drove him down on to his knees, and he thought he was going to be suffocated. He shouted for help, but he was so well muffled that I didn't hear him, and because I was standing on the far side of the huge, crumpled heap, which in places was still twenty or thirty feet high, I didn't realize what had happened. The result was that he had to cut his way out by slashing upwards with his knife.

By then I'd had enough. Feeling utterly exhausted and wanting only to lie down, I climbed back into the gondola through the top hatch, which was now on one side. The bunks were uninhabitable because they were nearly vertical, and the whole inside of the capsule was an awful mess. Not only had we shipped ice and water, but our kit had fallen out into a jumble, and as I scrambled in my boots left sand all over the formerly pristine white insulation on the walls. I was so worn out that I flopped down on one of the pilots' seats, which was lying more or less horizontal. It was incredibly uncomfortable, but all I wanted was to shut my eyes: apart from everything else, I think I had a touch of heatstroke.

BERTRAND

With the envelope down, I sat with my back against the keel of the gondola, letting sand run through my fingers, reflecting that we had flown over deserts for seven or eight days and were now safely down, in physical contact with one of those desolate wastes. I could have stayed there for a long time – except that the wind kept increasing until sand started to fly through the air.

Reaction set in. Like Brian, I felt exhausted and badly wanted to lie down, so I too climbed back inside and looked for a place to rest. The only thing I could think of was to cut through the safety harness in the bunk to release the mattress and to lay it on the face of the shelves along one side of the corridor, which had been vertical but was now horizontal. On that makeshift bed I stretched out and soon fell asleep.

BRIAN

I was so uncomfortable twisted down on the pilot's seat that I couldn't stay there very long; so I took a piece of foam rubber, which we had planned to strap around our bodies in the event of a nasty landing, and laid it next to where Bertrand was lying. I could only just balance on it, but at least it was better than the chair, and I lay there with my head right next to his.

All at once he began to swear atrociously in French – the first time I'd ever heard him cursing – because drops of water were falling on his head. Where they were coming from he couldn't make out, but it seems that ice must have formed inside the Kevlar shell of the gondola, behind the foam insulation. Every minute or two he would grab a cloth and wipe irritably at the surface above his head – only for the process to start again. Soon he was going full blast –

'*Merde! Quelle est la saloperie qui me tombe sur la tête?*' — but I couldn't help seeing the funny side of it and lay there giggling.

BERTRAND

Because we'd lost our main communications system, we retrieved our hand-held radios and switched them on. Of course, their range was much more limited than that of our bigger sets, and at first we couldn't get any contact. Unable to go back to sleep, because drops of water kept falling on me, I lay there awake until suddenly I heard voices talking half in Egyptian, half in French. I jumped outside and tried to call them on the VHF emergency frequency, but although I could still hear them talking I couldn't make them hear me.

At last, at around three o'clock local time — seven hours after touch-down — through the dust haze I saw two Hercules C-130 transports heading in our direction. Finally the crew responded and said they were being followed by a helicopter, which would reach us in five minutes. The Hercules began to circle us, a thousand feet up, and guided a huge Russian military MIL-17 helicopter, with space for thirty people, to our position. It landed next to us in a storm of sand.

The six-man crew was an Egyptian medical rescue team — very friendly and ready to give us all sorts of assistance. I couldn't help thinking that if we'd needed *medical* assistance we'd probably have been dead long ago, but we were delighted when they helped us carry our equipment into their aircraft. We kept a close eye on everything because all the items were very important to us: the official mail which we'd carried round the world, the computers with all the messages stored in them, the barograph and pieces of the envelope. As souvenirs, Brian and I had each cut out a piece which included the balloon's registration, HB-BRA.

Inside the helicopter, one of the Egyptians asked, 'Have you got everything you want to take?' Even though I said yes, two men jumped out, ran across to the gondola and grabbed everything they could. I protested that we didn't need the stuff immediately and that our team would come out to fetch it later, but they brought it anyway. Much of it never emerged from the helicopter. We lost half the mail, one of our flying suits, one survival pack, a life raft and more besides.

The pilots told us they proposed to fly to Asyut, refuel there and go straight on to Cairo, which would have taken three hours. That was a tough prospect as the machine was extremely noisy and vibrated severely. But after less than half an hour, when we came overhead Dakhla, we saw the Breitling plane on the ground and told the air crew that our friends were down there – whereupon they said their orders had changed and they were going to land there anyway.

So we came in towards this big oasis surrounded by thousands of palm trees, with some small pyramids of its own and, we heard later, hot springs that gush up from 5,000 feet or more beneath the surface of the earth. During the approach we realized that this was our return to the real world – for there on the tarmac was a swarm of people, obviously waiting for us. The helicopter came in down a glide path, like a fixed-wing aircraft, and taxied to the apron. Before we had even put our feet on the ground we were hemmed in by a rush of more than a hundred journalists, literally fighting to get in front of each other to take photographs.

Because of the struggling human barrier it was some time before we could reach our friends from Breitling and greet them. Eventually, with huge emotion, I reached Thedy and threw my arms round him. He had put so much into the project – not just money and energy but enthusiasm and his company's reputation – that I couldn't find words to thank him enough. I felt that, by succeeding, we had paid back some of the trust that Breitling had put in us, but in the heat of the reunion it was impossible to express such thoughts clearly. Also there was Thierry Lombard, a private banker from Geneva and a great benefactor of charitable organizations, a good friend who had always been in the right place at the right time to help and reassure us.

Ceremonies began at once. We were presented to the Governor of Dakhla and his officials. The Swiss ambassador, who had come from Cairo on the Breitling plane, handed me an official letter from the President of our country – a moving document which congratulated us on persevering through all difficulties, and said that the whole world had followed the flight, which had been a wonderful triumph for Switzerland. Caught up in such a surge of joy and emotion, Brian and I were constantly between laughter and tears. A journalist handed me a satellite phone to call Michèle in Cairo. When I heard her voice I found it difficult to speak, but I know my first words were, 'Can you imagine, *Chérie* – we made it!' These were the words I had dreamt of saying for five years, and I am sure the power of the moment will stay in my mind and my heart for all my life.

BRIAN

Two notable absentees were Stefano Albinati and Alan Noble. By the time we flew in, they had set off in a convoy of four-wheel-drive vehicles in search of us. Somebody called them back by iridium phone (which works through a satellite), but as they were already five hours out into the desert we had to wait all that time for them to return.

Meanwhile, the Governor invited us to his office to have a shower and a gigantic lunch of Egyptian specialities – stuffed tomatoes, chicken, lamb, rice, cucumber in yoghurt. After three weeks without a proper wash the shower was a rare delight, and after days without fresh fruit or vegetables the food looked wonderful, but I was so tired that I could hardly eat. Bertrand, on the other hand, pitched in with his usual gusto. As the meal did not begin until four o'clock and we'd had nothing to eat all day, he was starving.

Our gracious hosts could not have been kinder; but unfortunately, once we had eaten, they absolutely insisted that we did some sightseeing. There was nothing on earth we wanted less: our only desire was to get into the luxurious Breitling jet and fly off home. But the Governor took us in his air-conditioned car to see a water-pumping station – clearly his pride and joy – and we drove through the town with an escort of two police cars, their sirens wailing. Everything had become quite surreal: Bertrand and I still wearing our heavy flying suits and boots, punch-drunk with fatigue, keeping glazed smiles on our faces as details of hot-spring technology washed over us.

We were supposed to fly to Switzerland the same day, but it was already dark when Alan and Stefano returned from the desert, so plans were changed and it was decided that we would stay the night in Cairo. After yet another emotional reunion, we all jumped into the Breitling plane and just an hour later landed in Cairo in the midst of an incredible scrum. From every side people charged at us with microphones and cameras, and it was some time before Bertrand could even see Michèle and the children. Then the girls rushed at him and he swept them up into his arms, crying *'Bonjour, les filles!'* They were in a state of high excitement as they had seen the pyramids during the day and were now being reunited with their father.

The first individual I spoke to was the British ambassador, Sir David Blatherwick, who came up in an immaculate pinstripe suit and insisted on carrying my bags.

'You can't do that,' I protested.

'My dear boy,' he said. 'That's what I'm here for.'

I thought, 'This is great! I could really get to like this game.'

The next person I bumped into was Terry Lloyd, from ITN, who thrust a microphone in front of my mouth and shouted, 'How d'you feel?'

'Knackered!' I answered. Then I turned to the ambassador and asked, 'Can I say that on television?' He replied, 'I think you can say whatever you like.'

Our next move was to the Swissôtel, in town, and Sir David pressed me to travel there in his car, rather than in the official coach. When I said I thought I should stay with the rest of the team, he said, 'No, no, I must insist' – so off we went in a splendid black Rolls-Royce, with a Union Jack pennant flying from its bonnet. 'Such style!' I thought.

I soon saw why he wanted me on board: he was determined that his car should arrive at the hotel first and that the first pictures the TV cameras got would be of me descending from the British Embassy Rolls. Much as I enjoyed being fêted, after spending so long sealed in our private bubble in the sky I found it a shock to be plunged back into the harsh reality of the world, where politics ruled the roost.

BERTRAND

Because of the time difference, our arrival in Cairo coincided exactly with the television news in Europe. The airport was a madhouse, with everybody thrusting microphones and mobile telephones at us, demanding live interviews. Luckily, the Swiss ambassador realized that I would need some time alone with the family before the official press conference at the Swissôtel. So, most gallantly, he put us in his big black limousine, alone with his Egyptian chauffeur, for the twenty-minute drive into the city, while he himself went in the bus full of journalists.

At the hotel, pandemonium reigned. Outside there were camels, local musicians playing Bedouin music, and three hundred journalists wrestling with one another to get pictures. Brian and I each had five bodyguards forcing a passage for us through the crowd. It was an exotic and exciting scene, but by then we were both on autopilot, wearing fixed smiles and going wherever we were led.

In the big ballroom of the Swissôtel we sat at a table and gave our first proper press conference. We thanked Breitling for its inestimable support, praised the work of our team, and so on. One question made Brian bristle: 'What do you say to those who describe your flight as frivolous and a waste of money?' Brian answered, 'Before anyone asks questions of that nature, I suggest he looks at the history of the flight – and I think he'll find the question superfluous.'

Nobody asked technical questions; instead, interest quickly turned to the philosophical aspects of the flight. The reporters wanted to know how we had felt – what the human experience had been like. I had a chance to explain how lucky we had felt to be flying in a bubble of peace above a world in which so many people were fighting, suffering and committing atrocities. This, I think, immediately created an attractive image of the flight: the first articles described how we had been pushed gently round the earth by the wind, accompanied by the spirit of peace, without trying to control nature or prove ourselves stronger than the elements. Our message, the writers said, was one of tolerance and respect, as much for human beings as for the natural world. They seemed to catch the spirit of our flight extraordinarily fast.

The Egyptian Minister of Tourism came to congratulate us and said he was sorry we hadn't landed by the pyramids, because he had installed a whole lot of chairs for spectators to watch us come down and had laid on local musicians to serenade our descent. I tried to explain that the wind round Cairo had been too strong, but I don't think he really understood much about ballooning. Then, again, we had something to eat – another wonderful meal laid out in the Swissôtel. The moment we finished dinner, Michèle and the children had to board the journalists' plane for the flight back to Geneva because the Breitling aircraft was full.

Brian and I went off to snatch a few hours' sleep. In the middle of the night I woke up, terrified because I could not hear the roar of the burners. The room was pitch dark, and in my panic I thought, 'Brian's supposed to be flying the balloon. He must have fallen asleep.' I called out, 'Brian! Brian! The burners! Keep the balloon in the air!' I was convinced we must be going down. At last I sat up in bed, found the light switch and started to laugh out of sheer relief.

BRIAN

In the morning the whole team was in a state of euphoria. We woke quite early, had breakfast and boarded a bus for the airport. The Breitling aircraft was exceedingly luxurious: big enough to carry forty passengers, it was fitted out to seat only twelve. All the seats were upholstered in cream leather. The four at the front – two on each side – swivelled through 180 degrees. Behind them on one side was a sofa with two single seats opposite, and behind these were two more pairs of singles. During the flight a stewardess called Sandra served us a delicious meal of lobster and fillet steak and some incredibly good claret, Château Cheval Blanc. She also won my heart by coming up to me and saying, 'I've carried every kind of celebrity and pop star on this plane, and I've never asked for an autograph, but I'd be honoured if I could have yours.' So Bertrand and I both signed one of the menus and gave her a signed photograph.

The only jarring note was struck by the doctor whom Breitling had brought out in case we urgently needed medical treatment. Sitting down beside me, he quizzed me about my health. When he asked if I had any problems, I showed him the swelling on my hand and dropped my trousers to display the lump caused by the impact of the laptop. He dismissed those as mere contusions and pressed me for details of any other ailments from which I might be suffering. Shortness of breath? Giddiness? Rashes? Oedema? Anxiety? My answer to everything was no because there was nothing whatever wrong with me, but at the end of the consultation I began to wonder if I wasn't feeling ill purely as a result of all his suggestions.

There was so much to talk about that the four-hour flight seemed to pass in a flash. With all our friends – Thedy, Stefano, Thierry, Alan – we went through every stage of our voyage round the world and discussed our ideas about creating a foundation.

CHAPTER THIRTEEN

HEROES' WELCOME

BOTH-OF-US

We flew round the world in pursuit of adventure, not of celebrity. We flew for the passion of flying, of exploring all the skies of our planet. Of course we knew that the first people to succeed would enter the history books, but when we came back to earth we were astounded by the excitement that our circumnavigation had aroused. The hysterical reaction of the media in Cairo gave us a taste of what lay ahead: we were surprised to see that for many of the journalists this was the greatest adventure. Yet when we landed at Geneva at 12.30 p.m. on Monday, 22 March, we still had no inkling of what lay in store.

First came a fleeting moment of doubt because the airport seemed to be deserted. As we touched down Bertrand said, 'What a pity we didn't get back yesterday, at the weekend, because a lot more people would have been free to come and meet us.' While the plane taxied past the terminal building we had our faces glued to the windows – and saw not a soul. 'They could have given one of the cleaners a Swiss flag,' Brian muttered, 'and she could have come out on the balcony and waved it.'

The aircraft taxied for a long way, and then, at the far end of the airfield, to our amazement we realized that the tarmac was covered by an immense crowd. As the plane came to a halt we could see thousands of people waving – incredible numbers. Rain had been falling and umbrellas were still up, but as we arrived the downpour was stopping. Later we heard that the airfield had been thrown open to the public for the day, that the facility had been advertised on television and radio and in the press and that there had been a colossal security operation to screen such numbers, but in the heat of the moment we had no time to wonder how everyone had got there.

When the door of the aircraft opened, we heard a roar of cheers. We looked at each other as if to say, 'Do we really dare go out?' A moment later we were standing side by side on the top of the steps, waving furiously to communicate our joy. Below us, a sea of faces, all laughing and cheering; a forest of Swiss and British flags waving wildly. At the bottom of the steps on one side were our team, our wives and Bertrand's children, all with tears in their eyes, all waving and calling out. The noise was so great that we couldn't hear what they were shouting, but their delight and excitement were electrifying. We stayed at the top of the steps for what seemed an eternity, just to savour the moment.

When the time came to walk down the narrow ladder, Brian gestured and said, 'After you.' Bertrand replied, 'No – we'll go together.' So we put our arms round each other's shoulders and off we went, step by step, side by side, down the ladder. As long as we were walking down we were still on the flight, but already we felt that our lives would change for ever once we hit the tarmac.

Our feet touched down simultaneously – whereupon our families rushed at us. Bertrand's father came up and embraced him. Adolf Ogi, the Vice-President of Switzerland, whom Bertrand had only met on formal occasions, hugged him, congratulated him and addressed him by his Christian name. We had intensely emotional meetings with the staff from the control room, some of whom, extraordinary as it may seem, Bertrand had never met. John and Debbie, for instance, were quite new to him – and yet he knew their voices, their humour, their style, their personalities. It was equally wonderful for Brian to be able to thank his old friends for everything they had done. We took them all in our arms, overjoyed that we could associate them with the team's triumph.

The same was true of our magic weathermen, Luc and Pierre, who had become popular heroes in their own right through television and newspapers. Whenever the gondola's antennae froze up, preventing us transmitting pictures from the air, cameramen had gone to photograph the weathermen in the control centre, so their faces became well known – and before our plane came in they had gone round the crowd in a lap of honour. The whole scene was fantastically moving. There were so many people to thank.

BRIAN

My own reunion was overwhelming. Bertrand had met Michèle and the girls in Cairo, but this was the first time Jo and I had seen each other. I wasn't just meeting my wife again after a three-week separation: Jo had been an integral part of the Orbiter project. She had put up with all my bad moods during the difficult periods of *Orbiter 2*, and for months we had worked together all the hours that God sent on *Orbiter 3* – so that on top of our natural delight at seeing each other we were swept up by a tremendous feeling of joint achievement.

For me, our homecoming was the most emotional part of the whole flight. Never before in my life had I played a part in an undertaking on this scale. Ever since crossing the line I'd realized that what we had done would mean nothing until we were able to share the achievement with others. The emotion of the event lay in the sharing of it. So for me, our return to Geneva was the time when everything came to a head – the most extraordinary moment of my life.

Of course I had been desperately keen to be with Jo and our closest friends – John and Debbie, Brian and Cecilia. But I was also intensely moved by the obvious joy of all the Swiss who had come to greet us. Their faces were lit up with excitement and pleasure, and I felt they were really sharing our triumph. The fact that so many people were joining us in spirit lifted the experience to a higher plane.

BOTH-OF-US

The public had been corralled behind fences, but they all wanted to shake hands, so we allowed ourselves to be pushed – almost carried – into an open-topped car. Standing in the back, we were driven along the barrier, shaking as many hands as we could. Probably none of the crowd realized why our vehicle was a Peugeot – but behind the make there lay a little saga. The Peugeot car company had booked the VIP suite in the airport for an important meeting in the middle of March, but because our balloon was still flying and the control operation had to be maintained, the firm graciously withdrew and found another venue. In return, the airport manager, much relieved, asked them to lay on one of their cars for our homecoming. Even if the team's official cars were Chrysler Voyagers, this was no moment for petty rivalry.

It would have made no difference if we'd been in a dustcart. People were thrusting flowers at us, handing us drawings of the balloon done by their children, offering photographs of the take-off. After a tour of the crowd our driver carried on into an enormous hangar, and we realized that all the people in the open were just the ones who could not be fitted inside.

When we climbed on to the stage and saw Don Cameron, we hugged him, and Bertrand exclaimed, 'You built the most wonderful balloon ever made!'

'Well!' he retorted. 'We had the two best pilots in the world to fly it.'

As we took our places, confronted by thirty microphones, every-body was waving and shouting – so we stood on our chairs, holding hands aloft, overwhelmed by the excitement. Even the journalists were cheering. The applause seemed to go on for ever, and it was a long time before either of us could start to speak. Then Brian made a brilliant remark which deflated some of the tension: 'What an amazing coun-try,' he said, 'where nobody has to go to work on a Monday!'

Every television station in the world seemed to want to interview us. Our homecoming went out live on CNN, NBC, BBC, Sky News, TF1, Swiss Television – everywhere. People seemed surprised that, instead of boasting of how many records we had broken, we spoke about how we had gained respect for human life and nature. Soon the atmosphere was the same as in Cairo: rather than worry about technical details, everyone wanted to know what had been going on in our minds.

'What was the best moment of the flight?' someone asked.

'The time between take-off and landing,' Bertrand told him. 'It was a dream lasting twenty days.'

'What were you thinking all the time?'

'We didn't need to think,' said Bertrand. 'We just felt. We felt incredibly respectful for the miracle of life on the planet. We felt enormous admiration for the quality that human beings can achieve if they're not fighting rivals for more power, more territory, more money.'

'What about this invisible hand you mentioned?'

'We'd be dishonest if we claimed that we succeeded on our own,' Brian replied. 'We had the best balloon, the best possible back-up team and the best possible morale, but all that wasn't enough to account for our success. "The invisible hand" was the only name we could think of for the mysterious force which seemed to come to our aid so often.'

Bertrand picked up the theme. 'We also felt we were being helped on our way by the good wishes of millions of people. That's why we decided to dedicate the flight to the children of the world. They'll be the adults of tomorrow, and they must know how important it is to have peace and tolerance on earth.'

'Now you're heroes and famous all over the world,' somebody else asked, 'what are you going to do with your celebrity?'

During the flight we had never dared consider such matters, but now Bertrand answered openly, 'Yes, we do seem to be famous – otherwise you wouldn't be here! But it would be futile to use our fame just to promote ourselves. Rather, we want to use it to spread the message of peace which we conceived in the air. We're going to use the prize money from Budweiser to form a foundation which will promote the spirit of peace.'

Again and again we tried to emphasize that ours had been a team effort. Our balloon could well have been called *Team Spirit*, we said, because it was exactly that which enabled us to succeed. 'Without Breitling, we would have had nothing. Without Don Cameron and his team we would have had a lousy balloon instead of a wonderful one. Without Alan Noble and the control team, without Luc and Pierre, the flight would never have come off. Without the Swiss diplomats, we never would have been able to cross China.'

Then someone asked, 'Honestly, how did you manage to survive together for three weeks in such a small capsule?'

'By respecting each other and talking through every problem that came up,' Brian told him. 'We never got the slightest bit irritated with each other. We're both professionals, and we left our egos in the car park when we took off.'

Bertrand added, in a phrase that became famous, 'We took off as pilots, flew as friends, and landed as brothers.'

Then Richard Branson appeared on the platform with a magnum of champagne, which he shook up and squirted over us as if we were Grand Prix drivers. The meeting broke up into individual interviews, and these lasted until 11.30 p.m. – by which time we were both utterly exhausted.

Our phrase about the invisible hand set off a tremendous debate. Journalists began discussing what it was, or who it was, that had sped us on our way. Good, rational people said, 'Of course, they mean their two weathermen.' But later several people wrote to the newspapers saying, 'It's not the meteorologists. It's God.' Other people thought it was their prayers which had helped us. Obviously, all these factors contributed.

BRIAN

The joy of ordinary Swiss people was brought home to me when I got away from the crowd and walked down to the control centre for a cup of tea. Outside the door I noticed a fair-haired young man standing around and smiling at me nervously. When I came out, after nearly an hour, the boy was still there, and because he half-moved towards me as if wanting to say something, I stopped and talked to him.

'Mr Jones,' he said, 'can I have your autograph?'

'Yes, of course,' I replied, and I signed my name in a little book that he produced. As I was writing, his eyes filled with tears and he said, 'Mr Jones – you've made my dream come true.'

My eyes, also, were moist in that extraordinary moment, which summed up the way the flight had gripped people's imagination. There was no envy or jealousy: the success belonged not just to Bertrand and me, but to the nation, and somehow to the world.

At the first opportunity – in the shower at the Holiday Inn – I shaved off three weeks of beard. Bertrand had jokingly suggested that we should not shave before returning to Switzerland because he thought that if we came back looking fresh and shaved people would just think we'd been for a picnic. Anyway, in the event we had no opportunity to shave; but I hated my beard, and I lost no time in getting rid of it.

BOTH-OF-US

While all this was going on, the balloon was still lying in the desert, guarded – if that's the word – by a troop of the Egyptian coastguard. Melvyn James, head of the retrieve crew subcontracted by Breitling, remained overnight in Dakhla, and the next day he organized an expedition to rescue the gondola and as much as he could of the envelope. Several vehicles drove out, and he told his helpers not to touch anything before he arrived; but by the time he came on the scene they had already started stripping equipment out of the capsule – not least the toilet, which they had completely dismantled.

A powerful helicopter lifted the gondola back to Dakhla, where it was put on a truck and driven to Alexandria. Thence it came by sea to Marseilles. By the time it reached Switzerland a good deal of equipment had disappeared from it. Sadly enough, one casualty was the little singing football that had hung in the cockpit throughout our flight.

Later the gondola was put on exhibition in the fine transport museum in Lucerne; but its final home is the National Air and Space Museum at the Smithsonian Institution in Washington, where a big hall houses many milestones in aviation: the Wright brothers' *Kitty Hawk*, Lindbergh's *Spirit of St Louis*, Chuck Yeager's *X-1* (the first plane to break the sound barrier), and the Mercury, Gemini and Apollo space capsules. The Swiss Government would have liked to keep our gondola at home, but when it was suggested that the capsule should join the illustrious assembly in the United States, we felt it was the greatest honour anybody could confer. The gondola is the only piece of equipment in that fabulous display which is not American, so it constitutes a magnificent advertisement for Switzerland and Europe.

In the first few days after our return the Piccard household was deluged by bouquets of flowers, presents, bottles of wine, letters by the thousand. People were not only congratulating us: they were also expressing their thanks at having had the opportunity to dream with us.

As if to show how friendly the race had been, our competitors sent us moving letters – Steve Fossett, Richard Branson, Colin Prescott, Jacques Soukup, Dick Rutan, Kevin Uliassi. Barron Hilton, who had sponsored many round-the-world attempts, was also full of enthusiasm. One phrase of Dick Rutan's has stuck in our minds ever since: 'In some time, when the excitement is over, you'll both have the opportunity to sit down and realize how magnificent your achievement has been.'

Many letters contained invitations to events taking place over the next few days. In a single, unbelievable first week we went to the Aéro Club in France; to Belgium, for an audience with Crown Prince Philip; to New York, to receive the medal of the Explorers' Club; and to England to meet the Queen. There was also a ceremony in Bern, at which almost the whole Swiss Government gave an official welcome to our team – including Alan, the weathermen, the air controllers and representatives of Breitling. Breitling itself invited the fifty people most closely involved in the project to Rochat, the best restaurant in Switzerland, in the Hôtel de Ville in Crissier, where the firm gave us a wonderful evening and presented each one of us with a specially engraved watch.

In Paris, at a beautiful ceremony organized by the Jules Verne Adventure Association, attended by Buzz Aldrin, we gave back our treasured copy of La Vie, which both of us had signed, to Jean-Jules Verne himself. Then we received the Gold Medal of the Aéro Club of France – the oldest such club in the world. The presentation was made by the Club's President, Gérard Feldzer, but the arrangements were extraordinary, for the address was given by Jean-Pierre Haygneré, the French astronaut then orbiting the earth in the Mir space station. He performed the ceremony by remote control, speaking from space directly above France; Bertrand already knew him from former contacts, and it was wonderful to hear him congratulate us from such a god-like altitude. We also received the Gold Medal of Youth and Sport from the Minister, who said that she was giving it not because we had gone round the world but for the sentiments about peace and friendship which we had expressed when we returned.

In England, the Queen and the Duke of Edinburgh came to Camerons' factory in Bristol on 1 April. Because of the date we had thought the whole thing was a joke, and even when all the factory staff lined up we were fully expecting Don Cameron to say, 'April fool!' But the royal couple really did come, and on behalf of the British Balloon and Airship Club the Queen presented us with the Charles Green Salver, a splendid silver tray first given to the balloonist of that name in 1839. We were delighted that she took the trouble to have a few nice words with every member of the team.

That was also the first time we had seen Andy Elson and Colin Prescott since our flight. They were as friendly as could be: there were no hard feelings of any kind, and Andy said that, disappointed as he was not to have succeeded himself, he was glad it was us who had done so. He explained that it was the lack of spare batteries that had forced him to ditch, and altogether was very honest about his failure.

We cannot report every ceremony or transcribe every tribute that was made, but one speech caught the atmosphere of all the events. This was the one given by Max Bishop, General Secretary of the Fédération Aéronautique Internationale (FAI) at the splendid new Olympic Museum in Lausanne, where the main hall was packed – not least with dozens of children, sitting on the floor in front of the seats and on the stage. Before we received the Olympic Order from Juan Antonio Samaranch, President of the IOC, who had given us unfaltering support throughout the project, Max spoke first in his native English, then in perfect French, reducing both of us – and many others – to tears:

Mr President, Distinguished Guests, Ladies and Gentlemen,
We are here today to honour two great aviators, two outstanding sportsmen and two remarkable human beings. Bertrand Piccard, Brian Jones, we are all proud of you. We feel that we too have taken part in your adventure. We were with you in spirit when you soared up from your Alpine valley in Château d'Oex, not far from here; when you tiptoed through the Chinese Corridor; when you floundered over the Pacific; and when you finally sped over the Sahara to touch your balloon down, a symbol of late 20th-century technology, in Egypt, the cradle of an ancient civilization that fascinates you, and so many others. We all shared emotions with you: joy and fear, optimism and frustration, doubt, gratitude, and the final elation that you described so eloquently. Your balloon, on its three-week voyage round our

fragile planet, was a beacon of hope for all the world's peoples, and particularly for its children.

In your characteristically modest and unassuming way, you reminded us that hard work and perseverance pay — that not everything can be obtained instantaneously. You taught us that what some thought impossible could be achieved with patience, skill, courage and dedication. You showed us that, in this last year of a dark and turbulent century, incredible adventures are still possible, and that these strike a chord in the hearts of people around the world of all ages, inspiring us all to cast aside empty cynicism and set ourselves higher goals.

Your flight was an example of all that is best in the Olympic movement, an ideal that we in the FAI share. By drifting unobstructed over so many national frontiers, you showed these to be insubstantial barriers, dividing people who in reality share common causes and aspirations. By competing with your fellow round-the-world balloon contenders in an open and friendly fashion, you demonstrated fair play and respect for other competitors. By dedicating your flight to the world's children and establishing your charitable fund 'Winds of Hope', you have shown that great sporting achievements should not be selfish acts, but dedicated to others.

This last great aeronautical exploit of the 20th century ranks with the greatest in the archives of the FAI, which was founded in 1905 and which, by a happy coincidence, moved its headquarters from Paris to the Olympic capital, Lausanne, just a few months ago.

Among the records that the FAI has had the honour of ratifying we find:

Louis Blériot who, in 1909, crossed the Channel from Calais to Dover for the first time.

In 1910 George Chavez made the first crossing of the Alps.

In 1927 Charles Lindbergh succeeded in crossing the Atlantic, solo.

In 1931 a certain Auguste Piccard achieved the absolute ballooning altitude record.

Then Chuck Yeager beat the sound barrier in 1947.

Yuri Gagarin first flew in space in 1961, and Neil Armstrong walked on the moon in 1969.

The first non-stop, unrefuelled circumnavigation of the earth in an aeroplane was Dick Rutan's, in 1986.

And now we can add two names to the FAI's scroll of honour, to our cavalcade of heroes: Piccard and Jones.

But these are no ordinary heroes. Even in the company of the distinguished names I have mentioned, Bertrand Piccard and Brian Jones stand out for their humility and generosity of spirit, their ability to communicate their feelings to ordinary people, and their determination to help others. The men that you, Mr President, are honouring today are not only great airmen and athletes. More importantly, they are distinguished ambassadors for our air sports and for the Olympic ideal. Most important of all, they are excellent examples for the children of the world to look up to.

On behalf of all air sportsmen and women the world over, I salute you, Bertrand Piccard and Brian Jones. This is an honour you richly deserve. We wish you well in the important work of education, encouragement and support of others that lies ahead of you.

For both of us it was fascinating to be associated with the heroes of our childhood, with the explorers and aviators we had so much admired all our lives, and to receive the same honours and the same medals.

In Brussels we had a grand ceremony at the Royal Institute of Meteorology, where Luc normally worked, and we were officially welcomed by Prince Philip, Crown Prince of Belgium. Prince Philip's father and grandfather had been friends of Bertrand's forebears, so this was something of a Piccard family occasion.

For Bertrand, to acquire an Explorers' Club medal was a particular thrill because his father had been awarded one: he kept it in his living room, and as a child Bertrand was always looking at it. Now he was given the same prize. We flew to New York on Concorde because it was the only way to fit the trip in, and at the dinner 2,000 people gave us a standing ovation. We sat at the same table as the astronaut John

Glenn, who had given Bertrand his autograph at Cape Kennedy when he was a boy of eleven.

Another trip was to Washington, where we collected the Budweiser cheque for one million dollars. The company had specified that half the total should go to charity; we shared the rest with Breitling, who presented their share to the same charity. The presentation ceremony was held at the Smithsonian Institution, to which we rode in a carriage pulled by eight gigantic shire horses: we started in the park next to the Capitol and went up Independence Avenue to the museum, where a red carpet had been rolled out. A makeshift stage had been arranged underneath Lindbergh's *Spirit of St Louis* and in front of the Apollo 11 capsule – an amazing setting.

Yet another ceremony took place in Château d'Oex. Exactly two months after our landing we returned to our launch point in a special panoramic train. Thousands of people were waiting for us at the station. Together with Luc and Pierre, we rode in the basket of a balloon set on a trailer, and paraded through the village to inspect the monument created to commemorate our flight: a pyramid of light-coloured stone, surmounted by a bronze globe showing our trajectory, with little bronze balloons standing proud over our take-off and landing sites and an inscription recording details of the circumnavigation. Such was Brian's feeling for the local people that he got Bertrand to teach him one special sentence of French, which he spoke over the microphone to tremendous applause: '*Aujourd'hui, ma femme Joanna et moi, nous sommes rentrés à la maison.*' ('Today my wife Joanna and I feel we've come back home.')

BRIAN

Many people have asked how the flight changed us. There was an obvious physical effect in that we both lost weight: Bertrand shed nearly five kilos, dropping from 62 to 57 kilograms, his lowest for years. I lost about the same – 10 pounds. The difference between us was that I was happy to be lighter, whereas he was not. Part of the loss was due to the fact that we ate relatively little, and part to the fact that our muscles withered from lack of use. Our worst problem immediately after our return was exhaustion: the schedule of appearances was so hectic that we had no chance to recover.

While I was project manager for *Orbiter 3*, and during the lead-up to launch, I was totally focused on getting the balloon built and ensuring that its systems would operate as designed. I gave little thought to what it might be like to fly round the globe. The depth of my relationship with Bertrand, and all our talks about the wellbeing of the planet, elevated the whole experience to another plane.

There is no question that the flight changed my life. It made me more extrovert: the feeling that I wanted to share our story and tell everyone about it brought me out of the relatively private way of life I had followed before. The urge to spread the word is such that I now positively enjoy giving lectures about our circumnavigation. The flight got rid of some of my typically British reserve and brought my emotions closer to the surface. I feel closer to nature, and cry more easily now. Before my first British TV appearance, which went out from a London studio some ten days after our return, I was put in the green room to wait. The television news was in progress, showing scenes of the conflict in Kosovo. Before that moment we had been on the move so much that I had hardly been aware of the war; but now I found that the sight of refugees leaving their homes, and the evidence of massacres, brought tears to my eyes. Before our flight I would not have been so moved: I'd have taken in the refugees' plight, but then switched my attention to the next item on the programme. Now I was more deeply affected – and no bad thing, either.

To go from total obscurity to celebrity status in twenty days was exceedingly strange, but soon I began to see that most people in high places are no different from the rest of us. After our return Bertrand and I met a number of important personalities – from royalty to heads of state, former astronauts and film stars – and to my surprise I found all of them, without exception, incredibly nice. They had no affectations and gave themselves no airs: on the contrary, they were natural and friendly, and had time for us. It was a revelation for me to find that a hero like John Glenn, revered in aviation circles, has heroes of his own.

Another result of the flight was that it brought a new dimension to my already deep friendship with John and Debbie, Smiffy and C, and the other people on the team. Three weeks of shared danger, excitement and tension created a unique bond between us. Whenever we meet now and talk about the flight, there is a greater depth to the conversation than the mere words convey. We scarcely have any need to discuss what we were feeling at the time, or how close we came to each other: we all know, and the unspoken knowledge itself reinforces the bond.

As for Bertrand: the fact that the two of us shared such an experience certainly created a deep and lasting friendship. I always look forward to seeing him and enjoy his and Michèle's company. I love his children, and have promised myself that I will learn French so that I can communicate with them better. His phrase about our becoming brothers was accurate as well as memorable. He will always have a special place in my life.

BERTRAND

For me, the most striking fact about the whole flight was that we had such extraordinary luck. Why was the honour of succeeding granted to us? Why, when people were suffering all round the earth, when atrocities were being committed and wars fought, should we have been having the most fabulous time of our lives? We looked down on the planet with awe and admiration, and yet many questions remained unanswered.

Now, whenever I see a globe or a map of the world, I have an almost proprietorial feeling about it. Before the flight, I associated globes and maps with geography lessons. Now when I look at a globe and turn it on its axis, or observe every detail on it, I get a tremendous feeling of pleasure and strong emotions as memories of the flight flash through my head. I feel far more closely involved than before with the life of our planet and of those countries that we flew over. When King Hassan of Morocco dies, when starvation hits the Sudan, when war breaks out between Pakistan and India, I think, 'Well – I've been there. I know what the country looks like, and I feel closer to the people. In some way, flying round the world is like taking it in our arms.'

I emerged from the flight with much greater respect for life and for mankind. I now feel far more deeply concerned about ecology and wildlife as well as about the way people behave. When I say 'ecology', I don't mean fanatical attempts to rid nature of human beings in order to turn the world into a nature reserve. I mean the deep respect everyone should have for every form of life – from air, sand and water to trees, animals and humans. 'Respect' means the realization that there is valuable life, though in different forms, all around us and inside us. Neither is the goal to get rid of the high technology which we have been able to develop: instead the aim is to use it to understand nature better, rather than wanting to extend our power. For me such subjects are not just theoretical any more but completely practical concerns. I am so thankful at having had my dream come true that I feel I must pay back something to the planet.

One way of doing this has been to form our Winds of Hope charitable foundation. Our plan is to use the interest from the Budweiser money and other donations to make an annual award, every 21 March – the anniversary of the landing. This award will fund projects which provide concrete, lasting assistance to child victims of catastrophes, diseases or conflicts, whose sufferings are unreported by the media or forgotten by the general public.

We hope we can exploit the status we have achieved by meeting high-level officials and politicians, as well as thousands of ordinary mortals, so that people will listen to what we say. To give money to worthwhile projects is one thing, but we feel we can also promote selected projects personally by offering them the backing of our celebrity. We know that during the flight school classes all round the world were following our progress. Even in countries that we had no chance of overflying, children's attention was focused on the balloon. So, wherever we go, we should have an immediate affinity with the children, and through them with their teachers and government officials. We should also be able to score from the fact that we will have no secondary agenda: we will not be looking for further publicity – just for results.

I am not a professional adventurer. I have now returned to my job as a practising psychiatrist, and I enjoy giving talks and lectures about the flight. But what I have realized is that the whole flight turned out to be a metaphor for life. In life many people are afraid of the unknown, afraid of losing control, with the result that they try to over-control everything. Many of their problems arise from the fact that they expend a lot of energy seeking to control events over which they have no power. On the other hand, they fail to control those things which are within their power.

During the Breitling *Orbiter 3* project we learnt what we could control and what we couldn't. We could control the construction of gondola and envelope, the building of the team, the technical training of the crew. Once in the air, though, we could not control the weather or the wind. The only way to change our heading was to change our altitude.

On earth the situation is very similar. People become prisoners of their problems, their lives, their fate, as the balloon is prisoner of the wind. Exactly as in the balloon, if you want to change direction in life, you have to climb: by deliberately reaching upward, through philosophy, psychology or some spiritual discipline, you can achieve a different trajectory.

What I do with my patients now is exactly what we did in the balloon – except that in psychotherapy I'm not the pilot: I'm the weatherman, always trying to help the patient find the altitude at which he or she will discover the most suitable track. If you have the wrong altitude and the wrong heading, you get lost in storms, you get lost in suffering, you get lost in pain. So, although university taught me the theory of psychotherapy, ballooning has taught me a new, practical approach to the subject.

It is now very important for me to help my patients, or the people to whom I give talks, to realize that life itself is a great adventure. In life you have the same kind of storms that can destroy you when you are ballooning and you are anxious about the future. There are moments when you have no wind and you are depressed by your stagnation; at other moments, everything seems so easy and smooth that you wonder why other people find life (or ballooning) so difficult. When people are healthy, young and handsome, of course they think life is simple – but that's a mirage. In fact life is a huge and difficult adventure because you are facing the unknown: by definition, you never know what will happen, and the only ability you need to develop is that of adapting yourself to whatever happens. Although you cannot control what will come, you can control your reaction to it. When each new problem comes along, you have to dig inside yourself to find the resources to go further and learn new strategies for survival and evolution.

So now, although I am no longer in the round-the-world balloon, I feel myself in exactly the same situation in life. Just because we landed safely, the adventure is by no means finished. Our descent into Egypt was a practical return to earth, but the flight continues in life. That's why the greatest adventure of all is not flying around the world in a balloon: the greatest adventure is travelling through life itself.

Looking ahead, I expect that somebody will make a solo round-the-world attempt – and the most obvious candidate must be Steve Fossett. I also anticipate a round-the-world race, with all competitors taking off from the same place at the same time. They will try to fly faster than we did, and if they succeed their pleasure will be more short lived. Brian and I will not take part in such a race, but we will be glad to support it.

We are happy and proud that our team's achievement has become part of the history of aviation. But all the honours we received were no more than the icing on the cake. The cake – if I can put it like that – is the opportunity our flight gave us for constructive action in the future.

Meanwhile, I very often like to bring back into my mind how I sat in the Egyptian desert with my back against the gondola, feeling the wind get up. I remember how the warm wind blew on my face for the first time in three weeks, how the wind increased until I could feel it with my entire body. This was the wind – the wind of providence – which had carried Brian and me round the world, in harmony with nature. Henceforth, and for ever more, I will think of it as the Wind of Hope, and I will do all I can to hasten it on its journey round the earth.

ROUND-THE-WORLD ATTEMPTS

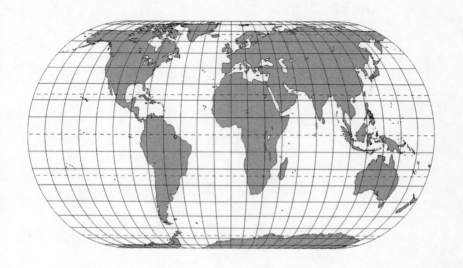

Year	Pilots	Balloon	Country of Origin	Take-off	Result
1981	Max Anderson	Jules Verne	USA	Egypt	Landed in India. Flew 2,763 miles, 47.30hours
1993	Henk Brink	Unicef Flyer	Holland		Never took off
1993	Larry Newman Don Moses Vladimir Dzhanibekov	Earthwind 1	USA	Reno, USA	Crashed shortly after take-off
1994	Larry Newman Richard Abruzzo Dave Melton	Earthwind 2	USA	Reno, USA	Frozen valve, landed same day
1995	Larry Newman Dave Melton George Saad	Earthwind 3	USA	Reno, USA	Anchor balloon burst during initial climb
1996	Steve Fossett	Solo Challenger	USA	S. Dakota, USA	Landed in Canada. Flew 1,819 miles, 51.13 hours
1997 7 Jan	Richard Branson Per Lindstrand Alex Ritchie	Virgin Global Challenger	Britain	Morocco	Flew 19 hours, landed in Algeria

Year	Pilots	Balloon	Country of Origin	Take-off	Result
1997 12 Jan	Bertrand Piccard Wim Verstraeten	Breitling Orbiter	Switzerland	Château d'Oex, Switzerland	Came down in Mediterranean after six hours
1997 15 Jan	Steve Fossett	Solo Spirit	USA	St Louis, USA	Landed in India. Duration record – 146.44 hours; distance record – 11,265 miles
1997 Dec	Richard Branson Per Lindstrand Alex Ritchie	Virgin Global Challenger	Britain	Morocco	Envelope broke away and flew on its own
1997 31 Dec	Kevin Uliassi	J-Renée	USA	Illinois, USA	Balloon burst after one hour
1998 1 Jan	Steve Fossett	Solo Spirit 2	USA	St Louis, USA	Landed in Russia. Flew 5,802 miles, 108.23 hours
1998 8 Jan	Bertrand Piccard Wim Verstraeten Andy Elson	Breitling Orbiter 2	Switzerland	Château d'Oex, Switzerland	Aborted take-off: envelope not inflated

Year		Pilots	Balloon	Country of Origin	Take-off	Result
1998	9 Jan	Dick Rutan Dave Melton	Global Hilton	USA	Albuquerque, USA	Balloon burst. Pilots parachuted
1998	28 Jan	Bertrand Piccard Wim Verstraeten Andy Elson	Breitling Orbiter 2	Switzerland	Château d'Oex, Switzerland	Landed 7 Feb in Burma. Flew 5,266 miles. Absolute duration record – 233.55 hours
1998	7 Aug	Steve Fossett	Solo Spirit 3	USA	Mendoza, Argentina	Crashed in Coral Sea, off Australia. Distance record – 14,236 miles
1998	Winter	John Wallington Dave Liniger	Remax	Australia	Alice Springs, Australia	Take-off announced but never made
1998	18 Dec	Richard Branson Per Lindstrand Steve Fossett	ICO Global Challenger	Britain	Morocco	Flew seven days. Ditched off Honolulu. Flew 12,404 miles, 177.57 hours

Year	Pilots	Balloon	Country of Origin	Take-off	Result
1999 Jan	Jacques Soukup Mark Sullivan Crispin Williams	Spirit of Peace	USA	Albuquerque, USA	Never took off because of Chinese block
1999 Jan	Kevin Uliassi	J-Renée	USA	Illinois, USA	Never took off because of Chinese block
1999 18 Feb	Andy Elson Colin Prescott	Cable & Wireless	Britain	Almería, Spain	Ditched off Japanese coast with power failure. Flew 11,495 miles. Absolute duration record – 425.41 hours
1999 1 Mar	**Bertrand Piccard Brian Jones**	**Breitling Orbiter 3**	**Switzerland**	**Château d'Oex, Switzerland**	**Three absolute world records: first round the world; distance record – 25,361 miles; duration record – 477.47 hours**